Configuring SAP Financial Accounting – Vol. II

SAP S/4HANA Finance

Narayanan Veeriah

Configuring SAP Financial Accounting – Vol. II

SAP S/4HANA Finance

Acknowledgements

I acknowledge the understanding and adjustments made by my family, especially my wife, for all the encouragement and letting me concentrate working on this book, as with previous other books. I thank Narayanan Krishnan, who helps in checking out the content for its correctness.

Preface

As with my other books on SAP, this book also follows a case-study approach to make your learning easy. Efforts have been taken, throughout the book, to guide you step-by-step in understanding how to configure your SAP system, to meet your exact business needs. Each configuration activity has been discussed with appropriate screen shots (from an SAP system) and illustrations to help you 'see' what is being discussed in that activity / step. You will see a lot of additional information, provided across the Chapters and the Sections, to help you understand better a topic or a setting or a concept. The entire content of the book, vide various Chapters, has been presented as in SAP IMG (Implementation Guide) for easy comprehension. You will come across with appropriate menu paths and Transactions, to help you to navigate the various activities.

This book is on *'Configuring SAP Financial Accounting'* in *SAP S/4HANA Finance (1909)*, has been published in two volumes: Vol. I and Vol. II.

The Vol. II (this book) covers:

- Configuring SAP Financial Accounting – Vol. I
- Case Study (Project Dolphin & Project Starfish)
- Chapter 10: Accounts Receivable and Accounts Payable
- Chapter 11: Contract Accounts Receivable and Payable
- Chapter 12: Bank Accounting
- Chapter 13: Asset Accounting

In the Chapter *'Configuring SAP Financial Accounting – Vol. I'*, we have captured the details of what is covered in Vol. I of this title, to give you an idea. You will see a brief Chapter-wise summary of that coverage with configuration highlights that has been discussed in each of those Chapters, from 1 to 9:

- Chapter 1: SAP HANA
- Chapter 2: SAP S/4HANA
- Chapter 3: SAP S/4HANA Finance
- Chapter 4: Case Study (Project Dolphin & Project Oyster)
- Chapter 5: Enterprise Structure
- Chapter 6: FI Global Settings I (Fields, Ledgers, Field Status Variant, Fiscal Year, Posting Period, Fiscal Year Variant, Parallel Accounting, Integration of SAP CO with SP FI, and Company Code Global Parameters)

- Chapter 7: FI Global Settings II (Documents, Inflation Accounting and Correspondence)
- Chapter 8: FI Global Settings III (Taxes including Extended Withholding Tax)
- Chapter 9: General Ledger Accounting

As mentioned already, this book follows a case-study approach with a story-board technique, that provides you with the required business background for a given configuration activity. The **Case Study Chapter** discusses two case-studies (*Project Dolphin and Project Starfish*) in its entirety, setting up the tone for further discussions in the remaining Chapters.

The **Chapter 10** deals with Accounts Receivable (FI-A/R) and Accounts Payable (FI-A/P), in detail. It covers customer and vendor accounts, business transactions associated with both FI-A/R and FI-A/P and the information system. In business transactions, you will see topics like incoming invoices, release for payment, payments (outgoing & incoming, manual and automatic), dunning, open item clearing, down payment processing, adjustment posting, interest calculation and closing operations.

The **Chapter 11** discusses Contracts Accounts Receivable and Payable (SAP FICA). With a separate case study (*Project Starfish*), you will understand the functionality and the configuration required for setting up of SAP FICA for a business.

In **Chapter 12,** you will understand Bank Accounting (FI-BL). You will learn about bank master data (bank directory, house bank, business partner's bank, bank distribution etc.), bank chains, payment transactions including manual & electronic bank statement, lockbox processing, cash journal and online payments.

The last Chapter (**Chapter 13**) covers Asset Accounting (FI-AA) in great detail. It covers the organizational structure, structuring fixed assets in FI-AA (including special forms of assets, asset classes etc.), integration of FI-AA with other SAP components including SAP FI-G/L, general & special valuation, depreciation, master data, transactions (like acquisitions, retirements, transfers, capitalization of assets under construction etc.), FI-AA information system, asset data transfer, preparations for going live and overview for experts.

In all, you can use this book as a desktop-reference for configuring SAP FI. As the Chapters have been progressively elaborated, with the help of a case-study, you will certainly find this as informative and easy to comprehend. The screenshots, in each of the Chapters, will help you understand the settings better and will enable for a better learning.

Hope you will enjoy learning SAP Financial Accounting, through this book!

Contents at a Glance

Table of Contents

Configuring SAP Financial Accounting – Vol. I

The book on *'Configuring SAP Financial Accounting' (S/4HANA Finance 1909)*, has been brought out in two volumes, Vol. I and Vol. II. What you have on your hand is the Vol. II. Before getting into the details of Vol. II, let us update you with the details as to what has been covered in Vol. I, so as to give you the required perspective and background.

The following is the content covered in Vol. I of the book:

8   FI Global Settings - III

9   General Ledger Accounting

Let us briefly understand what you will learn in each of the above Chapters, in Vol. I.

Chapter 1: SAP HANA

You will learn about the evolution of SAP, from SAP R/1 to the latest, the SAP HANA. You, then, will learn, in detail, about SAP HANA which is an in-memory, column-oriented, relational database management system with its primary function of storing / retrieving data, as requested by the applications and performing analytics as an application server.

You will, also, learn about SAP HANA's history and architecture, before moving on to learn about its benefits and editions ('on-premise' and 'in-cloud'). While learning about the 'on-premise' editions, you will understand that there are four variants namely standard, express, runtime and enterprise editions. In addition, you will understand that you could go in either for a public cloud (SAP HANA as a Service) or private cloud (SAP HANA Enterprise Cloud) in the case of 'in-cloud' editions. Finally, you will learn about the latest in SAP HANA, the SAP HANA 2.0 and its innovations and improvements.

Chapter 2: SAP S/4HANA

You will, in this Chapter, learn that SAP S/4HANA is the digital core of the modern business enterprise, which consolidates internal and external elements into a single structure connecting all the processes, and providing you with live information and insights. You will learn about the major benefits and its capabilities.

You will, also, learn about the deployment options (on-premise or in-cloud) of SAP S/4HANA with the associated advantages in each case, the release and maintenance strategy, the innovations that are brought into the release 1909, and the implementation considerations as to whether to go in for a greenfield project or system conversion. You will find out how you can integrate SAP S/4HANA with some of the key SAP solutions like SAP SuccessFactors Employee Central, SAP Ariba Network, SAP Hybris, SAP Fieldglass etc.

Chapter 3: SAP S/4HANA Finance

You will understand SAP S/4HANA Finance, in detail, in this Chapter.

First, you will learn about the overview of SAP S/4HANA Finance as to how it is different from the erstwhile and traditional ERP applications with its digital SAP HANA core, its new and improved set of comprehensive financial solutions that are designed to help business to meet the demands of today's digital economy, and its intuitive user interface and experience.

Second, you will learn about the major capabilities of SAP S/4HANA Finance in accounting and financial close, financial operations, planning and predictive analysis, treasury & risk management, and financial governance & compliance. You will understand how this new solution helps to overcome the age-old pains like delayed period-end and closing, inability to perform real-time inventory valuation, manual reconciliations, issues in integrating multiple A/P systems, difficulties to model and simulate business innovation, costs, and structural changes in the organization to assess the financial impacts etc.

Third, you will learn about the major benefits that will accrue to businesses from SAP S/4HANA Finance solution, with its single source of truth, flexible business processes and a plethora of best practices that you can leverage. You will further learn that you will be able save substantially as this solution will help in reducing the bank fees, A/R write-offs, audit cost, cash management cost, days required to close the books etc.

Chapter 4: Case Study

You will come across two case studies in this Chapter 4.

- Project Dolphin`1
- Project Oyster

The *Project Dolphin* is the main case study, that will cover most of the SAP FI configuration, and relates to BESTM Corporate. However, in this Chapter 4, you will not see the full case study but only the portions that are relevant for Chapters 5 to 9. In Vol. II of the book, the case study is covered in full.

The *Project Oyster* is a mini case study that has been used to discuss inflation accounting (Chapter 7), as a part of configuring SAP FI. You will not find this case study featured in this Vol. II, as it is not relevant for the Chapters discussed in this book.

However, you will see another case study, *'Project Starfish'* featured under 'Case Study' in this book, relating to SAP Contract Accounts Receivable and Payable.

Chapter 5: Enterprise Structure

You will start this Chapter with a discussion on the various organizational units (forming the enterprise structure), that you would need to create in the SAP system, to configure SAP FI and SAP CO; you will understand about all the organizational units that need to be mandatorily defined and what could be optional. You will, then, go on to understand about country localization: why it is necessary, how to do that etc. You will go through the steps to localize the SAP's sample organizational units to meet the specific requirements of the case study, for USA and India.

You, in the later Sections of the Chapter, will learn about defining the important organizational units like, company, company code, credit control area, business area, FM (financial management) area, segment, controlling area and profit center. While defining each of these organizational units, you will learn about the characteristics of that particular organizational unit, why it is important to have that defined, how to define etc. In the process, you will understand that the 'client' sits at the top of the SAP system, with one or more companies below, and each company comprising of at least one company code.

You will learn that a company code is the smallest mandatory central organizational unit, in SAP, for which you can maintain a complete and self-contained set of accounts, besides drawing up the external financial statements (balance sheet and profit & loss account) to meet the legal and statutory requirements of the country in which the company code operates. You will learn that you can have one or more credit control areas, defined to suit your credit management. Your will, further, learn that a business area in SAP FI represents an area of responsibility (or operations) of the business, and that it enables creation of financial statements below the level of a company code. You will also learn that a functional area in SAP FI classifies expenses of the business, based on the functions like, administration, marketing etc., performed by employees of the organization.

While learning about FM (financial management) areas that are used to structure the business organization from the perspective of SAP Cash Budget Management and SAP Funds Management, you will understand the difference between a functional area and a FM area. You will, then, go on to learn about the segments that are used in segment reporting to meet the statutory requirements IAS, IFRS and US GAAP; and, that these segments are based, normally, on the location of a business entity's assets or customers or a geographical segment.

You will understand that the controlling area (CO area) is a self-contained cost accounting entity (like a company code in FI) that is central to the organizational structure in SAP CO, and is used to subdivide your business from the cost-accounting viewpoint, for bringing out internal reporting. Finally, you will learn about defining the profit centers that are areas of responsibility within a company for revenues and expenses; while on profit centers, you will also learn about profit center groups and standard hierarchy.

In the last part of the Chapter, you will learn about assigning the various organizational units among themselves, to bring out the functional relationship between two units that will enable process and data flow in SAP. You will learn that you can assign one or more company codes to a company, one or more company codes to a credit control area, one or more FM areas to a company code and so on. In the case of assignment of company code to controlling area, you will learn that the assignment can be 1:1 or 1:n between the controlling area and company code(s). Lastly, you will see the assignment of profit centers (profit center groups and standard hierarchy) to a company code.

Chapter 6: FI Global Settings - I

As the first part of configuring the FI global settings, here in this Chapter, you will start your learning with the configuration of fields: you will understand the difference between standard and customer fields, learn how to define the customer fields and also learn about including the customer fields in the coding block to make them available in data-entry screens for transaction processing. You will, also, learn about field status, field status group (FSG) and field status variant (FSV). You will understand that an FSG is a collection of field statuses, defined in the company code data of G/L account, and is used to determine which fields are ready for data entry input (required or mandatory / optional), and which needs to be hidden. You will, also, learn that SAP uses 'link rules' to overcome conflicting field status situations. You will understand that you can group several FSGs in one field status variant (FSV), and then assign that FSV to a company code. By this, you learn that, you will be able to work with the same FSGs in multiple company codes.

You will, then, move on to understand the ledger concept in SAP. You will learn that there are two different ledger types: standard and extension ledgers. You will learn that a standard ledger is one that contains a full set of journal entries for all business transactions, and it can be designated either as a 'leading ledger' or 'non-leading ledger'. You will understand that you must designate one (only one) standard ledger as the 'leading ledger'. Along with the leading ledger, you will learn that, you can have other ledgers known 'non-leading ledger' and/or 'extension ledger'. You will, also, learn that the non-leading ledgers are parallel ledgers to the leading ledger, and they can be – for example - based on a local accounting principle. You will learn that an extension ledger is a non-leading ledger, created based on an underlying standard ledger, and the postings to the underlying ledger also apply for the extension ledger, even though the postings made explicitly to an extension ledger are visible only in that extension ledger but not in the underlying standard ledger. You, then, will learn about the 'universal journal' that is actually an enhanced financial document in S/4HANA, created whenever you post to SAP FI from any of the SAP modules. You will understand that ACDOCA is SAP FI's important new S/4HANA table that is based on the universal journal line items, containing all of the financial fields, as well as a lot of information from other sub-modules of SAP. You will, then, proceed to define and configure the ledgers in the system besides configuring the currency settings for the ledgers defined.

You, later, will learn about the fiscal year, posting period and special periods. You will learn about the different types of fiscal years (calendar, non-calendar and shortened fiscal years). You will learn that a 'calendar fiscal year' is nothing but a calendar year with 12 posting periods corresponding to the 12 calendar months, and a fiscal year that does not correspond to a calendar year is known as the 'non-calendar fiscal year'. You will understand that the posting periods may or may not correspond to the calendar months in a non-calendar fiscal year. You also will understand that a fiscal year that is less than 12 posting periods in duration, is called a 'shortened fiscal year', and is year-dependent and has always to be followed or preceded by a full fiscal year with 12 periods. You will, then, go on to learn and configure fiscal year variant (FYV), assigning company codes to FYV and finally will learn about opening and closing of posting periods through posting period variant (PPV).

You will move on to learn about parallel accounting. You will learn that unlike the erstwhile classic G/L, wherein parallel accounting has to be performed through the accounting approach, using several parallel G/L accounts and special-purpose ledgers, you can now use the alternative approach for parallel accounting in SAP G/L using the parallel ledger concept. You will learn how to define the accounting principles, and assign them to ledger groups.

You, then, will learn about the configuration settings that are required for the integration of CO with FI. In the process, you will learn to define the document types for postings in CO, assigning document types to mapping variants and defining the default values for CO postings.

You will, then, move on to check the configuration settings for the ledgers that have already been defined. You will learn that this check must run without errors before continuing, for example, with the migration of transaction data or any other activities. You will understand that as long as inconsistencies exist, you will not be able to post journal entries in the affected company codes / ledgers.

You will, finally, move on to configure the global parameters for company codes. You will learn that these company code global parameters control how a company code behaves in your SAP system, besides controlling the associated transaction processing. You will understand that you are required to configure about 35 global parameters, grouped into two categories: accounting organization and processing parameters. You will learn, in detail, about each of these parameters, and what value they need to be configured with and why. You also will learn about creating a new chart of accounts while configuring the company code global parameters.

Chapter 7: FI Global Settings - II

You will start this Chapter, with the discussion on documents in SAP. You will learn that the transaction, in SAP, is based on the document principle and a unique document is generated every time you make a posting in the system. You will understand the document structure: the document header and line items. You will, also, understand that you can post a document only when it is 'complete' with the debit=credit. Then, you will learn about the various document types, how they are used to differentiate business transactions, and how they control the posting to the appropriate account types (namely, vendor, customer, or G/L). You, then, go on to learn document number ranges: its assignment (internal and external), validity, change and deletion. You will, also, learn about copying one or more number range to company code(s) and to fiscal year(s). Then, you will learn about posting keys and how a posting key controls the entering / processing of a line item in a document. You will, also, learn about the (a) screen variants that are required for document entry, (b) rules for changing a document and (c) bar code entry. You will, then, move on to understand tolerance and tolerance groups, how to define a tolerance group, how to use tolerance group in document processing and how to assign users to a tolerance group. You will learn about defining texts / text identifiers for documents and their usage, in document processing. You will learn how to make the required settings to make the system propose default values like default document type / posting key (for a transaction), value date and fiscal year. You will go further, on to understand the details of recurring entries, account assignment models and defining the run schedules. You, also, will learn about document parking and how to change the posting date of a parked document. You, finally, will learn about account document archiving: using the account type life and document type life.

You will, then, move on to learn inflation accounting. You will learn that the inflation accounting is the process of adjusting the financial statements of a company to show the real financial position, during periods of high inflation. During the discussion, you will learn about defining and configuring the settings for inflation index, TBE variant, inflation key, inflation methods and inflation calculation.

You will, then, move on to discuss the correspondence in SAP. You will learn that the correspondence function is to set the system up for mailing letters, for corresponding with your business partners and for internal purposes. You will learn that the standard correspondence, in SAP, includes account statements, balance confirmations, document extracts, payment notifications and so on. You will go on to learn what is a correspondence type, how to define a new correspondence type, assigning print programs to correspondence types, how to denominate a particular company code as 'correspondence company code' and setting up of call-up functions to specify which correspondence types can be selected online, while executing certain business functions (like document entry, payment settlement etc).

You, at the end of the Chapter, will learn about the SAP Shared Services Framework and how to integrate SAP S/4HANA with SAP Shared Service Center.

Chapter 8: FI Global Settings - III

As the final set of FI global settings, you will learn the configuration relating to tax on sales and purchases, and withholding tax, in this Chapter.

You will learn that you can use SAP FI (FI-G/L, FI-A/P and FI-A/R) for tax management involving calculation, posting, adjustment, and reporting of taxes. You also will learn that you can manage tax at the national level or at the regional / jurisdictional level or at the combined national and regional levels. You will learn that you have to make the tax configuration at the country level, as all legal entities in the same country need to follow the same taxation policies while preparing their financial statements. You will understand that you can either define the tax rates internally within your SAP system or fetch them from an external taxation system as in US (like, Vertex), via interfacing. You will learn that SAP supports multiple taxation types like sales tax, tax on sales and purchases, and withholding tax.

You will understand that the 'tax on sales and purchases' (also known as 'sales and use tax') are levied on invoiced goods and services payable in accordance with the principles of VAT (value-added tax). You will, also, understand that while the 'sales tax' is levied on the sale of taxable goods on the transactions occurring within a state, the 'use tax', on the other hand, is imposed on the purchaser; the seller is not liable for this tax. You will further understand that the taxes on sales and purchases apply to 'input tax', 'output tax', 'additional tax', and 'acquisition tax'. You will, also, understand that you can calculate the taxes on sales and purchases through three different ways: non-jurisdiction method, jurisdiction method and jurisdiction method with external tax calculation. You will learn that the tax on sales and purchases is calculated through condition methods, in SAP, using a tax calculation procedure, tax codes, and jurisdiction codes, if any, and that the system posts the tax during document processing. You will, then, be taken through the various configuration settings – grouped into basic settings, calculation and posting – that you need to make, in the system, for tax on sales and purchases. You will understand that you can configure the SAP system to manage the tax sales and purchase for USA, either through manual calculation or automatically using an external tax application solution. You will learn how to configure the settings for external tax calculation using Vertex.

Moving on to withholding tax, you will learn that withholding tax is the tax that is charged at the beginning of the payment flow in some countries, and the party (vendor) that is subject to tax does not pay the withholding tax (to the tax authorities by himself), but a customer that is authorized to deduct reduces the payment amount by the withholding tax proportion and pays the tax, so withheld, directly to the appropriate tax authorities. You will learn that SAP supports both classic withholding tax and extended withholding tax (EWT). You will learn that EWT supports assignment of more than one withholding tax type to a business partner, and allows tax calculation for partial payments as well, besides enabling processing the tax from both the vendor and customer views. You will learn the various configuration settings (grouped under basic settings, calculation, posting and advanced compliance reporting) that enable you set up the EWT functionality in SAP, to meet your business requirements including compliance reporting to the tax authorities. At the end, you will understand how to make the changeover from classic withholding to EWT.

Chapter 9: General Ledger Accounting

Here, in this Chapter, you will start your discussion with the General Ledger (G/L). You will understand that G/L is the backbone of any accounting system holding the financial data of an organization. You will, then, understand what is SAP G/L Accounting, its purpose and functions. You will, also, understood, in detail, about the various features and functionalities (like extensibility, ledger concept, document splitting, parallel accounting, segment reporting etc) of SAP G/L Accounting. You will, also, learn about the pre-requisites for configuring SAP G/L Accounting, to meet your exact business needs.

You will, then, move on to learn G/L account master data: the preparations that you need to create master data, how to create, and the options you have in creating them. While looking at the preparations, you will learn about revising / editing the chart of accounts, assigning company codes to chart of accounts, creating account groups and so on. You will, also, learn to create sample accounts that would enable creation of G/L account master records quickly. In G/L account master records, you will learn about creating the records in company code area, chart of accounts area, and also in both the areas in a single step. You will learn to create the G/L accounts using different methods including the reference method. You will see how to create / edit the master records either individually or collectively for several accounts. You will, then, learn about the financial statement structures, with the definition and assignment of financial statement versions.

Later, you will move on to learn about the configuration settings required to set up various business transactions including document splitting, cross-company code transactions, open item clearing, bank interest calculation and adjustment posting including reversals. You will learn how to use the 'Document Splitting Wizard' to configure document splitting functionality in the system. While discussing the open item clearing, you will learn that an 'open item' is an uncleared transaction that can be cleared and closed by posting an offsetting amount to that account; you will learn to define the clearing rules, accounts for exchange rate differences, automatic clearing settings, tolerance groups for G/L accounts etc. In bank account interest calculation, you will learn that you can use the functionality, in SAP FI, to calculate interest on the balance of the G/L accounts that are managed on open item basis. During the configuration of bank interest calculation, you will come across with the fields that are relevant for this interest calculation; you will learn about interest indicator (that controls interest calculation), interest calculation period and interest rate definition; you will, also, learn about the settings required for interest calculation and posting. While discussing adjustment postings/reversal, you will learn that SAP allows you to reverse a document that was entered incorrectly; understood the difference between a regular reversal and a negative posting (also known as 'true reversal'): you will learn that in the case of a negative posting, the system reduces the transaction figures in customer, vendor and G/L Accounts, thereby keeping the transaction figures (after the reversal) unchanged at the original status, as if you had not posted the reversed document and its subsequent reversal.

In periodic processing, you will be introduced to the integrated business planning using SAP BPC for SAP S/4HANA. You, in closing operations, will learn about the intercompany reconciliation and the settings required to set that up for reconciliation of group receivables/payables (cross-system). You will, then, learn that to complete creation of financial statements, you need to perform foreign currency valuation; in the process, you will learn about valuation methods, valuation areas and the associated settings including how to activate delta logic, besides making the settings for automatic posting of foreign currency valuation. You will, further, learn that the system makes use of the 'reclassify' program, in closing operations, in analysing the GR/IR clearing account and thereby making the required adjustments. In 'allocation', you will understand that the allocation rules help you to determine how amounts and quantities should be allocated from the sender (object) to the receiver (object); you will, then, make the required configuration settings to make use of allocation in closing operations in SAP G/L Accounting. Finally, in closing operations, you will learn about the balance carry forward functionality which involves carrying forward the account balances into the new fiscal year; you will learn that to carry forward the account balances, you will use two separate programs: for G/L accounts, you will use program SAPFGVTR and for the customer / vendor accounts, you will use the program SAPF010.

You will, then, see what needs to be done to prepare the system to become 'productive' with SAP G/L Accounting; you will see, in detail, the settings required in new SAP implementations as well as existing SAP installations from which you will migrate to new SAP S/4HANA system.

Finally, in FI-G/L information system, you will learn about the settings that you can make to enhance the existing reports (both conventional as well as drilldown reports), besides creating your own reports. You will, also, learn about the Report Painter / Report Writer reports.

With this preamble, let us move on to the case studies in the next Chapter. These case studies will provide you with the required context for FI configuration discussed over various Chapters, from Chapter 10.

Case Study

You will come across two case studies in this book:
- Project Dolphin
- Project Starfish

The *Project Dolphin* is the main case study, that will cover most of the configuration in this book and will relate to BESTM Corporate. The *Project Starfish* relates to the configuration of SAP Contract Accounts Receivable and Payable (SAP FICA).

Let us discuss each of the projects in the Sections below:

Project Dolphin

BEST Machinery, also known as BESTM group, is the corporate group having companies operating out of both United States of America (USA) and India, among other countries. The case study is, however, limited to the operations in USA and India. BESTM group has three companies namely, BESTM Agro, BESTM Construction and BESTM Drives. All the three companies are operating out of USA from the same address as that of the corporate group at Glen Ridge, New Jersey:

- ✓ BESTM Agro is the flagship company and is made up of four company codes – two in USA and two in India. This company, through its various legal entities, is in the business of manufacturing, supplying and servicing tractors for agricultural and other uses, agricultural implements, lawn & garden mowers, and equipments required by the forestry industry.
- ✓ BESTM Construction manufactures and services all kinds of trucks and heavy machinery used in the construction industry like dump trucks, track & crawler loaders, excavators, dozers etc. It has two company codes both of which are operating out of USA.
- ✓ BESTM Drives is in the business of making and servicing industrial diesel engines including diesel generators, and drivetrain related equipments like transmissions, axles, gear drives etc. This company is comprising of two USA-based company codes.

BESTM group had been using a variety of software applications, built and bought over a period of years, to meet all their business requirements. Because of a plethora of applications, which were often different between USA and India, the corporate was finding it difficult to integrate the information that hampered their decision making. Calling for a lot of manual interventions and time-consuming reconciliations, they were finding it hard to close their books in time. Also, there were lot of redundancies and duplicity as the applications were not fully integrated. Hence, the corporate group was thinking of to go in for an ERP that would overcome all these shortcomings, and they wanted to bring in the latest in ERP so that they would have an enterprise solution that would not only be state-of-the-art, but also insulate them from becoming obsolete in the near future. Accordingly, the management had taken decision to implement the SAP S/4HANA suite of applications, and it was decided to deploy the application on-premise.

BESTM decided to partner with a leading IT firm to manage the implementation and the transition to SAP S/4HANA. The implementation was code named as *'Project Dolphin'*. The project team had several discussions and workshops with the BESTM management at various levels, and what you see in the following pages is the outcome of those discussions / workshops.

The project team will define three *companies* in SAP, as shown in Table 0.1:

Company	Company ID	Country	Currency
BESTM Agro	B1000	USA	USD
BESTM Construction	B2000	USA	USD
BESTM Drives	B3000	USA	USD

Table 0:1 BESTM - Companies

BESTM Agro company has the following legal entities (company codes) operating out of USA:
1. BESTM Farm Machinery
2. BESTM Garden & Forestry Equipments

BESTM Agro also operates in India through the following company codes:
1. BESTM Farm Machinery
2. BESTM Garden & Forestry Equipments

BESTM Construction company is made up of the following legal units functioning out of USA:
1. BESTM Trucks
2. BESTM Other Construction Equipments

BESTM Drives manages the following legal units:
1. BESTM Drives
2. BESTM Engines

All the *company codes*, except the ones in India, will have USD as their company code currency; the ones in India will have INR as the company code currency. All the company codes will use English as the official language. Each of these company codes will have 4-digit numerical identifier as indicated in the Table 0.2.

Company Code	Company Code ID	Country	Currency
BESTM Farm Machinery	1110	USA	USD
BESTM Garden & Forestry Equipments	1120	USA	USD
BESTM Farm Machinery	1210	India	INR
BESTM Garden & Forestry Equipments	1220	India	INR
BESTM Trucks	2100	USA	USD
BESTM Other Construction Equipments	2200	USA	USD
BESTM Drives	3100	USA	USD
BESTM Engines	3200	USA	USD

Table 0:2 BESTM - Company Codes, Country and Currency

There will be a total of four *credit control areas*: one each for the companies B2000 (BESTM Construction) and B3000 (BESTM Drives), and two credit control areas for company B1000 (BESTM Agro). These credit control areas will be denoted by a 4-character numeric identifier. The details of credit control area, currency etc will be as shown in Table 0.3

Company	Company Code	Credit Control Area (CCA)	CCA Currency	Default Credit Limit
B1000	1110	1100	USD	10,000
	1120			
	1210	1200	INR	700,000
	1220			
B2000	2100	2000	USD	20,000
	2200			
B3000	3100	3000	USD	30,000
	3200			

Table 0:3 BESTM – Credit Control Areas

Since it has been decided to default some of the credit control data while creating the customer master records in each of the company codes, a default credit limit has been mentioned per credit control area as denoted in the table above. BESTM wants the users not to be allowed to change the default credit control area during document posting.

BESTM group requires several *business areas* cutting across company codes (Table 0.4) to report and monitor the operations of different operational areas like agri. tractor business, agri. equipments, after-sales services, garden equipments etc.

Business Area	Business Area Identifier
Agri Tractor Business	ATRA
Agri Equipments	AEQP
After-sales Service	ASER
Garden Equipments	GEQP
Forestry Equipments	FEQP
Construction Machinery	CONM
Drives & Engines	DREN
Military Sales	MILI

Table 0:4 BESTM – Business Areas

BESTM group plans to create their own *functional areas* with easy-to-remember IDs. The project team shall copy the SAP supplied functional areas into the new ones, like BM20 (Production), BM25 (Consulting/Services), BM30 (Sales & Distribution) and so on. BESTM wants the project team to configure the system to derive the functional areas automatically.

BESTM requires the following four FM (Financial Management) areas:
- BF11: FM area for USA-based company codes of BESTM Agro
- BF12: FM area for India-based company codes of BESTM Agro
- BF21: FM area for USA-based company codes of BESTM
- BF31: FM area for USA-based company codes of BESTM Drives

BESTM requires the following business segments to be defined for segment reporting. BESTM wants to have a 10-character alpha-numeric ID segments, with the first three indicating the company code (say, B11/B12/B13 for company B1000, B21/B22 for company 2000 and so on), and the last seven characters, a meaningful abbreviation of the segment description.

- B11FMTRACT   Farm Tractors
- B12HARCOMB   Harvester Combines
- B12FMIMPLE   Farm Implements
- B12FORESTY   Forestry Equipments
- B13LANTRAC   Lawn Tractors
- B13LANMOWR   Lawn Mowers
- B13GRDNUTL   Garden Utility Vehicles
- B13GOLFSPR   Golf and Sports Equipments
- B21LODRDOZ   Loaders and Dozers
- B22EXCAVAT   Excavators and other Construction Equipments
- B31DRVTRAN   Drivetrain Components
- B32GENERAT   Generators
- B33INDSENGN   Industrial Diesel Engines
- B33MARENGN   Marine Engines

BESTM group has decided to have three controlling areas, BESTM Agro (B1000), BESTM Construction (B2000) and BESTM Drives (B3000) with USD as CO area currency. They will need to be denoted as B100, B200 and B300 respectively.

BESTM group has indicated that they need profit centers, defined in such a way, to represent the actual internal management as in Table 0.5:

Controlling Area	Profit Center Group	Profit Center
B100	Tractors	Farm Tractors
		Lawn Tractors
		Speciality Tractors
	Farm Equipments	Cultivators & Planters
		Harvesters
		Seeding / Fertilizing Equipments
		Sprayers & Liquid Systems
	Garden Equipments	Lawn Movers
		Garden Utility Vehicles
	Others	Misc. Farm / Garden Equipments
		Forest Machinery
		Others (B100)
B200	Light Machinery	Compact Machines
		Building Equipments
	Heavy Machinery	Heavy Equipments
		Road Machinery
		Mining Equipments
	Others	Miscellaneous Construction Machinery
		Others (B200)
B300	Drives	Gear Drives
		Pump Drives
		Transmissions
	Engines	Industrial Engines
		Commercial Marine Engines
		Pleasure Marine Engines
	Generators	Stationary Generators
		Portable Generators
	Others	Military Solutions
		Others (B300)

Table 0:5 BESTM – Profit Centers / Profit Center Groups

Looking at the SAP-supplied transaction types in the system, the Dolphin Project team has decided not to add any new transaction type for consolidation for BESTM. They have also decided not to add any new coding fields in the system. This has been finalised after a thorough study of the SAP defined standard coding fields.

The project team has decided to use a single field status variant (FSV), B100, in all the company codes of BESTM. They have further recommended that (a) 'Business Area' and 'Functional Area' fields to be set as 'required' for data entry, and (b) 'Payment Reference' field as 'optional entry' field.

The team has recommended to use different ledgers to meet the different statutory requirements of the company codes: (1) BESTM group of companies will use the SAP supplied standard ledger 0L as their leading ledger and that will meet the International Accounting Standards (IAS), (2) US-based company codes will use a non-leading ledger (BU) to meet the local accounting requirements (US GAAP) and (3) India-based company codes will use another leading ledger (BI) to meet India's legal reporting (Ind-AS). BESTM management is of the opinion that the project team combines the leading ledger (0L) and the non-leading ledger (BU) into a ledger group called B1 as the accounting principles of IAS (0L) and US GAAP (BU) are the same as there will almost be identical postings to both of these accounting principles.

BESTM wants to leverage the 'extension edger' functionality of SAP S/4HANA. Accordingly, the project team has proposed to define four extension ledgers: one for general purpose, the other for simulation, the third for prediction & commitment and the fourth for valuation purposes accounting for valuation differences. In all the cases, BESTM wants manual postings.

BESTM does not want to create new fiscal year variants (FYVs), but shall use the SAP supplied ones. Accordingly, FYV 'K4' will be used for all the US-based company codes and V3 will be used by India-based company codes. To simplify opening and closing of posting periods in the system without much complications, it has been decided to define separate posting period variant (PPV) per company code.

There will be two new charts of accounts defined in the system, BEUS for US-based company codes and BEIN for India-based company codes. The respective Financial Statement Version (FSV) will also be created in the same name as that of the chart of accounts. For all the US-based company codes, both the operative and country chart of accounts will be the same: BEUS. In the case of India-based company codes, the operative chart of accounts will be BEUS and the country chart of accounts will be BEIN. A suitable document entry screen variant that facilitates country-specific processing of withholding tax needs to be used in all the US-based company codes.

If there is a difference in currency translation due to exchange rate fluctuations during transaction posting, then, a maximum of 10% has to be allowed as the permitted deviation.

However, this will not be applicable to the tax postings as all the tax items have to be translated using the exchange rate from the document header. All the US-based company codes will use a single variant as the workflow variant. It has been decided to allow negative postings, thereby avoiding inflated trial balance.

BESTM wants to activate *Cost of Sales* (CoS) *accounting*, in all the company codes, to understand the outflow of economic resources engaged in making the company's revenue. It has also been decided that suitable configuration to be made to enable drawing up of financial statements per business area. Further, it has been requested that the system should clear the foreign currency open items into local currency using the prevailing exchange rate instead of using the original exchange rate; any gain/loss arising out of this, needs to be posted to the designated G/L accounts.

BESTM does not want the system to propose fiscal year during document change or document display functions, as it expects all the company codes to work with year-independent document numbers. However, the current date can be defaulted to as the 'value date' while entering the line items in a document.

Since USA makes use of the jurisdiction codes for tax calculation, BESTM wants the tax base to remain at the jurisdiction code level, for all the US-based company codes. For the company codes in India, the tax base has to be configured as the net of discount of the invoice amount.

BESTM does not want to define any new document type, and has decided to use the standard ones. It has also been decided to use the same document type for document reversals. To restrict the access to the closing operations, BESTM wants to make use of user authorization through document type CL. To make cross-verification easier, the project team has decided to make the 'Reference' field mandatory for data input for invoice postings and credit memos. There will be no change in the default document type / posting key for the common transactions. The posting date = system date, when posting a parked document.

BESTM does not want to define any new posting keys in the system. However, BESTM has requested to configure the posting keys in such a way that (a) 'Invoice Reference' to be made mandatory for all payment transactions, (b) 'Payment Reference' is optional for document reversals and (c) a valid reason to be mandatory for all payment difference postings.

BESTM wants numerical number ranges for all the document types, in all the company codes. The project team has decided to define a number range 91 (9100000000 to 9199999999) for document type CL in non-leading ledgers. All the number ranges are to have a validity of 9,999 years, so as to overcome any additional configurations every year.

BESTM management has indicated that it requires two additional tolerance groups, besides the null tolerance group, to be configured in the system: the tolerance group TGUS will be for all the US-based company codes, and TGIN for the India-based company codes. It is further stipulated that these special tolerance groups will have only a handful of employees assigned, in each company code, to handle special situations and high-value customers / vendors, as these additional groups will have liberal tolerances in comparison to the null group.

All the employees who are allocated to the tolerance group TGUS will be allowed to post accounting documents of maximum value USD 999,999,999 per document, with a limit of USD 99,999,999 per open item. However, they can process cash discounts at 5% per line item, with the system allowing a maximum payment difference of 3%, subject to an absolute maximum of USD 500. The cash discount adjustment amount will be USD 100.

As already indicated, the tolerance group TGIN will be for the two India-based company codes (1210 and 1220). The select employees who are part of this group will be allowed to post accounting documents of maximum value INR 999,999,999 per document with a limit of INR 99,999,999 per open item. However, they can process cash discounts at 5% per line item, with the system allowing a maximum payment difference of 3%, subject to an absolute maximum of INR 5,000. The cash discount adjustment amount will be INR 1,000.

The null tolerance group will be applicable for all the employees, and will be the default tolerance group for all the company codes of BESTM, both in USA and India:

- ✓ For all the US-based company codes, this null tolerance group will enable posting of accounting documents with values not exceeding USD 999,000 per document with a limit of USD 99,000 per open item. The maximum cash discount allowed is 2% per line item, and the maximum payment difference is 1%, with an amount cap of USD 50. The cash discount adjustment limit has to be set at USD 5.
- ✓ In the case of India-based company codes, the null group enables posting of accounting documents of value up to INR 1,500,000 per document with the line item limit of INR 1,000,000. The maximum cash discount allowed will be 2% per line item, with the maximum allowed payment difference of 1% with an amount cap of INR 1,000. The cash discount adjustment limit will be at INR 100.

BESTM wanted to know if they can go in for the summarization functionality of SAP. However, the project team, after careful consideration of the current and future data volume for each of the company codes, has advised the management that this functionality will be useful only in the case of exceptionally large volume of data, as in the case of – for example – companies operating in telecommunications, and not for BESTM entities.

BESTM wants to implement the following changes (Table 0.6) to the standard messages:

Message description	Changes to be made for	
	Online processing	Batch input processing
Amount is zero - line item will be ignored	Warning (W)	Switch off message (-)
Check whether document has already been entered under number & & &	Warning (W)	Error (E)
Vendor is subject to withholding tax	Note in window (I)	Switch off message (-)
Terms of payment changed; Check	Warning (W)	Warning (W)

Table 0:6 BESTM – Standard Messages and Changes Required for BESTM

BESTM has requested to explore the possibility of using validation rules for preventing posting of documents, based on certain pre-defined account assignment combinations. For example, they have indicated that for the cost center 11101101 and G/L account 11001099 combination, the validation rule set in the system should reject the posting. Similar combinations are to be built in for various cost center-G/L account combinations, as decided by the FI Manager of various company codes for BESTM. This is to prevent posting with incorrect account assignment combinations.

To enable auditing and other purposes, BESTM corporate has decided that the documents / accounts should not be archived until they cross a minimum life of 1000 days (about 3 years), as it was felt that SAP's default of 9,999 days may put pressure on system performance. However, it was clarified, that even after archiving, the documents / accounts need to be fetched faster from respective archives, at least, for another year (365 days).

The project management team has recommended to make use of standard correspondence types supplied by SAP. Accordingly, it has been decided not to create any new correspondence type except a few like SAP01, SAP06 and SAP08 which will be copied into new correspondence types namely YB01, YB06 and YB08 for use in cross-company code correspondence, for company codes 2100 and 2200. Also, the project team has recommended using standard print programs associated with the correspondence types, in all the company codes of BESTM but use different variants to meet individual company code's reporting requirements. To make use of 'cross-company code correspondence' functionality in respect of company codes 2100 and 2200, the company code 2100 needs to be designated as the 'correspondence company code' that will manage the correspondence for company code 2200 as well.

The BESTM management has recommended to make use of the standard settings in SAP for tax calculation and posting, for both India and USA. As regards USA, the team has planned to take care of the jurisdiction requirement of taxation, by interfacing with the external tax system, 'Vertex'. The project team will properly structure the tax jurisdiction code identification in the SAP system to make it fully compatible with Vertex. The project team, accordingly, indicated that the tax on sales and purchases, for all the US-based company codes, is to be calculated at the line item level. Any decision to tax a particular transaction has to come from Vertex. As the tax calculation is from this external tax application, no user is required to enter the tax amount in SAP system. If that is not the case, the system needs to issue a warning, if the tax amount entered by the user is different from the amount calculated automatically in Vertex. No new tax code will be defined by the project team. The posting date will be the baseline date, for tax calculation. The tax amounts should be translated using the exchange rate of the tax base amounts.

The BESTM management has requested the project team to complete the required configurations settings for *extended withholding tax* (EWT) in the system. They have requested the project team to make use of the standard (a) withholding tax keys, (b) reasons for exemptions and (c) recipient types in the system for EWT. The project team, per instructions from BESTM management, has decided to configure the message control to be valid for all users; no separate configuration will be done for individual users. For online transactions, the project team will configure message control in such a way to enable the system to issue warning messages, yet allowing users to correct errors, if any. For batch input processing, the project team will make use of standard message control settings of SAP, for all the message numbers relevant for withholding tax processing.

The Dolphin project team has decided to define the following withholding tax types to support invoice posting:

- 42: 1042 Compensation
- FW: 1099 Federal Withholding Tax
- IN: 1099 Independent Contractor Status
- SW: 1099 State Withholding Tax
- EW: Exempted from WT

BESTM has instructed the project team to make it possible to manually enter the withholding base amount / tax amount, to provide some flexibility in transaction posting. However, these fields should not be made as 'required' in the relevant field status settings, so as not to hold up a transaction. The management also indicated that the minimum / maximum amount settings to be done at the tax code level and not at the tax type level.

BESTM management has informed the project team to define the required withholding tax types for payment postings relating to government payments (1099-G). Accordingly, the project team has decided to define two withholding tax types for payment posting: GX - 1099G reporting excluding WT and GN - 1099G reporting including WT. Besides, BESTM made it clear to the project team that all the company codes will be using the exchange rate of payment, when translating the withholding tax from foreign currency to a local currency.

BESTM has indicated to the project team to make use of standard default withholding tax codes relating to 1099-MISC reporting. If any additional tax codes (to comply with 1099-G, 1099-INT etc) are required, BESTM suggested that the project team creates them in accordance with the reporting requirements in USA, to cover both the federal and state provisions.

The Dolphin project team has recommended to BESTM management to have separate G/L accounts (from 21613000 to 21614000), differentiated by withholding tax types. However, they also indicated that it may not be required to have these accounts separated according to the tax codes for all the third-party transactions. It has also been recommended to have a single account (21603000) for self-withholding tax. No explicit withholding tax certificate numbering is required for withholding tax reporting in USA as the requirement is fulfilled through TIN, EIN, and SSN numbers.

The project team has been instructed by the BESTM management to configure only one retained earnings account for each of the company codes. Accordingly, the G/L account 33000000 has been designated as the retained earnings account (in the chart of accounts area) of the operative chart of accounts BEUS.

The project team has suggested to the BESTM management to make use of sample accounts in creating some of the G/L account master records, to facilitate quicker and easier master data creation. Accordingly, it has been agreed to use sample accounts, in all the company codes, to create G/L account master records for bank accounts. The project team will create the required data transfer rules. Two sample rule types (or sample rule variants) will be created; one for the US-based company codes, and the other for Indian based company codes.

For the rule type for US-based company codes, following data transfer rules will be applicable:

- ✓ The FSG 'YB32' (bank accounts with obligatory value / due dates) set in the sample account, will be transferred to the newly created G/L account but the users will not be able to change the values in the newly created G/L accounts. So also, with the field 'Valuation Group'. However, the fields 'Exchange Rate Difference Key', 'Account Currency', 'Sort Key' and 'House Bank' will be configured in such a way that the non-blank value in the sample account will be transferred and can be overwritten, after transfer to the new G/L account master record that is being created.

For the rule type for all the Indian-based company codes, the above data transfer rules will also apply, except that the reconciliation account ('Recon. Account for Account Type') will be transferred from the sample account which can be changed, if required, after the transfer.

BESTM wants the project team to have thorough validation of all the G/L accounts of the chart of accounts BEUS, to ensure that (a) the accounts have been properly identified as B/S or P&L type, (b) the correct functional area has been assigned to them and (c) the account groups are correct for each of the accounts. Also, the short / long texts need to be properly modified; for example: instead of 'Bank1 Main Account', it should be changed to 'BoA Main Account'. Bank 2 should be renamed as 'Chase', Bank 3 as 'Citi', Bank 4 as 'PNC' and so on. BESTM requires a similar verification be done, in the company code area data as well, to ensure that the accounts have been correctly identified for open item management, line item display, balance in local currency etc.

BESTM wants to make use of document splitting functionality for all the company codes, both in US and India. Accordingly, the project team has suggested the following, which was later agreed upon with the BESTM management:

- ✓ The configuration will make use of SAP's default and standard document splitting method 0000000012; no new method will be defined. Also, no new item categories, document types, business transactions, and business transaction types will be defined as the project feels that the standard offerings from SAP will be enough to meet all the document splitting requirements of BESTM company codes. The 'Business Area', 'Profit Center' and the 'Segment' will be used as the document splitting characteristics, with a zero-balance setting. Additionally, the team will make appropriate settings for 'Segment', as BESTM requires a complete balance sheet, per segment, for which inaccuracies due to non-assigned postings cannot be tolerated. The characteristics 'Order', 'Cost Center' and 'WBS Element' need to be used as the document splitting characteristics for CO. The cash discount that is applied in the payment of an asset-relevant invoice should be capitalized to the asset.

The BESTM Corporate wants to take care of cross-company code transactions as the company code 1110 will be the central purchasing organization for all the company codes in US. Besides, the company code 1120 will make sales of their products through company code 1110 which will act as the merchandiser. A similar scenario was envisaged for India-based company codes, as well, with regard to the central purchasing by the company code 1210.

The Dolphin Project team has recommended, to the BESTM management, that there is no need to define any new clearing procedures. They also recommended not to change any of the default posting keys for these procedures, as tinkering with the standard posting keys may result in system-wide unforeseen discrepancies.

The project team suggested using a single set of accounts, to take care of automatic posting of the exchange rate differences realized in clearing open items: for loss it will be 72010000, and for the gains it will be 72510000. For valuation adjustments, the loss will be posted to 72040000 and the gains to 72540000; B/S adjustments will go to the G/L account 11001099.

The Dolphin Project team has recommended not to go for any additional clearing grouping criteria. The BESTM management, after some discussion with the project team, requested to configure four more user-criteria for grouping clearing items for automatic clearing, for more flexibility: 'Assignment Number', 'Business Area', 'Trading Partner' and 'Contract Number' for customer and vendor, and 'Segment' (in the place of 'Contract Number') for G/L accounts. The project team has suggested to configure two separate G/L accounts for posting of clearing differences: G/L account 52080000 will be configured for debits and 52580000 for credits.

The project team has been advised by the BESTM management to configure three G/L tolerance groups: a null tolerance group and two special tolerance groups:

a) The *null tolerance group* will be applicable for all employees, and will be the default tolerance group for all the company codes of BESTM, both in USA and India. This will have a tolerance of USD 1 (in absolute terms), with 0.5% as the limit for US-based company codes; the absolute limit will be INR 10 and the percentage limit will be the same at 0.5%, for Indian company codes.

Besides the null tolerance group, there will be two more special tolerance groups defined in the system: one for US-based company codes, and the other for India-based company codes:

b) BGLU: This will be for the selected employees of US-based company codes allowing a tolerance of USD 10, in absolute terms, both for debit and credit transactions; in percentage terms the limit will be 1%.

c) BGLI: This will be for the India-based company codes; the percentage will be the same at 1%, but the absolute amount in INR will be 100.

In all the three tolerance groups, lower of the absolute amount or percentage will apply.

BESTM has decided to use two different interest indicators, besides the standard. The new interest indicators will be used for calculating account balance interest on staff loan accounts; one indicator for US-based company codes and the other for India-based company codes.

BESTM management wants the two new interest indicators with the details as under:

✓ The interest calculation frequency is to be set at six months for the staff loans, for both India and USA. The Gregorian calendar needs to be used for interest calculations. The interest settlement should be configured to be on the last day of the month. The interest needs to be charged on a graduated scale for all the staff loan accounts, for US-based company codes, at 2% interest up to $10,000; 3% up to $25,000; and 4% in excess of $25,000; for India, the corresponding figures will be: 8% for loans up to INR 200,000, 9% up to INR 500,000 and 10.5% for above INR 500,000. The interest will have to be settled when the interest amount calculated is in excess of $10 and INR 100, respectively for US and India-based company codes. The interest needs to be paid within 10 days of interest posting to the respective accounts. The interest posting is to be made to the appropriate G/L accounts, one for interest paid (71100000) and another for interest received (70100000). The system should use the document type SA for interest posting.

In addition to allowing negative postings in all the company codes of BESTM, the project team has been asked to configure suitable 'document reversal reasons' in the system, to handle the reversal transactions. It has been clarified to the team that:

- If reversal is happening in the current period, then, the system should allow negative posting; but, should not allow to change posting date (of the document to be reversed).
- If reversal is to happen in a closed period, then, following conditions should be met:
  - Negative postings can be allowed, but without altering the posting date (of the document to be reversed).
  - Negative postings cannot be allowed, but the posting date (of the document to be reversed) can be altered.

BESTM Corporate wants to have single valuation method that will be used worldwide. However, there needs to be different valuation areas to take care of the different valuation needs and requirements of each of the accounting principles. Besides, the corporate also wants to make use of the 'delta logic' functionality in foreign currency valuation to ensure that the system does not execute any reversal postings, for the valuation postings in the subsequent period. Besides the default account assignment fields for foreign currency valuation, BESTM wants to include 'Functional Area' and 'Cost Center' as the additional account assignments to have more flexibility.

BESTM management has indicated to the project team that they want to set up appropriate adjustment accounts to post the results of P&L and B/S adjustments, so as to assign line items to specific account assignment objects like 'Business Area', 'Profit Center' etc. This is to avoid posting the adjustment line items to the original accounts.

In closing, for regrouping receivables and payables, BESM wants the configuration team to stick to the SAP's standard sort method. The team has been tasked to assign the suitable G/L accounts as adjustment accounts for this default sort method.

The BESTM management has indicated that they want additional account assignments during carryforward, in the case of B/S accounts, on 'Order Number' and 'Account Type', besides the standard account assignments in the system. In the case of P&L accounts, BESTM does not want to have any additional account assignments than that of the standard settings.

BESTM management has asked the Dolphin project manager to create a fairly large number of account groups like sold-to-party (0001), goods recipient (0002), payer (0003), bill to party (0004), one-time accounts OTA (0099) and consumer (0170). Besides, additional account groups are to be created, to suitably number the customer accounts that are transferred from the external system are also be created.

The project team has recommended to the BESTM management, to control the field status through accounts groups, for both customers and vendors. Accordingly, no new screen layout settings are to be defined for the company codes (of BESTM) or for transactions. As BESTM wants its company codes to participate in 'factoring', the project team has decided to activate A/R pledging for each of the company codes, both in USA and India. Also, the field 'Accts recble pledging ind.' is to be set as an 'optional' field in the customer account group and the company code (customers) screen layout.

BESTM requested the project team create six number ranges from B1 to B5, and B9, for both customers and vendors, with the specifications that B5 should be used for one-time accounts (OTA) and B9 for external numbering to accommodate the customer / vendor accounts transferred from the external systems.

BESTM wants the project team to manage 'Payment Terms', 'Alternate Payer' and 'House Bank' as the sensitive fields. Accordingly, these fields need to be brought under dual control to avoid any misuse.

BESTM management has indicated that they want to include additional fields like 'Alternative Payer', 'House Bank', 'Payment Terms', 'Reconciliation Account', 'Customer Classification', 'Payment Block' and 'Credit Control Area' in logging the changes made by users while changing the customer master records. However, they have indicated that they do not want to exercise restricting the changes to these fields as such action for some of the fields ('Alternative Payer', 'House Bank' and 'Payment Terms') are better handled by dual control of sensitive fields.

The project team has recommended to the BESTM corporate to stick to the line item display using the ABAP List View (ALV). Also, they have suggested not to define additional fields for customer / vendor line item display, as that may result in performance issues. Besides, they are also of the view that no additional settings would be required than the default ones, for processing open items.

BESTM management has asked the Dolphin project manager to create elaborate account groups like vendor (0001), goods supplier (0002), alternate payer (0003), invoice presented by (0004), forwarding agent (0005), special vendor (0010) and one-time vendors (0099) besides separate account groups to take care of vendor accounts that are transferred from the external system.

BESTM wants to have a strict control of unauthorized changes to some of the important fields in vendor master records. Accordingly, they wanted to bring 'Alternative Payee', 'Payment Block', Bank Account', 'Account with Vendor' and 'Tolerance Group' fields under dual control by denoting them as 'sensitive' fields. Only the supervisor or manager, will have the required authorization to confirm or reject the changes made to these sensitive fields.

BESTM management wants to include additional fields like 'Alternative Payee', 'House Bank', 'Reconciliation Account', 'ABC Indicator', 'Payment Block' and 'Interest Indicator' in logging the changes made by users, while changing the vendor master records. However, they have indicated that they do not want to exercise restricting the changes to these fields as such action for some of the fields ('Alternative Payee', 'House Bank' etc) are better handled by dual control. BESTM wants to go with default settings for parking document entry screens.

BESTM wants to have separate release approval groups, for customers / vendors, who have been classified into A, B and C buckets, for parking documents. They want to include fields like 'House Bank', 'Tolerance Group', 'Payment Terms', 'Payment Method', 'Alternative Payer' and 'Payment Block' to be checked by the system. If any changes are found for these fields, then, the system should cancel the document release. For vendors, the fields will include 'Alternate Payee', 'Interest Indicator', 'House Bank' and 'Payment Block'.

BESTM wants to have different set of payment terms for customers and vendors so that if there is a change that needs to be done for either customer or vendor, then, that can be carried out without affecting the other. However, there will a single payment term that will apply for both customers and vendors when the due date is immediate.

- For customers, the three payment terms will cover a credit period of 90 / 60 / 30 days:
  1) BC90: 15 Days 3%, 45/2%, 90 Net (there will be a discount of 3% if paid within 15 days, 2% discount for payment within 45 days, and no discount beyond that).
  2) BC60: 15 Days 3%, 30/2%, 60 Net.
  3) BC30: 15 Days 4%, 30 Net.
- Similar payment terms will be configured for vendors, but the key will be changed to BV90, BV60 etc.
- A common payment term B001 will also be configured for immediate payment without any discount, and this can be used for both customers and vendors.
- For instalment payments, BESTM wants the system to be configured with the payment terms key, BINS. The number of instalments will be three, with the first instalment at 20%, second at 30% and the third being 50%. All the instalments need to be paid within a maximum of 30 days, with 4% discount for early birds but within 15days.
- BESTM will be using default payment block reasons and will not require anything new.

BESTM wants to:

- Have a single G/L account (70040000) to manage all cash discounts received.
- Capture the difference between the originally calculated cash discount and the actual cash discount received, and post that difference, as an expense (discount lost) to a single G/L account (71040000).
- Use G/L account 44000000 for accounting overpayments / underpayments.
- Configure G/L accounts 72020000 and 72520000 for currency rounding off during clearing.
- Use G/L accounts 72010000 and 72510000, to handle to handle payment differences (gain/ loss), when working with alternative currencies for payment.
- Use G/L account 71000000 to take care of posting of vendor bank charges.
- Enable posting of translation gain/loss for clearing open items in foreign currency, in all the company codes both US-based and India-based.

BESTM does not want to propose a default blocking key via payment terms, for postings customer / vendor accounts.

BESTM wants to have two tolerance groups: a strict tolerance group (also known as 'null tolerance group') that will be for most the vendors and a liberal one that will be applied to specific vendors.

For all the US-based company codes:

- The 'null tolerance group' which will be the default, when a vendor is not assigned with a specific tolerance group. For this tolerance group, the permitted payment difference will be $50 for gains (1%) and $10 for losses (0.5%), with a maximum adjustment cash discount being $5. For automatic write-off of payment differences, the amount and percent values will be $5 and 0.25% respectively, both for revenue and expense.
- For the specific tolerance group, which will be termed as BEU1, the corresponding permitted payment difference is $500 for gains (2%) and $250 for losses (1%). The maximum cash discount that can be adjusted, will be $50. The amount and percentage values for automatic write-off of payment differences (revenue or expense) will be $25 and 0.5% respectively.

For all the India-based company codes the tolerance amount, tolerance percentage, and the cash discount amount that can be adjusted, the amount and percentage for automatic write-off of payment differences will be the same as that of US company codes but the amount will be in INR. The corresponding tolerance group will be termed as BEI1.

The project team has suggested to create new reason codes to cover situations like cash discount period exceeded, cash discount rate not kept to, cash discount deducted for net terms, discount period exceeded & rate incorrect, calculation error on customer side, debit paid twice, credit memo paid instead of reduction, credit memo reduced twice etc.

BESTM has indicated that the company code 1110 will need to be configured in such a way the it can carry out manual payments and other clearing procedures on behalf of company code 1120. Similarly, the cross-company code manual payments need to be enabled for the pair of company codes as shown in Table 0.7. Accordingly, the project team has decided to configure the settings to cover the clearing procedures like incoming payment, outgoing payment, credit memo and transfer posting with clearing.

Paying Company Code	Payments for
2100	2200
3100	3200
1210	1220

Table 0:7 Cross-Company Code Pairing for Manual Payments

BESTM suggested to the project team to configure 'create manual payment' application to cover both the scenarios of 'direct payment without an invoice' and 'payment of vendor open line items', with the system posting both the payment and document.

All the company codes in USA will have their primary accounts with Bank of America (BOFA), Citi Bank (CITIU) and Chase Manhattan (CHASU) and they will accordingly be designated as the house banks. In India, the company codes will have accounts with State Bank of India (SBIIN), HDFC bank (HDFCI) and ICICI bank (ICICI). Each bank account, within a house bank, will be assigned to a G/L account and there can be multiple bank accounts in a single house bank. BESTM has indicated to the project team to differentiate foreign currency account numbers by using a separate G/L account, per currency for bill discounting.

BESTM wants to designate the company code 1110 as the paying company code for themselves, and also for 1120. Similarly, company code 2100 will be the paying company code for 2200, and 3100 will be the paying company code for 3200. Similar arrangements will be made for India based company codes as well wherein the company code 1210 will pay for 1220. BESTM Corporate wants to continue with their existing practice of making payments to their vendors, six days after the invoices are due. BESTM has requested the project team to configure the payment program to enable payments per 'Business Area', but the project team suggested not to do that, instead suggested grouping of payments in the normal way by 'Currency', 'Payment Method', 'House Bank' etc, so as to have more flexibility; BESTM, after a long deliberation, has accepted to this idea and does not, now, require payment grouping per 'Business Area'. However, BESTM has requested that payment should cover the special G/L transactions like downpayments (including down payment requests), security deposits, guarantee etc, for both customers and vendors. Additionally, BESTM wants to ensure that maximum cash discount is always taken, when paying vendor invoices automatically.

BESTM wants to avoid large numbers of small payments. Accordingly, they need the system to be configured in such a way, that there will not be any automatic payment processing, including the debit memos, if the payment amount < $25 for all the US-based company codes and < INR 500 for company codes 1210 and 1220, for all incoming and outgoing payments. In all, wherein the payments proposed are less than these minimum, the system will accumulate them till the limit is crossed, and then pay as in the normal course. In case of bill of exchange (BoE) payments, BESTM wants the system to be configured to create one BoE per invoice.

BESTM wants does not want to define any new payment method. Instead, they have indicated that, they will go ahead using the default payment methods that have been configured in the standard system, for both USA and India.

As regards payments through automatic payment program, BESTM wants to have the system configured to reflect the following:

- All the line items that are due on a particular date, should be grouped and paid in a single payment. If line items are associated with a payment method explicitly, then, the system should pay those items; else, if the payment method is not specified explicitly in the line item, and if the system selects the payment method automatically, then, several items can be paid together. The 'extended individual payment' should be activated to make it possible to include and offset all available credit memos for a payment group. For payment methods like bank transfer, the system should make payments abroad, using the business partners' banks in their respective countries. The system should be able to make payments - for all payment methods - in other currencies, other than the company code currency. BESTM wants bank optimization using their own house banks and business partners' banks so as to optimize international payments.
- As regards payments, if the payment method is check, then, all in-country payments should not be less than $25 (for US-based company codes) and INR 500 for Indian company codes. If the payment is more than $5,000 (or INR 250,000) then, it has to be made through bank transfer or direct debit. For direct debit, bank transfer or card payment, there is no lower limit for payment. In cases of composite payments, BESTM wants the system to split the payment by grouping the invoices, with the appropriate credit memos, for payments exceeding $10,000 in the case of US-based company codes (or INR 500,000 for all the India-based company codes), for all the allowed payment methods, for both domestic and international payments.
- The BESTM Corporate has indicated to the project team that Bank of America will be the primary bank for all the payment methods, followed by Chase Manhattan and Citi

Bank, in that ranking order. It has been envisaged to provide an amount limit of $9,999,999,999 for Bank of America for facilitating automatic payment transactions (outgoing payments). The limit for the other two banks would be $999,999,999, in each case. In the case of incoming payments, there should not be any limit restriction. The value date should be 1 day after, for all the payments through electronic format; however, it would be 3 days after, for all the checks denominated in local currency. For house banks in India, the limits will be the same but denominated in INR.

- The project team has suggested not to go in for any additional search fields for payments (and line item display) as the standard fields are sufficient to be used as the criteria for maintaining proposal run, besides displaying the payment proposal / payment run.

BESTM wants to configure the system to take care of payment through payment cards as well. In the process, it has been outlined, that the system needs to be configured to retain the customer line items in FI department, during transfer of payment card data from SD department. This decision has been taken, consciously, after several deliberations knowing fully well that this will call for more database space; BESTM is ok with this, as the configuration will provide (a) the advantage of displaying the receivables on the debit side and (b) the ability to the department personnel to deal with any settlement problems of the payment cards.

The Dolphin project team has suggested to configure six dunning block reasons in the system: disputed (A), promised to pay (B), clarification required from SD side (C), blocked by legal department (D), other reasons (E) and blocked by invoice verification (R).

The project team has suggested to copy and adapt the SAPScript forms provided by SAP to meet dunning needs of BESTM group of company codes. Accordingly, there will be five forms that will be created anew by copying the standard ones: the form F150_BE_DUNN_01 (without interest) will be copied as ZF150_BE_DUNN_01 and will be used both for the single-level dunning procedure and also for the first dunning level of the 5-level dunning procedure. The standard form F150_BE_DUNN_02 (with interest) will be copied to create the other four levels for the 5-level procedure. Also, separate spool lists will be created by copying the standard LIST1S spool list, and five new spool lists will be created, prefixed with the company code name like 1110-1, 1110-2 etc.

The BESTM management has decided to have two dunning procedures, in each of the countries (USA and India) where the company is operating:

1. A dunning procedure that will be used to remind the VIP business partners, which will be *single level dunning procedure*. This will just be a 'payment reminder' and there will not be any charges / interest associated with this dunning.
2. The *multi-level dunning procedure* will be used for all other business partners. This will have a maximum of 5 dunning levels, with a dunning interval of 7 days. There

needs to be a cushion of three days for dunning levels 2 and 3, and five days for levels 4 and 5. Also, there will be a grace period of five days at the account level. Further, if the due date falls on a holiday, the dunning program should take the next working day as payment due date based on respective country's public calendar. The dunning charges, for the multi-level dunning procedure, will be as in the Table 0.8:

Amount Range	Dunning Level 1 Dunning Charges	Dunning Level 2 Dunning Charges	Dunning Level 3 Dunning Charges (%)	Dunning Level 4 Dunning Charges (%)	Dunning Level 5 Dunning Charges (%)
Up to $5,000	0	$5	0.10	0.15	0.20
$5,001 – $10,000	0	$10	0.15	0.20	0.25
$10,001 - $25,000	0	$10	0.20	0.25	0.30
$25,001 - $50,000	0	$15	0.25	0.30	0.35
$50,001 - $100,000	0	$20	0.30	0.35	0.40
Above $100,000	0	$50	0.35	0.40	0.50

Table 0:8 Dunning Charges for BESTM for US-based Company Codes

Besides the above charges, there will be an overdue interest charges, to be charged on the arrears, at the prevailing rates subject to a minimum of $50 for level 2, $100 for level 3, $250 for level 4 and $500 for level 5. Of course, there will be no interest on arrears for the level 1. The level 5 will be considered as *legal dunning level* and will use legal wording on the dunning notice; a separate legal dunning notice format will be used. BESTM wants the system to consider the interest indicator in the master record of a business partner, and not through the dunning procedure.

The charges and interest amount will be the same for India-based company codes as well, except that the amounts will be in INR.

When printing the dunning notice, the program should display the entire account balance, and should include all the open items, even if the dunning level is at the lowest. BESTM does not want to include any of the Special G/L items in the dunning list. Each company code will dun their business partners separately. However, they can group the overdues of a customer across other company codes.

BESTM has suggested to the project team to configure the item interest calculation in such a way that (a) the system should calculate the interest as and when it becomes due, but on the due date for net payment, (b) the value date should be the baseline date for net payment, (c) there would be a grace period of 5 days for payment without interest, after the receivable payments become due, (d) the system should calculate interest both on debit and credit items, using the respective interest rates and (e) there should not be any interest calculated on items that have been paid before the due date. In case of interest settlement, it has been directed that there should not be any interest settlement, if the interest amount is less than $10 for all US-based company codes, and INR 100 for India-based company codes. It was also suggested that the interest receivables should be created and posted with reference to the invoice for which interest was calculated.

The BESTM management has requested the project team to make use of SAP defined standard scenarios for determining the bank chain. This is because, they have been informed that defining new scenario may result in slow system performance, as secondary indexes have been created for the relevant database tables only for the standard scenarios provided by SAP. Also, that would call for contacting SAP to create the necessary indexes for implementing the new scenario. Hence the decision to go in for standard scenario. In doing so, it was requested to make use of 'Sender Bank Oriented' scenario.

BESTM has requested the project team to ensure creating general bank chains involving three intermediary banks per chain, with the sender's correspondent bank always at the top level (priority1), followed by any intermediary bank, and lastly with the correspondent bank of the recipient. While configuring the bank assignment per bank chain, it needs to be noted that the sender will be one of the company's house bank and the payment should be valid across currencies. The bank chain identifier should be easy to decipher with the company code figuring in that ID, along with a numeric chain identifier at the last 2 positions. For example, a chain ID 'BM1110-1' will indicate that it is the chain #1 belonging to the company code 1110.

The project team has recommended to the BESTM management to make use of the standard account assignment variant for manual processing of bank statements. Accordingly, it has been decided not to define any new variant in the system.

The project team suggested to use the BAI2 as the electronic bank statement (EBS) file format for BESTM group of company codes, as BAI2 is the most widely used standard in USA for EBS. BESTM wants to summarize the line items, in EBS, by 'Value Date' instead of creating payment advice per bank statement item.

The file format to be used, for all BESTM company codes, will be BAI2 for lockbox processing. Additionally, it was required that the configuration should enable (a) G/L account posting (debit bank, credit cash receipt account) with one posting per check to the bank account, (b) the system to execute incoming payments postings to customer accounts, (c) partial payments, if the incoming payment is not sufficient for full clearing and (d) change the customer's master record to include the new bank details, if any.

The Dolphin project team has recommended use of multiple cash journals, in each of the company codes of BESTM, to meet the differing requirements. All cash journals would be in the company code currency, of the respective company codes. Each cash journal would need to be assigned to separate G/L accounts enabling easy reconciliation. There needs to be separate number ranges for the different cash journals. Also, to differentiate incoming and outgoing cash payments, there needs to be different number ranges; this has been necessitated by the fact that SAP, by default, assigns continuous numbering for both incoming and outgoing transactions from a single number range. The project team has also recommended usage of PDF print forms, to print the check lot. Also, it was suggested to print not only the documents that have been posted in FI (G/L), but all the documents saved in the cash journal.

BESTM management has requested to configure the country-specific settings for USA and India, for asset accounting: The low value asset (LVA) cut-off limit should be $5,000 for USA and INR 5,000 for India. Also, it should be configured that the system capitalizes the assets under construction (AuC) without considering the down payments. Besides, it should be ensured that the system posts the gain / loss posting when an asset is retired.

BESTM wants to have two charts of depreciations, one for US and the other for India. As with chart of accounts, these new charts of depreciation will also be named as BEUS and BEIN respectively, for US and India.

The project management team has recommended to create easily identifiable new account determination keys to map to the various types of fixed assets for BESTM group of companies. It has been advised to create two account determinations for LVAs: one for collective management and another for individual management. They have also recommended to create new screen layout rules to customize the field status to suit BESTM requirements.

BESTM management has decided to define as many number ranges as that of asset account determination keys, so as to easily identify an asset just by a number. And, all the asset main numbers will be internal but the asset subnumbers will be external, to help in modeling and grouping the assets. BESTM does not want to have cross-company code number assignment for asset master records. Instead, it requires each company code to supply the number range intervals, for numbering their asset master records.

The project team has recommended to BESTM management to have as many asset classes as that of the asset determination keys. However, instead of creating a separate asset class for goodwill, an asset class in the name of 'intangible assets' will have to be created to cover all intangible assets including the goodwill, patent, copyright etc. For AuC, it should be configured for line item settlement. Except the LVA, all other asset classes should be configured to have the subnumber assigned externally. It has also been indicated that there is no need for creating exclusive asset classes for group assets; instead, any of the defined asset classes can be used to create a group asset as well.

The project team has recommended to make use of the control specifications for screen layout and account determination, at the asset class level rather than making the specifications at the chart of depreciation level. It has also been decided to use the SAP's default document type AF for all the depreciation related postings in all the company codes.

BESTM requested the project management team to configure the FSV to ensure that indicator 'Asset retirement' and the field 'Asset number / Subnumber' are set with a field status as 'required entry'. Similar settings need to be carried out for the asset posting keys as well.

BESTM, as it needs asset reporting at the 'Segment' / 'Profit Center' level, has requested to activate segment reporting in FI-AA. The project team has pointed out this activation would also help to carry out the consistency check when users make single / mass asset maintenance of 'Segment' and/or 'Profit Center' details while creating / changing asset master records. This is because, if this activation is not done, then the system will not do the consistency check, for these two fields, when maintaining the asset master.

BESTM management wants to make use of additional account assignment objects like 'Internal Order', 'Investment Order', 'Functional Area', 'Maintenance Order' etc during posting in asset accounting. It was also indicated that if an account assignment object is relevant to B/S, then, no user should be able to change the account assignment object in the asset master record, once the asset has been capitalized. Also, the account assignment object like 'Funds Center', 'Funds Center for Investment', 'Investment Order', 'Functional Area' etc should be prevented from being changed during a posting.

The BESTM management, after a detailed discussion with the implementation team, has decided not to create any new depreciation areas other than the ones that were copied from the country-specific chart of depreciation. It was also decided that all the company codes will use the book depreciation area (01) for updating the quantity information of LVAs. To meet some of the tax requirements in USA, BESTM has requested to specify the appropriate depreciation areas for managing the group assets as well. As in practice, the interest calculated on the capital tied up on fixed assets, needs to be managed in the cost accounting depreciation area, 20 in the case of BESTM.

BESTM has indicated that, when posting values are transferred from the book depreciation area (01) to other areas, all the APC-relevant values should be transferred in a manner that the user will have no option to make any change, later, during posting so as to minimise errors in the transferred values. BESTM has also requested the project team to configure adoption of depreciation terms from one depreciation area to another in such a way that the adopted depreciation terms cannot be changed, manually, later in the asset master.

BESTM management decided to have a uniform economic life policy for the asset classes across company codes, both in US and India. Accordingly, for example, the useful life of vehicles has been set at 10 years, computer hardware at 5 years, computer software at 2 years, furniture & fittings at 5 years, office equipments at 5 years and so on.

BESTM wants to round off, using arithmetic rounding method, the year-end net book value, and also the automatically calculated replacement value of assets. BESTM has indicated that they want to depreciate, all the fixed assets, until the book values become zero. Accordingly, the project team has decided not to use the 'memo value' functionality in the system.

BESTM company codes will use the same FYV that has been defined in SAP FI (G/L) in FI-AA as well. However, the project team has been asked to configure use of half months to take care of mid-month acquisition / depreciation of assets for all the US-based company codes.

Managing depreciation areas in the currency of corporate group, for legal consolidation, is a requirement for all the India-based company codes of BESTM as the local valuation will be in INR but the group consolidation in USD. Accordingly, suitable depreciation areas need to be defined for the chart of depreciation BEIN, which will be used by the India-based company codes1210 and 1220.

BESTM wants to the project team to define a multi-level depreciation method, with three levels for special depreciation. The three levels will correspond to three periods: first 5 years, next 3 years and the last 2 years. The depreciation percentage for these corresponding phases will need to set at 10%, 7% and 3% respectively.

BESTM requested the project management team not to define default values for the company codes and depreciation areas. Also, BESTM does not want to impose the condition that the acquisitions are allowed only in the year in which depreciation started.

BESTM has decided to have a cutoff value key defined for depreciating vehicles with 10 year validity. The scrap value percentage will vary at 5% for the first 5 years, 3% for the next 3 years and 2% for the last 2 years. The scrap value needs to be deducted from the base value and the start of calculation will be from the asset capitalization date.

BESTM has decided to make use of the standard depreciation keys that are pre-defined in the system. However, while handling multiple shift operations, it needs to be configured that the result is increased depreciation / expired useful life. Also, there need not be any stopping of depreciation during asset shutdown. As in line with the standard settings, BESTM wants to calculate the ordinary depreciation before the special depreciation.

In the case of special reserves, BESTM has asked the project team to configure the system, to use the net procedure, so that it posts the allocation amounts and write-off amounts, for the same asset, offsetting against each other instead of the gross method.

The project team has suggested to the BESTM management to use SAP supplied standard transaction types for handling unplanned depreciation, transfer of reserves, asset acquisition, asset revaluations etc.

BESTM, while configuring the depreciation area for revaluation of fixed assets, wants only the APC to be revalued but not the accumulated depreciation that had been debited to the asset in the earlier years. The revaluation of fixed assets for balance sheet purposes, will happen on 31st December, every five years, starting with 31-Dec-2020. The revaluation IDs will be numbered serially and revaluation will be handled in the cost accounting depreciation area.

BESTM, to make physical inventory easier, requires that all the assets be identified with valid 'Inventory number' in their respective asset master records. Accordingly, this field is to be made mandatory for input. Also, to keep track of asset history, they want the 'History indicator' field to be enabled, but not mandatory. Besides, they also insisted that 'Cost center', 'Business area' and 'Maintenance order' fields be made as 'optional' entry fields. During this discussion, the project team suggested to synchronize all the equipments with SAP Plant Maintenance application.

As regards the screen layout control of depreciation areas is concerned, BESTM has decided to make use of the standard versions supplied by SAP, without changing any of the field status thereon.

For making the selection screen specifications for some of the web transactions including 'My Assets', the project team has indicated that it will use most of the common fields, such as 'Asset', 'Asset Sub Number', 'Asset Class', 'Account Determination', 'Acquisition Year', 'Capitalized On', 'Evaluation Group 1/2/3', 'Asset Super Number', 'Vendor', 'Manufacturer', 'Description', 'Lease Start Date' etc, as the selection fields for the 'Cost Accountant' role. Similar definitions will be created for 'Cost Center Manager' and 'Employee Self-Service'.

While defining the account assignment category of asset purchase orders, BESTM has indicated to make the settings in such a way to have the 'Business Area' and 'Cost Center' as 'optional' entry fields (from their original status of 'suppressed') to have the details captured, wherever possible. In the case of integrated asset accounting, BESTM does not want to use different technical clearing accounts, but wants the system to use the one defined at the chart of accounts level. BESTM wants the project team to configure the system to prevent subsequent adjustments made to APC of an asset arising out of incorrect discount charged in 'net' invoice posting, relating to assets, in FI-A/P and the resulting capitalization. As BESTM uses P&L accounts to post the gain/loss arising out of asset retirements, the project team has been asked not to configure the transaction types to collect gain/loss on an asset itself. Also, BESTM does not want to configure this for asset classes as well.

BESTM does not, in general, need a cross-system depreciation areas to handle intercompany asset transactions, when asset transfer happens among the company codes situated either within US or within India, as all the US-based company codes use the same chart of depreciation BEUS and all the company codes in India use the same chart of depreciation BEIN. In each case, the chart of depreciation is the same and the depreciation areas have the same numbering and meaning. However, BESTM requires the cross-system depreciation area(s), to facilitate intercompany asset transfers between a company in US and another in India, as these company codes use two different charts of accounts (BEUS for US-based company codes and BEIN for India-based company codes). In this case, the depreciation areas, though have the same keys (for some of the areas), their meaning is different across the systems.

For AuC capitalization, the project team will copy the standard profile and create a new one so that settlement is made optional to some of the CO receivers like 'Cost Center', 'Order' etc. This is required to take care of settling debits to these receivers when debits were capitalized to AuC, by mistake. Also, BESTM wants to have the flexibility of settling by 'percentage', 'equivalence numbers' and 'amount'. Besides, it was suggested to have a validation to ensure that the settlement does not exceed 100% in a percentage settlement; above, or below, the system should issue a warning accordingly. Also, BESTM, in AuCs, does not want to ignore the down payments during line item settlement. Instead, they want capitalization of down payments from previous year, and the closing invoice from the current year, together.

BESTM wants to use the standard sort versions without defining anything new, for FI-AA Information System. However, they want to create a new simulation version, to simulate the depreciation in all asset classes, for book depreciation, to understand what happens when the depreciation key is LINS and the useful life is increased by 10% across asset classes. BESTM wants to use the default key figure groups, without going in for any new key figure group definition, for the Fiori apps 'Asset Balances' and 'Asset Transactions'. Also, BESTM will not be renaming any of the value fields meant for the 'asset explorer'. They are good with the short text supplied by SAP.

BESTM will not be requiring any new currency translation methods as they will use the standard ones supplied by SAP as default. BESTM will not be creating any new authorizations; rather, they will be using the standard ones supplied by SAP.

Project Starfish

'Digifone', an ABG group company, is USA's leading telecom service provider, providing pan America voice and data services across 2G, 3G, 4G (and the proposed 5G) platforms. Through a large spectrum of portfolio supporting data and voice, the company is committed to usher in customer delight in digital experience by connecting millions and millions across USA. The company is always in the forefront, developing cutting-edge infrastructure to deliver newer and smarter technologies, for both retail and enterprise customers.

Headquartered in Sacramento, California, the Digifone Corporate operates through two companies namely *Digifone* and *Digiband*. While 'Digifone' (D900) handles voice in the form of landline, mobile, wireless and satellite telephony besides taking care of customer requirements in the area of broadband connectivity, the other company 'Digiband' (D910) is involved more in the digital entertainment business including DTH (direct to home), OTT (over the top) platform besides creating digital consumer content for broadcasting.

As both the companies handle millions and millions of customers and transactions, the project team of Starfish has been appointed by the Digifone Corporate to implement SAP FICA so as to reap the benefits from functionalities like EBPP, flexible credit management, dispute handling etc.

ABG group, besides the two entities, Digifone and Digiband operating in telecommunications industry, has several other company codes that operate in different industries /sectors. Accordingly, the corporate group has decided to go in for SAP S/4HANA implementation without any specific industry flavour. Hence, for Digifone and Digiband, it has been recommended to activate Extended FI-CA rather than using IS-Telecommunications.

It has been clarified to the project team, by the Digifone Corporate, that the following has to be taken into account while configuring SAP FICA:

- The configuration should allow account assignment to a 'Profit Center' while processing items for a business partner.
- The tax items are to be updated in SAP G/L in accordance with their distribution to different G/L account assignments like 'Segment', 'Business Area', and 'Profit Center', but with no separate tax reporting.
- It should be possible to enter the 'Segment' in FICA documents, when it is not a derived field.
- The system should post the 'payments on account' in the same company code in which the bank posting was also created. Also, the system should account the 'payments on account' as downpayments.

- A payment, from a customer, can be used to clear a number of open items in the contract account, and the system should post the contract account automatically whenever payment orders are reversed.
- Besides extended withholding tax (EWT), the Cash Flow Analysis should also be made active.
- The outgoing payment and reconciliation should be carried out in SAP FICA itself, and only the totals posted to the G/L, so as to reduce the load on the SAP G/L Accounting side.
- A total invoice should contain all receivable items and there should be no retroactive clearing allowed in FICA.
- The disputes need to be handled via SAP Dispute Management (FIN-FSM-DM).
- The foreign currency valuation should be carried out in the first local currency.
- The 'factoring' should be enabled.
- The tax reporting date should be set to the posting date.

Digifone wants the project team to define a single company code group to include the two company codes D900 and D910, with the company code D900 as the paying company code.

Digifone management has suggested to the project team to use the standard date as the translation date for various processes including invoiced revenue, payment card settlements, deferred revenue and revenues that are not invoiced, for the local currency. In the case of 2nd and 3rd local currencies, the translation date will be the posting date.

Digifone has indicated to the project team that there needs to be two contract account categories, one for the regular 'post-paid' customers and the another for the 'pre-paid' customers. The contract account maintenance has to be online. It also wants the project team to ensure to group line items of different contract accounts for billing, together with the same dunning / payment deadline. On numbering, it has been suggested to provide for both internal as well as external numbering.

Digifone wants to post, via automatic account determination, the business transactions to separate G/L accounts for the transactions with third party customers (domestic and overseas) and affiliate companies. Accordingly, the project team has decided to define three account determination characteristics in the system.

Digifone wants to maintain number ranges, both for individual and mass maintenance, and has suggested to the project team to plan at least five number ranges exclusively for mass maintenance to facilitate parallel processing. As for as posting locks, appropriate lock reasons need to be defined to take care of posting and clearing locks and these locks would be valid for a period of one week during every month end. Digifone has also requested to configure the system in such way that all the document types should allow cross-company code postings. This is to facilitate billing / dunning a business partner who is no longer associated with a participating company but still owes some money. Also, the system should enable negative postings for transactions such as payment or interest. But, in the case of returns / payment reversals or clearing resets, the negative posting will have to be allowed only if it happens in the same fiscal year.

In the case of security deposits, Digifone has requested the project team to make sure that the assignment of security deposit to contract should be flexible enough to assign at the contract or contract account level. Also, when cash security deposit requests are transferred from one contract account / contract to another contract account / contract, the system should determine the due date, and the new date has to be based on the transfer date. Also, the interest is to be set as due as soon as an item is posted.

Digifone wants to create three kinds of lock reasons for interest calculation: locking the periodic interest, locking the interest calculation during clearing, and a total lock. These locks are to be valid for a period of one week from the start date. It has also been decided that during interest calculation, the system should calculate net interest, the due date should be the date of interest debit in the account, and there should be no rounding off of the interest calculated. Also, the system should create interest documents per contract instead of clubbing all the contracts and creating a single interest document.

The Digifone management has suggested to use the default settings provided by SAP, wherever possible, for dunning. Accordingly, the project team has decided to go ahead with the standard definitions for both dunning procedure categories and dunning level categories.

10 Accounts Receivable and Accounts Payable

Fully integrated with the SAP General Ledger Accounting (SAP G/L), the accounts receivable (FI-A/R) and accounts payable (FI-A/P) components of SAP help in dealing with your customers and vendors, respectively, for managing the amounts that your business would receive from (customers) and pay to (vendors). Besides SAP G/L, these modules are also integrated with SAP-SD, SAP-MM and FI-AA. These components help in managing the master data (of customers and vendors) and the various business transactions associated with the receivable and payable.

Allowing you to record and manage accounts receivable data of all customers, the '*Accounts Receivable*'(FI-A/R) component, takes care of all postings to A/R that are triggered in response to operative transactions in sales and logistics, besides updating the FI-G/L simultaneously. It updates different G/L accounts such as receivables, down payments, bills of exchange etc., depending on the transaction involved. It also clears customer line items with the incoming payments. With the functionality, you (a) can monitor open items by using, for example, due date lists and a flexible dunning function, (b) can adjust the correspondence forms, payment notices, balance confirmations, account statements, interest calculations etc., to suit your requirements, and (c) can assign incoming payments to receivables due. With its wide range of tools, you can evaluate balance lists, journals, balance audit trails and other standard reports.

The key features of FI-A/R are outlined in Table 10.1:

Key Feature	Details
Master data	You can manage and store your customer data as business partner data. You can create and change customer data using the business partner, so that you do changes, for example, in address data, only once.
Monitoring of receivables	Besides displaying overdue receivables and customer balances, you can process individual customer items.
Posting business transactions	You can post accounting data for customers in A/R and the data entered is transferred to G/L which is updated

	according to the transaction concerned like, receivable, down payment, bill of exchange (BoE) etc.
Clearing of open invoices	You can post incoming payments and clear customer open items either manually or automatically.
Evaluation of days receivable outstanding (DSO)	You can use this functionality to identify customers with the highest or the lowest days receivable outstanding (DSO).
Correspondence	Besides sending correspondence (such as payment notices, open item lists, balance confirmation or account statements) to your customers, you can adjust the forms for the correspondence according to your business needs.
Periodic activities and closing operations	You can prepare and carry out periodic activities (such as automatic payment, interest calculation or dunning) or activities that arise for closing.
Analytics	You can carry out evaluations and analyses for your customers, such as payment history, currency risk or DSO analysis.

Table 10:1 Key Features of FI-A/R

Integrated with SAP-MM, the *'Accounts Payable'* (FI-A/P) application component records and manages accounting data for all your vendors. As in the case of A/R, all postings made in A/P are also simultaneously recorded in FI-G/L with different G/L accounts recording different business transactions like payables, down payments, BoE etc. Interacting with SAP Cash Management application (a subcomponent of SAP Financial Supply Chain Management), A/P helps in updating the data from invoices for optimized liquidity planning. With its payment program, you can pay all your payables either through standard payment methods (check, wire transfer etc) using regular printed forms or through electronic form (by way of DME-data medium exchange on disk and EDI- electronic data interchange). As in the case of A/R, you can create dunning notices, if required, for outstanding receivables (for example, to receive payment for a credit memo). You may use due date forecasts and other standard reports to monitor the A/P open items. Using the functionality, you can also design balance confirmations, account statements, and other forms of reports to suit your specific business requirements in corresponding with you vendors. You can document the transactions in A/P, using balance lists, journals, balance audit trails, and other internal evaluations.

The key functionalities of FI-A/P are outlined in Table 10.2:

Key Feature	Details
Master data	You can manage and store your vendor data as business partner data. You can create and change vendor data using the business partner, so that you do changes (as in A/R), for example, in address data, only once.
Posting business transactions	You can post accounting data for vendors in A/P and the data entered is transferred to G/L which is updated according to the transaction concerned like, payable, down payment, bill of exchange etc.
Import of supplier invoices	You can import multiple supplier invoices all at once.
Analysis of payments to suppliers	Besides viewing the information about payments to suppliers, you can check the overdue / future payable amount. If you identify negative trends in the payable amount, you can notify the responsible persons to take action.
Management of cash discounts	You can use this feature to forecast the available cash discounts and to monitor the cash discount utilization in your responsible area. You can find out where you need to make better use of cash discounts in order to avoid cash discount loss in the future.
Reviewing of cleared overdue invoices	Use this feature to get details and statistical facts about cleared overdue invoices.
Evaluation of days payable outstanding (DPO)	This is similar to DSO functionality of A/R. You can use this functionality to identify suppliers with the highest or the lowest DPO.
Management of payments	Use this feature to create, post, and, if necessary, reverse payments.
Management of payment blocks	You can use this feature to set and remove payment blocks on invoices or supplier accounts. You can identify irregularities or potential fraud in invoices through integration with SAP Fraud Management for SAP S/4HANA.
Management of payment proposals	You use this feature to revise and release payment proposals. The system creates journal entries in FI.
Management of payment media	You use this feature to transfer the data required for electronic payment transactions to banks via a data medium per successful payment run.

Table 10:2 Key Features of FI-A/P

> **i** To be co-deployed with SAP S/4HANA, 'SAP Fraud Management for SAP S/4HANA' is not part of SAP S/4HANA Enterprise Management, but part of the add-on 'SAP Assurance and Compliance Software' for SAP S/4HANA, for which you need a separate license.

In this Chapter, we will discuss:

- Customer Accounts
- Vendor Accounts
- Business Transactions
- Information System

Let us start with the customer accounts, first.

10.1 Customer Accounts

Under customer accounts, we shall discuss the configuration settings relating to master data and line items. Let us, first, understand the settings and preparations that are required, before you can create a customer master data.

10.1.1 Master Data

As all transactions in SAP are posted to and managed in accounts. You need to create one master record for each customer account that you require in the system. Both the financial accounting (FI-A/R) and the sales (SAP SD) departments of your organization use the same master records. By creating and storing customer master data centrally, you enable their access throughout the organization, and this avoids (a) the need to enter the same information more than once and (b) the inconsistencies in master data that may creep in if not maintained centrally. If the address of one of your customers changes, for example, you have to enter this change only once; your accounting and sales departments will always have the updated details.

> **i** You should have implemented the SAP Sales and Distribution (SAP SD) application component in order to enter / process customer master records for processing the sales related business transactions.

A customer can be a person (individual), an organization or a group. A typical customer master data is made up of four areas (segments) as shown in Figure 10.1:

- General Data
- Company Code Data (FI area)
- Sales and Distribution Data (SD area)
- ETM Data

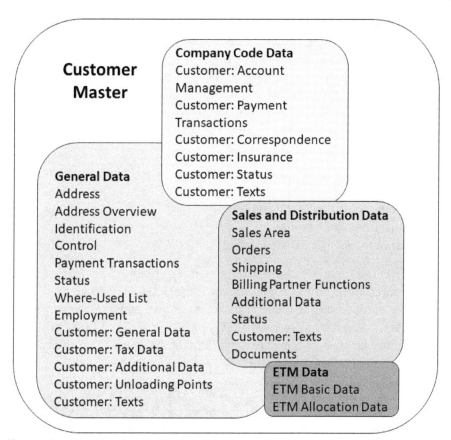

Figure 10.1 Customer Master Data Areas

The 'general data' such as the information relating to address, control data, payment transactions, status etc., will be at the Client level and hence is valid across all the company codes. The 'company code data' (account management, payment transactions, insurance, correspondence etc) is valid only for the specific company code in which the customer has been created. The 'sales and distribution data' is made up of information relating to sales area (sales organization, distribution channel and division), shipping, orders, billing, customer texts, billing partner functions, documents, additional data etc., and will be valid across sales areas. The 'ETM data' contains the industry specific equipment and tools data for customers.

> **i** The ETM (Equipment and Tools Management) data is used, basically, in engineering and construction industry, and it deals with optimal process flow in enterprise areas of (construction) companies or equipment rental companies etc., for planning, processing, settlement and evaluation of resources (materials and equipment). To use ETM, you should have implemented the SAP application components like Sales and Distribution (SD), Plant Maintenance (PM), Financial Accounting (FI) and Controlling (CO). It is also advisable to use the other SAP application components like Asset Accounting (AA) and Project System (PS).

The specifications that you make in a customer master record are used (a) as default values when you post items to the account (for example, the terms of payment you specify in the master record are defaulted for document entry), (b) for processing business transactions like dunning for which the date of the last dunning notice and the address are required for the automatic dunning process, (c) for working with master records so as to, for example, prevent unauthorized users (through appropriate authorization groups) from accessing an account, (d) for communication with the customer using the address details and (e) in the sales department for order processing, shipping, and billing.

You can create customer master data, in SAP, in three different ways:

- Central maintenance (for all the three areas)
- FI maintenance (for FI area alone)
- Sales data maintenance (for SD area alone)

The Table 10.3 outlines the menu path and Transaction for creating / changing / displaying customer master records from different maintenance areas (FI, SD and central). All these Transactions are now bundled into a single Transaction known as BP. However, if you still enter any of the earlier Transactions like FD01 / FD02 / FD03 or VD01 / VD02 / VD03 or XD01 / XD02 / XD03 to create / change / display customer master in FI area, SD area and centrally, the system redirects you to the new Transaction BP, automatically.

Maintenance Area	Activity	SAP Easy Access Menu	Transaction
Accounting (FI) Area Menu FDMN	Create Customer (Accounting)	SAP Menu > Accounting > Financial Accounting > Accounts Receivable > Master Records > Create	BP (earlier FD01)
	Change Customer (Accounting)	SAP Menu > Accounting > Financial Accounting > Accounts Receivable > Master Records > Change	BP (earlier FD02)
	Display Customer (Accounting)	SAP Menu > Accounting > Financial Accounting > Accounts Receivable > Master Records > Display	BP (earlier FD03)
Sales (SD) Area Menu VS00	Create Customer (Sales)	SAP Menu > Logistics > Sales and Distribution > Master Data > Business Partner > Customer > Create > Sales and Distribution	BP (earlier VD01)
	Change Customer (Sales)	SAP Menu > Logistics > Sales and Distribution > Master Data > Business Partner > Customer > Change > Sales and Distribution	BP (earlier VD02)
	Display Customer (Sales)	SAP Menu > Logistics > Sales and Distribution > Master Data > Business	BP (earlier VD03)

Centrally		Partner > Customer > Display > Sales and Distribution	
	Create Customer (Centrally)	SAP Menu > Accounting > Financial Accounting > Accounts Receivable > Master Records > Maintain Centrally > Create	BP (earlier XD01)
		SAP Menu > Logistics > Sales and Distribution > Master Data > Business Partner > Customer > Create > Complete	
	Change Customer (Centrally)	SAP Menu > Accounting > Financial Accounting > Accounts Receivable > Master Records > Maintain Centrally > Change	BP (earlier XD02)
		SAP Menu > Logistics > Sales and Distribution > Master Data > Business Partner > Customer > Change > Complete	
	Display Customer (Centrally)	SAP Menu > Accounting > Financial Accounting > Accounts Receivable > Master Records > Maintain Centrally > Display	BP (earlier XD03)
		SAP Menu > Logistics > Sales and Distribution > Master Data > Business Partner > Customer > Display > Complete	

Table 10:3 Customer Master Maintenance

> **i** In some companies, the accounting (FI) and sales (SD) departments maintain the general data together and their own FI and Sales areas separately. In other companies, customer master records are maintained centrally (for all the areas).

10.1.1.1   Preparations for Creating Customer Master Data

There are certain pre-requisites - like defining number ranges, creating customer account groups and maintaining field status - which you need to complete before you create master data for your customers:

- *Define Number Ranges*: As in G/L account master records, you need to have appropriate number ranges defined (refer Section 7.1.5 'Document Number Ranges', of Chapter 7 of Vol. I) for more details on number ranges) for the customer master records for the system to allocate a suitable number from a number range when creating a master record. In doing so, you also determine if the numbers are to be assigned internally by the system or to be supplied by the user who is creating the master record.

> **i** Pay attention in doing this exercise by taking into account the current number of existing customers and the expected increase of new customers in future, and define the number range intervals accordingly, so that you do not run out of numbers midcourse.

- *Create Account Groups*: We have already seen (in Section 9.3.1.4 'Account Groups', of Chapter 9 of Vol. I) that an account group is used to control the creation of master records as it determines which fields have to be filled compulsorily (mandatory) and which ones can be optionally filled when creating the master record, besides allocating a number (external or internal) to the master record. You normally create the master records using the same account group, if the accounts require the same master record fields and use the same number range. You will be creating customer master records, by entering the account group in the initial screen. In FI, once a customer account is created, its account group cannot be changed. However, when using partner functions in SD, in some cases, the account group of a customer can be changed from, say, 'ship-to address' to an 'ordering address'.

> **i** The number of account groups which you need depends on whether you use these groups for the layout of the screens. For example, you may want two account groups: one group for 'standard accounts' and another for 'one-time accounts'. The other consideration should be the number ranges. The number of 'number ranges' will give you an initial clue as to the number of account groups. If you have determined that you require five number ranges, for example, then, you must create at least five account groups. There should at least be one account group in the system.

- *Maintain Field Status*: As already outlined (in Section 6.2 'Field Status Variants', of Chapter 6 of Vol. I), the field status definitions determine the status of the fields on the screens for the master data. Though by default all the fields would be 'suppressed', the field status can be (a) optional - field visible, enabled for input but entry not mandatory, (b) required - field visible, enabled for input, entry mandatory and (c) suppressed - field invisible, hidden from display, no entry is possible. The field status is normally determined based on the account group. However, you may also determine the field status depending upon the processing type (transaction) with which you create the master record, and based on the company code in which you define the master record. It is also possible to vary the field status based on a posting key for a transaction. If there is a conflicting situation to arrive at the final field status, you already know that SAP follows the 'link rules' to overcome the situation.

Let us start with the first activity of defining the account groups.

10.1.1.1.1   Define Account Groups with Screen Layout (Customers)

Use this step to create the accounts groups that you will require for creating the master records of your customers. While defining the account groups, specify - per account group - the number range interval for the account numbers, the type of number assignment (external or internal), whether it is a one-time account and the field status. You can also define 'reference account groups' for one-time accounts, and use them to control the field status of the one-time account screen. When creating a one-time customer account, specify an account group: if not, all fields of the one-time account screen are ready for input during document entry.

> **i** If you create new account groups, do not forget to maintain the field status; else, all corresponding fields are shown. Always control the field status via the account groups; however, in exceptional cases, you may control the field status either via company code (refer Section 10.1.1.1.2) or transaction (refer Section 10.1.1.1.3).

As in the case of G/L account groups, (a) you can delete an account group, from the system, only if there are no master records referencing that account group; else, you cannot display or change the master record; (b) if you hide a field at a later stage in which you had already made an entry, the field contents are still valid; and (c) you can increase the upper limit of the number interval as long as there is no other overlapping interval.

> **i** Do not attempt to allocate the accounts to accounting clerks via the account groups or group customers together according to countries. Do this via special master record fields.

You can have several customer account groups like sold-to-party (0001), goods recipient (0002), payer (0003), bill to party (0004), one-time accounts OTA (0099), consumer (0170) and so on or create fewer number of account groups like domestic customers, export customers, one-time customers etc.

Project Dolphin

BESTM management has asked the Dolphin project manager to create a fairly large number of account groups like sold-to-party (0001), goods recipient (0002), payer (0003), bill to party (0004), one-time accounts OTA (0099) and consumer (0170). Besides, additional account groups are to be created, to suitably number the customer accounts that are transferred from the external system.

The project team has recommended to the BESTM management, to control the field status through accounts groups. Accordingly, no new screen layout settings are to be defined for the company codes (of BESTM) or for transactions. However, as BESTM wants its company codes to participate in 'Factoring', necessary field status needs to be configured: the field 'Accts recble pledging ind.' is to be set as an 'optional' field in the customer account group and the company code (customers) screen layout.

Use the menu path: SAP Customizing Implementation Guide > Financial Accounting > Accounts Receivable and Accounts Payable > Customer Accounts > Master Data > Preparations for Creating Customer Master Data > Define Account Groups with Screen Layout (Customers), to create new account groups. You may also use Transaction OBD2:

i.   On the resulting screen, click on 'New Entries' to create a new account group (Figure 10.2), and enter a 4-character identifier for the new 'Account Group', say 001B.

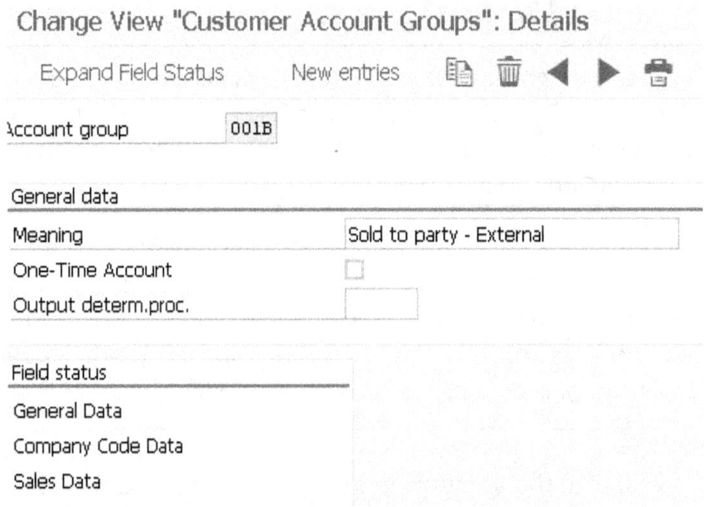

Change View "Customer Account Groups": Details

| Expand Field Status | New entries |

Account group   001B

General data

Meaning	Sold to party - External
One-Time Account	☐
Output determ.proc.	

Field status

General Data
Company Code Data
Sales Data

Figure 10.2 Customer Account Group - New

ii.   Under 'General Data', enter an explanation for the group in the 'Meaning' field, select 'One-Time Account' check-box if the account group is for creating one-time accounts, and enter a suitable output determination procedure (DB0001, DB0002 etc), if required, in 'Output determ.proc.' field.

> **i** The 'Output determ.proc.' field defines the output categories (for example, order confirmation and electronic mail message) that are allowed in a document, and the sequence in which the output categories appear in the document.

iii. Now, to manage the field status, place the cursor on 'General data', or Company code data' or 'Sales data' under 'Field status' block and click on 'Expand Field Status'. For example, as we need to ensure that the accounts receivable pledging indicator ('Accts recble pledging ind.') field is configured with 'optional entry' field status, for BESTM, double-click on 'Company Code Data' under 'Field Status' on the initial screen, double-click on 'Payment transactions' group on the next screen and ensure that the radio-button for 'Accts recble pledging ind.' is selected under 'Opt. entry' field status column (Figure 10.3).

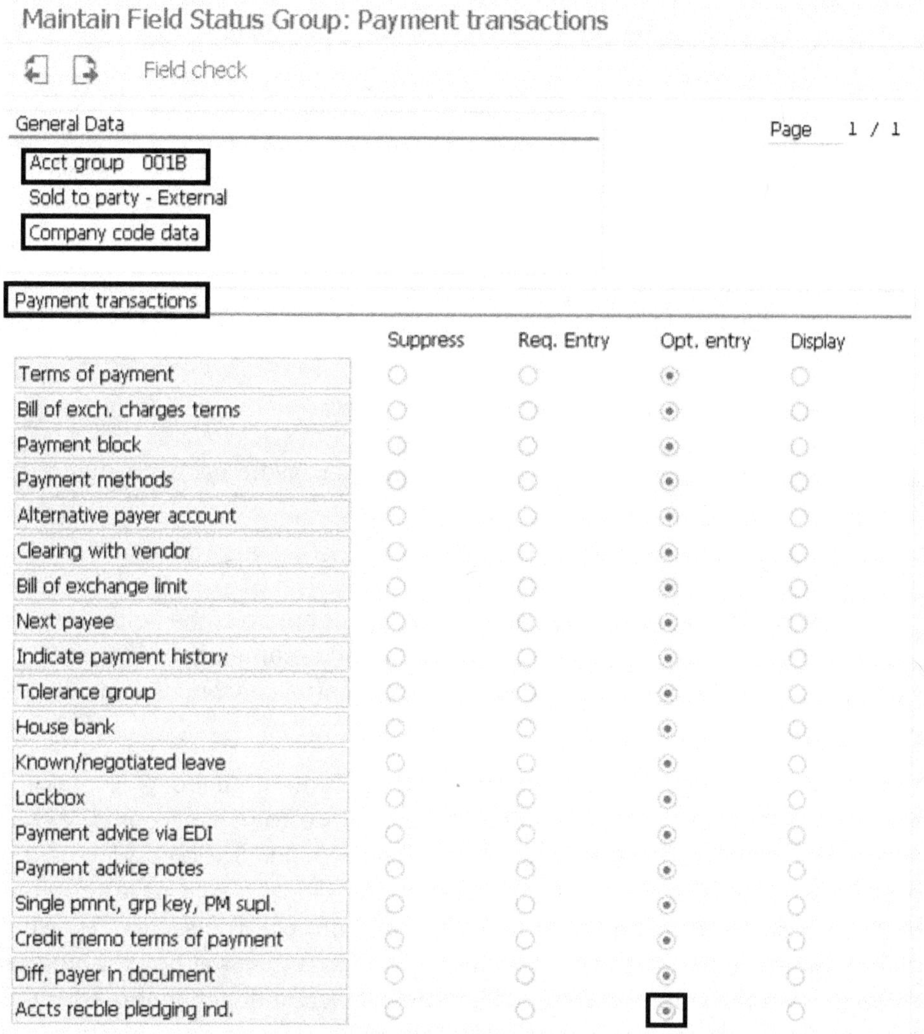

Maintain Field Status Group: Payment transactions

⬅ ➡   Field check

General Data   Page   1 / 1

Acct group   001B
Sold to party - External
Company code data

Payment transactions

	Suppress	Req. Entry	Opt. entry	Display
Terms of payment	○	○	◉	○
Bill of exch. charges terms	○	○	◉	○
Payment block	○	○	◉	○
Payment methods	○	○	◉	○
Alternative payer account	○	○	◉	○
Clearing with vendor	○	○	◉	○
Bill of exchange limit	○	○	◉	○
Next payee	○	○	◉	○
Indicate payment history	○	○	◉	○
Tolerance group	○	○	◉	○
House bank	○	○	◉	○
Known/negotiated leave	○	○	◉	○
Lockbox	○	○	◉	○
Payment advice via EDI	○	○	◉	○
Payment advice notes	○	○	◉	○
Single pmnt, grp key, PM supl.	○	○	◉	○
Credit memo terms of payment	○	○	◉	○
Diff. payer in document	○	○	◉	○
Accts recble pledging ind.	○	○	◉	○

Figure 10.3 Making AR Pledging Indicator Field as Optional

iv.   You can, similarly, maintain any other field statuses, as required.

v.   Once done, 'Save' the settings, and create/change other account groups, accordingly. Now you have created the required account groups (Figure 10.4) with the required field status, for BESTM.

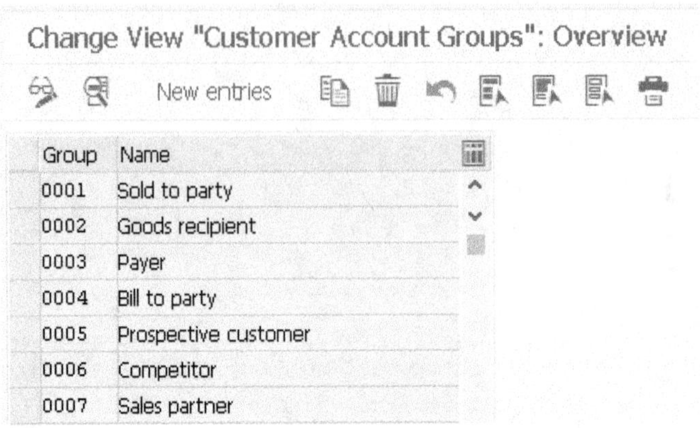

Group	Name
0001	Sold to party
0002	Goods recipient
0003	Payer
0004	Bill to party
0005	Prospective customer
0006	Competitor
0007	Sales partner

Figure 10.4 Customer Account Groups for BESTM

Let us move on to the next step of defining the screen layout per company code, for customer accounts.

10.1.1.1.2 Define Screen Layout per Company Code (Customers)

As already stated, you should try to control, as for as possible, the field status via the account groups. However, in exceptional cases, you may define company-code specific field status, for example, if the company codes are in different countries or some company codes do not use automatic payment processing for customers.

Use the menu path: SAP Customizing Implementation Guide > Financial Accounting > Accounts Receivable and Accounts Payable > Customer Accounts > Master Data > Preparations for Creating Customer Master Data > Define Screen Layout per Company Code (Customers), to define the necessary settings if fields are to have an alternative status depending on the company code. Once you are into the Transaction, specify the company code and determine the status of the fields as required. In the process, you can determine, depending on the company code, which company code-dependent master record fields (a) are ready for input, (b) require an entry and (c) are hidden. This specification is linked (via 'link rules') to the field status of the account group and a specification for the transaction. By the linkage, you can see which status the fields have on the entry screen for master data: the fields take on the status which has the highest priority: 'hiding' a field has the highest priority, followed by 'display', 'required' and 'optional' in that order.

In the standard system, you will see default settings that are valid for all the company codes as denoted by '*' in the 'Company Code' field (Figure 10.5). You may create new settings by clicking on 'New Entries' for specific company codes, or use the default settings as such or with some modifications. As we need to ensure that the 'Accts recble pledging ind.' field is managed as 'optional entry' for all the company codes of BESTM, double-click on the 'Company Code' row with '*', double-click on 'Payment transactions' on the next screen and ensure that this field is set to the 'optional entry' field status.

Change View "Field Selection per Co. Code (Custs)": Overview

Company Code	Company Name	
*	Default field status	

Figure 10.5 Defining Screen Layout per Company Code

Since all the company codes of BESTM needs to participate in factoring, you need to make sure that the field 'Accts recble pledging ind.' is set to 'optional entry' field status.

Let us, now, see how to configure the field status settings per activity (transaction).

10.1.1.1.3   Define Screen Layout per Activity (Customers)

Here, you determine, depending on the transactions (display, create or change) for customer master data, which master record fields are ready for input, require an entry and are hidden. As discussed previously, these specifications will be linked with the field status of the account group and the company code-dependent specification; the 'link rule' will determine which final status the fields have on the entry screen for master data. Again, try to control the field status via the account groups though you can define the field status for each transaction, in exceptional cases.

If fields are to have an alternative status depending on the transaction, you can determine the status of the fields for the required transaction using the menu path: SAP Customizing Implementation Guide > Financial Accounting > Accounts Receivable and Accounts Payable > Customer Accounts > Master Data > Preparations for Creating Customer Master Data > Define Screen Layout per Activity (Customers):

i.   On the resulting screen, you will see the listing of various transactions like create customer (accounting), change customer (accounting), delete customer (accounting), create customer (sales), create customer (centrally) and so on (Figure 10.6).

Change View "Customer Activity-Dependent Field Selection": Overview

Transaction	
Create Customer (Accounting)	
Change Customer (Accounting)	
Display Customer (Accounting)	
Create Customer (Sales)	
Change Customer (Sales)	
Display Customer (Sales)	
Create Customer (Centrally)	
Change Customer (Centrally)	

Figure 10.6 Defining Screen Layout per Transaction

ii.   Double-click on the required transaction, and change the field status to suit your requirements on the next 'Change View "Customer Activity-Dependent Field Selection": Details' screen. For example, you may want to make 'Reconciliation account' field with the status as 'required' from 'optional'. 'Save' when completed and continue modifying the field status for other transactions, as required.

With this, we are now ready to look at configuring the settings for message control.

10.1.1.1.4   Change Message Control for Customer Master Data

Using this configuration step, you can (a) determine whether a message is issued as a note in the dialog box or in the footer, (b) change warnings into error messages and (c) switch off warnings and error messages. You can maintain different specifications for online mode and background processing (batch input sessions). You can, further, make the corresponding specifications for a client or, if required, also for the individual user. SAP uses the work area F2 for switching on the duplicate check for customer (or vendor) master records: the system checks, using 'matchcode' fields, whether accounts with the same address already exist when creating a new account or changing the address. If the same data is found, then, the system displays the duplicates in a window. You may use the default settings (Figure 10.7) as such or change the settings using the menu path: SAP Customizing Implementation Guide > Financial Accounting > Accounts Receivable and Accounts Payable > Customer Accounts > Master Data > Preparations for Creating Customer Master Data > Change Message Control for Customer Master Data.

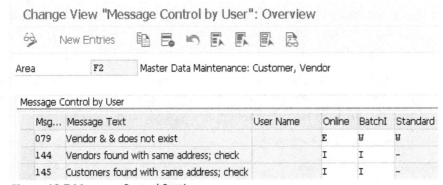

Change View "Message Control by User": Overview

New Entries

Area   F2   Master Data Maintenance: Customer, Vendor

Message Control by User

Msg...	Message Text	User Name	Online	BatchI	Standard
079	Vendor & & does not exist		E	W	W
144	Vendors found with same address; check		I	I	-
145	Customers found with same address; check		I	I	-

Figure 10.7 Message Control Settings

ℹ️ You may use the enhancement SAPMF02D to copy and create your own: by modifying the source code for a standard SAP transaction, and adding the elements you need, for checking the data entered, before saving.

The next activity is to define the accounting clerks.

10.1.1.1.5   Define Accounting Clerks

You can define the name of the accounting clerks under an identification code which you can later enter in the customer master records (Figure 10.8) - under 'Correspondence' block in the 'Customer: Correspondence' tab - that the accounting clerk supervises. The accounting clerk data can be printed on various forms (like payment forms, dunning notices, correspondence, interest calculation etc), and you can use this information for evaluations and correspondence as well.

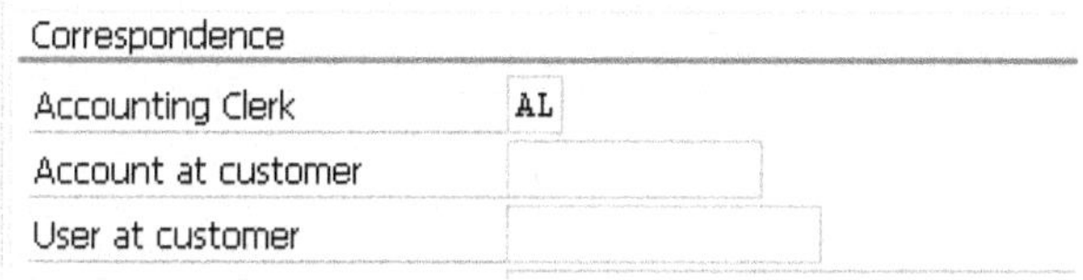

Correspondence	
Accounting Clerk	AL
Account at customer	
User at customer	

Figure 10.8 Accounting Clerk Field in Customer Master

Use the menu path: SAP Customizing Implementation Guide > Financial Accounting > Accounts Receivable and Accounts Payable > Customer Accounts > Master Data > Preparations for Creating Customer Master Data > Define Accounting Clerks or Transaction OB05. On the resulting screen, maintain the company code ('CoCd'), enter the identification code of the clerk in 'Clerk' field, enter the name in 'Name of Accounting Clerk' and provide the corresponding 'Office User' details (Figure 10.9).

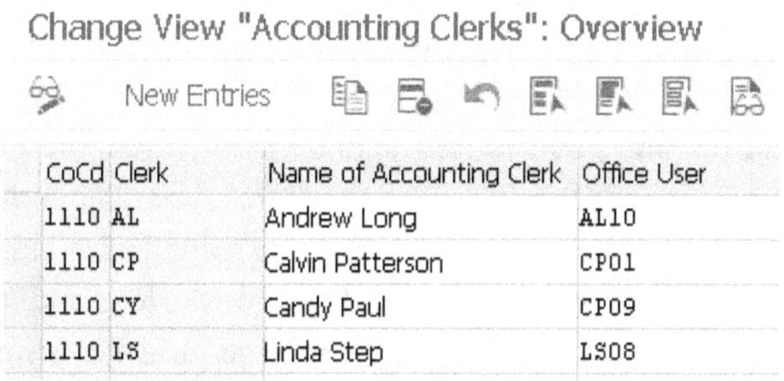

Change View "Accounting Clerks": Overview

New Entries

CoCd	Clerk	Name of Accounting Clerk	Office User
1110	AL	Andrew Long	AL10
1110	CP	Calvin Patterson	CP01
1110	CY	Candy Paul	CP09
1110	LS	Linda Step	LS08

Figure 10.9 Accounting Clerk Definition

> **i** The accounting clerk data is taken from the corresponding office user, from the structure FSABE. You therefore need to maintain the address data of the office user.

The next step is to define the industries.

10.1.1.1.6   Define Industries

Using this activity, you can define industries (also known as 'industry sector') by a 'industry key', and, later, you can group your customers together by industry, and use that information for evaluations; for example, to create a customer list according to industry.

Use the menu path: SAP Customizing Implementation Guide > Financial Accounting > Accounts Receivable and Accounts Payable > Customer Accounts > Master Data > Preparations for Creating Customer Master Data > Define Industries. You may also use Transaction OB44. On the resulting screen, click on 'New Entries' and maintain the required details on the next screen (Figure 10.10). You can also access this Transaction, on the SD side, using the menu path: SAP Customizing Implementation Guide > Sales and Distribution > Master Data > Business Partners > Customers > Marketing > Define Industry Sector For Customers.

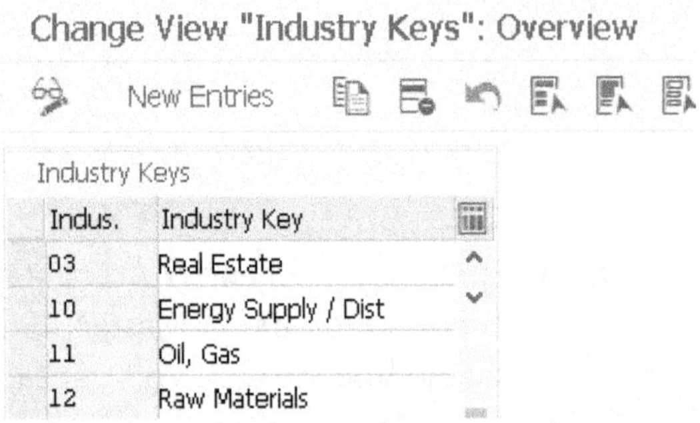

Change View "Industry Keys": Overview

New Entries

Industry Keys

Indus.	Industry Key
03	Real Estate
10	Energy Supply / Dist
11	Oil, Gas
12	Raw Materials

Figure 10.10 Defining Industries

> **i** The Standard Industrial Classification (SIC) include four-digit codes categorizing the industries that companies belong to, while organizing the industries by their business activities. The SIC codes were created by the U.S. government in 1937 to help analyze economic activity across various industries and government agencies. However, SIC codes were partly replaced in 1997 by a system of six-digit codes called the North American Industry Classification System (NAICS). The NAICS codes were adopted, in part, to standardize industry data collection and analysis in between Canada, the United States, and Mexico, under the North American Free Trade Agreement. Despite having been replaced, the government agencies and companies still use the SIC codes even now, for classifying the industry that companies belong to, by matching their business activity with similar companies.

Depending on the standards your organization uses (for example, SIC), you can configure SIC codes in SAP using the menu path: SAP Customizing Implementation Guide > Sales and Distribution > Master Data > Business Partners > Customers > Marketing > Define Industry Sector Codes. Once done, you may enter the appropriate code in the customer master record (Customer: General Data). You can assign more than one industry code to a customer (Figure 10.11).

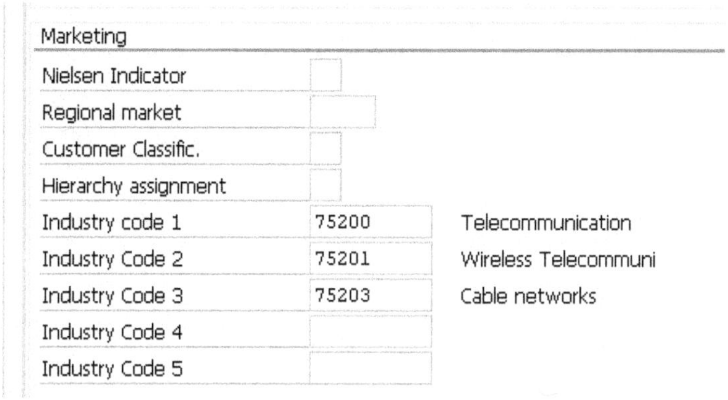

Marketing		
Nielsen Indicator		
Regional market		
Customer Classific.		
Hierarchy assignment		
Industry code 1	75200	Telecommunication
Industry Code 2	75201	Wireless Telecommuni
Industry Code 3	75203	Cable networks
Industry Code 4		
Industry Code 5		

Figure 10.11 Assigning Industry Code in Customer Master Record

With this, we can, now, move on to define the number ranges for the customer accounts.

10.1.1.1.7   Create Number Ranges for Customer Accounts

As in the case of G/L account master records, you also need to maintain the required number ranges for the customer master records that you will be creating in the system. Define as many number ranges that you may require and specify whether a range is external or internal. Make sure you provide sufficient interval, in each of the number ranges, so as not to run out of numbers in the middle. Refer Section 7.1.5 'Document Number Ranges' of Chapter 7 of Vol. I, for more details on number ranges.

Except for the customer master records that you will be transferring from the external system(s) for which you specify external number ranges, go ahead with the internal numbering for all other number ranges. You may not need several number ranges to exactly match the number of account groups, as you can use the same number range for more than one account group.

Project Dolphin

BESTM requested the project team create six number ranges from B1 to B5, and B9 with the specifications that B5 should be used for one-time accounts (OTA) and B9 for external numbering to accommodate the customer accounts transferred from the external systems.

Use the menu path: SAP Customizing Implementation Guide > Financial Accounting > Accounts Receivable and Accounts Payable > Customer Accounts > Master Data > Preparations for Creating Customer Master Data > Create Number Ranges for Customer Accounts or Transaction XDN1 to create the new number ranges:

i.   On the 'Edit Intervals: Customer, Object DEBITOR' screen, click on the 'Change Interval' button and maintain the required number ranges on the next screen (Figure 10.12) by entering the interval number ('No.'), 'From No.' and 'To Number'.

Edit Intervals: Customer, Object DEBITOR

N..	From No.	To Number	NR Status	Ext
B1	1600000031	1800000000	0	☐
B2	2500000011	2600000000	0	☐
B3	2600000031	2800000000	0	☐
B4	2800000021	3100000000	0	☐
B5	5500000011	6999999999	0	☐
B9	9600000000	9999999999	0	☑

Figure 10.12 Number Ranges for Customer Accounts

ii.   Select the 'Ext' check-box, if the interval is to be used for external numbering.

iii.   'Save' the settings.

Now that we have defined the required number ranges, the next step is to assign these number ranges to the appropriate account groups.

10.1.1.1.8   Assign Number Ranges to Customer Account Groups

Use this configuration step to assign a number range to an account group. As indicated already, you can assign the same number range to more than one account group.

Change View "Assign Customer Acct Groups->Number Range": Overview

Group	Name	Number range	
0001	Sold to party	B1	
0002	Goods recipient	B2	
0003	Payer	B3	
0004	Bill to party	B4	
0005	Prospective customer	B3	
0006	Competitor	B3	
0007	Sales partner	B3	
0012	Hierarchy node	B3	
001B	Sold to party - External	B9	
002B	Goods recipient - External	B9	
003B	Payer - External	B9	
004B	Bill to party - - External	B9	
0099	OTA	B5	

Figure 10.13 Assigning Number Ranges to Customer Account Groups

Use the menu path: SAP Customizing Implementation Guide > Financial Accounting > Accounts Receivable and Accounts Payable > Customer Accounts > Master Data >

Preparations for Creating Customer Master Data > Assign Number Ranges to Customer Account Groups or Transaction OBAR. On the resulting screen, enter the number range against each of the account groups and 'Save' the details (Figure 10.13).

The next activity is to define the A/R pledging indicator.

10.1.1.1.9   Define Accounts Receivable Pledging Indicator

You can use the A/R factoring (or pledging) indicator to select customer master records and line items, within a company code, to participate in the factoring procedure.

Project Dolphin

As BESTM wants customer master records and line items within a company code to participate in the factoring procedure, the project team has decided to activate A/R pledging for each of the company codes, both in USA and India.

In order to use the functionality:

i.   You need to activate the A/R factoring procedure in the required company code (s). You may do this by following the menu path: SAP Customizing Implementation Guide > Financial Accounting > Financial Accounting Global Settings > Global Parameters for Company Code > Activate Accounts Receivable Pledging Procedure per Company Code. Since BESTM wants to enable all the company codes to participate in factoring, select the 'AR Pledg.' check-box for all the company codes of BESTM group (Figure 10.14).

Change View "Accounts Receivable Pledging Active": Overview

Figure 10.14 Activating AR Pledging Indicator

ii.   You need to make sure that the accounts receivable factoring indicator ('Accts recble pledging ind.') field is set as an 'optional' or 'required' entry field in the customer account group and the company code (customers) screen layout. We have already completed this in Section 10.1.1.1.1 and 10.1.1.1.2 of this Chapter.

iii.   You also need to adapt a line layout variant for the customer line item display to take care of this. Alternatively, you can create your own line layout variant for the A/R factoring procedure. You can do this using the menu path: SAP Customizing Implementation Guide > Financial Accounting > Accounts Receivable and Accounts

Payable > Customer Accounts > Line Items > Display Line Items > Define Additional Fields for Line Item Display.

To define the A/R pledging indicator:

i. Use the menu path: SAP Customizing Implementation Guide > Financial Accounting > Accounts Receivable and Accounts Payable > Customer Accounts > Master Data > Preparations for Creating Customer Master Data > Define Accounts Receivable Pledging Indicator.

ii. On the resulting screen, click on 'New Entries' and maintain the details on the next screen as indicated in Figure 10.15. The 'AR Pled. Stat.' (Accounts Receivable Pledging Status) field indicates the type of A/R pledging procedure and assigns the factoring indicator ('AR Pled. Stat.') to the open (1) or closed (2) procedure. This pledging status appears as additional information in the customer master record and is therefore visible, to you, in the line item and open item list.

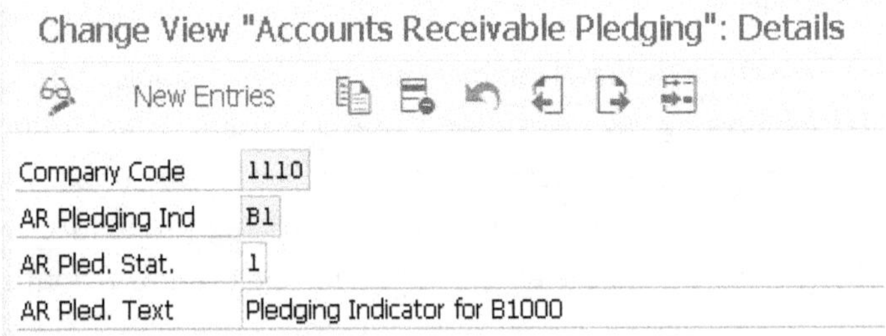

Change View "Accounts Receivable Pledging": Details

Company Code	1110
AR Pledging Ind	B1
AR Pled. Stat.	1
AR Pled. Text	Pledging Indicator for B1000

Figure 10.15 AR Pledging Indicator - Details

iii. Repeat the definition for all the company codes and 'Save' the details. We have, now, defined the A/R pledging indicator for all the company codes of BESTM Corporate (Figure 10.16).

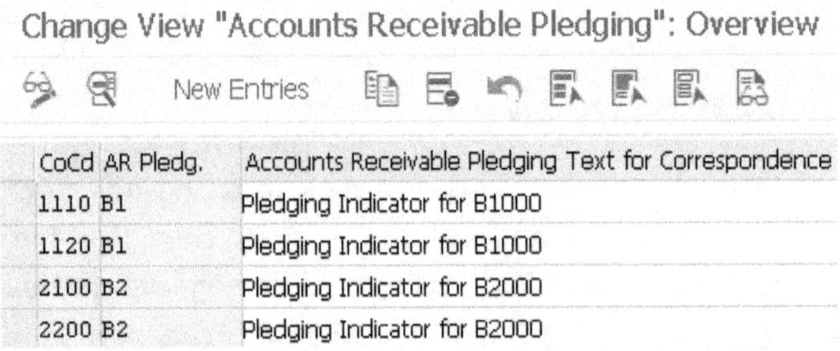

Change View "Accounts Receivable Pledging": Overview

CoCd	AR Pledg.	Accounts Receivable Pledging Text for Correspondence
1110	B1	Pledging Indicator for B1000
1120	B1	Pledging Indicator for B1000
2100	B2	Pledging Indicator for B2000
2200	B2	Pledging Indicator for B2000

Figure 10.16 AR Pledging Indicator for BESTM Company Codes

Once defined, and entered in the customer master record (Figure 10.17) under 'Additional Company Code Data' under the 'Customer: Payment Transactions' tab, the system automatically transfers the AR pledging indicator to the customer line item on posting; of course, you can also enter this manually.

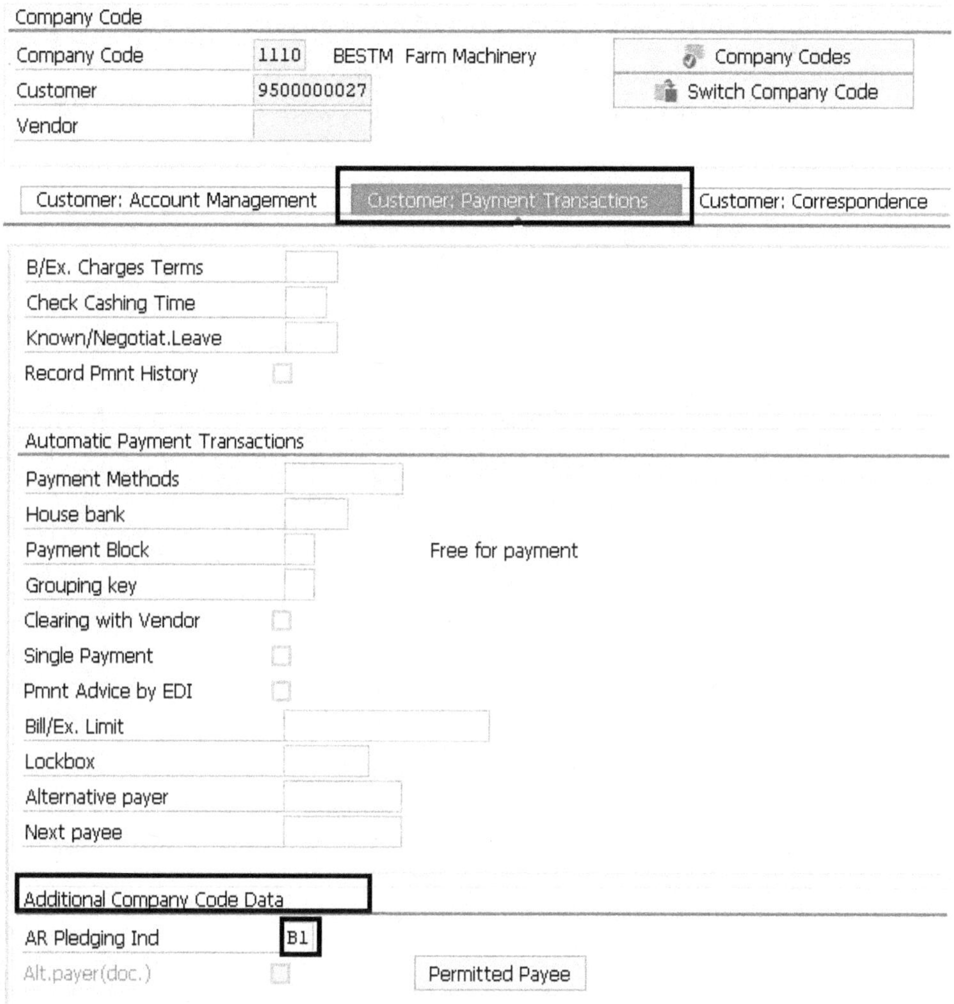

Figure 10.17 AR Pledging Indicator in Customer Master

With this, we are, now, ready to configure the sensitive fields for dual control.

10.1.1.1.10 Define Sensitive Fields for Dual Control (Customers)

Here, you define the 'sensitive fields' for dual control in the customer (or vendor) master records. If you define a field (say, payment terms) in the customer (or vendor) master record as 'sensitive', then, the system blocks corresponding customer (or vendor) account for the payment run if there is a change to the entry. The system will, however, remove the block when a second person, with proper authorization, checks the change and confirms the same.

Project Dolphin

BESTM wants the project team to manage 'Payment Terms', 'Alternate Payer' and 'House Bank' as the sensitive fields. Accordingly, these fields need to be brought under dual control to avoid any misuse.

To define the sensitive fields for dual control:

i.   Use the menu path: SAP Customizing Implementation Guide > Financial Accounting > Accounts Receivable and Accounts Payable > Customer Accounts > Master Data > Preparations for Creating Customer Master Data > Define Sensitive Fields for Dual Control (Customers). You may also use Transaction S_ALR_87003378.

ii.   On the resulting screen, click on 'New Entries' and select the required fields in 'Field name' and 'Save' the details when done (Figure 10.18). With these settings, now, if anyone changes the field content of any of these sensitive fields, the system brings up a message when saving the master record. Though the system will eventually allow to save the data, it will not allow this account to be included in any payment run unless the change is verified and confirmed (or rejected) by another user, other than the one who has changed the field contents.

Figure 10.18 Sensitive Fields for Dual Control

Suppose that you have changed the payment terms (for customer 9500000027) to 0001 from the previous value:

i.   The system pops-up a message that the changes you have done are yet to be confirmed (Figure 10.19).

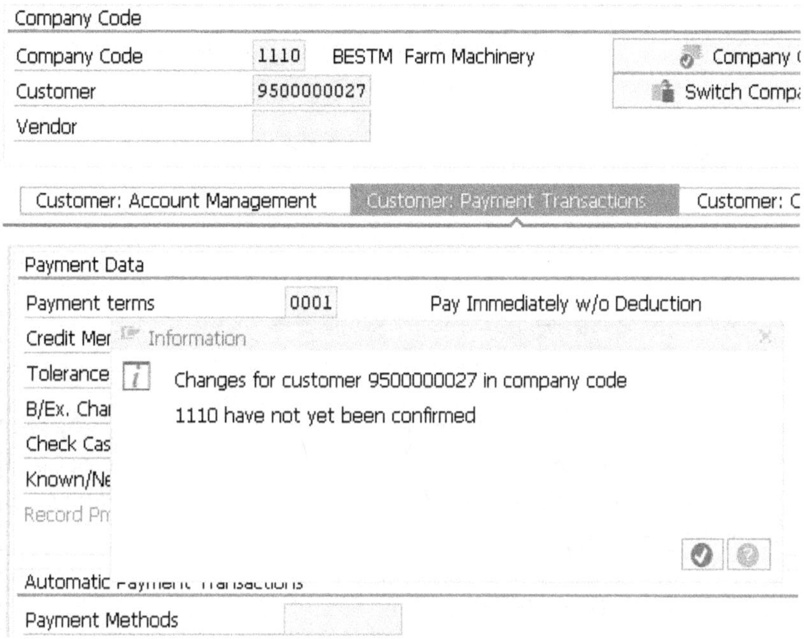

Figure 10.19 System Displaying a Message on the Changes to Sensitive Fields

ii.   You can use Transaction FD08 (for single records) and FD09 (for multiple customer master records) to view and confirm/reject the changes. On entering the Transaction FD08, for example, the system brings up the last record, and you can press 'Enter' to continue, if that is the record you want to review. The system will, now, bring up the next screen showing the 'Current Status' that there are field contents which needs to be confirmed (Figure 10.20).

Figure 10.20 System Displaying the Confirmation Status

iii.   You can click on 'Changes to sensitive fields' button to view which field's content has been changed to (Figure 10.21).

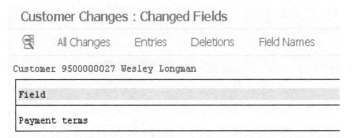

Figure 10.21 System Displaying the Changed Sensitive Field

iv.   The system shows that the contents of 'Payment terms' field has been modified. You may double-click on 'Payment terms' to view the changes: the system brings up the details indicating when the change was made, what was the old value and what is the new value (Figure 10.22).

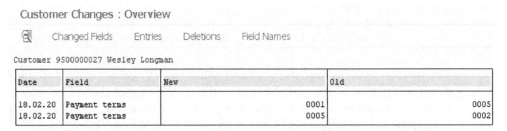

Figure 10.22 System Displaying the Details of Changes Made to Sensitive Fields

v.   If you go back to the previous screen, and try confirming the changes the system will not allow you to do so, if you are the same person who has made the changes in the first place. The system will bring up a message that you are not allowed to change but can only display the details (Figure 10.23).

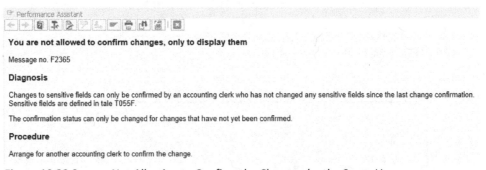

Figure 10.23 System Not Allowing to Confirm the Changes by the Same User

vi.   Now you need to approach another accounting clerk / supervisor, who has the necessary authorization, to confirm / reject the changes.

---

i You may also display the critical changes (and take action) using the SAP Easy Access menu path: SAP Menu > Accounting > Financial Accounting > Accounts Receivable > Information System > Reports for Accounts Receivable Accounting > Master Data > Display/Confirm Critical Customer Changes. You may also use Transaction S_ALR_87012183.

This completes our discussion on dual control of sensitive fields and also the preparations required for creating customer master records. Let us, now, look at the settings that you can make to exercise control on changing customer master records.

10.1.1.2   Preparations for Changing Customer Master Data

SAP uses the report RFDABL00 to display changes to the customer master record data, across accounts. The default 'select option' brings out the change date, the name of the person who made the change and the field group. However, you can choose additional fields for which you may want to see the changes for the general data, the company code data or the sales area data. You can also display the technical field names of the changed fields. Besides selecting additional fields, for which you want to see the changes, if any, you can also protect these individual fields via authorizations when maintaining master data.

You need to complete the preparations in two steps: in the first step, you need to define the field groups and in the second step, you will assign the required fields (to the field group you just defined) for which you want the program to display the changes. By establishing suitable authorization, you may also restrict the changes to these fields.

Project Dolphin

BESTM management has indicated that they want to include additional fields like 'Alternative Payer', 'House Bank', 'Payment Terms', 'Reconciliation Account', 'Customer Classification', 'Payment Block' and 'Credit Control Area' in logging the changes made by users while changing the customer master records. However, they have indicated that they do not want to exercise restricting the changes to these fields as such action for some of the fields ('Alternative Payer', 'House Bank' and 'Payment Terms') are better handled by dual control of sensitive fields.

Let us start with the first step of defining the field groups for customer master change.

10.1.1.2.1   Define Field Groups for Customer Master Records

Here, you will define field groups by entering a key and description for each field group. When you set the indicator 'No authorization', then, the system does not subject this group to the authorization check when maintaining master data; the system uses this field group only for selecting the fields via the report (RFDABL00) for displaying changes.

To define the required field groups:

i. Use the menu path: SAP Customizing Implementation Guide > Financial Accounting > Accounts Receivable and Accounts Payable > Customer Accounts > Master Data > Preparations for Changing Customer Master Data > Define Field Groups for Customer Master Records.

ii. On the resulting screen (Figure 10.24) click on 'New Entries' and enter a 1 or 2-digit numeric identifier for the new 'Field group', provide a 'Description' and select the 'No authorization' check-box to prevent any authorization checks on this field group, when changing the master records.

iii. 'Save' the details and create more field groups, if required.

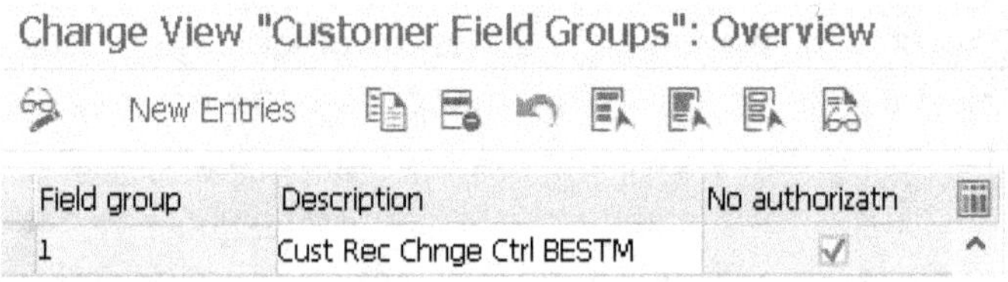

Change View "Customer Field Groups": Overview

New Entries

Field group	Description	No authorizatn
1	Cust Rec Chnge Ctrl BESTM	✓

Figure 10.24 Field Group for Customer Master Change Control

With the definition of field group, we are now ready to assign individual fields (to the field group) for which you want to show the changes, while displaying the customer master changes.

10.1.1.2.2   Group Fields for Customer Master Records

Using this activity, you will, now, assign the customer master record fields to the field group(s) that you have defined in the previous step. Once done, you can enter this field group in program RFDABL00 afterwards, to display the changes.

To include the fields to the field group:

i. Use the menu path: SAP Customizing Implementation Guide > Financial Accounting > Accounts Receivable and Accounts Payable > Customer Accounts > Master Data > Preparations for Changing Customer Master Data > Group Fields for Customer Master Records.

ii. On the resulting 'Change View "Customer field group fields": Overview' screen (Figure 10.25), click on 'New Entries', enter the field group identifier ('Field grp') and add the customer master fields ('Fld name') that you want to include in report RFDABL00, under this field group. 'Save' when completed; the system brings up the 'Field Label' for each of these fields.

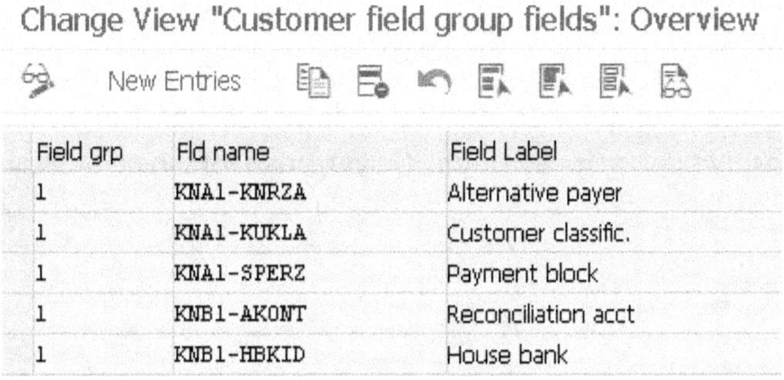

Change View "Customer field group fields": Overview

New Entries

Field grp	Fld name	Field Label
1	KNA1-KNRZA	Alternative payer
1	KNA1-KUKLA	Customer classific.
1	KNA1-SPERZ	Payment block
1	KNB1-AKONT	Reconciliation acct
1	KNB1-HBKID	House bank

Figure 10.25 Adding Fields to Field Group

Now that you have defined the field group and added the customer master record fields to the field group, you can use them in the selection screen of report RFDABL00. Use the SAP Easy Access menu path: SAP Menu > Accounting > Financial Accounting > Accounts Receivable > Information System > Reports for Accounts Receivable Accounting > Master Data > Display Changes to Customers or Transaction S_ALR_87012182 and maintain the entry (Figure 10.26) for the 'Field group' (01).

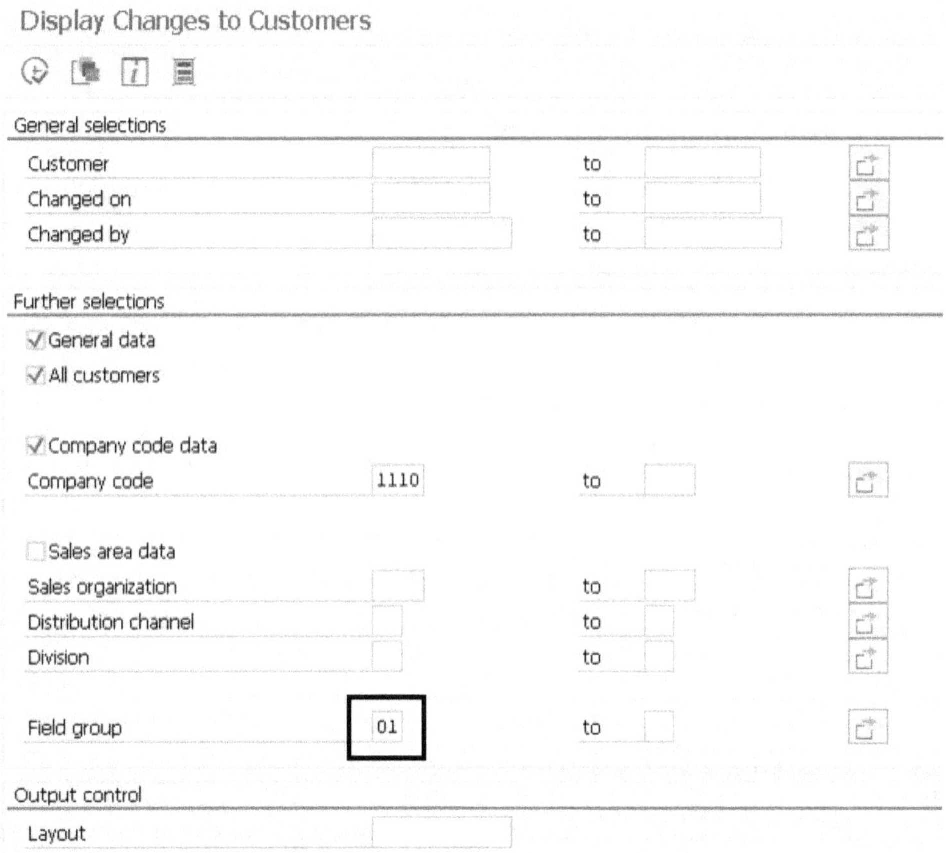

Display Changes to Customers

General selections

Customer		to	
Changed on		to	
Changed by		to	

Further selections

☑ General data
☑ All customers

☑ Company code data

Company code	1110	to	

☐ Sales area data

Sales organization		to	
Distribution channel		to	
Division		to	

Field group	01	to	

Output control

Layout	

Figure 10.26 Selection Screen of Report RFDABL00 Showing the Field Group

When you execute the report, the system brings up the list displaying the changes made to the fields, including the ones in the field group (01), for example. You can notice (Figure 10.27) that the system is displaying the changes for the additional fields (for example, 'Recon. Account'), besides the sensitive fields (for example, 'Payt terms) for which there were changes in the master record.

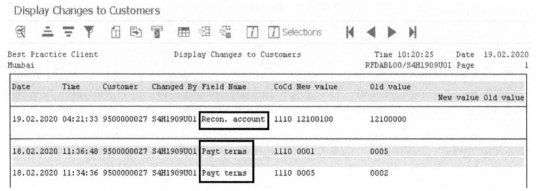

Figure 10.27 Report RFDABL00 Displaying Changes

This completes our discussion on the settings required to control changing of customer master records. Let us, now, see the deletion of customer master records.

10.1.1.3   Delete Customer Master Data

Using this configuration step, you can delete the customer master records through the standard SAP program SAPF019. The system deletes general customer master data for customers who are not created as customers in SAP SD.

You will be able to delete master records for accounts which do not have any transaction data. The other condition is that the company code for which you are trying to delete the master records should not have been flagged as 'productive'. Use this program only in the test phase.

To delete, use the menu path: SAP Customizing Implementation Guide > Financial Accounting > Accounts Receivable and Accounts Payable > Customer Accounts > Master Data > Delete Customer Master Data or Transaction OBR2. Maintain the required selection parameters on the resulting screen and run the program. As you can see, you will be using the same program to delete G/L (refer Table 9.7, in Section 9.6.1 of Chapter 9 of Vol. I) and vendor master records as well.

> **i** You can use the program SAPF019 to delete master data in FI. You can use it to delete customer master data, vendor master data and G/L account master data. You can run this for: (1) deleting general master data (in the case of G/L accounts, in one chart of accounts), (2) deleting master data dependent on company code and (3) deleting general master data and

master data dependent on company code. For each of the deletion run, you can specify whether or not the system should take into account the deletion flag in master records by selecting or deselecting the 'Delete per deletion flag only' check-box. The system checks the deletion block always at general data and company code-dependent data level: if there is a block at company code-dependent data level, then the general data is not deleted either. The 'deletion block' (NODEL) takes precedence over the 'deletion flag '(LOVEM).

In the case of customer master records, the program deletes general master data, bank details, VAT registration numbers, addresses, classifications, credit management (across control areas and centrally), unloading points, tax indicators, contact persons, licenses, partner function limit, shipping data, master data in the company code, dunning data and the linked data. As regards the vendor master records are concerned, the program deletes general master data, bank details, contact persons, VAT registration numbers, addresses, classifications, master data in the company code, dunning data and the linked data. In the case of G/L accounts, the program deletes, general master data in the chart of accounts, names in the chart of accounts, key word list in the chart of accounts, master data in the company code and sample accounts, if selected in the selection screen. Besides the above, the program also deletes the change documents for master data and the SAPScript text files.

The general master data can only be deleted if no other application makes reference to that account. If you want to delete only general master data, master data dependent on company code should not have been created in FI. If a customer or vendor is referenced by another customer or vendor (for example, via alternative payee), you can only delete the referenced master record by deleting the referencing master record at the same time. Also, you can delete master data in FI, only if no transactions have been posted to the corresponding accounts; if there are transaction figures in any of the selected accounts, then, you have to manually run the program SAPF020 (to reset transaction data from company code) before deleting that account.

After execution, the log lists every table which is processed in the program selection. You can also create a detail log, for each account type, to find out why certain data was not deleted. The detail logs show you what other company codes and applications use the data and how customers and vendors are linked to one another. Since deleting or displaying even smaller volumes of data can result in runtime problems, you should always run this program only as a background job.

This completes our discussion on preparations for creating / changing / deleting customer master records. Let is now see the settings required for line items.

10.1.2 Line Items

The settings that are required to be configured for customer line items can be grouped into three categories viz., (1) display open items, (2) open item processing and (3) correspondence.

10.1.2.1   Display Line Items

In the case of 'display open items', you will have to make the settings for the line item display using the ABAP List View (ALV). By default, the system displays the line items with the ALV. However, if you do not wish to use ALV, you can continue to use line item display without ALV, as a modification. To enable this, you have to complete the settings listed under the configuration step 'Display Line Items without ALV'. You can access this IMG node through the menu path: SAP Customizing Implementation Guide > Financial Accounting > Accounts Receivable and Accounts Payable > Customer Accounts > Line Items > Display Line Items > Display Line Items without ALV.

Project Dolphin

The project team has recommended to the BESTM Corporate to stick to the line item display using the ABAP List View. Also, they have suggested not to define additional fields for customer line item display as that may result in performance issues. Besides, they are also of the view that no additional settings would be required than the default ones, for processing open items.

You may use 'Define Additional Fields for Line Item Display' (menu path: SAP Customizing Implementation Guide > Financial Accounting > Accounts Receivable and Accounts Payable > Customer Accounts > Line Items > Display Line Items > Define Additional Fields for Line Item Display) to include additional fields (such as, 'User' or 'Quantity' etc) for display. However, consider carefully whether you really need to enhance the line item display, as such enhancements can reduce performance since the system has to read more table entries.

10.1.2.2   Open Item Processing

As in display of line items, you may make additional settings for open item processing. Follow the menu path: SAP Customizing Implementation Guide > Financial Accounting > Accounts Receivable and Accounts Payable > Customer Accounts > Line Items > Open Item Processing, and complete the individual configuration steps there on.

10.1.2.3   Correspondence

In the case of settings for correspondence, you can make new settings for correspondence using the menu path: SAP Customizing Implementation Guide > Financial Accounting > Accounts Receivable and Accounts Payable > Customer Accounts > Line Items > Correspondence, or check your existing settings to ensure completeness. We have already discussed the settings for correspondence (in Section 7.3 'Correspondence' of Chapter 7 of Vol. I) when we configured the FI global settings. Of course, you can check here, now, whether the settings are correct / complete. If you have not yet made any settings earlier, you can do so here.

10.1.2.3.1   Define Period Types for Customers

Additionally, you can create account statements automatically by entering a key (say, 1 for monthly statements, 2 for quarterly statements, 3 for half-yearly statements and so on) specifying with which frequency the account statements are to be created in the 'Bank Statement' field in the customer master and 'Account Statement' field in the vendor master records. You may specify this key as a selection criterion for the program for creating account statements periodically.

Use the menu path: SAP Customizing Implementation Guide > Financial Accounting > Accounts Receivable and Accounts Payable > Customer Accounts > Line Items > Correspondence > Define Period Types for Customers. On the resulting screen, enter the identifier for the frequency key ('Acct Stmnt') and provide an explanation in the 'Text' field (Figure 10.28).

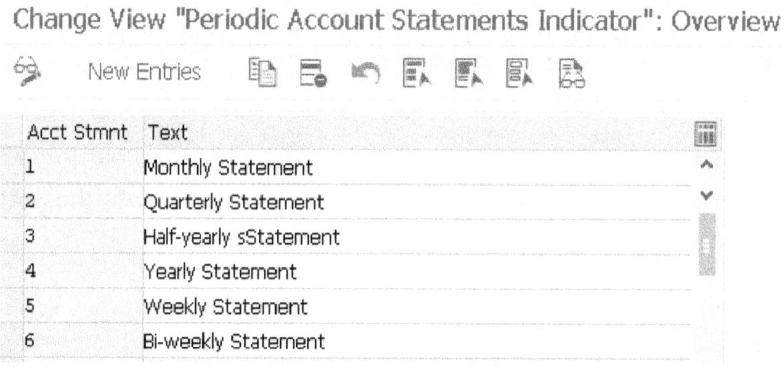

Change View "Periodic Account Statements Indicator": Overview

New Entries

Acct Stmnt	Text
1	Monthly Statement
2	Quarterly Statement
3	Half-yearly sStatement
4	Yearly Statement
5	Weekly Statement
6	Bi-weekly Statement

Figure 10.28 Periodic Account Statement Indicator

You need to determine the customer accounts for which you plan to generate periodic account statements. Once done, you need to enter the appropriate key (from the above definition) in the appropriate field in customer ('Bank Statement') / vendor master ('Account Statement') record (Figure 10.29). The system, now, creates the account statements, for all the customers / vendors whose master record is entered with this key, through the report program as per the periodicity defined in the key.

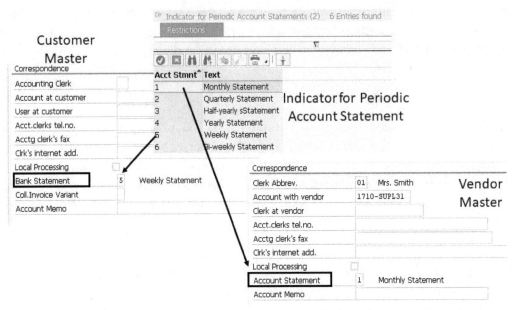

Figure 10.29 Periodic Account Statement Indicator in Customer / Vendor Master Record

This completes our discussion on the settings required for line items, and also the customer accounts. Let us, now, move on to discuss the vendor accounts in the next Section.

10.2 Vendor Accounts

As in the case of customer accounts, we shall see the settings that are required for vendor accounts in this Section. Besides master data and line items, we shall discuss the settings required for overdue payables as well here.

Let us start with the vendor master data.

10.2.1 Master Data

As in the case of customer accounts, you need to create one master record for each vendor account that you require in the system. Both the financial accounting (FI-A/P) and the purchasing (SAP MM) departments of your organization use the same master records. By creating and storing vendor master data centrally, you enable their access throughout the organization, and this avoids (a) the need to enter the same information twice and (b) inconsistencies in master data that may creep in if not maintained centrally. If the address of one of your vendors changes, for example, you only have to enter this change once and your accounting and purchasing departments will always have the updated details.

A vendor, like a customer, can be a person (individual), an organization or a group. A typical vendor master data is made up of three areas (segments) as shown in Figure 10.30:

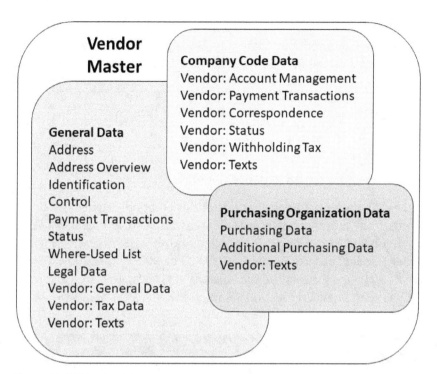

Figure 10.30 Vendor Master Data

- General Data
- Company Code Data (FI area data)
- Purchasing Organization Data (MM area data)

As in the case of a customer account, the 'general data' with the information such as address, control data, payment transactions, status, legal data etc., will be at the Client level and hence is valid across company codes. The 'company code data' (account management, payment transactions, withholding tax, correspondence etc) is valid only for the specific company code in which the vendor has been created. The 'purchasing organization data' is made up of information relating to purchasing organization, purchasing data (conditions, sales data, control data, default values for material etc), additional purchasing data and texts and will be valid for the purchasing organization.

The specifications you make in a vendor master record are used (a) as default values when you post items to the account (for example, the terms of payment you specify in the master record are defaulted for document entry), (b) for processing business transactions like payment processing for which the date of the last payment run is required for the automatic payment program, (c) for working with master records so as to, for example, prevent certain users (through appropriate authorization groups) from accessing an account, (d) for communication with the vendor using the address details and (e) in the purchasing department for material procurement activities.

> **i** You should have implemented the Materials Management (SAP MM) application component in order to enter / process vendor master records for processing the purchasing related business transactions.

You can create vendor master data, in SAP, in three different ways:

- Central maintenance (for all the three areas)
- FI maintenance (for FI area alone)
- Purchasing organization data maintenance (for MM area alone)

The Table 10.4 outlines the menu path and Transaction for creating / changing / displaying vendor master records from different maintenance areas (FI, MM and central). All these Transactions are now bundled into a single Transaction known as BP. However, if you still enter any of the earlier Transactions like FK01 / FK02 / FK03 or MK01 / MK02 / MK03 or XK01 / XK02 / XK03 to create / change / display vendor master in FI area, MM area and centrally, the system redirects you to the new Transaction BP automatically, after briefly displaying the earlier Transaction screen.

Maintenance Area	Activity	SAP Easy Access Menu	Transaction
Accounting (FI) Area Menu FDMN	Create Vendor (Accounting)	SAP Menu > Accounting > Financial Accounting > Accounts Payable > Master Records > Create	BP (earlier FK01)
	Change Vendor (Accounting)	SAP Menu > Accounting > Financial Accounting > Accounts Payable > Master Records > Change	BP (earlier FK02)
	Display Vendor (Accounting)	SAP Menu > Accounting > Financial Accounting > Accounts Payable > Master Records > Display	BP (earlier FK03)
Purchasing (MM) Area Menu ME00	Create Vendor (Purchasing)	SAP Menu > Logistics > Materials Management > Purchasing > Master Data > Vendor > Purchasing > Create	BP (earlier MK01)
	Change Vendor (Purchasing)	SAP Menu > Logistics > Materials Management > Purchasing > Master Data > Vendor > Purchasing > Change	BP (earlier MK02)
	Display Vendor (Purchasing)	SAP Menu > Logistics > Materials Management > Purchasing > Master Data > Vendor > Purchasing > Display	BP (earlier MK03)
Centrally	Create Vendor (Centrally)	SAP Menu > Accounting > Financial Accounting > Accounts Payable > Master Records > Maintain Centrally > Create	BP (earlier XK01)

		SAP Menu > Logistics > Materials Management > Purchasing > Master Data > Vendor > Central > Create	
	Change Vendor (Centrally)	SAP Menu > Accounting > Financial Accounting > Accounts Payable > Master Records > Maintain Centrally > Change	BP (earlier XK02)
		SAP Menu > Logistics > Materials Management > Purchasing > Master Data > Vendor > Central > Change	
	Display Vendor (Centrally)	SAP Menu > Accounting > Financial Accounting > Accounts Payable > Master Records > Maintain Centrally > Display	BP (earlier XK03)
		SAP Menu > Logistics > Materials Management > Purchasing > Master Data > Vendor > Central > Display	

Table 10:4 Vendor Master Maintenance

---

i As in the case of customer accounts, in some companies, accounting (FI) and Purchasing (MM) departments maintain the general data together but FI and Purchasing organization data separately. In other companies, vendor master records are maintained centrally (for all the areas).

10.2.1.1   Preparations for Creating Vendor Master Data

As in the case of customer master records, you need to complete certain pre-requisites - like defining number ranges, creating vendor account groups and maintaining field status - before you can create master data for your vendors. Since we have discussed them in details in Section 10.1.1.1, we are not repeating the details here. It is sufficient to note that you need to (a) decide on suitable numbering (internal / external) for the vendor master records with appropriate number range intervals, (b) have adequate vendor account groups for creation of vendor master records as the account group determines which fields have to be filled compulsorily (mandatory) and which ones can be optionally filled when creating the master records besides allocating a number (external or internal) to the master record and (c) have field status definitions - suitably defined for the account group (and also for the company code and/transactions) - to determine the status of the fields on the screens for the master data creation.

Let us start with the creation of (vendor) account groups.

10.2.1.1.1   Define Account Groups with Screen Layout (Vendors)

This is similar to the one that we have seen earlier for customers. Use this activity to define the required account groups for crating you vendors (suppliers). As in the case of customer, you can have more detailed classification of vendor account groups like domestic vendor (0001), goods supplier (0002), alternate payer (0003), invoice presented by (0004), forwarding agent (0005), special vendor (0010), one-time vendors (0099) and so on or you can have limited ones like domestic vendors, foreign vendors etc.

Project Dolphin

BESTM management has asked the Dolphin project manager to create elaborate account groups like vendor (0001), goods supplier (0002), alternate payer (0003), invoice presented by (0004), forwarding agent (0005), special vendor (0010) and one-time vendors (0099) besides separate account groups to take care of vendor accounts that are transferred from the external system.

The project team has recommended to the BESTM management, to control the field status through accounts groups. Accordingly, no new screen layout settings are to be defined for the company codes (of BESTM) or for transactions.

Use the menu path: SAP Customizing Implementation Guide > Financial Accounting > Accounts Receivable and Accounts Payable > Vendor Accounts > Master Data > Preparations for Creating Vendor Master Data > Define Account Groups with Screen Layout (Vendors) to create new account groups (Figure 10.31). You may also use Transaction OBD3.

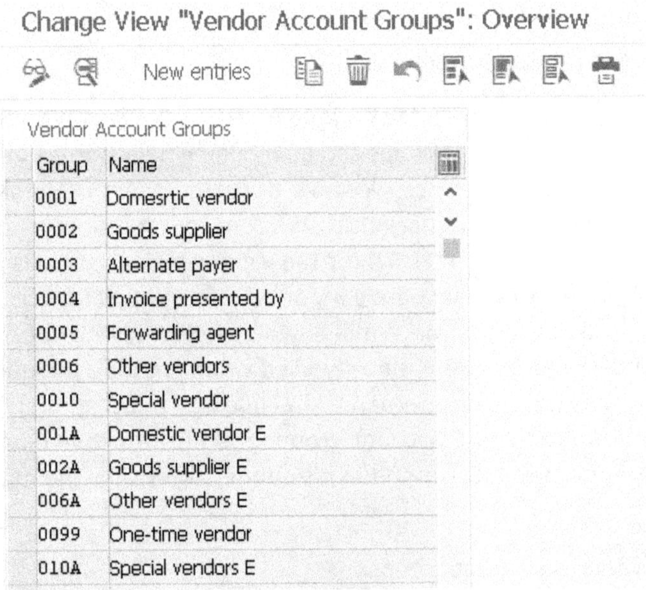

Change View "Vendor Account Groups": Overview

New entries

Group	Name
0001	Domesrtic vendor
0002	Goods supplier
0003	Alternate payer
0004	Invoice presented by
0005	Forwarding agent
0006	Other vendors
0010	Special vendor
001A	Domestic vendor E
002A	Goods supplier E
006A	Other vendors E
0099	One-time vendor
010A	Special vendors E

Figure 10.31 Vendor Account Groups

As in the case of customer account groups, you must have at least one vendor account group defined in the system without which you cannot create any vendor master record. As stated elsewhere, you will be able to delete an existing account group only if no master record is referencing that group. You also need to be cautious in changing its field status settings of an existing account group; else, you may run into serious issues. For example, if you change the field status of an already existing field (with the status 'display') to 'suppressed', then, you will not be able to see that field on the screen even though the earlier field contents would still be valid for that field.

10.2.1.1.2   Define Screen Layout per Company Code (Vendors)

As already discussed in Section 10.1.1.1.2, you should manage the field status via the account groups, except for special situations wherein you may define company-code specific field status, for example, if the company codes are in different countries or some company codes do not use automatic payment processing for vendors.

Project Dolphin

BESTM does not want to manage the field status via either company codes or processing type (= transaction); instead, it has to be through the account groups.

Use the menu path: SAP Customizing Implementation Guide > Financial Accounting > Accounts Receivable and Accounts Payable > Vendor Accounts > Master Data > Preparations for Creating Vendor Master Data > Define Screen Layout per Company Code (Vendors), to define the necessary settings, if fields are to have an alternative status depending on the company code. Once you are into the Transaction, specify the company code and determine the status of the fields as required. In the standard system, as in the case of customers, you will see default settings that are valid for all the company codes as denoted by '*' in the 'Company Code' field (Figure 10.32). You may create new settings by clicking on 'New Entries' for specific company codes, or use the default settings as such or with some modifications. We are not doing any change to the standard settings as BESTM wants to manage the field status via account groups.

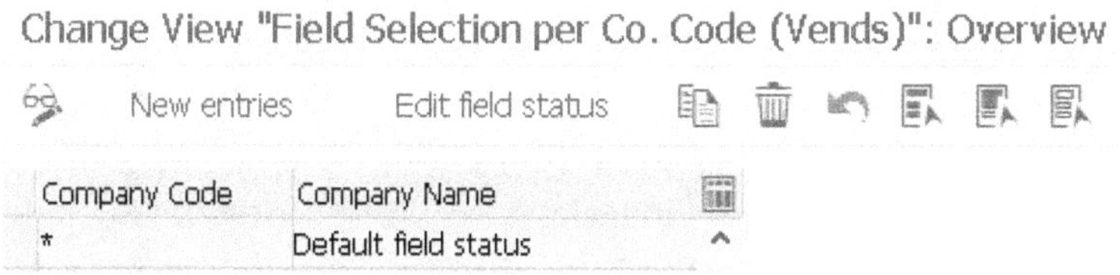

Change View "Field Selection per Co. Code (Vends)": Overview

Company Code	Company Name	
*	Default field status	

Figure 10.32 Defining Screen Layout per Company Code (Vendors)

10.2.1.1.3   Define Screen Layout per Activity (Vendors)

Here, you determine, depending on the transactions (display, create or change) for vendor master data, which master record fields are ready for input, require an entry and are hidden. As discussed previously, these specifications will be linked with the field status of the account group and the company code-dependent specification; the 'link rule' will determine which final status the fields have on the entry screen for master data. Since, for BESTM, the field status will be controlled via account groups, we will not be configuring this activity.

However, should you really need to control via transactions, you can do so by using the menu path: SAP Customizing Implementation Guide > Financial Accounting > Accounts Receivable and Accounts Payable > Vendor Accounts > Master Data > Preparations for Creating Vendor Master Data > Define Screen Layout per Activity (Vendors). On the resulting screen (Figure 10.33), you will see the listing of various transactions like create vendor (accounting), change vendor (accounting), delete vendor (accounting), create vendor (purchasing), create customer (centrally) and so on. You may double-click on the required transaction, and change the field status, as required, on the 'Change View "Transaction-Dependent Field Selection (Vendor)": Details' screen.

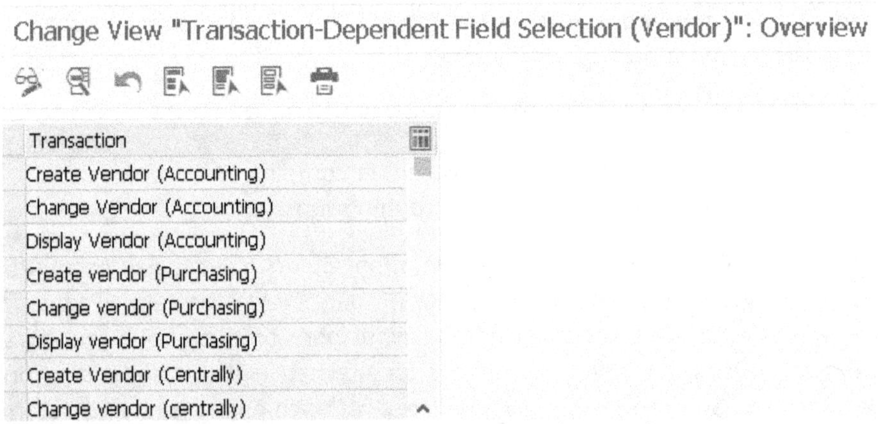

Figure 10.33 Defining Screen Layout per Transaction (Vendors)

We will not be discussing (a) change message control, (b) define accounting clerks and (c) define industries, again in this Section, as we have already discussed them in Section 10.1.1.1.4, 10.1.1.1.5 and 10.1.1.1.6 respectively, when we discussed the customer accounts. You do not need to repeat defining industries. However, you can define the accounting clerks who will handle vendor accounts, using the menu path SAP Customizing Implementation Guide > Financial Accounting > Accounts Receivable and Accounts Payable > Vendor Accounts > Master Data > Preparations for Creating Vendor Master Data > Define Accounting Clerks. Similarly, you can change the standard message control (or define new) by using the menu path: SAP Customizing Implementation Guide > Financial Accounting > Accounts Receivable and Accounts Payable > Vendor Accounts > Master Data > Preparations for Creating Vendor Master Data > Change Message Control for Vendor Master Data.

With this we are now ready to define the number ranges for vendor master records.

10.2.1.1.4   Create Number Ranges for Vendor Accounts

As with number ranges for customer accounts, you will use this configuration step to maintain the required number range intervals for the vendor accounts. You can have several number ranges with each range being allocated to a single account group, or have fewer number ranges wherein you will allocate more than one account group with the same number range. Refer Section 7.1.5 'Document Number Ranges' of Chapter 7 of Vol. I, for more details on number ranges.

Project Dolphin

BESTM wants numbering the vendor accounts similar to that of the customer accounts. Accordingly, the project team wants to create six number ranges from B1 to B5, and B9 with the specifications that B5 should be used for one-time vendors and B9 for external numbering to accommodate the vendor accounts transferred from the external systems.

The configuration is similar to the one that we have discussed in Section 10.1.1.1.7 when we defined the number ranges for customer accounts. Use the menu path: SAP Customizing Implementation Guide > Financial Accounting > Accounts Receivable and Accounts Payable > Vendor Accounts > Master Data > Preparations for Creating Vendor Master Data > Create Number Ranges for Vendor Accounts or Transaction XKN1 to create the required number ranges (Figure 10.34). While defining, select 'Ext' check-box if you need to denote one or more number ranges as external. For all the number ranges which are external, you will need to supply the account number while creating the master records; for all other cases, the system will automatically supply the number ranges, internally, from the respective number range intervals.

Edit Intervals: Vendor, Object KREDITOR

N..	From No.	To Number	NR Status	Ext
B1	1800000011	2500000000	0	☐
B2	2500000011	3100000010	0	☐
B3	3100000021	5000052999	0	☐
B4	5000054000	5500000010	0	☐
B5	5500000021	6700000000	0	☐
B9	9200000000	9599999999	0	☑

Figure 10.34 Number Ranges for Vendor Accounts

Now that we have defined the required number ranges, the next step is to assign these number ranges to the appropriate (vendor)account groups.

10.2.1.1.5   Assign Number Ranges to Vendor Account Groups

Use the menu path: SAP Customizing Implementation Guide > Financial Accounting > Accounts Receivable and Accounts Payable > Vendor Accounts > Master Data > Preparations for Creating Vendor Master Data > Assign Number Ranges to Vendor Account Groups or Transaction XKN2 to assign the number ranges to the vendor account groups (Figure 10.35). As already indicated, you can have a single number range assigned to more than one account group, if required. For example, in the case of BESTM, we have assigned the number range B3, B4 and B9 to more than one account group.

Change View "Assign Vendor Account Groups->Number Range": Overview

Group	Name	Number range
0001	Domesrtic vendor	B1
0002	Goods supplier	B2
0003	Alternate payer	B3
0004	Invoice presented by	B3
0005	Forwarding agent	B3
0006	Other vendors	B4
0010	Special vendor	B4
001A	Domestic vendor E	B9
002A	Goods supplier E	B9
006A	Other vendors E	B9
0099	One-time vendor	B5
010A	Special vendors E	B9

Figure 10.35 Assigning Number Ranges to Vendor Account Groups

With this, we are now ready define the sensitive fields for dual control.

10.2.1.1.6   Define Sensitive Fields for Dual Control (Vendors)

As in the case of customer accounts, you need to define the sensitive fields (if any) here, so that these fields will be brought under dual control for additional security. This means, that the user who changes the field content of a sensitive field will not be able to approve the same; but need to approach another user, with the required authorization, to confirm/reject the changes. Unless the changes are confirmed or rejected, you will not be able to include that account, for example, into certain transactions like say, payment run. Till the changes are verified, the system will pop-up with the message, indicating that the changes are yet to be actioned upon, when you enter any Transaction to edit the master record. It is a general practice that a sensitive field will be verified by the supervisor or senior accounting clerk in the accounts department.

Project Dolphin

BESTM wants to have a strict control to unauthorized changes to some of the important fields in vendor master records. Accordingly, they have indicated to the project team to bring 'Alternative Payee', 'Payment Block', Bank Account', 'Account with Vendor' and 'Tolerance Group' under dual control by denoting them as 'sensitive' fields. Only the supervisor or manager of the accounting clerk, will have the required authorization to confirm or reject the changes made to these sensitive fields.

Use the menu path: SAP Customizing Implementation Guide > Financial Accounting > Accounts Receivable and Accounts Payable > Vendor Accounts > Master Data > Preparations for Creating Vendor Master Data > Define Sensitive Fields for Dual Control (Vendors) or Transaction S_ALR_87003179 to define the sensitive fields (Figure 10.36).

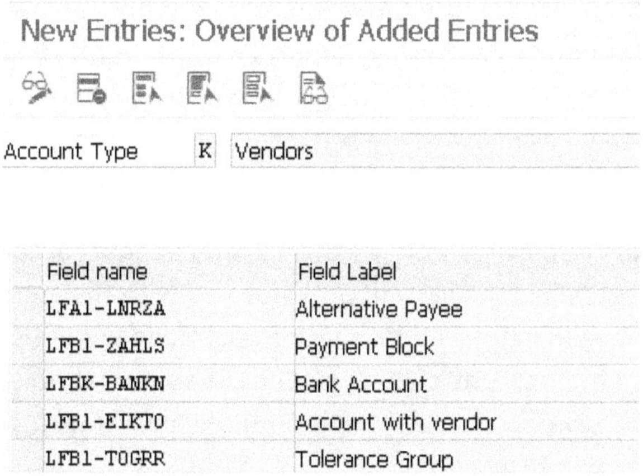

New Entries: Overview of Added Entries

Account Type   K   Vendors

Field name	Field Label
LFA1-LNRZA	Alternative Payee
LFB1-ZAHLS	Payment Block
LFBK-BANKN	Bank Account
LFB1-EIKTO	Account with vendor
LFB1-TOGRR	Tolerance Group

Figure 10.36 Sensitive Fields under Dual Control for Vendor Master

---

i You may use Transaction FK08 to confirm changes to sensitive fields of a single vendor or Transaction FK09 to confirm changes belonging to multiple vendors (Figure 10.37).

In the case of multiple accounts, you have the option to select (a) accounts not yet confirmed, (b) accounts refused and (c) accounts to be confirmed by yourself. In the case of option (b), you can display the accounts for which sensitive field changes have earlier been rejected. In option (c), the system displays only those accounts for which you have authorization to confirm changes. As a part of dual control, the system also checks to see if you were involved in such changes.

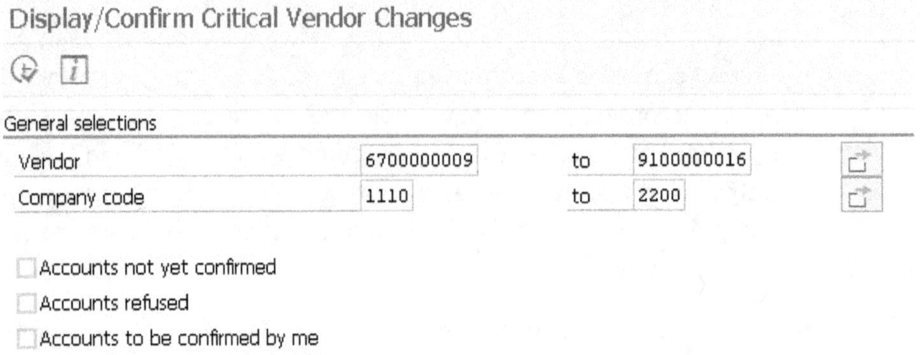

Display/Confirm Critical Vendor Changes

General selections

| Vendor | 6700000009 | to | 9100000016 | |
| Company code | 1110 | to | 2200 | |

☐ Accounts not yet confirmed
☐ Accounts refused
☐ Accounts to be confirmed by me

Figure 10.37 Confirming Changes to Sensitive Fields of Multiple Records

> **i** You may also use the SAP Easy Access menu path: SAP Menu > Accounting > Financial Accounting > Accounts Payable > Information System > Reports for Accounts Payable Accounting > Master Data > Display/Confirm Critical Vendor Changes or Transaction S_ALR_87012090, to display the critical changes made to the sensitive fields (and take action, if required). If you notice closely, you will see that this is nothing but the Transaction FK09.
>
> SAP uses the program RFKCON00 for displaying and changing the vendor account's confirmation status (LFA1-CONFS, LFB1-CONFS). The system provides you with the status as to whether sensitive fields have been changed in the vendor master record, and whether the changes have been confirmed or rejected by dual control. You will see the confirmation status represented by a coloured stoplight with Green (status: confirmed), Yellow (status: to be confirmed) and Red (status: rejected).

This completes our discussion on dual control of sensitive fields and also the preparations required for creating vendor master records. Let us, now, look at the settings that you can make to exercise control on changing vendor master records.

10.2.1.2   Preparations for Changing Vendor Master Data

This is exactly similar to that preparations for changing customer master data. SAP uses a similar report, as that of customer, RFKABL00 to display changes to the vendor master record data across various accounts. As in the case of customer accounts, first, you need to define one or more field groups, and then in the second step you will assign the additional fields to the field group(s) thus defined. Once done, when you run the report, you can include this field group in the 'select option' so as to enable the program to display changes made to these fields as well, besides the default display of, for example, date of change, person who has made the changes etc. Also, by establishing suitable authorization, you can restrict the changes to these fields.

Project Dolphin

BESTM management has indicated that they want to include additional fields Like 'Alternative Payee', 'House Bank', 'Reconciliation Account', 'ABC Indicator', 'Payment Block' and 'Interest Indicator' in logging the changes made by users while changing the vendor master records. However, they have indicated that they do not want to exercise restricting the changes to these fields as such action for some of the fields ('Alternative Payee', 'House Bank' etc) are better handled by dual control of sensitive fields.

Let us start with the first step of defining the field group(s) for vendor master change.

10.2.1.2.1   Define Field Groups for Vendor Master Records

Define the required field group(s) by entering a key and a description for each field group. Select the indicator 'No authorization', if you do not want the system to subject this group to the authorization check when maintaining master data; in this case, the system uses this field group only for selecting the fields via the report () for displaying changes.

To define the required field groups:

- i.   Use the menu path: SAP Customizing Implementation Guide > Financial Accounting > Accounts Receivable and Accounts Payable > Vendor Accounts > Master Data > Preparations for Changing Vendor Master Data > Define Field Groups for Vendor Master Records.
- ii.   On the resulting screen, click on 'New Entries' and enter a 1 or 2-digit numeric identifier for the new 'Field group', provide a 'Description' and select the 'No authorization' check-box to prevent authorization checks on this field group when changing the master records (Figure 10.38). 'Save' the details and create more field groups, if required.

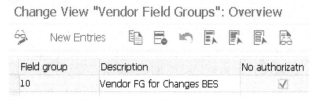

Figure 10.38 Field Group for Vendor Master Change Control

With the definition of field group, we are now ready assign individual fields (to the field group) for which you want to show the changes made, while displaying the vendor master changes.

10.2.1.2.2   Group Fields for Vendor Master Records

Assign the required vendor master record fields to the field group(s) that you have defined in the previous step. Once done, you can enter this field group in program RFKABL00 afterwards, on the selection screen, to display the changes.

To include the fields to the field group:

   i.   Use the menu path: SAP Customizing Implementation Guide > Financial Accounting > Accounts Receivable and Accounts Payable > Vendor Accounts > Master Data > Preparations for Changing Vendor Master Data > Group Fields for Vendor Master Records.

   ii.   On the resulting 'Change View "Fields of the Vendor Field Groups": Overview' screen, click on 'New Entries', enter the field group identifier ('Field grp') and add the vendor master record fields ('Fld name') that you want to include in report RFKABL00 under this field group. 'Save' when completed; the system brings up the 'Field Label' for each of these fields (Figure 10.39).

Change View "Fields Of The Vendor Field Groups": Overview

Field grp	Fld name	Field Label
10	LFA1-LNRZA	Alternative Payee
10	LFB1-AKONT	Reconciliation acct
10	LFB1-HBKID	House bank
10	LFB1-VZSKZ	Interest indicator
10	LFB1-ZAHLS	Payment Block

Figure 10.39 Assigning Fields to Field Group for Vendor Master Change Control

As you have now defined the field group (10) and added the vendor master record fields to that you can, now, use this field group in the selection screen of report RFKABL00. Use the SAP Easy Access menu path: SAP Menu > Accounting > Financial Accounting > Accounts Payable > Information System > Reports for Accounts Payable Accounting > Master Data > Display Changes to Vendors or Transaction S_ALR_87012089. On the resulting selection screen, you may enter 'Field group' (10), among other entries (Figure 10.40).

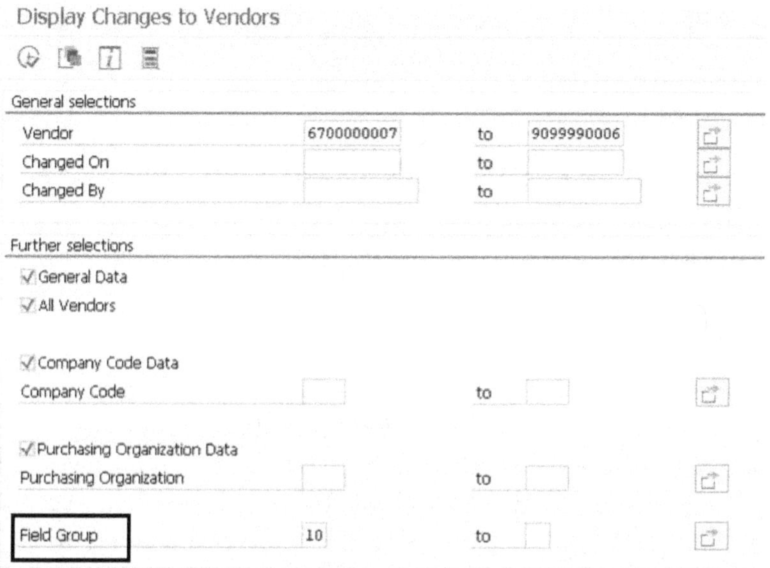

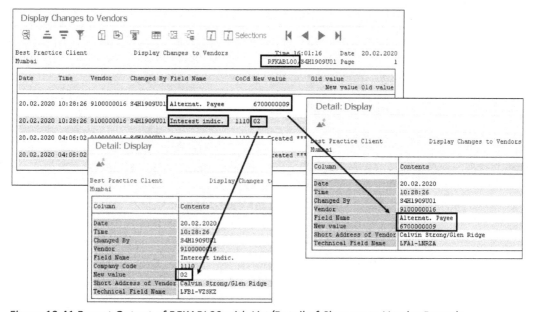

Figure 10.40 Selection Screen of Report RFDABL00 Showing the Field Group

When you execute the report, the system brings up a list displaying (Figure 10.41) the changes made to the fields, including the ones in the field group 10.

Figure 10.41 Report Output of RFKABL00 with List/Detail of Changes to Vendor Records

You can notice that the system is displaying the changes for the additional fields in the field group 10 (for example, 'Interest indic.' And 'Alternat. Payee'), besides the sensitive fields (if any) for which there were changes in the vendor master record.

This completes our discussion on settings required to control changing of vendor master records. Let us, now, see the deletion of vendor master records.

10.2.1.3   Delete Vendor Master Data

Using this configuration step, you can delete the vendor master records through the standard SAP program SAPF019. The system deletes general vendor master data for vendors who are not created as vendors through Purchasing in SAP MM. As discussed in Section 10.1.1.3, you will be able to delete master records for accounts which do not have any transaction data. The other conditions are similar to the deletion of customer master records.

To delete, use the menu path: SAP Customizing Implementation Guide > Financial Accounting > Accounts Receivable and Accounts Payable > Vendor Accounts > Master Data > Delete Vendor Master Data or Transaction OBR2. Maintain the required selection parameters on the resulting screen and run the program. As you can see, you will be using the same program to delete G/L (refer Table 9.7, in Section 9.6.1 of Chapter 9 of Vol. I) and customer master records as well. Refer to Section 10.1.1.3 for additional details on the program SAPF019.

This completes our discussion on preparations for creating / changing / deleting vendor master records. Let is, now, see the settings required for vendor line items.

10.2.2 Line Items

The settings that are required to be configured for vendor line items, are similar to the ones we have discussed for customers, and can be grouped into three categories viz., (1) display open items, (2) open item processing and (3) correspondence.

Let us start with the settings for displaying open items, for vendors.

10.2.2.1   Display Line Items

In the case of 'display open items', you will have to make the settings for the line item display using the ABAP List View (ALV). By default, the system displays the line items with the ALV. However, if you do not wish to use ALV, you can continue to use line item display without ALV as a modification. To enable this, you have to complete the settings listed under the configuration step 'Display Line Items without ALV'. You can access this IMG node through the menu path: SAP Customizing Implementation Guide > Financial Accounting > Accounts Receivable and Accounts Payable > Vendor Accounts > Line Items > Display Line Items > Display Line Items without ALV.

Project Dolphin

The project team has recommended to the BESTM Corporate to stick to the default and standard line item display settings using the ABAP List View. Also, they have suggested not to define additional fields for vendor line item display as that may result in performance issues. Besides, they also of the view that no additional settings would be required than the default ones, for processing open items.

You may use 'Define Additional Fields for Line Item Display' (menu path: SAP Customizing Implementation Guide > Financial Accounting > Accounts Receivable and Accounts Payable > Vendor Accounts > Line Items > Display Line Items > Define Additional Fields for Line Item Display) to include additional fields (such as, 'User' or 'Quantity' etc) for display. However, consider carefully whether you really need to enhance the line item display, as such enhancements can result in performance issues since the system has to read more table entries to bring up the display.

10.2.2.2   Open Item Processing

As in display of vendor line items, you may make additional settings for open item processing. Follow the menu path: SAP Customizing Implementation Guide > Financial Accounting > Accounts Receivable and Accounts Payable > Vendors Accounts > Line Items > Open Item Processing, and complete the individual configuration steps there on. We have not configured this, as BESTM wants to stick on to the default settings for the open item processing.

10.2.2.3   Correspondence

In the case of settings for correspondence, you can make new settings for correspondence using the menu path: SAP Customizing Implementation Guide > Financial Accounting > Accounts Receivable and Accounts Payable > Vendor Accounts > Line Items > Correspondence, or check your existing settings to ensure completeness. We have already discussed the settings for correspondence, (in Section 7.3 'Correspondence' of Chapter 7 of Vol. I), when we configured the FI global settings. You can check those settings, here, and make additional or new settings, if required.

10.2.2.3.1   Define Period Types for Vendors

The settings we have defined in Section 10.1.2.3.1, for customers, are valid as 'period types' for vendors as well. Use the menu path: SAP Customizing Implementation Guide > Financial Accounting > Accounts Receivable and Accounts Payable > Customer Accounts > Line Items > Correspondence > Define the 'Period Types' for Vendors, if you have not created these keys, earlier. Refer Section 10.1.2.3.1, for the configuration steps and how to use this key in vendor master records.

This completes our discussion on the settings required for line items. Let us move on to discuss defining the overdue thresholds for vendor account groups.

10.2.3 Define Thresholds for Vendor Account Groups

Here, you can define a threshold (in percentage) to flag when an overdue payment to a vendor should actually be termed as 'critically overdue'. The system flags an overdue payable amount as 'critically overdue', when the actual overdue payable amount to the total payable is equal to or greater than the defined threshold. You can differentiate the settings, per company code, and make that as more stringent or relaxed (called as 'exceptional threshold') that will then override the 'generic threshold' defined for a particular account group.

For example, as depicted in Figure 10.42, the 'generic threshold' for account group 0001 is 80%. However, since there is another entry for the same account group with the specification of company code (1110), the 'company code-vendor account group' entry of 70% is considered as the 'exceptional threshold'.

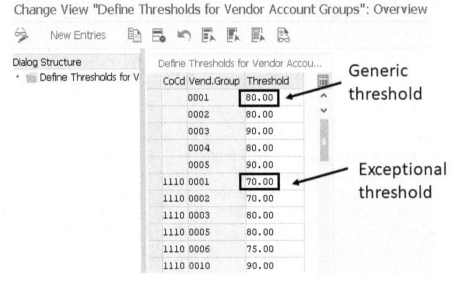

Figure 10.42 Overdue Thresholds for Vendor Account Groups

Now, consider a situation wherein the actual overdue payable amount is $7,690 against the total payable amount of $10,000, for a vendor, who has been assigned with the account group of 0001, in company code 1110:

- When there is both a generic entry and also a (more stringent) company code-specific entry, (for the account group 0001), with the overdue payable being 76.9%, the system flags the vendor's payable as 'critically overdue' based on the 'exceptional threshold' definition (70%), even though the 'generic threshold' definition (80%) does not make that as critically overdue.

- When there is no company code specific entry (for account group 0001), but only the generic entry (80%), then, this overdue is <u>not</u> be considered as 'critically overdue' as the actual overdue payable to the total payable is less than 80%.

With this, we have completed the discussion on settings required for both customer and vendor accounts. Let us move on to discuss the settings that you need to make for some of the important business transactions in both A/R and A/P.

10.3 Business Transactions

Let us discuss the configuration settings relating to important business transactions, here, in this Section. We shall discuss the following:

- Incoming Invoices/Credit Memos
- Release for Payment
- Outgoing Payments
- Outgoing Invoices/Credit Memos
- Incoming Payments
- Management of SEPA Mandates
- Payment with Payment Cards
- Dunning
- Open Item Clearing
- Down Payment Received
- Down Payment Made
- Adjustment Posting/Reversal
- Interest Calculation
- Closing

Let us begin with incoming invoices and/or credit memo receipt.

10.3.1 Incoming Invoices/Credit Memos

There are a couple of tasks which you need to complete including making/checking document settings, and making/checking settings for document parking. The first task will be to make or check the document settings.

10.3.1.1   Make and Check Document Settings

We have already completed the configuration of the important settings, in Vol. I, like defining document types (Section 7.1.2 of Chapter 7), defining posting keys (Section 7.1.6 of Chapter 7), defining screen variants for document entry (Section 7.1.7 of Chapter 7), defining document change rules (Section 7.1.8 of Chapter 7), defining texts and text IDs for documents / line items (Section 7.1.11 of Chapter 7), defining default values (Section 7.1.13 of Chapter

7), defining field status and assigning company codes to field status (Section 6.2 of Chapter 6), defining subscreens for coding blocks (Section 6.2.3 of Chapter 6) and so on.

Let us make or check the settings that are required for document parking.

10.3.1.2   Make and Check Settings for Document Parking

The settings for document parking include several configuration steps:

- Define Entry Screens for Parking Documents
- Create Workflow Variant for Parking Documents
- Assign Company Code to a Workflow Variant for Parking Documents
- Define Release Approval Groups for Parking Documents
- Define Release Approval Paths for Parking Documents
- Assign Release Approval Paths for Parking Documents
- Assign Release Approval Procedure for Parking Documents
- Define Users with Release Authorization for Parking Documents
- Reset Release Approval (Customers)
- Reset Release Approval (Vendors)

Let us discuss the settings one-by-one, in the following Sections.

Project Dolphin

BESTM wants to go with the standard default settings for parking document entry screens.

As BESTM has decided to go in with the standard settings for entry screens for parking documents, we have not defined anything new. On creating a workflow variant for parking documents, note that we have already discussed how to create a workflow variant in Section 6.8.1 of Chapter 6 of Vol. I, and defined the workflow US01 for posting / payment release. We, later, assigned the variant to the required company codes.

Let us look at the rest of the steps here, now.

10.3.1.2.1   Define Release Approval Groups for Parking Documents

Define the release approval groups and later enter them in the master records of your customers / vendors. You will need these approval groups for the next steps like assigning release approval paths / release approval procedures for parking documents. Based on the release approval path and amount specified, the system will determine the subworkflow to be triggered by the payment release; it also determines who needs to release the payment.

Project Dolphin

BESTM wants to have separate release approval groups, for customers / vendors who have been classified into A, B and C buckets, for parking documents.

To define new release approval groups:

i. Use the menu path: SAP Customizing Implementation Guide > Financial Accounting > Accounts Receivable and Accounts Payable > Business Transactions > Incoming Invoices/Credit Memos > Make and Check Settings for Document Parking > Define Release Approval Groups for Parking Documents.

ii. On the resulting screen, click on 'New Entries' and create the required entries and 'Save' the details (Figure 10.43).

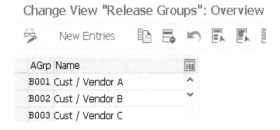

Figure 10.43 Release Groups

The next step is to define the release approval paths.

10.3.1.2.2   Define Release Approval Paths for Parking Documents

Define the release approval paths which you will need for the subsequent steps. Use the menu path: SAP Customizing Implementation Guide > Financial Accounting > Accounts Receivable and Accounts Payable > Business Transactions > Incoming Invoices/Credit Memos > Make and Check Settings for Document Parking > Define Release Approval Paths for Parking Documents. On the resulting screen, click on 'New Entries' and create the required entries and 'Save' the details (Figure 10.44).

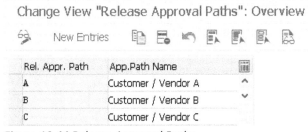

Figure 10.44 Release Approval Paths

The next step is to assign release approval paths for parking documents.

10.3.1.2.3   Assign Release Approval Paths for Parking Documents

Use this activity to assign a release approval path to a combination of 'workflow variants, document types and release approval groups'. Unless you complete this assignment, you will not be able to assign release approval procedures for parking documents, later.

Use the menu path: SAP Customizing Implementation Guide > Financial Accounting > Accounts Receivable and Accounts Payable > Business Transactions > Incoming Invoices/Credit Memos > Make and Check Settings for Document Parking > Assign Release Approval Paths for Parking Documents. On the resulting screen, click on 'New Entries' and create the required settings for each combination of 'workflow variant, document type, release group and release approval path' (Figure 10.45). Ensure to cover all the document types for which you may require release approval.

Change View "Release Approval Path Allocation": Overview

    New Entries

Workflow Variant	Doc. Type	Release Group	Rel. Appr. Path
US01	DR	B001	A
US01	DR	B002	B
US01	DR	B003	C
US01	DZ	B001	A
US01	DZ	B002	B
US01	DZ	B003	C
US01	KR	B001	A
US01	KR	B002	B
US01	KR	B003	C
US01	KZ	B001	A
US01	KZ	B002	B
US01	KZ	B003	C

Figure 10.45 Assigning Release Approval Paths for Parking Documents

With this, we are, now, ready to assign release approval procedures.

10.3.1.2.4   Assign Release Approval Procedure for Parking Documents

Here, you make the required settings to determine as to from which amount which release approval procedure (also known as 'subworkflow') is triggered for each combination of 'workflow variant and release approval path'. The procedure controls how the release is to be carried out and how many release levels are to be triggered.

> ℹ️ You may use SAP's standard settings wherein the subworkflows are predefined, or you may use them as reference templates to create your own.
>
> There are three such subworkflows for *document release*:
>
> 1. WS10000052 (single-level release) requires only one person to release the document.
> 2. WS10000053 (two-level release) requires two people to release (dual control).
> 3. WS10000054 (three-level release) requires three people (triple control) for the release.
>
> And, three more for *payment release*:
>
> a. WS00400011 (single-level release) requires only one person to release the payment.
> b. WS00400021 (two-level release) requires two people to complete the release (dual control).
> c. WS00400022 (three-level release) requires three people (triple control) for the release.

To complete the settings:

i. Use the menu path: SAP Customizing Implementation Guide > Financial Accounting > Accounts Receivable and Accounts Payable > Business Transactions > Incoming Invoices/Credit Memos > Make and Check Settings for Document Parking > Assign Release Approval Procedure for Parking Documents. You may also use Transaction OBWE.

ii. On the 'Change View "Subworkflow Allocation": Overview' screen, click on 'New Entries' and on the next screen (Figure 10.46):

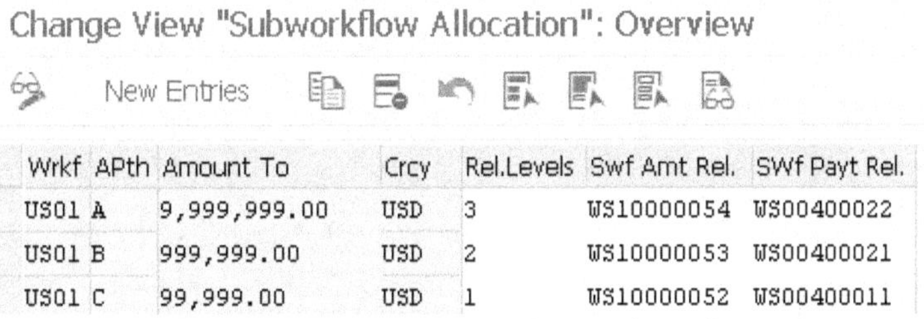

Change View "Subworkflow Allocation": Overview

🖉   New Entries   ▯▯ ▯▯ ▯ ▯▯ ▯▯ ▯▯ ▯▯

Wrkf	APth	Amount To	Crcy	Rel.Levels	Swf Amt Rel.	SWf Payt Rel.
US01	A	9,999,999.00	USD	3	WS10000054	WS00400022
US01	B	999,999.00	USD	2	WS10000053	WS00400021
US01	C	99,999.00	USD	1	WS10000052	WS00400011

Figure 10.46 Assigning Release Approval Procedures for Parking Documents

- Enter the workflow variant ('Wrkf').
- Enter the approval path ('APth').
- Enter the amount ('Amount To') up to which the release approval procedure is to be triggered. Note that the system determines (from the parked document) the amount in such a way that the subledger account with the highest amount is selected.
- Enter the number of release levels ('Rel. Levels') that you require for the 'workflow-release approval path' combination.

- Enter the document (amount) release workflow in 'Swf Amt Rel.' field. For example, if you want to have 3-level release, then, enter WS10000054.

> **i** If you do not want to use amount release, then, enter a blank workflow template (WS2000006).

- Also enter the appropriate payment release workflow (WS00400022) in 'Swf Payt Rel.' field.

Next, you can assign the persons authorized to release at each release level.

10.3.1.2.5   Define Users with Release Authorization for Parking Documents

Using this configuration step, for each combination of 'workflow and approval release path', define the levels and amount limits which can then be assigned to appropriate persons, for effecting the required releases. For example, in the case of 3-level release, you need to have three rows defined with the amount for each of the levels.

To define the settings:

i.   Use the menu path: SAP Customizing Implementation Guide > Financial Accounting > Accounts Receivable and Accounts Payable > Business Transactions > Incoming Invoices/Credit Memos > Make and Check Settings for Document Parking > Define Users with Release Authorization for Parking Documents. You may also use Transaction OBWF.

ii. On the resulting screen, click on 'New Entries' and define the amount limits for each level ('Lv') for each combination of workflow and approval release path (Figure 10.47).

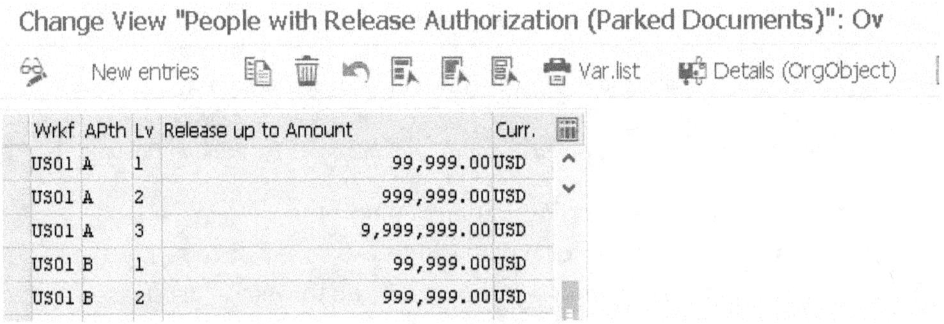

Change View "People with Release Authorization (Parked Documents)": Ov

Wrkf	APth	Lv	Release up to Amount	Curr.
US01	A	1	99,999.00	USD
US01	A	2	999,999.00	USD
US01	A	3	9,999,999.00	USD
US01	B	1	99,999.00	USD
US01	B	2	999,999.00	USD

Figure 10.47 Release Levels with Amount Limit

iii. Now, select the desired row and choose 'Goto -> Detail (OrgObject)' on the menu bar and create and/or assign the required organizational object for the level of release (Figure 10.48). Repeat and make the settings for all the levels, and 'Save' the details.

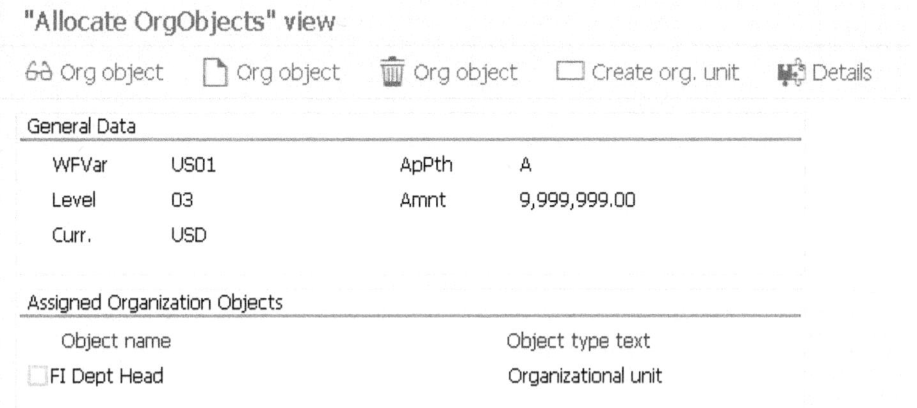

"Allocate OrgObjects" view

6ə Org object　　 Org object　　🗑 Org object　　☐ Create org. unit　　 Details

General Data

WFVar	US01	ApPth	A
Level	03	Amnt	9,999,999.00
Curr.	USD		

Assigned Organization Objects

| Object name | Object type text |
| ☐ FI Dept Head | Organizational unit |

Figure 10.48 Allocating Organization Object to Release Levels

The next action is to define the fields for reset release approval for customers.

10.3.1.2.6　Reset Release Approval (Customers)

Here, you can include the fields that are to be checked in case of changes to the customer document. If the system detects changes to any of the fields included here, then, the system cancels the document release and the process is reset.

Project Dolphin

The project has suggested to the BESTM management, to include fields like 'House Bank', 'Tolerance Group', 'Payment Terms', 'Payment Method', 'Alternative Payer' and 'Payment Block' to be checked by the system. If any changes are found for these fields, then, the system should cancel customer document release. For vendors, the fields will include 'Alternate Payee', 'Interest Indicator', 'House Bank' and 'Payment Block'.

To define the settings, use the menu path: SAP Customizing Implementation Guide > Financial Accounting > Accounts Receivable and Accounts Payable > Business Transactions > Incoming Invoices/Credit Memos > Make and Check Settings for Document Parking > Reset Release Approval (Customers). You may also use Transaction OBWG.

On the resulting screen, click on 'New Entries', select 'Customers' as the account type ('Acct type'), and enter the 'Field name'. You may select 'Incomplete' check-box, if you want the system to cancel the document release when someone attempts to change the contents of such fields when the document is incomplete. When you do not select the 'Incomplete' check-box, the system restarts the document release for such fields only when the document is complete (Figure 10.49).

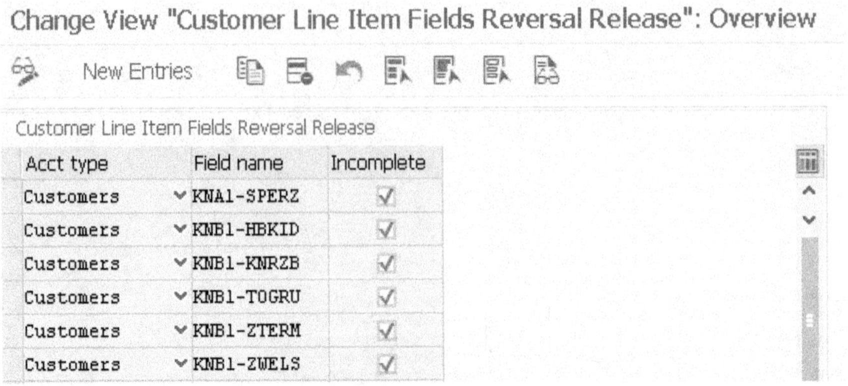

Change View "Customer Line Item Fields Reversal Release": Overview

New Entries

Customer Line Item Fields Reversal Release

Acct type	Field name	Incomplete
Customers	KNA1-SPERZ	☑
Customers	KNB1-HBKID	☑
Customers	KNB1-KNRZB	☑
Customers	KNB1-TOGRU	☑
Customers	KNB1-ZTERM	☑
Customers	KNB1-ZWELS	☑

Figure 10.49 Customer Line Item Fields for Resetting Document Release

Similarly, we need to define the vendor line items fields for reset of release approval.

10.3.1.2.7   Reset Release Approval (Vendors)

Here, you can include the fields that are to be checked in case of changes to the vendor documents. As in the case of fields that are included for reset release of customer document, if the system detects changes to any of the fields included here, then, the system cancels the document release and the process is reset.

To define the settings, use the menu path: SAP Customizing Implementation Guide > Financial Accounting > Accounts Receivable and Accounts Payable > Business Transactions > Incoming Invoices/Credit Memos > Make and Check Settings for Document Parking > Reset Release Approval (Vendors). You may also use Transaction OBWH. On the resulting screen, click on 'New Entries' and include the required fields (Figure 10.50).

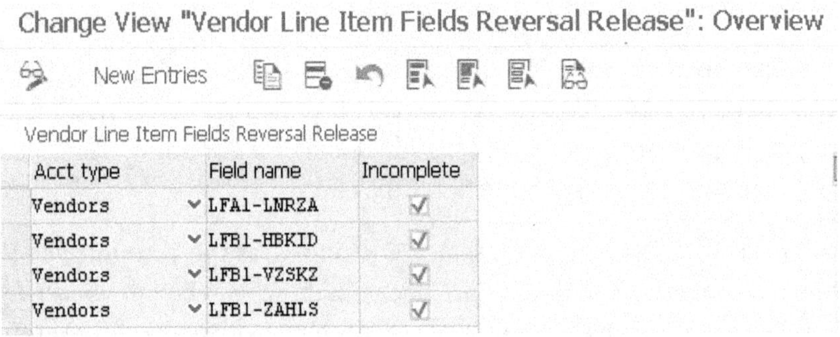

Change View "Vendor Line Item Fields Reversal Release": Overview

New Entries

Vendor Line Item Fields Reversal Release

Acct type	Field name	Incomplete
Vendors	LFA1-LNRZA	☑
Vendors	LFB1-HBKID	☑
Vendors	LFB1-VZSKZ	☑
Vendors	LFB1-ZAHLS	☑

Figure 10.50 Vendor Line Item Fields for Resetting Document Release

This completes our discussion on making / checking settings for document parking. Let us now understand terms of payment, in the next Section.

10.3.1.3   Maintain Terms of Payment

You will use the 'terms of payment' (or 'payment terms') to specify the payment conditions when you, for example, sell on credit. You can specify conditions such as the number of days before which the payment is to be made, whether there is a discount for early payment and what will be the discount amount in percentage. It is a common practice to offer higher discount with early repayments.

In SAP, using this configuration step, you can define the terms of payment in which you can specify the rules with which the system will determine the required terms of payment automatically. The system stores these rules using a 4-character key. Once defined, you can assign a key in business partner's master record. The system will, then, propose the terms of payment under this key when you enter a document for that vendor, for example; you may go ahead with the proposal or you can change, if required.

Though you may use the same key, for the terms of payment, for both customers and vendors who needs to be associated with the same payment terms, it is recommended to use different keys for customers and vendors thereby limiting the permitted account type within the terms of payment itself. By this, you can – for example – change the payment term for a customer without affecting the vendor having the same payment terms.

You may use the standard payment terms pre-defined in the system or you can create your own to meet your business requirements.

Project Dolphin

BESTM wants to have different set of payment terms for customers and vendors so that if there is a change that needs to be done for either customer or vendor, then, that can be carried out without affecting the other. However, there will a single payment term that will apply for both customers and vendors when the due date is immediate.

For customers, the three payment terms will cover a credit period of 90 days, 60 days, and 30 days.

1). BC90: 15 Days 3%, 45/2%, 90 Net (there will be a discount of 3% if paid within 15 days, 2% discount for within 45 days and no discount beyond that).
2). BC60: 15 Days 3%, 30/2%, 60 Net
3). BC30: 15 Days 4%, 30 Net

Similar payment terms will need to be configured for vendors but the key will be changed to BV90, BV60 etc. A common payment term B001 will also be configured for immediate payment without any discount, and this can be used for both customers and vendors.

To configure:

i.   Use the menu path: SAP Customizing Implementation Guide > Financial Accounting > Accounts Receivable and Accounts Payable > Business Transactions > Incoming Invoices/Credit Memos > Maintain Terms of Payment. You may also use Transaction OBB8.

ii.   On the resulting screen, click on 'New Entries' and make the required settings on the next screen (Figure 10.51):

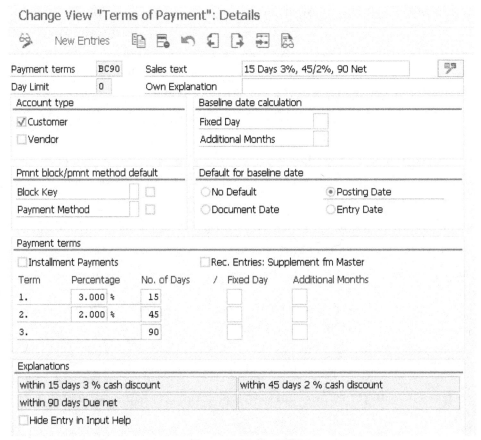

Figure 10.51 Configuring Payment Terms BC90 for BESTM

- Enter a 4-character key to identify the 'Payment terms'.
- Enter the appropriate 'Sales text' like '5 Days 3%, 45/2%, 90 Net'. When you enter in this format, then the system automatically fills the 'Explanations' (at the bottom of the screen) as 'within 15 days 3 % cash discount', 'within 45 days 2 % cash discount' and 'within 90 days Due net'.
- Enter a description in 'Own Explanation', if that will be different to the automatically created explanations. Only specify such an explanation, here, if

you want to use this text instead of the automatically created 'Explanations' by the system.

- Select the 'Account type': Select 'Customers' if this is only for customer accounts, or 'Vendors' if for vendors only, and select both the check-boxes if this will be valid for both customers and vendors.
- You may maintain additional details under 'Baseline date calculation': if you enter a calendar day number in 'Fixed Day' field, the system overwrites the day of the baseline date for payment of the line item; an entry in the 'Additional Month' will be added to the calendar month of the baseline date for payment. For example, if the baseline date is 02-15-2020, and you enter 02 in this field, then, the system calculates the baseline date as 04-15-2020.
- Under 'Pmnt block/pmnt method default', you may enter a default value for the payment blocking key in 'Block Key' field. The system proposes this block key along with the payment terms when you enter a document. If you leave the field as blank, then, it means, the document is free for payment.
- The check-box adjacent to 'Block Key' controls whether the payment block is transferred if the terms of payment key is changed in an invoice item: if set, the system transfer the payment block from the terms of payment when the item is first entered and also when the terms of payment key is changed; if not set, the system only transfers the payment block from the terms of payment when the item is first entered.
- You may enter a 'Payment Method' associated with this payment terms. If you want to control payment methods through customer / vendor master record, then, leave this field as blank.

> **i** In general, you enter the default payment methods in the customer / vendor master record. You can also enter a specific payment method to be applied for a particular open item in the that line item. However, in case, you want the system to apply specific payment method applied based upon payment terms, then, you can enter the same while configuring the payment terms in the 'Payment Method' field.

- Similar to the 'Block Key' check-box, the 'Payment Method' check-box controls whether the system transfers the payment method in an invoice item, if the payment terms key is changed. If set, the system transfers the payment method from the terms of payment when the item is first entered and also when the payment terms key is changed. If not set, then, the system only transfers the payment method from the terms of payment when the item is first entered.

- Select 'Posting Date' as the 'Default baseline date'. Do not select the 'No Default Option'; otherwise, you need to enter the baseline date, manually, every time you process a document.
- Maintain the details of 'Payment terms' as indicated in Figure 10.51. Instead of an entry in the 'No. of Days' field, you may also maintain 'Fixed Date' of 'Additional Months' in defining the payment terms.
- Do not select 'Installment Payments' for payment terms that are associated with normal payments.

> **i** Use the menu path SAP Customizing Implementation Guide > Financial Accounting > Accounts Receivable and Accounts Payable > Business Transactions > Incoming Invoices/Credit Memos > Define Terms of Payment for Installment Payments or Transaction OBB9 to define payment terms for instalment payment. Note to maintain a separate payment term key for instalment payment terms (using Transaction OBB8), before getting into Transaction OBB9. Refer Section 10.3.1.4, for more details on payment terms for instalment payments.

- Select 'Rec Entries: Supplement frm Master' check-box if you want the system to take the payment terms in a recurring entry from the customer / vendor master record, when there is no payment terms key available in the recurring entry original document.

iii.   'Save' the settings. Repeat the steps and define the other payment terms like BC60 and BC30 for use with BESTM customers (Figure 10.52).

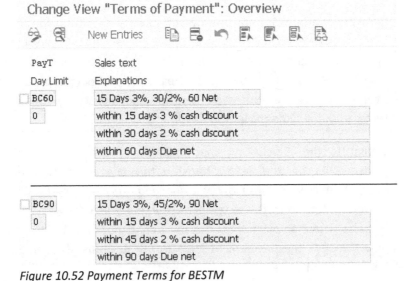

Figure 10.52 Payment Terms for BESTM

iv.   Also define payment terms with the keys BV90, BV60 and BV30 for BESTM vendors; in that case, select 'Vendors' check-box for 'Account type'. When defining the payment terms for vendors, you will not be able to maintain the 'Sales text'; instead, enter 'Own Explanation'.

v.   Finally, define the payment term B0001 to be used for both customers and vendors of BESTM.

The next step is to understand how to define the payment terms for instalment payments.

10.3.1.4   Define Terms of Payment for Installment Payments

When you have an invoice amount that is to be divided into partial amounts (instalments) with different due dates, then, you can use one or more payment terms to take care of the instalment payments. For instalment payment terms, you need to determine the amount of the instalment in percentage and the terms of payment for each instalment payment. When posting an invoice with terms of instalment payment, then, the system generates the corresponding number of line items as per your specifications for the instalments.

> **i** Maintain a separate terms of payment key as described in the previous Section 10.3.1.3 (Transaction OBB8) by selecting the 'Installment Payments' check-box. Then, define the percentage of each instalment and assign the key of the payment terms here in this step.

Project Dolphin

For instalment payments, BESTM want the system to be configured with the payment terms key BINS. The number of instalments will be three, with the first instalment at 20%, second at 30% and the third being 50%. All the instalments need to be paid within a maximum of 30 days, with 4% discount for early birds but within 15days.

Let us first define a new 'payment terms' for instalment payment for BESTM (BINS):

i.   Follow the steps listed in Section 10.3.1.3, and create a new entry: enter the payment term key as BINS, enter an appropriate 'Sales text'. Select 'Customer' check-box under 'Account type' and select the appropriate 'Default for the baseline date'. Do not enter anything, except selecting the 'Installment Payments' check-box. 'Save' the details.

As we have completed defining the new instalment payment term BINS, let us, now, configure the instalments, and to assign the payment terms:

ii.   Use the menu path: SAP Customizing Implementation Guide > Financial Accounting > Accounts Receivable and Accounts Payable > Business Transactions > Incoming Invoices/Credit Memos > Define Terms of Payment for Installment Payments. You may also use Transaction OBB9. On the resulting screen, click on 'New Entries' and make the required settings on the next screen (Figure 10.53):

Payment terms	Inst	Percent	Payt Term
BINS	1	20.000	BC30
BINS	2	30.000	BC30
BINS	3	50.000	BC30

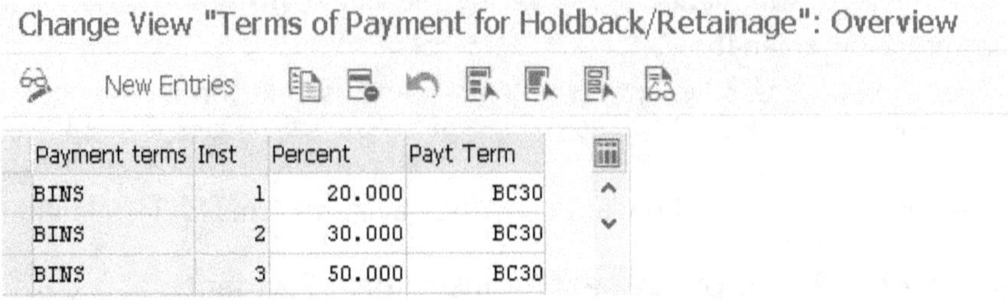

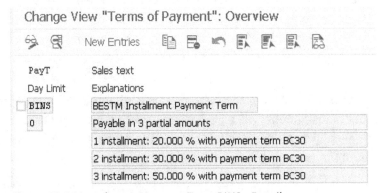

Figure 10.53 Defining Installments for Payment Terms BINS

iii. Repeat entering the details for other installments, and ensure that sum of all the installments are totalling to 100%. In the case of assigning the payment terms, you may assign different payment terms for each of the installments or assign a single one for all the installments. 'Save' the details.

iv. If you go back and open the payment term BINS, you will now see that the system has populated the 'Explanations' as depicted in Figure 10.54, indicating the percentage of instalment amount and the payment term (BC30).

Figure 10.54 Instalment Payment Term BINS - Details

Let us move on to the next configuration step to define the cash discount base for incoming invoices.

10.3.1.5 Define Cash Discount Base for Incoming Invoices

We have, already, discussed about the cash discount base (net and gross), in Section 6.8.1 of Chapter 6 of Vol. I, and made the required settings both for US-based company codes and India-based company codes while configuring the company code global parameters. Refer that Section for more details. Of course, You may use the menu path SAP Customizing Implementation Guide > Financial Accounting > Accounts Receivable and Accounts Payable >

Business Transactions > Incoming Invoices/Credit Memos > Define Cash Discount Base for Incoming Invoices, or Transaction OB70 or to view or change the settings.

This completes our discussion of settings required for incoming invoices / credit memos. Let us, now, move on to the configuration relating to release for payment.

10.3.2 Release for Payment

We have, already, discussed creating the required workflow variant (US01) for release of document / payment, when we discussed the company code global parameters in Section 6.8.1 of Chapter 6 of Vol. I. Later, we assigned this variant to all the required company codes. In Section 10.3.1.2 of this Chapter, we discussed the different steps that need to be configured for release approval of parked documents. We configured the release approval groups (B001, B002 and B003) and release approval paths (A, B and C), and later assigned release approval paths to each combination of 'workflow variant, document type and release group'; we also assigned release approval procedures (subworkflows) for each level of release to the combination of 'workflow and approval path' in which we assigned the workflow for both document release and payment release, and finally defined the users (with appropriate authorization) for approval of the releases.

The only activity that needs to be configured is the definition of payment block reasons for payment release. Let us do that now.

10.3.2.1   Define Payment Block Reason for Payment Release

You will be able to differentiate why invoices are to be blocked for payment in the system, by using 'payment block reasons' defined under 'block indicators'. The payment block reasons that you define here will be valid across company codes. Using the block indicators, you can prevent items from being processed manually with the clearing procedures (both incoming and outgoing payments). So, for each of the block indicators, you need to decide what changes can be allowed in the payment proposal and whether the blocked items can always be transferred or reversed.

---

i The default settings in the standard system include a number of payment block reasons like R (blocked by invoice verification', 'blank' (free for payment) etc.

Project Dolphin

BESTM will be using the default payment block reasons and will not require anything new.

If you want to define new payment block reasons, follow the menu path: SAP Customizing Implementation Guide > Financial Accounting > Accounts Receivable and Accounts Payable > Business Transactions > Incoming Invoices/Credit Memos > Release for Payment > Define Payment Block Reason for Payment Release, or Transaction OB27.

Change View "Payment Block Reasons": Overview

New Entries

Block Ind.	Description	Change in Pmnt Prop.	Manual Payments Block	Not Changeable
	Free for payment	☐	☐	☐
*	Skip account	☐	☐	☐
A	Blocked for payment	☑	☐	☐
B	Manual paym blocked	☑	☑	☐
N	Postprocess inc.pmnt	☐	☑	☐
P	Payment request	☐	☑	☑
R	Invoice verification	☑	☐	☐
V	Payment clearing	☐	☑	☐

Figure 10.55 Payment Block Reasons

On the resulting screen, click on 'New Entries' and maintain the required settings on the next screen (Figure 10.55):

- Enter single-character block indicator ('Block Ind.'), and provide a 'Description'.
- Use 'Change in Pmnt Prop.' check-box to indicate whether a change is allowed in the payment proposal. When not set, you can prevent – for example – changing of the block indicator that is set in invoice verification in the payment proposal. If set, you enable setting a new block reason or deleting the one that is already set during processing a payment proposal. Do not select this for FI-CA (Contract Accounts Receivable and Payable). We shall discuss SAP FI-CA in detail, in Chapter 11.
- If you select 'Manual Payments Block' check-box, then you are flagging the system from clearing that item through manual entry of incoming / outgoing payment. This indicator is also not relevant for FI-CA.
- The 'Not Changeable' check-box indicates, when set, that you cannot modify the payment block within a dialog transaction. That is, the user cannot rest the payment block. Again, this is also not relevant for FI-CA.

This completes our discussion on release for payment. Let us move on to discuss the outgoing payments in the next Section.

10.3.3 Outgoing Payments

The outgoing payments represent the payment you make to your external business partners (vendors or suppliers) and internal business partners (staff or group companies). Here, in this Section, we will discuss the (a) global settings for outgoing payments, the settings for (b) manual outgoing payments and (c) automatic outgoing payments.

10.3.3.1   Outgoing Payments Global Settings

There are various global settings that you need to complete to make your system to handle both the manual and automatic payments. These settings include:

- Define Accounts for Cash Discount Taken
- Define Accounts for Lost Cash Discount
- Define Accounts for Overpayments/Underpayments
- Define Accounts for Exchange Rate Differences
- Define Account for Rounding Differences
- Define Accounts for Payment Differences with Altern. Currency
- Define Accounts for Bank Charges (Vendors)
- Define Posting Keys for Clearing
- Enable Translation Posting
- Define Payment Block Reasons
- Define Default Values for Payment Block

Let us, first, start with the definition of cash discount taken (received).

10.3.3.1.1   Define Accounts for Cash Discount Taken

Define the G/L account number(s) for accounting the cash discount received. During open item clearing, the system posts the cash discount to the account(s) defined here. If necessary, you may differentiate the accounts by tax codes.

Project Dolphin

BESTM wants to have a single G/L account (70040000) to manage all the cash discounts that are received into.

Use the menu path: SAP Customizing Implementation Guide > Financial Accounting > Accounts Receivable and Accounts Payable > Business Transactions > Outgoing Payments > Outgoing Payments Global Settings > Define Accounts for Cash Discount Taken, or Transaction OBXU. Enter the chart of accounts (say, BEUS) on the resulting pop-up screen, and enter the appropriate G/L accounts on the next screen (Figure 10.56).

Configuration Accounting Maintain : Automatic Posts - Accounts

Posting Key   Rules

Chart of Accounts	BEUS	BESTM - US Standard Chart of Accounts
Transaction	SKE	Cash discount received

Account assignment

Account
70040000

Figure 10.56 G/L Account for Cash Discount Received

Let us move on to define the accounts for cash discount lost.

10.3.3.1.2   Define Accounts for Lost Cash Discount

Here, you will define the G/L account numbers for cash discount lost. In case of nett invoices posted, the system automatically posts the difference between the originally calculated cash discount and the actual cash discount received, as an expense, to this G/L account.

Project Dolphin

BESTM wants to capture the difference between the originally calculated cash discount and the actual cash discount received, and post that difference as an expense (lost discount) to a single G/L account (71040000).

Use the menu path: SAP Customizing Implementation Guide > Financial Accounting > Accounts Receivable and Accounts Payable > Business Transactions > Outgoing Payments > Outgoing Payments Global Settings > Define Accounts for Lost Cash Discount, or Transaction OBXV. For the chart of accounts BEUS, enter the appropriate G/L account on the next screen (Figure 10.57).

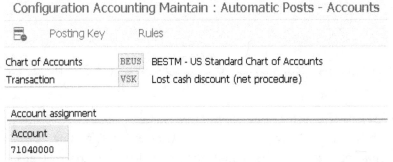

Configuration Accounting Maintain : Automatic Posts - Accounts

Posting Key   Rules

Chart of Accounts	BEUS	BESTM - US Standard Chart of Accounts
Transaction	VSK	Lost cash discount (net procedure)

Account assignment

Account
71040000

Figure 10.57 G/L Account for Cash Discount Lost

The next step is to define the accounts for handling over / under payments (payment differences).

10.3.3.1.3   Define Accounts for Overpayments/Underpayments

Use this configuration step to define revenue and expense G/L accounts to which the system posts the amount if (a) there is a difference payment difference resulting from an underpayment or an overpayment, (b) the difference is within the tolerance limits for automatic adjustment posting and (c) the difference cannot be handled adjusting the cash discount.

Project Dolphin

BESTM wants to use G/L account 44000000 for accounting overpayment and underpayments.

Use the menu path: SAP Customizing Implementation Guide > Financial Accounting > Accounts Receivable and Accounts Payable > Business Transactions > Outgoing Payments > Outgoing Payments Global Settings > Define Accounts for Overpayments/Underpayments, or Transaction OBXL. On entering the Transaction, enter the chart of accounts BEUS, and enter the appropriate G/L account on the next screen (Figure 10.58).

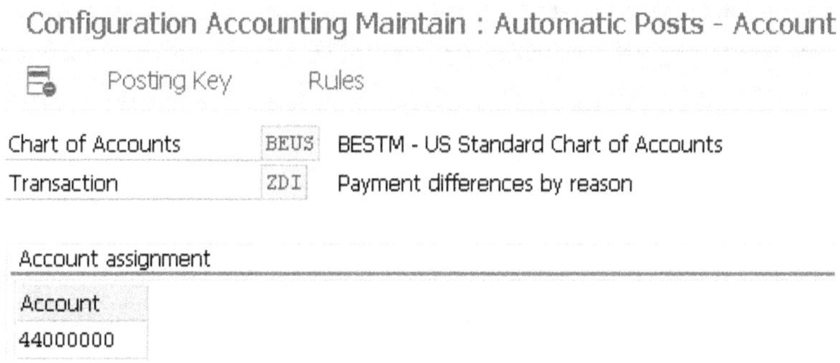

Configuration Accounting Maintain : Automatic Posts - Account

  Posting Key   Rules

Chart of Accounts   BEUS   BESTM - US Standard Chart of Accounts
Transaction   ZDI   Payment differences by reason

Account assignment
Account
44000000

Figure 10.58 G/L Account for handling Under / Over Payments

The next step is to define the accounts for exchange rate differences.

10.3.3.1.4   Define Accounts for Exchange Rate Differences

We have already configured this in Section 9.4.3.2 of Chapter 9 of Vol. I. We have defined a single set of G/L accounts to take care of automatic posting of the exchange rate differences realized in clearing open items: for loss it will be 72010000, and for the gains it will be 72510000. For valuation adjustments, the loss will be posted to 72040000 and the gains to 72540000; the B/S adjustments will go to the G/L account 11001099.

You may, of course, check the settings – if required – by using the menu path: SAP Customizing Implementation Guide > Financial Accounting > Accounts Receivable and Accounts Payable > Business Transactions > Outgoing Payments > Outgoing Payments Global Settings > Define Accounts for Exchange Rate Differences, or Transaction OB09. On the resulting screen, double-click on any of the G/L accounts (for the chart of accounts BEUS) and see the details of the accounts already configured.

Let us now define the account for handling rounding off differences.

10.3.3.1.5   Define Account for Rounding Differences

During clearing open items, the system posts the gains / losses realised from exchange rate differences. Hence, you need to define the appropriate revenue / expense G/L accounts for automatically posting of the gain / loss arising out of currency rounding off during clearing.

Project Dolphin

BESTM has asked the project team to configure G/L account 72020000 and 72520000 to handle currency rounding off during clearing.

Use the menu path: SAP Customizing Implementation Guide > Financial Accounting > Accounts Receivable and Accounts Payable > Business Transactions > Outgoing Payments > Outgoing Payments Global Settings > Define Account for Rounding Differences, or Transaction OB00. On the resulting screen (Figure 10.59), for the chart of accounts BEUS, define appropriate G/L accounts: one for revenue and one for expense, to take care currency rounding off.

Figure 10.59 G/L Accounts for handling Rounding Off Differences

You also need to define a separate set of G/L accounts to handle payment differences if you work with any alternative payment currencies in manual or automatic payments. Let us configure the same, next.

10.3.3.1.6   Define Accounts for Payment Differences with Altern. Currency

As in the previous case, define the appropriate G/L accounts (debit and credit) to handle payment differences (gain/ loss) when you work with alternative currencies for payment – both manual and automatic.

Project Dolphin

BESTM has asked the project team to use G/L account 72010000 and 72510000 to handle to handle payment differences (gain/ loss) when working with alternative currencies for payment.

Use the menu path: SAP Customizing Implementation Guide > Financial Accounting > Accounts Receivable and Accounts Payable > Business Transactions > Outgoing Payments > Outgoing Payments Global Settings > Define Accounts for Payment Differences with Altern. Currency, or Transaction OBXO. On the resulting screen, for the chart of accounts BEUS, define the appropriate G/L accounts, one for revenue and one for expense (Figure 10.60).

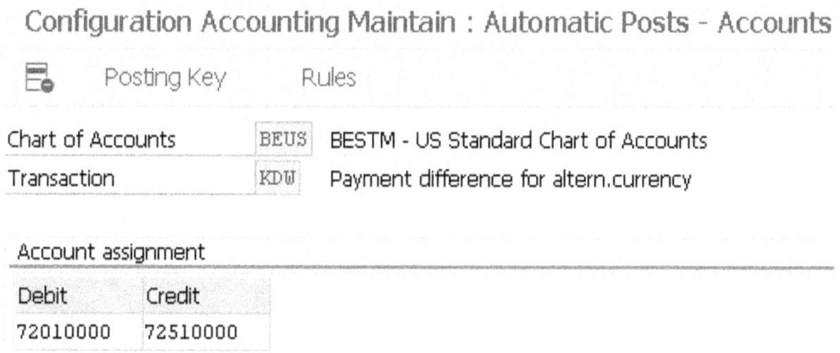

Configuration Accounting Maintain : Automatic Posts - Accounts

Posting Key	Rules

| Chart of Accounts | BEUS | BESTM - US Standard Chart of Accounts |
| Transaction | KDW | Payment difference for altern.currency |

Account assignment

Debit	Credit
72010000	72510000

Figure 10.60 G/L Accounts for Payment Differences with Alternative Currencies

The next activity is to define the G/L account to post vendor bank charges.

10.3.3.1.7   Define Accounts for Bank Charges (Vendors)

Define the G/L account number(s) for your bank charges accounts. Once defined, the system posts the charges that you specify for a bank item when settling payment to these accounts.

Project Dolphin

BESTM has asked the project team to use G/L account 71000000 to take care of posting of vendor bank charges.

Use the menu path: SAP Customizing Implementation Guide > Financial Accounting > Accounts Receivable and Accounts Payable > Business Transactions > Outgoing Payments > Outgoing Payments Global Settings > Define Accounts for Bank Charges (Vendors), or Transaction OBXK. On the resulting screen, double-click on 'Bank charges' (Transaction BSP) procedure, and define the appropriate G/L account(s), for the chart of accounts BEUS (Figure 10.61).

Figure 10.61 G/L Account for Bank Charges (Vendors)

The next step is to define the posting keys for clearing.

10.3.3.1.8   Define Posting Keys for Clearing

You can define the posting keys, here in this step, that you want the system to use for automatically created line items for clearing (procedures) and for the payment program. In the case of 'Transfer posting with clearing' transaction, additional document types have already been defined in the standard system. We have already discussed this in Section 9.4.3.1 of Chapter 9 of Vol. I, while discussing the open item clearing.

However, you can view the standard settings using the menu path: SAP Customizing Implementation Guide > Financial Accounting > Accounts Receivable and Accounts Payable > Business Transactions > Outgoing Payments > Outgoing Payments Global Settings > Define Posting Keys for Clearing, or Transaction OBXH for the various transactions as in Figure 10.62. You can double-click, on any of the rows ('Clearing Transaction'), to see the default posting key settings.

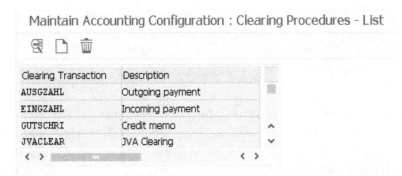

Figure 10.62 List of Clearing Transactions

> **i**   Do not to change the standard settings of posting keys for the clearing transactions.

The next step is to enable company codes for translation postings.

10.3.3.1.9   Enable Translation Posting

When you enable translation posting for a company code, you determine that the translation gain / loss for clearing open items, in foreign currency, is to be posted by the system to the appropriate accounts. The system posts the translations if the item to be cleared has already been revalued once during foreign currency valuation. The system, then, posts the valuation difference to a separate G/L account (translation account), with an offsetting entry to a clearing account.

Project Dolphin

BESTM wants the project team to enable posting of translation gain/loss for clearing open items in foreign currency, in all the company codes both US-based and India-based.

Use the menu path: SAP Customizing Implementation Guide > Financial Accounting > Accounts Receivable and Accounts Payable > Business Transactions > Outgoing Payments > Outgoing Payments Global Settings > Enable Translation Posting. On the resulting screen, enable translation posting by selecting the 'Post Translation' check-box for all the required company codes.

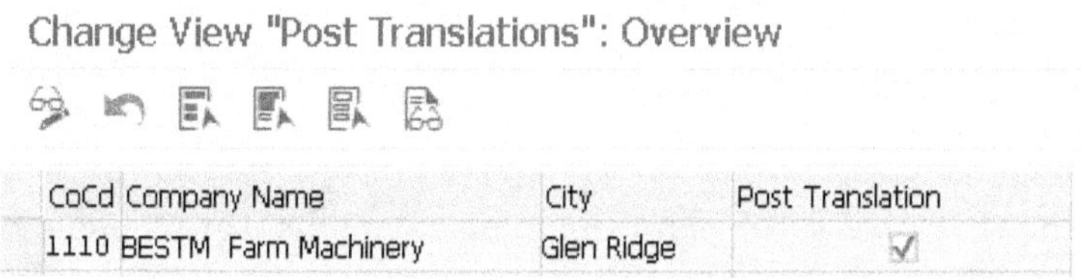

Change View "Post Translations": Overview

CoCd	Company Name	City	Post Translation
1110	BESTM Farm Machinery	Glen Ridge	☑

Figure 10.63 Enabling Company Code for Posting Translation Gain / Loss

The next step is to define the settings for payment block reasons.

10.3.3.1.10 Payment Block Reasons

There are two settings you need to make: one is to define the payment block reasons and the other is to define the default values for payment block.

10.3.3.1.10.1   Define Payment Block Reasons
We have already discussed payment block reasons in Section 10.3.2.1.

Let us, now, look at the last configuration step in global settings for outgoing payments: defining default values for payment block.

10.3.3.1.10.2   Define Default Values for Payment Block
Using this step, you can change the payment blocking key value that is proposed as a default, per payment terms, when entering postings to customer / vendor accounts.

Project Dolphin

BESTM does not want to propose a default blocking key via payment terms, for postings customer / vendor accounts.

Use the menu path: SAP Customizing Implementation Guide > Financial Accounting > Accounts Receivable and Accounts Payable > Business Transactions > Outgoing Payments > Outgoing Payments Global Settings > Payment Block Reasons > Define Default Values for Payment Block. On the resulting screen, enter the payment block key in 'Block Key' field that should be proposed as the default, for each of the payment terms. If you do not want the system to propose a default payment blocking key based on the terms of payment, you just need to leave this field as blank, as we have done for BESTM.

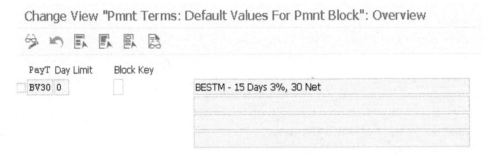

Figure 10.64 Default Block Key Configuration via Payment Terms

This completes our discussion on global settings for outgoing payments. Let us move on to discuss manual outgoing payments, in the next Section.

10.3.3.2   Manual Outgoing Payments

There are several settings you need to make to configure manual outgoing payments, including defining accounts for payment differences and checking payment block reasons. As you are aware, we have already configured the G/L account for taking care of payment differences, and defined the payment block reasons in <u>Section 10.3.3.1</u>, when configuring the global settings for outgoing payments. Let us now look at the remaining settings, in this Section, that include the following:

- Define Tolerances (Vendors)
- Define Reason Codes (Manual Outgoing Payments)
- Prepare Cross-Company Code Manual Payments
- Configure Manual Payments

Let us start with the definition of vendor tolerances.

10.3.3.2.1 Define Tolerances (Vendors)

We have discussed tolerance and tolerance groups, in detail, in Section 7.1.10, and have configured the employee tolerance groups in Section 7.1.10.1 of Chapter 7 of Vol. I. We have also discussed and configured the G/L account tolerance groups in Section 9.4.3.6 of Chapter 9 of Vol. I. Similar to those tolerance groups, let us, now, define the tolerance groups for vendors here. Actually, we should call this as the 'tolerance group for business partners' as you can use this for both customers and vendors, even though the configuration step states this as 'tolerances (vendors)'.

Specify the tolerances for vendors and use them for dealing with payment to vendors, in case of payment differences and residual items during payment settlement. Define one or more tolerance groups and allocate a tolerance group to each of your vendor masters. Per tolerance group, (a) specify the tolerances up to which the system posts the differences, automatically, either to a revenue account or an expense account while clearing the vendor open items, and (b) specify how to handle the terms of payment for residual items that may arise during clearing.

> **i** Since there is an employee tolerance defined and set in the system, during clearing, the system takes into account the lower of the specifications in employee tolerance and vendor tolerance.

Project Dolphin

BESTM wants to have two tolerance groups: a strict tolerance group that will be for most the vendors and a liberal one that will be applied to specific vendors.

For all the US-based company codes:

The strict tolerance group will be called as the 'null tolerance group' which will be the default when a vendor is not assigned with a specific tolerance group. For this tolerance group, the permitted payment difference will be $50 for gains (1%) and $10 for losses (0.5%), with a maximum adjustment cash discount being $5. For automatic write-off of payment differences, the amount and percent values will be $5 and 0.25% respectively, both for revenue and expense.

For the specific tolerance group, which will be termed as BEU1, the corresponding permitted payment difference is $500 for gains (2%) and $250 for losses (1%). The maximum cash discount that can be adjusted, will be $50. The amount and percentage values for automatic write-off of payment differences (revenue or expense) will be $25 and 0.5% respectively.

For all the India-based company codes:

The tolerance amount, tolerance percentage, and the cash discount amount that can be adjusted, the amount and percentage for automatic write-off of payment differences will be the same as that of US company codes but the amount will be in INR. The corresponding tolerance group for BEU1 will be BEI1.

Let us configure the tolerance group BEU1:

i.   Use the menu path: SAP Customizing Implementation Guide > Financial Accounting > Accounts Receivable and Accounts Payable > Business Transactions > Outgoing Payments > Manual Outgoing Payments > Define Tolerances (Vendors). You may also use Transaction OBA3.

ii.   Click on 'New Entries' on the resulting screen, to configure the settings (Figure 10.65):

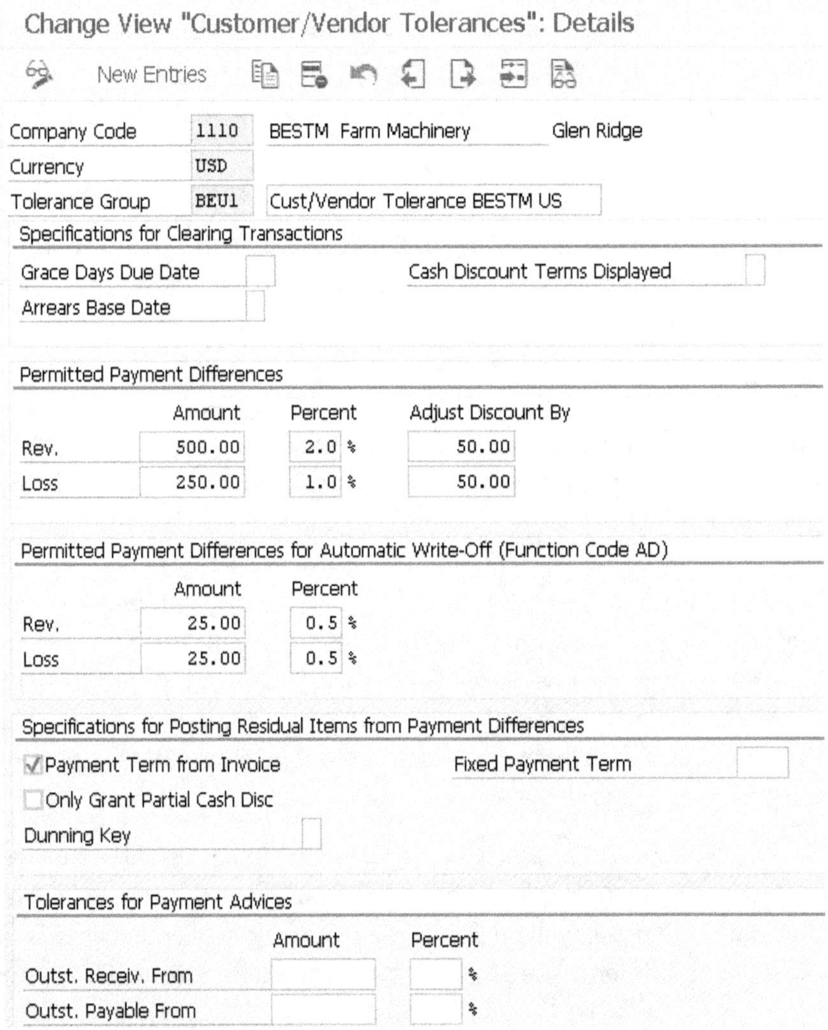

Figure 10.65 Customer/Vendor Tolerance Group BEU1 - Details

- Enter the 'Company code'. The system brings up the company code 'Currency' when you save the details.
- Enter an identifier for 'Tolerance Group' (BEU1), and provide a description.
- You may enter the 'Specifications for Clearing Transactions'. When you enter a number in 'Grace Days Due Date' field, then, the system adds this to the payment deadline, to arrive at the new deadline, to take care of cash discount. The system also takes into account the revised payment deadline(s) for accepting the net payment.
- Use a dropdown value in 'Arrears Base Date' to indicate how the system should arrive at the arrears baseline date. When left blank, the system determines the days in arrears based on document date. If you select '1', then the arrears baseline date will be the value date.
- Use 'Cash Discount Terms Displayed' field to specify whether cash discount terms are to be displayed or not. When left blank, or when you enter 0 or *, then system displays the current discount term; if you enter 1, 2, or 3, then, the system displays the respective cash discount terms. You can, of course, change the default, later, when processing an open item.
- Enter the absolute amount, tolerance percentage and cash discount adjustment amount, for revenue and loss, under 'Permitted Payment Differences'. The system allows the payment difference (in local currency) to your advantage (gain) up to the amount that is entered in the 'Amount' field in the 'Rev.' row which increases your profit when posted. As you can also maintain a percentage ('Percent') for the revenue row ('Rev.'), the system takes into account the lower of these two ('Amount' and 'Percent') into account for deciding the gain (and, of course, takes only the lower of employee or vendor tolerance). The system corrects the payment difference up to the amount specified in 'Adjust Discount By' field, when the cash discount is large enough for adjustment, with the cash discount posting, before posting the gain. The system creates the necessary line items for all these adjustments/postings. The explanation will be similar to the 'Loss' row except that the payment difference will be to your disadvantage (loss), and you profit decreases by this amount when the system posts the loss.
- Enter the values for 'Permitted Payment Differences for Automatic Write-Off (Function Code AD)' for both revenue and loss, both in amount and in percentage.
- You may also maintain the 'Specifications for Posting Residual Items from Payment Differences'. Select 'Payment Term from Invoice' check-box if you want the payment terms to be transferred from the original line item to residual items arising out of over / under payments. However, if you maintain

'Fixed Payment Term', then, the system will not transfer the payment terms from invoice. The check-box 'Only Grant Partial Cash Disc', when selected, indicates that the system should grant only a partial cash discount, if an outstanding receivable is posted due to an under payment during invoice clearing. Use the 'Dunning Key' filed to select an appropriate dunning level, to enable the system to enter that into the automatically generated residual line item.

- You may also maintain the 'Tolerances for Payment Advices'.

ii.   When completed 'Save' the details. This completes creation of the tolerance group BEU1 for company code 1110. You may go back to the previous screen and copy this group to all other US-based company codes of BESTM.

iii.   Similarly, create the null tolerance group for BESTM US-based company codes, by following the steps listed above. Also, create the other tolerance groups – BEI1 and null tolerance group for India-based company codes (Figure 10.66).

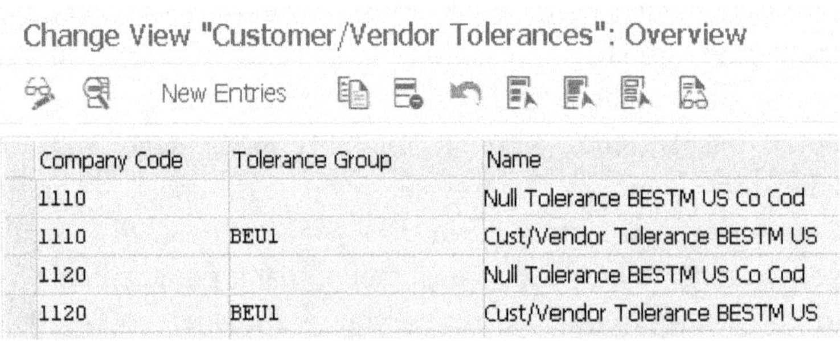

Change View "Customer/Vendor Tolerances": Overview

New Entries

Company Code	Tolerance Group	Name
1110		Null Tolerance BESTM US Co Cod
1110	BEU1	Cust/Vendor Tolerance BESTM US
1120		Null Tolerance BESTM US Co Cod
1120	BEU1	Cust/Vendor Tolerance BESTM US

Figure 10.66 Customer/Vendor Tolerance Groups for BESTM

Let us now move on to discuss the next configuration activity under manual outgoing payments, namely, defining reason codes.

10.3.3.2.2   Define Reason Codes (Manual Outgoing Payments)

You will use 'reason codes' to handle business situations like, when the cash discount period has been exceeded, or if cash discount has been taken when payment is net due etc. Define the reason codes, per company code, for handling payment differences in the form of residual items, partial payments and/or postings on account. For each of the reason codes, you can decide for which of the company codes it is valid, for which correspondence type (say, payment notice) it is connected to and an explanation in the form of both short and long text. You can also set the clearing indicator, for each of the reason codes, so that the payment difference is cleared using a separate G/L account. If you do not set the indicator, then, the system generates a new item as an outstanding receivable in the customer's account.

Project Dolphin

The project team has suggested to create new reason codes to cover situations like cash discount period exceeded, cash discount rate not kept to, cash discount deducted for net terms, discount period exceeded & rate incorrect, calculation error on customer side, debit paid twice, credit memo paid instead of reduction, credit memo reduced twice etc.

To configure new reason codes:

i. Use the menu path: SAP Customizing Implementation Guide > Financial Accounting > Accounts Receivable and Accounts Payable > Business Transactions > Outgoing Payments > Manual Outgoing Payments > Overpayment/Underpayment > Define Reason Codes (Manual Outgoing Payments) or Transaction OBBE.

ii. Enter the company code on the resulting 'Determine Work Area: Entry' pop-up screen. On the resulting screen, click on 'New Entries' and on the next screen (Figure 10.67):

Change View "Classification of Payment Differences": Overview

New Entries

Company Code   1110   BESTM Farm Machinery   Glen Ridge

RCd	Short Text	Long Text	CorrT	C	D	Do...
B50	Cash discount period	Cash discount period exceeded	SAP50			
B51	Cash discount rate	Cash discount rate not kept to	SAP51			
B52	Cash discount f. net	Cash discount deduction for net t...	SAP52			
B53	Cash discount retro.	No csh disc.retrograde calc.frm cr...	SAP53			
B54	Disc.period and rate	Disc.per.exceeded and disc.rate i...	SAP54			
B55	Pmnt on acct	General payment on account	SAP55			
B56	Pmnt advice error	Pmt adv.on acct is missing or inco...	SAP56			
B57	Calculation error	Customer calculation error	SAP57			
B58	Debit reduced	Debit reduced instead of paid	SAP58			
B59	Debit paid twice	Debit paid twice	SAP58			
B60	Credit memo paid	Credit memo paid instead of redu...	SAP60			
B61	Credit memo twice	Credit memo reduced twice	SAP60			

Figure 10.67 Reason Codes for Manual Outgoing Payments

- Enter a 3-character identified for the reason code ('RCd').
- Enter a 'Short Text' and a 'Long Text'.
- Select the appropriate correspondence type ('Corr T') from the drop-down list like SAP01 (payment notice with line items), SAP02 (payment notice

without line items, SAP06 (account statement), SAP11 (customer credit memo), SAP12 (failed payments), SAP19 (customer invoice) etc.

- Select check-box 'C' if the payment differences with this reason code are to be charged off via a separate G/L account.
- Select check-box 'D' if payment differences with this reason code should lead to a disputed item when creating a residual item.

> **i** The 'disputed items' will not increase the total A/R against a customer. You can display them separately in the line item display as well as in credit management. The system does not take into account the disputed items, in credit reviews, against the oldest open items or against that percentage of open items with a specific number of days in arrears.

- When you set 'Do Not Copy Text' indicator, then, the system does not copy the text of the reason code into the segment text of the residual item / partial payment. You need to select this check-box only when you want to manually enter the segment text.

iii.   'Save' when completed, and create any other reason code(s) that will be required for you specific business need (Figure 10.67).

With this, we can, now, move on to the last activity of preparing for cross-company code manual payments.

10.3.3.2.3   Prepare Cross-Company Code Manual Payments

Use this configuration activity to maintain the company codes which carry out manual payments and other clearing procedures, on behalf of other company codes in a corporate group. The pre-requisite is that you should have maintained the clearing accounts for cross-company transactions while configuring the G/L Accounting (Refer Section 9.4.2 of Chapter 9 of Vol. I). Maintain the specifications for each clearing procedure like incoming payment (EINGZAHL), outgoing payment (AUSGZAHL), credit memo (GUTSCHRI) and transfer posting with clearing (UMBUCHNG).

The specifications you make here for cross-company code payments are valid only for manual payments, and they will not have any impact on the automatic payment program.

Project Dolphin

BESTM has indicated that the company code 1110 will need to be configured in such a way the it can carry out manual payments and other clearing procedures on behalf of 1120. Similarly, the cross-company code manual payments need to be enabled for the following other pairs of company codes:

Paying Company Code	Payments for
2100	2200
3100	3200
1210	1220

Accordingly, the project team has decided to configure the settings to cover the clearing procedures like incoming payment, outgoing payment, credit memo and transfer posting with clearing.

To make the settings:

i.   Use the menu path: SAP Customizing Implementation Guide > Financial Accounting > Accounts Receivable and Accounts Payable > Business Transactions > Outgoing Payments > Manual Outgoing Payments > Prepare Cross-Company Code Manual Payments or Transaction OB60.

ii. On the 'Change View "Company Code Allocation For Manual Payments": Overview' screen, click on 'New Entries' and make the required settings on the resulting screen:

   - Enter the 'Company code' that will pay for the company code entered in 'Payments For' field.
   - Select the appropriate clearing transaction ('Clearing trans.').
   - Enter the company code for which the payments will be made, in 'Payments For' field.
   - Repeat the entries for all the required clearing transactions for a given pair of company codes, and complete for all the required pairs of company codes.

iii. 'Save' the details when completed (Figure 10.68).

Change View "Company Code Allocation For Manual Payments": Overview

New Entries

Company Code	Clearing Trans.	Payments For
1110	AUSGZAHL	1120
1110	EINGZAHL	1120
1110	GUTSCHRI	1120
1110	UMBUCHNG	1120
2100	AUSGZAHL	2200
2100	EINGZAHL	2200

Figure 10.68 Settings for Cross-Company Code Manual Payments

The next step is to configure the manual payments.

10.3.3.2.4   Configure Manual Payments

Here, you can configure the settings for 'Create Manual Payment' application which allows you to create manual payments for the two scenarios: (a) direct payment without an invoice and (b) payment of open vendor line items.

Project Dolphin

BESTM suggested to the project team to configure 'create manual payment' application to cover both the scenarios of direct payment without an invoice and payment of vendor open line items, with the system posting both the payment and document.

To configure:

i.   Use the menu path: SAP Customizing Implementation Guide > Financial Accounting > Accounts Receivable and Accounts Payable > Business Transactions > Outgoing Payments > Manual Outgoing Payments > Configure Manual Payments.

ii.   On the resulting screen (Figure 10.69), click on 'New Entries' and maintain the details:

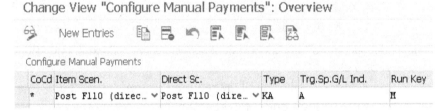

Figure 10.69 Configuring Manual Payments

- Enter the company code in 'CoCd' field; a * indicates that the settings made here will be valid across company codes.
- Select the appropriate item scenario ('Item Scen.') from the drop-down list to decide the behaviour of the payments that you create with the 'Create Manual Payment' application:
  - ➢ Select 'Post F110 - direct and item scenarios' option to cover both the scenarios. Here, the system creates the document (only in the direct scenario) and executes the payment with the payment program; and, posts both the document and the payment.

    You may also look at the other two options:

  - ➢'Post down payment request only' for direct payment scenario in which the system creates document for direct payment but does not post the payment.
  - ➢'Start payment media workbench – direct and item scenarios' in which the system creates the document (only in the direct scenario),

> executes the same with the payment program, runs the payment media workbench to create a payment file, and - of course - posts both document and payment.
>
> - Select the appropriate direct scenario process step as well for the 'Direct Sc.' field. Here, also, select 'Post F110 - direct and item scenarios' option to cover both the scenarios.
> - Select the appropriate document type ('Type'), select also the target special G/L indicator ('Trg.Sp.G/L Ind.') to derive the account for posting the down payment request, and enter the identifier for payment run in the 'Run Key' field.

ii.   'Save' when completed.

This completes our discussion on configuring the system for manual outgoing payments. With this we are, now, all set to discuss the most important aspect of outgoing payments: configuring the automatic outgoing payments by payment program.

10.3.3.3   Automatic Outgoing Payments

With the payment program, in SAP, you can manage, automatically, both the incoming and outgoing payments. Supporting several payment methods including check, bill of exchange (BoE), direct debit, bank transfer, card payment etc., the payment program is delivered in the standard SAP system with the appropriate print forms and print programs to take care of any country-specific payment requirements of the world. Using this program, you can clear open items of customers and vendors, manage intercompany payments, process domestic and overseas payments, prevent a payment by payment block etc. You can create DME (data medium exchange) file for transferring the payment data through electronic format. Via the payment program, you can print the check, payment list and payment forms. By configuring the program suitably, you can manage the 'what, when and how' of payments.

You have to determine, by suitable configuration, (a) which company codes are to be included in payment transactions and which company code makes payments, (b) which payment methods are to be used, (c) whether you need to use payment method supplements (c) from which bank accounts payment is to be generated, and (d) with which form the payment is to be made.

The configuration includes the following activities:

- Set Up All Company Codes for Payment Transactions
- Set Up Paying Company Codes for Payment Transactions
- Set Up Payment Methods per Country for Payment Transactions
- Set Up Payment Methods per Company Code for Payment Transactions
- Set a Payment Medium Format per Company Code

- Set Up Bank Determination for Payment Transactions
- Define Value Date Rules
- Assign Payment Method to Bank Transaction
- Define Payment Groupings
- Prepare Automatic Postings for Payment Program
- Prepare Automatic Posting for Payment Requests
- Select Search Fields for Payments
- Select Search Fields for Line Item Display

You may carry out the individual steps as in IMG or use Transaction FBZP to configure the same through an interface (Figure 10.70).

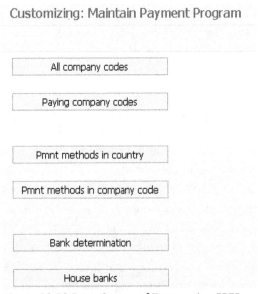

Customizing: Maintain Payment Program

All company codes

Paying company codes

Pmnt methods in country

Pmnt methods in company code

Bank determination

House banks

Figure 10.70 Entry Screen of Transaction FBZP

Before we proceed to set up the configuration for automatic payment program, we need to define a house bank without which you will not be able to complete the payment program settings at a later stage.

10.3.3.3.1   Define House Banks

The bank that you will use for making payments is known as the 'house bank', in SAP. You can have more than one house bank in a company code. You need to enter a house bank in the master record of customer / vendor for the payment program to use that bank. If not, you have to maintain a rule by which the payment program can determine the house bank automatically.

A 'bank directory' consists of master data of all the banks that you have created either manually or automatically. For automatic creation of bank master data, complete the configuration step SAP Customizing Implementation Guide > Cross-Application Components > Bank Directory > Bank Directory Data Transfer > Transfer Bank Directory Data – International or Transfer Bank Directory Data - Country-Specific. Once you have created the bank directory, you may designate one or more banks to be your house bank. Refer Section 12.1.1 of Chapter 12, for more details on bank directory.

Project Dolphin

All the company codes in USA will have their primary accounts with Bank of America (BOFA), Citi Bank (CITIU) and Chase Manhattan (CHASU) and they will accordingly be designated as the house banks. In India, the company codes will have accounts with State Bank of India (SBIIN), HDFC bank (HDFCI) and ICICI bank (ICICI). Each bank account in a house bank will be assigned to a G/L account and there can be multiple bank accounts in a single house bank. BESTM has indicated to the project team to differentiate foreign currency account numbers, by using a separate G/L account per currency for bill discounting.

To define a new house bank:

i. You can use the SAP IMG menu path: SAP Customizing Implementation Guide > Financial Accounting > Bank Accounting > Bank Accounts > Define House Banks, to create your house banks, or SAP Easy Access Menu Path: SAP Menu > Accounting > Financial Accounting > Banks > Master Data > House Banks and House Bank Accounts > Manage House Banks and House Bank Accounts to create both house banks and accounts within a house bank. You can also use Transaction FI12.

> ℹ️ To create only house banks, you may use SAP Easy Access Menu Path: SAP Menu > Accounting > Financial Accounting > Banks > Master Data > House Banks and House Bank Accounts > Manage House Banks or Transaction FI12_HBANK.

ii. On the resulting screen, select the company for which you want to define the house banks and double-click on 'House Banks' on the left hand side 'Dialog Structure'.

iii. On the resulting 'Change View "House Banks": Overview' screen, click on 'New Entries' and on the next screen (Figure 10.71):
   - Enter an identifier, for the 'House bank', of length not exceeding 5-characters. For example, BOFAU for Bank of America, CITIU for Citi Bank etc.
   - Under 'House Bank Data', enter 'Bank Country' (say, US) where the house bank is located and enter a 'Bank Key'. The bank key can be up to 15 characters long and is a unique ID identifying the bank both domestically and internationally. This is the SWIFT (Society for Worldwide Interbank Financial

Telecommunication) code for overseas banks. You can also derive the 'Bank Key' from IBAN.

- Enter the 'Communications data'.
- Expand 'Address' and provide the details like bank name, region, street, city etc

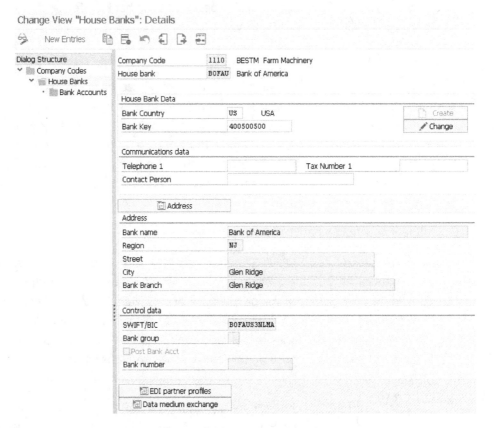

Figure 10.71 New House Bank Creation

- In 'Control data' block, enter the SWIFT/BIC code, enter a 'Bank group' that you can use in bank chain to optimize payments.

A SWIFT (Society for Worldwide Interbank Financial Telecommunication) code is used to identify a bank branch internationally for routing financial transactions. Used as the BIC (Bank Identifier Code), the SWIFT is a combination of letters and numbers and can have a total length of 8 or 11. It, however, does not have the account number information of the beneficiary who will receive the money. For example, the SWIFT code of HDBC bank, Hyderabad branch, India is HDFCINBBHYD: the first 4-characters (say HDFC) of a SWIFT will denote the bank and will always be in letters, the next 2-characters (say, IN) denote the country , the next 2-character (say, BB) can be characters or a mix of characters and numbers denoting the location, and the last 3-characters (say, HYD) denoting the branch with the last 3-characters being optional.

IBAN (International Bank Account Number), was developed originally in Europe for standardizing international numbering for individual bank accounts across the world, for simplifying bank transactions. All the European banks use IBAN, though its usage is becoming popular in other countries as well excluding USA and Canada where they do not use IBAN but recognise the system for routing international payments. The IBAN is made up of a number string with the two letters denoting the country, followed by two check digits, and with up to 35 alphanumeric characters containing the bank identifier / bank code and account number. The alphanumeric characters are known as the BBAN (Basic Bank Account Number). The national banking association of a country is free to decide the length of the BBAN to make it as a standard for that country. As a result, the length of IBAN varies from country to country: for example, the IBAN for UK, Ireland and Germany is 22, 27 for France, 28 for Poland and so on. IBAN cannot contain any space in between two digits / characters, when transmitted electronically (for example: DE89370400440532013999). However, it is denoted in groups of 4-characters separated by single spaces (with the last group of any variable length) when printed. An example of IBAN in print format for Germany will be DE89 3704 0044 0532 0139 99: DE is the country code, 89 is the check digit, 37040044 is the bank code (also called as BLZ code) and the last 0532013999 denoting the account number.

How IBAN is different from SWIFT?

The SWIFT code identifies a specific bank (branch) in international financial transactions. The IBAN, on the other hand, identifies not only the bank/branch but also the individual account involved in the international transaction.

- You may maintain the other details for DME, and EDI partner profiles.

> **i** If you are creating the house bank for the first time, you will see that the 'Create' button is enabled; else, you will see only the 'Change' button active.

- As we are creating the house bank for the first time, click on 'Create', and 'Save' the details.

iv.   Repeat the steps and create all other house banks that you may require.

v.   When completed, go back to the previous screen, and you will see all the house banks that you have created for a specific company code (Figure 10.72).

Figure 10.72 House Banks for Company Code 1110

vi.   Now, select the row containing a house bank and double-click on 'Bank Accounts' on the left hand side 'Dialog Structure' to create the required bank accounts for that bank.

vii. Click on 'Create Bank Account' and maintain the required details on the next screen:

- Enter an account identifier ('Account ID') of length not more than 5 characters. This 'Account ID' together with the house bank ID ('House bank') uniquely defines a bank account.
- Enter a proper 'Description' for the account ID.
- Under 'Bank Account Data' block: enter a 'Bank Account Number' of length not exceeding 18 characters. You may, if required, generate the IBAN number to fill this field. You may also enter an alternative account number ('Alternative acc no.') and enter the 'Currency' in which this account is to be maintained. Enter a 'Control key' which, for example, determines the type of account in most of the countries: in USA, 01 is used to denote checking account, 02 savings account, 03 loans and so on. Enter the 'G/L Acct' number in which the transaction figures from this bank account will get updated in the SAP system. You may also maintain a 'Discount Acct' which will be the G/L account to which you can post the credit memos arising out of BoE at this house bank account.
- 'Save' when completed. You have now, for example, created a bank account called 'BA100 at the house bank 'BOFAU' (checking account1 at Bank of America) as shown in Figure 10.73.

Figure 10.73 Creating a Bank Account at House Bank

viii.   Repeat the steps and create all other bank accounts at this specific house bank.

ix.   Go back to the previous screen and create all the required bank accounts for the various house banks (Figure 10.74).

Figure 10.74 Accounts at a House Bank

Now that we defined the required house banks (and the bank accounts) for BESTM, let us continue with our discussion on configuring the automatic payment program. The first step will be to set up all the company codes for payment transactions.

10.3.3.3.2   Set Up All Company Codes for Payment Transactions

Using this configuration step, you will make the settings for all company codes that are involved in the payment transactions. Per company code, you will define: (a) the paying company code (the company code that pays for itself and also for other company code), (b) if separate payment is required per business area, (c) if payment method supplements are to be used, (d) the cash discount and tolerance which the payment program uses to determine the appropriate cash discount strategy, and (e) the special G/L transactions that need to be settled, if any.

Project Dolphin

BESTM wants to designate the company code 1110 as the paying company code for themselves and also for 1120. Similarly, company code 2100 will be the paying company code for 2200, and 3100 will be the paying company code for 3200. Similar arrangements will be made for India based company codes as well wherein the company code 1210 will pay for 1220. BESTM Corporate wants to continue with their existing practice of making payments to their vendors, six days after the invoices are due. BESTM has requested the project team to configure the payment program to enable payments per 'Business Area', but the project team suggested not to do that, instead suggested grouping of payments in the normal way by 'Currency', 'Payment Method', 'House Bank' etc, so as to have more flexibility; BESTM, after a long deliberation, has accepted this idea and does not now require payment grouping per 'Business Area'. However, BESTM has requested that payment should cover the special G/L transactions like down payments (including down payment requests), security deposits, guarantee etc., for both customers and vendors. Additionally, BESTM wants to ensure that maximum cash discount is always taken, when paying vendor invoices automatically.

To make the required settings:

i.   Use the menu path: SAP Customizing Implementation Guide > Financial Accounting > Accounts Receivable and Accounts Payable > Business Transactions > Outgoing Payments > Automatic Outgoing Payments > Payment Method/Bank Selection for Payment Program > Set Up All Company Codes for Payment Transactions.

ii.   On the resulting screen, click on 'New Entries' and on the next screen (Figure 10.75):

- Enter the 'Company code' for which you are maintaining the settings (say, 1120).
- In 'Control Data', enter the 'Sending company code' that is known to your customer / vendor as the one that is sending the payment. It can be paying company code or different. If this field is left blank, then the system understands that the paying company code is the same as that of the sending company code. However, when the sending company code (1120) is not the paying company code (1110), then, the system incorporates the sending company code in the payment transfer medium or payment advice as your business partners (say, vendor) normally expect the sending company code to send the payment. Also, the sending company code decides grouping of items from different company codes: the items are grouped into one payment for all the company codes that have the same paying company code and sending company code.
- Enter the 'Paying company code' (say, 1110). This is the company code that pays on behalf of other company codes; for example, here, the company code 1110 is the paying company code for 1120. In a setting like this, which is also

known as 'centralized payment', the system automatically creates the inter-company postings in the system.

- Select 'Separate Payment per Business Area' check-box only if you want to group payments per business area. If selected, you will not be able to use the payment program's default grouping based on the currency / payment method / bank (mentioned in the line item).

Change View "Company Codes": Details

  New Entries

Company Code	1120	BESTM Garden & Forestry E		🔍 Paying company code

Control Data

Sending company code	1120	BESTM Garden & Forestry E
Paying company code	1110	BESTM Farm Machinery
Separate Payment per Business Area	☐	
Pyt Meth Suppl.	☐	

Cash discount and tolerances

Tolerance Days for Payable	6
Outgoing Pmnt with Cash Disc.From	%
Max.Cash Discount	☑

Vendors

Sp. G/L Transactions to Be Paid	AFH
Sp. G/L Trans. for Exception List	

Customers

Sp. G/L Transactions to Be Paid	AFGHP
Sp. G/L Trans. for Exception List	

Figure 10.75 Setting up All Company Codes for Payment Transactions

- Select 'Pyt. Meth Suppl.' check-box if payments are to be separated according to a pre-set characteristic. When selected, you can pre-define a 'payment method supplement' for customers / vendors of the company code. The payment method supplement is a 2-character identifier with the first character standing for priority (say, 2 for salary & wages, 4 for remittance of taxes etc) and the 2nd character denoting the execution method (say, N for clearing via electronic file). So, a payment method supplement 4N, for example, indicates that the tax remittance should be via electronic file.

> **i** You can use a 'payment method supplement' to group payments, in countries like Russia, and you can print the thus separated payments by sorting them. Though the system will default the payment method supplement during document entry, from the customer / vendor master, you can overwrite them during payment processing.

- Under 'Cash discount and tolerances' data block, enter the 'Tolerance Days for Payable' if required. Enter 6 for BESTM group of companies, as they plan to pay only six days after the invoice becoming due.

> **i** The system adds up the number of days specified in 'Tolerance Days for Payable' field, when calculating the cash discount period / due date for net payment. Suppose that an invoice is due on 20th Mar 2020 and you have maintained a tolerance of 6 days here in this field, then, the system arrives at the invoice due date as 26th Mar 2020 and the invoice will not be paid until that date even though the invoice due is on 20th Mar 2020.

- You can use the 'Outgoing Pmnt with Cash Disc. From' field to specify the lower limit for payments with cash discount deduction. When maintained, the system pays (after deducting the cash discount) only items having cash discount percentage rate more than (or equal to) the one specified in this field. If cash discount percentage rate is less than the one entered by you in this field, then, the system makes the payment only at the due date for net payment.

> **i** Enter 99 in the 'Outgoing Pmnt with Cash Disc. From' field, to delay the payment as long as possible and to ensure that the payment is always net.

- Select 'Max. Cash Discount' check-box to ensure that maximum cash discount is always deducted when paying your vendor invoices automatically.
- For both vendors and customers, enter the special G/L transactions that need to be paid through the payment program: enter A (down payment), F (down payment request) and H (security deposit) for vendors; for customers, enter A (down payment), F (down payment request), G (Guarantee), H (security deposit), and P (payment request). You may also maintain an exception list.
- 'Save' the settings.

iii.   Repeat the steps and configure all the company codes; in each case, identify clearly the paying and sending company codes.

With this we are now ready to configure the 2nd step in automatic payment program: setting up the paying company code for payment transactions.

10.3.3.3.3   Set Up Paying Company Codes for Payment Transactions

Using this configuration activity, you can specify the minimum amount for creating an incoming or outgoing payment. Besides this, you can also maintain the forms and sender details for payment advices and sheets accompanying EDI.

Project Dolphin

BESTM has indicated that they want to avoid large numbers of small payments. Accordingly, BESTM wants the system to be configured in such a way that there will not be any automatic payment processing, including the debit memos, if the payment amount is less than $25 for all the US-based company codes and INR 500 for company codes 1210 and 1220, for all incoming and outgoing payments. In all cases, wherein the payments proposed are less than these minimum thresholds, the system will accumulate them till the limit is crossed and then pay as in the normal course. In the case for bill of exchange (BoE) payments, BESTM wants the system to be configured to create one BoE per invoice.

Use the menu path: SAP Customizing Implementation Guide > Financial Accounting > Accounts Receivable and Accounts Payable > Business Transactions > Outgoing Payments > Automatic Outgoing Payments > Payment Method/Bank Selection for Payment Program > Set Up Paying Company Codes for Payment Transactions:

i.   On the resulting screen, click on 'New Entries' and on the next screen (Figure 10.76), enter the paying company code in 'Paying co. code' field (say, 1110).

ii.   You will see 'Use in Company Codes' button to the right of the 'Paying co. code' field. When you click on that, the system brings up a pop-up screen listing the company codes (1110 and 1120, in our case) for which this 'Paying co. code' (1110, in our case) is used for payment.

iii. Enter appropriate settings for the 'Control Data':

- Specify the minimum amount for both incoming payments and outgoing payments, below which the system will not process automatic payments. So, the system generates a debit memo, for an incoming payment, only when it is more than the amount entered in 'Minimum Amount for Incoming Payment' field; else, the system prints the amounts in an exception list and accumulates them for processing at a later date. In the case of outgoing payments, the system processes the payment only if the payment is more than or equal to the amount entered in 'Minimum Amount for Outgoing Payment' field; else, here, also such line items that are less than the threshold limit is printed in an exception list and accumulated for payment in future.

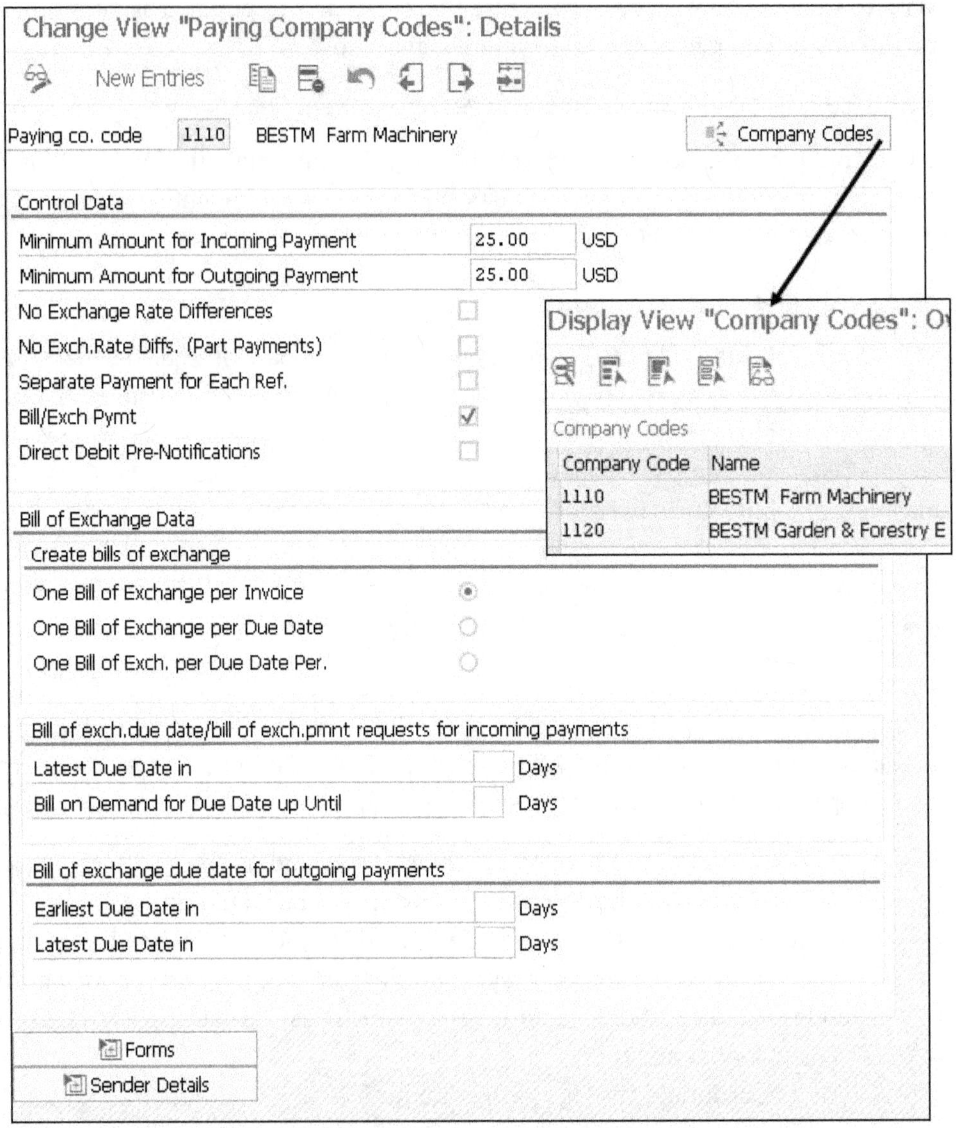

Figure 10.76 Setting up Paying Company Codes for Payment Transactions

- You may select 'No Exchange Rate Differences' check-box enabling the system not to post exchange rate differences, if any, for foreign currency line items, during automatic payment processing. Else, the system determines exchange rate difference (using foreign exchange translation), and posts the same automatically per payment.

- The behaviour of 'No Exch.Rate Diffs (Part Payments)' flag is similar to that of 'No Exchange Rate Differences' check-box except that this applies only to partial payments.

- Select 'Separate Payment for Each Ref.' check-box to settle invoices and credit memos having the same payment reference in one payment. Used in countries like Norway, Finland etc, you should set this flag only if payment methods need a payment reference for each payment.

> **i** You cannot generate an outgoing payment for payment references referring to credit memos, when separate payments are made by payment reference. Also, when you make payments, by payment reference, the system will not offset between a customer and a vendor, unless the payment reference in a customer line item is also the same payment reference in a vendor line item.

- Select 'Bill/Exch Pymt' check-box to enable display of bill of exchange (BoE) fields during payment transaction. You will select this if you want use BoE, BoE payment requests, or the check/BoE procedure in the paying company code. If not selected, but if you have already made the settings for payment transactions with BoE, then, the system deletes all those settings.

> **i** Only when you select 'Bill/Exch Pymt' check-box, the system brings up additional details on the screen under 'Bill of Exchange Data'.

- Under 'Create bills of exchange', select the appropriate radio-button. You need to select the first one namely 'One Bill of Exchange per Invoice' for BESTM's paying company codes. In the case of BoE due date or BoE payment requests for incoming payments, you need to maintain the due date in the appropriate fields.
- Maintain the form and sender details by expanding the data blocks 'Forms' and 'Sender Details'.
- 'Save' the settings.

iv. Repeat the steps and configure the appropriate settings for all other paying company codes of BESTM Corporate.

With this, let us move on to configure the payment methods, for each country, for the payment transactions.

10.3.3.3.4   Set Up Payment Methods per Country for Payment Transactions

A 'payment method', in SAP, specifies how payment is made when you enter it in customer / vendor master record, line items, or payment run (parameter). There are several payment methods supported in SAP, including check (or cheque), bill of exchange, bank transfer, direct debit etc.

Per payment method per country, you have to specify (a) if the payment method is to be used for incoming payment or outgoing payment, (b) the characteristics for classifying the payment method that includes type of payment method (like, check, bank transfer, bill of exchange etc) and other features including, for example, if the payment method is valid for personnel payments, (c) the master record control settings as to, for example, entering the bank details (say, account number, SWIFT code etc), entering the address / postal details etc, (d) the parameters for posting like document type for posting, clearing document type to be used etc, and (e) the settings for payment medium. You also need to maintain the currencies that can be used per payment method per country. If you do not specify any currency, then, you can use that payment method, in that country, for payments in all currencies.

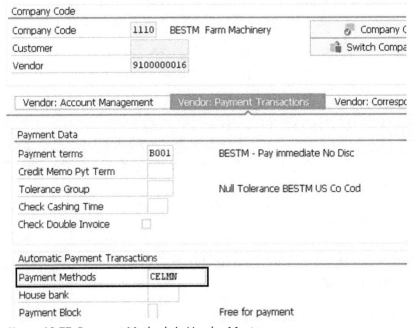

Figure 10.77 Payment Methods in Vendor Master

i You will maintain the payment method in a couple of places: in the customer / vendor master record, in a line item of customer / vendor, and also while maintaining the payment run parameter ('Payment Methods' under 'Payment Control') for executing the automatic payment run.

You need to enter the payment method in vendor (or customer) in the 'Payment Methods' field under 'Automatic Payment Transactions' to enable the system to pick up the appropriate payment method for that business partner for automatic payments. You can maintain more than one payment method in the master record. However, the order in which you maintain the payment methods is important: the system will try making payment using the first method, then uses the second one if the first one is not successful and so on. Consider, for example, you have maintained (Figure 10.77) CELMN as the payment methods: now, the system will consider the payment method C with the first priority before considering E, L, M and so on in the order it has been maintained.

Though you can maintain more than one payment method in a customer / vendor master record, you can enter only one payment method (from those mentioned in the master record) in a line item. The payment method entered in the line item takes precedence; it will override the payment methods in the master record, irrespective of the order in which they have been entered into. For example, you have maintained M (direct debit) as the payment method in a vendor line item, and you have maintained CELMN as the payment methods in vendor master. Now, the payment method M (entered in the line item) has the priority over the other methods (CELMN) even though M is not at the first place in the 'Payment Methods' field in the master record.

Take care not to enter a payment method in the 'payment run parameter' that is conflicting with the payment methods already maintained in the master record or line item. Else, the system will not process the automatic payment. For example, if you enter T [Bank transfer (ACH CTX)] as the payment method, in payment run parameter, but have maintained M as the payment method in a line item and CELMN as the payment methods in vendor master, then, the system will not process the line item for payment as the payment method in payment run parameter is in conflict with the payment method maintained in line items and master record.

The standard system comes delivered with the default settings of applicable payment methods for each of the countries (Figure 10.78). You may use that as such.

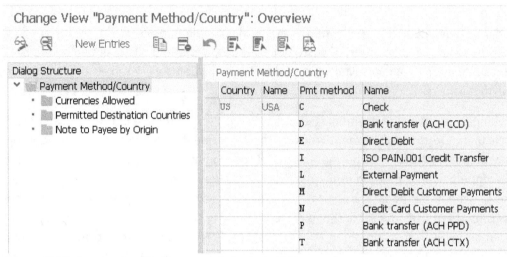

Figure 10.78 Country-Specific Payment Methods for USA

Project Dolphin

BESTM wants does not want to define any new payment method. Instead, they have indicated that, they will go ahead using the default payment methods that have been configured in the standard system for both USA and India.

However, if you want to define a new payment method for a country, you may do so as detailed below:

i.   Use the menu path: SAP Customizing Implementation Guide > Financial Accounting > Accounts Receivable and Accounts Payable > Business Transactions > Outgoing Payments > Automatic Outgoing Payments > Payment Method/Bank Selection for Payment Program > Set Up Payment Methods per Country for Payment Transactions. You may also use Transaction OBZ3.

> ℹ️ When you use Transaction OBZ3, you will see a slightly different user interface, for the first two screens, than the one you will be seeing when you use the menu path (Figure 10.78).

ii.   On the resulting screen, click on 'New Entries' and maintain the required settings as shown in Figure 10.79, on the next screen.

iii. Once you have maintained the settings for the new payment medium, you may double-click on 'Currencies' on the left hand side 'Dialog Structure' to specify the currencies for which you intend to use this new payment medium. As mentioned already, you just need to leave this as blank if you want this payment medium valid for all currencies.

iv.   Double-click on 'Permitted Destination Countries' on the left hand side 'Dialog Structure', to maintain the destination countries in which you want to use this payment method. As in the case of currency settings, you can leave this table empty so that the payment method is valid for all countries

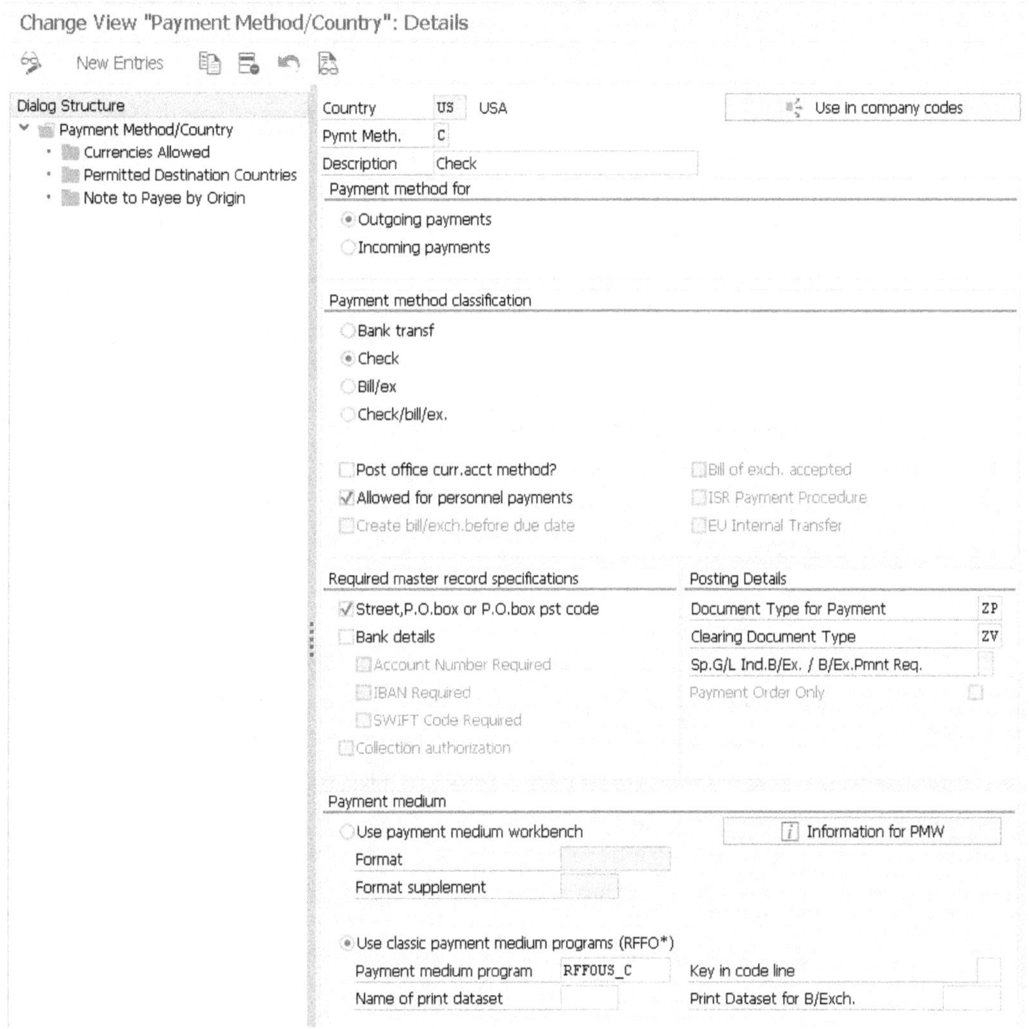

Change View "Payment Method/Country": Details

New Entries

Dialog Structure
- Payment Method/Country
  - Currencies Allowed
  - Permitted Destination Countries
  - Note to Payee by Origin

Country   US   USA   Use in company codes
Pymt Meth.   C
Description   Check

Payment method for
- ● Outgoing payments
- ○ Incoming payments

Payment method classification
- ○ Bank transf
- ● Check
- ○ Bill/ex
- ○ Check/bill.ex.

☐ Post office curr.acct method?   ☐ Bill of exch. accepted
☑ Allowed for personnel payments   ☐ ISR Payment Procedure
☐ Create bill/exch.before due date   ☐ EU Internal Transfer

Required master record specifications   **Posting Details**
☑ Street,P.O.box or P.O.box pst code   Document Type for Payment   ZP
☐ Bank details   Clearing Document Type   ZV
  ☐ Account Number Required   Sp.G/L Ind.B/Ex. / B/Ex.Pmnt Req.
  ☐ IBAN Required   Payment Order Only
  ☐ SWIFT Code Required
  ☐ Collection authorization

Payment medium
○ Use payment medium workbench   ⓘ Information for PMW
  Format
  Format supplement

● Use classic payment medium programs (RFFO*)
  Payment medium program   RFFOUS_C   Key in code line
  Name of print dataset   Print Dataset for B/Exch.

Figure 10.79 Details of Payment Method Settings for 'Check' for USA

ⓘ If bank details are required for a payment method, and, for example, if you have selected 'EU Internal Transfer' check-box for the payment method (in step ii), then, you have to enter an EU country or one of the exception countries as the destination country in step (iii) without which you will not be able to process the payment using this payment method.

---

v.   'Save' the settings when completed.

i We have already seen that you can maintain the payment methods in a couple of places. If that is the case, then, how the system selects the appropriate payment method for a particular payment run?

Scenario 1: Payment method is maintained in all the three places: payment run parameter, line item and customer / vendor master.

Suppose you have maintained C as the payment method in payment run parameter and also in the line item. However, you have maintained multiple payment methods (ELMNC) in customer / vendor master. Now, the payment program selects C as the payment method as this is maintained both in the line item and also in payment run parameters notwithstanding the payment methods mentioned in business partner's master record.

Scenario 2: Payment method is maintained in two places: payment run parameter and customer / vendor master. No payment method is maintained in the line item.

Suppose you have maintained C as the payment method in payment run parameter and have maintained multiple payment methods (ELMNC) in customer / vendor master. Since there is no payment method maintained in the line item, the program verifies if the payment method entered in the business partner's record is the same in payment run parameters also. If there is a single payment method in master record and if it is the same in the payment run parameter also, then the program uses that method. If more than one payment method has been entered in the master record, then the program proceeds as under: (a) the program checks the first payment method in the master record (E, in our case) and compares that with the payment method maintained in the payment run parameter (C, in our case); if both are same, then, the program uses that payment method, else (b) the payment program checks the second entry of payment method in the master (L), and compares that again with the method in the payment run parameters (C); if both are same, then, the program uses that payment method, else (c) the program checks the 3rd method and the iteration goes on.

With this, we are now ready to configure the next step: setting up the payment methods per company code.

10.3.3.3.5   Set Up Payment Methods per Company Code for Payment Transactions

Specify, here in this configuration activity, which payment methods you want to use per (paying) company code. You can also determine the conditions under which a payment method should be used. You can specify the amount limits (for payments) per payment method, maintain the specifications for grouping items for payment (say, making a single payment for all the marked items), enter the settings for foreign/foreign currency payments, make the specifications for optimizing bank selection, enter the appropriate settings for the system to select the correct form for the payment medium and maintain the specifications for issuing payment advice notes, if any.

While maintaining the amount limits for payment methods, always specify a maximum amount; else, you will not be able to use that payment method. In case you maintain the payment method in an open item, then, the system ignores the amount entered here, in this configuration, as the limit for payment method.

Project Dolphin

As regards payments through automatic payment program, BESTM wants to have the system configured to reflect the following:

All the line items that are due on a particular date should be grouped and paid in a single payment. If line items are associated with a payment method explicitly, then, the system should pay those items; else, if the payment method is not specified explicitly in the line item and if the system selects the payment method automatically, then, several items can be paid together. The 'extended individual payment' should be activated to make it possible to include and offset all available credit memos for a payment group. For payment methods like bank transfer, the system should make payments abroad using the business partners' banks in their respective countries. The system should be able to make payments – for all payment methods - in other currencies, other than the company code currency. BESTM wants bank optimization using their own house banks and business partners' banks so as to optimize international payments.

As regards payments, if the payment method is check, then, all in-country payments should not be less than $25 (for US-based company codes) and INR 500 for Indian company codes. If the payment is more than $5,000 (or INR 250,000) then, it has to be made through bank transfer or direct debit. For direct debit, bank transfer or card payment, there is no lower limit for payment. In cases of composite payments, BESTM wants the system to split the payment by grouping the invoices with the appropriate credit memos, for payments exceeding $10,000 in the case of US-based company codes (or INR 500,000 for all the India-based company codes), for all the allowed payment methods, for both domestic and international payments.

To configure the payment method per company code, for payment transactions:

i.   Use the menu path: SAP Customizing Implementation Guide > Financial Accounting > Accounts Receivable and Accounts Payable > Business Transactions > Outgoing Payments > Automatic Outgoing Payments > Payment Method/Bank Selection for Payment Program > Set Up Payment Methods per Company Code for Payment Transactions.

ii.   On the resulting screen, select 'New Entries' and maintain the required settings per payment method per company code (Figure 10.80), on the next screen:

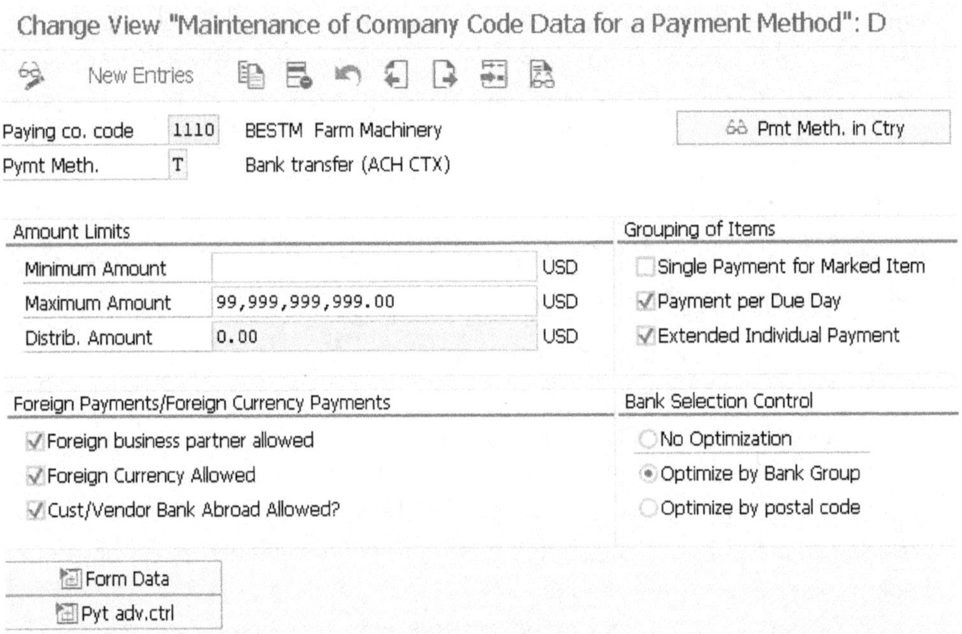

Change View "Maintenance of Company Code Data for a Payment Method": D

| 👓 | New Entries | 📄 | 📑 | ↩ | ⬅ | ➡ | ⬌ | 📊 |

| Paying co. code | 1110 | BESTM Farm Machinery | | 👓 Pmt Meth. in Ctry |
| Pymt Meth. | T | Bank transfer (ACH CTX) | | |

Amount Limits

Minimum Amount		USD
Maximum Amount	99,999,999,999.00	USD
Distrib. Amount	0.00	USD

Grouping of Items

☐ Single Payment for Marked Item
☑ Payment per Due Day
☑ Extended Individual Payment

Foreign Payments/Foreign Currency Payments

☑ Foreign business partner allowed
☑ Foreign Currency Allowed
☑ Cust/Vendor Bank Abroad Allowed?

Bank Selection Control

◯ No Optimization
◉ Optimize by Bank Group
◯ Optimize by postal code

📋 Form Data
📋 Pyt adv.ctrl

Figure 10.80 Payment Method Configuration Per Company Code

- Enter the paying company code (1110), and select the payment method (T).
- Enter the amount limits (minimum and maximum). If a payment is below the 'Minimum Amount' or above the 'Maximum Amount', then, the system will not process the payment using this payment method. If you have maintained payment methods in the customer/vendor master record under the 'Payment Methods' field under 'Automatic Payment Transactions' data block in the 'Vendor (Customer): Payment Transactions' tab in the Company Code area, then, the system ignores the maximum / minimum amount entries entered here, if it contradicts with the payable amount to that business partner.
- When you make an entry in 'Distrib. Amount' field, then, the system analyses the payments exceeding this amount to see if it is possible to split those payments into more than one payment but not exceeding this amount. The system makes the payment method check independent of the payment method specification in the document item. However, this limit in the 'Distrib. Amount' field will not have any effect on payment proposal processing. The 'Distrib. Amount' field settings cannot be used together with 'Enhanced Individual Payment' and also with 'Payment per Due Day'.

> **i** Consider that the amount limit to be split and distribute for the payment method 'External Payment' is, $10,000.
>
> *Scenario: 1*. You have two invoices $15,000 & $11,000 and four credit memos $2,800, $2,200, $700 & $800. You, now, have the group of document items totalling $19,500 to be paid together. Once the system checks the 'External Transfer' as the payment method successfully, it creates two payment documents: one for $10,000 (clearing invoice of $15,000 and credits of $2,800 & $2,200), and another for $9,500 (clearing invoice of $11,000 and credits of $700 & $800).
>
> *Scenario: 2*. You have two invoices $15,000 & $11,000 and two credit memos $1,800, $900. Now, you have these group of documents totalling $23,300 to be paid together. The check, for the payment method 'External Payment', will not be successful as not all the invoice items, for this payment, can be reduced by the corresponding credit memos to the maximum distribution limit of $10,000. To proceed, you may select a different payment method. Else, the system puts them in the exception list as no suitable payment method is found.
>
> *Scenario: 3*. You have two invoices $15,000 & $11,000 and a credit memo $6,000. Now, you have these group of documents totalling $20,000 to be paid together. The check, for the payment method 'External Payment', will not be successful as no proportional distribution of credit to invoices can be made (system does not bifurcate $6,000 to distribute to invoices as $5,000 and $1,000).

iii.   Under 'Grouping of Items':

- When you select 'Single Payment for Marked Item' check-box, then, it makes the system to pay the open items, that contain this payment method, individually. So, all the items with explicit payment method are paid individually. However, you can pay several items together, when the payment method is not specified explicitly, but instead is selected by the payment program.

- Select 'Payment per Due Day' check-box to group payments that are due on a particular due date. You can use this to leverage to get maximum cash discount. When not selected, then, the payment program groups – irrespective of due date - all the payments per vendor / customer. For example, if the due date of a vendor line item is earlier than the payment run's posting date, the system replaces the due date with the payment run's posting date, so that all items that are overdue on the posting date are grouped and paid together with a single payment. Suppose, if such a grouping results in a credit balance, then, the system groups those items that have debit balances with different due dates and then makes the payment.

> **i** If you set the 'Single Payment' indicator in the customer / vendor master record (Figure 10.81), then, the system pays every customer/ vendor open item separately during automatic payment. That is, the system does not group open items together for payment.

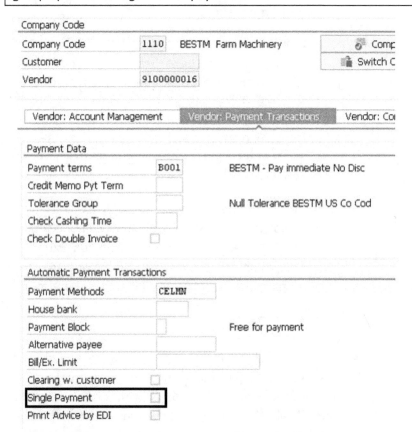

Figure 10.81 Configuring 'Single Payment' in Vendor Master

- You can use the 'Extended Individual Payment' to process open items of a payment group (to be defined separately) individually according to pre-defined rules. You can include and offset all available credit memos for the payment group. However, in case of individual payments, you can offset only credit memos with invoice reference; you cannot offset credit memos without invoice reference. You can form new payment groups with the rules like, items with the opposite payment direction (say, credit memos - F110) have to be offset with the other items, invoice-related credit memos to be offset always with the related invoice, credit memos w/o invoice reference can be grouped together with any of the invoices for a payment group etc.

iv.   For configuring 'Foreign Payments / Foreign Currency Payments':

- Select 'Foreign business partner allowed' to enable the payment method to be used for payments with customers/vendors abroad.
- Select 'Foreign Currency Allowed' flag to use the payment method for payments in foreign currency. Set this indicator if you can transmit the currency key to the bank using the payment medium used.

> **i** Do not select this check-box for checks with the local currency key or for payment methods for domestic DME, wherein the currency field is not defined in the format description.

- Select 'Cust/Vendor Bank Abroad Allowed?' check-box to route the payment from a bank of the customer/vendor who is abroad. You cannot use this payment method if you do not set this flag and when the customer/vendor does not have a bank account in paying company code's country. You will normally select this for payment methods such as bank transfer (T), and external transfer. However, as a prerequisite, you need set up the required bank settings in customer / vendor master records.

> **i** SAP supports a variety of bank transfers. The bank transfers happen via different variants of ACH (Automated Clearing House) transactions. ACH enables automatic fund transfer, across banks and financial institutions through e-payments.
>
> SAP supports various formats of ACH:
>
> 1. ACH-CCD where CCD refers to 'Cash Concentration and Disbursement' for corporate credits and debits. This is the most common automated payment for corporate (business) accounts.
>
> 2. ACH-PPD: with the PPD standing for 'Prearranged Payment and Deposit', this is mainly used to pay (or receive) from consumer (personal) accounts, for example, payroll payment to employee accounts.
>
> 3. ACH-CTX: here the CTX stand for 'Corporate Trade Exchange' and ACH-CTX is used mainly by corporates and government for money transfer.

v.   Select the suitable option under 'Bank selection control'. You have three options including 'No Optimization'. The 'Optimize by Bank Group' option lets the system to select the most appropriate pair of your bank and that of your business partner's for a payment method like bank transfer. When you select 'Optimize by postal code', the system makes use of the postal code and arrives at the bank that is geographically nearer to the business partner's location. However, to make use of this option, you need to define the range of postal codes serviced by the bank(s).

vi.   Maintain the required settings for 'Form Data' and also for the payment advice ('Pyt.adv.ctrl.').

vii.   'Save' the settings, when completed. Repeat, and make the settings for all the payment methods that you will use in a particular company code (Figure 10.82).

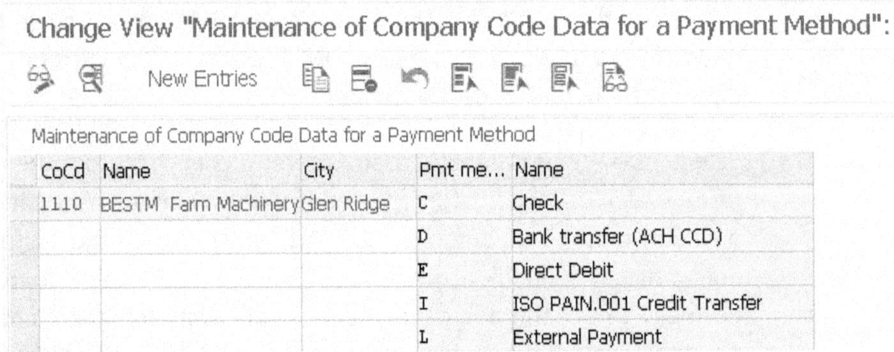

Change View "Maintenance of Company Code Data for a Payment Method":

New Entries

Maintenance of Company Code Data for a Payment Method

CoCd	Name	City	Pmt me...	Name
1110	BESTM Farm Machinery	Glen Ridge	C	Check
			D	Bank transfer (ACH CCD)
			E	Direct Debit
			I	ISO PAIN.001 Credit Transfer
			L	External Payment

Figure 10.82 Configuring Payment Methods Per Company Code

viii.   Repeat the steps for configuring the payment methods for all the paying company codes.

With this, we are, now, ready to set up the payment medium format for paying company codes.

10.3.3.3.6   Set a Payment Medium Format per Company Code

The system uses the payment medium format to control how payments (and debit memos) to the bank are created. The specifications, per payment medium format, is published by the banks or the central banking committees of the country. Use this step to specify which payment medium format is to be used for each combination of 'company code-payment method-house bank'. Per payment medium format, you can also decide if you also want to add a note to payee.

Use the menu path: SAP Customizing Implementation Guide > Financial Accounting > Accounts Receivable and Accounts Payable > Business Transactions > Outgoing Payments > Automatic Outgoing Payments > Payment Method/Bank Selection for Payment Program > Set a Payment Medium Format per Company Code. On the resulting screen, click on 'New Entries' and define the required settings:

    i.   Enter the paying company code ('CoCd'), and enter a payment method ('PM').

    ii.   Enter the house bank ('House bk') and select the suitable payment medium format ('Payt Mdm Format'). Enter the appropriate format supplement ('Addit.') which lets you differentiate between the collection and direct debiting procedures in the case of debit memos. The supplement will either be printed in the coding line of the payment medium or transferred into the appropriate field during DME.

    iii. Enter the 'Alternative Format Type' which specifies how payment files from the back-end system should be transferred to the house bank. When you select 'SAP Multi-Bank Connectivity', the system automatically sends the payment files to your house bank via SAP Multi-Bank Connectivity. When left blank, the system does not send the payment files.

    iv. You may also maintain a note to payee by selecting a row containing the 'company code-payment method-house bank' combination, and double-clicking on 'Note to Payee' on the left hand side 'Dialog Structure'.

    v.   Repeat the steps for all the house bank-payment method combinations and 'Save' the details (Figure 10.83).

Change View "PMW Format": Overview of Selected Set

New Entries

		Dialog Structure	PMW Format				
PMW Format		CoCd	PM	House bk	Payt Mdm Format	Addit.	Alternative Format Type
Note to Payee		1110	D	BOFAU	US_ACH	CCD	SAP Multi-Bank Connectivity
		1110	E	BOFAU	US_ACH_DD	CTX	SAP Multi-Bank Connectivity
		1110	I	BOFAU	US_CGI_XML_CT		SAP Multi-Bank Connectivity
		1110	M	BOFAU	US_ACH_DD	CTX	SAP Multi-Bank Connectivity
		1110	P	BOFAU	US_ACH	PPD	SAP Multi-Bank Connectivity
		1110	T	BOFAU	US_ACH	CTX	SAP Multi-Bank Connectivity

Figure 10.83 Configuring Payment Medium Format Per Company Code

    vi. Repeat the settings for all the paying company codes.

The next step is to set up the bank determination for payment transactions.

10.3.3.3.7   Set Up Bank Determination for Payment Transactions

Here, you can make settings that determines how the payment program selects the banks or bank accounts for making the payments. In the process, (a) you specify which house banks are permitted and rank them in a list, (b) per house bank and payment method (and currency, if required), you then specify which bank account is to be used for payments, (c) per account at a house bank, you, then, enter the amounts that are available for the payment run; you can maintain separate amounts for incoming and outgoing payments, (d) you also specify how many days should elapse between the posting date of the payment run and the value date at the bank; this will dependent on the payment method, bank account, payment amount, and currency, and finally (e) you define the charges that are printed on the BoE forms, if any.

---

i In determining the bank account, the system first runs 'classic bank account determination'. It uses the 'enhanced settings' only if it cannot determine an account in classic bank account determination.

In the classic view, you can enter only one bank account with its account determination for each combination of 'house bank-payment method-currency'. The settings of classic bank account determination may not be sufficient: (a) when posting the open items wherein you have already defined which bank account is to be used, and (b) when you want to define a ranking of multiple accounts for the same house bank. So, in both these cases you need to define the account determination exclusively in the 'Bank Accounts (Enhanced)' view.

Project Dolphin

The BESTM Corporate has indicated to the project team that Bank of America will be the primary bank for all the payment methods, followed by Chase Manhattan and Citi Bank in that ranking order. It has been envisaged to provide an amount limit of $ 9,999,999,999 for Bank of America for facilitating all the automatic payment transactions (outgoing payments). The limit for the other two banks would be $ 999,999,999 in each case. In the case of incoming payments, there should not be any limit restriction imposed. The value date should be 1 day after, for all the payments through electronic format; however, it would be 3 days after for all the checks denominated in the local currency. For house banks in India, the limits will be the same but denominated in INR.

To configure the settings for bank determination:

i. Use the menu path: SAP Customizing Implementation Guide > Financial Accounting > Accounts Receivable and Accounts Payable > Business Transactions > Outgoing Payments > Automatic Outgoing Payments > Payment Method/Bank Selection for Payment Program > Set Up Bank Determination for Payment Transactions. You may also Transaction REMMHBACC.

ii. On the 'Display View "Bank Selection": Overview' screen, select the row under 'Bank selection' and double-click on 'Ranking Order' on the left hand side 'Dialog Structure'.

iii. On the next screen, click on 'New Entries' and maintain the settings on the resulting screen (Figure 10.84):

- Enter the payment method ('PM'), currency ('CrCy'), ranking order ('Rank Order') and the house bank ('House bk'). The ranking order is the sequence used in selecting a particular house bank. The house bank with a ranking order of 1 will be the first bank to be picked up, by the system, for the payment run for that payment method.

> **i** You can use the 'House bk' to denote the house bank that would pay the BoE created with a check/bill of exchange payment. Also, you can use 'Acct for Bill/Exch' field to store the bank account at the local bank against which a BoE should be paid from the check/bill of exchange payment.

Change View "Ranking Order": Overview

New Entries

Dialog Structure						
∨ Bank Selection	Paying company code		1110	BESTM Farm Machinery		
• Ranking Order						
• Bank Accounts	Ranking Order					
• Bank Accounts (Ent	PM	Crcy	Rank.Order	House bk	House bk	Acct for Bill/Exch.
• Available Amounts	C		1	BOFAU		
• Value Date	C		2	CHASU		
• Expenses/Charges	C		3	CITIU		

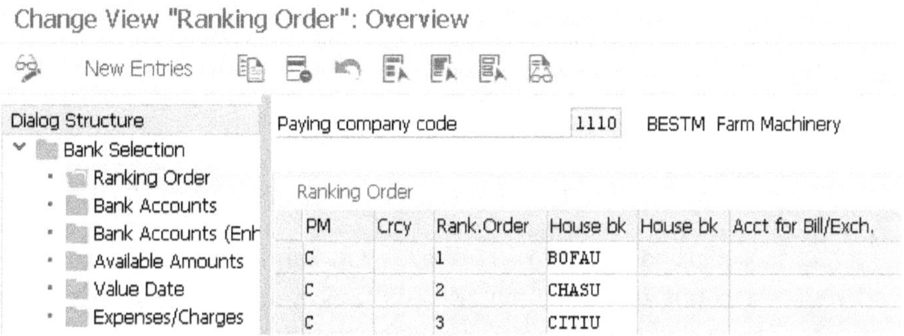

Figure 10.84 Configuring Bank Determination – Ranking Order

- Repeat the entries to cover all payment methods, currency and house banks that you may require in the ranking list. Since you can assign multiple currencies and several house banks to a single payment method, you may need to repeat the entries for a particular payment method to cover all scenarios.

> **i** If you want a particular house bank and a particular currency to be valid for all payment methods, then you need to leave the payment method ('PM') field as blank. You can also leave the currency ('Crcy') field as blank so that the particular row will be valid for all currencies for the given 'payment method-house bank combination'. For a single payment method, you can maintain a maximum of 9,999 house banks with the appropriate ranking order.

iv. Now, double-click on 'Bank Accounts' on the left hand side 'Dialog Structure' and maintain the required accounts by clicking on 'New Entries' (Figure 10.85):
- Enter the house bank, payment method, currency (you can leave this as blank to make the settings valid for all currencies), account identifier at the bank ('Account ID') and the G/L account ('Bank Subaccount') to which the transactions will be posted to in the SAP system.

- Repeat and maintain the settings for all the house banks for the given payment method / currency combination. You will be able to maintain only one account per 'house bank- payment method-currency' combination and this is known as the 'classic bank account determination'.
- Repeat the steps and maintain for all the payment methods.

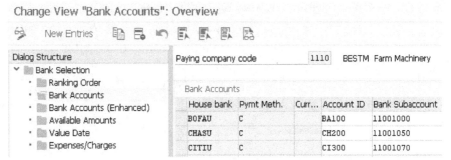

Figure 10.85 Configuring Bank Determination – Bank Accounts

v.   Similar to the step (iv) above, you can maintain the settings for 'enhanced bank account determination'. When the system is unable to select the appropriate account in the classic bank account determination, then, it will use the settings maintained here. To configure, double-click on 'Bank Accounts (Enhanced)' on the left hand side 'Dialog Structure'.

vi. Now, you may maintain the settings for available amounts. Double-click on 'Available Amounts' on the left hand side 'Dialog Structure', click on 'New Entries' and maintain the details on the next screen (Figure 10.86):

Figure 10.86 Configuring Bank Determination – Availabe Amounts

- Enter the house bank and the account ID at that house bank.
- You need to enter the 'Days' only if you have BoE payments to be posted before their due date. In such a case, the value date of BoE on the bank account is expected within the number of days entered here. Enter 999 in all other cases, so that the system will not take this value into account.
- Enter the currency.

- Maintain the amount limit for outgoing payment ('Available for outgoing payment'). The amount entered here in this field is only used for payments with which the bank debit entry is expected during the number of days ('Days') displayed.

> 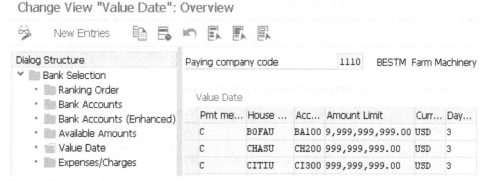 For example, the system checks to see if this amount ('Available for outgoing payment') in the account is sufficient for making an outgoing payment from this house bank using that payment method. If the amount in the bank account is insufficient for the outgoing payment, the payment program moves on to select another bank account, based on the ranking order, to determine if there is a sufficient amount in that bank account to cover the entire payment. If yes, then the payment is processed; else (that is, when the amount is not sufficient), the system will not process the payment. Note that when the amount in a particular account is insufficient for payment, the system will not draw the shortfall from other bank account but moves to the other bank account to make the payment in full.

- Also enter the incoming payment ('Scheduled incoming payment'), if required. This limit applies only to incoming payments for which the bank credit memo is expected during the number of days ('Days') displayed. You may also leave this as blank (as in the case of BESTM) to receive any amount as incoming payment without a limit.

vii. Repeat and maintain the settings for all the ('House bank'- 'Account ID'-'Currency') combinations.

viii. Now, double-click on 'Value Date' on the left hand side 'Dialog Structure', click on 'New Entries' and maintain the details on the next screen (Figure 10.87):

Change View "Value Date": Overview

New Entries

Dialog Structure	Paying company code		1110	BESTM Farm Machinery		
∨ Bank Selection						
· Ranking Order	Value Date					
· Bank Accounts						
· Bank Accounts (Enhanced)	Pmt me...	House ...	Acc...	Amount Limit	Curr...	Day...
· Available Amounts	C	BOFAU	BA100	9,999,999,999.00	USD	3
· Value Date	C	CHASU	CH200	999,999,999.00	USD	3
· Expenses/Charges	C	CITIU	CI300	999,999,999.00	USD	3

Figure 10.87 Configuring Bank Determination – Value Date

- Enter the payment method, house bank, and account ID at the house bank.
- Enter the 'Amount Limit' up to which the settings specified here will be valid.

- In the 'Days to value date' field, enter the number of days before a debit and/or a credit memo transaction is accounted for in the bank account. The system will add the days you enter here to the posting date to arrive at the date that is relevant for cash management and forecast. For example, if the payment method is bank transfer, direct debit etc., then you can expect payments to be accounted at the bank on the next day; hence, you may enter 1 in this field. On the other hand, if the payment method is, say, check then there could be a delay of more than 1 day and it may even dependent on the amount of the check.

> **i** For example, if you enter 3 in this 'Days to value date' field, then, the system adds this to the posting date (say, 15-Mar-2020) of the payment run date to arrive at the value date as 18-Mar-2020. If you do not enter a value in this field, then, the posting date of the payment run = value date.
>
> You can maintain the 'Check Cashing Time' in the customer / vendor master record (Figure 10.88). The system uses this value to arrive at the value date. If you keep this 'Check Cashing Time' as blank, then, the payment program uses the value entered in 'Days to value date' field in the payment program.

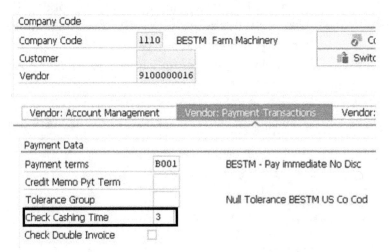

Figure 10.88 'Check Cashing Time' Field in Vendor Master

ix.   Double-click on 'Expenses/Charges' on the left hand side 'Dialog Structure' and maintain the charges that are printed on the BoE forms, if any (not required in all the countries, but in vogue in country like Spain).

This completes the configuration for bank determination.

> **i** So, how the payment program determines the correct house bank for the payment?
>
> First, the payment program tries identifying a house bank for a given 'payment method-currency' combination. If it is unable to find a house bank, for the given 'payment method-currency' combination, it tries to find a house bank for the same payment method but without the currency stipulation. If it is successful, then it goes ahead with the bank. Then, secondly, it iterates to find out the suitable account at the selected house bank. Finally, it checks if the amount limit at the selected house bank account is sufficient for the payment. The program, during this process, finds only one house bank that matches the criteria; if more than one bank is found, then, it makes use of the 'ranking order' to select the house bank with the highest ranking order and uses that bank for the payment. This is, of course, assuming that there is no bank optimization either via postal code or bank group. If there is such an optimization, the selection will be based on the results of optimization.
>
> If the payment program does not find a house bank fulfilling all the three criteria - house bank, house bank account and available amount limit – it tries to locate another house bank that fulfils these requirements for the given payment method. If it cannot find a house bank, then it concludes that the payment cannot be made using that payment method. Now, it starts all over, and begins checking for another payment method currency combination. This iteration goes on till the program finds suitable house bank for a given payment method.

Let us, now, move on to discuss how to configure the value date rules.

10.3.3.3.8 Define Value Date Rules

We have already discussed, in the previous Section, the effect of adding the days in 'Days to value date' for specific 'payment method-house bank-account ID' combination (while configuring the value date in bank determination for payment transactions) and also the effect of entering the 'Check Cashing Time' in business partner's master record. Let us see, now, in this Section, how you can make certain specifications for some of the bank transactions like incoming checks, BoE etc., per house bank and per account.

Use the menu path: SAP Customizing Implementation Guide > Financial Accounting > Accounts Receivable and Accounts Payable > Business Transactions > Outgoing Payments > Automatic Outgoing Payments > Payment Method/Bank Selection for Payment Program > Define Value Date Rules. You may also use Transaction OBBA.

On the resulting pop-up screen, maintain the company code and proceed to configure the settings on the next screen. When fully configured, the system adds / subtracts the specified days as deviation from the reference date ('R') which may be the document date or posting date or due date. After this, the system checks the date thus arrived with a factory calendar and decides the value date for that transaction.

> **i** You may configure the system to arrive at the value date by defining either the value date rules (as above) or value date settings as in setting up the bank determination for payment transactions that we discussed in the previous Section (10.3.3.3.7). Both are not required.

We will not be configuring this for BESTM as we have already configured the value date in bank determination wherein we have maintained the 'Days to value date'.

The next step is to assign the payment method to bank transactions to use the value date rules that have been defined previously.

10.3.3.3.9   Assign Payment Method to Bank Transaction

Once you have defined the value date rules, you need to assign the payment method to each house-bank related transaction using the menu path: SAP Customizing Implementation Guide > Financial Accounting > Accounts Receivable and Accounts Payable > Business Transactions > Outgoing Payments > Automatic Outgoing Payments > Payment Method/Bank Selection for Payment Program > Assign Payment Method to Bank Transaction. You may also use Transaction OBBB.

With this, we are ready to discuss payment groupings.

10.3.3.3.10   Define Payment Groupings

Using this activity, you can define the grouping keys which you can use to settle a customer or vendor's open items together. Per grouping key, you may specify up to three fields (like, ZUONR – Assignment Number) from the database tables BSIK (vendors) or BSID (customers). The system, then, settles the items containing the same entries in these specified fields. You can, then, enter the appropriate grouping key in the customer/vendor master record.

You will use grouping key if you do not want all the open items of a customer / vendor to be paid together; instead, you want only those items which belong together, as defined in the grouping key, to be grouped into a single payment. For example, if you use SAP Loan Management, you may define a payment grouping so that the system uses that key for grouping open items with the same loan number together.

Project Dolphin

BESTM has indicated that they do not want to use payment grouping; Instead, wanted to make use of the default grouping of open items of customers / vendors in the automatic payment program.

To define a payment grouping key, which you can enter later in the customer / vendor master, you may use the menu path: SAP Customizing Implementation Guide > Financial Accounting > Accounts Receivable and Accounts Payable > Business Transactions > Outgoing Payments > Automatic Outgoing Payments > Payment Method/Bank Selection for Payment Program > Define Payment Groupings. You may also use Transaction OBAP.

The next activity is to prepare automatic posting for payment program.

10.3.3.3.11 Prepare Automatic Postings for Payment Program

Define the posting keys and special G/L indicators for postings that are required for the automatic payment program. You can just go ahead with the default settings. However, you may use this configuration step to check if the settings are correct.

Use the menu path: SAP Customizing Implementation Guide > Financial Accounting > Accounts Receivable and Accounts Payable > Business Transactions > Outgoing Payments > Automatic Outgoing Payments > Automatic Posting > Prepare Automatic Postings for Payment Program. You may also use Transaction OBXC.

On the resulting screen, you will see three procedures namely, ZBA (Payment program: bank posting), ZWE (Payt program: bill exch/bill payt reqst) and ZWO (Payt program: bank bill liability) under the payment program group ZAH. You may double-click on any of the procedures to check the associated settings (Figure 10.89).

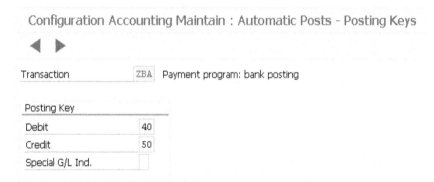

Figure 10.89 Automatic Posting Settings for Payment Program

In the next step, let us define the posting keys and special G/L indicator for automatic posting of payment requests.

10.3.3.3.12   Prepare Automatic Posting for Payment Requests

This is similar to the previous step except that you will be defining the posting keys and special G/L indicator for automatic posting of payment requests through the automatic payment program. Here, also you can just go along with the standard settings without changing anything.

> ℹ️ A request for payment ('payment request') activates a payment by the payment program, and the system pays the same when it is due.

Use the menu path: SAP Customizing Implementation Guide > Financial Accounting > Accounts Receivable and Accounts Payable > Business Transactions > Outgoing Payments > Automatic Outgoing Payments > Automatic Posting > Prepare Automatic Posting for Payment Requests. You may also use Transaction OBXP (Figure 10.90).

Configuration Accounting Maintain : Automatic Posts - Posting Keys

Transaction   ZAF   Payment requests

Posting Key
Debit   29
Credit   39
Special G/L Ind.   P

Figure 10.90 Automatic Posting Settings for Payment Requests

The next task is to include additional search fields for payments.

10.3.3.3.13   Select Search Fields for Payments

Here, you can define the search fields which will be used by the system to search and find individual payments or line items that are paid. You can use these search fields as the filter criteria for maintaining the payment proposal run and also for the display of the proposal run / payment run. The standard SAP system comes delivered with several search fields which will meet most of the normal business requirements.

Project Dolphin

The project team has suggested to the BESTM management not to go in for any additional search fields for payments (and line item display) as the standard fields are more than sufficient to be used as the criteria for maintaining proposal run besides displaying the payment proposal / payment run.

You may use the menu path: SAP Customizing Implementation Guide > Financial Accounting > Accounts Receivable and Accounts Payable > Business Transactions > Outgoing Payments > Automatic Outgoing Payments > Payment Run Display > Select Search Fields for Payments. You may also use Transaction O7FC. On the resulting screen, you may retain all or delete some or rearrange the order of appearance (Figure 10.91). If you want to add a new field, use the 'Insert after' button after positioning the cursor suitably, and select the fields by clicking on, for example, 'Standard Fields' on the resulting pop-up screen.

Maintain Field Selection Configuration: Detail Screen

🗑   Insert after...   Select

Payment proposal Payment Find

Fields

Field name	Description
HBKID	House bank
HKTID	Account ID
RWBTR	Amount Paid
RBETR	Amount Paid in Local Currency
LIFNR	Vendor
KUNNR	Customer
RZAWE	Payment Method
WAERS	Currency
PAYGR	Grouping

Figure 10.91 Standard Search Fields for Payments in Payment Run

The next step is to look at the standard settings of search fields for line item display in automatic payment program execution.

10.3.3.3.14   Select Search Fields for Line Item Display

This is similar to the previous activity except that the system uses the search fields for displaying the line items paid. As in the case of search fields for payments, you can use these search fields, as the filtering criteria, for maintaining the proposal run besides using them for the display of proposal run or payment run.

You may use the menu path: SAP Customizing Implementation Guide > Financial Accounting > Accounts Receivable and Accounts Payable > Business Transactions > Outgoing Payments > Automatic Outgoing Payments > Payment Run Display > Select Search Fields for Line Item Display. You may also use Transaction O7FE. On the resulting screen, you may retain all or delete some or rearrange the order of appearance (Figure 10.92). If you want to add a new field, use the 'Insert after' button after positioning the cursor suitably, and select the fields by clicking on, for example, 'Standard Fields' on the resulting pop-up screen.

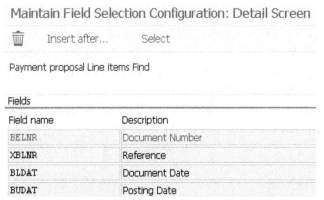

Figure 10.92 Standard Search Fields for Line Item Display in Payment Run

This completes our discussion on automatic outgoing payments. In the next section, let us discuss about the configuration settings for outgoing invoices / credit memos.

10.3.4 Outgoing Invoices/Credit Memos

Most of the settings here are similar to the ones that we discussed in Section 10.3.1 (incoming invoices / credit memos). The unique steps for outgoing invoices / credit memos are:

- Define Cash Discount Base for Outgoing Invoices
- Define Tax Accounts for Outgoing Invoices
- Define Posting Key for Outgoing Invoices/Credit Memos

Let us start with the definition of cash discount base for outgoing invoices.

10.3.4.1   Define Cash Discount Base for Outgoing Invoices

Here, you will be determining, per company code, if the tax amount is to be taken into account in arriving at the base amount for calculating the cash discount amount. We have already configured this for BESTM 's company codes while discussing the company code global parameters in Section 6.8.1 of Chapter 6 of Vol. I. However, you may use the menu path SAP Customizing Implementation Guide > Financial Accounting > Accounts Receivable and Accounts Payable > Business Transactions > Outgoing Invoices/Credit Memos > Define Cash Discount Base for Outgoing Invoices, or Transaction OB70 to check and confirm (Figure 10.93).

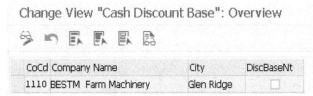

Figure 10.93 Cash Discount Base for Outgoing Invoices

Next, let us define the tax accounts for outgoing invoices.

10.3.4.2   Define Tax Accounts for Outgoing Invoices

Using this configuration step, you can define to which G/L accounts the system should post the different tax types to, in automatic postings.

Use the menu path SAP Customizing Implementation Guide > Financial Accounting > Accounts Receivable and Accounts Payable > Business Transactions > Outgoing Invoices/Credit Memos > Define Tax Accounts for Outgoing Invoices, or Transaction OB40:

i.   On the resulting screen, you will see the list of procedures like input tax (109), output tax (190) etc., which have already been configured for the automatic posting. You just need to maintain the G/L accounts for the required transactions like 109, 190 etc.

ii.   Select a transaction / procedure, and double-click on the same to reach the posting rules screen. Click on 'Posting Key' and define the keys (debit 40, credit 50) if that has not been defined earlier. 'Save' and click on 'Accounts' and enter the G/L account in 'Account Assignment' (Figure 10.94).

iii.   Repeat maintaining the posting key settings and G/L account entry for the other procedures as well.

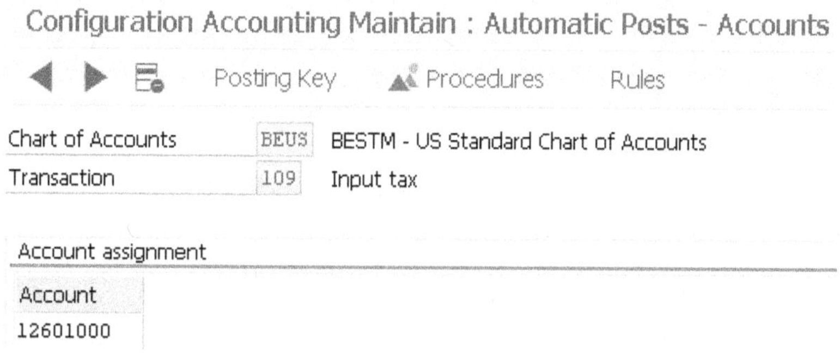

Configuration Accounting Maintain : Automatic Posts - Accounts

◀ ▶ 🗒   Posting Key   🏔 Procedures   Rules

| Chart of Accounts | BEUS | BESTM - US Standard Chart of Accounts |
| Transaction | 109 | Input tax |

Account assignment

| Account |
| 12601000 |

Figure 10.94 Tax Accounts for Outgoing Payments

With this, let us understand the final configuration for outgoing invoices/credit memos, next.

10.3.4.3   Define Posting Key for Outgoing Invoices/Credit Memos

You define the posting keys, here, for customer / vendor and G/L account items which you can use to enter for outgoing invoices and credit memos.

To configure, use the menu path: SAP Customizing Implementation Guide > Financial Accounting > Accounts Receivable and Accounts Payable > Business Transactions > Outgoing Invoices/Credit Memos > Outgoing Invoices/Credit Memos – Enjoy > Define Posting Key for Outgoing Invoices/Credit Memos, or Transaction OBXW. On the resulting screen (Figure 10.95), double-click on the appropriate 'Procedure' (say, 'Customer Item on Outgoing Invoice' – Transaction AGD) and confirm that you can use default posting keys as set by SAP (01 for debit, 11 for credit). Come back to the previous screen, and double-click on other 'Procedures' to check the posting keys for transactions AGS and AGX.

Configuration Accounting Maintain : Automatic Posts - Procedures

Group   **AGR**   Outgoing invoices

Procedures

Description	Transaction	Account Determ.
Customer Item on Outgoing Invoice	AGD	☐
G/L Account Item on Outgoing Invoice	AGS	☐
Customer item with special G/L indicator	AGX	☐

Figure 10.95 Posting Key Definition for Outgoing Invoice/Credit Memo

This completes our discussion on the settings required for outgoing invoices/credit memos. Let us, now, move on to discuss the settings that are unique to incoming payments.

10.3.5 Incoming Payments

As in the case of outgoing payments that we discussed in Section 10.3.3, you can group the configuration settings for incoming payments into the following three categories:

1. Incoming Payment Global Settings
2. Manual Incoming Payments
3. Automatic Incoming Payments

Let us start with the global settings for incoming payments.

10.3.5.1   Incoming Payment Global Settings

We have already discussed most of the settings like defining (a) accounts for overpayments/underpayments, (b) accounts for exchange rate differences, (c) accounts for rounding differences and (d) accounts for bank charges, (e) posting keys for clearing transactions, (f) the settings for enabling translation, (g) payment block reasons and (h) the default values for payment while discussing the global settings for outgoing payments in Section 10.3.3.1. Hence, we are not repeating them here again. However, we shall define the accounts that are required for posting the cash discount granted.

10.3.5.1.1   Define Accounts for Cash Discount Granted

Define the G/L account number(s) for posting the cash discount amount granted when clearing open items. If necessary, as in the case of cash discount taken (in incoming payments) you may differentiate the G/L accounts by tax codes.

To configure, use the menu path: SAP Customizing Implementation Guide > Financial Accounting > Accounts Receivable and Accounts Payable > Business Transactions > Incoming Payments > Incoming Payments Global Settings > Define Accounts for Cash Discount Granted, or Transaction OBX1. On the resulting pop-up, enter the chart of accounts (BEUS, for BESTM) and on the next screen enter the G/L account for the system to post the cash discount expenses (Figure 10.96).

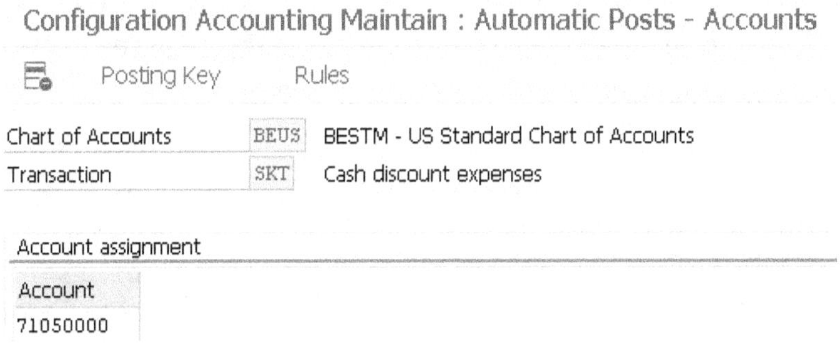

Configuration Accounting Maintain : Automatic Posts - Accounts

Posting Key   Rules

| Chart of Accounts | BEUS | BESTM - US Standard Chart of Accounts |
| Transaction | SKT | Cash discount expenses |

Account assignment

| Account |
| 71050000 |

Figure 10.96 G/L Account for Posting Cash Discount Taken

With this, let us move on to understand the configuration requirements for manual incoming payments.

10.3.5.2   Manual Incoming Payments

Here also, the configuration settings are similar to the ones that we have already discussed in Section 10.3.3.2, for manual outgoing payments. The settings include defining & assigning tolerance groups, settings to take care of clearing differences and preparing for cross-company code transactions. As regards 'Defining Tolerance Groups for Employees), we have already completed this in Section 7.1.10.1 of Chapter 7 of Vol. I.

Let us move on to discuss the automatic incoming payments, next.

10.3.5.3   Automatic Incoming Payments

We have already covered automatic incoming payments while we configured the automatic outgoing payments in Section 10.3.3.3.

With this, let us move on to discuss how to manage SEPA mandates in the system.

10.3.5.4   Management of SEPA Mandates

SEPA (Single Euro Payments Area) is an initiative by the EU (European Union). It is to make the cross-border electronic payments as inexpensive and easy like a local payment within a country. All the customers, businesses, and the government in the EU can undertake SEPA payments in the form of instant debit / credit by leveraging the SEPA architecture. The SEPA payments are free and is expected help international business in the EU. There are about 40 member countries including the 28 EU member states and others like Liechtenstein, Iceland, Norway, Switzerland, Vatican City, Monaco, San Marino and Andorra.

> **i** Since we are discussing FI configuration from the point of US and India, in this book, we will not be discussing this in detail here. However, we shall give you a brief idea as how to configure the SEPA mandates should you work with an EU member state.

In SAP, you can enter a SEPA mandate for each of your bank accounts. The SEPA mandate is an authorization issued by your business partner (as debtor) for payment to be collected by you (as creditor). It will be in the form of a direct debit.

Towards configuring the SEPA mandates, the first step is to make the general settings.

10.3.5.4.1   General Settings

Here, you will activate SEPA mandate management in the system. In the process, you can specify a subscreen for displaying additional data, register your own function modules that make data supplements and further checks, and finally define a form name for printing SEPA mandates.

Change View "SEPA Mandate Management: General Settings": Details

New Entries

Applic.   Financial Accounting

SEPA Mandate Management: General Settings

☑ Active

Function Modules for Data Enhancement and Checks

Address Data	_
Creditor ID	_
Mandate Ref.	FI_APAR_MANDATE_PREFIX_MNDID
Enrichment	_
Check	_
Follow-up	_
Authorization	_
Parameters	_

Subscreen for Additional Data in the Detail Display

Program Name
Screen number

SEPA Form for Printing

Form Type	Smart Forms
Form Name	SEPA_AR

Other Parameters

Parameter	Val.
External Assignment of the Mandate Reference	ENABLED
Internal Assignment of the Mandate Reference	ENABLED
External Assignment of Creditor ID	ENABLED
Internal Assignment of Creditor ID	ENABLED
Function Module for Controlling the Assignment	
Maximum Number of Logged Usages	
Minimum Number of Logged Usages	
Function Module for Settable Button 1	FFO_SEPA_MANDATE_BUTTON_PARA
Function Module for Settable Button 2	
Function Module for 'Print Mandate' Button	FFO_SEPA_MANDATE_BUTTON_PARA
Show 'Create Attachment' Button	ENABLED
Show 'Save and Print' Button	ENABLED

Figure 10.97 Activating SEPA Mandate Management

To configure, use the menu path: SAP Customizing Implementation Guide > Financial Accounting > Accounts Receivable and Accounts Payable > Business Transactions > Incoming Payments > Management of SEPA Mandates > General Settings, or Transaction FI_APAR_SEPA_CUST. On the resulting screen, click on 'New Entries' and:

- Select the appropriate application ('Applic.').
- Activate SEPA Mandate Management.
- Add, your own program/screen details for displaying additional data, if any.
- Select the 'Form Type' and enter the 'Form Name' for printing SEPA form.

When 'Saved', the system brings up the appropriate functional modules for data enhancement and checks besides filling in the 'Other Parameters' (Figure 10.97).

The next task is to define the available function modules for generating SEPA mandate IDs.

10.3.5.4.2   Define Available Function Modules for Generating Mandate IDs

Use the menu path: SAP Customizing Implementation Guide > Financial Accounting > Accounts Receivable and Accounts Payable > Business Transactions > Incoming Payments > Management of SEPA Mandates > Number Ranges for Mandates > Define Available Function Modules for Generating Mandate IDs, or Transaction SEPA_MND_FM_MT. You can use the standard settings, or you may enter your own function modules, if necessary, on the next screen (Figure 10.98).

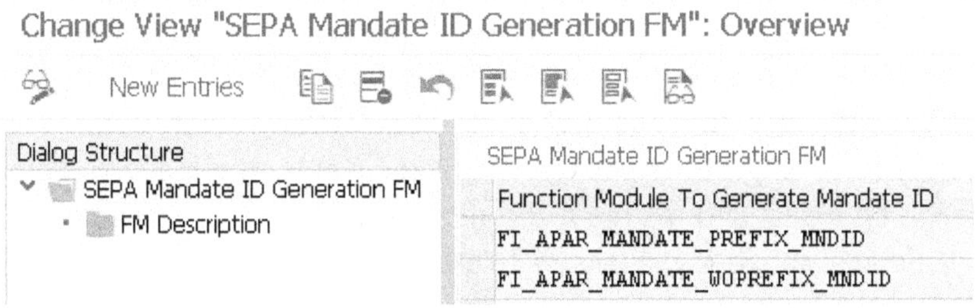

Change View "SEPA Mandate ID Generation FM": Overview

New Entries

Dialog Structure

SEPA Mandate ID Generation FM

SEPA Mandate ID Generation FM
- FM Description

Function Module To Generate Mandate ID

FI_APAR_MANDATE_PREFIX_MNDID

FI_APAR_MANDATE_WOPREFIX_MNDID

Figure 10.98 Function Module Configuration for Generating SEPA Mandate ID

The next step is to select the appropriate function module to generate the SEPA mandate ID.

10.3.5.4.3   Select Function Module for Generating Mandate IDs

You can select the appropriate function module to generate the SEPA mandate IDs with or without the paying company code as the prefix. You can use either of the SAP-delivered standard function modules: FI_APAR_MANDATE_PREFIX_MNDID (to generate mandate IDs with the paying company code as the prefix) or FI_APAR_MANDATE_WOPREFIX_MNDID (to generate mandate IDs without a prefix).

From the function modules made available in the previous task, you can select the appropriate one in this step, by using the menu path: SAP Customizing Implementation Guide > Financial Accounting > Accounts Receivable and Accounts Payable > Business Transactions > Incoming Payments > Management of SEPA Mandates > Number Ranges for Mandates > Select Function Module for Generating Mandate IDs, or Transaction SEPA_MND_FM_CUST. On the resulting screen, click on 'New Entries' and select the appropriate function module on the next screen, and 'Save' the details (Figure 10.99).

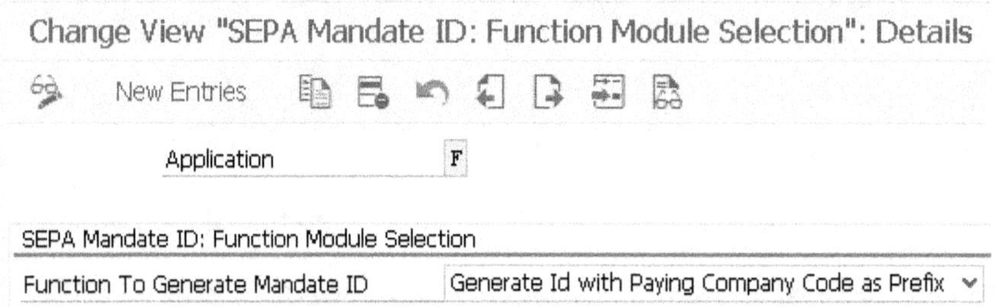

Change View "SEPA Mandate ID: Function Module Selection": Details

New Entries

| Application | F |

SEPA Mandate ID: Function Module Selection

| Function To Generate Mandate ID | Generate Id with Paying Company Code as Prefix ∨ |

Figure 10.99 Selecting the Function for Generating SEPA Mandate ID

The next step is to define the number ranges for SEPA mandates.

10.3.5.4.4   Define Number Range Intervals

As in any other case of defining a number range for a company code, define the required number range intervals for SEPA mandates for all the paying company codes.

Use the menu path SAP Customizing Implementation Guide > Financial Accounting > Accounts Receivable and Accounts Payable > Business Transactions > Incoming Payments > Management of SEPA Mandates > Number Ranges for Mandates > Define Number Range Intervals, or Transaction SEPA_NR_MT. On the resulting screen, enter the (paying) 'Company Code', click on 'Change Intervals' and maintain the required number range(s) on the next screen under suitable number range key(s) (Figure 10.100).

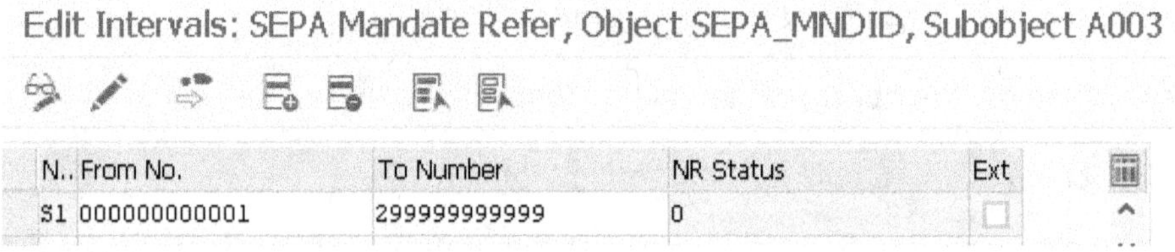

Edit Intervals: SEPA Mandate Refer, Object SEPA_MNDID, Subobject A003

N..	From No.	To Number	NR Status	Ext	
$1	000000000001	299999999999	0	☐	^

Figure 10.100 Number Ranges for SEPA Mandate

Let us, now, assign the number range that we have defined in the previous Section to SEPA mandates.

10.3.5.4.5   Assign Number Range Intervals

Here, you need to assign the number range interval for each combination of ('Account Group - 'B2B' Boolean-Payment Type'). The B2B Boolean decides if the mandate is for business to business or otherwise. The 'Payment Type' will identify if it is for a single usage or recurring usage. When you create the mandate in this way, the system checks the 'Account Group', the 'B2B' Boolean, the 'Payment Type' of the mandate and assigns the next available number in the number interval as the mandate ID, when it finds a match.

To configure the settings, use the menu path: SAP Customizing Implementation Guide > Financial Accounting > Accounts Receivable and Accounts Payable > Business Transactions > Incoming Payments > Management of SEPA Mandates > Number Ranges for Mandates > Assign Number Range Intervals, or Transaction SEPA_NR_CUST. On the resulting screen, select the 'Account Group', 'B2B' and the 'Payment Type'. Then, for each combination of these three variables, enter the number range interval key in 'Number Range Interval'. 'Save' and repeat the settings for all the required account groups (Figure 10.101).

Change View "SEPA Mandate ID: Number Range Customizing": Overview

New Entries

SEPA Mandate ID: Number Range Customizing

Account Group	B2B	Payment Type	Number Range Interval
0001	Yes	One-Time Mandate	S1
0001	Yes	Recurring Use Man…	S1

Figure 10.101 Number Ranges Assignment for SEPA Mandate

You may also need to configure 'Status Management' (defining non-permitted status changes and reason codes for status change) and 'Returns from the Bank' (configuring how to process the returned debit memos in electronic account statement processing and which changes are to be made in the mandate when debit memos are returned by the bank).

This completes our discussion on managing SEPA mandates in the system. Let us move on to discuss the payments with payment cards.

10.3.6 Payments with Payment Cards

You can use 'Payment Cards' - credit card, debit card, charge card, deferred charge card etc - as a form of payment that offers your vendors with an almost-risk-free payment guarantee, as the payment includes an authorization from the card issuing bank (or financial organization) during payment transaction processing

SAP offers you with a wide range of functions both in SD and FI modules, for payment with payment cards. It provides you with all the basic tools that you may need to handle payment cards in different of business processes.

On the SD side, you configure the payment card types, payment card categories, payment card plan types, authorization & settlement of payment cards, account determination for payments through payment cards and so on. You can configure all these and much more following the menu path: SAP Customizing Implementation Guide > Sales and Distribution > Billing > Payment Cards.

On the FI side, you will need to configure only two settings:

1. Make Central Settings for Payment Cards
2. Assign G/L Account to Cash Clearing Account

Let us look at these two settings, here, in this Section, and let us start with the central settings for payment cards.

10.3.6.1   Make Central Settings for Payment Cards

Here, in this configuration step, you can decide whether to retain the customer line items in the accounting document when transferring data from SD component to FI. The advantage of going in for this is that you can re-create the receivables against a customer automatically (that is, the cleared items are reset) without the need for creating them again by a new posting. You can, then, process these customer items in the dunning / payment program. You can also specify the type of settlement document (that clears the G/L open items and creates line items in a cash clearing account) when the settlement is made by the payment card company. Additionally, you can specify the document type for resetting cleared items when the card company cannot make a settlement.

Project Dolphin

BESTM wants to configure the system to take care of payment through payment cards as well. In the process, it has been outlined, that the system needs to be configured in such way to retain the customer line items in FI department during transfer of payment card data from SD department. This decision has been taken, consciously, after several deliberations knowing fully well that this will call for more database space; BESTM is ok with this, as the configuration will provide (a) the advantage of displaying the receivables on the debit side and (b) the ability to the department personnel to deal with any settlement problems of the payment cards.

You configure the settings by following the menu path: SAP Customizing Implementation Guide > Financial Accounting > Accounts Receivable and Accounts Payable > Business Transactions > Payments with Payment Cards > Make Central Settings for Payment Cards. You may also use Transaction OBZH.

On the resulting screen (Figure 10.102):

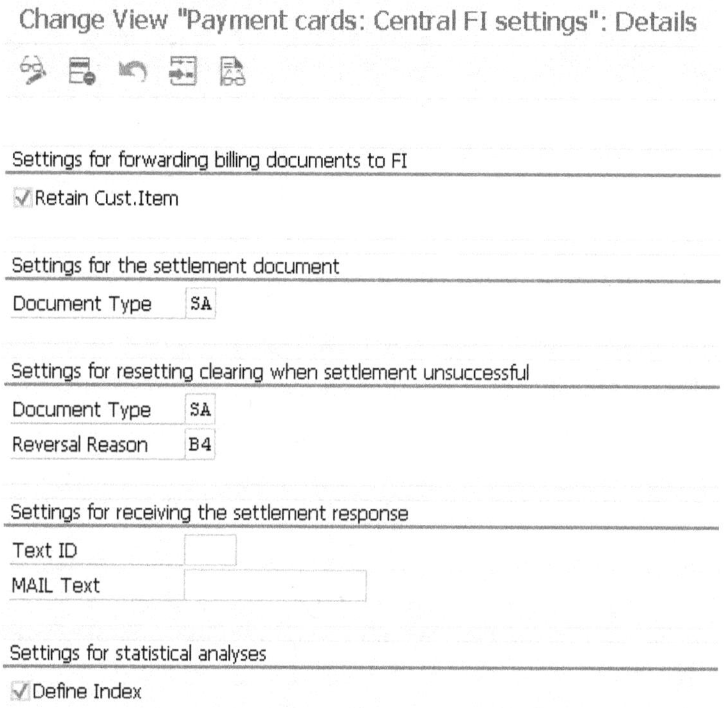

Change View "Payment cards: Central FI settings": Details

⚙ 🗐 ↺ 📲 📑

Settings for forwarding billing documents to FI
☑ Retain Cust.Item

Settings for the settlement document
Document Type   SA

Settings for resetting clearing when settlement unsuccessful
Document Type   SA
Reversal Reason B4

Settings for receiving the settlement response
Text ID
MAIL Text

Settings for statistical analyses
☑ Define Index

Figure 10.102 Central FI Settings for Payment Cards

i.   Select the 'Retain Cut. Item' check-box under 'Settings for forwarding documents to FI' to retain the customer line item details on FI side while transferring the data from SD. The system, then, clears the customer item as soon as the document is posted, creates a corresponding identical cleared payment item, and also creates an open 'account receivables from payment card transactions' item. Because of this, a simple document with two line items (customer/revenue) now becomes four line items (customer/customer/payment card receivable/revenue). If you do not select the check-box, then, the system replaces the customer line item with a receivable from payment card transactions in the corresponding SAP G/L account.

> **i** Even though you would require more database space when you set the 'Retain Cut. Item' indicator, as the system creates additional line items, the advantage is that you will be able to display receivables on the debit side, besides the ability to deal with any settlement problems easily.

ii.   Enter an appropriate 'Document Type' for the settlement document and also for handling resetting clearing when the settlement is unsuccessful. Also, enter an appropriate 'Reversal Reason' (for example, B4-payment card settlement failed) under 'Settings for resetting clearing when settlement unsuccessful'. The system defaults to this 'Document Type' (entered her in 'Settings for the settlement document') on the initial screen of the settlement program RFCCSSTT in the 'Journal Entry Type' field under 'Data for Clearing Entry' block (Transaction FCC1); you can, of course, over-write the same.

iii.   You may enter a 'Text ID and 'MAIL Text' for using the standard texts as settlement responses. If you do no enter a text module here, in the 'MAIL Text' field, then, this message is only for statistical purposes.

iv.   Set the 'Define Index' indicator to enable the system to enter the number of the settlement run in the (already cleared) customer line item. Then, it becomes possible for you to display all customer line items of a specific settlement run, for more than one account, when carrying out the evaluations.

The next step is to assign a G/L account to cash clearing account.

10.3.6.2   Assign G/L Account to Cash Clearing Account

Assign the G/L account that the system will use to record the open items, per card type, to a cash clearing account. That is, you will use this G/L account to record all the receivables that you report to the credit card company using a settlement program; the settlement program, then, posts these reported open items against the cash clearing account and clears them.

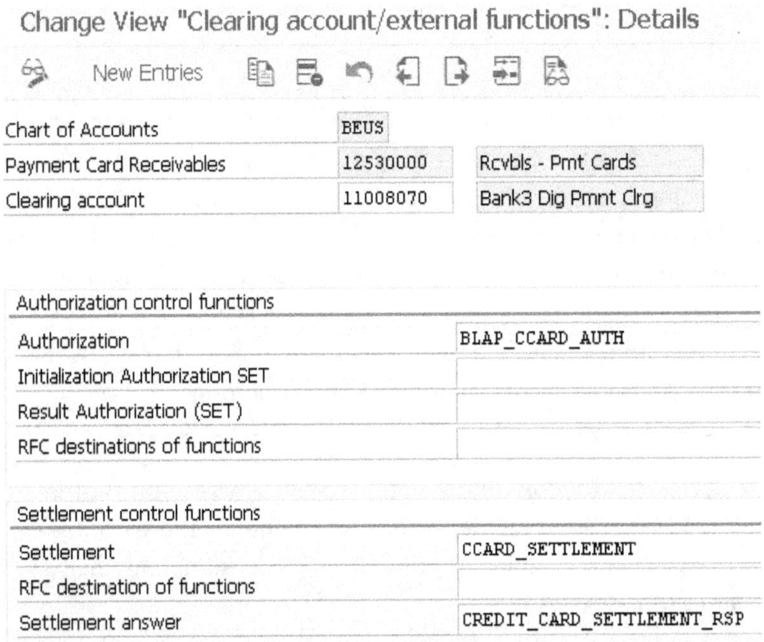

Figure 10.103 G/L Account Assignment to Clearing Account (Payment Cards)

Follow the menu path: SAP Customizing Implementation Guide > Financial Accounting > Accounts Receivable and Accounts Payable > Business Transactions > Payments with Payment Cards > Assign G/L Account to Cash Clearing Account or use Transaction OBZI to maintain the required G/L account(s).

On the resulting screen, click on 'New Entries' and maintain the chart of accounts, G/L account for 'Receivable' and 'Clearing'. You may also maintain the necessary settings for 'Authorization control functions' and 'Settlement control functions'. 'Save' the details (Figure 10.103).

This completes our discussion on the settings required on the FI side for payment with payment cards. Let us move on to discuss dunning, in the next Section.

10.3.7 Dunning

'Dun' is to make a (persistent) demand for a payment of an outstanding debt. 'Dunning', in SAP, is the process of reminding your business partners (who are falling behind the payments) to pay the outstanding payment. It is, essentially, sending a notice of reminder ('dunning notice'). Using the dunning program, you can automatically dun your business partners. The program selects the overdue open items of an account, ascertains the 'dunning level' of the account and creates a dunning notice using the pre-defined dunning notice format and text, and finally saves the dunning data so determined for the line items / account which will be looked upon during the next dunning.

Normally, you use the program to dun your customers; but, you can also dun your vendors, if the vendor has a debit balance (arising from a credit memo). You can enable the program to offset between credit and debit balances and raise the dunning notice for the balance, when your customer is also a vendor. You can use the program do dun all the customers / vendors or only a select few. Again, you can dun the customers across several company codes ('cross-company code dunning'), in a single dunning run. If you have your business partners with head office / branch organization structure, you can configure the dunning program to dun, for example, the head office but send dunning notice to the branch office(s). The dunning program uses the currency (local or foreign) in which you have posted all the open items in an account. If the open items of an account are not posted in the same currency, then, the dunning program uses the local currency of the company code; it displays the items in document currency in the dunning notice, but shows the totals in local and foreign currency.

It is possible that you can dun a 'one-time' account as well, like any other account. While dunning the one-time accounts, the system groups all the items of a one-time account having the same address into a single dunning notice. Even though the program enters the dunning date and dunning level in both the account master record and in the line item of the one-time account, the system determines the dunning interval solely by what is entered in the line item notwithstanding the entry in the master record.

You can use the dunning history to understand all of the dunning runs that you have executed and the dunning notices that you have sent. You can view the details by account type, company code, and/or customer or vendor.

You can use the following attributes to control the dunning process in the system:

- *Dunning Procedure*: You use the dunning procedure to control how the system carries out dunning. You can define more than one dunning procedure. You may connect the dunning procedure to a customer / vendor master or to a dunning area. The control parameters of a dunning program include dunning frequency, dunning levels, minimum dunning amounts (overdue threshold), dunning charges, dunning text etc.
- *Dunning Level*: The system calculates the dunning level based on the number of days an open item is in arrears. Alternatively, you can have the system to calculate the dunning levels based on the dunning amount or percentage paid. It is possible that you can determine more than one dunning level per dunning procedure.
- *Dunning Area*: A 'dunning area' is an organizational unit (for example, a division or sales organization etc) within a company code that you can use, as the responsibility area, for dunning. Once defined, you may assign a dunning area to an open item. With dunning areas defined, you can dun open items separately per dunning area. However, it is optional to define a dunning area.

The dunning process is made up of several sub-processes like (1) creating the dunning proposal, (2) editing the dunning proposal and (3) printing the dunning notices, which you need to need to carry out the in the proper order:

1) *Creating Dunning Proposal*: When you start the dunning program, you will enter the parameters for the dunning run: the dunning date, the date up to which the program should select the posted documents, the company code(s) and also the optional account restrictions to select the required account(s). Now, during the dunning run, the dunning program determines the (a) accounts and items that must be dunned, (b) dunning level, and (c) other details required for dunning. With these details, the dunning program creates a dunning proposal (list).

> **i** You can create the dunning proposal list as often as you require. The system does not update the dunning data for the item / account until the dunning notices are actually printed.

2) *Editing Dunning Proposal*: While editing a dunning proposal, you essentially carry out activities like setting / resetting the dunning blocks, and changing the dunning levels. You can manually increase or decrease the dunning level of an item or account in the proposal. You can block an item / account from dunning. Similarly, you can unblock an item / account so that it will be included in the dunning proposal. As all the changes are logged, you can look at the log and confirm that the changes are taken into account before accepting the proposal. If not, you can go ahead and still edit. It is also possible that you can view the sample print out of the dunning notices, on the screen, to see and understand how the notices will look like when actually printed.

---

i While editing a dunning proposal, though you can lower the dunning level by any number of levels (for example, from level 4 to 2 or 1), you can only raise by one level, at a time, to its next higher level (for example, you can raise the level from 2 to 3 but not from 2 to 4). You will, normally, undertake lowering / raising the dunning level only when you unblock an item / account in the dunning proposal.

---

3) *Printing Dunning Notices*: Once you complete the editing of dunning proposal, and execute the program, (a) the print program prints the dunning notices and (b) the dunning program stores the relevant dunning data (like dunning level, dunning date etc) in the line items and in the master record of the customer / vendor. While printing the dunning notices, the system uses the pre-defined dunning formats together with the appropriate dunning texts, for that dunning level of that dunning procedure. You will be able to restart printing, if there is an interruption.

With this understanding of dunning in SAP, let us move on to configure the required settings of BESTM. SAP has grouped these settings into three categories:

1. Basic Settings for Dunning
2. Dunning Procedure
3. Printout

Let us start with the basic settings for dunning.

10.3.7.1   Basic Settings for Dunning

The basic settings are the global settings for dunning in the system. They include:

- Define Dunning Areas
- Define Dunning Keys
- Define Dunning Block Reasons
- Define Dunning Forms

Let us discuss the dunning areas, first.

10.3.7.1.1 Define Dunning Areas

As already pointed out, defining a 'dunning area' is optional. You will use dunning areas if there are different organizational units (distribution channel or business area or sales organization, for example) that are responsible for carrying out dunning within the company code. If you want to use dunning area, then, you can use the same or different dunning procedures for these areas.

> **ℹ** When you want the system to make use of dunning areas for handling dunning, then, you need to maintain the dunning area ('Area') with the dunning procedure ('Procedure') in the master record of the business partner by clicking on 'Dunning Areas' button (Figure 10.104). Else, the system will use the standard dunning procedure ('Dunning Procedure') but, you can enter the dunning area in the line item; the system will update the dunning area automatically into the master record.
>
> Note that the 'Dunning Areas' button will be visible only when you have defined one or more dunning area; this enables you to enter the dunning area-specific dunning procedure.

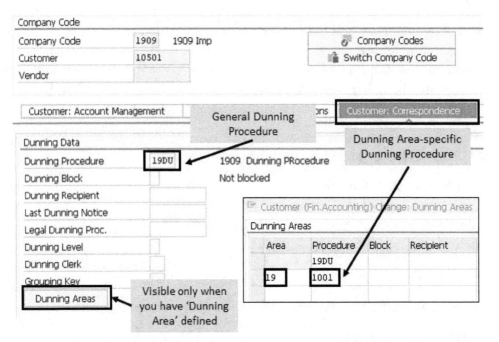

Figure 10.104 Mantaining Dunning Area in a Customer Master Record

Project Dolphin

BESTM does not want to dun its business partners through dunning areas. Instead, all the dunning will be carried out at the company code level for all the customers / vendors.

Though we will not be defining dunning areas for BESTM, you may still want to know how to define them. To define a dunning area, use the menu path: SAP Customizing Implementation Guide > Financial Accounting > Accounts Receivable and Accounts Payable > Business Transactions > Dunning > Basic Settings for Dunning > Define Dunning Areas. You may also use Transaction OB61. On the resulting screen, click on 'New Entries' and define the required dunning areas per company code on the next screen.

Let us move on to define the dunning keys

10.3.7.1.2   Define Dunning Keys

The 'dunning keys', which are company code independent, enable you to limit the dunning level for an item. While configuring a dunning key, you can, also, decide if some of the items with a specific dunning key are to be displayed separately in the dunning notice.

> **i** Consider an example that you have an incoming payment and when posting you made a residual item to carryforward, as the payment resulted in a payment difference. Now, as you want to display this residual item in a separate section in the dunning notice, you can accomplish this by defining a separate dunning key. You can also print the text for the dunning key in the dunning notice.

Project Dolphin

The management of BESTM wants to have five dunning keys defined. The first three keys should be used to initiate the respective dunning levels, 1, 2 and 3. The 4th dunning key will be for denoting the payments made with a separate line item display. The 5th key will be used for denoting residual items arising out of payment differences and will also be displayed separately.

To configure the dunning keys:

i.   Use the menu path: SAP Customizing Implementation Guide > Financial Accounting > Accounts Receivable and Accounts Payable > Business Transactions > Dunning > Basic Settings for Dunning > Define Dunning Keys, or Transaction OB17.

ii.   On the resulting screen (Figure 10.105), click on 'New Entries' and define the required dunning keys ('Dunn.Key') and provide a description in 'Text' field.

iii.   Select 'Print sep' check-box to display the items separately on the dunning notice.

iv.   Per dunning key, you also need to enter the maximum dunning level ('Max. Level') that will be triggered for that key.

Change View "Dunning Keys": Overview

New Entries

Dunn.Key	Max. Leve	Print sep	Text
1	1	☐	Triggers maximum dunning level 1
2	2	☐	Triggers maximum dunning level 2
3	3	☐	Triggers maximum dunning level 3
4		☑	Payment has been made, separate line item
5		☑	Residual item from payment differences

Figure 10.105 Defining Dunning Key

With this, we can now move on to discuss the last step in dunning basic settings: defining the dunning block reasons.

10.3.7.1.3   Define Dunning Block Reasons

The 'dunning blocks' or 'dunning block reasons' help you to prevent an account or an item from being dunned. You will define a dunning block reason using a blocking key and will enter the same in the 'Dunning block' field of customer / vendor master record (Figure 10.106) or in the line item. During a dunning run, the system checks for this dunning block key in the master record or line item, and excludes the blocked accounts and/or items in the dunning run proposal. You can see the details blocked accounts / items, printed in an exception list, with the reason for the block.

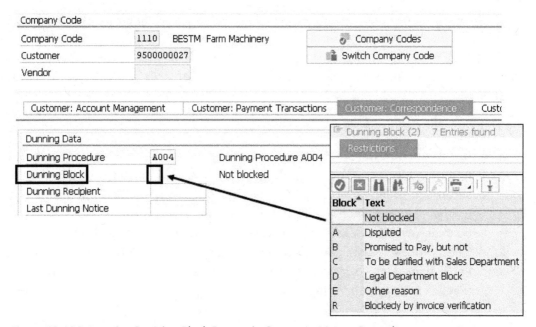

Figure 10.106 Entering Dunning Block Reason in Customer Master Record

Project Dolphin

The Dolphin project team has suggested to configure six dunning block reasons in the system: disputed (A), promised to pay (B), clarification required from SD side (C), blocked by legal department (D), other reasons (E) and blocked by invoice verification (R).

To configure the dunning block reasons:

i. Use the menu path: SAP Customizing Implementation Guide > Financial Accounting > Accounts Receivable and Accounts Payable > Business Transactions > Dunning > Basic Settings for Dunning > Define Block Reasons, or Transaction OB18.

ii. On the resulting screen, click on 'New Entries' and define the required 1-character block keys ('Block') and provide a description in 'Text' field (Figure 10.107). The blank in the 'Block' field will indicate that the item/account is not blocked and is free for dunning.

Change View "Dunning Block Reasons": Overview

New Entries

Block	Text
	Not blocked, free for dunning
A	Disputed
B	Promised to Pay
C	To be clarified with Sales Department
D	Legal Department Block
E	Other reason
R	Blockedy by invoice verification

Figure 10.107 Defining Dunning Block Reasons

With this, let us look at defining the dunning forms which you will be using to configure the dunning procedure.

10.3.7.1.4   Define Dunning Forms

SAP provides you with the option of using either 'SAP Smart Forms' or 'SAPScript' forms for use as the dunning forms. The standard dunning forms cater to different situations like forms that have the provision for including the dunning interest or plain forms which you will normally use for 1st level of dunning (or 'payment reminders'). Depending upon whether you want to have different layout or want to include interest etc., you will select the appropriate form for a given level of dunning. You may need more than one form, and it is recommended to copy the standard forms in SAP to create your own.

Project Dolphin

The project team has suggested to copy and adapt the SAPScript forms provided by SAP to meet the business needs of BESTM group of company codes. Accordingly, there will be five forms that will be created anew by copying the standard ones: the form F150_BE_DUNN_01 (without interest) will be copied as ZF150_BE_DUNN_01 and will be used both for the single-level dunning procedure and also for the first dunning level of the 5-level dunning procedure. The standard form F150_BE_DUNN_02 (with interest) will be copied to create the other four levels for the 5-level procedure. Also, separate spool lists will be created by copying the standard LIST1S spool list, and five new spool lists will be created prefixed with the company code name like 1110-1, 1110-2 etc.

To copy and create new dunning forms for BESTM:

i.   Use the menu path: SAP Customizing Implementation Guide > Financial Accounting > Accounts Receivable and Accounts Payable > Business Transactions > Dunning > Printout > Define Dunning Forms (with SAPScript), or Transaction SE71.

Figure 10.108 Defining a New Dunning Form (SAPScript) by Copying the Standard Form

ii.   On the resulting screen, enter the form that you want to copy (say, F150_BE_DUNN_01), and click on 'Change'.

iii. On the next screen (Figure 10.108), click on 'Form > Save As' and input the name of the new form (say, ZF150_BE_DUNN_01).

iv.   Click 'Activate'. You have now created the new form ZF150_BE_DUNN_01. This is the form for dunning notice without interest.

v.   You can, now, copy the other form F150_BE_DUNN_02 (with interest), to create the new forms ZF150_BE_DUNN_02, ZF150_BE_DUNN_03, ZF150_BE_DUNN_04 and ZF150_BE_DUNN_05.

This completes our discussion of configuring the basic settings required for dunning. We shall, now, move on to discuss the settings relating to dunning procedure.

10.3.7.2   Dunning Procedure

The 'dunning procedure' controls how the dunning program duns the business partners. It contains specifications like dunning frequency / dunning interval with which the program duns the open items, specifications relating to grace days and minimum number of days which will be required to determine the open items to be dunned, details of the number of dunning levels with the level determining the wording of the dunning notice and the specifications as to whether to dun standard and/or Special G/L transactions.

You need to complete the following settings to complete configuring the dunning procedures in the system:

- Define Dunning Procedures
- Define Dunning Groupings
- Define Interest Rates

Let us start with the definition of dunning procedures.

10.3.7.2.1   Define Dunning Procedures

As already outlined, you control the dunning program via the specifications maintained in the dunning procedure. It is possible that you may need more than one dunning procedure to take care of your dunning needs. For example, you may have business partners who need to be reminded only once and in such a situation you will need a dunning procedure with only one dunning level; on the other hand, you may have some customers who need to be followed up several times to get back your receivables, and in such a case you may need a multi-level dunning procedure with the wording in the dunning notice progressively changing to stricter and legal tone with every increase in the dunning level. The dunning procedures are company code independent.

Project Dolphin

The BESTM management has decided to have two dunning procedures in each of the countries where the company is operating. Accordingly, they have asked the project team to configure the following, both for India and USA:

1. A dunning procedure that will be used to remind the VIP business partners, which will be single level dunning procedure. This will just be a 'payment reminder' and there will not be any charges / interest associated with this dunning.

2. Another dunning procedure – multi-level dunning procedure – that will be used for all other business partners. This will have a maximum of five dunning levels, with a dunning interval of seven days. There needs to be a cushion of three days for dunning levels 2 and 3 and five days for levels 4 and 5. Also, there will be a grace period of five days at the account level. Further, if the due date falls on a holiday, the dunning program should take the next working day as the payment due date based on respective country's public calendar. The dunning charges, for the multi-level dunning procedure, will as set out in the Table 10.5.

Amount Range	Dunning Level 1 Dunning Charges	Dunning Level 2 Dunning Charges	Dunning Level 3 Dunning Charges (%)	Dunning Level 4 Dunning Charges (%)	Dunning Level 5 Dunning Charges (%)
Up to $5,000	0	$5	0.10	0.15	0.20
$5,001 – $10,000	0	$10	0.15	0.20	0.25
$10,001 - $25,000	0	$10	0.20	0.25	0.30
$25,001 - $50,000	0	$15	0.25	0.30	0.35
$50,001 - $100,000	0	$20	0.30	0.35	0.40
Above $100,000	0	$50	0.35	0.40	0.50

Table 10:5 Dunning Charges for Multi-level Dunning Procedure of BESTM

Besides the dunning charges, there will be an overdue interest charges, to be charged on the arrears, at the prevailing rates subject to a minimum of $50 for level 2, $100 for level 3, $250 for level 4 and $500 for level 5. Of course, there will be no interest on arrears for the level 1. The level 5 will be considered as legal dunning level and will use legal wording in the dunning notice; a separate legal dunning notice format will have to be used. BESTM wants the system to consider the interest indicator in the master record of a business partner and not through the dunning procedure.

When printing the dunning notice, the program should display the entire account balance and should include all the open items even if the dunning level is at the lowest. BESTM does not want to include any of the Special G/L items in the dunning list.

Each company code will dun their business partners separately. However, they can group the overdues of a customer across other company codes.

The charges and interest amount will be the same for India-based company codes as well, except that the amounts will be in INR.

To define the required dunning procedures for BESTM:

Use the menu path: SAP Customizing Implementation Guide > Financial Accounting > Accounts Receivable and Accounts Payable > Business Transactions > Dunning > Dunning Procedure > Define Dunning Procedures, or Transaction FBMP. On the resulting screen, click on 'New Procedure' and, on the next screen (Figure 10.109):

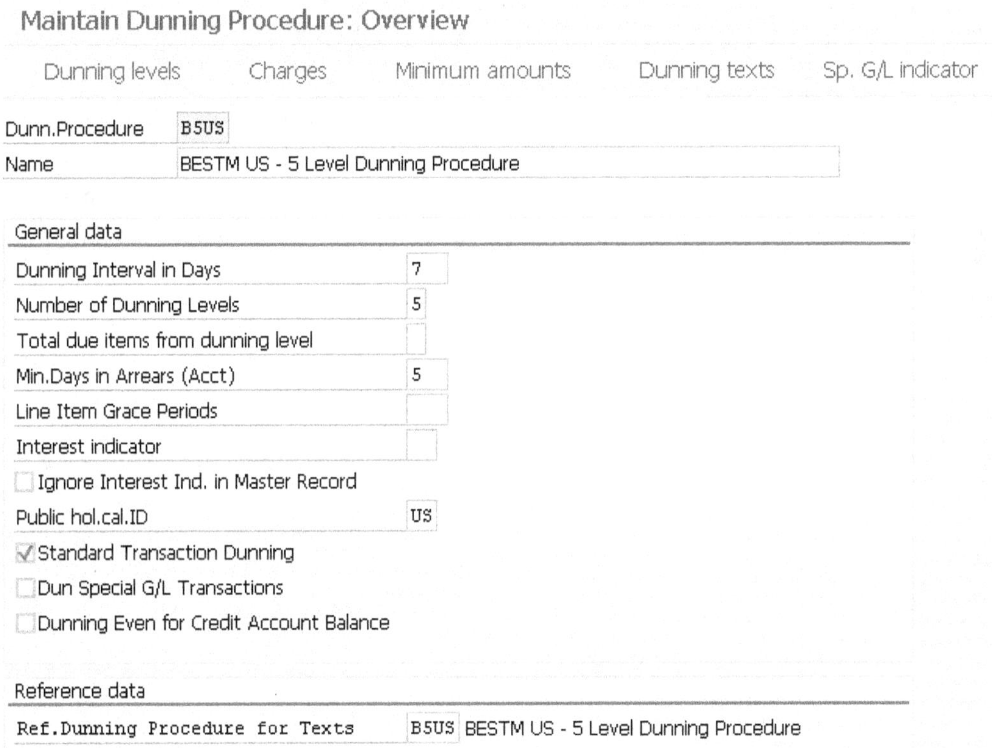

Maintain Dunning Procedure: Overview

Dunning levels	Charges	Minimum amounts	Dunning texts	Sp. G/L indicator

Dunn.Procedure   BSUS
Name   BESTM US - 5 Level Dunning Procedure

General data

Dunning Interval in Days	7
Number of Dunning Levels	5
Total due items from dunning level	
Min.Days in Arrears (Acct)	5
Line Item Grace Periods	
Interest indicator	
☐ Ignore Interest Ind. in Master Record	
Public hol.cal.ID	US
☑ Standard Transaction Dunning	
☐ Dun Special G/L Transactions	
☐ Dunning Even for Credit Account Balance	

Reference data

Ref.Dunning Procedure for Texts   BSUS BESTM US - 5 Level Dunning Procedure

Figure 10.109 New Dunning Proceudre – Overview

   i.   Enter the identifier for the new dunning procedure in 'Dunn.Procedure', and provide a description in the 'Name' field.
   ii.   Under 'General Data':
         • Enter the 'Dunning Interval in Days'. During every dunning run, the system will check to see if the run date is at least this number of days since the last dunning run. If not, then, the program will not select the account/ items for dunning, even if they are overdue. For BESTM, the interval will be 7.

- Enter the highest dunning level that you want for this dunning procedure in the 'Number of Dunning Levels' field. For BESTM, this will be 5.

> **i** You cannot have more than nine dunning levels in a dunning procedure.

- You will enter the dunning level from which you want the program to total all the items, in 'Total due items from dunning level' field. Not required in most of the countries.
- Enter the grace period, in days, at the account level in 'Min.Days in Arrears (Acct)' field. This denotes the number of days that should be crossed, at least by one item in an account, so as to create a dunning notice. This grace period does not influence the way the system calculates the overdue.

> **i** For example, consider that you have entered 5 in 'Min.Days in Arrears (Acct)' field. Now, suppose that there is an open item in the account 1235545 that is due on 20-Mar-2020. When you run the dunning on 24-Mar-2020, the program will not select this account for dunning because as the line the item has not crossed the minimum days of 5 in arrears (that is, the grace period) after becoming due. But, if you run the dunning program on 26-Mar-2020, then, the program selects this account for dunning as the item has crossed the minimum days in arrears of 5 days.

- Enter the days in 'Line Item Grace Periods', if any. The system will consider the grace period per line item, entered here, while determining the due date for the dunning run. So, any item whose days in arrears is less than or equal to the grace period entered here will be considered as not due yet for that dunning notice, and hence will not be selected for dunning.
- Enter the 'Interest Indicator' for item interest calculation. If you do not enter anything here, then, the entry maintained in the master record is taken into account. Even if you enter an indicator here, the entry in the master record has the highest priority. As BESTM wants to control the interest through the entry in master record, we are not maintaining a value here.
- Select 'Ignore Interest Indi. in Master Record' check-box if you want the system to take into account the entry in the 'Interest Indicator' field notwithstanding what has been maintained in the master record.

> **i** The system ignores the interest indicator entered in the master record if you have selected the 'Ignore Interest Indi. in Master Record' check-box and have maintained a value in the 'Interest Indicator' field; it uses the interest indicator in the dunning procedure to calculate the dunning interest. However, if you have not maintained an interest indicator either in the master record or in dunning procedure but you have selected the 'Ignore Interest Indi. in Master Record' check-box, then, this setting does not have any impact and the program will not calculate the dunning interest.

- Enter the country-specific public calendar ID in the 'Public hol.cal.ID' field to enable the system to make use of the relevant calendar to arrive at the due date that will be printed on the dunning notice, when the due date falls on a public holiday.
- Select 'Standard Transaction Dunning' to ensure that the dunning program selects only the standard G/L transactions for dunning.
- Select 'Dun Special G/L Transactions', if you want the system to include the Special G/L items as well along with the standard items for dunning.
- When you do not select 'Dunning Even for Credit Account Balance' check-box, the dunning program selects only the debit balance items for dunning.

> **i** If you set 'Dunning Even for Credit Account Balance' flag, then, the system does not check the account balance as to credit or debit. But, it ensures that the total of the overdue items is in debit to create a dunning notice; else, it does not create the dunning notice.

iii. Under 'Reference data', enter the dunning procedure which is used as the reference to determine the forms for dunning notices in the 'Ref. Dunning Procedure for Texts' field. When left blank, the system fills this field, automatically, with the selected dunning procedure. You can simplify the maintenance of the form names for various dunning procedures which have the same number of dunning levels and the same form layout, by referencing to a particular procedure.

iv. 'Save' the details and proceed to configure the other settings.

v. Click on 'Dunning Levels' button to maintain the settings relating to dunning levels on the next screen (Figure 10.110):

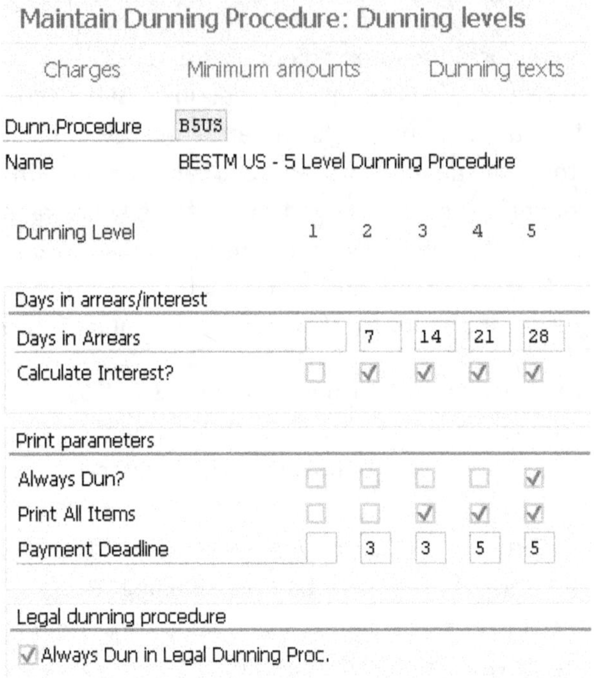

Maintain Dunning Procedure: Dunning levels

Charges   Minimum amounts   Dunning texts

Dunn.Procedure   BSUS
Name   BESTM US - 5 Level Dunning Procedure

Dunning Level	1	2	3	4	5

Days in arrears/interest

	1	2	3	4	5
Days in Arrears		7	14	21	28
Calculate Interest?	☐	☑	☑	☑	☑

Print parameters

	1	2	3	4	5
Always Dun?	☐	☐	☐	☐	☑
Print All Items	☐	☐	☑	☑	☑
Payment Deadline		3	3	5	5

Legal dunning procedure

☑ Always Dun in Legal Dunning Proc.

Figure 10.110 New Dunning Proceudre – Dunning Level

- Enter the 'Days in Arrears' for each dunning level. You will notice that based in the configuration in the previous step, the system has already filled up this field for each dunning level. If you have entered any 'Line Item Grace Periods' previously, then, the system adds this to each level to arrive at the days in arrears.
- Select 'Calculate Interest?' check-box for all the dunning levels for which you want the program to calculate the dunning interest. For BESTM, we have selected the check-box for all the levels except dunning level 1.

vi.   Under 'Print parameters':

- Select 'Always Dun?' check-box, for the appropriate dunning levels, to indicate that a dunning notice needs to be printed, even if no change has been made to the dunning proposal since the last dunning run. Select this flag for the highest dunning level.

> **i** You will consider that a dunning proposal has changed if at least one of the items has reached another dunning level or a new item has been included or there is a change in the dunning level of the account in question.

- Select 'Print All Items' check-box, to determine if you want the dunning program to print all open items in the dunning notices that have the particular dunning level. You will, normally, enable this for higher dunning levels so as to give the customer/vendor an idea of the overall account balance.

> ℹ️ Even if you select 'Print All Items' check-box, note that the blocked items (for dunning) or items for which you have allowed automatic debit, are not displayed. Also, this indicator does not have any effect, if you have opted for separate dunning notices per dunning level for your company code(s).

- In 'Payment Deadline' field, enter the number of days that will be added to the dunning run date to arrive at the payment deadline date, per dunning level. The system also takes into account the public calendar for the country, if you have maintained that in the earlier configuration step, when arriving at the payment deadline so that it does not fall on an official holiday.

vii. Under 'Legal dunning procedure', select 'Always Dun in Legal Dunning Proc.', if you want to send a dunning notice irrespective of the fact that there have not been any further account movements since the last dunning.

> ℹ️ The system usually sends a further dunning notice only when there is some account movement since the last dunning and when you have entered legal dunning procedure in the customer/vendor master record.

Maintain Dunning Procedure: Charges

Dunning levels   Minimum amounts   Dunning texts   🗒

Dunn.Procedure   B5US
Name   BESTM US - 5 Level Dunning Procedure

Charges

Dunn.Level	From Dunn. Amt	Dunn.charge		Dunn.chrge %
2	1.00	5.00	USD	
2	5,001.00	10.00	USD	
2	10,001.00	10.00	USD	
2	25,001.00	15.00	USD	
2	50,001.00	20.00	USD	
2	100,001.00	15.00	USD	
3	1.00		USD	0.10
3	5,001.00		USD	0.15
3	10,001.00		USD	0.20

Figure 10.111 New Dunning Proceudre – Dunning Charges

viii.   Now, click on 'Charges' and enter the 'Currency' on the resulting pop-up screen. Press 'Continue' and maintain the required dunning charges either as amount ('Dunn.charge') or percentage ('Dunn.chrge %') on the next screen (Figure 10.111) per dunning level and for each amount range ('From Dunn. Amt.'). Use the 'Page Down' key to add more rows, if required.

ix.   Click on 'Minimum amounts', enter the 'Currency' on the resulting pop-up screen, and maintain the required settings on the next screen (Figure 10.112):

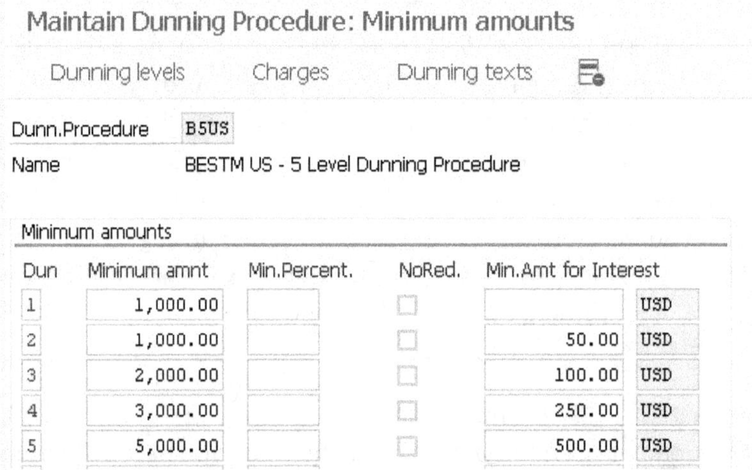

Maintain Dunning Procedure: Minimum amounts

| Dunning levels | Charges | Dunning texts | |

Dunn.Procedure   BSUS

Name   BESTM US - 5 Level Dunning Procedure

Minimum amounts

Dun	Minimum amnt	Min.Percent.	NoRed.	Min.Amt for Interest	
1	1,000.00		☐		USD
2	1,000.00		☐	50.00	USD
3	2,000.00		☐	100.00	USD
4	3,000.00		☐	250.00	USD
5	5,000.00		☐	500.00	USD

Figure 10.112 New Dunning Proceudre – Minimum Amounts

- Enter the minimum amount ('Minimum amnt') of the overdue items which is necessary for the dunning program to set a dunning level. If this minimum amount is not reached in a dunning level, then, the program assigns these items in this dunning level to the next lowest level, besides checking whether a dunning notice can then be created in this dunning level. When you have entered both 'Minimum amnt' and 'Min.Percent.', then, the program would look at the minimum percentage but subject to the minimum amount specified for that dunning level.

- Select 'NoRed.' Check-box if you do not want the system to reduce the dunning level of items for which the 'Minimum amnt' or 'Min.Percent.' is not reached. In such a case, these items will not be included in the dunning proposal and will not be dunned.

- Enter the absolute minimum of dunning interest that needs to be charged for a dunning level in the 'Min.Amt for Interest' field.

x.   Now, click on 'Dunning Texts' button. On the resulting pop-up screen, enter the 'Company Code' and select the 'Account type' (say, Customer) and proceed. On the next screen (Figure 10.113):

Maintain Dunning Procedure: Dunning texts

Dunning levels   Charges   Minimum amounts

Dunn.Procedure	B5US
Name	BESTM US - 5 Level Dunning Procedure
Company Code	1110 BESTM Farm Machinery
Account type	D Customer

Dun	Area	Form	List Name	Adv.	Form ID
Normal dunning procedure					
1		ZF150_BE_DUNN_01	1110-1	☐	
2		ZF150_BE_DUNN_02	1110-2	☐	
3		ZF150_BE_DUNN_03	1110-3	☐	
4		ZF150_BE_DUNN_04	1110-4	☐	
5		ZF150_BE_DUNN_05	1110-5	☐	
				☐	
				☐	

Legal dunning proceedings			
	ZF150_BE_DUNN_LE	1110-L	Display form

Figure 10.113 New Dunning Proceudre – Dunning Texts

- Under the 'Normal dunning procedure' block, enter the dunning level ('Dun'), and maintain the dunning form name ('Form') and the list name ('List Name') for all the dunning levels. We have adapted the default dunning forms for BESTM and renamed them starting with Z (refer Section 10.3.7.1.4). The form for 1st dunning level is without interest, but for other levels the form is with interest.

> **i** In the 'List Name', you enter the name for the spool list for printing the dunning notices. As you can store the dunning notices for different company codes or different dunning levels in the spool as separate lists, it makes sense to specify a different name. Of course, if you do not specify anything here, then, the system uses the standard spool list 'LIST1S'.

- Select 'Adv.' check-box to generate payment advice for that dunning level.
- You may also enter the 'Form ID' for the accompanying media.
- Repeat the settings for 'Account type' = Vendor (K) for the selected company code, and do similar settings for all other company codes.

xi.   Go back to the initial screen, and go to the menu 'Environment > Company Code Data'. Click on 'New Entries' and maintain the details as depicted in Figure 10.114.

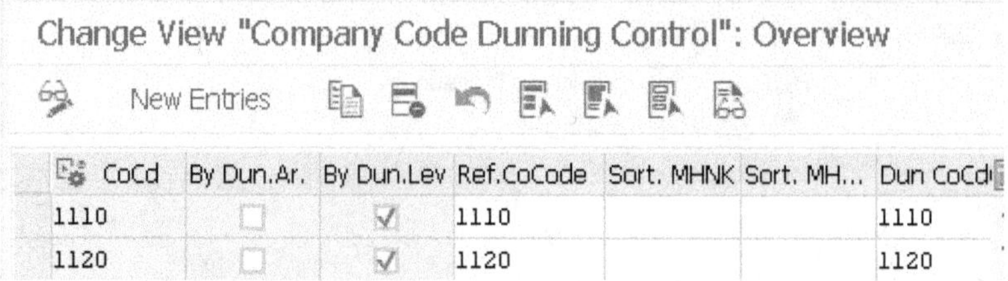

Change View "Company Code Dunning Control": Overview

New Entries

CoCd	By Dun.Ar.	By Dun.Lev	Ref.CoCode	Sort. MHNK	Sort. MH...	Dun CoCd
1110	☐	☑	1110			1110
1120	☐	☑	1120			1120

Figure 10.114 New Dunning Proceudre – Company Code Dunning Control

- Enter the company code ('CoCd') for which you are maintaining the settings, select the appropriate check boxes ('By Dun.Ar.' or 'By Dun.Lev') and enter the reference company code ('Ref.CoCode') if any. The reference company code is the one that will provide the required dunning forms.
- Enter the sorting variant: K1 for MHNK and P1 for MHND. You will not be able to use these sort variants K1 and P1, when you plan to dun by dunning level.
- Also enter the dunning company code ('Dun CoCd') if the company code entered in column 1 is not responsible for dunning (useful in cross-company code dunning).

> **i** While printing the dunning notice, the system updates the dunning level in the customer master record. If you are dunning by dunning level ('By Dun. Lev' check-box selected), and sort the print in descending order (using the sort variants K1 and/or P1), this may lead to an incorrect dunning level being entered in the customer master record.

xii.   'Save' the details. This completes defining the multi-level dunning procedure for BESTM. Repeat the settings and define the single level dunning procedure as well for BESTM.

With this, let us understand how to use the dunning groups for dunning.

10.3.7.2.2   Define Dunning Groups

By default, the dunning program groups the dunning notices per customer / vendor. However, you can plan to group the open items of your business partners according to certain pre-defined criteria and dun those items together. For example, you may want to send your business partner a separate dunning notice per leased property; for this, you can define a grouping key referring to the contract number field and dunning all the open items, with the same contract number, together.

We will not be using this configuration for BESTM. However, it may help to understand that you can configure this by using the menu path: SAP Customizing Implementation Guide > Financial Accounting > Accounts Receivable and Accounts Payable > Business Transactions > Dunning > Dunning Procedure > Define Dunning Groups, or Transaction OBAQ.

With this we are now ready to configure the last configuration setting, under dunning procedure.

10.3.7.2.3   Define Interest Rates

While you have discussed entering an interest indicator when configuring the dunning procedure (Section 10.3.7.2.1), you can use this configuration step to define interest rate % (debit / credit), valid from and the currency, per interest indicator. Even though we have not entered an interest indictor in the dunning procedure for BESTM mentioning that the interest calculation will be controlled through the master record, you can use this step to maintain the rates for the interest indicator which you will enter in the master record of customer or vendor. We have already defined (vide Section 9.4.4.6.1 of Chapter 9 of Vol. I) two arrears (or item) interest indicators – one for US (1U) and another for India (1I) for which you can maintain the interest rates.

Use the menu path: SAP Customizing Implementation Guide > Financial Accounting > Accounts Receivable and Accounts Payable > Business Transactions > Dunning > Dunning Procedure > Define Dunning Interest Rates, or Transaction OB42. On the resulting screen, click on 'New Entries' and maintain the interest rates for both the indicators, 1U and 1I to be used in US and India respectively (Figure 10.115).

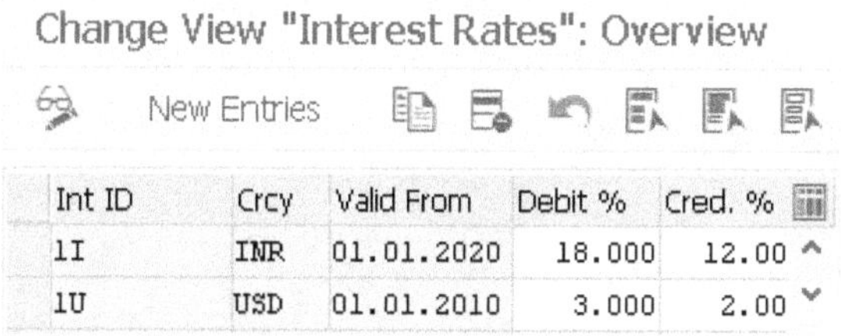

Change View "Interest Rates": Overview

Int ID	Crcy	Valid From	Debit %	Cred. %
1I	INR	01.01.2020	18.000	12.00
1U	USD	01.01.2010	3.000	2.00

Figure 10.115 Dunning Interest Rates

With this, we are now ready to discuss the settings that are required for dunning printouts.

10.3.7.3   Printout

Under this, we will be discussing the configuration relating to the settings for printing dunning notices. The dunning notices (forms) can be either in the form of SAPScript or SAP Smart Forms. The settings include:

- Define Dunning Forms (with SAPScript)
- Define Dunning Forms (with SAP Smart Forms)

- Assign Dunning Forms
- Define Sender Details for Dunning Forms

10.3.7.3.1   Define Dunning Forms (with SAPScript)

We have already discussed this in Section 10.3.7.1.4.

10.3.7.3.2   Define Dunning Forms (with SAP Smart Forms)

Since we will be using only the SAPScript-based dunning forms, we will not be discussing in detail about defining the dunning forms based on SAP Smart Forms.

If you want to define dunning forms which are based on Smart Forms, you may use the menu path: SAP Customizing Implementation Guide > Financial Accounting > Accounts Receivable and Accounts Payable > Business Transactions > Dunning > Printout > Define Dunning Forms (with SAP Smart Forms), or Transaction SMARTFORMS. The standard Smart Form supplied by SAP is named as F150_DUNN_SF (Figure 10.116). You may copy and adapt the same, to meet your own requirements.

Figure 10.116 Dunning Form F150_DUNN_SF (Smart Form)

The next step is to assign the dunning forms

10.3.7.3.3   Assign Dunning Forms

Here, you need to specify, per 'dunning procedure–company code–account type', the forms that you want to use for the normal and legal dunning procedures. Remember we have already configured most of these settings while defining the dunning procedure vide Section 10.3.7.2.1. Here, you just need to identify the form type: whether it is SAPScript, SAP Smart Form and so on.

Use the menu path: SAP Customizing Implementation Guide > Financial Accounting > Accounts Receivable and Accounts Payable > Business Transactions > Dunning > Printout > Assign Dunning Forms. On the resulting screen:

i.   Select the dunning procedure (say, B5US) and double-click on 'Forms for normal dunning procedure' on the left hand side 'Dialog Structure'. Maintain the company code (say, 1110) and the account type (say, Customer) on the resulting pop-up screen and proceed to the next screen (Figure 10.117).

Figure 10.117 Assigning Dunning Forms for Normal Dunning Procedure

ii.   You will notice that the system has already populated the 'Form Object Name' and the 'List Name' for each of the dunning levels. You just to need to select the form type ('FormTyp') as SAPScript and 'Save' the details.

iii.   Repeat and select the form type for legal dunning procedure as well (Figure 10.118)

Figure 10.118 Assigning Dunning Forms for Legal Dunning Procedure

Now, we are ready to complete the final step in configuring the dunning printout, and defining the sender details for dunning forms.

10.3.7.3.4   Define Sender Details for Dunning Forms

Define which standard texts are to be used for the header / footer / sender address, in the letter window of the dunning notice. Create the standard texts and specify the same for each of the company codes.

To configure, use the menu path: SAP Customizing Implementation Guide > Financial Accounting > Accounts Receivable and Accounts Payable > Business Transactions > Dunning > Printout > Define Sender Details for Dunning Forms. You may also use Transaction S_ALR_87001305. On the resulting pop-up screen, enter the 'Company Code' and continue. On the next screen (Figure 10.119), click on 'New Entries' and:

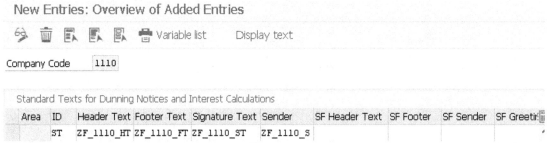

Figure 10.119 Configuring Sender Details for Dunning Forms

    i.   Leave the 'Area', which is nothing but the dunning area, as blank as we are not dunning per dunning area for BESTM.

    ii.   Select the appropriate 'ID'. ST for standard text.

    iii.   All the fields without a prefix of SF denotes the fields for SAPScript form: enter the identifier for 'Header Text' (say, company logo, telephone etc), 'Footer Text' (say, details like signatory, salutation of the signatory etc), 'Signature Text' and for 'Sender' as well. The 'Sender' provides the details of the company code that sends the dunning notices.

    iv.   You may maintain / display the text using the 'Display text' button. Alternatively, you can use Transaction SO10, to maintain the required texts.

    v.   Repeat the steps and configure similar texts for other company codes as well, and 'Save' all the details.

    vi.   If you are using Smart Forms for dunning notices, then, you need to maintain the text IDs in all the fields that are prefixed with SF.

This completes our discussion on the settings that are required for printing the dunning notices. Let us proceed to list the dunning program configuration, you have carried out so far, to verify and modify, if required.

10.3.7.4   Generate List for Dunning Program Configuration

Using this, you can generate the list displaying the dunning program configuration in the system, per company code, per dunning procedure. The list will come handy to check the settings and make a change, if required. The system uses the program SAPMSSY0 to bring out the details.

Dunning Program Configuration Documentation

Dunning Procedure	B5US	BESTM US - 5 Level Dunning Procedure		
USD	25,001.00	0.00	0.30	%
USD	50,001.00	0.00	0.35	%
USD	100,001.00	0.00	0.40	%

Dunning Procedure   B5US   BESTM US - 5 Level Dunning Procedure

Minimum amounts in dunning level 4

Currency	Minimum Amount	Min. Percentage Rate	Min. Amt for Interest
USD	3,000.00	0.00 %	250.00

Dunning Procedure   B5US   BESTM US - 5 Level Dunning Procedure

Dunning texts in dunning level 4

Ref. Dunning Procedure for Texts   B5US
Ref. Company Code   1110

Acct Type	Dunn. area	Form	List Name
D		ZF150_BE_DUNN_04	1110-4

Dunning Procedure   B5US   BESTM US - 5 Level Dunning Procedure

Dunning level general data   5

Days in Arrears	028
Calculate Interest?	X
Payment Deadline	05
Print All Items	X
Always Dun?	X

Dunning Procedure   B5US   BESTM US - 5 Level Dunning Procedure

Dunning charges in dunning level 5

Currency	Dunning Amount	Dunning Charge	Dunn. chrge in percent	
USD	1.00	0.00	0.20	%
USD	5,001.00	0.00	0.25	%
USD	10,001.00	0.00	0.30	%
USD	25,001.00	0.00	0.35	%
USD	50,001.00	0.00	0.40	%
USD	100,001.00	0.00	0.50	%

Dunning Procedure   B5US   BESTM US - 5 Level Dunning Procedure

Figure 10.120 System Generated Configuration List for Dunning Program

To generate the list, use the menu path: SAP Customizing Implementation Guide > Financial Accounting > Accounts Receivable and Accounts Payable > Business Transactions > Dunning > Generate List for Dunning Program Configuration. You may also use Transaction OBL6.

On the resulting screen, enter the 'Dunning procedure' and 'Company code' and click on 'Execute'. The system brings out all the details of the settings that you have maintained for the dunning procedure (say, B5US) for the entered company code (say, 1110), on the next screen (Figure 10.120). You will see all the details for basic settings, the configuration details for the dunning procedure, details of forms used etc. Scan through the list, and, if you see a setting that is incorrect or a setting that has not been maintained, revisit the appropriate configuration step to correct or maintain the same.

With this, we have completed all the required settings for configuring the dunning program in the system. In the next Section, let us understand how the system actually carries out the dunning process.

10.3.7.5   Dunning Process Flow

1) Use the SAP Easy Access menu path: SAP Menu > Accounting > Financial accounting > Accounts Receivable (or Accounts Payable) > Periodic processing > Dunning or use Transaction F150, and begin the dunning process by ***Maintaining the Dunning Parameters*** for the dunning run:
    a. First enter the basic parameters like the dunning run execution date ('Run On') and an identifier for the dunning run ('Identification').
    b. Now, on the 'Parameters' tab, maintain the 'Dunning Date' (that will be printed in the dunning notice), posting cut-off date for selection of documents ('Docmnts Posted up To'), 'Company code', and 'Amount Restrictions' (for customer / vendor).
    c. You may also make further restrictions in 'Free Selection' tab, wherein you may enter up to eight additional selection criteria for accounts and documents: you can use document fields (from tables BSID and BSIK), customer master record fields (from tables KNA1, KNB1 and KNB5) and vendor master record fields (from tables LFA1, LFB1 and LFB5) as selection criteria.
    d. When completed, 'Save' the details. The system will, now, display the current status of the dunning run in the 'Status' tab.
2) Now, on the 'Dunning' initial screen, click on 'Schedule' to schedule the dunning run for a later date / time or run the program immediately. If you do not select the 'Dunn.Print with Scheduling' check-box, then, the system prints the dunning notices immediately after the dunning run, and you will not be able to edit the dunning proposal manually or to delete a dunning proposal which has been created.

3) During the **Creation of Dunning Proposal List**, the system determines the accounts and items to be dunned in two steps:

   a. First, the dunning program checks the *accounts*. The dunning program checks whether an *account* needs to be dunned:

      i. It checks the fields 'Dunning Procedure' and 'Last Dunning Notice' (date of last run) in the customer master record to determine whether the arrears date or the date of the last dunning run is in the past.

      ii. It checks whether the account is blocked for dunning, based on the entry in the 'Dunning Block' field in the customer master record.

Following these two checks, the program determines if an account in question is released for dunning or rejected.

   b. Second, when the account is released for dunning, then, the dunning program processes all *open items* that were posted to this account on or before the date entered in the 'Docmnts Posted up To' field maintained in the dunning parameters:

      i. The program checks each open item, in an account, to decide if the item:

         • Is blocked for dunning?

         • Is overdue according to the date of issue, the base date, the payment conditions, and the number of grace days granted.

Following these checks, the open item in question is either released for dunning or rejected.

   c. If the open item is released for dunning, the dunning program, now, arrives at:

      i. How many days the open item is overdue?

      ii. Which dunning level the open item has according to the dunning levels specified in the dunning procedure?

From the above, the program determines the open items with specific dunning levels for an account, and sets the highest dunning level to the account, based on the highest dunning level of an open item of the account, even though there are several items with different dunning levels.

   d. Once the dunning program has ascertained which open items to dun and the dunning level for the account, it processes each account by making the following checks:

i. Does the customer (or vendor) have a debit balance with regard to overdue items and all open items?
   - If NOT, the account is not dunned.
ii. If YES, is the total amount to be dunned and the percentage of all open items more than the minimum amount and percentage defined in the dunning procedure?
   - If NOT, the account is not dunned.
iii. If YES, is the dunning level for the account or the overdue items higher than it was for the last dunning run?
   - If NOT, the account is not dunned.
iv. If YES, are there any new open items to be dunned (with a previous dunning level = 0)?
   - If NOT, the account is not dunned.
v. If YES, does the dunning procedure for this level specify that dunning be repeated?
   - If NOT, the account is not dunned.
vi. If YES, the account is released for dunning, and the program goes on to check the next account as described above.

e. Now, the program creates a list (dunning proposal list) of all the accounts and open items that have been proposed for dunning and assigns a dunning level to the account according to the highest dunning level of an open item in the account.

4) You can, now, **Edit the Dunning Proposal List** to manually raise or lower the dunning level of an item or account. You can also block or unblock an item, account, or document from being dunned. You can look at the log to confirm the changes you have made to the dunning proposal; if you are not satisfied or want to make further changes, you can edit further till you incorporate all the changes. You can also display the sample printout of the dunning notice on the screen; you will be able to display only the first 10 dunning notices.

5) Now, you are ready to **Print the Dunning Notices**. The program selects the dunning form / text based upon the dunning levels. After you activate the print run, the program prints the dunning notices besides updating the important details, such as 'Dunning Level' and 'Last Dunning Notice', in the customer (or vendor) master. You can, always, restart an interrupted printing. You can optically archive the dunning notices while they are getting printed.

This completes our discussion on dunning. We can, now, move on to discuss the configuration settings required for open item clearing.

10.3.8 Open Item Clearing

We have already discussed, in detail, about open item clearing in Section 9.4.3 of Chapter 9 of Vol. I, when we discussed the SAP G/L Accounting. In that, we have defined the necessary accounts for posting exchange rate differences, defined the posting keys for clearing transactions, the settings for automatic clearing, the tolerance groups to handle clearing differences etc. Also, we have defined the appropriate accounts for handling rounding off differences vide Section 10.3.3.1.5 of this Chapter. Hence, no more setting is required here for handling the clearing of open items.

With this, we are now ready move on to discuss the settings required for handling down payment received.

10.3.9 Down Payment Received

The 'down payment received' denotes the advance amounts that you receive from your customers, and accounted in FI-A/R. The down payment received is also known as 'customer down payments'. To manage down payments received, you need to complete the following configuration steps in the SAP system:

- Define Reconciliation Accounts for Customer Down Payments
- Define Tax Accounts for Down Payments Received
- Define Account for Tax Clearing

Let us start with the configuration of reconciliation accounts for customer down payments.

10.3.9.1   Define Reconciliation Accounts for Customer Down Payments

Use this step to define the G/L accounts for managing the *customer down payments* (or down payment requests). In this case, the system automatically posts to these accounts instead of to the normal A/R reconciliation account. Maintain the required G/L account, per account type (D = customer) and Special G/L indicator (A, F, etc.) combinations. Ensure if a down payment or down payment request is to be displayed either as gross or net in the alternative reconciliation account, via appropriate specification in the 'Tax Category' field.

To configure, use the menu path: SAP Customizing Implementation Guide > Financial Accounting > Accounts Receivable and Accounts Payable > Business Transactions > Down Payment Received > Define Reconciliation Accounts for Customer Down Payments, or Transaction OBXR. On the 'Maintain Accounting Configuration: Special G/L – List' screen, you will see the list of Special G/L transactions (Figure 10.121).

Figure 10.121 Special G/L List for Customer

Double-click on the appropriate row (say, Account Type =D, Special G/L Indicator = A, Down Payment) and maintain the chart of accounts on the resulting pop-up screen. On the next screen (Figure 10.121):

i.   Maintain the reconciliation account(s) for the Special G/L account (s).

ii.   You will use the 'Planning level' field to control the displays in SAP Cash Management.

iii. The key you enter in the 'Output tax clearing' field determines the account to which the clearing entry is made. If the down payment is to be displayed gross in the business partner's account (in the case of down payments with taxes on sales/purchases), then, the system requires a clearing entry (as an offsetting entry) for the taxes on sales/purchases.

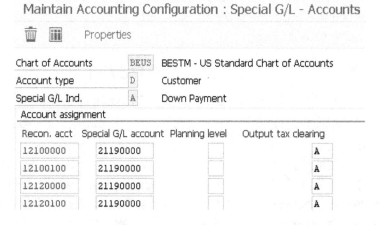

Figure 10.122 Reconciliation / Special G/L Accounts for Customer Down Payments

In the next step, let us define the tax accounts to manage down payments received.

10.3.9.2   Define Tax Accounts for Down Payments Received

Using this step, you will define the tax accounts, for down payments received, so that the system can use these accounts in automatic postings.

Use the menu path: SAP Customizing Implementation Guide > Financial Accounting > Accounts Receivable and Accounts Payable > Business Transactions > Down Payment Received > Define Tax Accounts for Down Payments Received, or Transaction OB40. On the resulting screen, double-click on the appropriate procedure, enter the chart of accounts on the pop-up screen and maintain the required G/L accounts on the next screen.

With this, let us complete the final configuration step for down payment received namely, defining the accounts for tax clearing.

10.3.9.3   Define Account for Tax Clearing

Here, you define an output tax clearing account that is needed, if you display down payments (gross) in the customer account. Besides the account, you can also specify a key for the differentiation which groups the Special G/L indicator, the account type and the reconciliation account together.

Use the menu path: SAP Customizing Implementation Guide > Financial Accounting > Accounts Receivable and Accounts Payable > Business Transactions > Down Payment Received > Define Account for Tax Clearing, or Transaction OBXB. On the resulting screen, you will see several procedures listed for down payments (group = ANZ). Double-click on the appropriate procedure ('Output tax clearing on down payments' - transaction MVA) and maintain the required G/L account(s) on the next screen (Figure 10.123).

Figure 10.123 Account for Output Tax Clearing on Down Payments

You may click on 'Rules' to look at the automatic posting settings (Figure 10.124). You can also click on 'Posting Key' to see the associated keys for debit / credit posting.

Configuration Accounting Maintain : Automatic Posts - Rules

◀ ▶   Accounts   Posting Key

| Chart of Accounts | BEUS | BESTM - US Standard Chart of Accounts |
| Transaction | MVA | Output tax clearing on down payments |

Accounts are determined based on

| Debit/Credit | ☐ |
| Output tax clearing | ☑ |

Figure 10.124 Automatic Posting Rules for Output Tax Clearing on Down Payments

This completes the settings that are required for configuring down payment received. With this, we can now proceed to discuss the settings that you need to make for down payments made by you.

10.3.10   Down Payment Made

As with the customer down payments (or down payments received), the down payments made represent the advance or down payments you make to your vendors or suppliers. These are also known as *vendor down payments* and are managed in FI-A/P. As with the customer down payments, you need to make the following settings for vendor down payments:

- Define Alternative Reconciliation Account for Down Payments
- Define Account for Tax Clearing

First, let us define the alternative reconciliation account for down payments.

10.3.10.1   Define Alternative Reconciliation Account for Down Payments

Here, you define an account in which you manage the vendor down payments in the G/L. The system, then, makes the down payment posting to this account automatically instead of to the normal A/P reconciliation account. The configuration is similar to that of the settings discussed in Section 10.3.9.1 of this Chapter.

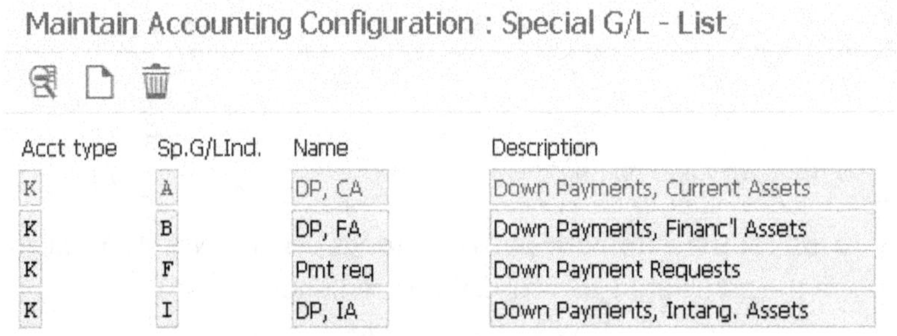

Maintain Accounting Configuration : Special G/L - List

🗃 🗋 🗑

Acct type	Sp.G/LInd.	Name	Description
K	A	DP, CA	Down Payments, Current Assets
K	B	DP, FA	Down Payments, Financ'l Assets
K	F	Pmt req	Down Payment Requests
K	I	DP, IA	Down Payments, Intang. Assets

Figure 10.125 Special G/L List for Vendor

Here, you will use the menu path: SAP Customizing Implementation Guide > Financial Accounting > Accounts Receivable and Accounts Payable > Business Transactions > Down Payments Made > Define Alternative Reconciliation Account for Down Payments, or Transaction OBYR. On the resulting screen (Figure 10.125), you will see the various Special G/L transactions for vendor (Account type = K).

Double-click on the appropriate transactions (say, down payment made, current assets) and maintain the required accounts on the next screen (Figure 10.126), for the selected chart of accounts (say, BEUS).

Maintain Accounting Configuration : Special G/L - Accounts

🗑 🗑   Properties

Chart of Accounts	BEUS	BESTM - US Standard Chart of Accounts
Account type	K	Vendor
Special G/L Ind.	A	Down Payments, Current Assets

Account assignment

Recon. acct	Special G/L account	Planning level	Input tax clearing
21100000	12110000		A
21100100	12110000		A
21200000	12110000		A

Figure 10.126 Reconciliation / Special G/L Accounts for Vendor Down Payments

With this, we can now define the accounts for tax clearing for down payments made.

10.3.10.2   Define Account for Tax Clearing

Similar to the one we defined for customer down payment in Section 10.3.9.3, you need to define the accounts for tax clearing for down payments made. Use the menu path: SAP Customizing Implementation Guide > Financial Accounting > Accounts Receivable and Accounts Payable > Business Transactions > Down Payments Made > Define Account for Tax Clearing, or Transaction OBXB.

Configuration Accounting Maintain : Automatic Posts - Accounts

◀ ▶ ☐ ⬚ ⬚   Posting Key   Procedures   Rules

| Chart of Accounts | BEUS | BESTM - US Standard Chart of Accounts |
| Transaction | VVA | Input tax clearing on down payments |

Account assignment

Input tax ...	Account
A	12111000
M	16010500
V	12111000

Figure 10.127 Account for Input Tax Clearing on Down Payments

On the resulting screen, double click on transaction VVA 'Input tax clearing on down payments' and maintain the accounts on the next screen (Figure 10.127) for the chart of accounts (say, BEUS).

This completes our discussion on the settings required for configuring down payments made. We shall discuss adjustment postings / reversals in the next Section.

10.3.11   Adjustment Posting/Reversal

We have already discussed the adjustment postings / reversal, in detail, in Section 9.4.5 of Chapter 9 of Vol. I, wherein we have defined the settings for permitting negative postings and also the reversal reasons. With this we are now ready to discuss the interest calculation, in the next Section.

10.3.12   Interest Calculation

We have already discussed the interest calculation in Section 9.4.4 of Chapter 9 of Vol. I, when we talked about the bank interest calculation. We completed some of the settings including defining the interest indicator, preparing the system for balance interest calculation etc. Hence, let us, now, discuss about the remaining settings that relate to item interest calculation, here, in this Section. We shall discuss the settings under the following four groups:

1. Interest Calculation Global Settings
2. Interest Calculation
3. Interest Posting
4. Printout

Let us start with the first group of settings, namely the global settings for interest calculation.

10.3.12.1   Interest Calculation Global Settings

The global settings for interest calculation include the following configuration steps:

- Define Interest Calculation Types
- Define Number Ranges for Interest Forms
- Prepare Item Interest Calculation
- Prepare Account Balance Interest Calculation

Let us get started with the first activity of defining the interest calculation types.

10.3.12.1.1 Define Interest Calculation Types

We have already completed this step vide Section 9.4.4.6.1 of Chapter 9 of Vol. I, wherein we have defined two indicators (1I and 1U) for item (or arrears) interest calculation, and two (2I and 2U) more for balance interest calculation.

The next step is to define the number ranges for the interest forms.

10.3.12.1.2 Define Number Ranges for Interest Forms

You can define the number ranges for the interest forms, per company code, following the menu path: SAP Customizing Implementation Guide > Financial Accounting > Accounts Receivable and Accounts Payable > Business Transactions > Interest Calculation > Interest Calculation Global Settings > Define Number Ranges for Interest Forms, or Transaction FBN1. This required only if you have not maintained the number ranges for the accounting documents (object: RF_BELEG), earlier, while configuring the company code global parameters. We have completed this in Vol. I of Chapter 7 (Section 7.1.5.5), while making the settings for documents.

The next step is to prepare the system for item interest calculation.

10.3.12.1.3 Prepare Item Interest Calculation

This is similar to the one we have did in Section 9.4.4.6.2 of Chapter 9 of Vol. I, wherein we completed the settings for preparing for account balance interest calculation. As in that case, here also, you will make the general settings (like, item selection, interest determination, post-processing, output control, posting etc) for the individual interest indicators (say, 1U and 1I) for the item (or arrears) interest calculation. All these settings relate to the standard SAP program RFINTITAR.

Project Dolphin

BESTM has suggested to the project team to configure the item interest calculation in such a way that (a) the system should calculate the interest as and when it becomes due but on the due date for net payment, (b) the value date should be the baseline date for net payment, (c) there would be a grace period of 5 days for payment without interest after the receivable payments become due, (d) the system should calculate interest both on debit and credit items using the respective interest rates and (e) there should not be any interest calculated on items that have been paid before the due date. In case of interest settlement, it has been directed that there should not be any interest settlement if the interest amount is less than $10 for all US-based company codes, and INR 100 for India-based company codes. It was also suggested that the interest receivables should be created and posted with reference to the invoice for which interest was calculated.

Let us make the settings using the menu path: SAP Customizing Implementation Guide > Financial Accounting > Accounts Receivable and Accounts Payable > Business Transactions > Interest Calculation > Interest Calculation Global Settings > Prepare Item Interest Calculation.

On the resulting screen, click on 'New Entries' and make the appropriate settings on the next screen (Figure10.128):

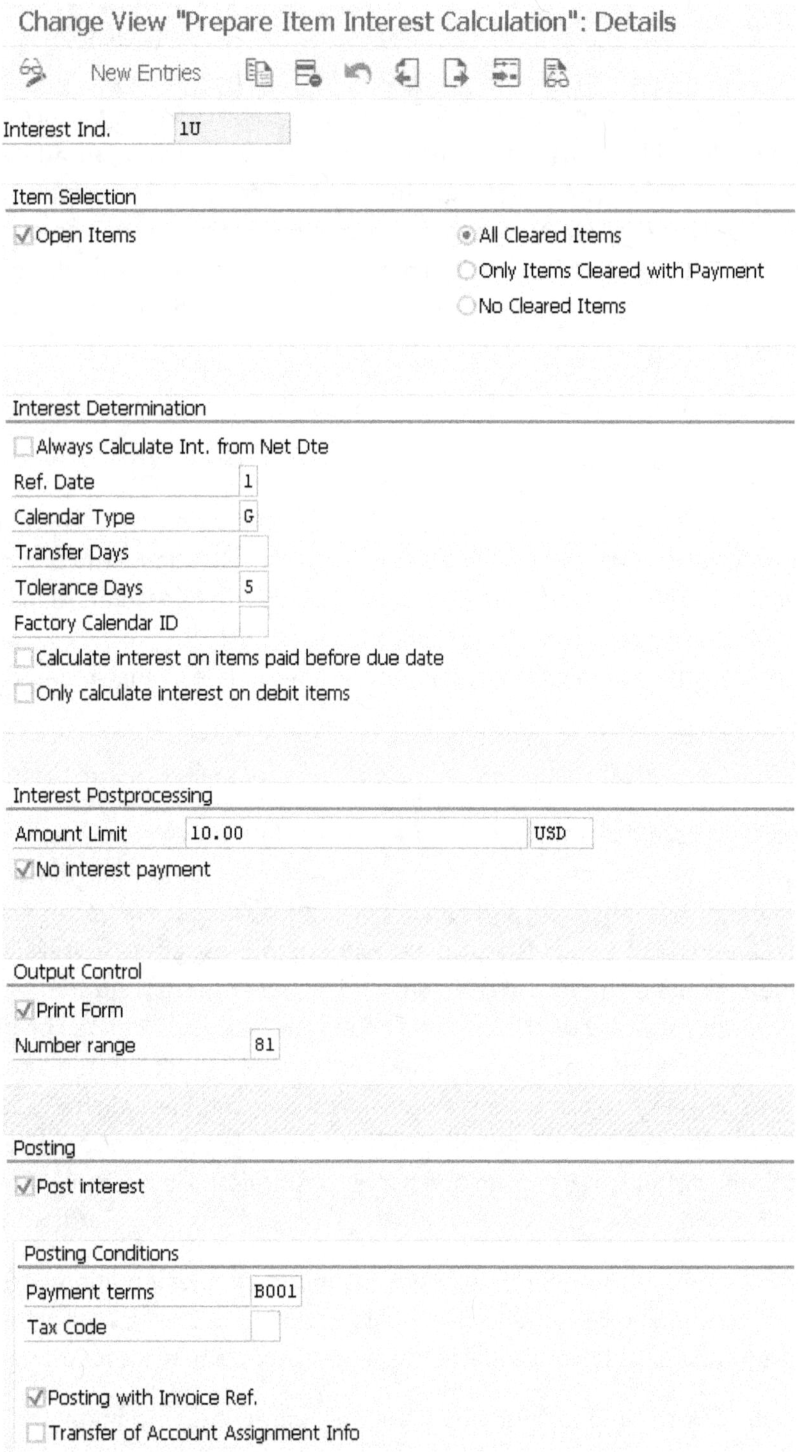

Change View "Prepare Item Interest Calculation": Details

New Entries

Interest Ind.   1U

Item Selection

☑ Open Items

◉ All Cleared Items
○ Only Items Cleared with Payment
○ No Cleared Items

Interest Determination

☐ Always Calculate Int. from Net Dte

Ref. Date	1
Calendar Type	G
Transfer Days	
Tolerance Days	5
Factory Calendar ID	

☐ Calculate interest on items paid before due date
☐ Only calculate interest on debit items

Interest Postprocessing

Amount Limit   10.00   USD

☑ No interest payment

Output Control

☑ Print Form

Number range   81

Posting

☑ Post interest

Posting Conditions

Payment terms	B001
Tax Code	

☑ Posting with Invoice Ref.
☐ Transfer of Account Assignment Info

Figure 10.128 Configuring Item Interest Indicator (1U)

i.   Enter the interest indicator (say, 1U) for item interest calculation ('Interest Ind.').

ii.   Under 'Item Selection', select the 'Open Items' check-box, and also select the 'All Cleared Items' radio-button.

iii. On the 'Interest Determination' block:

- Do not select 'Always Calculate Int. from Net Dte' check-box. Else, the system will calculate interest only as of the due date for net payment.
- Enter the value date in the 'Ref Date' field. Enter 1 here as you will want the system to refer to the baseline date for net payment as the value date.
- Enter the 'Calendar Type'. Let this be 'G'.
- Leave the 'Transfer Days' field as blank. The system recognizes the 'transfer days' are only for incoming payments, and these days have no meaning for open items.
- Enter 'Tolerance Days', if any. When entered, the system does not calculate the interest, for these many grace days, on customer receivable even after they become due. It will be 5 for BESTM.
- Select the 'Calculate interest on items paid before date' check-box if you want the system to calculate the credit interest (using credit interest rates) for items that are paid before their due date subject to the condition that the paid items were not subject to cash discount. We shall not select this for 1U.
- You have to select 'Only calculate interest on debit items' check-box, if you want the system to calculate interest only on debit items ignoring the credit ones.

> **i** When 'Only calculate interest on debit items' check-box is not selected, the system calculates interest on credit items as well, by treating them as debit items by applying the same (debit) interest. This is because, if the credit memo is not cleared immediately by the invoice, but cleared later, both the invoice and credit memo will become overdue and will eventually balance out in terms of interest.

iv.   In the 'Amount Limit' field, under 'Interest Postprocessing', enter the amount limit and the respective 'Currency' in the adjacent field. If the system-calculated interest is below this threshold per currency per account, then the system does not generate an interest settlement. Select the 'No Interest Payment' check-box, if you do not want the system to create an interest settlement when an interest payment is produced.

> **i** The system produces an interest payment when the credit interest (on items paid before the due date) is greater than the debit interest.

v.   Under 'Output Control', do not select the 'Print Form' check-box if you want only an account-level overview; else, select the flag. Enter the 'Number Range' for the interest forms.

vi.   Under 'Posting', select the 'Post interest' check-box enabling the system to post the interest.

vii.   Under 'Posting Conditions' you may also maintain the 'Payment terms' and 'Tax Code'. Select the 'Posting with Invoice Ref.' check-box, so that, the system creates the interest receivable and posts the same with reference to each of the invoices for which interest is calculated; the system creates a separate line item that contains the corresponding invoice reference.

> **i** In the case of account balance interest calculation, the system posts the interest by a batch input session, only when you 'run' the session. On the other hand, in the item interest calculation, the system posts the interest when you start the program as an 'update' run.

viii.   'Save' the settings, and create the other item interest indicator 1I for BESTM.

The next step is to make the settings for account balance interest calculation

10.3.12.1.4   Prepare Account Balance Interest Calculation

We have already made the required settings for preparing the system for account balance interest calculation vide Section 9.4.4.6.2 of Chapter 9 of Vol. I.

This completes our discussion on the global settings for interest calculation. Let us move on to the settings required for interest calculation.

10.3.12.2   Interest Calculation

The configuration steps under this group, include the following:

- Define Reference Interest Rates
- Define Time-Based Terms
- Enter Interest Values
- Define Fixed Amounts for Interest Calculation

Let us start with the definition of reference interest rates.

10.3.12.2.1   Define Reference Interest Rates

We have already created the required reference interest rates for account balance interest calculation in Section 9.4.4.7.1 of Chapter 9 of Vol. I. Let us define the same for item interest calculation, here. Use the menu path: SAP Customizing Implementation Guide > Financial

Accounting > Accounts Receivable and Accounts Payable > Business Transactions > Interest Calculation > Interest Calculation > Define Reference Interest Rates, or Transaction OBAC. Click on 'New Entries' and create the required reference interest rates: one for credit and another for debit, on the next screen (Figure 10.129).

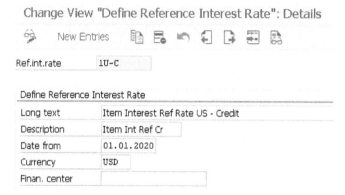

Change View "Define Reference Interest Rate": Details

Figure 10.129 Reference Interest Rate – Item Interest Calculation – Credit

The next step is to define the time dependent terms for each of the reference interest rates that we have defined in the previous step.

10.3.12.2.2   Define Time-Dependent Terms

As discussed in Section 9.4.4.7.2 of Chapter 9 of Vo. I, here, you specify how the interest rate is to be determined for each of the item interest indicators per currency and per validity date. Use the menu path: SAP Customizing Implementation Guide > Financial Accounting > Accounts Receivable and Accounts Payable > Business Transactions > Interest Calculation > Interest Calculation > Define Time-Dependent Terms. You may also use Transaction OB81.

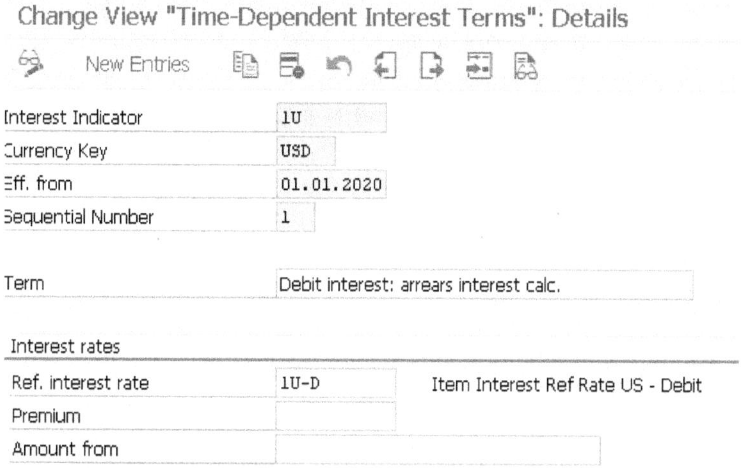

Change View "Time-Dependent Interest Terms": Details

Figure 10.130 Time Dependent Interest Terms of Interest Indicator 1U

On the resulting screen, click on 'New Entries' and make the required settings for the item interest indicator 1U, for both credit and debit reference interest rates (Figure 10.130). Note that you need to select the appropriate 'Term' (for example, 'Debit interest: arrears interest calc') corresponding to the 'Ref. interest rate' (for example, 1U-D). Repeat and complete the configuration for the other item interest indicator 1I as well.

When fully configured, you have all the settings defined for both item and balance interest indicators as shown in Figure 10.131.

Change View "Time-Dependent Interest Terms": Overview

🔧 🔧   New Entries   📄 📇 ↩ 📋 📋 📋 📇

Int.Ind.	Currency	Eff. from	Seq.no.	Trans. Type	Amount from
1U	USD	01.01.2020	1	Credit interest: arrears interest calc.	0.00
1U	USD	01.01.2020	2	Credit interest: arrears interest calc.	0.00
2I	INR	01.01.2020	1	Debit interest: balance interest calc.	0.00
2I	INR	01.01.2020	2	Debit interest: balance interest calc.	200,000.00
2I	INR	01.01.2020	3	Debit interest: balance interest calc.	500,000.00
2U	USD	01.01.2020	1	Debit interest: balance interest calc.	0.00
2U	USD	01.01.2020	2	Debit interest: balance interest calc.	10,000.00
2U	USD	01.01.2020	3	Debit interest: balance interest calc.	25,000.00

Figure 10.131 Time Dependent Interest Terms for BESTM

The next step is to maintain the interest values per validity for the reference interest rates that we have defined in the earlier step.

10.3.12.2.3   Enter Interest Values

We, in Section 9.4.4.7.3 of Chapter 9 of Vol. I, have entered the interest values for account balance reference interest rates. Now, using the menu path: SAP Customizing Implementation Guide > Financial Accounting > Accounts Receivable and Accounts Payable > Business Transactions > Interest Calculation > Interest Calculation > Enter Interest Values or Transaction OB83, you may maintain the interest rates (both debit and credit) for the various item interest reference interest rates.

Change View "Reference Interest Rate Values": Overview

🔧   New Entries   📄 📇 ↩ 📋 📋 📋 📇

Reference Interest Rate Values

Reference	Desc.	Valid From	Int. Rate
1I-C	Item Int Ref Cr	01.01.2020	12.0000000
1I-D	Item Int Ref Dr	01.01.2020	18.0000000
1U-C	Item Int Ref Cr	01.01.2020	2.0000000
1U-D	Item Int Ref Dr	01.01.2020	3.0000000

Figure 10.132 Interest Rate Values for Reference Interest Rates for Item Interest

On the resulting screen, click on 'New Entries' and enter the percentage of interest associated with each of the reference interest rates (like 1U-C, 1U-D, 1I-C and 1I-D) for the item interest calculation (Figure 10.132).

With this, let us complete the last step in making the settings for interest calculation, that is defining the fixed amounts for interest calculation.

10.3.12.2.4   Define Fixed Amounts for Interest Calculation

Using this configuration step, you can specify a fixed amount as a surcharge or minimum amount for the interest calculation. The fixed amount entered here will depend on the country of the company code, the interest indicator, and a validity date. The system applies this minimum amount, once for each invoice, for which interest has been calculated. You also make this applicable for each of the installments amounts that is due.

Use the menu path: SAP Customizing Implementation Guide > Financial Accounting > Accounts Receivable and Accounts Payable > Business Transactions > Interest Calculation > Interest Calculation > Define Fixed Amounts for Interest Calculation. On the resulting screen, click on 'New Entries' and maintain the details (Figure 10.133) on the next screen:

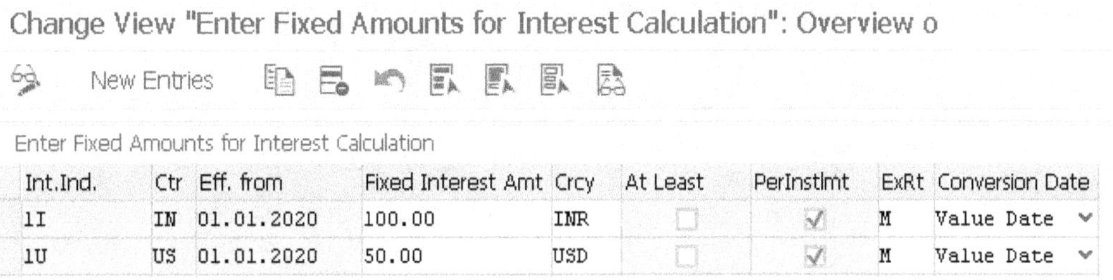

Change View "Enter Fixed Amounts for Interest Calculation": Overview o

New Entries

Enter Fixed Amounts for Interest Calculation

Int.Ind.	Ctr	Eff. from	Fixed Interest Amt	Crcy	At Least	PerInstlmt	ExRt	Conversion Date
1I	IN	01.01.2020	100.00	INR	☐	☑	M	Value Date ˅
1U	US	01.01.2020	50.00	USD	☐	☑	M	Value Date ˅

Figure 10.133 Fixed Amounts for Interest Calculation

   i.   Enter the interest indicator (Int.Ind.'), select the country ('Ctr') and fill in the effective date ('Eff.from').

   ii.   Enter the fixed interest amount ('Fixed Interest Amt') and select the currency ('Crcy').

   iii. Select the 'At Least' check-box to make this as the minimum amount. If you do not select this check-box, then, this is considered as a surcharge and added to the interest calculated by the interest program.

   iv. When you select the 'PerInstlmt' check-box, the settings are applied for each of the instalments from the business partner.

   v.   Specify the exchange rate type ('ExRt') and the 'Conversion Date' to be used for currency translation, in case of items posted in a foreign currency.

   vi. Repeat the settings for the other item interest indicator, 1I, and 'Save' the details.

> **i** Consider that you have entered $50 in the 'Fixed Interest Amt' field.
>
> *Scenario 1*: You have not selected 'At Least' check-box. Supposing that the system calculates the overdue interest as $9.97, the system adds $50 as the surcharge and customer has to pay a total interest of $59.97.
>
> *Scenario 2*: You have selected 'At Least' check-box. Supposing that the system calculates the overdue interest as $9.97, the system makes the minimum interest as $50 to be paid by the customer. However, if the overdue interest arrived at is (say, $55.67) more than the minimum amount (say, $50) the system does not add extra charge and the customer will be paying only $55.67.

This completes our settings for interest calculation in the system. Let us move on to see the settings that you will have to make for interest posting.

10.3.12.3   Interest Posting

You need to complete the following configuration steps, under this category:

- A/R: Calculation of Interest on Arrears
- Interest on Arrears Calculation (Vendors)
- A/R: Balance Interest Calculation
- A/P: Balance Interest Calculation

Let us get started with the first step: A/R: Calculation of Interest on Arrears.

10.3.12.3.1   A/R: Calculation of Interest on Arrears

Here, you will define the settings for posting the interest calculated as interest on arrears. The system carries out the account determination via the posting interface 0002 (interest on arrears). Make the required specifications for (a) account determination & posting keys, (b) G/L accounts and (c) document type.

In the case of account determination & posting keys, decide which account determination keys you need to use for the two business transactions: interest earned (1000) and interest paid (2000). The other account determination keys like company code, interest indicator and business area are all optional. Then, per account determination key, you also need to maintain the debit / credit posting key and the posting details (account symbols). Use the account symbol 1000 for customer posting. For each of the G/L accounts, you will have to specify the account allocation for interest received and interest paid; if required, you can make separate entries for different currencies. You can use the document type DA as recommended in the standard system.

Use the menu path: SAP Customizing Implementation Guide > Financial Accounting > Accounts Receivable and Accounts Payable > Business Transactions > Interest Calculation > Interest Posting > A/R: Calculation of Interest on Arrears. You may also use Transaction OBV1. On the resulting screen, you will see the default specifications from SAP; do not make any changes to the standard account determination settings (Figure 10.134).

Maintain Account Determination: Posting Specifications

Accounts   Symbols   ☐ 🗑

| Application | 0002 | Interest on A/R arrears |

Posting specifications

| Business transaction | 1000 | Interest indicator | + |
| Company code | + | Business area | + |

Debit	01	1000	Customer account	✓ Comp
Credit	50	0001	Interest revenue	✓ Comp

| Business transaction | 1100 | Interest indicator | + |
| Company code | + | Business area | + |

Debit	01	1000	Customer account	✓ Comp
Credit	50	0001	Interest revenue	✓ Comp

| Business transaction | 2000 | Interest indicator | + |
| Company code | + | Business area | + |

Debit	40	0002	Interest expense	✓ Comp
Credit	11	1000	Customer account	✓ Comp

| Business transaction | 2100 | Interest indicator | + |
| Company code | + | Business area | + |

Debit	40	0002	Interest expense	✓ Comp
Credit	11	1000	Customer account	✓ Comp

Figure 10.134 A/R: Calculation of Interest on Arrears – Account Determination Settings

Now, you may click on 'Accounts' on the 'Maintain Account Determination: Posting Specifications' screen, to maintain the required G/L accounts on the next screen (Figure 10.135) for your chart of accounts (say, BEUS). A '+' in 'Currency' field indicates, that the settings are valid for all the currencies. A masking entry of ++++++++, in the 'G/L Acct' field establishes (assuming that you want to replace the G/L account) the actual G/L account which is to be posted to, after possible modifications.

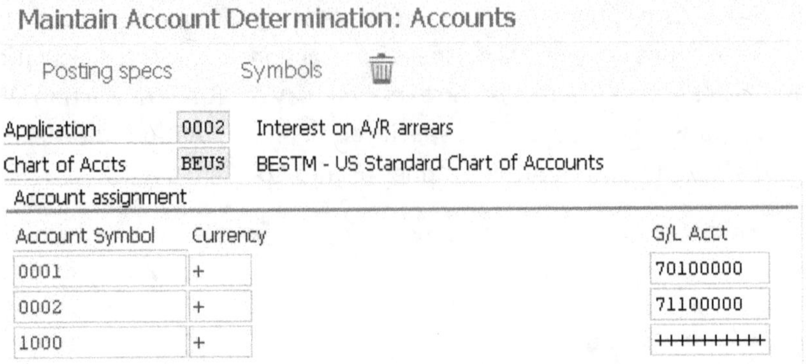

Maintain Account Determination: Accounts

Posting specs   Symbols   🗑

| Application | 0002 | Interest on A/R arrears |
| Chart of Accts | BEUS | BESTM - US Standard Chart of Accounts |

Account assignment

Account Symbol	Currency	G/L Acct
0001	+	70100000
0002	+	71100000
1000	+	++++++++++

Figure 10.135 A/R: Calculation of Interest on Arrears – G/L Accounts

You can, also, click on 'Symbols' to see the account symbols and their descriptions.

The next step is to understand the settings relating to arrears interest calculation for vendors.

10.3.12.3.2 Interest on Arrears Calculation (Vendors)

This is similar to the previous step, except that the settings relate to vendors. Here, you will use the menu path: SAP Customizing Implementation Guide > Financial Accounting > Accounts Receivable and Accounts Payable > Business Transactions > Interest Calculation > Interest Posting > Interest on Arrears Calculation (Vendors). You may also use Transaction OBV9.

Here, the system carries out the account determination via the posting interface 0009 (interest on A/P arrears).

The next step is to look at the settings for A/R balance interest calculation.

10.3.12.3.3 A/R: Balance Interest Calculation

This is also similar to the previous step discussed in Section 10.3.12.3.1 except that the posting interface will be 0005 (customer interest scale). You will use the menu path: SAP Customizing Implementation Guide > Financial Accounting > Accounts Receivable and Accounts Payable > Business Transactions > Interest Calculation > Interest Posting > A/R: Balance Interest Calculation. You may also use Transaction OBV3.

As in the previous step, you can click on 'Accounts' from the main posting specifications screen to maintain the required G/L accounts for each of the account symbols (Figure 10.136).

Figure 10.136 *A/R Balance Interest Calculation – G/L Accounts*

The various 'Account symbols' are as shown in the Figure 10.137.

Maintain Account Determination: Account Symbols

Accounts	Posting specs

Application   0005   Customer interest scale

Account symbols

Account Symbol	Description
0001	Interest received
0002	Interest paid
0011	Pt vl.min.int.earned

Figure 10.137 *A/R Balance Interest Calculation – Account Symbols*

With this, we can see the settings required for A/P balance interest calculation, next.

10.3.12.3.4 *A/P: Balance Interest Calculation*

This is similar to the previous step, except that the posting interface will be 0006 (vendor interest scale). The menu path: SAP Customizing Implementation Guide > Financial Accounting > Accounts Receivable and Accounts Payable > Business Transactions > Interest Calculation > Interest Posting > A/P: Balance Interest Calculation or Transaction OBV4, will take you to the main posting specifications screen with the default standard settings from SAP which need not be changed. As in previous steps, you just to need to maintain the required G/L accounts by clicking on 'Accounts'.

With this, we are, now, ready to see the last set of settings for configuring interest calculation: interest printout.

10.3.12.4   Printout

There are two configuration activities relating to the printout settings for interest notices:

- Assign Forms for Interest Indicators
- Define Sender Details for Interest Forms

Let us start with the first activity of assigning appropriate forms for interest notices/printouts.

10.3.12.4.1   Assign Forms for Interest Indicators

Specify which form you want the system to use, for printing the letter on interest on arrears or account balance interest, for each of the interest indicators. The system uses the forms configured, here, if no other form has been specified when calculating interest.

Use the menu path: SAP Customizing Implementation Guide > Financial Accounting > Accounts Receivable and Accounts Payable > Business Transactions > Interest Calculation > Printout > Assign Forms for Interest Indicators. You may also use Transaction OB84.

On the resulting screen, click on 'New Entries' and maintain the appropriate form per interest indicator per company code; the form can be 'SAPScript Form' or a 'Smart Form'. Repeat the entries to cover all the company codes and all the interest indicators (Figure 10.138).

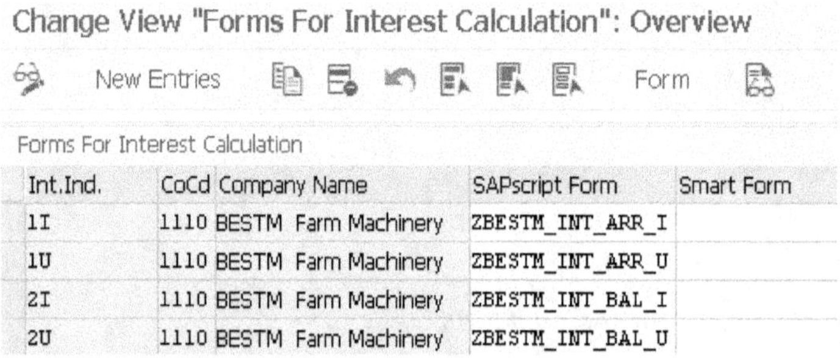

Change View "Forms For Interest Calculation": Overview

New Entries   Form

Forms For Interest Calculation

Int.Ind.	CoCd	Company Name	SAPscript Form	Smart Form
1I	1110	BESTM Farm Machinery	ZBESTM_INT_ARR_I	
1U	1110	BESTM Farm Machinery	ZBESTM_INT_ARR_U	
2I	1110	BESTM Farm Machinery	ZBESTM_INT_BAL_I	
2U	1110	BESTM Farm Machinery	ZBESTM_INT_BAL_U	

Figure 10.138 Forms for Interest Calculation

The next activity is to define the sender details for the interest forms.

10.3.12.4.2   Define Sender Details for Interest Forms

This step is the same as what we have already discussed in <u>Section 10.3.7.3.4</u>, when we talked about the printout settings for dunning / interest notices. You will define the standard texts for the header, the footer, and the sender address in the letter window for each company code. You may use the menu path: SAP Customizing Implementation Guide > Financial Accounting > Accounts Receivable and Accounts Payable > Business Transactions > Interest Calculation > Printout > Define Sender Details for Interest Forms.

This completes our discussion on settings required for interest calculation. Let us, next, see the settings associated with closing operations.

10.3.13   Closing

You can group the configuration settings for various closing activities, for FI-A/R and FI-A/P, under the following three categories:

1. Count
2. Valuate
3. Reclassify

Let us start with the first category of settings.

10.3.13.1   Count

We have already discussed the required settings for 'Cross-System Intercompany Reconciliation' when we discussed the 'Check/Count' as a part of closing operations in G/L Accounting in Section 9.5.2.1 of Chapter 9 of Vol. I. However, you can make the required settings for balance confirmation correspondence here.

10.3.13.1.1 Balance Confirmation Correspondence

You can make settings relating to the reply address for balance confirmation besides specifying the selection criteria for balance confirmation, here. Let us start with the definition of reply address, per company code, for handling balance confirmations.

10.3.13.1.1.1   Define Reply Addresses for Balance Confirmation

Define the address to which you want your customers or vendors to send their balance confirmation reply. Normally, this address will be different from the company code address. You can define several addresses, for every company code. Once defined, you can specify the required ID, for every run of the balance confirmation.

You may use the menu path: SAP Customizing Implementation Guide > Financial Accounting > Accounts Receivable and Accounts Payable > Business Transactions > Closing > Count > Balance Confirmation Correspondence > Define Reply Addresses for Balance Confirmation. On the resulting screen, click on 'New Entries' and enter the company code ('CoCd') and 'Address ID' on the next screen (Figure 10.139). When you 'save', the system will prompt you to provide the address details for the new address ID. You can define more than one such address ID, per company code.

Figure 10.139 Address Data for Reply Addresses for Balance Confirmation

We can now complete the next step to add more selection criteria fields, for balance confirmation.

10.3.13.1.1.2   Specify Selection Criteria for Balance Confirmation

Here, you can choose the additional selection criteria which you may need for the balance confirmation (for the report SAPF130D), besides the standard ones.

Use the menu path: SAP Customizing Implementation Guide > Financial Accounting > Accounts Receivable and Accounts Payable > Business Transactions > Closing > Count > Balance Confirmation Correspondence > Specify Selection Criteria for Balance Confirmation or Transaction FSSP:

   i.   On the resulting screen, enter the 'Account Type' and press 'Enter' to continue.
  ii.   On the next 'Change Selection Criteria for Balance Confirmation' screen, the system brings up the list of fields from which you can select the additional fields, to add to the existing selection criteria for the report.
 iii.   On this screen, place the cursor on the field which you want to add and click on 'Select' button or press F9 to add. Repeat to add more fields, and 'Save' when completed.

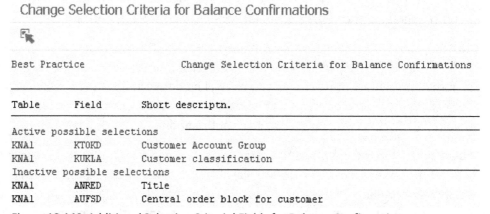

Figure 10.140 Additional Selection Criterial Fields for Balance Confirmation

When you run the report SAPF130D (Transaction F.17), you can see that the two fields (Customer Account Group - NA1KTOKD, and Customer Classification - NA1KUKLA), which we just included, have now been added to the selection criteria screen (Figure 10.141).

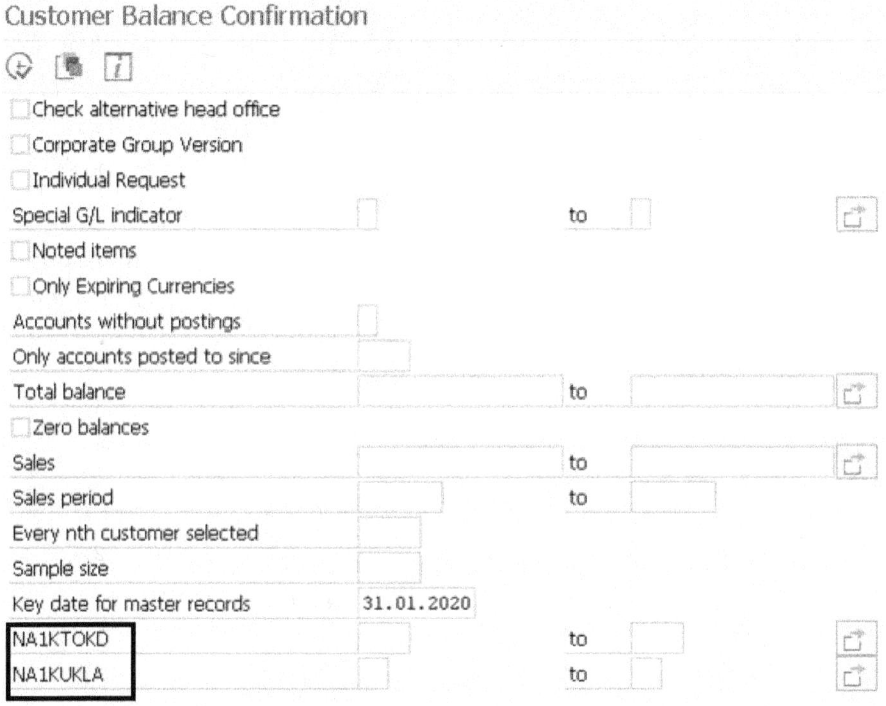

Customer Balance Confirmation

Check alternative head office
Corporate Group Version
Individual Request
Special G/L indicator   to
Noted items
Only Expiring Currencies
Accounts without postings
Only accounts posted to since
Total balance   to
Zero balances
Sales   to
Sales period   to
Every nth customer selected
Sample size
Key date for master records   31.01.2020
NA1KTOKD   to
NA1KUKLA   to

Figure 10.141 Additional Selection Criteria Fields for Balance Confirmation (Transaction F.17)

With this, we are now ready to discuss the settings for the next closing operation, 'valuate'.

10.3.13.2 Valuate

Under valuate, you need to make settings for foreign currency valuation and general valuation. Let us start with the foreign currency valuation.

10.3.13.2.1 Foreign Currency Valuation

We have already discussed and made the required settings for foreign currency valuation in Section 9.5.2.2 of Chapter 9 of Vol. I. Let us, now, make the settings for general valuation.

10.3.13.2.2 Valuations

The following are the settings that you need to make, as a part of 'valuate' closing operation:

- Define Value Adjustment Key
- Define Interest Calculation Types
- Define Accounts
- Determine Base Value
- Determine Values for Line Item Display

Let us start with the first step of defining value adjustment key.

10.3.13.2.2.1   Define Value Adjustment Key

The value adjustment key determines (a) whether you want to execute a valuation for a different valuation area, (b) the percentage of the provision for the value adjustment calculation and (c) whether the calculation is to be based on country and due date. Using this configuration step, you can define a value adjustment key based on country or due date. Once defined, you then enter the value adjustment key in the customer master record.

Use the menu path: SAP Customizing Implementation Guide > Financial Accounting > Accounts Receivable and Accounts Payable > Business Transactions > Closing > Valuate > Valuations > Define Value Adjustment Key. On the resulting screen, click on 'New Entries' and maintain the required settings on the next screen (Figure 10.142):

Change View "Maintain Accumulated Depreciation Key": Overview of Se

New Entries

Maintain Accumulated Depreciation Key

Value Adj. Key	Valuati...	Ctr	Days	Future	Debit...	Valuate Manually	Ext....	PT
B0			60	☐	3.000	☐		Net amount
B0			90	☐	5.000	☐		Net amount
R1	B2	US	30	☐	3.000	☐		Net amount
R1	B2	US	60	☐	5.000	☐		Net amount
R1	B2	US	90	☐	7.000	☐		Net amount

Figure 10.142 Value Adjustment Keys

i.   Enter the value adjustment key ('Value Adj. Key'), and the type of valuation ('Valuation'). If you leave the 'Valuation' field as blank, then it is valid for all the valuations; if you fill in a particular valuation (say, B2 – For IAS/US GAAP) that you have defined earlier, then, the valuation adjustment entry is valid only for that GAAP.

ii.   Enter the country ('Ctr'), and the 'Days' of overdue which is the difference between key date and the due date for net payment. Based on the overdue days, you may have a graduated scale of debit interest which you will enter in 'Debit Int. Rate' field.

iii. Select 'Valuate Manually' check-box, if you want to determine the provision for unsecured receivables manually; in that case, you do not need to enter the percentage interest rate. Though the system selects the open item during valuation, the interest is not calculated automatically.

iv.   If you do not want a standard valuation adjustment, but want to use some external valuation, then enter that detail in 'Ext. Valuation'. Select the appropriate posting type ('PT') for the adjustment posting. Let this be 'Net amount'.

v.   Repeat and define all the value adjustment keys for different overdue duration and 'Save' the settings.

With this, we are ready to discuss the next step of defining interest calculation types.

10.3.13.2.2.2 Define Interest Calculation Types

We have already defined the interest calculation types both for item (arrears) interest and account balance interest calculation, vide Section 10.3.12.1.1 of this Chapter.

We can now move on to define the accounts for valuation adjustments.

10.3.13.2.2.3 Define Accounts

Here, in this step, you will define an adjustment account and a target account, per reconciliation account, for the transactions 'Receivables discounting' (B02) and 'Flat-rate individual value adjustment' (B03). The system makes the postings, per business area, and the documents are reversed in the following period.

Use 'Transaction' B98 (User-defined valuation I) and B99 (User-defined valuation II) if you want to use your own algorithms. In the case of posting procedure 'Flat-rate individual value adjustment' (B03), you define a write-off account for the value adjustment (correction account) and an account for writing off receivables and payables (target account). In the case of 'Receivables discounting' (B02) posting procedure, define a write-off account for discounting (correction account) and an account for expenses from value adjustment on receivables (target account).

Use the menu path: SAP Customizing Implementation Guide > Financial Accounting > Accounts Receivable and Accounts Payable > Business Transactions > Closing > Valuate > Valuations > Define Accounts. You may also use Transaction OBB0. On the resulting screen, you will see the different valuation procedures for the value adjustment group HWA (Figure 10.143).

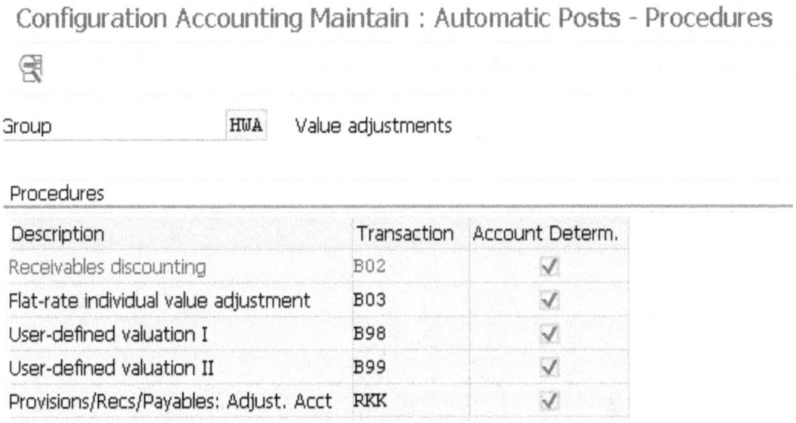

Configuration Accounting Maintain : Automatic Posts - Procedures

Group   HWA   Value adjustments

Procedures

Description	Transaction	Account Determ.
Receivables discounting	B02	✓
Flat-rate individual value adjustment	B03	✓
User-defined valuation I	B98	✓
User-defined valuation II	B99	✓
Provisions/Recs/Payables: Adjust. Acct	RKK	✓

Figure 10.143 Value Adjustment Procedures

Double-click on a selected 'Procedure' and enter the chart of accounts (say, BEUS). On the next screen (Figure 10.144), enter the adjustment G/L account and target G/L account, for each of the reconciliation accounts and 'Save' the details.

Figure 10.144 Account Assignment for a Value Adjustment Procedure

You may click on 'Posting Key' to look at the default posting keys in the standard system for the automatic postings. The next step is to determine the base value amount for the valuation methods.

10.3.13.2.2.4   Determine Base Value

Here, in this step, you will define the base amount for valuation per value adjustment method. For example, for the valuation method 3 'Flat-rate individual value adjustment (B03)', the discounted local currency amount (basis = 2) will be used as the base amount. Similarly, for the valuation method 2 'Receivables discounting (B02)', the system will use the foreign currency valuation (basis = 1). If you do not enter a value in 'Base Amt' field, then, the system uses the local currency.

Use the menu path: SAP Customizing Implementation Guide > Financial Accounting > Accounts Receivable and Accounts Payable > Business Transactions > Closing > Valuate > Valuations > Determine Base Value. On the resulting screen (Figure 10.145), click on 'New Entries' and maintain the basis ('BaseAmt') per valuation 'Method'.

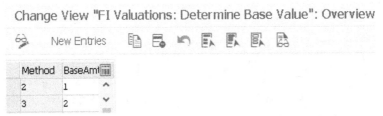

Figure 10.145 Base Value Determination per Valuation Method

The final configuration step, in valuations, is to determine the values for line item display.

10.3.13.2.2.5   Determine Values for Line Item Display

Here, in this step, you can determine which values you want the system to display in the 'Valuation difference' field in the line item display. Per 'valuation area, currency type and valuation method' combination, you can display up to six values in the line item display.

Use the menu path: SAP Customizing Implementation Guide > Financial Accounting > Accounts Receivable and Accounts Payable > Business Transactions > Closing > Valuate > Valuations > Determine Values for Line Item Display. On the resulting screen, click on 'New Entries', enter the 'Table' (say, BSBV), select the 'Field Name' and maintain the other details like currency type, 'Valuation' (local GAAP or IAS etc) and the valuation 'Method' (for example, 'Flat-rate individual value adjustment'). 'Save' the details and repeat to maintain other values (up to a maximum of six).

This completes our discussion on the settings required for 'valuate' closing operation. Let us see the next item in closing, namely 'reclassify'.

10.3.13.3   Reclassify

We have already discussed the settings required under 'reclassify' for transferring and sorting A/R and A/P while configuring the SAP G/L Accounting, vide Section 9.5.2.3 in Chapter 9 of Vol. I.

This completes our discussion on the configuration settings for closing operations. This also completes our discussion on configuring business transactions in FI-A/P and FI-A/R.

Let us move on to discuss the configuration settings required for information system.

10.4 Information System

You will come across several evaluations that are defined for customers and vendors, in the standard SAP system. You can make a selection from the standard evaluations to suit your needs, and you can enhance the same by including additional characteristics. However, you cannot define new evaluations, here. Use the drilldown reports to define new reports.

You need to complete the configuration settings discussed in the following Section to make use of the standard evaluations. Let us first discuss the standard evaluations.

10.4.1 Standard Evaluations

Maintain the appropriate configuration by completing the following steps:

- Copy Standard Evaluations
- Select Standard Evaluations
- Enhance Standard Evaluations

Let us start with the copying of standard evaluations.

10.4.1.1   Copy Standard Evaluations

You need to copy the standard evaluations from the source system (client 000) to your productive system. Use the menu path: SAP Customizing Implementation Guide > Financial Accounting > Accounts Receivable and Accounts Payable > Information System > Accounts Receivable > Standard Evaluations > Valuations > Copy Standard Evaluations. You can also use Transaction FY01.

On the resulting screen, click 'Yes' on the 'Customizing Transfer' pop-up screen, to copy the standard evaluations to your productive SAP client. The system carries out the copying and brings up a log on the next screen. Use Transaction SCC3, and double-click on the log entry on the resulting screen to view the details (Figure 10.146) of what has been copied.

Client Copy/Transport Log Analysis

Details   File Log

Target Client	400
Source Client (incl. Auth.)	000
Source Client User Master	000
Copy Type	Local Copy
Profile	SAP_UCUS
Status	Completed
User	SAP*
Start on	02.10.2019 / 07:23:57
Last Entry on	02.10.2019 / 09:18:52
Statistics for this run	
- Number of Tables	113145 of 113146
- Deleted Rows	24
- Copied Rows	4968078

Figure 10.146 Copying Standard Evaluations

Now that we have copied and made available the standard evaluations in the target client, we can continue to set up the system for standard evaluations. The next step will be selecting the standard evaluation views that you may require for your business.

10.4.1.2   Select Standard Evaluations

To complete selection of standard evaluations to meet your reporting needs of A/R and A/P information system, you need to complete a 3-step procedure that includes (1) evaluation views, (2) evaluation types and (3) evaluations.

You will use the 'evaluation view' to determine what volume of data is to be evaluated. For this, you have to create a selection variant for the relevant account types (D and K) for the specified data retrieval program (RFDRRSEL for customer standard evaluations, and RFKRRSEL for vendor standard evaluations).

> **i** Using the *evaluation view*, you can make an organizational distinction between the evaluations. For example, you may need two subgroups for meeting the requirements as in the case of BESTM. One subgroup will be for use by company codes in USA, and the other for use by the company codes in India. For both the subgroups, you can define separate selection variants (specifying the appropriate company codes), for each of the data retrieval reports, covering customer and vendor evaluations.

Once you have maintained the evaluation views, you can then define which 'evaluation types' you want to use per evaluation view. The standard SAP system provides you with the following evaluation types:

- Currency risk
- DSO analysis (for customers)
- Due date structure
- Overdue items
- Payment history (for customers)
- Terms offered/terms taken (for customers)

Finally, under 'evaluations', you determine the characteristics (say, country, industry, or accounting clerk), for each evaluation type, the system should use to format the evaluations. For this, you need to enter a 'Selection variant' for the program for 'Selection' under 'Reports' for the given 'Evaluation Version' (Figure 10.150). Using the variant, you specify (a) the grouping field, which groups together the selected data and (b) the maximum number of accounts (or documents) that are to be displayed in the ranking lists of the evaluation. In the standard system, for example, selection variants are provided for the company code, business area and country fields.

Let us configure the settings for the selection of standard evaluations.

Use the menu path: SAP Customizing Implementation Guide > Financial Accounting > Accounts Receivable and Accounts Payable > Information System > Accounts Receivable > Standard Evaluations > Valuations > Select Standard Evaluations. You may also use Transaction OBDF.

i. On the resulting screen, you will see two standard evaluation views (for customer and vendor) defined already by SAP. Copy these to create two new customer evaluation views (one for US and another for India) and two new vendor evaluation views (one for US and another for India). When you copy the system creates all the associated evaluation types and evaluations for each evaluation views (Figure 10.147).

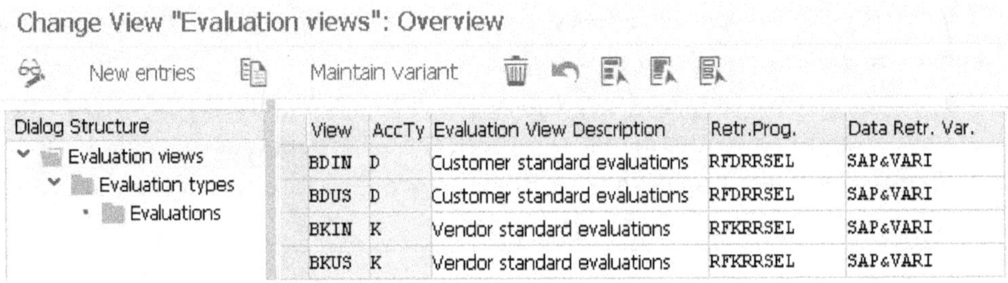

Change View "Evaluation views": Overview

View	AccTy	Evaluation View Description	Retr.Prog.	Data Retr. Var.
BDIN	D	Customer standard evaluations	RFDRRSEL	SAP&VARI
BDUS	D	Customer standard evaluations	RFDRRSEL	SAP&VARI
BKIN	K	Vendor standard evaluations	RFKRRSEL	SAP&VARI
BKUS	K	Vendor standard evaluations	RFKRRSEL	SAP&VARI

Figure 10.147 Evelution Views for BESTM

ii. Now, select a specific row and double-click on 'Evaluation types' on the left hand side 'Dialog Structure'. You will see the various evaluation types on the 'Change View "Evaluation types": Overview' screen (Figure 10.148). You can decide which are all the evaluation types you need, and delete the ones which you may not need. For BESTM, we are not deleting anyone but retain all the six evaluation types, as required by the management of BESTM.

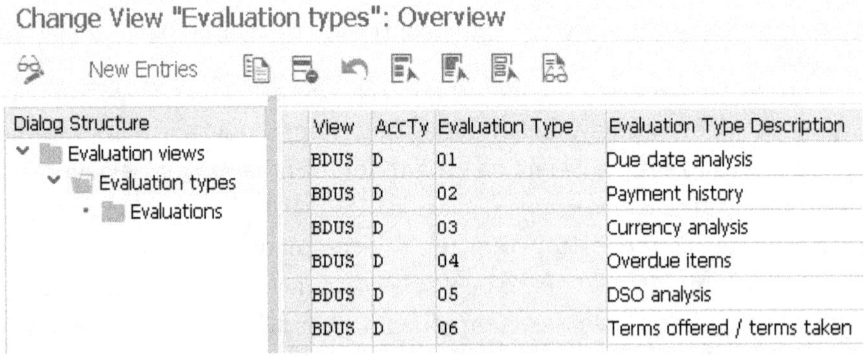

Change View "Evaluation types": Overview

View	AccTy	Evaluation Type	Evaluation Type Description
BDUS	D	01	Due date analysis
BDUS	D	02	Payment history
BDUS	D	03	Currency analysis
BDUS	D	04	Overdue items
BDUS	D	05	DSO analysis
BDUS	D	06	Terms offered / terms taken

Figure 10.148 Customer Evelution Types for BESTM

iii. You may highlight any of the rows and double-click on 'Evaluations' on the left hand side 'Dialog Structure' to see the evaluations that are associated with that evaluation type. On the next screen (Figure 10.149), you will see the different evaluations (known as 'Version') for the evaluation type (it is being called as evaluation category 'EvalCat' here) 02 – Payment history, for example.

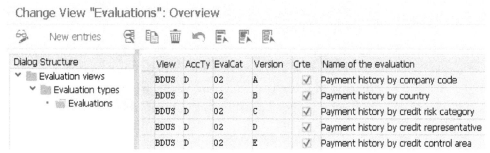

Figure 10.149 Customer Evaluations for BESTM

iv.   Select a row and click on 'Details' to view the settings associated with that evaluation on the next screen (Figure 10.150):

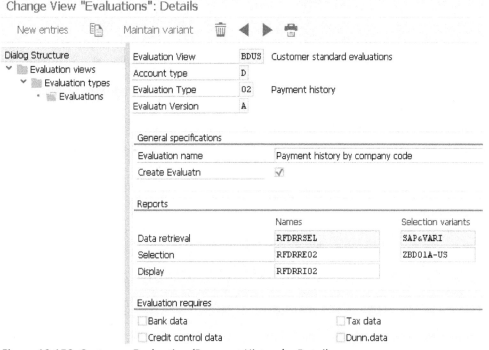

Figure 10.150 Customer Evaluation 'Payment History' – Details

- Under 'General specifications', you will see the 'Evaluation' name. You will also notice the 'Create Evaluatn' check-box, which when selected instructs the system to generate the evaluation during next evaluation run.
- You will see the name of the reports (for data retrieval, selections and display) and the associated 'Selection variants' under the 'Reports' data block. Note that we have created a new variant ZBD01A-US, with all the company codes of BESTM in USA, for the 'Selection' report RFDRRE02. You can customize the

'Selection variant' to include all or select company codes or credit control areas, for example.

- We have not selected any of the flags like 'Bank data', 'Tax date', 'Credit control data' or 'Dunn.data' under 'Evaluation requires' data block, as reading the data of these respective areas may have a negative effect on the system performance when creating evaluations.

You can also enhance the standard evaluations. Let us look at that, now.

10.4.1.3   Enhance Standard Evaluations

You may use SAP enhancement RFDRRANZ for enhancing the standard evaluations. For example, you may want to group the evaluations from the A/R information system, according to the 'Customer classification' field (KNA1-KUKLA). You can use the enhancement route to achieve this. Similarly, for A/P, you have to use the enhancement RFKRRANZ. For example, you may want to group the evaluations from the A/P information system according to the 'Industry' field (LFA1-BRSCH). Again, you can use the enhancement route to achieve this.

In either case, Use the menu path: SAP Customizing Implementation Guide > Financial Accounting > Accounts Receivable and Accounts Payable > Information System > Accounts Receivable > Standard Evaluations > Valuations > Enhance Standard Evaluations. You may also use Transaction CMOD. On the resulting screen, create a new 'Project' or use an existing one, use SAP enhancement RFDRRANZ, activate and modify the source code EXIT_ RFDRRANZ_0001 to enhance the standard evaluation to suit your exact business needs (Figure 10.151)

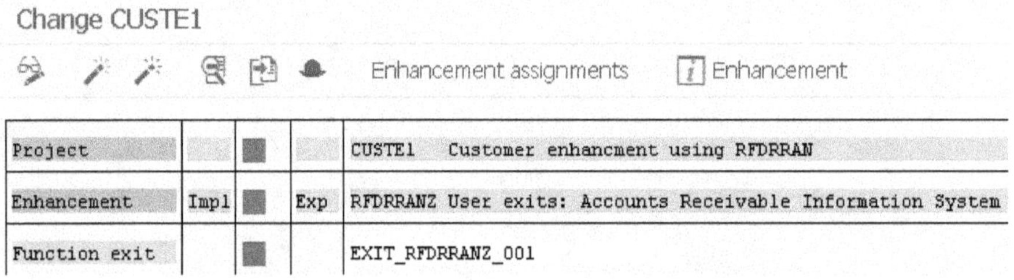

Change CUSTE1

⊗ ⚘ ⚘ ⬚ ⬚ ☁   Enhancement assignments   ⓘ Enhancement

Project		■		CUSTE1 Customer enhancment using RFDRRAN	
Enhancement	Impl	■	Exp	RFDRRANZ User exits: Accounts Receivable Information System	
Function exit		■		EXIT_RFDRRANZ_001	

Figure 10.151 Enhancement of Standard Evaluation – Customer

> ℹ️ What we have discussed in Section 10.4.1 is common for both A/R and A/P though you will see two different entries in IMG as 'Accounts Receivable > Standard Evaluations' and 'Accounts Payable > Standard Evaluations'.

This completes our discussion on standard evaluations of both customers and vendors, and also completes our discussion on information system for A/R and A/P. And, by this we have completed this Chapter discussing the configuration settings for FI-A/R and FI-A/P.

10.5 Conclusion

We started this Chapter with the understanding that the accounts receivable (FI-A/R) and accounts payable (FI-A/P) components of SAP, integrated fully with the SAP General Ledger Accounting (SAP G/L), help you in dealing with the customers and vendors, respectively, for managing the amounts that your business would receive from (customers) and pay to (vendors).

We discussed both the customer and vendor accounts, and you understood the preparations in terms of account groups, screen layout, message control, number ranges etc., for creating the master records of the business partners. You understood that a typical customer master record is made up of four data segments namely the general data, the company code area data, the sales & distribution area data and the ETM (Equipment and Tools Management) data. You, further, understood that you can create the customer master record, in SAP, in three different ways: central maintenance (for all the areas), FI maintenance (for FI area or company code area alone) and sales data maintenance (for SD area alone). Similar to the customer master data, you saw that a vendor master record is made up of three distinct data segments: general data, company code area data and purchasing organization data. And, you also saw that you can create the vendor data also in three ways, as in the case of customer master records: centralised creation (for all the three area), FI maintenance (company code area data alone) and purchasing organization data maintenance (for MM area alone). You learned how the account groups play a major role in maintenance of these master data, both for customer and vendor. You also saw how to change or delete a customer / vendor master.

In the case of customers, besides the general specifications, you understood what are the sensitive fields and the need for dual control of these fields. You learned about the settings that are required, for both customers and vendors, for displaying line items, for open item processing and for correspondence.

Under business transactions, you have been exposed to the various configuration settings that you have to make for handling incoming / outgoing invoices, incoming / outgoing payments, processing down payments, open item clearing, adjustment posting/reversal, dunning, interest calculation and closing activities. You also learned about the settings that are required for document parking, and its subsequent release using approval groups, approval path and approval procedure.

You learned in details about the global settings that are required for outgoing / incoming payments, during which you understood defining of various accounts for handling discount (taken / given), overpayments / underpayments, exchange rate differences, rounding off differences, translation settings, payment block reasons, payment terms and so on. You also learned about the settings required for both manual and automatic payments. While discussing manual outgoing payments, you learned about the vendor tolerances, reason codes and also on how to prepare the system for handling cross-company code manual payments. In configuring the automatic payment program, which can handle both incoming and outgoing payments, you saw how to set up: the house banks, all / payment company codes for payment transactions, the different payment methods etc. You understood how the system determines a suitable bank for a given payment transactions, besides understanding the value date rules, payment groupings, automatic payment posting etc. You did understand how the automatic payment program works from selecting the open item payables, to selecting the appropriate payment method, house bank, account and finally making and posting the payments, besides creating the payment media for electronic data transfer.

You learned about SEPA mandates and the associated configuration. You also learned about the payments through payment cards and the settings that you may need to make on the FI side of payment card integration with SAP SD.

You learned dunning in detail. You saw the basic settings, including dunning areas, dunning keys, dunning block reasons and dunning forms. You understood when you need to configure dunning, per dunning area. While discussing the dunning procedure, you saw that this is at the heart of the dunning program controlling how the program duns the business partners. You, further, saw that the dunning procedure contains specifications like dunning frequency / dunning interval, grace days, minimum number of days for open items to be dunned, the number of dunning levels (with the level determining the form and text of the dunning notice) and also the specifications as to whether to dun standard and/or Special G/L transactions. For the dunning notice printouts, you understood defining of dunning forms and maintaining the sender details for those forms.

In interest calculation, you learned about the item (or arrears) interest calculation, the settings associated with that in terms of interest calculation types, reference interest rates, time-dependent terms, interest values etc. You also learned about the automatic account determination settings for item and balance interest calculation for both A/R and A/P. You did learn about the forms for interest printout and the associated settings.

While discussing the configuration settings for closing operations, you learned about settings for balance confirmation, settings for valuation in terms of valuation adjustment keys and determination of base value for valuation.

Towards the end of the Chapter, you learned about the settings you will require to make use of SAP's standard evaluations, for customers and vendors, as a part of A/R and A/P information system. You learned how to copy the standard evaluations to your productive system, how to select and enhance the required standard evaluations to meet your business reporting.

This completes our discussion on accounts receivable (FI-A/R) and accounts payable (FI-A/P). We shall discuss 'Contract Accounts Receivable and Payable' in the next Chapter.

11 Contract Accounts Receivable and Payable

The Contract Accounts Receivable and Payable (SAP FICA or FI-CA) is a subledger accounting in SAP. It is for processing large document volumes in terms of master data and business transactions, with both typical and improved/additional A/R functionalities. You can use SAP FICA to take care of businesses in certain industries like public sector, utilities, insurance, telecommunications etc., wherein you need the capability to handle large volume of business partners and documents for processing, without having to face any performance issue. It offers highly automated range of functions for managing business processes through SAP Industry Solution (SAP IS). Suitable for worldwide implementation, SAP FICA can handle various statutory requirements of taxation and accounting, together with country-specific processes like payment transactions, across the world.

SAP FICA is tightly integrated with SAP's other components like FI (Financial Accounting), CO (Controlling) (CO), CRM (Customer Relationship Management), SD (Sales and Distribution), FSCM (Financial Supply Chain and Management), Funds Management (PSM-FM), Cash Management, Flexible Real Estate Management (RE-FX) etc. It has the capability to deal with customers and payments over the internet by using SAP Biller Direct and EBPP (Electronic Bill Presentment and Payment).

The industry-neutral FICA (came into being in 2002) is also known as Extended FI-CA. As a subledger, you can use the Extended FI-CA as an alternate to the regular FI-A/R and FI-A/P applications, even if you do not operate in any of the high transaction volume industries / businesses.

However, on the downside, the weak point of SAP FICA is its limited reporting functionality because of the huge data size. For this reason, it may be necessary that you need to go in for the installation of SAP BW (Business Information Warehouse) together with SAP FICA.

For our discussion on SAP FICA, in this Chapter, we shall limit to the following topics:

- Organizational Units
- Basic Functions
- Business Transactions
- Integration

> **i** Note that we will not be covering the entire A to Z of configuration for SAP FICA, in this Chapter. We shall only try to give you some understanding and settings for FICA.

Let us start with the organizational units.

11.1 Organizational Units

Before going ahead with the configuration of other settings to make use SAP FICA component for your business, you need to suitably configure the required organizational units for FICA. You have to complete the following configuration activities:

- Set Up Company Codes for Contract Accounts Receivable and Payable
- Define Company Code Groups
- Assign Company Codes to Company Code Groups
- Enter Translation Date for Postings in Foreign Currency

> **i** We will not be using our regular case study of 'Project Dolphin' to demonstrate how to configure SAP FICA, as BESTM's line of business does not call for usage of SAP FICA. Instead, we shall discuss the settings using another case study called 'Project Starfish'. We have already completed configuring the enterprise structure, company code global parameters, chart of accounts, G/L master data etc for Digifone (Project Starfish), and will not repeat those settings, here, as they are similar to what we have discussed for Project Dolphin in the respective Chapters.

Project Starfish

'Digifone', an ABG group company, is USA's leading telecom service provider, providing pan America voice and data services across 2G, 3G, 4G (and the proposed 5G) platforms. Through a large spectrum of portfolio supporting data and voice, the company is committed to usher in customer delight in digital experience by connecting millions and millions across USA. The company is always in the forefront, developing cutting-edge infrastructure to deliver newer and smarter technologies, for both retail and enterprise customers.

Headquartered in Sacramento, California, the Digifone Corporate operates through two companies namely Digifone and Digiband. While Digifone handles voice in the form of landline, mobile, wireless and satellite telephony besides taking care of customer requirements in the area of broadband connectivity, the other company 'Digiband' is involved more in the digital entertainment business including DTH (direct to home), OTT (over the top) platform besides creating digital consumer content for broadcasting.

As both the companies handle millions and millions of customers and transactions, the project team of Starfish has been appointed by the Digifone Corporate to implement SAP FICA so as to reap the benefits from functionalities like EBPP, flexible credit management, dispute handling etc.

ABG group, besides the two entities, Digifone and Digiband operating in telecommunications industry, has several other company codes that operate in different industries /sectors. Accordingly, the corporate group has decided to go in for SAP S/4HANA implementation without any specific industry flavour. Hence, for Digifone and Digiband, it has been recommended to activate Extended FI-CA rather than using IS-Telecommunications.

We have already defined the Digifone Corporate with a company ID of D1000. Under this company, we have configured two company codes: Digifone (D900) and Digiband (D910).

Let us now start with the first configuration activity of setting up the company codes for FICA.

11.1.1 Set Up Company Codes for Contract Accounts Receivable and Payable

Here, we will define the settings for the two company codes of Digifone Corporate, to use SAP FICA component; in the process, we will also make the required configuration to control the postings in FICA for these company codes.

Project Starfish

It has been clarified to the project team, by the Digifone Corporate, that the following has to be taken into account while configuring SAP FICA:

The configuration should allow account assignment to a 'Profit Center' while processing items for a business partner. The tax items are to be updated in SAP G/L, in accordance with their distribution to different G/L account assignments like 'Segment', 'Business Area', and 'Profit Center', but with no separate tax reporting. It should be possible to enter the 'Segment' in FICA documents when it is not a derived field. The system should post the 'payments on account' in the same company code in which the bank posting was also created. Also, the system should account the 'payments on account' as down payments. A payment, from a customer, can be used to clear a number of open items in the contract account, and the system should post the contract account automatically whenever payment orders are reversed. Besides extended withholding tax, the Cash Flow Analysis should also be made active. The outgoing payment and reconciliation should be carried out in SAP FICA itself, and only the totals posted to the G/L so as to reduce the load on the SAP G/L Accounting side. A total invoice should contain all receivable items and there should be no retroactive clearing allowed in FICA. The disputes need to be handled via SAP Dispute Management (FIN-FSM-DM). The foreign currency valuation should be carried out in the first local currency. The 'Factoring' should be enabled. The tax reporting date should be set to the posting date.

To configure setting up of company codes for FICA:

Use the menu path: SAP Customizing Implementation Guide > Financial Accounting > Contract Accounts Receivable and Payable > Organizational Units > Set Up Company Codes for Contract Accounts Receivable and Payable. You may also use Transaction S_KK4_74002390. On the resulting screen, click on 'New Entries' and make the settings on the next screen (Figure 11.1):

i.   Enter the company code (D900, for example).

ii.   Under 'Account Assignments for G/L Accounting' data block:

- Select 'Allowed' for the field 'Profit Center in Business Partner Items', so as to allow account assignment to a profit center while posting items for a business partner.

- The 'Tax Items' field will be used to specify if tax items are updated in SAP G/L in accordance with their distribution to different G/L account assignments like segment, business area, and profit center. The distribution is normally proportional to the amounts in the revenue or expense items with the same tax code. If tax items are to distributed in combination with separate recording of tax data, then, you have to indicate that specifically here in the 'Tax Items' field by selecting the option 2 'Distribution Active, Separate Tax Reporting Data'.

- Select 'Segment Posting Optional' check-box, to enter the segment in FI-CA documents when it is not a mandatory / derived field.

iii. Under 'Posting and Processing of Payments' data block:

- The check-box 'Pymts on Acct in Stnd. Co. code', when selected, indicates that the system will create the business partner items in the standard company code (say, D900) in cases of 'payment on account' (POA). In this case, when you reset clearing, the system posts the payment to an account that is involved in clearing as POA, and the system determines the standard company code as the company code for posting. If you do not select the check-box, the system posts the POA in the same company code (say, D910) in which the bank posting was also created; when you reset clearing, the payment amount is posted in a company code involved in clearing.

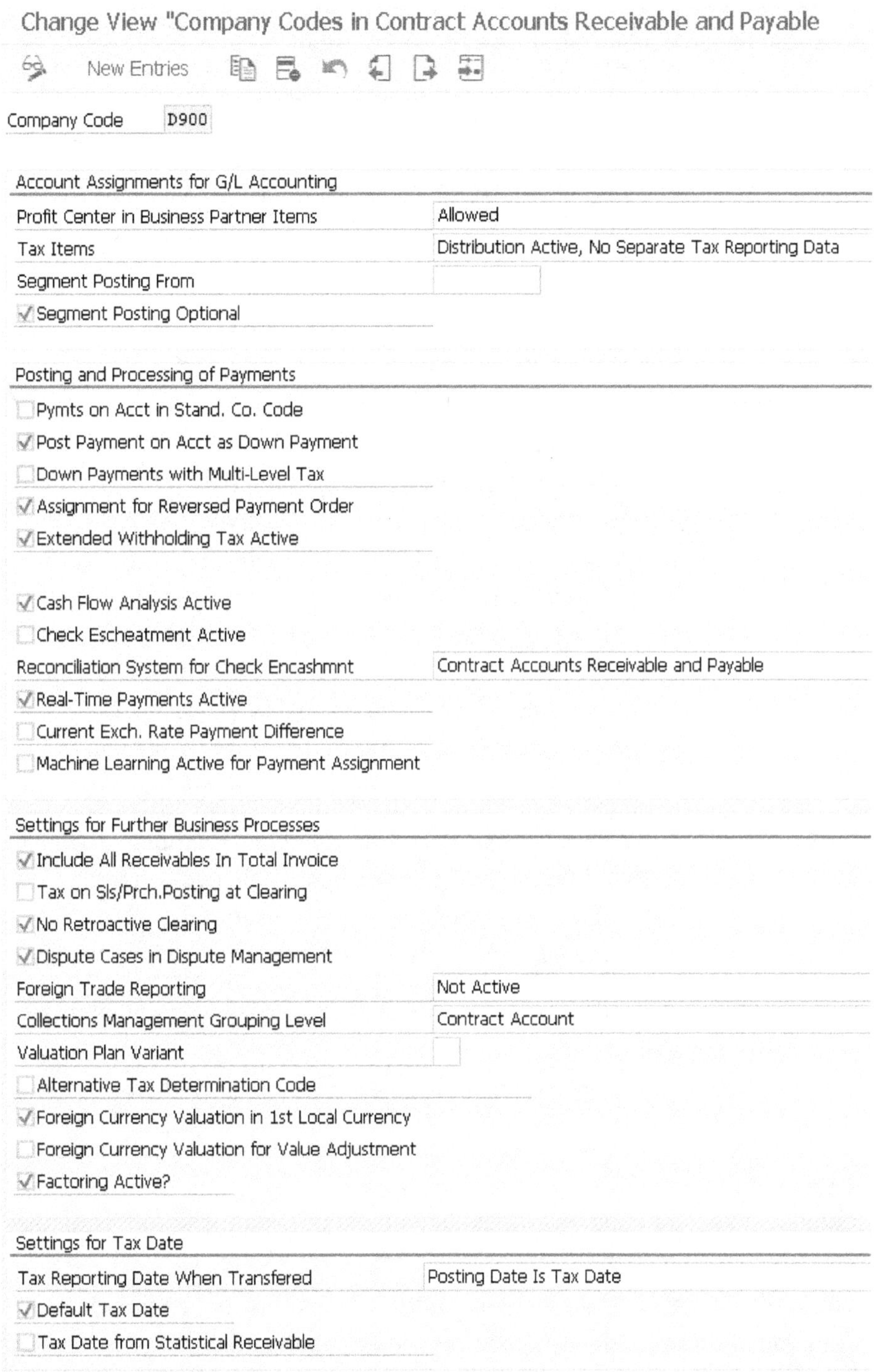

Change View "Company Codes in Contract Accounts Receivable and Payable

    New Entries

Company Code   D900

Account Assignments for G/L Accounting

Profit Center in Business Partner Items	Allowed
Tax Items	Distribution Active, No Separate Tax Reporting Data
Segment Posting From	
☑ Segment Posting Optional	

Posting and Processing of Payments

☐ Pymts on Acct in Stand. Co. Code
☑ Post Payment on Acct as Down Payment
☐ Down Payments with Multi-Level Tax
☑ Assignment for Reversed Payment Order
☑ Extended Withholding Tax Active

☑ Cash Flow Analysis Active
☐ Check Escheatment Active

Reconciliation System for Check Encashmnt	Contract Accounts Receivable and Payable

☑ Real-Time Payments Active
☐ Current Exch. Rate Payment Difference
☐ Machine Learning Active for Payment Assignment

Settings for Further Business Processes

☑ Include All Receivables In Total Invoice
☐ Tax on Sls/Prch.Posting at Clearing
☑ No Retroactive Clearing
☑ Dispute Cases in Dispute Management

Foreign Trade Reporting	Not Active
Collections Management Grouping Level	Contract Account
Valuation Plan Variant	

☐ Alternative Tax Determination Code
☑ Foreign Currency Valuation in 1st Local Currency
☐ Foreign Currency Valuation for Value Adjustment
☑ Factoring Active?

Settings for Tax Date

Tax Reporting Date When Transfered	Posting Date Is Tax Date

☑ Default Tax Date
☐ Tax Date from Statistical Receivable

Figure 11.1 Setting Up Company Code D900 for FICA

- When you select the check-box 'Post Payment on Acct as Down Payment', system posts 'payments on account' as down payments.
- The 'Assignment for Reversed Payment Order' check-box, when selected, indicates that a payment (in the payment order lot) can be used clear a number of open items in the contract account. Hence, the system posts the contract account automatically, where payment orders are reversed. When not selected, the system creates a 'clarification case' and assigns the payment receipt to the customer's account when you process the clarification case.
- Select 'Extended Withholding Tax Active' check-box.
- Select 'Cash Flow Analysis Active' check-box, so as to enable the system to record additional data for analysing cash flows, and that this data is transferred to the G/L.
- For the field 'Reconciliation System for Check Encashmnt', you have the option to select either G/L or FICA. If you select G/L, the system posts the checks to the G/L accounts individually, with their number specified. On the other hand, if you select FICA, then, the outgoing payment and reconciliation is carried in FICA itself and the system uses the FICA check management and the corresponding clarification tables, with only the totals posted to the G/L.
- When you select 'Real-Time Payments Active' check-box, then, you can enter and process real-time payments of the company code.

> **i** You will use 'real-time payment methods' in the case of externally-initiated payments (for example, online payments) to handle immediate forwarding / confirmation, of the payment data, by the bank. Note that these real-time payment methods are not processed by the payment run.

iv.   Make necessary settings under 'Settings for Further Business Processes' and 'Settings for Tax Date'.

v.   'Save' when completed and make similar setting for the other company code D910.

With this, we are now ready to configure the second step in setting up the organization for FICA, namely, defining the company code groups.

11.1.2 Define Company Code Groups

You need to define the company codes to be used, for each contract account. You can summarise these company codes in non-overlapping company code groups. You need to denominate a company code, of the group, as the paying company code for that group.

Project Starfish

Digifone wants the project team to define a single company code group to include the two company codes D900 and D910, with the company code D900 as the paying company code.

Use the menu path: SAP Customizing Implementation Guide > Financial Accounting > Contract Accounts Receivable and Payable > Organizational Units > Define Company Code Groups. On the resulting screen, click on 'New Entries' and define the company code group(s) and the paying company code, per company code group (Figure 11.2).

Change View "Company Code Groups": Overview

Company Code Group	Name	Paying Compa...
DIGI	FICA Group for Digifone	D900

Figure 11.2 Company Code Groups

The next step is to assign the company codes to the company code group that you have just defined.

11.1.3 Assign Company Codes to Company Code Groups

Use the menu path: SAP Customizing Implementation Guide > Financial Accounting > Contract Accounts Receivable and Payable > Organizational Units > Assign Company Codes to Company Code Groups. On the resulting screen, click on 'New Entries' and assign the company codes to the company code group(s) as shown in Figure 11.3.

Change View "Company Codes for Company Code Groups": Overview

Company Codes for Company Code Groups

Company Code Group	Company Code
DIGI	D900
DIGI	D910

Figure 11.3 Assign Company Code to Company Code Groups

The last step in configuring the FICA organization is to define the appropriate translation date for foreign currency postings.

11.1.4 Enter Translation Date for Postings in Foreign Currency

Here, you define, per company code, which date the system should use for the translation of a foreign currency into the various local currencies, for posting of deferred revenue, non-invoiced revenue amounts, and invoiced revenue from Convergent Invoicing. The settings made here enable the use of multiple parallel currencies for mapping various accounting principles.

Project Starfish

Digifone management has suggested to the project team to use the standard date as the translation date for various processes including invoiced revenue, payment card settlements, deferred revenue and revenues that are not invoiced, for the local currency. In the case of 2nd and 3rd local currencies, the translation date will be the posting date.

Use the menu path: SAP Customizing Implementation Guide > Financial Accounting > Contract Accounts Receivable and Payable > Organizational Units > Enter Translation Date for Postings in Foreign Currency. On the resulting screen, click on 'New Entries' and maintain the appropriate translation date for the local currency (Figure 11.4).

Change View "Date for Currency Exchange (Company Code-Specific)": Over

New Entries

Date for Currency Exchange (Company Code-Specific)

CoCd	Process ID	Translation Date for Local Currency	Translation Date for Local Currency 2	Translation Date
D900	Invoiced Revenue	Standard Date	Posting Date	Posting Date
D900	Payment Card Settlement	Standard Date	Posting Date	Posting Date
D900	Event-Based Deferred Revenu…	Standard Date	Posting Date	Posting Date
D900	Revenue Not Invoiced	Standard Date	Posting Date	Posting Date

Figure 11.4 Translation Date for Foreign Currency Postings

With the configuration of FICA organizational units complete, we can, now, move on to discuss the next group of settings namely, the basic functions.

11.2 Basic Functions

Under basic functions, you need to maintain a number of configuration settings that are relevant for contract partners, contract accounts, master agreement, posting of transactions, settings for SAP Fiori and so on.

Before venturing into other settings, you first need to specify the application area, industry instance and subapplication. You also need to make the general settings for master data. Let us start with application area specification.

11.2.1 Application Area

SAP recommends that you use only one application area (say, Extended FI-CA, Convergent FI-CA, Insurance Company, Telecommunications etc) from the several options available in the system. This will make all users to work, automatically, with the specified application area which the system stores in the user defaults.

Use the menu path: SAP Customizing Implementation Guide > Financial Accounting > Contract Accounts Receivable and Payable > Basic Functions > Application Area. On the resulting screen, click on 'New Entries' and select the appropriate application area (Extended FI-CA) in our case for Project Starfish) and activate the same (Figure 11.5).

Change View "Application Area in Contract Accounts Receivable/Payable"

New Entries

Application Area in Contract Accounts Receiva...

Appl. area	Activ
Extended FI-CA	✓

Figure 11.5 Application Area Activation

The next step is to specify the industry instance for the selected application area.

11.2.2 Specify Industry Instance of Contract Accounts Receivable and Payable

Here, you need to enter the industry solution with which you want to use FICA. The system, then, will use the industry instance to determine the corresponding metric for system measurement. Of course, you need to make the settings only if you use FICA as a part of SAP Charging and Billing for High Tech / Telecommunications / Banking.

The other step to complete is to activate the appropriate subapplication in FICA.

11.2.3 Activate Subapplication

The subapplication is used by the individual industry components that use FICA for the contract master data. For example, in the case of IS-Utilities, the primary contract will be energy contract and the additional ones will be SD contract (C) and provider contract (P); for IS-Telecommunications the primary contract will be the provider contract (P) and so on.

Use the menu path: SAP Customizing Implementation Guide > Financial Accounting > Contract Accounts Receivable and Payable > Basic Functions > Activate Subapplication. On the resulting screen, you have to activate 'Provider Contract' if your application area is, for example, 'Telecommunications'.

Finally, you need to make the general settings for master data.

11.2.4 General Settings for Master Data

Here, you can choose if an address entered in a business partner (to which the correspondence is sent) is also for an additional correspondence recipient to the contract account.

Use the menu path: SAP Customizing Implementation Guide > Financial Accounting > Contract Accounts Receivable and Payable > Basic Functions > General Settings for Master Data. On the resulting screen, select 'Address Selection for Add. Correspondence Recipient' check-box, to activate the selection options of an address entered in a business partner for the additional correspondence recipient.

With these preliminary settings completed, let us now look at the other settings that you need to configure for the basic functions in FICA. Let us start with the settings required for configuring contract partner.

11.2.5 Contract Partner

A 'contract partner' is one that is connected with your company through 'contract accounts' and through the conclusion of contracts. Accordingly, you can assign contract accounts to a 'business partner' (a person, organization or a group of persons), and bill for the services when you have created this business partner in the role of contract partner.

You need to make the general settings including defining the default values for payment methods. You will also make the settings for processing variants, checking for duplicates and follow-up actions. Besides these normal settings, you can activate additional checks for handling master data changes of business partner.

11.2.5.1   Activate Additional Checks for Master Data Changes to Business Partner

As additional checks, you can activate the use of business partner shadow table for mass runs, to check the dependencies between master data objects during master data changes, the summarization of spool requests at job level for printing correspondence etc.

Use the menu path: SAP Customizing Implementation Guide > Financial Accounting > Contract Accounts Receivable and Payable > Basic Functions > Contract Partner > Activate Additional Checks for Master Data Changes to Business Partner. You may also use Transaction S_KK4_74002225.

On the resulting screen (Figure 11.6):

i.   Select 'BP Shadow Table' check-box to enable the system to store an extract of the business partner data, in a shadow table, to improve system performance. Accordingly, for mass runs like payment and/or dunning runs, the system uses the shadow table for the required data and updates that during business partner maintenance. If you already have business partner data, in SAP, you have to fill the table, first, by using Transaction GPSHAD_NEW. However, if you are reactivating this shadow table, you need to deactivate this field, and run the report RFKKGPSH_DELETE to delete all existing entries in this table so as to prevent the system to read obsolete data, if any.

> **i** Note that the use of shadow table, though improves the system performance for mass runs, may increase the volume of the business partner data by around 20%.

ii.   Select 'Last BK Details' check-box, only if you want the system to always save the last bank details found for a business partner in the shadow table. When you use the business partner shadow table, the system, by default, always saves the first bank details found for a business partner in the business partner record in the shadow table. If you are already using shadow table, then, this setting only has an effect on those business partners that you create (or change) after you have selected the 'Last BK Details' check-box.

Change View "Central Technical Settings for Contract Accounts Rec.& Pa

Central Technical Settings for Cont

☑ BP Shadow Table
☐ Last BK Details
☑ Check dependency
☑ Spool Aggr.
☑ Central Tax Data Table
☐ Changed BP

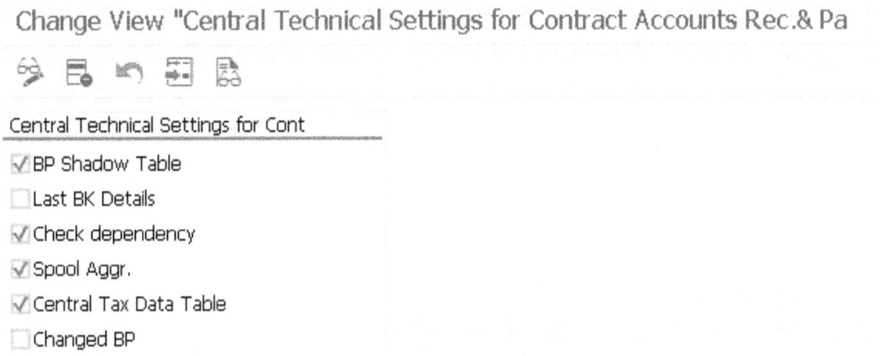

Figure 11.6 Activating Additional Checks for Master Data Changes

iii.   Select 'Check dependency' check-box to activate additional checks when changes are made to the master data of a business partner.

> **i** For example, you have maintained the bank details in a contract account for a business partner. These bank details have subsequently been deleted from the master record and the contract account does not, now, contain any bank details. When you set the 'Check dependency' flag, then, the system automatically checks for such dependencies; if a dependency exists, then, the system brings up a dialog box in which you may remove the dependencies, if required.

iv.   When you select 'Spool Aggr' check-box, the system summarises the pool requests at the job level during correspondence printing. By default, the system creates one spool request per processing interval.

> **i** Consider that in a correspondence printing run, you have 100 processing intervals that are processed by 15 jobs. If you do not select the 'Spool Aggr' flag, there will be 100 spool requests; if selected, there will only be 15 spool requests.

v.   Select 'Central Tax Data Table' for a country like USA, for telecommunications companies that need to calculate and store telecommunications taxes. This is important, because in a customer invoice, usually voice calls and other data services are grouped together for a given time period, say, one month. When you want to tax each service differently, this can result in a large number of tax types. So, the detailed tax data per billing document can be huge. In the standard system, this data is stored in database tables DFKKOPUSTAXIN01 … 12 (input parameters for tax calculation) and DFKKOPUSTAXOUT01 … 12 (detailed data of calculated tax). The system determines which table is used (based on the month of the CPU date of the document). And, this approach of dividing up the data enables you to delete and archive data more quickly.

vi.   When you select 'Changed BP' check-box, it activates the notification of changes to the bank details ID of contract partners by events 1025 and 1052, if you distribute time-dependent contract partner changes to interested applications using report BUPTDTRANSMIT.

With this let us move on to discuss the settings for basic functions for contract accounts.

11.2.6 Contract Accounts

A 'contract account' is a structure, in FICA, used to bill the posting data for contracts or contract items for which the same collection/disbursement agreements apply. The contract accounts are managed on an open item basis, and are governed by master data.

You can divide the master data in a contract account into two parts: one that is the same for all business partners in the contract account (in other words, cross-business partner) and the other that is business partner-specific. You can set the business partner-specific data differently for different business partners. In the contract account master record, you can define, per business partner, the procedures (for example dunning, payment etc) that apply when posting and processing the line items of a given contract account. You will be able block, through 'lock reasons', automatic master data changes through certain business transactions.

> **i** You must assign at least one business partner to each contract account. Depending on the industry, you may also be allowed to assign several business partners to a contract account.

You assign contracts to the contract accounts for which there is a business partner. Each contract is normally assigned to one contract account; however - as in the case of Utilities, Insurance, Telecommunications etc – one contract account may have several contracts assigned to it.

A 'contract account category' defines certain attributes for a contract account. When you create a contract, you need to assign a contract account category to that. The contract account category controls the fields that appear when you create a contract account. We shall see more on contract account category, later in Section 11.2.6.2.

The settings you need to make under contract accounts include the following:

- Define Number Ranges
- Configure Contract Acct Categories and Assign Number Ranges
- Define Contract Account/Business Partner Relationships
- Define Account Categories
- Define Account Determination Characteristics

Let us start with the first activity of defining number ranges for contract account categories.

11.2.6.1   Define Number Ranges

Use the menu path: SAP Customizing Implementation Guide > Financial Accounting > Contract Accounts Receivable and Payable > Basic Functions > Contract Accounts > Number Ranges and Contract Account Categories > Define Number Ranges or Transaction FPN2, and define the number range for the contract account (Figure 11.7). Later, in the next step, you can assign the defined number ranges to the contract account categories.

Edit Intervals: Contract Account, Object FKK_KONTO

N..	From No.	To Number	NR Status	Ext
D1	100000000001	399999999999	0	☐
D2	400000000000	699999999999	0	☐

Figure 11.7 Number Ranges for Contract Account Categories

> **i** Note that the contract account number ranges (object: FKK_KONTO) are valid across clients. If you have contract accounts that are transferred from external systems with the same number, then, you should define number ranges with external number assignment, to take care of these contract accounts.

With the number ranges defined, we are ready to configure the contract account categories and assign them with the appropriate number ranges.

11.2.6.2   Configure Contract Acct Categories and Assign Number Ranges

Using this configuration step, you can define the 'contract account categories', as grouping characteristics, for accounts that display the same control features. While configuring the attributes for contract account categories, you will specify – for example – if one or more business partners can be assigned to a contact account, whether a contract account can have one or more contracts, if you can process a contract account online etc. You will, then, allocate these categories to the contract accounts while defining the master data.

Project Starfish

Digifone has indicated to the project team that there needs to be two contract account categories, one for the regular 'post-paid' customers and the another for the 'pre-paid' customers. The contract account maintenance has to be online. It also wants the project team to ensure to group line items of different contract accounts for billing together with the same dunning / payment deadline. On numbering, it has been suggested to provide for both internal as well as external numbering.

Use the menu path: SAP Customizing Implementation Guide > Financial Accounting > Contract Accounts Receivable and Payable > Basic Functions > Contract Accounts > Number Ranges and Contract Account Categories > Configure Contract Acct Categories and Assign Number Ranges or Transaction S_KK4_74002420. Click on 'New Entries' on the resulting screen, and define the settings on the next screen (Figure 11.8):

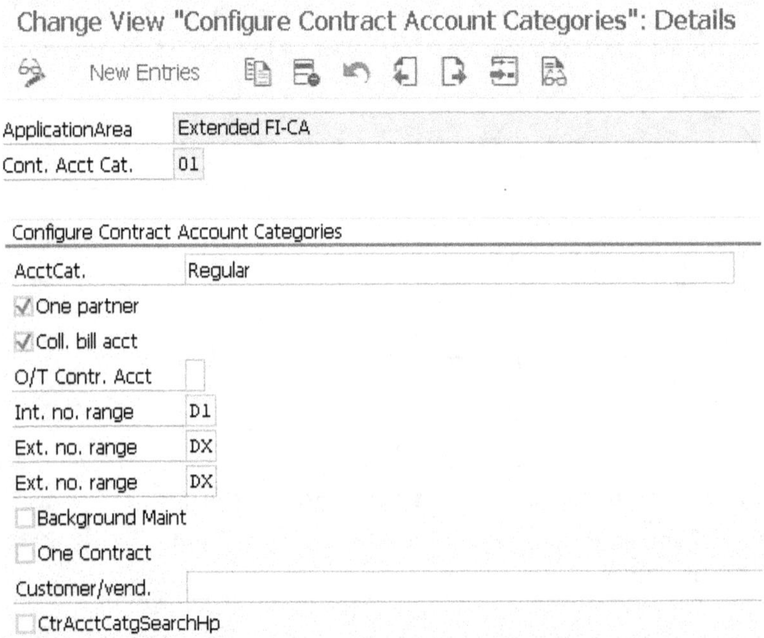

Figure 11.8 Configuring Contract Account Categories

i.   Enter the 'Application Area' (Extended FI-CA) and enter an identifier for the new contract account category (say, 01).

ii.   Under 'Configure Contract Account Categories' data block:

- Enter the description for the contract account category in 'AcctCat' field.
- The 'One partner' check-box, when selected, allows only one business partner to be assigned to a contract account of this contract account category.
- The 'Coll.bill acct' check-box, when selected, indicates that a contract account of this type is a collective bill account. When set, you can group line items of different contract accounts together for dunning, for example. You will select this for company codes in telecommunication industry, for example, so that you can send a consolidated bill to the business partner for all services like landline, mobile, broadband, DTH etc. However, you should not set this for IS-Insurance and IS-Public.
- Use 'O/T Contr. Acct.' field to indicate if a contract account of this contract account type is a one-time account.
- Enter the number range number. You can enter both internal number range ('Int. no range') and external number range ('Ext. no range') to enable applying internal or external numbers to the contracts.
- If you select 'Background Maint' check-box, then, you cannot maintain contracts online.
- Select 'One Contract' check-box, if you want only one contract for this account category.

 The 'Customer/vend.' field is no longer in use in SAP FICA.

iii.   'Save' the details and create all the required contract account categories.

Now that we have configured the contract account categories, let us move on to define the contract account/business partner relationship so that you can assign a business partner to a contract account.

11.2.6.3   Define Contract Account/Business Partner Relationships

You will use the 'contract account relationships' to define the role of the business partner in a contract account. The role can, for example, be of account holder, payer etc. The account relationship serves to differentiate between several business partners belonging to a single contract account. During automatic payment clearing, for example, this enables you to specify that a 'payment on account' is always assigned to the holder of the account. You can assign the account holder relationship to only one business partner per contract account. If you flag a contract account category as one-time account , you can, of course, maintain several business partners as the account holder with a contract account.

Use the menu path: SAP Customizing Implementation Guide > Financial Accounting > Contract Accounts Receivable and Payable > Basic Functions > Contract Accounts > Contract Account Relationships > Define Contract Account/Business Partner Relationships or Transaction S_KK4_74002305. On the resulting screen, create the required new entries (Figure 11.9). For account holder relationship, select 'AH' check-box.

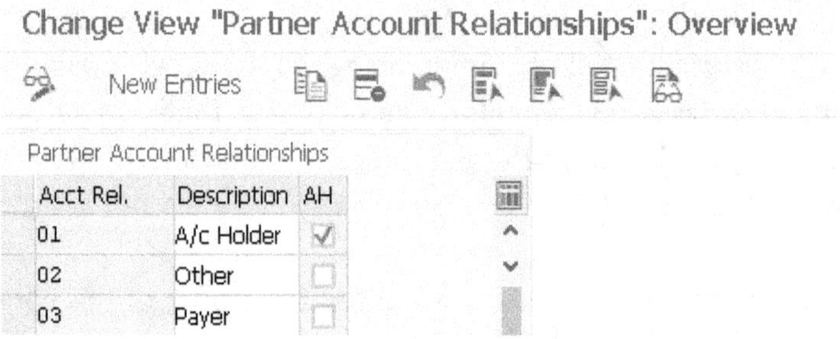

Change View "Partner Account Relationships": Overview

New Entries

Partner Account Relationships

Acct Rel.	Description	AH
01	A/c Holder	☑
02	Other	☐
03	Payer	☐

Figure 11.9 Contract Account / Business Partner Relationship

The next configuration activity is to define the account characteristics.

11.2.6.4   Define Account Categories

You will use 'account category' in the determination of specification for 'security deposits' (see Section 11.3.1 for more details). The system uses these account categories to determine the additional data for cash security deposits. Use the menu path: SAP Customizing Implementation Guide > Financial Accounting > Contract Accounts Receivable and Payable > Basic Functions > Contract Accounts > Define Account Categories. On the resulting screen, create new entries by entering the 'Account Class' and a description ('Text').

With this, we are ready to configure the last step in contract accounts: defining the account determination characteristics.

11.2.6.5   Define Account Determination Characteristics

Here in this step, you can create the account determination IDs that you want to use in the contract account and in the posting areas. Via the account determination ID and the company code (division, main and possibly the subtransaction), the system determines the correct G/L account to be posted with. When you post a document, the account determination ID is determined automatically from the contract account.

Project Starfish

Digifone wants to post, via automatic account determination, the business transactions to separate G/L accounts for the transactions with third party customers (domestic and overseas) and affiliate companies. Accordingly, the project team has decided to define three account determination characteristics in the system.

Use the menu path: SAP Customizing Implementation Guide > Financial Accounting > Contract Accounts Receivable and Payable > Basic Functions > Contract Accounts > Define Account Determination Characteristics. You may also use Transaction S_KK4_74002395. On the resulting screen, create new entries by entering the 'Account Determ. ID' and a description ('Text') as shown in Figure 11.10.

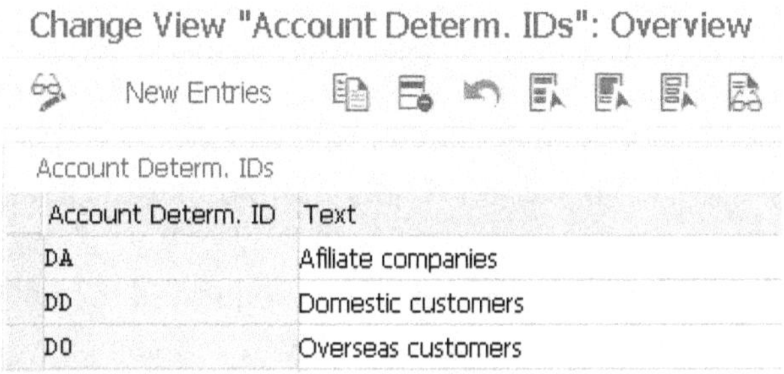

Change View "Account Determ. IDs": Overview

| | New Entries | | | | | | | |

Account Determ. IDs

Account Determ. ID	Text
DA	Afiliate companies
DD	Domestic customers
DO	Overseas customers

Figure 11.10 Account Determination IDs

With this let us move on to define the number ranges for master agreement.

11.2.7 Master Agreement

You need to define the number ranges for master agreement, besides configuring other settings like field attributes per activity, specifying authorization types, defining field groups for authorization check and defining filters for billable items.

11.2.7.1 Define Number Range

Use the menu path: SAP Customizing Implementation Guide > Financial Accounting > Contract Accounts Receivable and Payable > Basic Functions > Master Agreements > Define Number Range. You may also use Transaction FPN_MA. On the resulting screen (Figure 11.11), create the required number ranges for the master agreements (object: FKK_MAA).

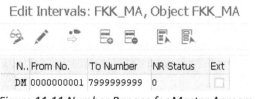

Edit Intervals: FKK_MA, Object FKK_MA

N..	From No.	To Number	NR Status	Ext
DM	0000000001	7999999999	0	☐

Figure 11.11 Number Ranges for Master Agreements

With this, let us move on to configure the settings for postings and documents, as a part of basic functions.

11.2.8 Postings and Documents

There are several settings that you need to make under this configuration group. In most of the cases you can use the standard / default settings, and we shall define only the settings that you need to explicitly set up. The ones you need to configure include:

- Maintain Document Number Ranges
- Define Lock Reasons for Posting Locks
- Define Rounding Rules for Currencies

Project Starfish

Digifone wants to maintain number ranges, both for individual and mass maintenance, and has suggested to the project team to plan at least five number ranges exclusively for mass maintenance to facilitate parallel processing. As for as posting locks, appropriate lock reasons need to be defined to take care of posting and clearing locks, and these locks would be valid for a period of one week during every month end. Digifone has also requested to configure the system in such way that all the document types should allow cross-company code postings. This is to facilitate billing / dunning a business partner who is no longer associated with a participating company, but still owes some money. Also, the system should enable negative postings for transactions such as payment or interest. But, in the case of returns / payment reversals or clearing resets, the negative posting will have to be allowed only if it happens in the same fiscal year.

Let us start with the maintenance of document number ranges.

11.2.8.1   Maintain Document Number Ranges

Define the number ranges, here, in this step, that you want the system to use for posting documents. Once defined, you can assign the number ranges to the document types. You may require separate number ranges for individual and mass processing. This is because, during mass processing the system makes use of parallel processes that cannot access the same number range at any given time.

> **i** For individual processing, the number range key should have the first character as a number, and the assignment can be internal or external. For mass processing, the first character has to be a letter and the number assignment should only be internal. Additionally, you need to assign as many number ranges for mass processing as that of the number of parallel processes, as each process would need its own number range.

Use the menu path: SAP Customizing Implementation Guide > Financial Accounting > Contract Accounts Receivable and Payable > Basic Functions > Postings and Documents > Basic Settings > Maintain Document Number Ranges. You may also use Transaction FPN1. On the resulting screen, create the required number range intervals for the object FKK_BELEG (Figure 11. 12).

Edit Intervals: FI-CA documents, Object FKK_BELEG

N..	From No.	To Number	NR Status	Ext
11	700000000000	899999999999	0	☐
D1	000300000000	199999999999	0	☐
D2	200000000000	299999999999	0	☐
D3	300000000000	399999999999	0	☐
D4	400000000000	499999999999	0	☐
D5	500000000000	599999999999	0	☐

Figure 11.12 Document Number Range Intervals

We can now move on to the next step, namely, defining of lock reasons for posting locks.

11.2.8.2   Define Lock Reasons for Posting Locks

The 'lock reasons', you define here, can be assigned at the contract account / business partner level in the master record of the contract account. You can also enter the posting lock (essentially, the clearing lock) in the line item and prevent clearing.

Use the menu path: SAP Customizing Implementation Guide > Financial Accounting > Contract Accounts Receivable and Payable > Basic Functions > Postings and Documents > Basic Settings > Define Lock Reasons for Posting Locks.

Change View "Posting Locks": Overview

Posting Locks

PBck	Descript.	Post./Clrg	AGrp	Period	Number
1	Pstg & Clg Lock	Posting and clearing lock	⌄	Weeks ⌄	1
2	Posting Lock	Posting lock only	⌄	Weeks ⌄	1
3	Posting Lock	Clearing lock only	⌄	Weeks ⌄	1

Figure 11.13 Lock Reasons for Posting Lock

On the resulting screen (Figure 11.13), create the required posting locks under lock categories like 'posting and clearing lock', 'posting lock' or 'clearing lock'. You may also restrict access by maintaining an authorization in 'AGrp'. You can also mention the 'Period' (days / weeks / months / years) for which the lock should be valid and enter the number of periods in the 'Number' field.

> **i** If you enter a from-date for a lock, then, the system adds the number of periods you entered in the 'Number' field here to that date. If not, then the system adds the number of periods you entered here, to the system date (today's date).
>
> For example, you have entered the 'Period' as 'Week' and the 'Number' as 1. When maintaining this lock (with this lock reason) on, say, 10-Mar-2020, you enter neither a from-date nor a to-date. Now, the system determines the start of the lock as 10-Mar-2020, and the end date as 17-Mar-2020.

With this, we are now ready to discuss the rounding rules for currencies.

11.2.8.3   Define Rounding Rules for Currencies

Define the rounding unit and rules for currencies, in which you make the postings, in a multiple of the smallest unit of currency. The system will use these settings, if a cash discount is to be posted by the payment program or receivables posting during invoicing or posting of charges or interest.

Use the menu path: SAP Customizing Implementation Guide > Financial Accounting > Contract Accounts Receivable and Payable > Basic Functions > Postings and Documents > Basic Settings > Define Rounding Rules for Currencies. Create the specifications, per company code and per currency. Enter the rounding unit for both debit and credit, and also select the rounding methodology (a + indicates that the system will always round up the value) as shown in Figure 11.14.

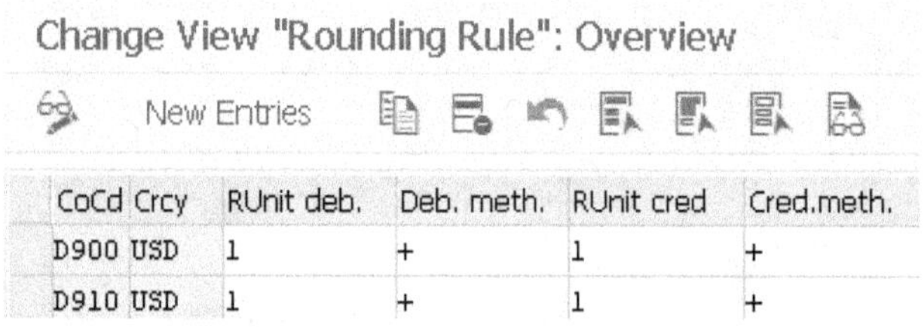

Change View "Rounding Rule": Overview

   New Entries

CoCd	Crcy	RUnit deb.	Deb. meth.	RUnit cred	Cred.meth.
D900	USD	1	+	1	+
D910	USD	1	+	1	+

Figure 11.14 Rounding Rule

The next activity is to maintain the document types and assigning the number ranges to them.

11.2.8.4   Maintain Document Types and Assign Number Ranges

Define the document types that you want to use for the business transactions in FICA. Use the menu path: SAP Customizing Implementation Guide > Financial Accounting > Contract Accounts Receivable and Payable > Basic Functions > Postings and Documents > Document > Maintain Document Assignments > Document Types > Maintain Document Types and Assign Number Ranges.

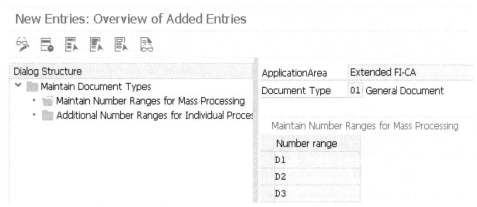

Change View "Maintain Document Types": Overview

New Entries

Dialog Structure
- Maintain Document Typ
  - Maintain Number Rai
  - Additional Number R

ApplicationArea

Maintain Document Types

D..	Description	Number r...	Cross-Company	Not Manually	Negative Posting	Doc. Type Res
01	General Document	01	✓	☐		400
02	Payment	11	✓	✓	Negative Posting	400
03	Charges	11	✓	☐	Negative Posting, except for Aperiodic Reset	400
04	Reversal	11	✓	☐	Negative Posting, except for Aperiodic Reset	400
05	Clearring	11	✓	☐	Negative Posting, except for Aperiodic Reset	400
06	Returns	11	✓	✓		400
07	Dunning Notice	01	✓	✓		300

Figure 11.15 Maintaining Document Types.

On the resulting screen, click on 'New Entries' and maintain the required document types (Figure 11.15). Per 'Document type', enter the 'Description', the number range ('Number range'), select if you want allow for cross-company code postings ('Cross-Company'), indicate if the document can be used for manual posting ('Not Manually'), indicate if negative posting is allowed ('Negative Posting') and specify the document resident life for archiving ('Doc. Type Res. Time').

Now select a row, and double-click on 'Maintain Number Ranges for Mass Processing' on the left hand side 'Dialog Structure'. Click on 'New Entries' and enter the number ranges (Figure 11.16). Recall that we have defined five number ranges for facilitating parallel processing during mass processing. You may also maintain additional number ranges for individual processing.

New Entries: Overview of Added Entries

Dialog Structure
- Maintain Document Types
  - Maintain Number Ranges for Mass Processing
  - Additional Number Ranges for Individual Proces

ApplicationArea	Extended FI-CA
Document Type	01 General Document

Maintain Number Ranges for Mass Processing

Number range
D1
D2
D3

Figure 11.16 Number Ranges for Mass Processing

With this, we can move on to maintain the document type for collective bills.

11.2.8.5   Maintain the Document Type Specifications for Collective Bills

Use the menu path: SAP Customizing Implementation Guide > Financial Accounting > Contract Accounts Receivable and Payable > Basic Functions > Postings and Documents > Document > Maintain Document Assignments > Document Types > Maintain the Document Type Specifications for Collective Bills. On the resulting screen (Figure 11.17), enter the 'Document Type' for collective bills (posting area = 0700).

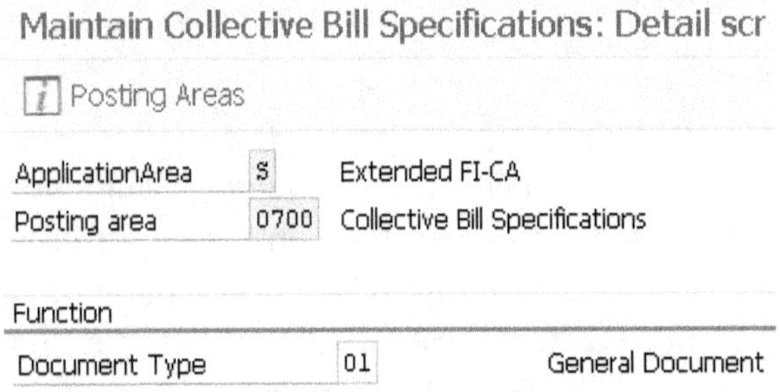

Maintain Collective Bill Specifications: Detail scr

> Posting Areas

ApplicationArea	S	Extended FI-CA
Posting area	0700	Collective Bill Specifications

Function

Document Type	01	General Document

Figure 11.17 Document Type for Collective Bills

The next step is to maintain the transactions for non-industry FICA solution.

11.2.8.6   Maintain Transactions for Non-Ind. Contract Accounts Receivable and Payable.

You have to maintain the settings for transactions for non-industry FICA solution, in the following activities:

- Define and Parameterize External Transactions
- Assign External Transactions

Let us understand the settings for the first activity.

11.2.8.6.1   Define and Parameterize External Transactions

Here, you define the external main and subtransactions for your company and assign the parameters (such as company code and statistics key) for document control, to these transactions. The main and subtransactions control the determination of item attributes, processing of items and account determination. You can use the standard settings delivered by SAP, without making any change.

Use the menu path: SAP Customizing Implementation Guide > Financial Accounting > Contract Accounts Receivable and Payable > Basic Functions > Postings and Documents > Document > Maintain Document Assignments > Maintain Transactions for Non-Ind. Contract Accounts Receivable and Payable > Define and Parameterize External Transactions.

On the resulting screen (Figure 11.18), you can see the main transactions ('MTra') like M001, M002 etc., for the application area S (Extended FI-CA).

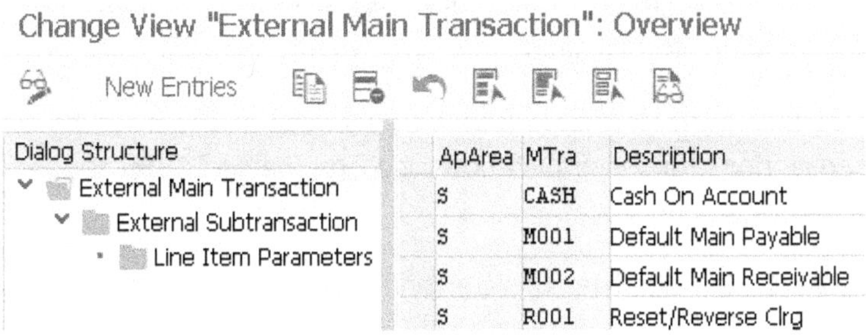

Change View "External Main Transaction": Overview

New Entries

Dialog Structure	ApArea	MTra	Description
External Main Transaction	S	CASH	Cash On Account
External Subtransaction	S	M001	Default Main Payable
Line Item Parameters	S	M002	Default Main Receivable
	S	R001	Reset/Reverse Clrg

Figure 11.18 External Main Transactions

You can look at the subtransactions for each of the main transactions by selecting the appropriate main transaction and double-clicking on 'External Subtransaction' on the left hand side 'Dialog Structure'. Then, for each of these subtransactions you can see the standard line item parameters.

You will use the next step to assign external transactions to the internal main / subtransactions predefined in SAP.

11.2.8.6.2   Assign External Transactions

Use this step, to assign the external main and subtransactions that you have defined to the internal main and subtransactions predefined in SAP. Using external transactions, the system controls the determination of the different attributes of the item, the account determination, and the further processing of documents. This enables you to also process documents created in the system, such as those arising for charges and postings on account, using the concept of main and subtransactions. During posting, the system reads the internal transactions for the external transactions, assigns them to one another, and then notes the external transaction in the new item created.

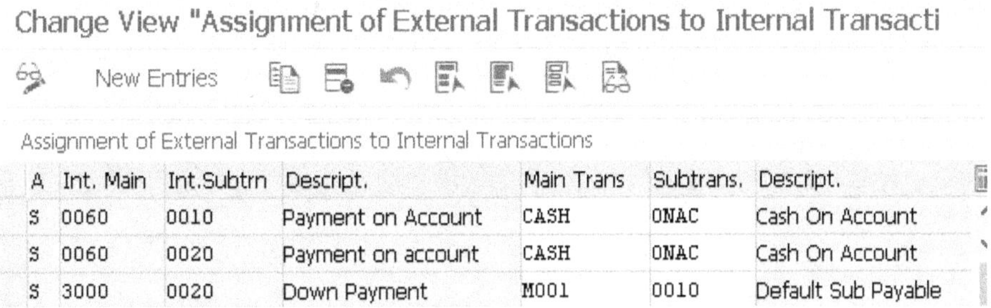

Change View "Assignment of External Transactions to Internal Transacti

New Entries

Assignment of External Transactions to Internal Transactions

A	Int. Main	Int.Subtrn	Descript.	Main Trans	Subtrans.	Descript.
S	0060	0010	Payment on Account	CASH	ONAC	Cash On Account
S	0060	0020	Payment on account	CASH	ONAC	Cash On Account
S	3000	0020	Down Payment	M001	0010	Default Sub Payable

Figure 11.19 Assignment External Transactions to Internal Transactions

Use the menu path: SAP Customizing Implementation Guide > Financial Accounting > Contract Accounts Receivable and Payable > Basic Functions > Postings and Documents > Document > Maintain Document Assignments > Maintain Transactions for Non-Ind. Contract Accounts Receivable and Payable > Assign External Transactions.

On the resulting screen, you will see the default mapping of external main / subtransactions to the internal main / subtransactions for the application area External FI-CA (S). You may use the default settings as such (Figure 11.19).

With this, we can now move on to perform the consistency check for transactions.

11.2.8.7   Perform Consistency Check for Transactions

Here, you can check the configurations that you have defined, so far, for consistency. The system displays a list showing correct / incorrect transactions. You may click on the long text and correct the inconsistencies, if any.

Use the menu path: SAP Customizing Implementation Guide > Financial Accounting > Contract Accounts Receivable and Payable > Basic Functions > Postings and Documents > Document > Maintain Document Assignments > Perform Consistency Check for Transactions. On the resulting screen (Figure 11.20), you will see the log showing the inconsistencies, if any, which you can correct before proceeding further.

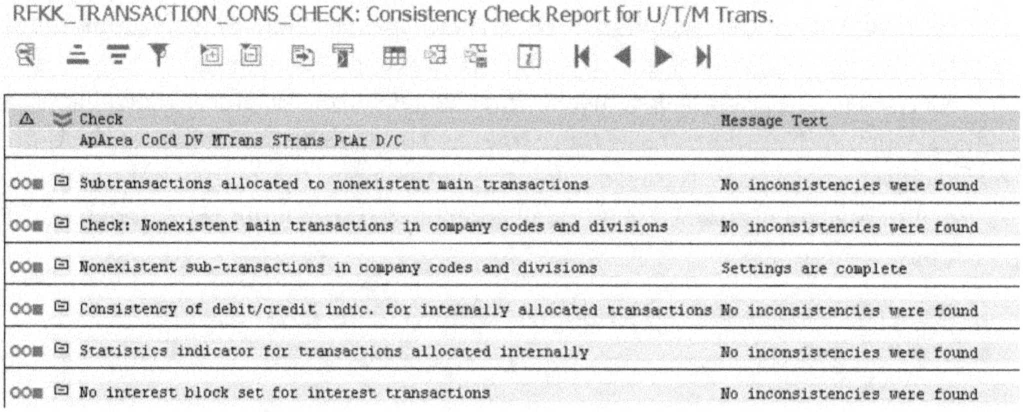

RFKK_TRANSACTION_CONS_CHECK: Consistency Check Report for U/T/M Trans.

⚠ ≷ Check	Message Text
ApArea CoCd DV MTrans STrans PtAr D/C	
OO▣ ▣ Subtransactions allocated to nonexistent main transactions	No inconsistencies were found
OO▣ ▣ Check: Nonexistent main transactions in company codes and divisions	No inconsistencies were found
OO▣ ▣ Nonexistent sub-transactions in company codes and divisions	Settings are complete
OO▣ ▣ Consistency of debit/credit indic. for internally allocated transactions	No inconsistencies were found
OO▣ ▣ Statistics indicator for transactions allocated internally	No inconsistencies were found
OO▣ ▣ No interest block set for interest transactions	No inconsistencies were found

Figure 11.20 Consistency Check for Transactions

With this, we can now move on to discuss the settings required for Fiori applications.

11.2.9 Settings for Fiori Applications

Here, for making the required settings for Fiori applications, you need to complete the following configuration steps:

- Assign Number Range Intervals to Fiori Apps
- Enter Number Ranges for Worklists

Let us start with the assignment of number range intervals.

11.2.9.1   Assign Number Range Intervals to Fiori Apps

Here, you will assign number range intervals to the Fiori apps that you plan to use. These number range intervals are for the creation of worklists in FICA (back-end). You need to assign only one number range to each Fiori app.

Use the menu path: SAP Customizing Implementation Guide > Financial Accounting > Contract Accounts Receivable and Payable > Basic Functions > Settings for Fiori Applications > Basic Settings > Assign Number Range Intervals to Fiori Apps.

On the resulting screen, click on 'New Entries' and enter the number range ('NR') for each of the Fiori application ID ('App ID') you select (Figure 11.21).

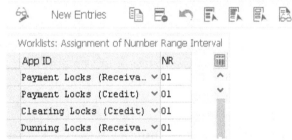

Figure 11.21 Number Range Interval for Fiori Apps

The next task is to set up the number ranges for worklists that are created by Fiori apps.

11.2.9.2   Enter Number Ranges for Worklists

Use the menu path: SAP Customizing Implementation Guide > Financial Accounting > Contract Accounts Receivable and Payable > Basic Functions > Settings for Fiori Applications > Basic Settings > Enter Number Ranges for Worklists.

On the resulting screen (Figure 11.22), maintain the required number ranges for the worklists created by Fiori apps.

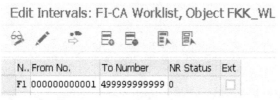

Figure 11.22 Number Ranges for Worklists

The other steps you need to complete for setting up the Fiori apps for FICA include defining the actions for worklists and defining the clearing reasons.

This completes our discussion on configuring the basic functions in FICA. We shall, now, move on to discuss the settings required for some of the important business transactions in FICA.

11.3 Business Transactions

Under business transactions, we shall see the configuration settings relating to the following:

- Security Deposits
- Payments
- Interest Calculation
- Dunning

Let us start with the settings required for security deposits.

11.3.1 Security Deposits

While configuring the settings for security deposits, you need to complete the following activities:

- Define Number Ranges for Security Deposits
- Define General Parameters for Security Deposits
- Define Specifications for Clearing of Cash Security Deposits
- Define Specifications for Cash Security Deposit Int. Calc. (Mass Proc.)

Let us start with the number range definition for security deposits.

11.3.1.1   Define Number Ranges for Security Deposits

Use the menu path: SAP Customizing Implementation Guide > Financial Accounting Global Settings > Contract Accounts Receivable and Payable > Business Transactions > Security Deposits > Define Number Ranges for Security Deposits. You may also use Transaction FPSECO.

On the resulting screen, maintain the required number ranges for the object FKK_SEC. We have defined S1 as the number range with internal number assignment. With the number ranges defined for security deposits, we can proceed to define the general parameters for security deposits.

11.3.1.2 Define General Parameters for Security Deposits

Using this configuration activity, you can maintain the general parameters for security deposits, per application area. While doing so, you must use a number range with internal number assignment (say, S1), and a document type to post the request document, when cash security payments are made. You can also create a setting in which the start date / return date is determined. You can also define default values for the return of cash security deposits.

Project Starfish

In the case of security deposits, Digifone has requested the project team to make sure that the assignment of security deposit to contract should be flexible enough to assign at the contract or contract account level. Also, when cash security deposit requests are transferred from one contract account or contract to another contract account / contracts, the system should determine the due date and the new date has to be based on the transfer date. Also, the interest is to be set as due as soon as an item is posted.

Use the menu path: SAP Customizing Implementation Guide > Financial Accounting Global Settings > Contract Accounts Receivable and Payable > Business Transactions > Security Deposits > Define General Parameters for Security Deposits.

On the resulting screen, click on 'New Entries' and maintain the appropriate settings on the next screen (Figure 11.23):

i.   Select the 'Application Area' (Extended FI-CA).

ii. Under 'Assignment to Contract', select the 2nd option 'Contract fld optional' so that the user can decide whether to create a cash security deposit, at contract level or contract account level.

iii. Under 'General settings', enter the number range (S1) that you have defined in the previous step and the system will bring up 'From number', 'To number' and 'Current Number' when you 'Save'.

iv. Under 'Cash sec. deposit', select 'Recalc. Due Date after Transfer'. Now, when you transfer cash security deposit requests from one contract account (or contract) to another contract account (or contract), the system will re-determine the due date and the new date will be based on the transfer date and the terms of payment in the contract account. Also enter the 'Document Type' and 'Rev.doc. type'.

v.   Enter the details for 'Return parameter' and 'Save' the settings.

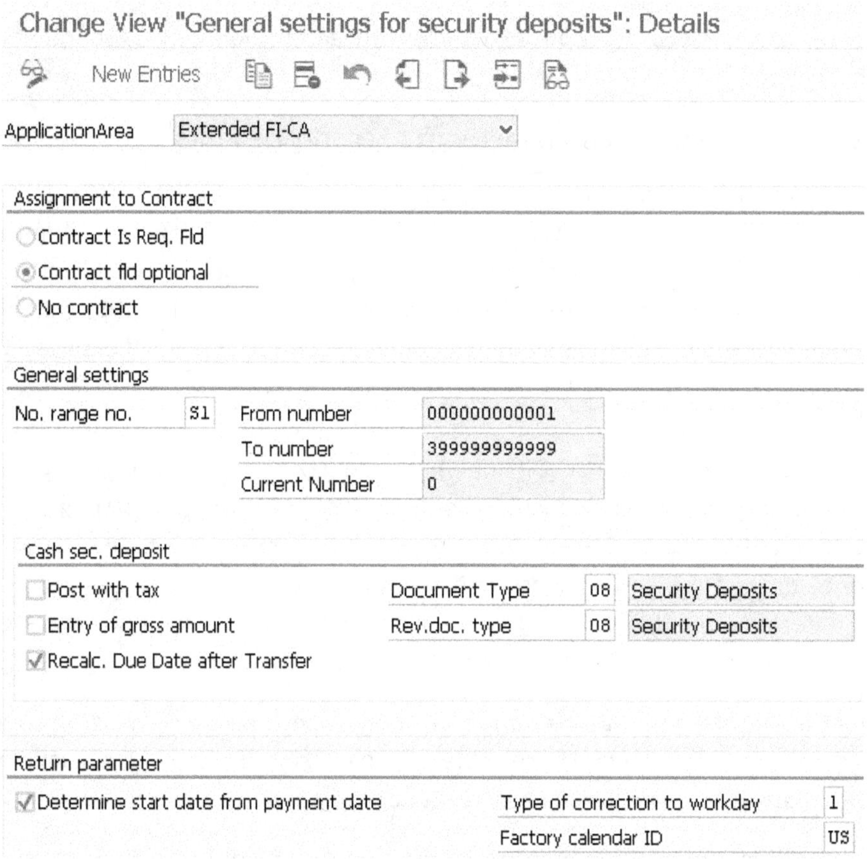

Figure 11.23 General Settings for Security Deposits

Now, you can move on to define the specifications for clearing cash security deposits.

11.3.1.3   Define Specifications for Clearing of Cash Security Deposits

Here, you define a document type and a main and subtransaction for postings for the clearing of cash security deposits.

Use the menu path: SAP Customizing Implementation Guide > Financial Accounting Global Settings > Contract Accounts Receivable and Payable > Business Transactions > Security Deposits > Define Specifications for Clearing of Cash Security Deposits.

On the resulting screen, for the posting area 0801 (specifications for clearing security deposits), maintain the document type, main transaction and the subtransaction.

> **i** The 'posting areas', in SAP FICA, bundle configuration settings under a technical key based on business subprocesses. The system stores these settings in a common table under this technical key, making possible the generic interpretation offering several advantages (especially for tables with a large number of key field), like hiding the fields that are not used, defining separate access sequences when using multiple key fields, using * for generic entry when you do not want entries for all key value fields and so on.

The other setting you need to make is the specification for mass processing of interest calculation on security deposits.

11.3.1.4   Define Specifications for Cash Security Deposit Int. Calc. (Mass Proc.)

Here, you need to define a document type for the mass activity of posting interest on security deposit.

Use the menu path: SAP Customizing Implementation Guide > Financial Accounting Global Settings > Contract Accounts Receivable and Payable > Business Transactions > Security Deposits > Define Specifications for Cash Security Deposit Int. Calc. (Mass Proc.) or Transaction FQI7.

On the resulting screen (Figure 11.24), for the posting area 1083 (Mass Activity Interest on Cash Security Deposit), maintain the document type and also the payment terms due. You have to select 'True' or 'False' value for 'Pmnt.terms due' flag: if you select 'True', then, the system determines the default value for the interest due date from the payment conditions though you can overwrite that manually.

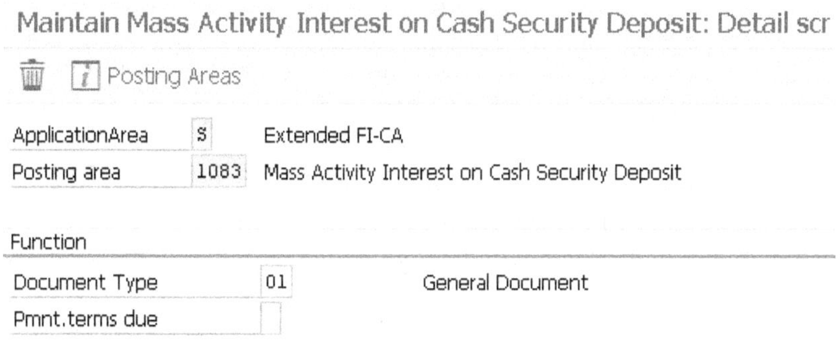

Maintain Mass Activity Interest on Cash Security Deposit: Detail scr

🗑 [i] Posting Areas

ApplicationArea	S	Extended FI-CA
Posting area	1083	Mass Activity Interest on Cash Security Deposit

Function

Document Type	01	General Document
Pmnt.terms due		

Figure 11.24 Settings for Mass Activity of Interest Posting on Security Deposits

> **i** Note that the interest is normally due as soon as an item is posted. However, it is sometimes advisable to determine the interest due date from the payment conditions. In this case, interest will often come due with other items. The 'Pmnt.terms due' flag is not used by all application areas, but used in Utilities and Telecommunications industries.

Besides the above, you may also need to complete other configuration activities like creating special definitions for security deposits, request reasons, defining status on non-cash security deposits, reversal reasons for security deposits etc.

With this, let us move on to discuss the configuration relating to payments under business transactions.

11.3.2 Payments

Under payments, you need to make settings for various configuration categories like processing incoming/outgoing payments, incoming / outgoing payment creation, reporting incorrect bank data, release of payment workflow and archiving. We may not be discussing all the configuration steps under the above categories, but limit our discussions to the following activities:

- Define Default Values for Payment Order Lots
- Define Bank Clearing Accounts for Payment Lots
- Define Clarification Account
- Define Clearing Account for Check Deposit
- Define Transactions for Electronic Bank Statement Transfer

Let us start with the definition of default values for payment order lots.

11.3.2.1   Define Default Values for Payment Order Lots

Here, you need to define a document type, a clearing reason and a selection category. The system suggests these specifications when you enter payment order lots and use them for posting clearing documents.

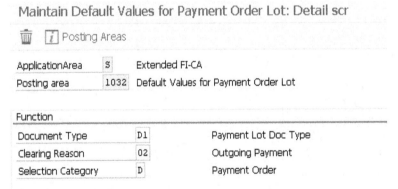

Figure 11.25 Default Values for Payment Order Lot

Use the menu path: SAP Customizing Implementation Guide > Financial Accounting Global Settings > Contract Accounts Receivable and Payable > Business Transactions > Payments > Processing Incoming and Outgoing Payments > Define Default Values for Payment Order Lots or Transaction FQ1032. On the resulting screen, enter the document type (D1), clearing reason (02) and a selection category (D) and 'Save' the settings (Figure 11.25).

With this, we can move on to define the bank clearing accounts for payment lots.

11.3.2.2   Define Bank Clearing Accounts for Payment Lots

Use the menu path: SAP Customizing Implementation Guide > Financial Accounting Global Settings > Contract Accounts Receivable and Payable > Business Transactions > Payments > Processing Incoming and Outgoing Payments > Define Bank Clearing Accounts for Payment Lots or Transaction S_KK4_74002161. On the resulting screen, click on 'New Entries' and maintain the required settings on the next screen (Figure 11.26):

Figure 11.26 Settings up of a Bank Clearing Account for Payment Lots

   i.   Enter the company code, G/L for the bank clearing account, house bank, and the account at the house bank.
  ii.   Select the appropriate check-boxes, for 'Debit/Credit', select 'No Restriction' and 'Save' the details. Repeat the settings for the other company code D910.

With this, we can now move to define the clarification account.

11.3.2.3   Define Clarification Account

You define a 'clarification account' that is nothing but a clearing account (a temporary account). The system automatically posts the incoming payment to this account, if the selection parameters are not sufficient to select open items for payment or to locate a contract account for posting a payment or to locate a contract account for posting a payment on account.

Use the menu path: SAP Customizing Implementation Guide > Financial Accounting Global Settings > Contract Accounts Receivable and Payable > Business Transactions > Payments > Processing Incoming and Outgoing Payments > Define Clarification Account or Transaction FQZJ.

On the resulting screen, click on 'Create' and enter the clarification account for the given chart of accounts, company code, bank clearing account and currency (Figure 11.27).

Maintain Incoming Payment Interim Account: Overview

🔲 📄 🗑 �📋 Single copy   Change chart/accts   📋 Mass copy

ApplicationArea	S	Extended FI-CA
Posting area	1040	Incoming Payment Interim Account
Chart of Accts	YCOA	Standard Chart of Accounts

Account Determination

Company ...	Currency	Bank cleari...	Document...	Clarif. Acct
*	*	*	02	0011101030

Figure 11.27 Settings up of a Clarification Account

> ℹ️ An * in 'Company Code', 'Currency' and 'Bank clearing acct' indicates that the clarification account entered here – 0011101030 - is valid across company codes, currencies, and bank clearing accounts. However, it is possible that you can transfer posting to another clarification account, during clarifying an incoming payment, if you feel that the cash is to be clarified from another department, for example. But, note that you need to transfer the entire amount and not partial.

Similar to bank clearing account for payment lots which we defined in Section 11.3.2.2, let us, now, define the clearing account for check deposit.

11.3.2.4   Define Clearing Account for Check Deposit

Use the menu path: SAP Customizing Implementation Guide > Financial Accounting Global Settings > Contract Accounts Receivable and Payable > Business Transactions > Payments > Processing Incoming and Outgoing Payments > Define Clearing Account for Check Deposit or Transaction FQZT. On the resulting screen, enter the appropriate G/L (say, 0011002070 for company code D900) in the 'Clearing Account' field.

With this, let us move on to the next configuration step: defining the transactions for electronic bank statement transfer.

11.3.2.5   Define Transactions for Electronic Bank Statement Transfer

Using this configuration step, you need to enter an external transaction code of the electronic account balance that is to be transferred to the system and classify this as a payment, return, payment order lot or post-dated check.

Use the menu path: SAP Customizing Implementation Guide > Financial Accounting Global Settings > Contract Accounts Receivable and Payable > Business Transactions > Payments > Processing Incoming and Outgoing Payments > Define Transactions for Electronic Bank Statement Transfer. You may also use Transaction S_KK4_74002160.

On the resulting screen, click on 'New Entries' and maintain the required settings on the next screen. Per 'Transaction Type' (say, 17BAI, CBBAI2, etc), maintain the 'External Transaction' (say, 115, 165, 195 etc), assign the proper sign in '+-sign' field, and enter the 'Business Transaction' (say, 01-incoming payments, 02-returns, 03-payment order etc).

Let us now move on to define the accounts for payment program.

11.3.2.6   Define Accounts for Payment Program

You may define the numbers of the bank accounts or bank subaccounts that you want the payment program for posting. The payment program will make additional postings, if any, such as cash discount or exchange rate differences.

Use the menu path: SAP Customizing Implementation Guide > Financial Accounting Global Settings > Contract Accounts Receivable and Payable > Business Transactions > Payments > Incoming/Outgoing Payment Creation > Define Accounts for Payment Program. You may also use Transaction FQZL.

Maintain Payment Program Bank Accounts: Detail scr

◀ ▶ 🗑 ⓘ Posting Areas

ApplicationArea	S	Extended FI-CA
Posting area	1061	Payment Program Bank Accounts

Key

Paying Company Code	D900	Digifone
House bank	*	
Payment Method	*	
Currency	*	
Account ID	*	

Function

Bank Subaccount	0011001000	Bank1 Main Account
Business Area		
Check Clearing Acct	0011001070	Bank1 Check Clearing
Expiration Date		
Profit Center		

Figure 11.28 Bank Accounts for Payment Program

On the resulting screen, click on 'New Entries' and maintain the details for the posting area 1062 (payment program bank accounts). For the company code entered in 'Paying Company Code' field, you can maintain individual house bank, payment method, currency etc., as separate entries or maintain a * in these fields to indicate that the 'Bank Subaccount' (say,

0011001000) and the 'Check Clearing Acct' (say, 0011001070) will be valid for all house banks, payment methods, currency etc., for the company code, say, D900 (Figure 11.28).

This completes our discussion on the settings required to set up payments in FICA.

Let us now move on to discuss the settings required for interest calculation

11.3.3 Interest Calculation

The interest calculation settings are similar to that of specifications that we have discussed, already, for both item interest and balance interest calculation vide Chapter 9 (of Vol. I) and Chapter 10 (Section 10.3.12). However, we shall discuss some of the settings unique to SAP FICA which we have not discussed so far. These settings include the following:

- Define Interest Lock Reasons
- Define Specifications for Interest Calculation
- Activate Additional Functions for Interest Calculation
- Define Clearing Reasons for which Interest is not Calculated
- Define Specifications for the Mass Run

Project Starfish

Digifone wants to create three kinds of lock reasons for interest calculation; locking the periodic interest, locking the interest calculation during clearing and a total lock. These locks are to be valid for a period of one week from the start date. It has also been decided that during interest calculation, the system should calculate net interest, the due date should be the date of interest debit in the account, and there should be no rounding off of the interest calculated. Also, the system should create interest documents per contract, instead of clubbing all the contracts and creating a single interest document.

Let us start with the first activity of defining interest lock reasons.

11.3.3.1   Define Interest Lock Reasons

Here, you will define the reasons for interest lock, and later, allocate the defined reasons to individual document items.

Use the menu path: SAP Customizing Implementation Guide > Financial Accounting Global Settings > Contract Accounts Receivable and Payable > Business Transactions > Interest Calculation > Item Interest Calculation > Define Interest Lock Reasons.

On the resulting screen, click on 'New Entries' and define the required lock reasons (Figure 11.29): enter an ID for the 'Interest lock reason', provide a 'Name' for the ID and select the appropriate 'Int. Lock'. Also, enter authorization group (if required), enter the 'Period' (Day

/Week/Month/Year) and enter the periods for which this lock will be valid in 'Number'. If, for example, you have selected 'Week' in 'Period' and entered 1 in 'Number', then, the lock will be valid for 1 week from the start date.

Change View "Blocking Reasons for Interest Calculation": Overview

🔁   New Entries   📋 📇 ↩ 📑 📑 📑 📑

Blocking Reasons for Interest Calculation

Interest lock reason	Name	Int. Lock	Au...	Period	Number
1	Periodic Int lock	Locked for Period... ⌄		Weeks ⌄	1
2	Clearing Int Lock	Locked for Intere... ⌄		Weeks ⌄	1
3	Total lock	Locked for All Ty... ⌄		Weeks ⌄	1

Figure 11.29 Interest Lock Reasons

With this, we can, now, move on to define the specifications for interest calculation.

11.3.3.2   Define Specifications for Interest Calculation

Using this activity, you need to define the specifications, such as the document type and the statistical key, for the posting of interest documents.

Use the menu path: SAP Customizing Implementation Guide > Financial Accounting Global Settings > Contract Accounts Receivable and Payable > Business Transactions > Interest Calculation > Item Interest Calculation > Define Specifications for Interest Calculation. You may also use Transaction FQI4.

On the resulting screen, for the posting area 1080 (Interest Calculation Specifications). On the resulting screen, create new entries: enter the 'Document Type' (03), enter the 'Statistical Key' (G), leave the fields 'Rounding' and 'Pmnt.terms due' blank, and select 'True' for 'Doc.per Contr. Acct' (to make individual interest documents per contract) as in Figure 11.30.

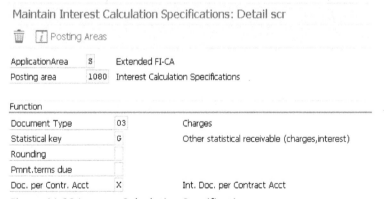

Maintain Interest Calculation Specifications: Detail scr

🗑 ⅈ Posting Areas

ApplicationArea	S	Extended FI-CA
Posting area	1080	Interest Calculation Specifications

Function

Document Type	03	Charges
Statistical key	G	Other statistical receivable (charges,interest)
Rounding		
Pmnt.terms due		
Doc. per Contr. Acct	X	Int. Doc. per Contract Acct

Figure 11.30 Interest Calculation Specifications

We can, now, activate the additional functions, in FICA, for interest calculation.

11.3.3.3   Activate Additional Functions for Interest Calculation

You can define whether additional functions like (a) calculation of interest based on net amounts and (b) calculation of interest on the original items for cleared installment plan items, are to be used for calculating interest on line items.

Use the menu path: SAP Customizing Implementation Guide > Financial Accounting Global Settings > Contract Accounts Receivable and Payable > Business Transactions > Interest Calculation > Item Interest Calculation > Activate Additional Functions for Interest Calculation. You may also use Transaction FQI4Z.

On the resulting screen, for the posting area 1084 (Additional Functions for Interest Calculation), make the appropriate settings (Figure 11.31): select 'Yes' for 'Net Int.' to calculate net interest, and leave 'Int. Inst. Plan' field as blank ('No'). If you select 'Yes' for 'Int. Inst. Plan' field, then, it deactivates the interest calculation function in installment plan transactions.

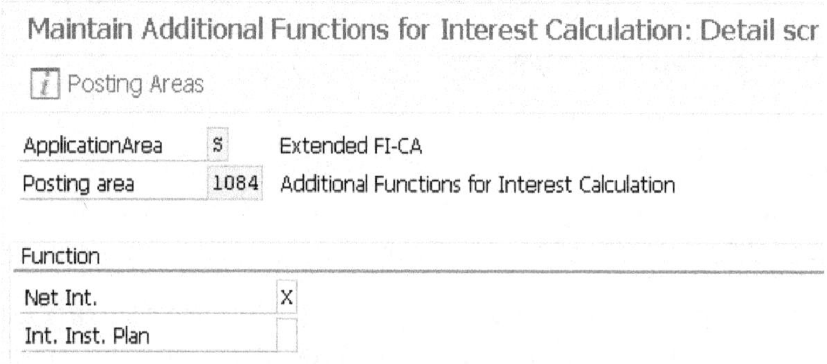

Maintain Additional Functions for Interest Calculation: Detail scr

i Posting Areas

| ApplicationArea | S | Extended FI-CA |
| Posting area | 1084 | Additional Functions for Interest Calculation |

Function	
Net Int.	X
Int. Inst. Plan	

Figure 11.31 Activating Additional Functions for Interest Calculation

The last activity which we need to discuss under the settings for interest calculation is, defining the specifications for mass run.

11.3.3.4   Define Specifications for the Mass Run

Here, in this step, you define a document type for the interest posting for the interest run, and also decide whether you want to post interest from the mass run statistically or you want the posting to update the G/L.

Use the menu path: SAP Customizing Implementation Guide > Financial Accounting Global Settings > Contract Accounts Receivable and Payable > Business Transactions > Interest Calculation > Item Interest Calculation > Define Specifications for the Mass Run. You may also use Transaction FQI6. This is similar to the previous configuration step that we discussed in Section 11.3.3.2. Make the required settings as shown in Figure 11.32.

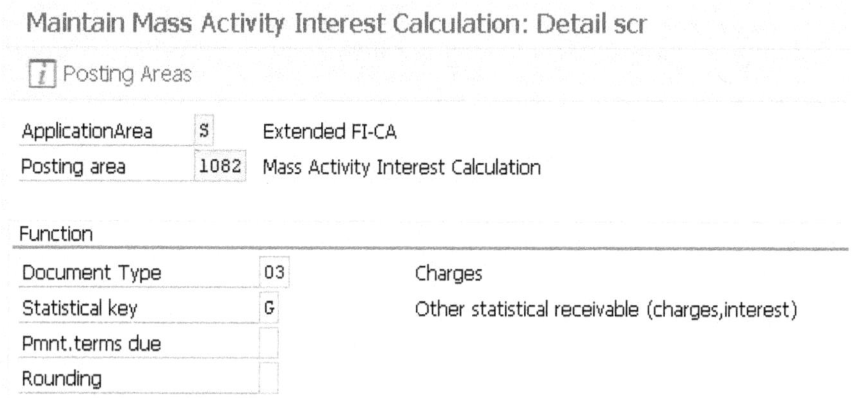

Maintain Mass Activity Interest Calculation: Detail scr

[i] Posting Areas

| ApplicationArea | S | Extended FI-CA |
| Posting area | 1082 | Mass Activity Interest Calculation |

Function

Document Type	03	Charges
Statistical key	G	Other statistical receivable (charges,interest)
Pmnt.terms due		
Rounding		

Figure 11.32 Specifications for Mass Run

This completes our discussion on the additional settings required for interest calculation in FICA. Let us, now, move on to discuss the dunning configuration in FICA.

11.3.4 Dunning

We have already discussed dunning, in detail, in Section 10.3.7 of Chapter 10. Let us see the settings that are relevant with respect to FICA, here:

- Define Dunning Procedure Categories
- Define Dunning Level Categories
- Configure Dunning Procedure
- Define Dunning Grouping

Project Starfish

The Digifone management has suggested to use the default settings provided by SAP, wherever possible. Accordingly, the project team has decided to go ahead with the standard definitions for both dunning procedure categories and dunning level categories.

Let us start with the definition of dunning procedure categories.

11.3.4.1   Define Dunning Procedure Categories

You can create the dunning procedure categories, here, which you can use, later, while configuring the dunning procedure.

Use the menu path: SAP Customizing Implementation Guide > Financial Accounting Global Settings > Contract Accounts Receivable and Payable > Business Transactions > Dunning > Dunning by Dunning Procedure > Define Dunning Procedure Categories.

On the resulting screen, you will see the standard settings from SAP which you can use as such (Figure 11.33). However, if you need new procedure categories, click on 'New Entries' and define your own.

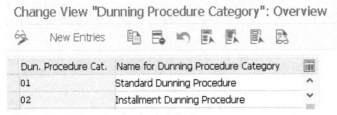

Change View "Dunning Procedure Category": Overview

New Entries

Dun. Procedure Cat.	Name for Dunning Procedure Category
01	Standard Dunning Procedure
02	Installment Dunning Procedure

Figure 11.33 Dunning Procedure Category

The next task is to define the dunning level categories.

11.3.4.2   Define Dunning Level Categories

Use the menu path: SAP Customizing Implementation Guide > Financial Accounting Global Settings > Contract Accounts Receivable and Payable > Business Transactions > Dunning > Dunning by Dunning Procedure > Define Dunning Level Categories.

On the resulting screen, you will see the standard settings from SAP which you can use as such (Figure 11.34).

Change View "Dunning Level Categories": Overview

New Entries

Dunning Level Cat.	Text for dunning level type
01	Reminder
02	Legal proceedings
03	Last Dunning Notice
04	Repeated Dunning
05	Qualified Dunning Notice

Figure 11.34 Dunning Level Category

With this, we can now define the dunning procedure to be used by the company codes of Digifone.

11.3.4.3   Configure Dunning Procedure

This is similar to the dunning procedure definition that we have discussed in Section 10.3.7.2 of Chapter 10. Here also, you will define the required dunning procedures and per procedure, you will, then, maintain the dunning levels, amount limits, dunning activities and minimum interest amount.

Use the menu path: SAP Customizing Implementation Guide > Financial Accounting Global Settings > Contract Accounts Receivable and Payable > Business Transactions > Dunning > Dunning by Dunning Procedure > Configure Dunning Procedure.

On the resulting screen, click on 'New Entries' and maintain the required settings (Figure 11.35):

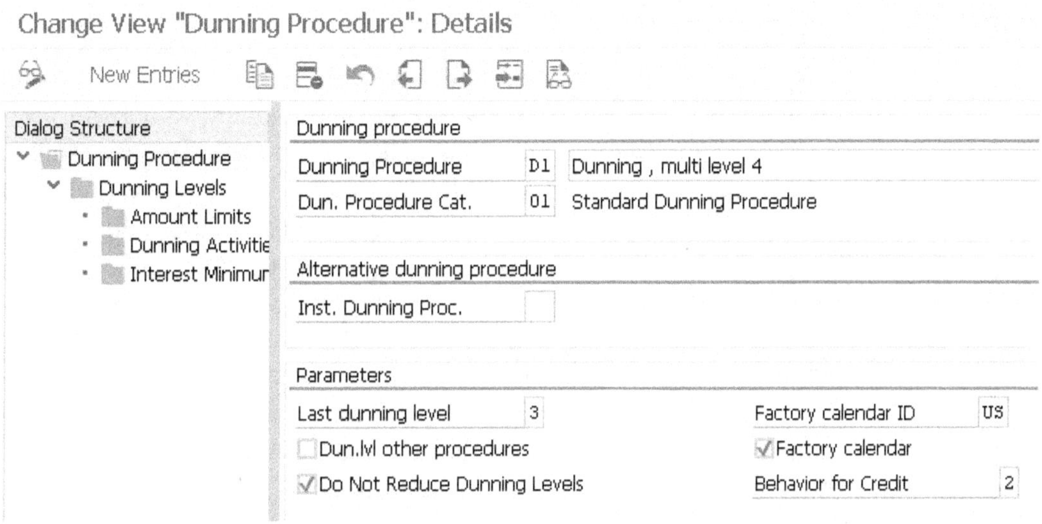

Figure 11.35 Dunning Procedure Configuration

i.   Enter the identifier for the dunning procedure (D1) and the explanation for the same.

ii.   Enter the dunning procedure category as to whether it is a standard procedure (01) or an instalment procedure (02).

iii.   Enter the 'Parameters':

- Select the appropriate parameter for 'Last dunning level'. The entry in this field determines how the dunning program is to react where open receivables exist for a business partner, and have already reached the highest dunning level in an earlier payment run. You have the options to enter a value from 0 to 4: if 0 - the system does not create any further dunning notice, and no log is created, 1 – no further dunning notice, but, the system makes an entry in the dunning log, 2 - if a further dunning run is carried out, then, those open receivables to which the highest dunning level already applied before the dunning run was carried out are dunned again at this same level, 3 - those open receivables to which the highest dunning level already applied before the dunning run was carried out are excluded from the dunning run, and 4 – dunning only the new items.

- Do not select 'Dun.lvl other procedures'; otherwise, when you change the dunning procedure (for an already dunned item), it will be now dunned with the lowest dunning level.
- The flag 'Do Not Reduce Dunning Level', when set, results in the dunning level (of the items in the dunning run) being not lowered during the next run, when the item was partially paid.

> **i** Consider, for example, that a receivable has reached the 4th dunning level but was partially paid. The system, subsequently, groups this residual amount with other items in one dunning notice. However, as a result of the partial payment, the amount limit for the 4th dunning level is no longer reached and the dunning notice created therefore receives dunning level 3. But, if you set the indicator, then, the item that has been partially paid receives dunning level 4.

- For the field 'Behaviour for Credit' you have three options: 0 - dun all items, ignore credit for dunning balance, 1- dun all items, consider credit balance for dunning and 2 – do not dun, if there is credit. Select the appropriate one.
- Enter the 'Factory calendar ID' and select the 'Factory calendar' check-box, to take into account the holidays for calculating the dunning frequency, payment deadline, and the arrears days.

iv. 'Save' the details. And, configure dunning levels. Later, per dunning level, maintain the amount limits, dunning activities and minimum interest amount.

The next activity is to define the dunning grouping.

11.3.4.4   Define Dunning Grouping

Define the dunning grouping, which you can allocate later to the contract accounts.

Use the menu path: SAP Customizing Implementation Guide > Financial Accounting Global Settings > Contract Accounts Receivable and Payable > Business Transactions > Dunning > Dunning by Dunning Procedure > Define Dunning Grouping.

On the resulting screen, enter an identifier and a description for the dunning grouping. Then, for the dunning group identifier, maintain the required dunning grouping fields (Figure 11.36).

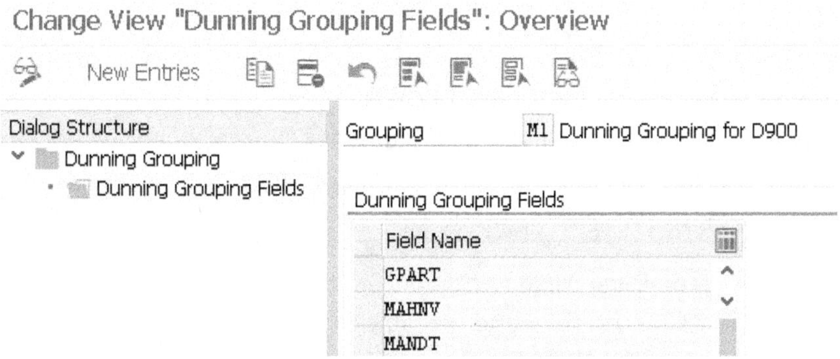

Change View "Dunning Grouping Fields": Overview

New Entries

Dialog Structure
˅ Dunning Grouping
   • Dunning Grouping Fields

Grouping   M1 Dunning Grouping for D900

Dunning Grouping Fields

Field Name	
GPART	
MAHNV	
MANDT	

Figure 11.36 Dunning Grouping Fields

This completes our discussion on configuring the settings for dunning for FICA for Digifone. Let us move on to discuss the FICA's integration settings with G/L.

11.4 Integration

Though FICA integration covers settings with various components and sub-components of SAP including SAP SD, CRM, CO, Cash Management, Flexible Real Estate Management (RE-FX), revenue accounting, billing management, business intelligence, convergent charging, FSCM, enterprise services etc., we will limit the discussion here, in this Section, to G/L integration.

11.4.1 General Ledger Accounting

Here, we shall see the settings necessary for integrating FICA with SAP G/L Accounting. We shall discuss:

- Define Posting Specifications for General Ledger Transfer
- Enter Additional Posting Specifications for General Ledger Transfer
- Define Direct G/L Transfer for Document Origins

Let us start with the first task of defining the posting specifications for G/L transfer.

11.4.1.1   Define Posting Specifications for General Ledger Transfer

Per chart of accounts and company code, you need to define the posting key (for debit / credit postings) and the document type, for posting the G/L account documents, during the transfer of totals records to FI-G/L. The document type, you specify here, will be used in all postings in the G/L. Besides, you also specify if adjustment postings are posted in the G/L as negative postings.

> ℹ️ Note that the number of items that you can include in a G/L document is limited. If the number of items to be posted, during the transfer of totals records to the G/L, exceeds this number, it is necessary that the system splits these documents. Normally, the G/L documents created by a document split do not have a balance of zero. You reach a balance of zero for these documents, by posting to a transfer account.

Use the menu path: SAP Customizing Implementation Guide > Financial Accounting Global Settings > Contract Accounts Receivable and Payable > Integration > General Ledger Accounting > Define Posting Specifications for General Ledger Transfer. You may also use Transaction FQZE.

On the resulting screen, for the posting area 0100, you can maintain the appropriate settings (Figure 11.37): enter the G/L account for transferring the totals from FICA ('Transfer Account'), maintain the debit /credit posting keys, enter the 'Document type' (SA), select 1 in 'Negative Posting' field to allow negative postings, and enter 'Segment' if required.

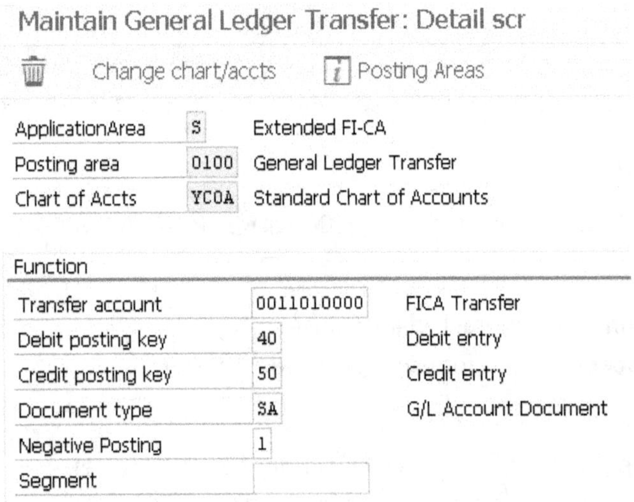

Maintain General Ledger Transfer: Detail scr

🗑️ Change chart/accts   ℹ️ Posting Areas

ApplicationArea	S	Extended FI-CA
Posting area	0100	General Ledger Transfer
Chart of Accts	YCOA	Standard Chart of Accounts

Function

Transfer account	0011010000	FICA Transfer
Debit posting key	40	Debit entry
Credit posting key	50	Credit entry
Document type	SA	G/L Account Document
Negative Posting	1	
Segment		

Figure 11.37 Posting Specification for G/L Transfer

The next activity is to enter the ledger-specific transfer accounts

11.4.1.2   Enter Additional Posting Specifications for General Ledger Transfer

Here, in this configuration step, you can enter a profit center and business area for posting to the transfer account, if needed. Remember that you can enter the segment, while configuring the previous activity 'Define Posting Specifications for General Ledger Transfer' (Section 11.4.1.1) or you can derive the segment from the profit center you maintain here, now.

Use the menu path: SAP Customizing Implementation Guide > Financial Accounting Global Settings > Contract Accounts Receivable and Payable > Integration > General Ledger Accounting > Enter Additional Posting Specifications for General Ledger Transfer. You may also use Transaction FQZE1. On the resulting screen, enter the 'Profit Center' and/or 'Business Area' that you want the system to derive while posting the transactions.

With this let us move on to defining direct G/L transfer for FICA document origins.

11.4.1.3   Define Direct G/L Transfer for Document Origins

It is possible that you can directly update the FICA document in SAP G/L Accounting. Towards that, you can define the document origins for which you can post the G/L document immediately with the FICA document. Use the menu path: SAP Customizing Implementation Guide > Financial Accounting Global Settings > Contract Accounts Receivable and Payable > Integration > General Ledger Accounting > Define Direct G/L Transfer for Document Origins.

This completes our discussion on integrating FICA with other SAP applications / sub-applications.

11.5 Conclusion

You learned that the Contract Accounts Receivable and Payable (SAP FICA or FI-CA) is a subledger accounting in SAP, meant for processing large document volumes in terms of master data and business transactions with improved/additional A/R functionalities, and is generally used in certain industries like public sector, utilities, insurance, telecommunications etc. You understood that you can use the industry-neutral FICA (also known as Extended FI-CA) as an alternate to the regular FI-A/R and FI-A/P applications, even if you do not operate in any of the high-transaction-volume industries / businesses.

You learned how to set up FICA in SAP to meet specific business requirements. In the process, you learned configuring the required organizational units to depict the enterprise structure on the FICA side. Later, you learned about setting up the system for handling the important basic functions including activating the application / subapplication, defining general settings for master data, and the settings for contract partner, contract accounts and postings.

While configuring the settings for business transactions, you learned the specifications you need to make for handling security deposits, payments, dunning and interest calculation. Finally, you learned about the important settings for integration of FICA with SAP G/L Accounting.

This completes our discussion on SAP FICA, and we are now ready to move on to discuss bank accounting in the next Chapter.

12 Bank Accounting

Bank Accounting (FI-BL) is a component within SAP that helps you in handling the accounting transactions that you process with your bank(s). A subapplication and not a subledger, you will use FI-BL for managing bank master data, cash balance (check and bill of exchange management), and also for creating / processing of payments, both incoming and outgoing. With this component, you will be able to define all the required country-specific parameters for both manual and electronic payment processing (including lockbox processing in USA), besides maintaining the specifications for payment forms, payment data media etc.

We shall discuss the following aspects for bank accounting in this Chapter:

- Bank Master Data
- Bank Chains (Multi-Stage Payment Methods)
- Payment Transactions

Let us start our discussion with bank master data.

12.1 Bank Master Data

SAP stores bank master data, centrally, in the bank directory. Besides maintaining the bank master data, you will also define your own bank (known as 'house banks') details and those for your business partners (that you will maintain in the business partner's master record). We shall describe, here in this Section, how you can maintain bank master data and also outline the factors that you should consider when transferring bank master data automatically.

We shall discuss the following:

- Bank Directories
- House Banks
- Business Partner's Banks
- Bank Distribution
- Checks for Bank Master Data

Let us start with the bank directories.

12.1.1 Bank Directories

Containing the bank master data, the 'bank directory' includes the bank address data and control data (such as the SWIFT Code, IBAN etc) for all the banks that you will be transacting with. This includes your house banks and also the banks of your business partners. If you also deal with post office banks, then, you need to identify them separately.

You can create bank directories in two ways: automatically and manually. You normally use the automatic option of creating the bank directory to start with, and once the directory is in place, you may resort to manual processing to add and/or update the existing directories.

Let us look at how to automatically create the bank directory.

12.1.1.1   Automatic Creation of Bank Directory

When creating the bank directory automatically, you can choose to create a bank directory containing the master data of international banks and/or local banks of a particular country.

In the case of creating a directory with data of international banks, use the menu path: SAP Customizing Implementation Guide > Cross-Application Components > Bank Directory > Bank Directory Data Transfer > Transfer Bank Directory Data – International or Transaction BIC2. You will, essentially, be using SAP's report program RFBVBIC2 to transfer bank master data, from a file that uses the format 'BICplusIBAN Directory'. You need to maintain the required upload parameters (for example, file structure, file path, file name etc), country selection specifications, data administration parameters etc, when you execute this Transaction.

 SAP has replaced the erstwhile Transaction of BIC with BIC2.

For creating a directory with country-specific bank master data, you have to transfer bank master data from an ASCII file (country-specific format) to the SAP System using the report program RFBVALL_0. Use the menu path: SAP Customizing Implementation Guide > Cross-Application Components > Bank Directory > Bank Directory Data Transfer > Transfer Bank Directory Data - Country-Specific or Transaction BAUP. You will notice that some data of your house bank(s) are also getting transferred during the process; you need to use the configuration activity 'Define House Banks' to add the missing data, later.

You may use Transaction BA01 to access the pre-defined country-specific file formats in the standard SAP system (Figure 12.1). You may use them as such. However, if you need to define a new country-specific file format for the program RFBVALL_0, you first need to copy the sample function module FILL_BNKA_FIELDS_SAMPLE. Then, enter your own statements in the copied function module. Never change the function module FILL_BNKA_FIELDS_SAMPLE.

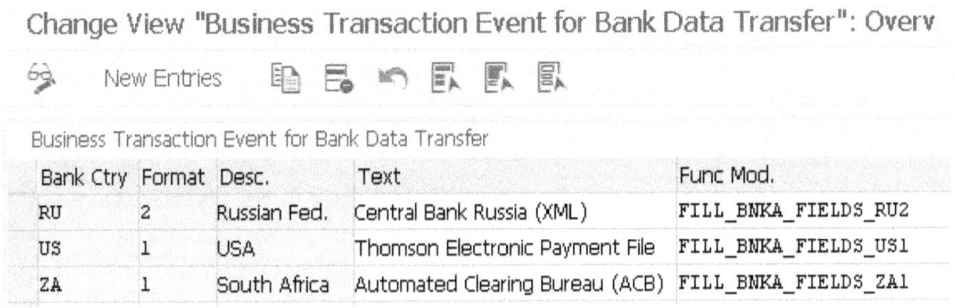

Change View "Business Transaction Event for Bank Data Transfer": Overv

   New Entries   🖹 🗟 ↰ 🖹 🖹 🖹

Business Transaction Event for Bank Data Transfer

Bank Ctry	Format	Desc.	Text	Func Mod.
RU	2	Russian Fed.	Central Bank Russia (XML)	FILL_BNKA_FIELDS_RU2
US	1	USA	Thomson Electronic Payment File	FILL_BNKA_FIELDS_US1
ZA	1	South Africa	Automated Clearing Bureau (ACB)	FILL_BNKA_FIELDS_ZA1

Figure 12.1 Country-Specific ASCII File Format for Bank Directory Creation

Let us move on to discuss the manual creation of bank directory, in the next Section.

12.1.1.2   Manual Creation of Bank Directory

To create the bank master records manually, you need to use the SAP Easy Access menu path: SAP Menu > Accounting > Financial Accounting > Banking > Master Data > Bank Master Record. You may also use Transaction FI01.

You can also create bank master records of business partner's banks while maintaining the vendor or customer master records. Once maintained, these records are added to the bank directory automatically.

12.1.1.3   Archiving / Deleting Bank Master Data

Use 'archiving' to archive bank master data that you no longer require. During archiving, the system deletes the selected bank master data from the database, and stores that in an archive file which you can transfer to an archiving system.

You cannot delete the bank master data just like that: you first need to set a 'deletion indicator' for the bank master data that is to be deleted. To set up the deletion indicator, you may use SAP Easy Access menu path: SAP Menu > Accounting > Financial Accounting > Banks > Master Data > Mark for Deletion, or Transaction FI06. The essential condition to delete a bank master data is that there should not be any reference existing, in the system, for that bank; that is, the bank which is to be deleted should not be appearing in the master data of any customer or vendor, and it should not have been defined as your house bank.

ⓘ To delete bank master data that you have copied for testing, use the program SAPF023 after ensuring that there is no productive company code in the bank country. Always run this program in the batch mode, as there could be run-time problems even with small amount of data. In this case of deleting the test data, the system will not check if the deletion indictor is set or not.

With this, we are, now, ready to discuss the house banks.

12.1.2 House Banks

We have already discussed the house banks, in detail, in <u>Section 10.3.3.3.1</u> of Chapter 10. Besides creating house banks, we also saw how to create the accounts in house bank.

We can, hence, move on to discuss the business partner's bank in the next Section.

12.1.3 Business Partner's Bank

We have already seen, vide <u>Section 12.1.1.2</u>, that you can branch out to maintain the business partner's bank master data while creating / changing the bank master data relating to business partners like vendor or customer. For example, you can maintain the 'Bank Details' under 'Payment Transactions' tab of a customer master record (Figure 12.2). Per business partner's bank, you may enter the bank 'ID', country key ('Ctry'), 'Bank Key', bank account number ('Bank acct'), etc. When there are multiple banks for a given business partner, you may use the 'ID' (field BKVID) to specify the particular bank in a line item enabling the system to use that bank for the payment transactions.

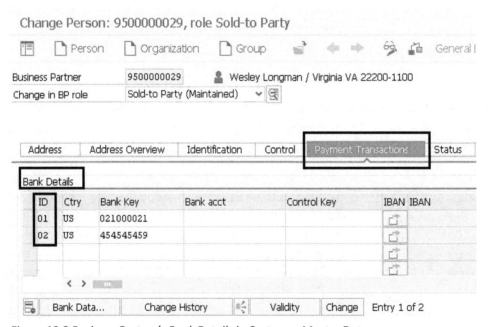

Figure 12.2 Business Partner's Bank Details in Customer Master Data

With this, let us move on to discuss bank distribution.

12.1.4 Bank Distribution

You can create / change bank data in different systems belonging to an SAP system group, so that every system, in the group, always has the current data. When you save bank data in one system, the same is sent on to other systems through ALE business processes via a consolidation system. The local systems send all changes to the consolidation system and *vice versa*.

In order to distribute bank master data and the related company addresses, you need to make the required settings using the menu path: SAP Customizing Implementation Guide > Cross-Application Components > Bank Directory > Distribution of Banks > Make Settings for Distributing Bank Master Data. Once you are in the Transaction, you need to complete the following configuration activities:

- Make Settings for Logical Systems
- Maintain Distribution Model (Transaction BD64)
- Generate Partner Profiles (Transaction BD82)
- Define Consolidation System for Bank Data Distribution

But there may be situations, in which the bank data is not properly distributed, due to non-availability of the target system, incomplete / incorrect Customizing etc. In such a case, you may use the report RFBANK_ALE, to distribute bank data that you have already created in one of the systems to the others. Use the menu path: SAP Customizing Implementation Guide > Cross-Application Components > Bank Directory > Distribution of Banks > Distribute Banks or Transaction FI08. During the process, the system creates the bank if it is not there already in the target system. On the other hand, if the bank exists, the system updates the target system with the changed data (address data, bank identifier, SWIFT code etc), if any. When a bank data becomes obsolete, you can set a deletion flag in the local system for the relevant bank. The system then copies this deletion flag to other systems.

With this, let us move on to discuss how to set up the checks for bank master data.

12.1.5 Checks for Bank Master Data

It is possible that you can specify 'check rules' for country-specific bank master data definitions. Once specified, these rules apply to the bank number, or the bank key and bank account number. Per country key, you can specify the length of the bank number and bank account number. Then, the check rule determines whether (a) the entry is numeric or alphanumeric, (b) the length specified is only a maximum length, or must be strictly adhered to and (c) gaps are permitted in the bank account number or bank number. Besides these mandatory checks, you can also maintain additional country-specific checks to avoid input errors.

The standard SAP system comes with country-specific settings based on ISO standards. You may view the standard settings by using the menu path: SAP Customizing Implementation Guide > SAP NetWeaver > General settings > Set Countries > Set Country-Specific Checks or Transaction OY17. On the resulting screen, double-click on a specific row to view the default settings for that country (Figure 12.3).

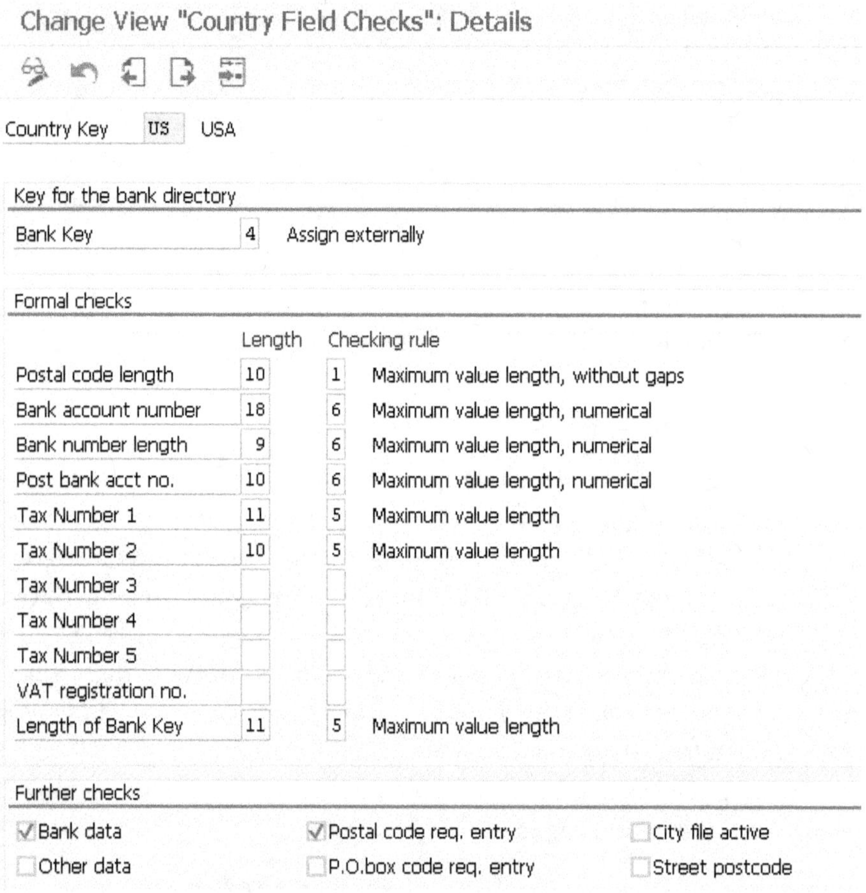

Change View "Country Field Checks": Details

Country Key   US   USA

Key for the bank directory

Bank Key   4   Assign externally

Formal checks

	Length		Checking rule
Postal code length	10	1	Maximum value length, without gaps
Bank account number	18	6	Maximum value length, numerical
Bank number length	9	6	Maximum value length, numerical
Post bank acct no.	10	6	Maximum value length, numerical
Tax Number 1	11	5	Maximum value length
Tax Number 2	10	5	Maximum value length
Tax Number 3			
Tax Number 4			
Tax Number 5			
VAT registration no.			
Length of Bank Key	11	5	Maximum value length

Further checks

☑ Bank data   ☑ Postal code req. entry   ☐ City file active
☐ Other data   ☐ P.O.box code req. entry   ☐ Street postcode

Figure 12.3 Country-Specific Checks for Bank Master Data

This completes our discussion on bank master data. Let us, now, discuss the bank chains (also known as the 'multi-stage payment methods'), next.

12.2 Bank Chains (Multi-Stage Payment Methods)

Earlier - before SAP introduced the concept of 'bank chain' - when making a payment to your business partner abroad, you used to specify the house bank and the business partner's bank for processing the payment. The house bank will be the starting point and the business partner's bank will be the end point in the payment transaction. It was the house bank that would determine via which bank (intermediary bank) the payment would be made.

Now, with the bank chain functionality, it is possible that you can define the bank chain by yourself for faster payments besides reducing bank charges. It is now possible that you can select up to three intermediary banks in the bank chain.

> **i** To make use of bank chain functionality, you must implement automatic payments either in SAP-FI (refer Section 10.3.3.3 of Chapter 10) or SAP-TR applications.

With the bank chain functionality, for each payment, the payment program determines a combination of intermediary banks (that you have previously defined). The order of the banks in the bank chain depends on the 'scenarios' which are represented by several factors including house bank, vendor's bank details, customer's bank details, currency and payment method supplement. When you carry out a payment run, the system determines the bank chain according to your settings in Customizing / master data. However, if you change an entry – for example, the house bank or the partner's bank – while editing the payment proposal, then, the system re-determines the bank chain. Also, the system determines the bank chain only for payment methods that call for processing via bank chain; the system will not use a bank chain for payments through checks, for example.

Let us start with the definition of scenario for bank chain implementation.

12.2.1 Define Scenario

A 'scenario' specifies the way in which the system determines the bank chain. It can be (a) general scenario (or general search) which is not dependent upon business partner bank details, (b) business-partner dependent scenario (or recipient-search) or (c) a scenario specifying which fields in which order. The standard SAP system comes delivered with several scenarios which you can use as such without making changes. However, should you want to create a new scenario, copy an existing one and make modifications there on.

Project Dolphin

The BESTM management has requested the project team to make use of SAP defined standard scenarios for determining the bank chain. This is because, they have been informed that defining new scenario may result in slow system performance, as secondary indexes have been created for the relevant database tables only for the standard scenarios provided by SAP. Also, that would call for contacting SAP to create the necessary indexes for implementing the new scenario. Hence the decision to go in for standard scenario. In doing so, it was requested to make use of 'Sender Bank Oriented' scenario.

Use the menu path: SAP Customizing Implementation Guide > Financial Accounting > Bank Accounting > Bank Chains > Define Scenario. You may also use Transaction FIBC. On the resulting screen (Figure 12.4), you will see several scenarios. You will notice that the check-box 'Gen.Search' has been selected wherever payments are independent of partner's bank details, and the check-box 'Rec.Search' selected (like, scenario 0004) if payments are dependent on partner's bank details. If both the check-boxes are selected, when determining the bank chain, the system first runs a search for a recipient-specific (that is, partner-dependent) bank chain, and then for a general bank chain. The scenario 0001 is for no bank chain determination.

Change View "Scenario definition": Overview

New Entries

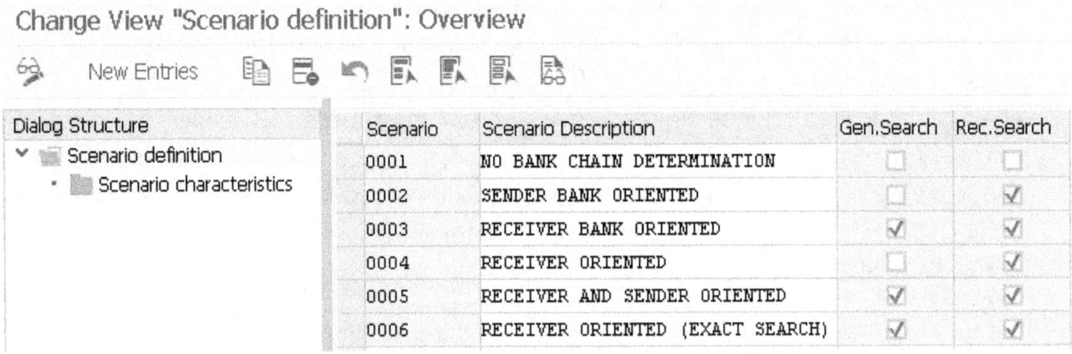

Scenario	Scenario Description	Gen.Search	Rec.Search
0001	NO BANK CHAIN DETERMINATION	☐	☐
0002	SENDER BANK ORIENTED	☐	☑
0003	RECEIVER BANK ORIENTED	☑	☑
0004	RECEIVER ORIENTED	☐	☑
0005	RECEIVER AND SENDER ORIENTED	☑	☑
0006	RECEIVER ORIENTED (EXACT SEARCH)	☑	☑

Dialog Structure
- Scenario definition
  - Scenario characteristics

Figure 12.4 Standard Scenario for Bank Chain Determination

Select a scenario row (say, 0003) and double-click on 'Scenario Characteristics' on the left hand 'Dialog Structure' to view the characteristics associated with that scenario (Figure 12.5).

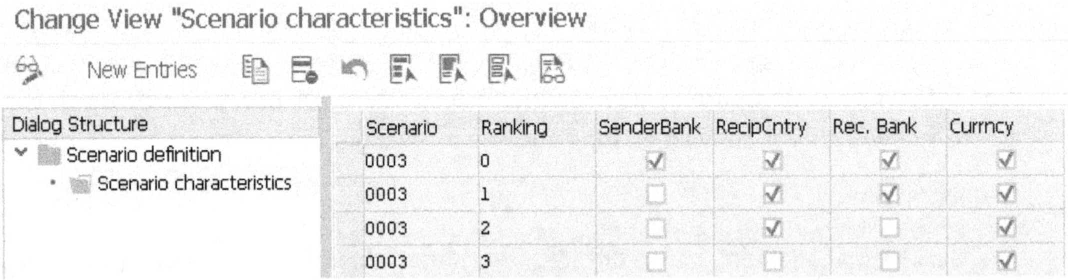

Change View "Scenario characteristics": Overview

New Entries

Scenario	Ranking	SenderBank	RecipCntry	Rec. Bank	Currncy
0003	0	☑	☑	☑	☑
0003	1	☐	☑	☑	☑
0003	2	☐	☑	☐	☑
0003	3	☐	☐	☐	☑

Dialog Structure
- Scenario definition
  - Scenario characteristics

Figure 12.5 Scenario Characteristics for Scenario 0003

If you pay attention to Figure 12.5, you will notice that the system determines the appropriate bank chain starting from 'Ranking' 0 and going all the way down to 'Ranking' 3.

The next step is to activate the bank chain.

12.2.2 Activate Bank Chain

Using this configuration step, you can activate the bank chain functionality in the system. By this, you are specifying that a bank chain is to be determined by the system for payment. You will select the appropriate scenario, here, for the bank chain determination. Use the menu path: SAP Customizing Implementation Guide > Financial Accounting > Bank Accounting > Bank Chains > Activate Bank Chain. You may also use Transaction FIBD. On the resulting screen, enter the appropriate scenario (say, 0002) and 'Save' (Figure 12.6).

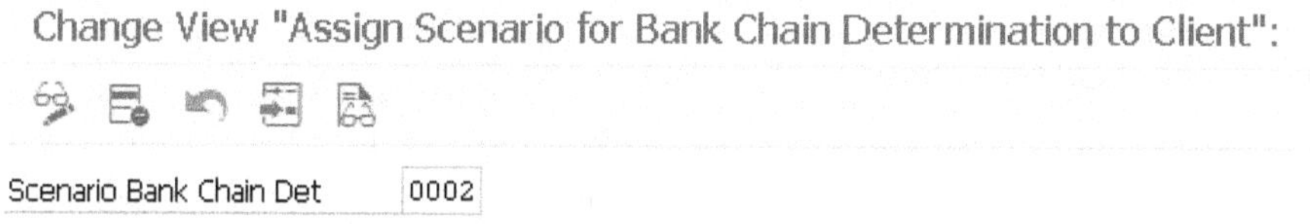

Change View "Assign Scenario for Bank Chain Determination to Client":

Scenario Bank Chain Det   0002

Figure 12.6 Scenario for Activating Bank Chain Determination

With this, we are now ready to discuss the settings for general bank chain.

12.2.3 Create General Bank Chain

You can define general bank chains using this configuration activity. Once defined, you can use the general bank chain, that is not dependent on business partner's bank details, to process your payment transactions. In this activity, you will define the sequence of banks and the accounts from which you will make the payments.

Project Dolphin

BESTM has requested the project team to ensure creating general bank chains involving three intermediary banks per chain, with the sender's correspondent bank always at the top level (priority1), followed by any intermediary bank and lastly with the correspondent bank of the recipient. While configuring the bank assignment per bank chain, it needs to be noted that the sender will be one of the company's house bank and the payment should be valid across currencies. The bank chain identifier should be easy to decipher with the company code figuring in that ID along with a numeric chain identifier at the last 2 positions. For example, a chain ID 'BM1110-1' will indicate that it is the chain #1 belonging to the company code 1110.

Use the menu path: SAP Customizing Implementation Guide > Financial Accounting > Bank Accounting > Bank Chains > Create General Bank Chain, or Transaction FIBB. On the resulting screen, click on 'New Entries' and maintain the required settings (Figure 12.7):

Change View "Bank chains": Overview

New Entries

BankChn ID	No.	Typ	Corr. Ctry	Corr.Bank Key	Bank Acct	IBAN
BM1110-1	1	1	CA	057003681	0015676668	
BM1110-1	2	2	CA	888888889	0039006700	

Dialog Structure
* Bank chains
* Assignment

Figure 12.7 Defining a General Bank Chain for Company Code 1110

i.   Enter an identifier for the bank chain in 'BankChn ID' field, select the order (of priority) of the intermediary bank in 'No.' field, select the type of the bank ('Typ') as to sender's correspondent bank (1) or intermediary bank (2) or correspondent bank of recipient (3) etc., select the country key of the correspondent bank ('Corr. Ctry'), enter the identifier of the correspondent bank ('Corr.Bank Key'), enter the bank account number at the correspondent bank ('Bank Acct') and IBAN, if required.

ii. Repeat the settings for 'No.' = 2 and 3, if required. 'Save' the settings. We have now defined a general bank chain for company code 1110 of BESTM.

iii. Now, select a row on the 'Change View 'Bank chains": Overview' screen, and double-click on 'Assignment' on the left hand side 'Dialog Structure'. On the resulting screen, click on 'New Entries', and maintain the settings, per bank chain ID, as indicated in Figure 12.8:

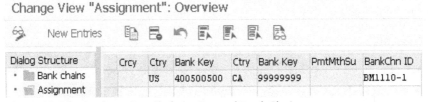

Change View "Assignment": Overview

New Entries

Dialog Structure
* Bank chains
* Assignment

Crcy	Ctry	Bank Key	Ctry	Bank Key	PmtMthSu	BankChn ID
	US	400500500	CA	99999999		BM1110-1

Figure 12.8 Assignment Details for a General Bank Chain

- Enter a currency key or leave that as blank to be valid for all currencies.
- Enter the sender bank's country key (say, US), and enter the 'Bank Key' of the sender (say, 400500500).
- Similarly, enter the recipient bank's country key (say, CA), and the key of the recipient bank.
- You may also enter the payment method supplement, if any.

iv. You can 'Save' the settings and define similar settings for other bank chain IDs.

v.   Repeat and define the settings for other general bank chains for all the paying company codes.

This completes our discussion on how to define a general bank chain. Let us now move on to discuss defining the bank chains for customers/vendors (partner's bank chain).

12.2.4 Define Bank Chains for Customers / Vendors

Use the SAP Easy Access menu path: SAP Menu > Accounting > Financial Accounting > Banks > Master Data > Bank Chain > Business Partners > Edit. You may also use Transaction FIBPU. On the resulting screen, enter either customer or vendor under 'Business Partner', enter the house bank details under 'House Bk' and maintain 'Other limitations' if required. You may also select the appropriate payment direction ('Payment direct.') as to outgoing payment or incoming payment (Figure 12.9).

Edit bank chains for creditors/debtors

Business partner

| Vendor | |
| Customer | 9500000029 |

House bk

Company code	1110
House bank	BOFAU
Account	BA100

Other limitations

| Payment currency | |
| Payment method supplement | |

Payment direct.

⦿ Outgoing payment
◯ Incoming payment

Figure 12.9 Edit Bank Chain for Creditors / Debtors – Initial Screen

When you 'Execute', the system lists all the partner banks associated with that customer / vendor on the next screen (Figure 12.10). At this point, no bank chain exists for the partner.

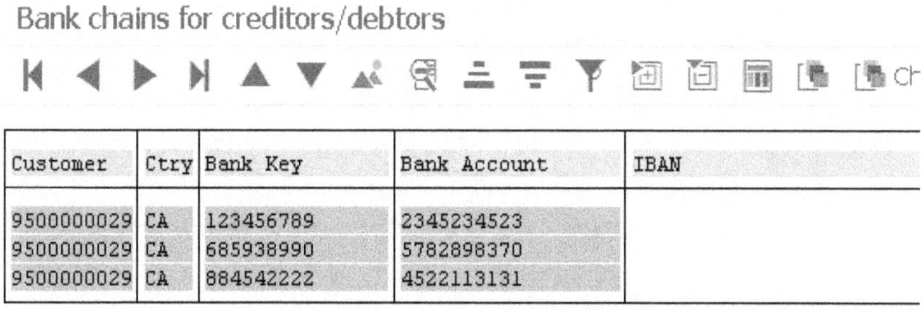

Bank chains for creditors/debtors

Customer	Ctry	Bank Key	Bank Account	IBAN
9500000029	CA	123456789	2345234523	
9500000029	CA	685938990	5782898370	
9500000029	CA	884542222	4522113131	

Figure 12.10 List of Banks Associated with the Partner

Now, select a row and click on 'Go To > Bank Chain' on the menu bar or double click on the row to create the bank chain. The system will throw a pop-up informing that the bank chain does not exist and the system is creating that chain now (Figure 12.11).

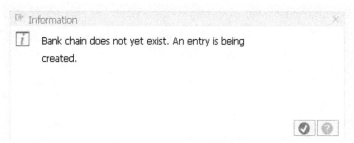

Figure 12.11 Pop-up showing Bank Chain being Created

Click 'Continue' and see that the system has now created the new bank chain for the customer (or vendor) as shown in Figure 12.12. You may click on 'Bank chain assignment' on the left hand side 'Dialog Structure' to add the necessary details.

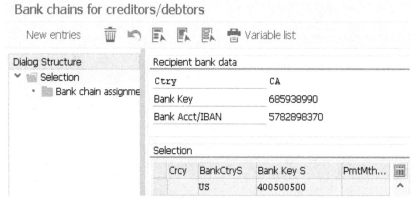

Figure 12.12 New Bank Chain for Customer

The way we created a new bank chain for a customer, you can create a bank chain for a vendor as well.

> **i** When creating a bank chain for a partner, note to enter either customer or vendor <u>and not both</u> while on the initial screen of Transaction FIPU (Figure 12.9).

Similar to that of creating bank chains for partner's banks, you can also define bank chains to handle incoming payments into your house banks. Let us discuss the same, next.

12.2.5 Bank Chains for House Banks

While you can create bank chains for partners to handle both incoming and outgoing payments, you can create bank chain for your house banks but to handle only the incoming payments.

Use the SAP Easy Access menu path: SAP Menu > Accounting > Financial Accounting > Banks > Master Data > Bank Chain > House Banks > Edit. You may also use Transaction FIBHU. On the resulting screen, maintain the required entries and note to select the 'Incoming payment' under 'Payment direct.' data block (Figure 12.13).

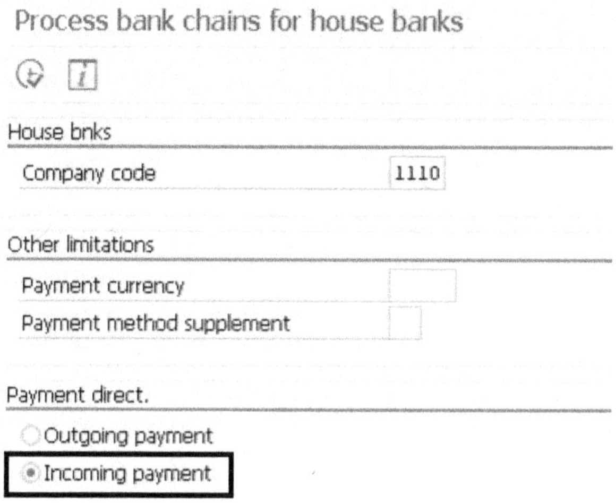

Figure 12.13 New Bank Chain for House Bank – Initial Screen

When you 'Execute', the system brings up all the associated house banks with that company code, and you can select a particular house bank row and double-click on the same to create the bank chain; you need to maintain the appropriate settings, later, on the resulting screen as to sender's bank country, sender's bank key etc.

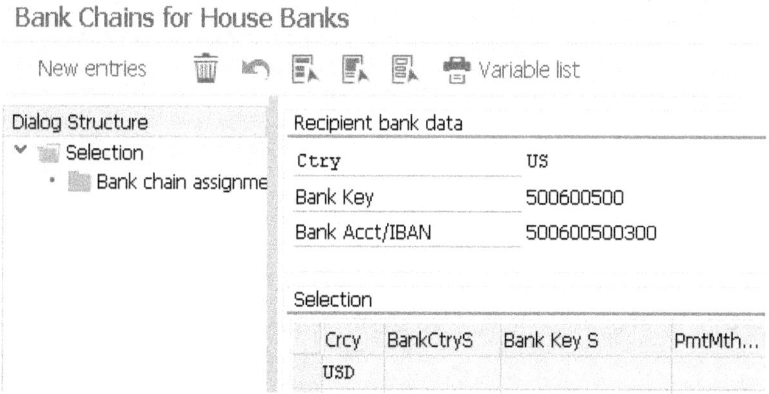

Figure 12.14 New Bank Chain for a House Bank

By default, the system creates an entry with these details as blank (Figure 12.14) indicating that it is valid for all the senders in all the countries but in the specified currency (USD in our case). As in the case of partner bank chain, you may complete the 'Bank chain assignment' settings, later.

With this, we can now look at defining a bank chain for cash management.

12.2.6 Bank Chain for Cash Management

You can also define bank chains exclusively for cash management. Use the SAP Easy Access menu path: SAP Menu > Accounting > Financial Accounting > Banks > Master Data > Bank Chain > Bank account carry over > Edit. You may also use Transaction FIBTU.

The steps are similar to the definition of bank chain for house banks except that you will enter the company code / house bank / account details for both the dispatching and receiving house banks as indicated in Figure 12.15.

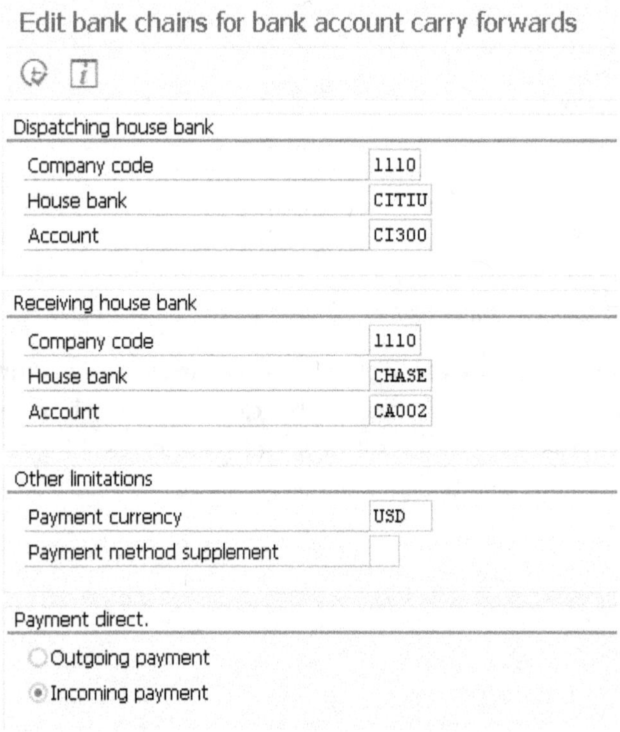

Edit bank chains for bank account carry forwards

Dispatching house bank

Company code	1110
House bank	CITIU
Account	CI300

Receiving house bank

Company code	1110
House bank	CHASE
Account	CA002

Other limitations

Payment currency	USD
Payment method supplement	

Payment direct.

○ Outgoing payment
◉ Incoming payment

Figure 12.15 New Bank Chain for Cash Management

With this, we have come to the last step of configuration in bank chain that will involve settings for including the bank chain information on payment lists.

12.2.7 Including Bank Chains on Payment Lists

By default, the system does not print the details of bank chain(s) in a payment or exception list. However, you can make technical modifications to get that printed. Create a customer include, say, CI_INCLUDE CI_REGUH_LST with the following attributes, using the ABAP workbench:

Field	Date Element	Type	Length	Short Description
CHAINTEXT	CHAINTEXT	CHAR	92	Bank chain as text

Note that the ABAP dictionary structures REGUH_LST (header information) and REGUP_LST (line item information) contain the output fields provided by program RFZALI20.

After creating and saving the customer include, you need to use the Business Transaction Event 00002110, to enter data in the field CHAINTXT that you added using CI_INCLUDE. For that, you need to use the 'Function Builder' and copy the sample function module SAMPLE_INTERFACE_00002110 and enter the required source text (from function module FI_BL_BANKCHAIN_RFZALI20, for example) in your new function module. The field CHAINTEXT will be filled in this function module and then made ready for output. Since all the command lines are deactivated in this module, you need to create a product for the 'Publish & Subscribe' interface. When done, enter Event 00002110, the product, and the function module SAMPLE_INTERFACE_00002120 and 'Save' your entries.

The system will now output the bank chain details, as text, in the payment / exception list.

This completes our discussion on bank chains. We are now ready to discuss the payment transactions associated with bank accounting.

12.3 Payment Transactions

Under payment (business) transactions, in bank accounting, we shall be discussing the following functions:

- Manual Bank Statement
- Electronic Bank Statement
- Lockbox
- Cash Journal
- Online Payments

Let us start our discussion with the manual bank statement.

12.3.1 Manual Bank Statement

Using the manual bank statement functionality, of FI-BL, you can manually enter the bank account statements that you receive from the banks. You will do the statement entry in two steps: in the first step, you will enter the account line items, using the various tools and in the second step you will post these line items. During entry of the line items, the system, besides appropriate account determination, also checks for data consistency. While posting the line items, you can create a maximum of two postings per line item: a bank account posting (say, debit bank account and credit bank clearing account) and a subledger posting (say, debit bank clearing account and credit customer account with clearing).

You shall use the menu path: use the SAP Easy Access menu path: SAP Menu > Accounting > Financial Accounting > Banks > Input > Bank Statement > Manual Entry. You may also use Transaction FF67.

Towards configuring manual bank statement functionality to suit your specific business needs, you need to complete the following activities:

- Create and Assign Business Transactions
- Define Posting Keys and Posting Rules for Manual Bank Statement
- Define Variants for Manual Bank Statement

> **i** Though 'Define Posting Keys and Posting Rules for Manual Bank Statement' has been listed as the second activity in the IMG, we need to complete this first before taking up 'Create and Assign Business Transactions' activity.

Let us start with the definition of posting keys and posting rules.

12.3.1.1   Define Posting Keys and Posting Rules for Manual Bank Statement

Using this configuration step, you will define all the posting rule(s), using a key, that you may need for bank statement entry. This posting rule key determines the posting rules for G/L and subledger accounting. The 'posting rule' represents the business transactions, like incoming check, credit memo etc, that appear on the bank statement.

Use the menu path: SAP Customizing Implementation Guide > Financial Accounting > Bank Accounting > Business Transactions > Payment Transactions > Manual Bank Statement > Define Posting Keys and Posting Rules for Manual Bank Statement, or Transaction OT84. On entering the Transaction, you need to input the chart of accounts (say, BEUS) for which you are going to maintain the settings:

i. The first task, is to create the 'account symbols'. Click on 'New Entries' and create the 'Account Symbol' along with the 'Description' (Figure 12.16). In the system, the posting details contain account symbols instead of accounts with the symbols leading to an account, after modifications, if any.

Change View "Create Account Symbols": Overview

New Entries

Dialog Structure
* Create Account Symbols
* Assign Accounts to Account Symbol
* Create Keys for Posting Rules
* Define Posting Rules

Create Account Symbols

Account Symbol	Description
BANKFEES	Bank Fees
BOEPAY	BoE Payable
BOERECDIS	BoE Rec.Discounting
BOERECPRE	BoE Rec.Presentation
CASHIN	Cash Inbound

Figure 12.16 Creating Account Symbols

ii. The second task, is to assign the appropriate accounts to each of these account symbols. Double-click on 'Assign Accounts to Account Symbol' on the left hand side 'Dialog Structure' and maintain the appropriate G/L accounts (Figure 12.17):

Change View "Assign Accounts to Account Symbol": Overview

New Entries

Dialog Structure
* Create Account Symbols
* Assign Accounts to Account Symbol
* Create Keys for Posting Rules
* Define Posting Rules

Chart of Accts   BEUS
Description   BESTM - US Standard Chart of Accounts

Assign Accounts to Account Symbol

Acct Symbol	Acct Mod.	Currency	G/L Account	Description
BANK	+	+	++++++++++	Bank Account
BANKFEES	+	+	71000000	Bank Fees
BOEPAY	+	+	++++++055	BoE Payable
BOERECDIS	+	+	++++++066	BoE Rec.Discour

Figure 12.17 Assigning Accounts to Account Symbols

* Per 'Acct Symbol', you can maintain the account modification ('Acct Mod.'), 'Currency' and the 'G/L Account'. The 'Acct Mod.' field helps in controlling account determination for bank subaccounts. Using this field, you can direct the posting to a differentiated bank subaccount, instead of a standard one.

> **i** If you do not want to use any account modification, you can leave this field as blank or you can enter the mask +.

- You can leave the 'Currency' field as blank (or use +) if you do not want to use different currencies in the G/L account.
- In the 'G/L Account' field, you can enter the exact G/L number or account determination using masking for modification. You can also specify a currency for further modifications.

> **i** As for as possible, it is recommended not to use the exact G/L number. An entry with a masking like +++++++++55 indicates that the postings will be to a specific bank subaccount ending with 55. A full masking like ++++++++ will lead postings to any of the G/L accounts belonging to that particular account symbol 'BANK'.

iii.   The third task, is to create the required keys for the posting rules. Double-click on 'Create Keys for Posting Rules' on the left hand side 'Dialog Structure' and define the required posting rules using a 'Posting Rule' key (Figure 12.18). You will use these keys to specify the rules for posting in the G/L and subledger.

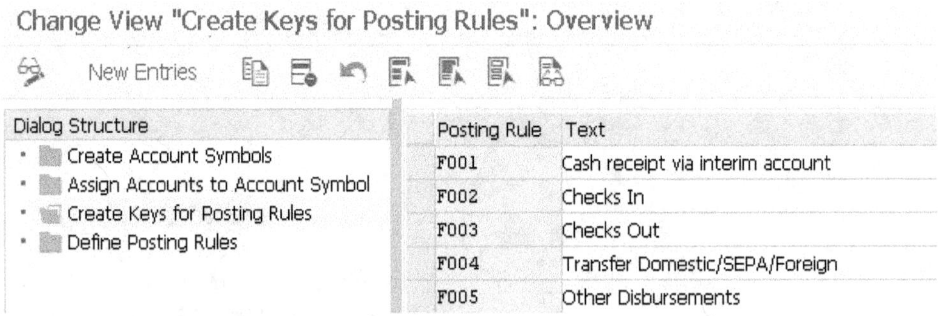

Figure 12.18 Creating Keys for Posting Rules

iv.   The final task, is to define the posting rules for the posting rule keys that you have defined in the previous task. Select a posting rule row and double-click on 'Define Posting Rules' on the left hand side 'Dialog Structure'. On the resulting screen, click on 'New Entries' and maintain the required details (Figure 12.19):

- Maintain the 'Posting Key', Special G/L indicator (if any) and 'Account Symbol' for both debit and credit postings. You may also select 'Compression' check-box to compress line items before posting.
- Select the appropriate 'Document Type', 'Posting Type' (1 is for posting to G/L, 2 for posting to subledger on debit side, 3 for posting to subledger on credit side etc) and enter a posting key to be used to generate an on-account posting in the 'Post on Acct Key' field. You may also enter a 'Reversal Reason', if required.

> **i** Valid both for manual and electronic bank statements, the 'Post on Acct Key' field enables the posting program to attempt an on-account posting when a clearing fails.

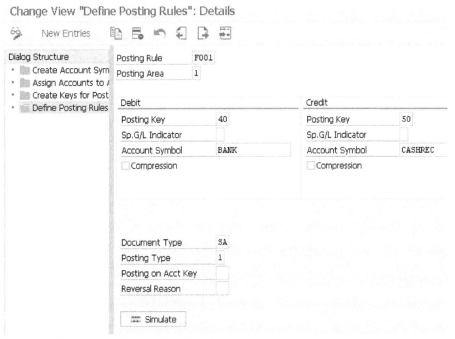

Figure 12.19 Defining Posting Rule Details

- You may press 'Simulate' for simulating the account determination. 'Save' the details and define the posting rule details for all the posting rule keys (Figure 12.20) per 'Posting Area' (1 = bank account and 2 = subledger account).

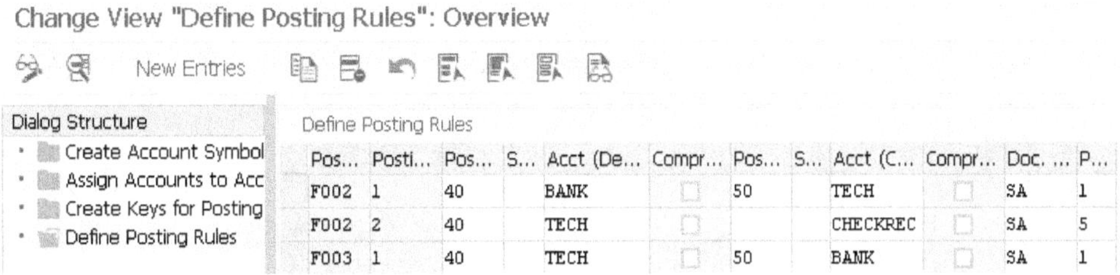

Change View "Define Posting Rules": Overview

Pos...	Posti...	Pos...	S...	Acct (De...	Compr...	Pos...	S...	Acct (C...	Compr...	Doc. ...	P...
F002	1	40		BANK	☐	50		TECH	☐	SA	1
F002	2	40		TECH	☐			CHECKREC	☐	SA	5
F003	1	40		TECH	☐	50		BANK	☐	SA	1

Figure 12.20 Posting Rule Details - Overview

With this, we are now ready to create and assign business transactions to posting rules.

12.3.1.2   Create and Assign Business Transactions

Here, in this step, you will store an indicator, per business transaction, and allocate a posting rule to that business transaction. It is possible that more than one business transaction to refer to a single posting rule.

> **i** For example, consider that you assign different indicators to the business transactions 'credit memo (domestic)', 'credit memo (foreign)' and 'credit memo (rent). Since, the posting logic is the same for all the three transactions, you can assign all of them with the same 'posting rule' (credit memo). Now, in this case, if you do not specify a modification key, then, the system directs all the postings represented by the posting rule 'credit memo' to a standard account. However, if you want, for example, to direct 'credit memo (foreign)' to a different account, then, you need to create an account modification.

Use the menu path: SAP Customizing Implementation Guide > Financial Accounting > Bank Accounting > Business Transactions > Payment Transactions > Manual Bank Statement > Create and Assign Business Transactions, or Transaction OT52. On the resulting screen (Figure 12.21), click on 'New Entries' and maintain the settings that include the business transaction indicators, posting rule etc., for the transaction type ('Trans. Type') 1 which is nothing but the manual bank statement. Per business transaction (we are using the standard ones), you will have to maintain the posting rule ('Post. Rule') that you have defined earlier, a +/- indicator, an account modifier and an interpretation algorithm.

Change View "Manual Bank Statement Transactions": Overview

🐷   New Entries   🖺 🖥 🔄 🗒 🗒 🗒 🗒

Trans. type   1

Tran	+-	Post. Rule	Acct mod	Int algthm	Text
F001	+	F001	+	1	Cash inflow via interim account
F002	+	F002	+		Check credit memo through bank
F003	–	F003	+	13	Check out
F004	–	F004	+	19	Transfer Domestic/SEPA/Foreign
F005	–	F005	+		Other disbursements
F006	+	F006	+		Other receipts

Figure 12.21 Manual Bank Statement Transactions - Overview

The account modifier ('Acct mod') helps to direct the posting to a different bank subaccount instead of to a standard bank subaccount. The 'interpretation algorithm' enables to find separate outgoing payments using the reference information returned by the bank: while an entry of 000 in 'Int algthm' field denotes that there is no algorithm used for that business transaction, an entry, for example, of 013 indicates that an algorithm by name 'Outgoing Check: Check Number = or <> Payment Doc.No.' is being used for the business transaction F003 (check out).

Let us, now, move on to define the variants for processing manual bank statements.

12.3.1.3   Define Variants for Manual Bank Statement

Create separate 'account assignment variants' for the manual bank statement, to adapt the arrangement and/or the selection of account assignment fields to suit your company-specific requirements. The standard SAP comes delivered with one variant (SAP01), as the default. You can work with that, or you can create your own by copying and adapting the same. If you plan not to use the default one, you can deactivate the same. But, you have to activate all your new variants before using them.

Project Dolphin

The project team has recommended to the BESTM management to make use of the standard account assignment variant for manual processing of bank statements. Accordingly, it has been decided not to define any new variant in the system.

Use the menu path: SAP Customizing Implementation Guide > Financial Accounting > Bank Accounting > Business Transactions > Payment Transactions > Manual Bank Statement > Define Variants for Manual Bank Statement, or Transaction OT43. On the resulting screen, you will see the standard variant SAP01 which has already been activated. You can double-click on that, to see the details on the next screen (Figure 12.22).

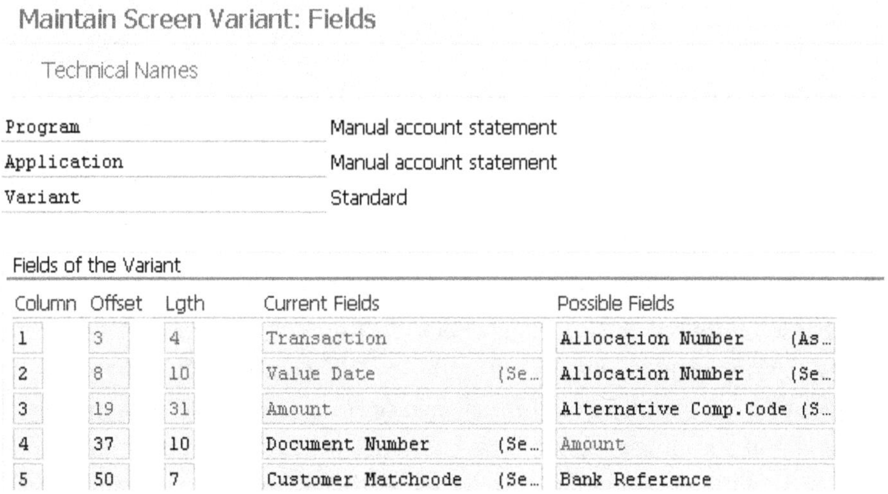

Maintain Screen Variant: Fields

Technical Names

Program	Manual account statement
Application	Manual account statement
Variant	Standard

Fields of the Variant

Column	Offset	Lgth	Current Fields		Possible Fields	
1	3	4	Transaction		Allocation Number	(As...
2	8	10	Value Date	(Se...	Allocation Number	(Se...
3	19	31	Amount		Alternative Comp.Code	(S...
4	37	10	Document Number	(Se...	Amount	
5	50	7	Customer Matchcode	(Se...	Bank Reference	

Figure 12.22 Standard Variant for Manual Bank Statement

If you want to create a new one, on the initial screen, select the standard variant and click on 'Copy', enter a name for the new variant on the pop-up and 'Continue'. On the next screen, you can select any of the 'Possible Fields' on the right hand side, to include under 'Current Fields'.

> **i** The fields that have already been included in the 'Current Fields' block are marked in blue colour. You will not be able to delete 'Transaction', Value Date' and 'Amount' fields as they have been predefined as the required fields.

This completes our discussion on configuring the system for handling manual bank statements. Let us, now, move on to discuss the settings that you need to make for working with the electronic bank statements.

12.3.2 Electronic Bank Statement

You can use the 'Electronic Bank Statement' (EBS) functionality, of FI-BL, to support you in the processing of incoming payments. You have the option of getting the bank statement data from your banks electronically. There are various standards and formats that are used in such a transfer of data, from a bank to your company. It is possible to manually postprocess and post any bank statement item that was not updated directly, in the system (using Transaction FEBA_BANK_STATEMENT).

SAP supports many international file formats for EBS. It supports two groups of formats: (a) the formats that can be further processed by SAP directly, such as SWIFT MT940 and BAI, and (b) the formats that can be converted (using a report) to the MulitCash format, for further processing.

> **i** BAI file formats (BAI and BAI2) for EBS has been developed by the Bank Administration Institute (BAI) of USA, for cash management balance reporting. The BAI (or BAI1) is no longer the preferred choice, since the introduction of BAI2 in 1987 which is widely used in USA. Though supported by several global banks, BAI2's usage outside USA is limited.
>
> BAI (or BAI1) and BAI2 formats differ mainly in their level of information detail. If you use BAI, you will not be able separate out the incoming check line items by invoice subtotal reference, as one check total amount has all invoices listed in it. This calls for 100% matching of the entire check amount with the total amount for all invoices listed. Else, SAP will post the check 'on account' or will make it 'unprocessed' if no customer account and documents could be identified. And, this will lead to manual intervention to clear payments against the open items. BAI2, on the other hand, splits the check total into separate invoice references and

associated payment amounts, thus, allowing for enhanced clearing even with partial payments.

A SWIFT MT940 or simply MT940 is an EBS standard, structured on SWIFT Customer Statement message representing the day-end statement data file, from a bank / financial institution containing details of all transactions posted to account(s).

MultiCash is another EBS format, from a German company (Omikron), and is widely recognized by various banking institutions, in Europe, for communication with customers' ERP systems. The format consists of two files: AUSZUG.txt (header information) and UMSATZ.txt (transaction details).

Using the EBS functionality, you can handle a variety of tasks including:

- Bank statement overview
- Displaying bank statements
- Functional enhancements
- Importing bank statements
- Posting and clearing
- Postprocessing bank statements
- Processing of returned debit memos
- Receiving a bank statement via EDI

To configure EBS to meet your specific requirements, you first need to complete the global settings. Let us do that now.

12.3.2.1 Make Global Settings for Electronic Bank Statement

There a total of six steps that form the global settings for EBS. They are:

1. Create Account Symbols
2. Assign Accounts to Account Symbols
3. Create Keys for Posting Rules
4. Define Posting Rules
5. Create A Transaction Type
6. Assign Bank Accounts to Transaction Type

Of the six, we have already completed the first four, in Section 12.3.1 when we configured the system for handling manual bank statement. Let us complete the remaining settings, now.

Project Dolphin

The project team suggested to use the BAI2 as the EBS file format for BESTM group of company codes, as BAI2 is the most widely used standard in USA for EBS. BESTM wants to summarize the line items, in EBS, by value date instead of creating payment advice, per bank statement item.

Use the menu path: SAP Customizing Implementation Guide > Financial Accounting > Bank Accounting > Business Transactions > Payment Transactions > Electronic Bank Statement > Make Global Settings for Electronic Bank Statement, or Transaction OT83:

   i.   Specify the chart of accounts (say, BEUS) on entering the Transaction.

   ii.   On the resulting screen, double-click on 'Create Transaction Type' on the left hand side 'Dialog Structure', then click on 'New Entries'. On the next screen, enter the 'Trans. Type' and provide a 'Name' (Figure 12.23).

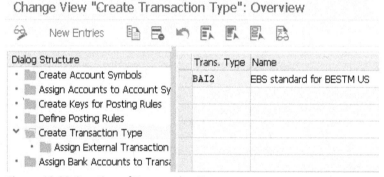

Figure 12.23 Creation of Transaction Type

   iii.   Now, double-click on 'Assign External Transaction Types to Posting Rules' on the left hand side pane, after selecting the row containing the transaction type entry (BAI2).

   iv.   On the resulting screen, click on 'New Entries' and maintain the required details on the next screen (Figure 12.24).

Trans. Type   BAI2

Name   EBS standard for BESTM US

Assign External Transaction Types to Posting Rules

Ex...	+...	Postin...	Interpretation Algorithm	Pla...	Processing Type
115	+	F002	001: Standard Algorit... ∨		Dummy entry - not assignable ∨
165	+	F001	001: Standard Algorit... ∨		Dummy entry - not assignable ∨
195	+	F017	001: Standard Algorit... ∨		Dummy entry - not assignable ∨
214	+	F009	001: Standard Algorit... ∨		Dummy entry - not assignable ∨
246	+	F009	001: Standard Algorit... ∨		Dummy entry - not assignable ∨

Figure 12.24 Assigning External Transaction Types to Posting Rules

Per 'External Transaction':

- Enter the appropriate +/- sign (for the incoming amount), specify the 'Posting Rule', and select the suitable 'Interpretation Algorithm'.

> **i** The 'external transaction code', also known as 'business transaction code', is what a bank enters as the transaction type in the account: for example, 020 transfer order, 051 bank transfer (Cr), 052 recurring entry credit memo etc. The SAP system requires this code, to identify (the business transaction) and convert the same into its own system-internal transaction codes (posting rules), that will, then, trigger specific posting transactions.

- You can also enter a transaction for planning type in 'PT Transaction' field (CL – cash concentration, AB – confirmed advice, DI – general planning etc) to generate SAP Cash Management payment advices for the relevant bank transactions.
- The 'Processing Type' field, is a country-specific parameter and is used only in countries like UK; for all other countries, including US, you need to enter the value 'Dummy entry – not assignable' in this field.
- Repeat the entries for all the external transactions and 'Save' the details.

Now, we can assign bank accounts to the transaction type. Double-click on 'Assign Bank Accounts to Transaction Types' on the left hand side 'Dialog Structure' and maintain the required details by clicking on 'New Entries' (Figure 12.25):

Assign Bank Accounts to Transaction Types

Bank Key	Bank Account	Trans. ...	Curre...	Pl...	Su...	Co...	Cash Mana...	W...	N..	Dunn...	Days
400500500	400500500100	BAI2			✓	1110	CHECKSIN	Bank	✓		

Figure 12.25 Assigning Bank Accounts to Transaction Types

- Enter the 'Bank Key' (say, 400500500), 'Bank Account' (say, 400500500100), and enter BAI2 in 'Transaction Type' field.
- You need to maintain a value in 'Currency Class' field, only if you want to import bank statements which have a currency key not in line with the currency keys in the ISO standard; else, you leave that as blank.
- If required, you may enter a 'Planning type'.
- Select the 'Summarization' check-box to summarize the items by value date; else, the system will create payment advice, per bank statement item. When selected, as in BESTM, this makes the system to summarize line items by value date.
- Enter the 'Company Code' (say, 1110).

- For 'Cash Management Account Name' field, enter a unique mnemonic name (distinct within a company code), that will replace the account number in transactions and reports in SAP Cash Management.
- You may also enter a 'Worklist' that you can use for searching open items in several bank subaccounts during postprocessing.
- If you select 'No Automatic Clearing' check-box, the system does not clear the open item automatically, when the 'amount' is the only selection criteria for clearing an open item.
- Enter a 'Dunning Block', if required. And this block will be active, until the expiry of number of days entered in 'Days Until Deletion' field before the bank statement report RFEBKA00 can delete it.

> **i** For example, you have entered 1 in 'Days Until Deletion' field. The daily bank statement notifies a payment for invoice X345. Now, the dunning block is active for one day, and will be deleted by the bank statement that arrives on the next day. Since it also contains the payment, the system clears the invoice and the customer will not be dunned.

This completes our discussion of the configuration settings that are required for using EBS functionality in the system to meet BESTM's specific requirements. Let us now move on to discuss lockbox processing.

12.3.3 Lockbox

Used only in USA, you can use the 'lockbox' functionality of FI-BL, to collect / process incoming payments (in the form of checks) faster. Here, instead of you collecting the checks, for the incoming payments from your customers, and then sending them to your bank for clearing, you arrange for creating one or more lockboxes (usually PO box) with your bank to collect these checks, for processing. You, then, inform your customers that they can send their check payments, directly, to the lockbox(es) thus set up. At periodical intervals (at least once a day), the bank collects the payment checks from the lockbox(es) and processes them for crediting into your company's account(s) with the bank. In the process, the bank captures the data from the payment advice and amounts of the customer(s) and sends you the electronic lockbox file (or a statement form), at regular intervals, which you can import into SAP for further processing at your end.

Now, using a lockbox clearing account, you post all the payments directly to your bank G/L account. This clearing account will have a non-zero balance until all the amounts are applied to the A/R of the customers. However, the bank account will show the correct balance. You post the incoming payments to the respective bank accounts besides clearing the appropriate

A/R open items. If the incoming payment is not enough to fully clear an open item, you can postprocess the items, using Transaction FLB1. While postprocessing, you can branch to 'payment advice processing' where you can change, add or delete clearing information. With appropriate reasons codes for classifying the deductions, you can, then, post a deduction as a residual item to the customer account or to a G/L account. Once done with the payment advice processing, you can go back to automatic posting.

Before you can configure lockbox processing, you need to define the required lockboxes for the house bank(s) a company code.

12.3.3.1   Define Lockboxes for House Banks

Define one or more lockboxes at your house bank(s), using the menu path: SAP Customizing Implementation Guide > Financial Accounting > Bank Accounting > Bank Accounts > Define Lockboxes for House Banks, or Transaction OB10.

On the resulting pop-up screen, double-click on 'Define Lockbox Accounts at House Banks' activity. On the next screen, click on 'New Entries' and define the required lockbox(es) for the house bank(s) of a company code (Figure 12.26). Repeat and define the lockboxes for all US-based company codes of BESTM.

Change View "Lockboxes For Our House Banks": Overview

New Entries

CoCd	Lockbox	House bk	LBox No
1110	LOCK1	BOFAU	11101
1110	LOCK2	CHASU	11102
1110	LOCK3	CITIU	11103

Figure 12.26 Defining Lockboxes for House Banks

With the lockboxes defined and in place, we can now look at configuring the lockbox processing procedure. In the configuration, you will essentially store the specifications for the lockbox procedure. Once done, this will enable the 'Lockbox program' to process the electronic file (of payment transactions) from the bank, create G/L posting for cash received and clear A/R open items. You need to complete the following activities to configure the lockboxes:

- Define Control Parameters
- Define Posting Data

Let us start with the first task of defining the control parameters for processing the lockboxes.

12.3.3.2   Define Control Parameters

Using this activity, you will specify the control data for the lockbox procedure 'LOCKBOX'. This control data is required for importing lockbox files (BAI or BAI2) sent by banks.

Project Dolphin

The file format to be used, for all BESTM company codes, will be BAI2 for lockbox processing. Additionally, it was required that the configuration should enable (a) G/L account posting (debit bank, credit cash receipt account) with one posting, per check, to the bank account, (b) the system to execute incoming payments postings to customer accounts, (c) partial payments, if the incoming payment is not sufficient for full clearing and (d) change the customer's master record to include the new bank details, if any.

Use the menu path: SAP Customizing Implementation Guide > Financial Accounting > Bank Accounting > Business Transactions > Payment Transactions > Lockbox > Define Control Parameters. You may also use Transaction OBAY.

On the resulting screen, click on 'New Entries' and maintain the required control parameters (Figure 12.27):

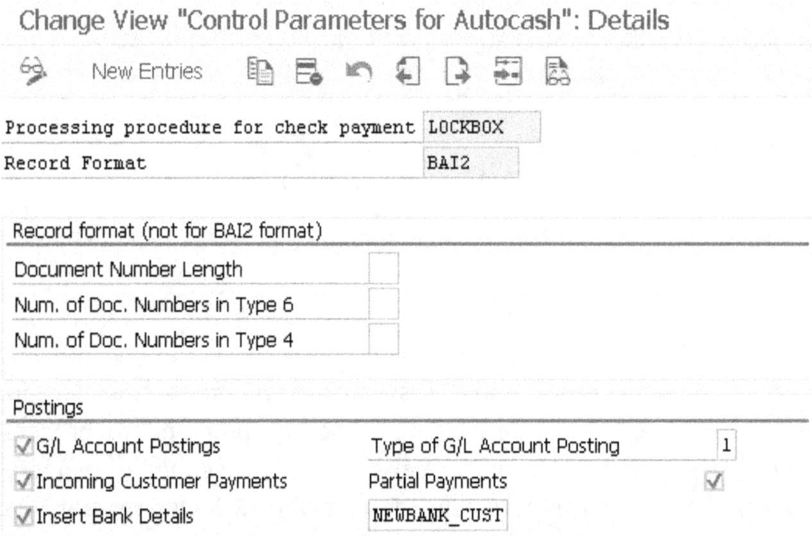

Change View "Control Parameters for Autocash": Details

🔍   New Entries   📄 📄 ↩ ⬅ 🗗 🗗 🗗

| Processing procedure for check payment | LOCKBOX |
| Record Format | BAI2 |

Record format (not for BAI2 format)

Document Number Length	
Num. of Doc. Numbers in Type 6	
Num. of Doc. Numbers in Type 4	

Postings

☑ G/L Account Postings	Type of G/L Account Posting	1
☑ Incoming Customer Payments	Partial Payments	☑
☑ Insert Bank Details	NEWBANK_CUST	

Figure 12.27 Control Parameters for Lockbox Processing

i.   Enter the 'Processing procedure for check payment'. The default procedure will be LOCKBOX. The system will process the entire lockbox data file with this procedure. If the file contains multiple lockbox accounts, then, the system will process all these accounts, via the same procedure.

ii.   Enter the 'Record Format'. You may enter either BAI or BAI2. If you want to use BAI, then, you also need to maintain the record format. We recommend using BAI2 for obvious advantages.

iii.   Under 'Record format (not for BAI2 format)' data block, enter the details if your 'Record Format' is BAI:

- Enter 10 in 'Document Number Length'
- For 'Num. of Doc. Numbers in Type 6', specify the maximum number of document numbers that can be transferred in record type 6. Known as the 'lockbox detail record', the 'Type 6', record carries data for each check or remittance and identifies information carried on each check.
- For 'Num. of Doc. Numbers in Type 4', specify the maximum number of document numbers that can be transferred in record type 4. The 'Type 4' is known as the 'lockbox overflow record', which identifies additional information (to be applied to each remittance) such as invoice numbers, and invoice amounts.

> **i** When you use BAI2, you do not need to specify the length of the document or the number of document numbers in record types 4 and 6, respectively, as BAI2 file is been designed in such a way that each document number is on a different record type 4, with its corresponding payment and deduction amounts.
>
> Though the BAI and BAI2 are standard formats, it is possible that they can vary with bank. The format you receive from a bank needs to be mapped to reconcile with the SAP delivered data dictionary layout for proper processing. If the format provided by your bank does not reconcile, and if the bank refuses to change the format, it is recommended to go in for custom ABAP coding to reformat the file; alternatively, you can modify the SAP data dictionary (which will, of course, call for a repair with every future release).

iv.   Under 'Postings':

- Select the 'G/L Account Postings' check-box to enable G/L account postings (debit bank, credit cash receipt account).
- For 'Type of G/L Account Posting', SAP supports three options: 1 – one posting per check (to the bank account), 2 – one posting per lockbox (check total) and 3 – one posting per batch number. Select 1, as BESTM wants to have one posting per check to the bank account.
- Select 'Incoming Customer Payments' field to enable the system to execute incoming payments postings to customer accounts.

- Select 'Partial Payments' check-box, to specify that payments received can be posted as partial payments if the payment is insufficient for full clearing (the default setting is to generate residual items with such payment receipt).
- When 'Insert Bank Details' check-box is selected, the system will create a batch input session to insert the new bank details (if any) to the customer master record.

v. 'Save' the details.

With the control parameters defined for lockbox processing, let us move on to configure the settings for posting the data.

12.3.3.3   Define Posting Data

Here, you have to maintain the information needed to process lockbox data and generate postings. Per unique destination/origin ('Destination' and 'Source' are routing information and defined by your bank), you need to create the posting information for the following:

- G/L posting - Debit bank account (incoming checks) and credit payment clearing account
- A/R posting - Debit payment clearing account and credit customer account

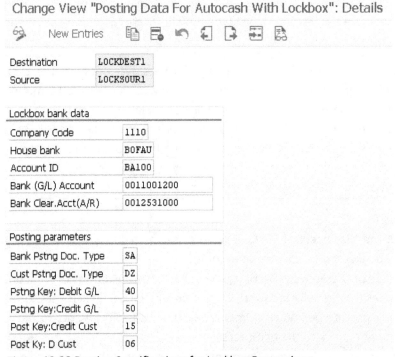

Figure 12.28 Posting Specifications for Lockbox Processing

To configure, use the menu path: SAP Customizing Implementation Guide > Financial Accounting > Bank Accounting > Business Transactions > Payment Transactions > Lockbox > Define Posting Data. You may also use Transaction OBAX. On the next screen (Figure 12.28):

i.   Enter the 'Destination' and the 'Source'.

ii.   Under 'Lockbox bank data', enter the company code, house bank, account ID for the lockbox, bank G/L account (lockbox clearing) and the G/L account for A/R clearing account.

iii. Enter the 'Posting parameters' as shown in Figure 12.28. When completed 'Save' the details, and create similar posting specifications for other lockboxes as well.

This completes our discussion on lockbox processing. We may, now, move on to discuss the setting up of the cash journal in the system.

12.3.4 Cash Journal

A subledger in FI-BL, you will use a 'cash journal' to manage your company's cash transactions. With the proper configuration, the system automatically calculates and displays the opening & closing balances, the receipts and payments totals. You can also carry out postings to G/L accounts, as well as vendor and customer accounts. You can set up several cash journals for each company code. You need to run separate cash journal for each currency.

Using the single-screen UI, you can enter, display, and change cash journal documents on one screen. You may use Transaction FBCJ or the SAP Easy Access menu path: SAP Menu > Accounting > Financial Accounting > Banks > Input > Kassenbuch (Cash Journal), to access the cash journal (Figure 12.29).

Figure 12.29 Cash Journal - Overview

You can carry out the following activities, in a cash journal:

- *Entering, saving, and posting cash journal entries*: you can save cash journal entries locally in the cash journal. The system also calculates the balances. The system, then posts the saved cash journal entries to the G/L.
- *Displaying follow-on documents*: you will be able to display the follow-on documents arising out of the cash journal entries that are posted.
- *Defining cash journal business transactions*: Usually you define (cash journal) business transactions in Customizing (refer Section 12.3.4.8). However, you can also define new business transactions, on the fly, while making entries in the cash journal.
- *Printing the cash journal*: you can print all the cash journal entries that have been posted in the time period displayed.
- *Printing receipts*: you can print the cash journal entries that have been saved.
- *Deleting cash journal entries saved*: with proper authorization, you can delete cash journal entries that have been saved.
- *Displaying all cash journal documents that have been deleted*: you can display all the cash journal documents that have been deleted within a specific time period.
- *Changing the cash journal*: you can change the cash journal and the company code, while you are processing entries in a cash journal.

You have to complete the following configuration activities to set up the cash journal in the system, to meet your company's specific requirements:

1. Create G/L Account for Cash Journal
2. Define Amount Limit
3. Define Document Types for Cash Journal Documents
4. Define Number Range Intervals for Cash Journal Documents
5. Define Numbering Groups
6. Define Number Ranges for Numbering Groups
7. Set Up Cash Journal
8. Maintain Business Transactions
9. Set Up Print Parameters for Cash Journal

Project Dolphin

The Dolphin project team has recommended the use of multiple cash journals, in each of the company codes of BESTM, to meet the different requirements. All the cash journals would be in the company code currency of the respective company codes. Each cash journal would need to be assigned to separate G/L accounts enabling easy reconciliation. There needs to be separate number ranges for the different cash journals. Also, to differentiate incoming and outgoing cash payments, there needs to be different number ranges; this has been necessitated by the fact that SAP, by default, assigns continuous numbering for both incoming and outgoing transactions from a single number range. The project team has also recommended usage of PDF print forms, to print the check lot. Also, it was suggested to print not only the documents that have been posted in FI (G/L), but all the documents that are saved in the cash journal.

Let us start with the first activity of creating G/L account for cash journal.

12.3.4.1   Create G/L Account for Cash Journal

Create a G/L account, per cash journal, for the required company codes. While doing so, ensure that the account created can only be posted automatically, and that it displays the account currency.

> **i** As you can run several cash journals in a company code, you need to understand how SAP controls the postings of cash journal entries to the G/L accounts:
>
> You can have all the cash journals defined with the company code (or local currency), or you can run cash journals in currencies other than the local currency.
>
> When you have more than one cash journal, but with the same currency, then, you need to have different G/L accounts as the system cannot post all the cash journals to a single G/L account. However, if you run more than one cash journal, but each with a different currency, then you can use a single G/L account to receive these postings from these journals.

Use the menu path: SAP Customizing Implementation Guide > Financial Accounting > Bank Accounting > Business Transactions > Cash Journal > Create G/L Account for Cash Journal. You may also use Transaction FS00. On the resulting screen, create a G/L account (if you have not already created the same earlier while creating the G/L account master data, discussed in Section 9.3.2 of Chapter 9 of Vol. I) to enable a cash journal to post into that (Figure 12.30).

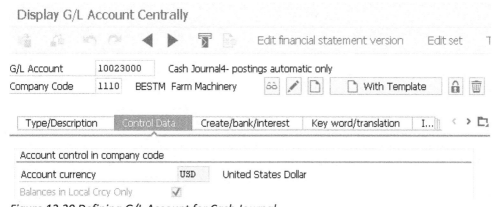

Figure 12.30 Defining G/L Account for Cash Journal

Make sure that, you do not select 'Balances in Local Crcy Only' check-box, if you want to run more than one cash journal, with different currencies, in this G/L account. We have selected this check-box as we will not be running cash journals with different currencies.

The next step is to define the amount limit for the cash journal with a specific validity.

12.3.4.2   Define Amount Limit

You define the limit values, here in this activity, with validity, which when reached and exceeded, the system displays an information pop-up for the user. You do not need to enter a company code, here, as the setting will be valid for all the company codes (in the same client), where the currency entered is the first local currency for all these company codes.

Use the menu path: SAP Customizing Implementation Guide > Financial Accounting > Bank Accounting > Business Transactions > Cash Journal > Define Amount Limit. On the resulting screen, maintain the settings (Figure 12.31).

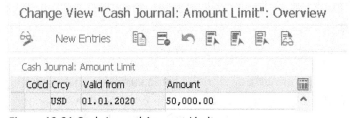

Figure 12.31 Cash Journal Amount Limit

The next task is to define the document types for cash journal documents.

12.3.4.3   Define Document Types for Cash Journal Documents

Use this configuration step, you define the required document types. You need to have separate document types defined and available for G/L account postings, outgoing payments to vendors, outgoing payments to customers, incoming payments from vendors and incoming payments from customers.

Use the menu path: SAP Customizing Implementation Guide > Financial Accounting > Bank Accounting > Business Transactions > Cash Journal > Define Document Types for Cash Journal Documents. You may also use Transaction OBA7. We have already defined these document types when we discussed documents in Section 7.1.3 of Chapter 7 of Vol. I.

Let us move on to the next step in the configuration of cash journal, namely, defining the number range intervals for cash journal documents.

12.3.4.4   Define Number Range Intervals for Cash Journal Documents

Here, you will be defining a number range interval for cash journal documents so that each cash document receives a unique number that does not clash with the G/L document number. See if you have already defined the number range interval 01 in the system. Else, define that, now, using the menu path: SAP Customizing Implementation Guide > Financial Accounting > Bank Accounting > Business Transactions > Cash Journal > Define Number Range Intervals for Cash Journal Documents. You may also use Transaction FBCJC1. We have already defined this number range 01 for all the company codes of BESTM (Figure 12.32).

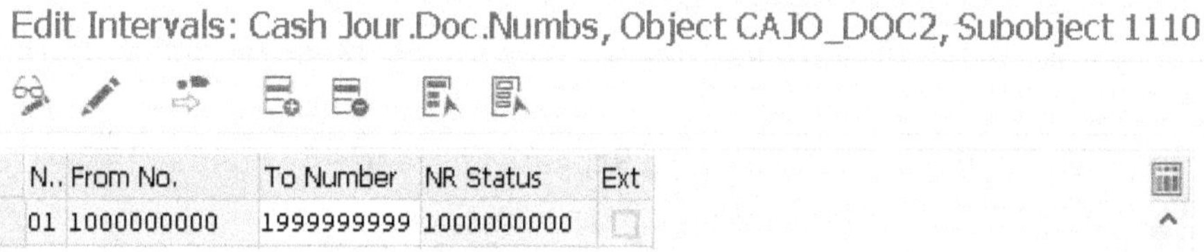

Edit Intervals: Cash Jour.Doc.Numbs, Object CAJO_DOC2, Subobject 1110

N..	From No.	To Number	NR Status	Ext
01	1000000000	1999999999	1000000000	☐

Figure 12.32 Number Range Interval for Cash Journal

With this, we are now ready to define the numbering groups.

12.3.4.5   Define Numbering Groups

By default, the system numbers the cash journal documents (both incoming and outgoing) sequentially, from a single number range. However, you can define different numbering groups, with their own number ranges, so that the system numbers incoming and outgoing cash payments, using these separate number ranges.

Use the menu path: SAP Customizing Implementation Guide > Financial Accounting > Bank Accounting > Business Transactions > Cash Journal > Define Numbering Groups. On the resulting screen, define the required numbering groups for cash journals (Figure 12.33).

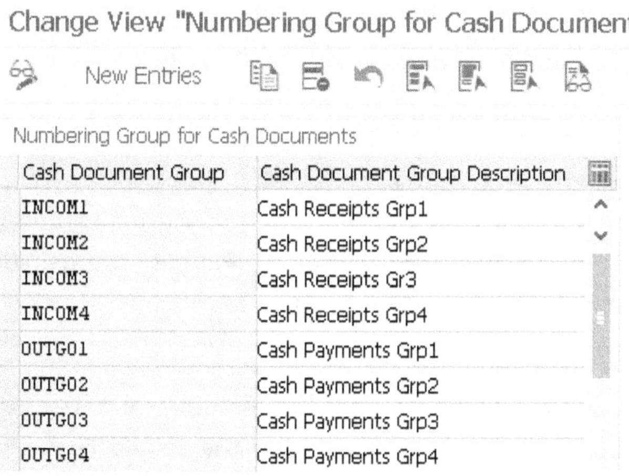

Change View "Numbering Group for Cash Documents": Overview

Numbering Group for Cash Documents

Cash Document Group	Cash Document Group Description
INCOM1	Cash Receipts Grp1
INCOM2	Cash Receipts Grp2
INCOM3	Cash Receipts Gr3
INCOM4	Cash Receipts Grp4
OUTGO1	Cash Payments Grp1
OUTGO2	Cash Payments Grp2
OUTGO3	Cash Payments Grp3
OUTGO4	Cash Payments Grp4

Figure 12.33 Numbering Groups for Cash Documents

If you have more than one cash journal, then you need to define two numbering groups, per journal, so that the numbering is unique. For example, we are running four cash journals for the company code 1110; accordingly, we have defined four numbering groups for incoming, and another four for outgoing cash payments.

With this, we can now move on to define the number ranges to be used by the numbering groups.

12.3.4.6   Define Number Ranges for Numbering Groups

Use the menu path: SAP Customizing Implementation Guide > Financial Accounting > Bank Accounting > Business Transactions > Cash Journal > Define Number Ranges for Numbering Groups. On the resulting screen, enter the 'Cash Document Group' (say, OUTGO1) and create the number range interval under the NR key 01. Repeat and create the number ranges for the other cash document groups as well (Figure 12.34).

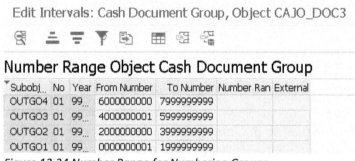

Figure 12.34 Number Range for Numbering Groups

> **i** Use only 01 as the number range interval number ('NR') for the number range objects while numbering the 'numbering groups'.

With the settings we have done so far, we can, now, set up the cash journals.

12.3.4.7   Set Up Cash Journal

Use this configuration step to set up the required cash journal(s), per company code. As discussed already, you can run more than one cash journal, and the journal can be in any currency and not necessarily in the company code currency alone. Per cash journal, identify the G/L account that will be posted to from the entries of the cash journal.

Use the menu path: SAP Customizing Implementation Guide > Financial Accounting > Bank Accounting > Business Transactions > Cash Journal > Set Up Cash Journal or Transaction FBCJC0. On the resulting screen, click on 'New Entries' and maintain the details (Figure 12.35):

Change View "Maintain View for Cash Journals": Overview

New Entries

Maintain View for Cash Journals

CoCd	CJ ...	G/L Account	Crcy	Cash Jnl...	D..	D..	D..	D..	D..	Cash ...	Cash ...	N..	Check Split	Cash journal name	AGrp	Subst.	Simultan.
1110	0001	10020000	USD	☐	SK	KZ	KZ	DZ	DZ	OUTG01	INCOM1		No Spli... ⌄	CASH JOURNAL 1		☐	✓
1110	0002	10021000	USD	☐	SK	KZ	KZ	DZ	DZ	OUTG02	INCOM2		No Spli... ⌄	CASH JOURNAL 2		☐	✓
1110	0003	10022000	USD	☐	SK	KZ	KZ	DZ	DZ	OUTG03	INCOM3		No Spli... ⌄	CASH JOURNAL 3		☐	✓
1110	0004	10023000	USD	☐	SK	KZ	KZ	DZ	DZ	OUTG04	INCOM4		No Spli... ⌄	CASH JOURNAL 4		☐	✓

Figure 12.35 Setting Up Cash Journals for Company Code 1110

i. Enter the company code ('CoCd'), and enter the cash journal number ('CJ Number'). If you do not enter a cash journal number, then, the system numbers the same serially.

ii. Enter the 'G/L Account'. You can assign the same G/L to more than one cash journal, if different journals use different currencies; else, you can assign only one G/L to a cash journal even if there are multiple journals but using the same local currency of the company code.

iii. Select 'Cash Jnl Closed' check-box, to prevent posting to this cash journal.

iv. Enter the appropriate document type for G/L account posting, vendor payment, vendor receipt, customer payment and customer receipt.

v. Enter the numbering group for payments ('Cash Payt Grp.') and receipts ('Cash Rcpt. Grp').

vi. Select the suitable option for 'Check Split'. Select the 'Offsetting Items of Totals Document Split' option, if you want to split only the offsetting item of the totals posting or the option 'All Items of Totals Document Split', if you want to split both the posting item and offsetting item of the totals, or 'No Split of Line Items of Totals Document' as the option for the CHECK SPLIT field if you don't want any split.

vii. Enter the 'Cash journal name' for the journal that you are defining.

viii. Select the 'Simultan.' check-box to allow simultaneous access to the different processing modes.

> **i** When you have selected the 'Simultan.' check-box, and, if a cash journal is already in use, you can open the same cash journal in 'Save Only' mode; now, you can save entries in the cash journal but cannot delete, post, or reverse documents. When this flag was not set, and, if a cash journal is already in use, you can open the same journal in 'Display Only' mode only.

ix. 'Save' the details, and repeat to define other cash journals for the company code, and define the journals for other company codes as well.

With this, we are now ready to configure the business transactions that you will use in the cash journals.

12.3.4.8   Maintain Business Transactions

You can create the required business transactions here, that you can use, later, in your cash journals for making the entries. Alternatively, it is also possible that you can create these business transactions, online, while making entries in a cash journal.

You will, for each business transition, make other settings like, business transaction blocker, account modification etc.

Use the menu path: SAP Customizing Implementation Guide > Financial Accounting > Bank Accounting > Business Transactions > Cash Journal > Maintain Business Transactions. You may also use Transaction FBCJC2.

Change View "Maintain View for Cash Journal Transaction Names": Overvi

New Entries

Maintain View for Cash Journal Transaction Names

CoCd	Tr...	B..	S..	T..	G/L Acc...	Tx	Cash journal business trans.	B...	Acct ...	T...	Bus. tran. long text
1110	0003	K					VENDOR		✓		VENDOR
1110	0004	D					CUSTOMER		✓		CUSTOMER
1110	0007	E		1	65100000		OFFICE SUPPLIES				OFFICE SUPPLIES
1110	0008	C		2	11001010		CASH TRF BANK TO CASH JOU				Cash Transfer - Bank to Cash Journal
1110	0009	B		1	11001080		CASH TRF CASH JOUR TO BAN				Cash Ttransfer - Cash Journal to Bank
1110	0010	E		1	61003000		HOTEL EXPNESES				Hotel expneses
1110	0011	E		1	61005000		GROUND TRANSPORTATION				Ground transportation
1110	0012	E		1	61008000		MISC TRAVEL EXPENSES				Miscellaneous travel expenses
1110	0013	E		1	65100000		OFFICE SUPPLIES ADHOC				office supplies adhoc

Figure 12.36 Business Transactions for Cash Journal

On the resulting screen, click on 'New Entries' and maintain the details (Figure 12.26):

i. Enter the company code in which you will use the cash journal, say, 1110.

ii. You will identify a business transaction using a business transaction number that is assigned by the system automatically, in the 'Trans. Number' field (for example, 0003, 0004 etc).

iii. Enter the business transaction type in 'Bus. Tran. Type'. The system uses this to categorise the business transaction like, E (expense), R (revenue), B (cash transfer – cash journal to a bank), C (cash transfer – bank to cash journal), D (customer – incoming / outgoing payment) and K (vendor – incoming / outgoing payment).

iv. You may enter 'Special G/L Indicator' if any.

v. Enter the transaction classification (1 cash payment, 2 cash receipts, 3 check receipts and 4 check/cash receipts) in 'Trans. Classifn.' field.

vi. Enter the appropriate G/L account.

vii. Enter an appropriate automatic 'Cash journal business trans.' identification name (language-dependent).

viii. Select 'BusTraBlkd' check-box, if you no longer want to use this business transaction for cash journal postings.

ix. Select the 'Acct Mod.' indicator to enable changing (during document entry) the default G/L account that has already been assigned to the business transaction in configuration. Also, if no G/L account was maintained during configuration, you can enter a G/L account, during document entry. Leave the 'G/L Account' field blank during configuration, for transaction types D and K, as the system applies the reconciliation account.

x. 'Save' and create all other required business transactions in all the company codes.

With this, we are now ready to configure the last configuration activity for cash journal, that is: setting up of the print parameters for cash journal.

12.3.4.9   Set Up Print Parameters for Cash Journal

Here, you will set up the required parameters for the print program to print the cash journal / cash journal receipts.

Use the menu path: SAP Customizing Implementation Guide > Financial Accounting > Bank Accounting > Business Transactions > Cash Journal > Set Up Print Parameters for Cash Journal. You may also use Transaction FBCJC3.

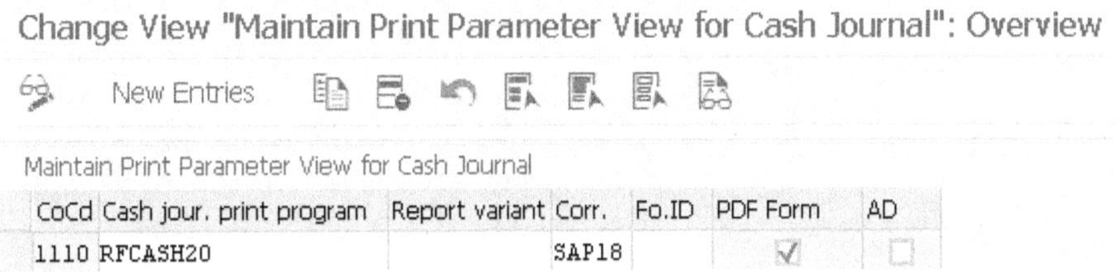

Change View "Maintain Print Parameter View for Cash Journal": Overview

🗞 New Entries   🗋 🗟 🔄 🖺 🖺 🖺 🖺

Maintain Print Parameter View for Cash Journal

CoCd	Cash jour. print program	Report variant	Corr.	Fo.ID	PDF Form	AD
1110	RFCASH20		SAP18		☑	☐

Figure 12.37 Print Parameters for Cash Journal

On the resulting screen, click on 'New Entries' and maintain the details (Figure 12.37):

i. Enter the company code (say, 1110) and enter the name of the cash journal print program (RFCASH20). You may also enter a 'Report Variant', if any.

ii. In 'Corr.' field, you need to enter the ID for correspondence (for example, SAP18 – cash document), and enter a form identifier in 'Fo.ID' field. Entering a form ID enables the system to access the specific form, from a selected group of forms.

iii. Select 'PDF Form' check-box to print a check lot in the cash journal in a PDF format.

iv. You may use the check-box 'AD' to determine if the system should print the cash journal receipt on the basis of the FI accounting document, or on the basis of the cash journal document. When selected, the system prints only the documents that have been posted in FI (G/L); else, the system prints all of the documents saved in the cash journal.

v.   'Save' the settings. You have, now, completed configuring the payment program to print the cash journal documents.

This completes our discussion on cash journal.

Let us, now, move on to discuss the configuration required for entering / processing of online payments, in the next Section.

12.3.5 Online Payments

As part of electronic payment processing, you can enter online payments in the system. SAP provides you with three Transactions (1 – free form payment, 2 – vendor payment request and 3 – customer payment request) for entering online payments. You may access these Transactions using SAP EASY Access menu path: SAP Menu > Accounting > Financial Accounting > Bank Outgoings > Online Payments > Free Form Payment (Transaction FIBLFFP) / Vendors – Payment Request (Transaction FIBLAOP) / Customers – Payment Request (Transaction FIBLROP). When you enter online payments in these Transactions, the system creates payment requests that you can display, release, or reverse. You can process released payments by executing the payment program for payment requests (Transaction F111).

You can use 'free-form payments' to trigger payments or debit memos without referencing to a business transaction. When you create a free-form payment, neither the master data of the business partner needs to be in the system, nor does the amount of the payment transaction have to be represented by an open item. You can either enter the payment recipient with name, address and bank details directly, or you can adopt this information from the vendor or customer master record. You do not need to repeat entering the recipient data, as you can save the same in a variant.

However, in the case of customer / vendor payment requests, you need to specify the recipient of a payment or the payer for a debit memo (by entering a customer or vendor account). The system, then, automatically adopts the name, address, and bank details from the corresponding master record, and posts the payment to the correct account.

To configure the system for processing online payments, complete the following activities:

- Define Process Steps
- Define Document Types
- Define Identification for Cross-Payment Run Payment Media

Let us start with the first activity of defining the process steps.

12.3.5.1   Define Process Steps

Here, in this activity, you will define – per origin - the order in which the steps of the online entry for payment requests need to happen: starting with entering a payment request, through processing by the payment program, and finally to the creation of the payment media via the Payment Medium Workbench (PMW). If you do not make any settings, the process ends with the creation of the payment requests released for payment. The standard SAP has the following three origins defined in the system:

- Customer payment requests (FI-AR-PR)
- Vendor payment requests (FI-AP-PR)
- Free form payments (FI-BL)

Use the menu path: SAP Customizing Implementation Guide > Financial Accounting > Bank Accounting > Business Transactions > Payment Transactions > Online Payments > Define Process Steps. Click on 'New Entries' and maintain the details (Figure 12.38):

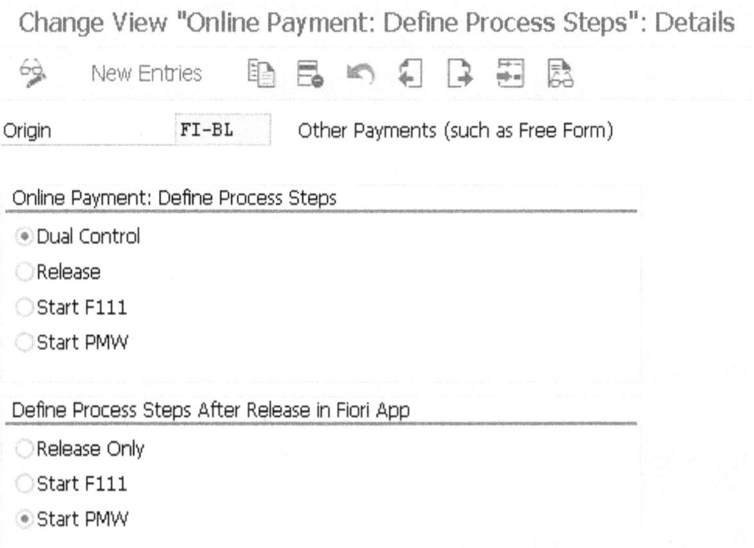

Change View "Online Payment: Define Process Steps": Details

⚙ New Entries   🖹 🖻 🔙 🔙 🔜 🔁 🔁

Origin   FI-BL   Other Payments (such as Free Form)

Online Payment: Define Process Steps
- Dual Control
- Release
- Start F111
- Start PMW

Define Process Steps After Release in Fiori App
- Release Only
- Start F111
- Start PMW

Figure 12.38 Defining Process Steps for Online Payments

   i.   Select the 'Origin'; FI-BL - Other Payments (such as Free Form).

   ii.   Select the appropriate radio-button under 'Online Payment: Define Process Steps' data block: when you select 'Dual Control', you will see the system bringing up another data block, 'Define Process Steps After Release in Fiori App'.

   iii.   Select 'Start PMW' under 'Define Process Steps After Release in Fiori App' data block.

   iv.   'Save' when completed, and complete the settings for other origins (FI-AP-PR and FI-AR-PR), if required.

The next step is to define the document types for online payments.

12.3.5.2   Define Document Types

Define, here, the document type that is permitted for the accounting documents arising out of online payments.

> **i** If you do not specify a document type, then, the program uses the document type that you have defined for the payment method during configuration of the payment program.

Use the menu path: SAP Customizing Implementation Guide > Financial Accounting > Bank Accounting > Business Transactions > Payment Transactions > Online Payments > Define Document Types. On the resulting screen, click on 'New Entries' and enter the 'Document type' per 'Origin' on the next screen (Figure 12.39).

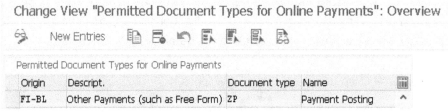

Figure 12.39 Document Type for Online Payments

With this, let us move on to complete the final configuration activity for setting up online payments.

12.3.5.3   Define Identification for Cross-Payment Run Payment Media

Here, you define the IDs that you will use to summarize payments from different payment runs, in one payment medium. Process the payment runs using the program 'SAPFPAYM_MERGE' to create the cross-payment-run payment media. You can summarize payments into two groups: *Group 1* - payments from the payment program for FI-A/R & FI-A/P (Transaction F110), and payments from payment requests (Transaction F111) including online payments and payments, and *Group 2* – personnel payments, payments from FI-TV. However, the system will not allow you to summarize payments from Group 1 with payments from Group 2 in one payment medium.

Use the menu path: SAP Customizing Implementation Guide > Financial Accounting > Bank Accounting > Business Transactions > Payment Transactions > Online Payments > Define Identification for Cross-Payment Run Payment Media.

Enter the appropriate 'Payment Run Indictor' (say, R for FI-BL) on the resulting pop-up screen, and press 'Continue'. On the next screen, click on 'New Entries' and enter the following details (Figure 12.40):

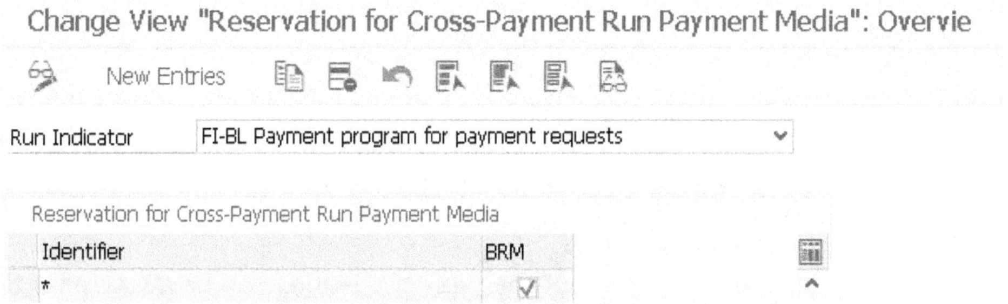

Change View "Reservation for Cross-Payment Run Payment Media": Overvie

New Entries

Run Indicator   FI-BL Payment program for payment requests

Reservation for Cross-Payment Run Payment Media

Identifier	BRM
*	☑

Figure 12.40 Identification Cross-Payment Run Payment Media

i.   Enter an 'Identifier'. You may enter the first five characters of the run ID (generic with the wildcard character + for one character, and * for a character string). For example, if you select FI-BL payment program for payment requests and enter M* then all payment runs for Transaction F111 are reserved for the creation of cross-payment run payment media that begin with the letter M.

You can also number these IDs sequentially (say 0*, 1*, 2*...9*). The IDs together with the corresponding online payment settings, enable the system to post the payment documents that belong together (in individual payment runs) with the program SAPFPAYM_MERGE grouping the payment media.

> **i** If you enter * or leave the 'Identifier' field as a blank, then, all payment runs (for the selected 'Run Indicator') are summarized for cross-payment run payment media. Here, you can use the BAdI FIBL_MPAY_RESERVATION to exclude, for example, company codes or countries from the function during execution.

ii. Select 'BRM' check-box to interface with Bank Communication Management. When selected, the system presents and process the payments in one or more payment runs in a 'payment status monitor' which serves as a repository for incoming status messages from SWIFT and from individual banks.

This completes our discussion on configuring the online payments, and also setting up the payment transactions in FI-BL.

12.4 Conclusion

You learned that 'Bank Accounting' (FI-BL) is a subapplication component (not a subledger) within SAP that enables handling the accounting transactions that you process with your bank(s). You understood that by using FI-BL, you can manage bank master data besides creating and processing of incoming and outgoing payments.

As a part of master data, you learned about the bank directories and how to create them, both manually and automatically. You, also, learned about the creation of house banks and business partner's banks. In the process, you learned about distributing the bank master data and also specifying the check rules for country-specific bank master data definitions.

You understood what a bank chain (or multi-stage payment method) is and learned how to create various types of bank chains: general bank chain, bank chain for customers / vendors, bank chains for house banks and bank chains for cash management.

In payment transactions, you learned the configuration required for manual and electronic bank statements. You, also, learned about lockbox and lockbox processing that is specific to USA. Besides understanding the lockbox functionality, you learned how to set that up in the system. You, then, learned about the settings required for running cash journals in the system; you learned that you can have several cash journals in a company code and that the currency of a cash journal need not be that of the company code currency alone. Lastly, you learned about the settings that are required for entering and processing online payments.

This completes our discussion on bank accounting, and we are ready to discuss Asset Accounting (FI-AA) in the next Chapter.

13 Asset Accounting

Asset Accounting (FI-AA), in SAP, is a subsidiary ledger to SAP G/L Accounting that you can use to manage fixed assets of your business entity. It provides information on various transactions, from acquisition to retirement, of fixed assets. You can use this component to manage different types of assets including 'Assets under Construction' (AuC) and intangible assets. As no country-specific valuation rules are hard-coded in the system, you can use FI-AA internationally, in any country and in any industry. However, you can make this component country-specific and company-specific with the appropriate settings that you make in Customizing.

FI-AA allows you to manage asset values in parallel currencies using different types of valuations, simplifying consolidation preparations for multi-national groups. Using parallel valuation, you can flexibly assign the depreciation areas of FI-AA to the ledgers of SAP G/L Accounting and enable the system posting the parallel values with the actual values in real time; it posts separate documents for each valuation (that is, each accounting principle). With the basic functions covering the entire life cycle of an asset, from the initial purchase / acquisition to retirement, you can use FI-AA to automatically calculate depreciation and interest between two points in time. You can also use the forecasting and simulation functionalities to carry out 'what if' analysis.

FI-AA is tightly integrated with the several applications / functionalities within SAP including material management (SAP MM), plant maintenance (SAP PM), production planning (SAP PP), project systems (SAP PS), investment management (SAP IM) etc that enables direct transfer of data to and from other applications. With these integrations, for example, when an asset is purchased or produced in-house, you can directly post the invoice receipt (IR) or goods receipt (GR), or the withdrawal from the warehouse, to assets in the FI-AA component. Also, it is possible that you can pass on depreciation and interest directly to SAP FI. Though you carry out the technical management of assets, in the form of functional locations / equipment in SAP PM, you can settle the maintenance activities requiring capitalization, to FI-AA.

Besides providing for managing the assets and their values, FI-AA also offers you with the functionality to structure these assets to reflect the organizational structure of your enterprise. This ensures that an asset is clearly and always assigned to an organizational unit at any given point in time.

Let us now understand the new asset accounting in S/4HANA and how it is different from the classic asset accounting.

13.1 New Asset Accounting in S/4HANA

The FI-AA in SAP S/4HANA is also known as 'new Asset Accounting. Actually, it is not really 'new' in the sense that it has been available for a while since SAP ECC EHP6. However, with SAP S/4HANA, it is mandatory to activate that for SAP S/4HANA Finance – whether it is a new implementation or a migration.

Though the core functionalities of new Asset Accounting are the same as that of the 'classic Asset Accounting', there has been several changes and improvements: for example, you will no longer be able to post the asset master data and values together, and post the summary transactions later to SAP FI; instead, similar to A/P and A/R, you can create the master data first and post the value to the asset and also simultaneously to the G/L. This is because, most of the asset tables have since been replaced with the introduction of new Asset Accounting; both asset and financial actuals are now stored in a single table, ACDOCA. The other notable change in new Asset Accounting is that all accounting principles post in real-time without the need for posting them periodically.

As the asset and G/L values are now in the same table (ACDOCA), you do not need to worry about the consistency of data and the reconciliation transactions that were required earlier. Since all ledgers post in real-time, the periodic posting transaction has become redundant. Besides, since the asset postings are now transferred to SAP FI at the asset level and with the availability of more information per asset, it is, now, possible to run asset reports, by asset number, from the SAP G/L. Also, you do not need to wait for the period to close, to see values in the parallel ledgers. Even, the planned depreciation is always up to date.

With the new functionalities in Depreciation Calculation Program (DCP), the system, now, updates the planned depreciation every time you post an asset transaction. As a result, the asset explorer and asset reports, now, show you the values that are up-to-date. Because of this, the month-end depreciation runs are faster as the system just need to post the already calculated (planned) values. The system still posts collective documents for depreciation, instead of one document per asset; the DCP posts a separate line item in SAP G/L per asset, facilitating more detail than earlier.

As regards the Transactions in new Asset Accounting, the new ones now contain an L suffixed to the erstwhile Transactions to signify that you can post to different ledger groups: for example, the old Transaction ABAA is now ABAAL, Transaction ABUM is now ABUML and so on. However, if you still try any of the old Transactions in S/4HANA, you will automatically be redirected to the new Transaction.

As regards to the tables in new Asset Accounting, even though you will not see the existence most of the old tables (ANEK, ANEP, ANLC, ANLP etc), the programs will still work. This is because, along with the improvements in new Asset Accounting, SAP has introduced the 'compatibility views' which are created from the new tables such as ACDOCA, but linked to the old tables such as ANEP, ANEK etc., enabling reading of data from the old tables.

> **i** We shall also refer the 'new Asset Accounting' simply as Asset Accounting (FI-AA) throughout this book.

In this Chapter, we shall be discussing the following aspects of FI-AA:

- Organizational Structures
- Structuring Fixed Assets in FI-AA
- Integration
- General Valuation
- Depreciation
- Special Valuations
- Master Data
- Transactions
- Information System
- Asset Data Transfer
- Preparations for Going Live
- Overview for Experts

Let us start with the organizational structures.

13.2 Organizational Structures

To represent your organizational structure that is relevant to FI-AA, and to classify your assets according to asset accounting criteria, you have to define the FI-AA organizational objects like chart of depreciation, FI company code, asset class etc. Then, you need to assign all the assets, of the business enterprise, to these organizational objects thus defined:

- FI-AA uses the same company codes as that of SAP G/L Accounting; but, you need to define these company codes further, in FI-AA, with the specifications needed for asset accounting. Unless you do this, you will not be able to use an FI company code in asset accounting.
- If you have, earlier, specified in SAP G/L Accounting configuration that you need business area balance sheets, then, you need to assign the assets (in master data maintenance), to the business areas for adopting the business area automatically from the cost center. With such an assignment, the system makes appropriate account assignments postings - including depreciation and gain / loss postings on asset retirement - to the respective business area.
- If you use segment reporting, you need to enter the profit center and/or segments directly in the asset master record. This unique 'asset-segment assignment' helps in creating asset reports relating to profit centers and segments.
- You can assign a fixed asset to a 'plant', for a set time frame. And, you can change the assignment to a different plant by changing the asset master record. Though a plant has no asset accounting relevance, you can use that as a sort and selection criterion for the asset reports.
- As in the case of plant, you can also assign a fixed asset to a 'location' for a set time. Since an 'address' is attached to a location, you can indirectly assign an asset to an address as well; so, all assets with the same location must have the same address.
- For internal accounting, you need to assign assets to cost centers; you assign (in the asset master) each asset to exactly one cost center. With this, you can post all depreciation and interest for the asset, plan all future depreciation and interest, and statistically post gain or loss from asset sales.

Let us look at the various configuration activities that you need to complete to define the asset accounting organizational structures:

- Check Country-Specific Settings
- Copy Reference Chart of Depreciation/Depreciation Areas
- Assign Chart of Depreciation to Company Code
- Specify Number Assignment Across Company Codes

To start with, let us look at the country-specific settings that are required to fulfil the statutory requirements of a country.

13.2.1 Check Country-Specific Settings

SAP comes delivered with most of the country-specific settings for FI-AA to meet the legal requirements of a country in which your company code operates. All the country-specific system defaults are company code dependent. As a one-time exercise, the system will assign the settings you make here, to the company code, as soon as you initially assign a chart of depreciation to the company code.

---

i Note that the default country-specific settings may not be complete in all respects. And, you may need to additionally configure a few settings that does not come as default; for example, the cut-off value for low value assets (LVA).

Use the menu path: SAP Customizing Implementation Guide > Financial Accounting > Asset Accounting > Organizational Structures > Check Country-Specific Settings, to check the default country-specific settings, and to add additional settings, if any. You may also use Transaction OA08.

Project Dolphin

BESTM management has requested to configure the country-specific settings for USA and India as indicated below:

The low value asset (LVA) cut-off limit should be $5,000 for USA and INR 5,000 for India. Also, it should be configured that the system capitalizes the assets under construction (AuC) without considering the downpayments. Besides, it should be ensured that the system posts the gain / loss posting when an asset is retired.

On the resulting screen, you will see the list of countries for which SAP has provided with the default settings. If the 'Country vers. available' check-box has been selected for any country, then, it indicates that a separate country version is available. Double-click on the selected country row, and check the default settings on the next screen. If required, you can make additional settings (Figure 13.1):

   i.   Under 'Amount entries', you will see that the system has pre-filled the currency for US.

   - Enter the amount limit, in the 'Max. LVA Amount: for Posting' field, up to which an asset will be considered as a low value asset (LVA).

> **i** In the case of collectively managed LVAs, the amount is the acquisition amount divided by the quantity of assets.

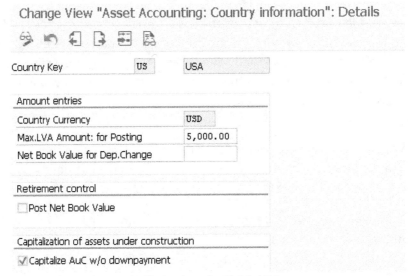

Figure 13.1 Country-Specific Settings for FI-AA: USA

- If you enter an amount in the 'Net Book Value for Dep. Change' field, then, the system changes over the calculation of depreciation to the changeover key defined in the depreciation key, as soon as the net book value (NBV) is less than this amount. Use an appropriate depreciation key, with an internal calculation key defined with changeover method 3 ('Changeover as soon as the net book value is less than the changeover amount'), for this changeover to happen; else, if you use any other changeover methods, the system ignores the amount entered here. This is valid only for depreciation area 01 (master/ book depreciation).

ii.   Select the 'Post Net Book Value' check-box under 'Retirement control', if you want the system to post the NBV at the time of retirement of an asset; the system posts the NBV to the account for clearing of revenue from asset sales or for clearing of revenue from asset sales to affiliated companies. By default, the check-box is not selected as the system posts a gain/loss, for an asset retirement (by sale or scrapping).

> **i** Posting of NBV during asset retirement is not allowed in most of the countries, including USA. Hence, you should not select this, in general. However, you need to select this flag for a country like France, where it is mandatory to post the NBV upon an asset's retirement.

iii.   When you select the 'Capitalize AuC w/o downpayment' check-box, the system ignores downpayments during the line item settlement of AuC, and transfers the total amount of the closing invoice to the capitalized asset using the appropriate transaction type based on the year of the closing invoice.

> **i** When the 'Capitalize AuC w/o downpayment' check-box is not selected, and if you capitalize a downpayment from a previous year along with the closing invoice from the current year, then, the system transfers the amount of the downpayment from the previous year, using a transaction type for old assets data. Then, it transfers the difference between the total amount (of the closing invoice) and the downpayment, using a transaction type for new acquisitions.

With this, we are now ready to complete the next configuration activity of creating a new chart of depreciation by copying from a reference chart of depreciation.

13.2.2 Copy Reference Chart of Depreciation/Depreciation Areas

Using this activity, you will define a new chart of depreciation that you will later assign to each of the company codes in FI-AA. However, before we start this activity to define a chart of depreciation, let us first understand what a chart of depreciation is.

The 'chart of depreciation' is a list of 'depreciation areas' arranged according to business and legal requirements, and it enables you to manage all rules for the depreciation and valuation of assets in a particular country (or economic region). With the chart of depreciation, you can calculate values for assets for different needs, both internal and external: say, book depreciation and cost-accounting depreciation. It is possible that you can flexibly define the keys for the automatic depreciation of assets per chart of depreciation. These keys are based on different elements for calculation of depreciation like calculation methods, period controls etc that are used client-wide. The chart of depreciation also supports special calculations of asset values like investment support through special keys.

> **i** You can manage values for assets, in parallel, in up to 99 depreciation areas in FI-AA.

When you create a new chart of depreciation, by copying from a reference chart, then the system copies all depreciation areas into the new chart. You can, then, delete the depreciation areas that you may not need from the newly defined chart. Alternatively, you can keep all the depreciation areas but activate them later whenever you want. Besides the depreciation areas, the system also copies some of the depreciation area-specific restrictions for the transaction types that were necessary in 'classic Asset Accounting'. As you will not be posting with the restricted transaction types in the new Asset Accounting, you may delete these redundant restrictions for the transaction types defined in table TABWA.

> ℹ️ SAP comes delivered with sample (or reference) charts of depreciation, with predefined depreciation areas, to meet the statutory requirements of countries like USA, UK, Spain, Germany, Austria etc. These reference charts are named as 0US, 0DE, 0GB etc. You can use these charts, as reference, to create your own. Remember, you cannot use the reference chart of depreciation as such, without creating a new one.

Once defined, you will assign a chart of depreciation to each of the company codes to make them available for FI-AA.

Let us now look at creating a new chart of depreciation by copying a reference chart in the system:

Project Dolphin

BESTM wants to have two charts of depreciations, one for US and the other for India. As in the case of chart of accounts, these new charts of depreciation will also be named as BEUS and BEIN respectively for US and India charts of depreciation.

Use the menu path: SAP Customizing Implementation Guide > Financial Accounting > Asset Accounting > Organizational Structures > Copy Reference Chart of Depreciation/Depreciation Areas.

i.   On the resulting pop-up screen, double-click on the first activity 'Copy Reference Chart of Depreciation'. You may also use Transaction EC08.

Figure 13.2 Creating New Chart of Depreciation (BEUS)

On the 'Organizational object: Chart of depreciation' screen, click on 'Copy org.object'. On the resulting pop-up screen, enter 'From Chart of dep' (say, 0US) and 'To Chart of dep' (say, BEUS) and click on 'Continue'. Press 'Continue' on the 'Transport number ranges and addresses' pop-up screen and press 'Yes' for 'Do you really want to transport number ranges?'. The system copies the reference chart of depreciation 0US to the new one, BEUS (Figure 13.2). Do a similar copy for creating a chart of depreciation for India (BEIN) by copying the reference chart, 0IN.

ii.   The next task is to provide the description for the newly created charts of depreciation. On the initial 'Select Activity' pop-up screen, double-click on the 'Specify Description of Chart of Depreciation' activity, and on the next screen, enter the 'Description' for BEUS and BEIN charts of depreciation (Figure 13.3).

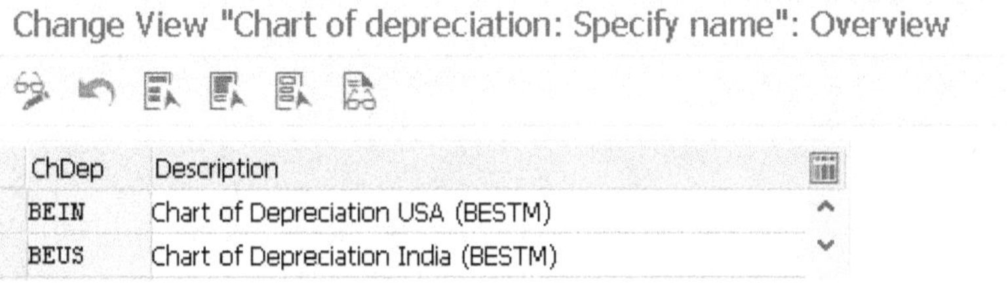

Change View "Chart of depreciation: Specify name": Overview

ChDep	Description	
BEIN	Chart of Depreciation USA (BESTM)	^
BEUS	Chart of Depreciation India (BESTM)	v

Figure 13.3 Providing Description for Newly Created Chart of Depreciation

iii.   The next activity is to copy / delete the depreciation areas, in the newly created chart of depreciation. From the initial 'Select Activity' pop-up screen, double-click on the 'Copy/Delete Depreciation Areas' activity. On the resulting pop-up, enter the chart of depreciation (BEUS) and proceed. On the next screen, the system brings up all the depreciation areas that have been copied from the reference chart (Figure 13.4). You can directly reach the 'Change View "Define Depreciation Areas": Overview' if you use Transaction OADB. You can rename depreciation areas, copy to create new ones and delete the unwanted areas.

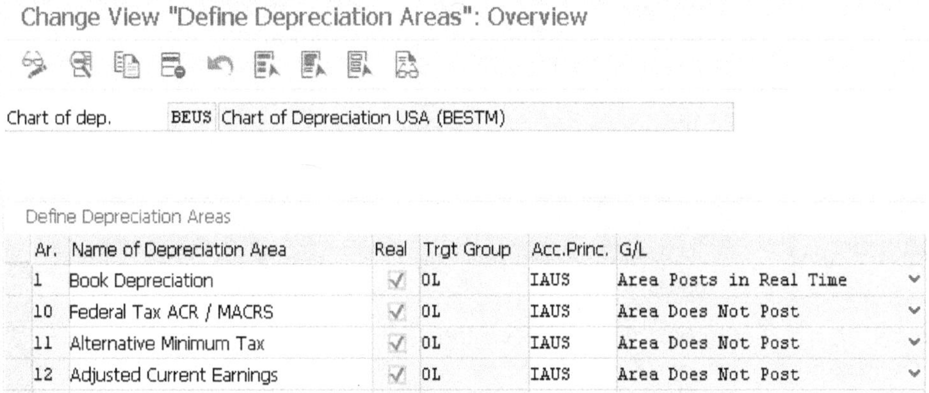

Change View "Define Depreciation Areas": Overview

Chart of dep.   BEUS Chart of Depreciation USA (BESTM)

Define Depreciation Areas

Ar.	Name of Depreciation Area	Real	Trgt Group	Acc.Princ.	G/L	
1	Book Depreciation	✓	0L	IAUS	Area Posts in Real Time	v
10	Federal Tax ACR / MACRS	✓	0L	IAUS	Area Does Not Post	v
11	Alternative Minimum Tax	✓	0L	IAUS	Area Does Not Post	v
12	Adjusted Current Earnings	✓	0L	IAUS	Area Does Not Post	v

Figure 13.4 List of Depreciation Areas for Chart of Depreciation BEUS

You may double click on a particular depreciation area (say, 1) and see / change the depreciation area details on the next screen (Figure 13.5):

a) You can change and/or provide a meaningful long and short text for the depreciation area.

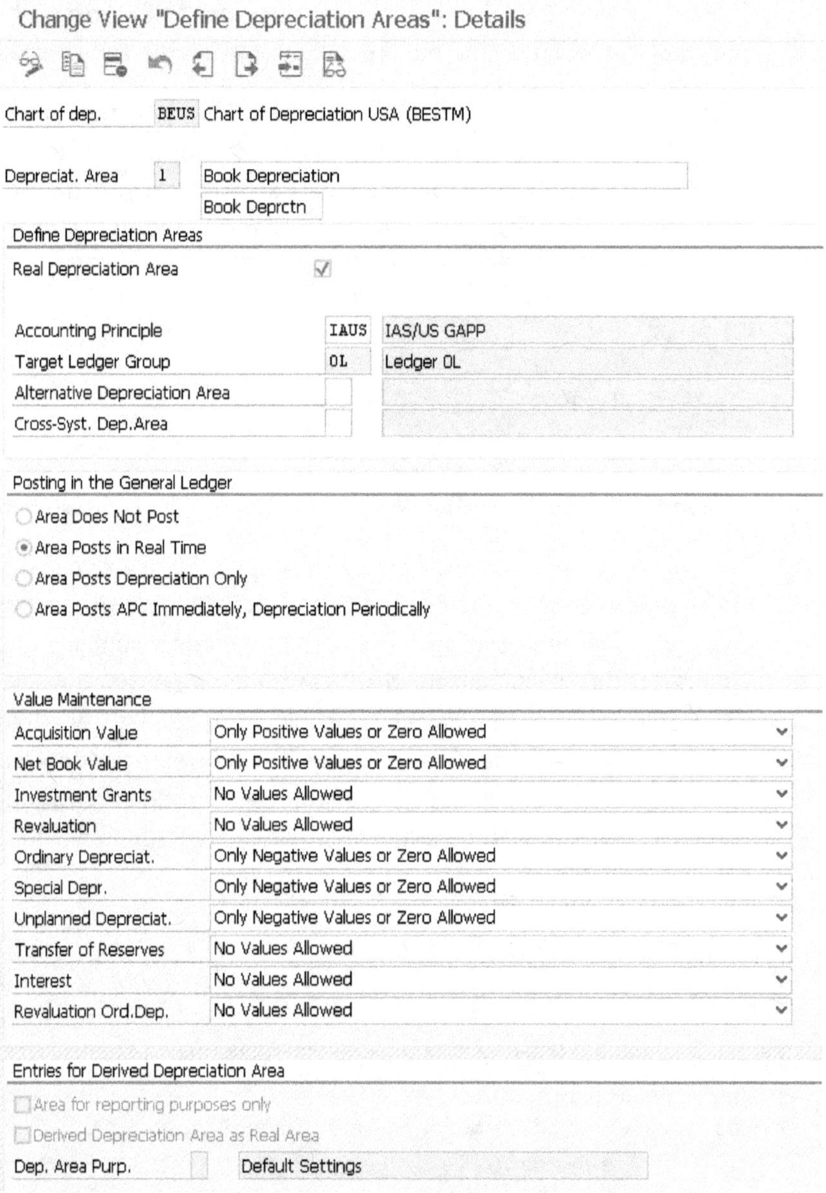

Change View "Define Depreciation Areas": Details

Chart of dep.   BEUS Chart of Depreciation USA (BESTM)

Depreciat. Area   1   Book Depreciation
                        Book Deprctn

Define Depreciation Areas

Real Depreciation Area   ☑

Accounting Principle	IAUS	IAS/US GAPP
Target Ledger Group	OL	Ledger OL
Alternative Depreciation Area		
Cross-Syst. Dep.Area		

Posting in the General Ledger

○ Area Does Not Post
◉ Area Posts in Real Time
○ Area Posts Depreciation Only
○ Area Posts APC Immediately, Depreciation Periodically

Value Maintenance

Acquisition Value	Only Positive Values or Zero Allowed	∨
Net Book Value	Only Positive Values or Zero Allowed	∨
Investment Grants	No Values Allowed	∨
Revaluation	No Values Allowed	∨
Ordinary Depreciat.	Only Negative Values or Zero Allowed	∨
Special Depr.	Only Negative Values or Zero Allowed	∨
Unplanned Depreciat.	Only Negative Values or Zero Allowed	∨
Transfer of Reserves	No Values Allowed	∨
Interest	No Values Allowed	∨
Revaluation Ord.Dep.	No Values Allowed	∨

Entries for Derived Depreciation Area

☐ Area for reporting purposes only
☐ Derived Depreciation Area as Real Area
Dep. Area Purp.   [ ]   Default Settings

Figure 13.5 Depreciation Area 01 – Details

b) Under 'Define Depreciation Areas' data block:
- Select 'Real Depreciation Area' check-box to indicate that this is not a derived depreciation area. When selected, the system updates the values in this area, in the database, each time a posting is made enabling immediate evaluation.
- Select the 'Accounting Principle' and the system automatically brings up the associated 'Target Ledger Group'.
- In 'Alternate Depreciation Area', you may enter the depreciation area from which the system uses the account determination when posting to parallel accounting. If you use ledger approach, specify the depreciation area that posts APC in real time (to the ledger group containing the leading ledger). If you use accounts approach, you should usually leave the field blank.
- Leave the 'Cross-Syst. Dep. Area' field as blank for the time being. We shall define this later (see Section 13.9.4.1.1).

c) For 'Posting in the General Ledger' select the appropriate radio-button: you have four options like 'Are Does not Post', 'Area Posts in Real Time', 'Area Posts Depreciation Only' and 'Area Posts APC Immediately, Depreciation Periodically'. We have selected 'Area Posts in Real Time' for the depreciation area 1 as this is for book depreciation.

d) Under 'Value Maintenance', you need to select the appropriate value for each of the parameters as shown in Figure 13.5. Per parameter, you can select one among the four options: 1 – only positive values or zero allowed, 2 – only negative values or zero allowed, 3 – all values allowed and 4 – no value allowed.

e) You will have to make the appropriate settings under 'Entries for Derived Depreciation Area' if you are configuring a depreciation area that is a derived one.

f) 'Save' the details, and continue with the settings for other depreciation areas.

With this, we are now ready to assign the chart of depreciation to company codes, in the next step.

13.2.3 Assign Chart of Depreciation to Company Code

By assigning a chart of depreciation to a company code that you have already defined in your FI enterprise structure, you make that company code available for FI-AA.

As in the case of 'chart of accounts and company code relationship', you can have more than one company code using a single chart of depreciation but, you cannot have one company code using more than one chart of depreciation. The essential condition for more than one company code to use a single chart of depreciation is that they should all be (a) operating in the same country / economic zone, or (b) belonging to the same industry even if they are in different countries, or (c) operating with the same set of valuation rules / requirements even if they are in different countries. Normally, you will use the different charts of depreciation if the company codes are in different countries.

The assignment of a company code to a chart of accounts is independent from its assignment to a chart of depreciation. That is, several company codes can use the same chart of accounts, although they have different charts of depreciation (and vice versa).

Use the menu path: SAP Customizing Implementation Guide > Financial Accounting > Asset Accounting > Organizational Structures > Assign Chart of Depreciation to Company Code. You may also use Transaction OAOB.

On the resulting screen, enter the chart of depreciation against each of the company codes: for BESTM, we have assigned the chart of depreciation BEUS for all the US-based company codes (Figure 13.6) and BEIN for all the India-based company codes.

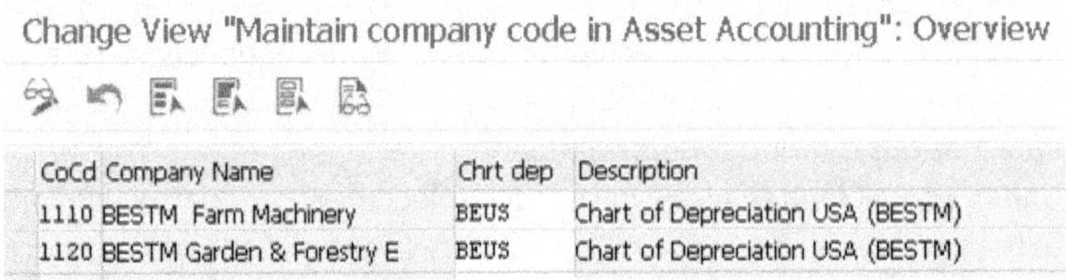

Change View "Maintain company code in Asset Accounting": Overview

CoCd	Company Name	Chrt dep	Description
1110	BESTM Farm Machinery	BEUS	Chart of Depreciation USA (BESTM)
1120	BESTM Garden & Forestry E	BEUS	Chart of Depreciation USA (BESTM)

Figure 13.6 Assignment of Chart of Depreciation to Company Codes

The next task is to specify the company code, for each of the FI-AA company codes, from which the system will use number interval for numbering the asset master records.

13.2.4 Specify Number Assignment Across Company Codes

For every company code in FI-AA, you can determine from which (other) company code the system should use the number range intervals, for numbering the asset master records. It is possible that you can assign the main asset number across company codes (cross-company code assignment), if required.

 Generally, the numbering of asset master records is carried out per company code.

Project Dolphin
BESTM does not want to have cross-company code number assignment for asset master records. Instead, it requires each company code to supply the number range intervals for numbering their asset master records.

Use the menu path: SAP Customizing Implementation Guide > Financial Accounting > Asset Accounting > Organizational Structures > Specify Number Assignment Across Company Codes. You may also use Transaction AO11.

On the resulting screen (Figure 13.7), you will see that, by default, the system has entered the same company code as the number range supplying company code ('No.CoCd') for each of the FI-AA company codes. You can keep that as such when you do not want cross-company code number assignment. Else, enter the number range supplying company code (say, 9000) against other company codes (say, 9100 and 9200) to make a cross-company code assignment of main asset number: in this case, the system will make use of number ranges from company code 9000 to number the main assets belonging to the company code 9100 and 9200.

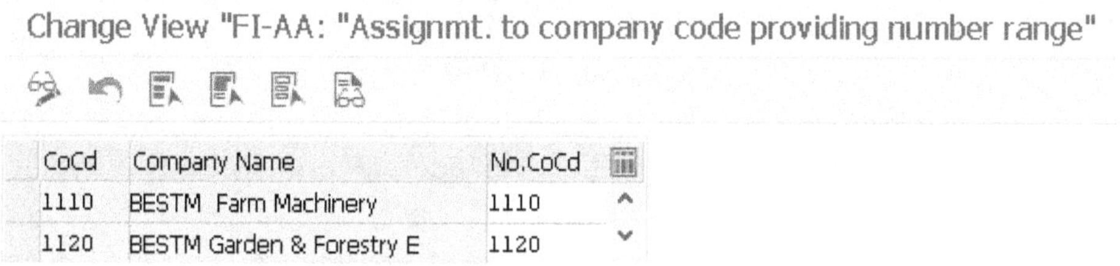

Change View "FI-AA: "Assignmt. to company code providing number range"

CoCd	Company Name	No.CoCd	
1110	BESTM Farm Machinery	1110	^
1120	BESTM Garden & Forestry E	1120	v

Figure 13.7 Number Range Assignment for Company Codes

Though configuring asset classes comes under 'Organization Structures', we will not be discussing that now. To understand asset classes, we first need to look at how to structure fixed assets in FI-AA that we shall discuss in the next Section. Once we understand the fixed assets structuring, we shall discuss about configuring the asset classes.

13.3 Structuring Fixed Assets in FI-AA

The term 'assets' represents different types of assets, and in a balance sheet (B/S) you normally represent them as (a) tangible assets, (b) intangible assets and (c) financial assets. Every asset type, in SAP, is represented by one or more asset classes (we shall define asset classes, in detail, later in Section 13.3.1), with each asset class serving as a kind of sample master record for the assets in that asset class. The asset classes contain certain control indictors. In general, all the asset classes, of an asset type, will use the same account determination and the same screen layout.

With this, let us look at the special forms of assets.

13.3.1 Special Forms of Assets

Let us understand, in this Section, some of the special forms of assets that are supported by SAP in FI-AA:

- *Assets under Construction (AuC)*: The AuC is a special form of tangible asset that you usually display as a separate B/S item and therefore it needs a separate account determination in the asset class. You can manage AuC as (a) any other asset using an individual master record or (b) collectively (comprising of several assets) on one master record. In most of the countries, ordinary depreciation is not allowed for AuC. You can achieve this by selecting a depreciation key that does not allow ordinary depreciation in the book depreciation area. However, for some AuC, it is possible to perform special tax depreciation: for this, you need to enter the corresponding keys in the asset class, to be used as mandatory default values.

- *Low Value Assets (LVA)*: As against regular fixed assets, you depreciate the LVAs completely in the year of their acquisition. You do not, normally, carry out individual assessment of their values as they individually have little value. Hence, you often manage them, collectively, in a single asset master record. For 'collective management' of LVAs, you need to activate the same by entering a UoM in the asset master record. You need to set the maximum amount for LVAs when defining the depreciation area at company code level while doing the Customizing. You will also specify if you want to manage the LVAs either through 'individual check' (*individual management*) or 'quantity check' (*collective management*) for the verification of the maximum amount for LVAs. In the case of 'individual check', when posting the acquisition, the system compares the entire APC (acquisition and production costs) of the asset with the LVA maximum amount specified earlier. However, in the case of 'collective check', when the system posts the acquisition, the system checks the entire APC of the asset, divided by the total quantity, against the LVA maximum amount.

- *Leased Assets*: The 'leased assets' create special accounting requirements for the lessee. During the term of the lease, the leased assets remain as the property of lessor (or manufacturer). They represent, therefore, a special form of rented asset. Such assets, legally and from a tax perspective, are the responsibility of the lessor, and are not relevant for assessing the value of the asset portfolio of the lessee. However, in certain countries, you are required to capitalize leased assets, depending on the type of financing involved. Depending on the legal terms and the conditions of the lease, the leased assets can be capitalized and depreciated ('capital lease') or they can flow into the P&L as periodic rental expenses ('operating lease'). In FI-AA, besides entering all the essential leasing contract information in the asset master record, you can assign a leasing type (that you have defined in Customizing) in the asset master. The leasing type contains all the information for the acquisition posting.

- *Intangible Assets*: Similar to the tangible assets, you can manage the intangible assets (such as, goodwill, brand recognition, copyrights, patents, trademarks etc) also in the system. SAP does not provide any special system functions for handling the needs of intangible assets. As with other assets, you must assign the account control of the asset class for the intangible assets to the corresponding B/S item. If you want to post down payments, for intangible assets, then, you must specify (in Customizing) in the asset class that posting is allowed with the transaction type group 'down payments'. As you will not normally retire the intangible assets, you cannot post any retirement posting. However, you can specify (in the asset class for intangible assets) that a retirement is simulated when the book value reaches zero. In this way, you can ensure that the intangible assets appear in the retirement column of the 'asset history sheet' (we shall discuss asset history sheet, in detail, in Section 13.10.7).

- *Technical Assets*: You can manage technical data of an asset only to a limited extent in the asset master record, in FI-AA. However, you can enter a virtually unlimited amount of technical description using the 'long text' function. In addition, it is possible to link any number of original documents (blueprints, bills of material etc) to the asset master record, using the document management system (DMS). If you need to create separate master records for technical assets, you, then, need to deactivate the book depreciation area for these fixed assets so as to prevent any posting. You can, also, enter detailed technical information for the maintenance of equipment in the Plant Maintenance (SAP PM) component: enter this information in the functional location in the equipment master record.

- *Real Estate*: You will not be using FI-AA component for rental contract management of residential buildings, or detailed land register management for real estate. Instead, for these types of activities, you need to use the Flexible Real Estate Management (RE-FX) component of SAP.

With this, we are ready to understand how you can structure the fixed assets in FI-AA.

13.3.2 Structuring Fixed Assets in FI-AA

You can structure fixed assets, in FI-AA, at three different levels as shown in Figure 13.8:

- Balance sheet structure level
- Classification structure level
- Asset-related structure level

At the 'balance sheet structure level', you can structure your fixed assets according to balance sheet criteria. Therefore, you can arrive at a 3-level hierarchy for your assets as shown under:

1) G/L ledger account (level 1)
2) Balance sheet item (level 2)
3) Financial statement version (level 3)

At the 'classification structure level', you can structure fixed assets using 'asset classes' in FI-AA. With the asset classes, you can structure assets according to a country's legal requirements or as per the demands of accounting. With every asset belonging to an asset class, you will use the 'account determination' (in the asset class) to assign an asset to an item in the B/S.

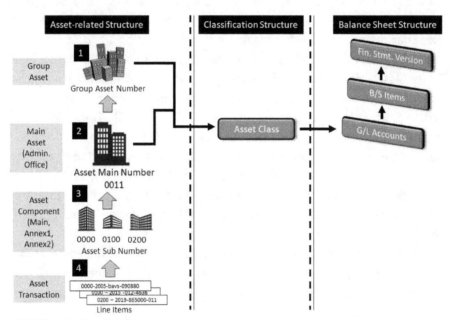

Figure 13.8 Structuring Fixed Assets

At the 'asset-related structure level', you can set up a maximum of 4-level hierarchy in FI-AA. However, it is not mandatory to have 4-levels. If required, and feasible, you can just have your assets represented by the asset main number, and in this case the asset will be known as a *'simple asset'*. In case you plan to use the 4-level hierarchy then you will structure the assets as detailed below:

- The *'group asset'*, at the top in a 4-level hierarchy, enables grouping a number of assets together for the purpose of uniform evaluation and depreciation. Like any other asset, you will assign a group asset also to an asset class. The concept of group asset is mostly used in USA to meet some tax requirements.

> ℹ️ Note that the asset class of a group asset need not be the same as that of the asset classes of the underlying assets that form the group asset.

- The *'asset main number'*, at the 3rd level, just below the group asset, represents an asset that you will like to evaluate independently, as a single unit. When you do not have group assets in the hierarchy, then, you will assign the asset main number directly to an asset class.
- Below the asset main number, at the 2nd level, you can subdivide your main asset into several component parts, each represented by an *'asset subnumber'*. With this structuring, you can use the subnumbers to depreciate subsequent acquisitions to main asset separately from the original asset.
- At the lowest level, you have the 'line items' that represent the transaction data (such as, acquisitions or retirements), per depreciation area, belonging to the asset master record.

With this, let us move on to discuss how to represent fixed assets in FI-AA.

13.3.3 Representing Fixed Assets in FI-AA

You normally use the term 'asset' to represent both simple assets as well as complex assets. A *'complex asset'* normally consists of a number of component assets. In a complex asset, you will use a main asset number to represent the asset as a whole (say, CNC lathe1), and use asset subnumbers to represent the various parts / components (say, headstock, CNC lathe bed, chuck, tailstock, tailstock quill, tool turret, control panel etc) of an asset.

In SAP, the system allows a 12-character alpha-numeric number for the main asset and a 4-character numbering for the asset subnumbers. When you create an asset master record, the system automatically creates at least one subnumber, even if there is no sub-asset. The system marks the first master record as the 'asset main number'. When you use internal subnumber assignment, this main number always has an asset subnumber = 0000. You can create any number of additional subnumbers for an asset main number. The system manages the values at the subnumber level, for every individual depreciation area, in the year segments. The system posts the individual transactions directly to the subnumbers, as line items.

- *Simple Asset*: A 'simple asset' is represented by only one asset master record. This master record has the subnumber as 0000. You will post the subsequent acquisitions to this master record. You can meet the most essential business and legal demands with year segments and transaction data. For a simple asset, you cannot separate the accumulated depreciation and book values from closed fiscal years according to their acquisition year. Also, you cannot depreciate the subsequent acquisitions individually.

- *Complex Asset*: A 'complex asset' consists of several sub-assets or component assets. You will denote the whole asset using an asset main number and represent each of the sub-assets using an asset subnumber. This is because, you may want to monitor the sub-assets individually from some accounting point of view: while it may be necessary for uniform depreciation of the entire asset in the book depreciation and tax depreciation areas, you may need to depreciate the sub-assets separately for, say, cost-accounting perspective.

> **i** Use external numbering, as for as possible, for asset subnumbers for meaningful modelling of the specific structure of the asset.

You may want to manage the various asset components of a large asset, in the system, as subnumbers because, (a) the development values of component assets may be different for each of the sub-asset numbers, (b) you may need a different cost accounting assignment for some of the sub-assets, (c) you may want to divide the asset based on certain technical aspects (for example, to link with SAP Plant Maintenance), and/or (d) you may want to represent investment support as negative for the sub-assets.

- *Group Asset*: As already outlined in Section 13.3.2, a 'group asset' (for example, administrative building) is made up of several assets (for example, administrative office1, administrative offcie2 etc) grouped only for some special purposes in evaluation and reporting. You will represent a group asset using a separate master record.

> **i** Specify, while configuring the IMG node 'Specify Asset Classes for Group Assets' (Transaction OAAX), if a particular asset class is meant strictly for group assets: select the 'Class consists entirely of group assets' check-box (refer Section 13.5.5.2)
>
> Also, while configuring the IMG activity 'Specify Depreciation Areas for Group Assets' (Transaction OAYM), select the 'Grp.asset' check-box, if you want to manage assets at the group asset level, in the respective depreciation areas (refer Section 13.5.5.1)

- *Asset Super Number*: The 'asset super number' offers some advantages of a group asset, without being as complex as that of a group asset. You can use asset super number to assign a number of assets to a single object. You assign assets to an asset super number by entering the common asset super number in the asset master record. You can either create the asset super number as a separate master record, or simply use it as a 'sort' criterion. If you want to manage master data at the asset super number level, you must create a statistical asset master record (without values) for the asset super number.

> **i** You cannot calculate asset values for the assets at the asset super number level.

- *Negative Assets*: Managing assets as 'negative assets' enables you, for example, (a) to collect investment support on negative assets, or (b) to represent investment support as a negative subnumber to the respective main number or (c) to collect credit memos on special assets. For handling a negative asset, you need to specify an asset class that allows assets with negative APC but with positive depreciation; make this specification using an indicator, in the detail screen of the depreciation areas, in the asset class.

With this, we are ready to discuss the asset classes.

13.3.4 Asset Classes

Valid across company codes of a client, you can use the 'asset classes' to structure your assets according to the legal and accounting requirements of your business enterprise. You can define any number asset classes (like, buildings, vehicles, AuC, machinery, furniture & fittings etc) in the system. The asset class establishes the link (through the account determination key) between asset master records and the G/L accounts in SAP FI (Figure 13.9).

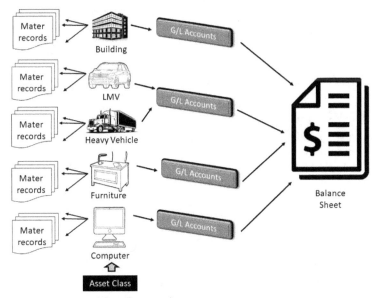

Figure 13.9 Structuring Asset Classes

> **i** Several asset classes can use the same account determination key.

Called as 'sample master record', the asset class, besides providing default values to all the asset master records in that class, also enables and simplifies creation of new asset master records. You can set the screen / tab layout together with the field status characteristics for each of the asset classes. You can also control asset numbering through the asset classes. In almost all the asset reports, you will use asset class as a 'sort' criterion.

By assigning any number of charts of depreciation to each asset class, you can have country-specific depreciation terms for each combination of 'asset class-chart of depreciation'. And, these depreciation terms can become the default values in the given chart of depreciation.

> **i** Even though an asset class with the default values can be used across company codes in a client, it is also possible to specify certain general master data that is dependent on a chart of depreciation, and to use that to provide default data.

An asset class is made up of three sections as shown in Figure 13.10:

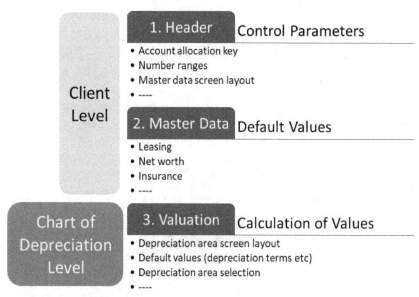

Figure 13.10 Asset Class Sections

1. A 'header section' comprising of control parameters (like account determination key, number & subnumber assignment, special functions etc) for master data maintenance and account determination.
2. A 'master data section' with default values (like, net worth tax, insurance etc) for the administrative data in the asset master record.

3. A 'valuation section' with control parameters (like, depreciation area screen layout, depreciation terms, useful life, index series, control indicator: amount / quantity check for LVA, allowing negative values etc) for valuation and default depreciation terms for each depreciation area.

With this background on asset class, let us look at configuring them (as a part of organizational structuring) in the system. The first activity is to specify the account determination.

13.3.4.1   Specify Account Determination

Here, you will define the account determination keys and their description for use in FI-AA. Stored in the asset class, the account determination links an asset master record with the FI-G/L accounts to be posted for an accounting transaction using the asset class. You can specify various accounts for each depreciation area to post to.

> **i** The number of account determinations should be at least equal to your asset types that are represented as B/S items.

Project Dolphin

The project management team has recommended to create easily identifiable new account determination keys to map to the various types of fixed assets for BESTM group of companies. It has been advised to create two account determinations for LVAs: one for collective management and another for individual management. They have also recommended to create new screen layout rules to customize the field status to suit BESTM requirements.

Change View "FI-AA: Account determination": Overview

New Entries

Acct. determ.	Name of Account Determination
B1000	Buildings
B2000	Plant and Machinery
B3000	Vehicles
B4100	Office Equipment
B4200	Furniture and Fixtures
B5100	Computer Hardware
B5200	Computer Software
B6000	Assets under Construction (AuC)
B7000	Low Value Assets (LVA) - Collective Management
B7100	Low Value Assets (LVA) - Individual Management
B8000	Intangible Assets

Figure 13.11 Account Determination Keys

Use the menu path: SAP Customizing Implementation Guide > Financial Accounting > Asset Accounting > Organizational Structures > Asset Classes > Specify Account Determination, or Transaction S_ALR_87009195. On the resulting screen, click on 'New Entries' and define the account determination keys ('Acct.determ.') and the description ('Name of Account Determination') as shown in Figure 13.11.

The next task in configuring asset classes, is to specify the screen layout rules.

13.3.4.2   Create Screen Layout Rules

The screen layout determines the field status in the asset master record. Accordingly, you will use the screen layout to determine if fields are to be of 'required entry' or 'optional entry', or if they are to be 'suppressed'. Here in this activity, you create only the keys and descriptions of the screen layout controls. You will carry out the definition of the field group rules, for the screen layouts, while configuring 'Screen Layout' under 'Master Data' (refer Section 13.8.2).

You can enter a *'screen layout rule'* in one of the two places: either in the part of the asset class that is valid for the entire client, or in the part of the asset class that is valid only for the chart of depreciation. Accordingly, the screen layout rule is, then, valid either for all assets in the asset class, or for all assets in the 'asset class/chart of depreciation' combination. You may use the SAP supplied screen layout rules for the most commonly used asset types, or you may create your own. We have created new screen layout rules to be in line with the different asset types for BESTM.

Use the menu path: SAP Customizing Implementation Guide > Financial Accounting > Asset Accounting > Organizational Structures > Asset Classes > Create Screen Layout Rules or Transaction S_ALR_87009209. On the resulting screen, click on 'New Entries' and create the keys for 'Screen Layout Rule' and also a description ('Name of screen layout rule'). All the screen layout rules for BESTM will start with the letters BE (Figure 13.12).

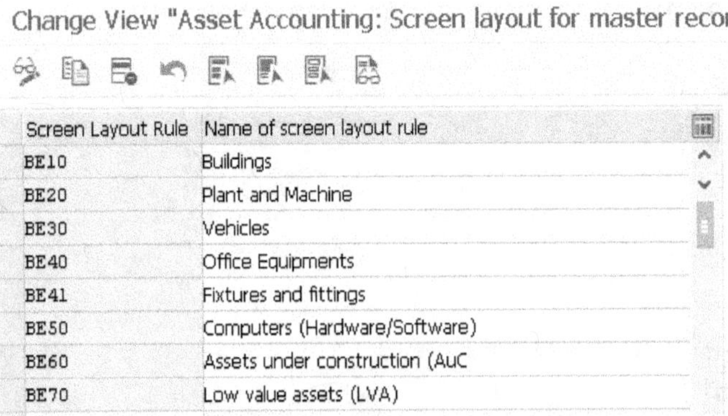

Change View "Asset Accounting: Screen layout for master record": Overv

Screen Layout Rule	Name of screen layout rule
BE10	Buildings
BE20	Plant and Machine
BE30	Vehicles
BE40	Office Equipments
BE41	Fixtures and fittings
BE50	Computers (Hardware/Software)
BE60	Assets under construction (AuC
BE70	Low value assets (LVA)

Figure 13.12 Screen Layout Rules

The next step is to define the number range interval for the asset classes.

13.3.4.3   Define Number Range Interval

Define the number ranges, that you will require, per company code, for assigning the main asset numbers. You specify the required number range intervals to cover your entire portfolio of assets. The number assignment of asset subnumbers is controlled by the asset class. You can specify there, in the asset class, whether the assignment of subnumbers is to be internal or external. You do not need to define the number ranges for the assignment of asset subnumbers.

> **i** Always opt for internal numbering for the asset main numbers, and external for asset subnumbers.

Project Dolphin

BESTM management has decided to define as many number ranges as that of asset account determination keys, so as to easily identify an asset just by a number. And, all the asset main numbers will be internal but the asset subnumbers will be external to help in modeling and grouping the assets.

Use the menu path: SAP Customizing Implementation Guide > Financial Accounting > Asset Accounting > Organizational Structures > Asset Classes > Define Number Range Interval. You may also use Transaction AS08. On the resulting screen, enter the 'Company Code' and click on 'Change Intervals'. On the next screen, create the required number ranges (Figure 13.13). And, repeat defining the number ranges for all the company codes of BESTM, both in USA and in India.

Edit Intervals: Asset Number, Object ANLAGENNR, Subobject 1110

N..	From No.	To Number	NR Status	Ext
B1	100000000000	199999999999	0	☐
B2	200000000000	299999999999	0	☐
B3	300000000000	399999999999	0	☐
B4	400000000000	499999999999	0	☐
B5	500000000000	599999999999	0	☐
B6	600000000000	699999999999	0	☐
B7	700000000000	799999999999	0	☐
B8	800000000000	899999999999	0	☐

Figure 13.13 Number Range Intervals for Main Asset (Company Code 1110)

With this, we are now ready to define the asset classes.

13.3.4.4   Define Asset Classes

From the previous discussion on asset classes at the start of the Section 13.3.1, we know that defining asset classes is fundamental to SAP FI-AA. We already know that the asset class is the most important way of structuring your fixed assets in the system, as it forms the linkage between your asset masters and the respective G/L accounts.

---

i Though the number of asset classes you may need depends upon the type of assets in your organization's asset portfolio, you will normally need no more than 50 asset classes at the maximum. Try to have assets with the same depreciation terms in the same asset class.

Project Dolphin

The project team has recommended to BESTM management to have as many asset classes as that of the asset determination keys that have been defined earlier. However, instead of creating a separate asset class for goodwill, an asset class in the name of 'intangible assets' will have to be created to cover all intangible assets including the goodwill, patent, copyright etc. For AuC, it should be configured for line item settlement. Except the LVA, all other asset classes should be configured to have the subnumber assigned externally.

Use the menu path: SAP Customizing Implementation Guide > Financial Accounting > Asset Accounting > Organizational Structures > Asset Classes > Define Asset Classes or Transaction OAOA.

On the resulting screen, click on 'New Entries' and define all the required settings for the asset class, say B1000, on the next screen (Figure 13.14):

   i.   Enter the key for the 'Asset Class', and provide both the description and and 'Short Text'.

   ii.   Under 'Asset Type', enter the appropriate account determination ('Account Determ.') and also the screen layout rule ('Scr.layout rule') that you have defined earlier.

   iii.   Enter the appropriate 'Number range', under 'Number assignment', from the number ranges that you have defined earlier. Select the 'External sub-no' check-box if you want all the subnumbers for this asset class are to be externally numbered, as required by BESTM.

   iv.   Select the first radio-button option 'No AuC or Summary Management of AuC' under 'Status of AuC' as this asset class is not for AuC. However, in the case of an asset class for AuC (say, B6000 in our case), you need to select the appropriate radio button ('Line item settlement' for BESTM).

   v.   Do not select the check-box 'Asset class is blocked' for now. When selected, this will prevent new assets from being created in this asset class.

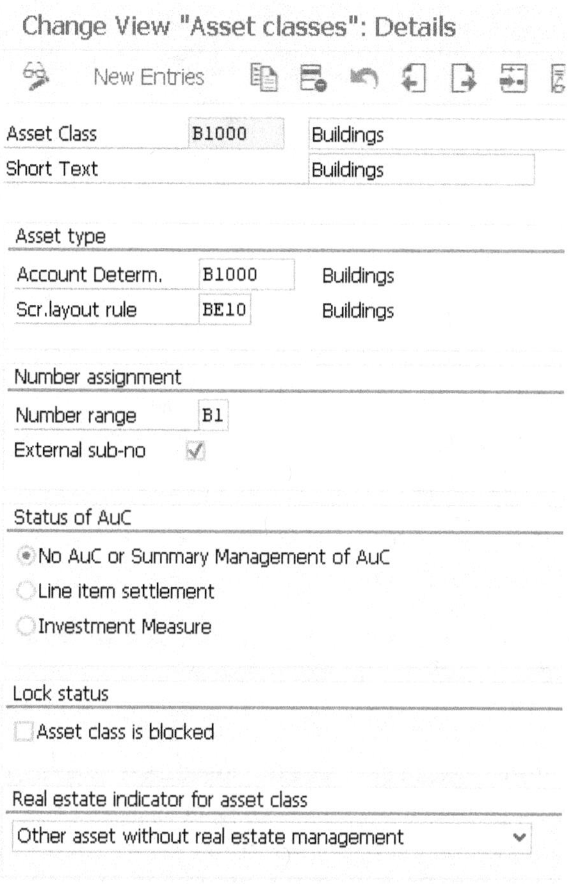

Change View "Asset classes": Details

🔁   New Entries   📋 📑 ↩ ⏪ ⏩ ⏭ 📊

| Asset Class | B1000 | Buildings |
| Short Text | | Buildings |

Asset type

| Account Determ. | B1000 | Buildings |
| Scr.layout rule | BE10 | Buildings |

Number assignment

| Number range | B1 |
| External sub-no | ☑ |

Status of AuC

◉ No AuC or Summary Management of AuC
◯ Line item settlement
◯ Investment Measure

Lock status

☐ Asset class is blocked

Real estate indicator for asset class

| Other asset without real estate management | ⌄ |

Figure 13.14 Asset Class B1000 – Detail Screen

vi.   Since this is not an asset class for real estate asset, you will select 'Other asset without real estate management' value for the 'Real estate indicator for asset class'. Select 'Real estate – property or buildings' value, if you want to manage the assets of this asset class in SAP-RE as real estate or buildings.

vii.   'Save' when completed, and create all other asset classes as well (Figure 13.15).

Change View "Asset classes": Overview

Class	Short Text	Asset Class Description
B1000	Buildings	Buildings
B2000	Plant	Plant & Machinery
B3000	Vehicles	Vehicles
B4100	Office Equipment	Office Equipment
B4200	Furniture	Furniture & Fixtures
B5100	Computer Hardware	Computer Hardware
B5200	Computer Software	Computer Software
B6000	AuC	Assets under Construction (AuC)
B7000	LVA - Collective	Low Value Assets - Collective Management
B7100	LVA - Individua	Low Value Assets -Individual Management
B8000	Intangible Assets	Intangible Assets

Figure 13.15 Asset Classes for BESTM

The last configuration step under asset classes is to specify the chart of depreciation dependent screen layout and account assignment.

13.3.4.5   Specify Chart-of-Dep.-Dependent Screen Layout/Acct Assignment

In general, the control specifications (the screen layout and the account determination) for the asset class applies throughout the client; that is, it is valid for all the charts of depreciation. Hence, it is sufficient to make control specifications at the asset class level as we have done in the earlier step. However, should you need to control the specifications, per country, using the chart of depreciation, then you need to carry out this configuration step for a given asset class. When done, the system will ignore the general control specifications but will make use of the settings made here.

Project Dolphin

The project team has recommended to make use of the control specifications for screen layout and account determination at the asset class level rather than making the specifications at the chart of depreciation level.

As we want to make use of the control specifications (for the screen layout and account determination) at the asset class level, for all BESTM company codes, we will not be configuring this step here.

However, should you want to do that you may use the menu path: SAP Customizing Implementation Guide > Financial Accounting > Asset Accounting > Organizational Structures > Asset Classes > Specify Chart-of-Dep.-Dependent Screen Layout/Acct Assignment or Transaction ANK1. On the resulting screen, select the appropriate asset class and double-click on 'Chart-of-depreciation-dependent-data' on the left-hand side 'Dialog Structure' and enter the chart of depreciation on the next screen and 'Save'.

This completes our discussion on configuring the asset classes, and thereby configuring the organizational structures. Let us, now, move on to discuss the integration of FI-AA with other SAP application components including SAP FI.

13.4 Integration

It possible that you can make account assignment to FI-AA from the application components like SAP MM (Materials Management), PM (Plant Maintenance), SAP PP (Production Planning) and IM (Investment Management). Let us see some of these integrations in the discussion below:

13.4.1 FI-AA Integration with SAP MM

The integration of FI-AA with SAP MM component enables the following:

- When you post to an asset while entering a purchase requisition (PR) or an outline agreement, the system checks (with reference to the planned delivery date) to ascertain whether the fixed asset actually exists and whether you can post to it. The system carries out the same checks if you post to a fixed asset when entering a purchase order (PO). During the process, the system ensures – for example - that you do not exceed the upper limit for LVAs.
- Also, when you have account assignment to an asset during a material reservation, the system checks whether the asset actually exists. Accordingly, any material withdrawal (with account assignment to an asset) results in capitalization of the purchase or production costs of the material to the fixed asset.
- Depending on the purchase order (PO), you can post the GR for a PO as valuated or non-valuated: if the GR is valuated, then, the system capitalizes the invoiced value of the goods (based on the PO) to the fixed asset; else, the system posts the non-valuated GR to a clearing account. See Section 13.9.1.2 for defining the account assignment category for asset POs.
- Depending upon when invoice receipt (IR) happens vis-à-vis the GR, the system handles the asset capitalization differently: (a) if the IR is before GR, the system capitalizes the invoice amount (without tax & discount) to the asset or (b) if the IR is after GR, then, the system capitalizes the difference between the invoice amount (minus tax & discount) and the posted invoiced value of goods, provided that the GR was valuated. However, in the case of IR after a non-valuated GR, the system capitalizes the total invoice amount (minus tax & cash discount).

> **i** You have to determine, beforehand, if you want the system to deduct the cash discount at IR; you can configure this through an appropriate document type.

13.4.2 FI-AA Integration with SAP PP/PM

Since you can enter fixed assets as the 'receivers' for the settlement of maintenance orders, you can settle maintenance activities that require capitalization to assets. In this case, the system will propose the asset that is assigned to the given equipment (or functional location) as the settlement receiver.

13.4.3 FI-AA Integration with SAP IM

You normally need to settle the costs collected on the investment measure to different receivers, when you settle capital investment measures. The system carries out most of this process, automatically, using the control parameters and settlement rules that you have entered. Accordingly, you can do (a) periodic settlement at the close of the period or (b) full settlement or partial capitalization of the investment measure at its completion:

- During 'periodic settlement', the system allocates the actual costs on the order or WBS completely or partially to one or more receivers. Also, it generates automatic offsetting postings that credit the order or WBS element. The original debit postings to the order or WBS element still exist on the receivers after the settlement.
- The system makes a 'full settlement' when the investment measure is completed. At that time, the system settles the debits that were transferred to the AuC to the completed assets. It is possible that you can make a correction, at this point, and make a final settlement of these debits to the correct cost centers, if debits were incorrectly transferred earlier to the AuC. However, the system allows this only for debits that were posted during the current fiscal year but not for previous fiscal years, since they were already listed under AuC in the B/S for the previous year.

Besides the above, the integration of FI-AA with other FI application components enables you to (a) post asset acquisitions and retirements that are integrated with A/P and A/R, (b) make account assignment of downpayments to assets by them in FI, and (c) post depreciation from FI-AA to the appropriate G/L accounts.

Let us now understand the integration of FI-AA with SAP G/L Accounting, in the next section.

13.4.4 FI-AA Integration with SAP G/L Accounting

Using FI-AA, you can automatically update all relevant accounting transactions that are posted to assets, and all the changes to asset values that are automatically calculated by the system (particularly depreciation), to SAP G/L Accounting. The system makes these updates in real-time for the leading depreciation areas of an accounting principle; for other depreciation areas (such as depreciation areas for special reserves), the system makes periodic updates.

We shall now discuss the configuration steps that are required to make the integration of FI-AA with SAP G/L Accounting:

- Define How Depreciation Areas Post to General Ledger
- Assign G/L Accounts
- Define Technical Clearing Account for Integrated Asset Acquisition
- Integrated Transactions: Alternative Document Type for 'Accounting Principle-Specific' Documents
- Specify Posting Key for Asset Posting
- Change the Field Status Variant of the Asset G/L Accounts
- Assign Input Tax Indicator for Non-Taxable Acquisitions
- Specify Financial Statement Version for Asset Reports
- Specify Document Type for Posting of Depreciation
- Specify Intervals and Posting Rules
- Segment Reporting
- Additional Account Assignment Objects

Let us start with the first step of defining how depreciation areas post to the G/L.

13.4.4.1   Define How Depreciation Areas Post to General Ledger

Here, in this step, you will specify the depreciation areas that post their APC transactions and/or depreciation to the G/L. The system posts the APC transactions of the depreciation areas to the G/L online, automatically. You always have to use periodic processing to post depreciation to the G/L. In the standard settings, the book depreciation area (1) posts the APC transactions and depreciation, in real-time, to the G/L.

Use the menu path: SAP Customizing Implementation Guide > Financial Accounting > Asset Accounting > Integration with General Ledger Accounting > Define How Depreciation Areas Post to General Ledger.

i.   On the resulting pop-up screen, enter the chart of depreciation to proceed.

ii.   On the next screen, you will see the list of depreciation areas and how they are posting to the G/L. If you look closely, you will notice that we have already completed this when we maintained the depreciation areas (activity: 'Copy/Delete Depreciation Areas') as a part of the IMG activity 'Copy Reference Chart of Depreciation/Depreciation Areas' vide Section 13.2.3. You can, of course, use this step now to change, if required, the way a depreciation area posts to the G/L.

> ℹ️ It is normally sufficient to post APC transactions and depreciation from one depreciation area automatically to the G/L online. This will always be the book depreciation area (1 or 01). However, you might need additional areas that post automatically to the G/L (a) when you want to post depreciation that differs from book depreciation to expense accounts (or cost elements) for meeting cost-accounting requirements, or (b) when you need special valuations for the B/S as in the case of special reserves, for example, or (c) when you need to meet the special requirements for legal consolidation of your corporate group or (d) when you are using the ledger approach, in SAP G/L Accounting, and you want to specify additional depreciation areas from which APC transactions are posted automatically online to the G/L.

With this, we are now ready to carry out the next step of specifying the B/S accounts, special reserve accounts, and the depreciation accounts for FI-AA.

13.4.4.2   Assign G/L Accounts

Per account determination and per depreciation area, you need to specify the B/S accounts, depreciation accounts and the special reserve accounts, using this configuration step.

Use the menu path: SAP Customizing Implementation Guide > Financial Accounting > Asset Accounting > Integration with General Ledger Accounting > Assign G/L Accounts. You may also use Transaction AO90:

   i.   On the resulting pop-up screen, enter the chart of depreciation (BEUS) and proceed further.

   ii.   On the next screen, select the chart of accounts row (BEUS) and double-click on 'Account Determination' on the left-hand side 'Dialog Structure' (Figure 13.16).

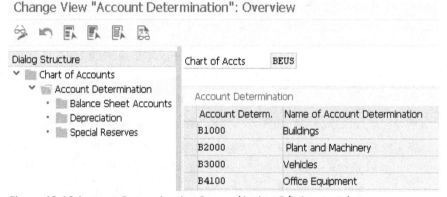

Figure 13.16 Account Determination Screen (Assign G/L Accounts)

   iii.   Select a row under 'Account Determination' (say, B1000, Buildings), and double-click on 'Balance Sheet Accounts' on the left-hand side 'Dialog Structure'. The system brings up the next screen listing the depreciation areas. Double-click on a depreciation area, and enter the appropriate G/L accounts for the B/S on the next screen (Figure 13.17).

Figure 13.17 B/S Accounts for Account Determination B1000 for Dep. Area 01

iv.   Similarly, per depreciation area maintain the G/L accounts for 'Depreciation' and 'Special Reserves' by double-clicking on the appropriate option on the left-hand side 'Dialog Structure'.

v.   Repeat the G/L account assignment for all the other account assignments like B2000, B3000 etc.

> **i** In the case of a special depreciation area, if you enter G/L accounts for gains and losses for reserves, the system will not post the revenue from writing off reserves for special depreciation. Instead, the system includes this amount in the gain/loss, when there is revenue from write-off of special reserves due to an asset sale. The system, then, balances the loss by a posting to an offsetting account, and posts the sum/difference between the revenue from the write-off of the special reserve and the loss to these accounts.

We can now move on to define the technical clearing account for integrated asset acquisition.

13.4.4.3   Define Technical Clearing Account for Integrated Asset Acquisition

In an integrated asset acquisition posting, the system divides the business transaction into an operational part and a valuating part: (a) for the 'operational part' (vendor invoice), the system posts a document valid for all accounting principles against the technical clearing account, and (b) for each 'valuating part' (asset posting with capitalization of the asset), the system generates a separate document that is (valid only for the given accounting principle) also posted against the technical clearing account.

ℹ️ By this, the system ensures that the 'technical clearing account for integrated asset acquisitions' has a zero-balance (for each accounting principle and account assignment object) in the chart of depreciation. To ensure zero balance, the system prevents you from making manual postings to the account.

Note that this technical clearing account, since it has a zero-balance, will not appear in the B/S itself, but in the notes to the financial statement.

Use the menu path: SAP Customizing Implementation Guide > Financial Accounting > Asset Accounting > Integration with General Ledger Accounting > Define Technical Clearing Account for Integrated Asset Acquisition. On the resulting screen, enter the technical clearing account for integrated asset acquisition against the chart of depreciation (Figure 13.18).

Figure 13.18 Technical Clearing Account for Integrated Asset Acquisition

Now that we have defined the technical clearing account for integrated asset acquisition, we also need to define alternate document types for integrated asset transactions.

13.4.4.4   Integrated Transactions: Alternative Doc. Type for Acctg-Princpl-Spec. Docs

We have already seen, in the previous Section, that in an integrated asset acquisition posting, the system divides the business transaction into an operational part and a valuating part. For the operative part, the system posts a document that is valid for all accounting principles (ledger-group independent document). And, for each valuating part, the system generates a separate document that is valid only for the given accounting principle (ledger-group-specific documents per accounting principle).

When document splitting is active, then, the system cannot always pass on the document type (of the entry view) to the valuating documents, because in the document type defined, the items have been designated as required, but they exist only in the operational document, and not in the valuating document. So, you need a different document type, to take care of the valuation postings. Also, you may require that the valuating documents be posted with a different document type (than that of the operational documents). Hence, you need to specify alternative document types for accounting-principle-specific documents:

13.4.4.4.1   Alternative Document Type for Acctg-Principle-Specific Documents

Use the menu path: SAP Customizing Implementation Guide > Financial Accounting > Asset Accounting > Integration with General Ledger Accounting > Integrated Transactions: Alternative Doc. Type for Acctg-Princpl-Spec. Docs > Alternative Document Type for Acctg-Principle-Specific Documents, and specify the general (company code independent) document types for the valuating documents to take care of the different account principles.

If necessary, you can further differentiate the valuating documents per company code, which you can achieve through the following activity:

13.4.4.4.2   Define Separate Document Types by Company Code

Use the menu path: SAP Customizing Implementation Guide > Financial Accounting > Asset Accounting > Integration with General Ledger Accounting > Integrated Transactions: Alternative Doc. Type for Acctg-Princpl-Spec. Docs > Define Separate Document Types by Company Code, and specify the company code dependent document types for the valuating documents to take care of the different account principles.

The next step, is to specify the posting keys for asset accounting.

13.4.4.5   Specify Posting Key for Asset Posting

Using this configuration step, you can define the posting keys which the system will use for automatic postings, when posting to FI-AA. You do not need to define your own keys as you can use the SAP supplied standard posting keys (Figure 13.19).

Configuration Accounting Maintain : Automatic Posts - Posting Keys

◀ ▶

| Transaction | ANL | Asset posting |

Posting Key	
Debit	70
Credit	75

Figure 13.19 Posting Keys for Asset Posting

You can see that these standard posting keys, for each of the posting procedures, by using the menu path: SAP Customizing Implementation Guide > Financial Accounting > Asset Accounting > Integration with General Ledger Accounting > Specify Posting Key for Asset Posting or Transaction OBYD:

- ANL – Asset Posting (posting keys: 70 debit and 75 credit)
- ANS – G/L Account Posting from Asset Posting (posting keys: 40 debit and 50 credit)

The next step is to define/change the field status variant (FSV) of the asset G/L Accounts.

13.4.4.6   Change the Field Status Variant of the Asset G/L Accounts

We have already defined the FSV for BESTM company codes vide Section 6.2 of Chapter 6. We have defined the FSV, B100, and have assigned the company codes of BESTM to that. Here, in this, activity we shall be viewing/editing the same to make sure that we have the appropriate field status for enabling asset accounting related postings.

Project Dolphin

BESTM requested the project management team to configure the FSV to ensure that indicator 'Asset retirement' and the field 'Asset number / subnumber' are set to with a field status as 'required entry'. Similar settings need to be carried out for the asset posting keys as well.

Use the menu path: SAP Customizing Implementation Guide > Financial Accounting > Asset Accounting > Integration with General Ledger Accounting > Change the Field Status Variant of the Asset G/L Accounts.

    i.   On the resulting 'Select Activity' pop-up screen, double-click on the 'Define Field Status Variants' activity (Figure 13.20):

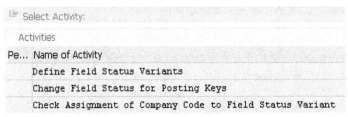

Figure 13.20 'Select Activity' Pop-Up Screen

- On the next screen (you may also reach this screen directly by using Transaction OBC4), select the appropriate FSV (B100), and double-click on the 'Field status group' on the left-hand side 'Dialog Structure'.
- The system will bring up all the field status groups (FSGs) of FSV B100. Double-click on the FSG YB07 [Asset accts (w/o accumulated depreciatn)].

- On the resulting 'Maintain Field Status Group: Overview' screen, double-click on 'Asset Accounting' under the 'Select Group' block.
- On the next screen, ensure that the 'Asset retirement' indicator and the 'Asset number / subnumber' fields are set to required entry ('Req. Entry'). 'Save' the settings (Figure 13.21).

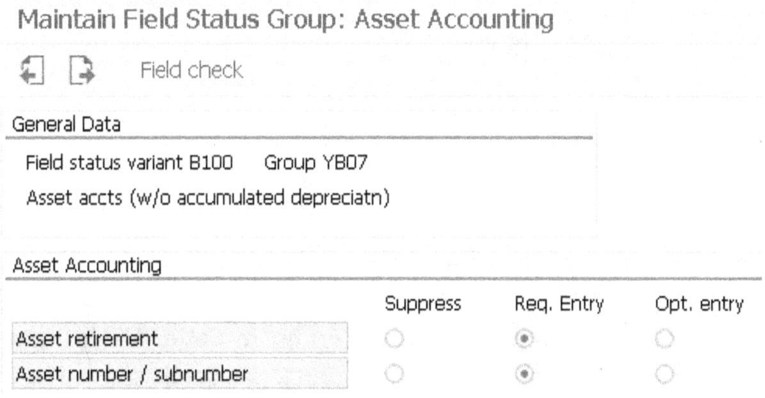

Maintain Field Status Group: Asset Accounting

⬅   ➡   Field check

General Data

Field status variant B100   Group YB07
Asset accts (w/o accumulated depreciatn)

Asset Accounting

	Suppress	Req. Entry	Opt. entry
Asset retirement	○	◉	○
Asset number / subnumber	○	◉	○

Figure 13.21 Field Status for Asset Accounting – FSV B100

ii. Go back to the initial 'Select Activity' pop-up screen (Figure 13.20), and double-click on the activity 'Change Field Status for Posting Keys'. The system brings up the list of postings keys on the next screen, 'Maintain Accounting Configuration: Posting Keys – List' (you may also reach this screen directly if you use Transaction OB41):

- Double-click on posting key 70 (debit asset), and you will see the posting key's configuration on the next screen.
- Now, click on 'Maintain Field Status' and the system takes you to the 'Maintain Field Status Group: Overview' screen. On this screen, now, double-click on 'Asset Accounting' under the 'Select Group' block.
- On the next screen ensure that the 'Asset retirement' indicator and the 'Asset number / subnumber' fields are set to required entry ('Req. Entry').
- 'Save' the settings (Figure 13.22).
- Go back to the previous screen, 'Maintain Accounting Configuration: Posting Keys – List', and double-click on the posting key 75 (credit asset) and repeat the above steps to set the FSV of the 'Asset retirement' indicator and the 'Asset number / subnumber' fields to required entry.
- 'Save' the details.

Maintain Field Status Group: Asset Accounting

Field check

General Data

Posting keys   ;70 Debit asset

Asset Accounting

	Suppress	Req. Entry	Opt. entry
Asset retirement	○	◉	○
Asset number / subnumber	○	◉	○

Figure 13.22 Field Status for Asset Accounting – Posting Key 70

iii.   Again, go back to the initial 'Select Activity' pop-up screen (Figure 13.20), and double click on the 'Check Assignment of Company Code to Field Status Variant' activity. On the resulting 'Change View "Assign Company Code -> Field Status Variant": Overview' screen, you will notice that the FSV B100 has been assigned to the company codes of BESTM (Figure 13.23). If not, assign the FSV to all the asset accounting company codes of BESTM, now.

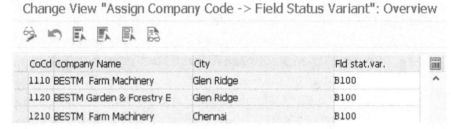

Change View "Assign Company Code -> Field Status Variant": Overview

CoCd	Company Name	City	Fld stat.var.	
1110	BESTM Farm Machinery	Glen Ridge	B100	^
1120	BESTM Garden & Forestry E	Glen Ridge	B100	
1210	BESTM Farm Machinery	Chennai	B100	

Figure 13.23 Assigning Asset Accounting Company Codes to FSV

With this, we can, now, move to assign the input tax indicator to non-taxable asset acquisition transactions.

13.4.4.7   Assign Input Tax Indicator for Non-Taxable Acquisitions

Specify an input tax indicator, for non-taxable asset acquisition, per company code so as to enable the system to make use of this indicator when posting acquisitions that are not subject to tax, but posted to accounts that are tax-relevant.

---

i You will, for example, come across an acquisition transaction from your in-house production wherein the acquisition itself is non-taxable but the transaction should be posted to an account that is tax-relevant.

Use the menu path: SAP Customizing Implementation Guide > Financial Accounting > Asset Accounting > Integration with General Ledger Accounting > Assign Input Tax Indicator for Non-Taxable Acquisitions. You may also use Transaction OBCL.

On the resulting screen, for each of the asset accounting company codes, enter the non-taxable tax code (Figure 13.24) for input tax ('Input Tax Code'). We have already discussed this, in detail, in Section 8.1.3.3 ('Assign Tax Codes for Non-Taxable Transactions') of Chapter 8, when we configured the settings for tax posting under 'Tax on Sales and Purchases'.

Change View "Allocate Co.Cd. -> Non-Taxable Transactions": Overview

CoCd	Company Name	City	Input ...	Outpu...	Jurisdict. Code
1110	BESTM Farm Machinery	Glen Ridge	I0	00	7700000000
1120	BESTM Garden & Forestry E	Glen Ridge	I0	00	7700000000

Figure 13.24 Assigning Input Tax Code for Non-Taxable Acquisitions

The next step for configuring the FI-AA integration with SAP G/L Accounting, is to specify the financial statement version for asset reports.

13.4.4.8   Specify Financial Statement Version for Asset Reports

Here, in this step, you need to specify, per depreciation area, which financial statement version the system should use as the default version.

We have already defined the required financial statement versions, in Section 9.3.3.1 of Chapter 9 while configuring the SAP G/L Accounting. We have defined two versions: BEIN as the financial statement version for use by India-based company codes and BEUS for US-based company codes.

Use the menu path: SAP Customizing Implementation Guide > Financial Accounting > Asset Accounting > Integration with General Ledger Accounting > Specify Financial Statement Version for Asset Reports or Transaction OAYN.

On the resulting screen, 'Change View "Company code selection": Overview', select the appropriate company code (say, 1110) and double-click on 'Assign financial statement version' on the left-hand side 'Dialog Structure'. The system brings up all the depreciation areas, for the company code 1110, on the next screen. Enter the appropriate financial statement version ('FS Vers'), say, BEUS (for US-based company codes of BESTM) against each of the depreciation areas, and 'Save' the settings (Figure 13.25).

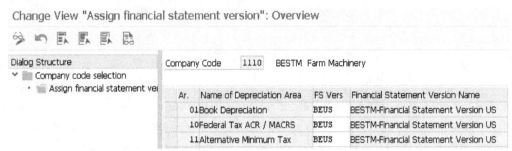

Figure 13.25 Assigning Financial Statement Version for Asset Reports

Repeat and assign the financial statement version, for all the depreciation areas for all the asset accounting company codes.

With this, we can move on to the next step in the configuration, namely, specifying the document type for depreciation posting.

13.4.4.9   Specify Document Type for Posting of Depreciation

Here, you need to specify the document type that the system should use for depreciation related postings to the SAP G/L Accounting.

Project Dolphin

The project team has decided to use the SAP's default document type AF for all the depreciation related postings in all the company codes of BESTM, both in India and in US.

Use the menu path: SAP Customizing Implementation Guide > Financial Accounting > Asset Accounting > Integration with General Ledger Accounting > Post Depreciation to General Ledger Accounting > Specify Document Type for Posting of Depreciation or Transaction OAYN.

On entering the Transaction, you will see the 'Select Activity' pop-up screen (Figure 13.26).

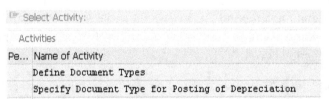

Figure 13.26 'Select Activity' Pop-Up screen for Defining / Assigning Document Types

You know that we have already configured the required document types, including AF, vide Section 7.1.2 of Chapter 7. However, you can double-click on the 'Define Document Types' activity to ensure that the already defined document type AF is with internal number assignment enabling automatic posting of the depreciation through batch input (Figure 13.27). You may also use this activity, now, to define new document type(s), if required. You may use Transaction OBA7 to reach the 'Change View "Document Types": Overview' screen directly.

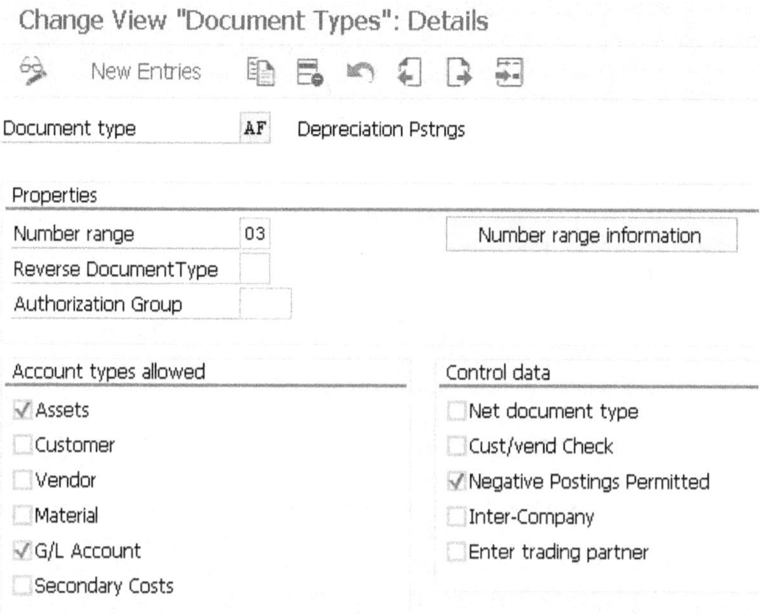

Change View "Document Types": Details

New Entries

Document type   AF   Depreciation Pstngs

Properties

Number range	03
Reverse DocumentType	
Authorization Group	

Number range information

Account types allowed

- ☑ Assets
- ☐ Customer
- ☐ Vendor
- ☐ Material
- ☑ G/L Account
- ☐ Secondary Costs

Control data

- ☐ Net document type
- ☐ Cust/vend Check
- ☑ Negative Postings Permitted
- ☐ Inter-Company
- ☐ Enter trading partner

Figure 13.27 Document Type AF - Details

Let us, now, proceed to specify the document type AF, per company code, for posting depreciation: double-click on the 'Specify Document Type for Posting of Depreciation' activity on initial the pop-up screen, and ensure that the document type AF has been specified for all the asset accounting company codes of BESTM (Figure 13.28) on the next screen. You may also reach this screen directly via Transaction AO71.

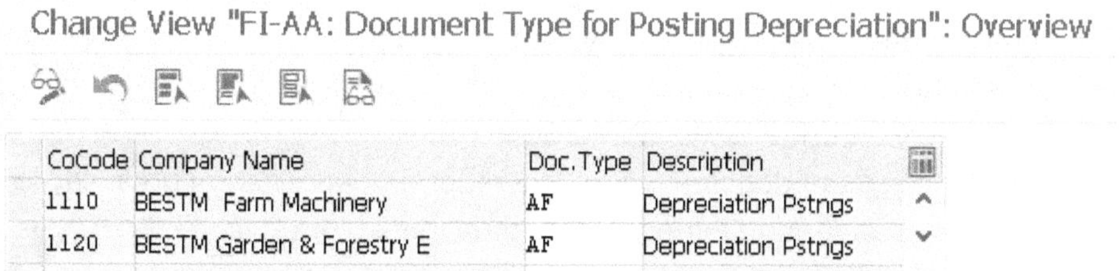

Change View "FI-AA: Document Type for Posting Depreciation": Overview

CoCode	Company Name	Doc.Type	Description	
1110	BESTM Farm Machinery	AF	Depreciation Pstngs	▲
1120	BESTM Garden & Forestry E	AF	Depreciation Pstngs	▼

Figure 13.28 Specifying Document Type AF for Depreciation Posting

The next task is to specify the intervals and posting rules for depreciation posting.

13.4.4.10   Specify Intervals and Posting Rules

An asset transaction (depreciation, interest and revaluation) will not immediately lead to an update of the depreciation and value adjustment accounts for the financial statements. The system posts the planned depreciation directly to FI, periodically, whenever you run the depreciation posting run. Besides various depreciation types, interest and revaluation, the system also posts the allocation and write-off of special reserves during this posting run. The system does not create documents for each asset, during the posting of depreciation; instead, it creates only collective documents.

> **i** Though it is difficult to provide a precise information on the performance of depreciation posting run, since it depends on your system configuration, you can safely estimate that the system can perform about 16,000 depreciation calculation, per hour. Even with collective documents, the number of documents the system needs to post in a depreciation run is function of number of G/L accounts to be posted, number of combinations of account assignments and number of account determinations. And, remember that the 'update run' of the depreciation posting run has always to be in the background, for performance reasons.

You can specify the posting cycle (discussed in this Section) and the additional account assignment levels (such as, cost center or order) for the depreciation posting run, per company code and per depreciation area. We shall discuss about specifying account assignment types for account assignment objects, later, in Section 13.4.4.12.

Here, in this configuration activity, you specify the posting rules for posting the depreciation values to SAP FI component. In doing so, you need to specify the period (posting periodicity or cycle) and the method for posting the depreciation run. Specify these details, per depreciation area, and per company code.

Use the menu path: SAP Customizing Implementation Guide > Financial Accounting > Asset Accounting > Integration with General Ledger Accounting > Post Depreciation to General Ledger Accounting > Specify Intervals and Posting Rules or Transaction OAYR:

i.   On the entering the Transaction, the system brings up the list of company codes for making a selection. Select the company code (say, 1110), and double-click on 'Posting rules' on the left-hand side 'Dialog Structure'.

ii.   On the resulting screen, double-click on the required depreciation area (say, 1) and enter the settings under the 'Period and method' data block (Figure 13.29):

- Select the appropriate posting radio-button: select 'Monthly posting'. If you select 'Bi-monthly posting', for example, then, the system posts the depreciation in every alternate posting period.

> **i** Note that the radio button, 'Bi-monthly posting', 'Quarterly posting' and 'Semi-annual posting' will be disabled if your posting periods in FI is not 12.

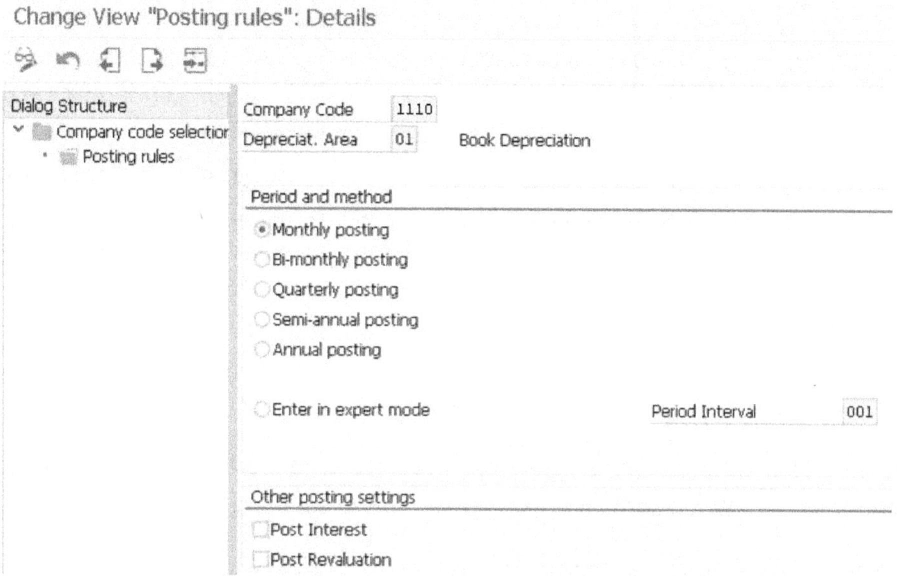

Change View "Posting rules": Details

Dialog Structure
∨ 📁 Company code selection
  • 📁 Posting rules

Company Code   1110
Depreciat. Area   01   Book Depreciation

Period and method
⦿ Monthly posting
○ Bi-monthly posting
○ Quarterly posting
○ Semi-annual posting
○ Annual posting

○ Enter in expert mode   Period Interval   001

Other posting settings
☐ Post Interest
☐ Post Revaluation

Figure 13.29 Posting Rules for Depreciation Posting

- Depending upon the period you select, the system fills up the 'Period Interval' automatically. For example, when you select 'Monthly posting', then the 'Period Interval' will be 001, for 'Bi-Monthly posting' it will be 002, for 'Quarterly posting' it will be 003, for 'Semi-annual posting' it will be 006 and for 'Annual posting' the value in 'Period Interval' will be 012. The 'Period Interval' denotes the interval between two depreciation posting runs.

> **ℹ** You can post the depreciation posting runs, resulting from valuation changes (due to year-end closing and taking place after the fiscal year end), as 'unplanned depreciation' posting runs in the special periods of the given fiscal year version.

- Select 'Enter in expert mode' radio-button, if you want to make your entry for the settings function in an 'expert mode', instead of using the simplified method. When you activate this, you need to enter the 'Period interval' manually.

iii. Under 'Other posting settings':

- Select 'Post Interest' check-box, if you want the system to post the imputed interest (for cost-accounting), in addition to the depreciation in this depreciation area, during the depreciation posting run. You will select this only for the depreciation areas that handle interest.

- Select 'Post Revaluation' check-box, if you want to post the revaluation of APC and the accumulated ordinary depreciation, of this depreciation area, in SAP G/L during the depreciation posting run, in addition to the depreciation.
- Select 'Below-Zero Acct When Planned Life Ends' check-box, if you want to the system to continue posting of depreciation, for this depreciation area, even after the expiry of the useful life. Here, the system will post this below-zero depreciation to the account specified in the account determination earlier.

iv. Complete the settings for other depreciation areas of the selected company code (say, 1110) and repeat the steps for defining for all the company codes of FI-AA of BESTM.

The next step is to discuss the settings required to enable segment reporting, as part of configuring the integration of FI-AA with SAP G/L Accounting

13.4.4.11   Segment Reporting

Here, you need to complete two configuration tasks:

- Activate Segment Reporting
- Fill Master Data for Segment Reporting

Let us start with the first activity of activating segment reporting in FI-AA.

13.4.4.11.1 Activate Segment Reporting

Use this configuration step to activate segment reporting for FI-AA. When activated, the system includes the 'Profit Center' and 'Segment' fields in the asset master record. As these fields are empty initially, you need to use the IMG activity 'Fill Master Data for Segment Reporting' (discussed in the next Section), to fill the asset master data with the relevant values.

Once you activate segment reporting, when you post/maintain the asset master data, the system checks whether the asset master records have been maintained consistently; that is, it must be possible for the system to derive the profit center and the segment uniquely from the CO account assignments and from the asset master records.

> **i** When you activate 'segment reporting' you can perform reporting at the profit center and segment levels. Note that once activated, you will not able to deactivate this.

Project Dolphin

BESTM, as it needs asset reporting at the segment / profit center level, has requested to activate segment reporting in FI-AA. The project team has pointed out this activation would also help to carry out the consistency check when users make single / mass asset maintenance of segment and/or profit center details while creating / changing asset master records. This is because, if this activation is not done, then the system will not do the consistency check, for these two fields, when maintaining the asset master.

Use the menu path: SAP Customizing Implementation Guide > Financial Accounting > Asset Accounting > Integration with General Ledger Accounting > Segment Reporting > Activate Segment Reporting. On the resulting screen, select the 'Segment Rptng Active' check-box and 'Save' the settings (Figure 13.30).

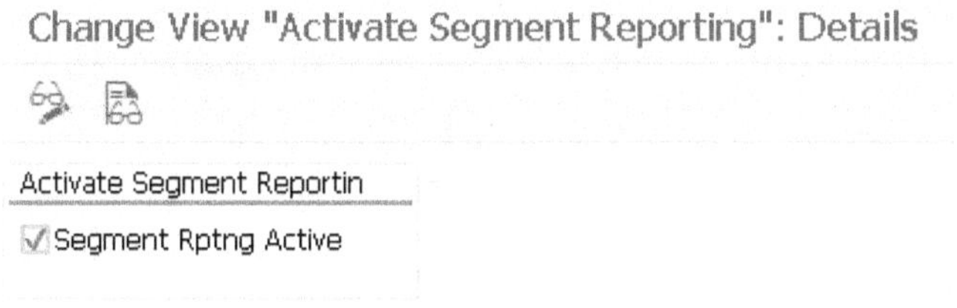

Change View "Activate Segment Reporting": Details

Activate Segment Reportin

☑ Segment Rptng Active

Figure 13.30 Activating Segment Reporting in FI-AA

With the activation of segment reporting for FI-AA, we can configure the system to fill the required master data for segment reporting.

13.4.4.11.2 Fill Master Data for Segment Reporting

You can use this configuration activity to fill the 'Profit Center' and 'Segment' fields in existing asset master data.

Use the menu path: SAP Customizing Implementation Guide > Financial Accounting > Asset Accounting > Integration with General Ledger Accounting > Segment Reporting > Fill Master Data for Segment Reporting. You may also use Transaction FAGL_R_AA_ASSET_UPDT.

On the resulting screen, enter the 'Selection Criteria' and 'Further Selections', if required. First, run the program in 'Test Mode'. In a test run, the system lists all fixed assets corresponding to your selection: (a) highlighted in green - the assets to which the system can uniquely assign a profit center and a segment and (b) highlighted in red - the assets to which the system cannot uniquely assign a profit center and a segment.

Now, the system selects all active fixed assets with a CO object in their master data, and checks whether data can be derived consistently. When successful, you can remove the tick in 'Test Mode' check-box and make a production run ('Update Mode'); the system assigns a profit center and a segment to fixed assets wherever a unique assignment can be made; else (where a unique assignment cannot be made), the system issues an error message. Though the online processing of this activity is limited to about 1,000 assets, you can run the program multiple times in 'update' mode.

---

i Instead of using this configuration activity to fill the 'Profit Center' and 'Segment' fields of the master data, you can also edit the master data using a single / mass change. However, we recommend that you carry out this activity because a consistency check is not carried out when you make single / mass change. Alternatively, you can do the mass maintenance in combination with this configuration.

With this we can, discuss the additional account assignment objects.

13.4.4.12   Additional Account Assignment Objects

As a part of configuring additional account assignment objects, towards integrating FI-AA with SAP G/L Accounting, you need to complete the following configuration steps:

- Activate Account Assignment Objects
- Specify Account Assignment Types for Account Assignment Objects
- Process Error Table
- Display of Active Account Assignment Objects

Let us start with the first activity of activating account assignment objects

13.4.4.12.1   *Activate Account Assignment Objects*

Here, you make the settings for additional account assignment objects like investment order, functional area, maintenance order etc, that you may use during posting in FI-AA. During this configuration, you will (a) activate the account assignment objects that you need, (b) specify whether the account assignment object is relevant to the B/S and (c) specify whether the account assignment object you enter, during posting, has to agree with the account assignment object entered in the asset master record.

Project Dolphin

BESTM management wants to make use of additional account assignment objects like internal order, investment order, functional area, maintenance order etc during posting in asset accounting. It was also indicated that if an account assignment object is relevant to B/S, then, no user should be able to change the account assignment object in the asset master record, once the asset has been capitalized. Also, the account assignment object like funds center, funds center for investment, investment order, functional area etc should be prevented from being changed during a posting.

Use the menu path: SAP Customizing Implementation Guide > Financial Accounting > Asset Accounting > Integration with General Ledger Accounting > Additional Account Assignment Objects > Activate Account Assignment Objects.

On the resulting screen, against the required account assignment objects ('AcctAsgnOb') select the appropriate check-boxes (Figure 13.31):

Change View "Account Assignment Elements for Asset Accounting": O

Account Assignment Elements for Asset Accounting

AcctAsgnOb	Account Assignment Object Name	Active	Bal. Sheet	Agreement
CAUFN	Internal Order	✓	☐	☐
EAUFN	Investment Order	✓	☐	✓
FISTL	Funds Center	✓	✓	✓
FISTL2	Funds Center for Investment	✓	✓	✓
FKBER	Functional Area	✓	✓	✓
FKBER2	Functional Area for Investment	✓	✓	✓
GEBER	Fund	✓	✓	✓
GEBER2	Fund for Investment	✓	✓	✓
GRANT_NBR	Grant	☐	✓	✓
GRANT_NBR2	Grant for Cap. Investment	☐	✓	✓
IAUFN	Maintenance Order	✓	☐	☐

Figure 13.31 Additional Account Assignment Objects for FI-AA

i. Only when you select the 'Active' check-box, the account assignment object will be made active for you to be able to post to it in FI-AA.
ii. Select 'Bal. Sheet' check-box, if the account assignment object is relevant to B/S. When selected, once the asset has been capitalized, you will be no longer able to change the account assignment object in the asset master record. However, you can make the required changes, by transferring such assets to a new asset master record.
iii. Select 'Agreement' check-box, if you want to prevent the account assignment object from being changed during a posting. This ensures that account assignment is only possible to the account assignment object entered, earlier, in the asset master record.

> **i** Make sure that the account assignment objects, that you want to use, are available for input, by making appropriate field status for posting keys 70 (debit asset) and 75 (credit asset). You can check and maintain the correct field status using Transaction OB41. We have already discussed this in Section 13.4.4.6.

With this are now ready to move on to the second configuration step under additional account assignment configuration. That is, to specify the account assignment type per account assignment object.

13.4.4.12.2 Specify Account Assignment Types for Account Assignment Objects

There are two 'account assignment types' (1. APC balance sheet posting and 2. account assignment of depreciation) possible for the additional account assignment objects that you have defined in the previous Section. Now, in this step, you can assign the appropriate account assignment type to these account assignment objects. These assignments depend on company code, depreciation area and transaction type. When you want to assign both the account assignment types to an account assignment object, then you need to make two table entries for that object. However, it is not possible to make two account assignment type entries for some of the objects like investment order (EAUFN), funds center for investment (FISTL2) etc, where you can make only one assignment i.e., APC balance sheet posting.

SAP has provided you with the following default settings:

- A generic (*) entry for company code, valid for all the company codes.
- Two generic (*) entries for depreciation areas, 0 and 1. The settings for depreciation area 0 are valid for all depreciation areas <u>other than 1</u>; the settings for generic depreciation area 1 are valid in all company codes for depreciation area 1 (book depreciation).

You can either make a generic entry or a specific entry for the transaction type. If you use both generic transaction types and 'normal' transaction types in the table, the system gives priority to the non-generic entries before generic entries. The system also gives priority to the non-generic company code over the non-generic transaction type. In all these situations, then the system proceeds as under, until it finds a suitable record as shown in Figure 13.32.

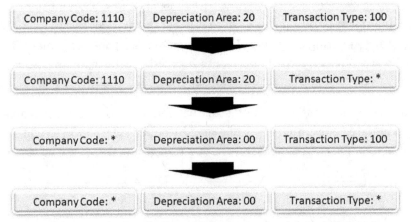

Figure 13.32 How the System Determines the Appropriate Account Assignment

You need to configure the settings, for the account assignment type, in the account assignment object as described below:

First, for the generic company code and the generic transaction type. Then, for the generic company code and non-generic transaction types. Third, for non-generic company codes and the generic transaction type. Finally, for non-generic company codes and non-generic transaction types (Figure 13.33). Activate the account assignments that you need. You do not need to delete the ones that you do not need; just deactivate them, you can activate them, later, if you need.

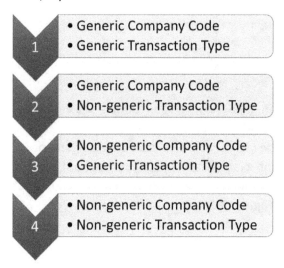

Figure 13.33 Configuration Order for Account Assignment Type

Use the menu path: SAP Customizing Implementation Guide > Financial Accounting > Asset Accounting > Integration with General Ledger Accounting > Additional Account Assignment Objects > Specify Account Assignment Types for Account Assignment Objects. You may also use Transaction ACSET:

i.   On the resulting screen, you will see the SAP default generic entry for the company codes (Figure 13.34).

Figure 13.34 Generic Entry for the Company Code

ii.   Select this row generic company code row, and double-click on 'Depreciation Area' on the left-hand side 'Dialog Structure'. You will see the two generic depreciation area entries (00 and 01) on the next screen (Figure 13.35).

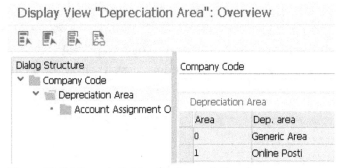

Figure 13.35 Generic Entries for Depreciation Area

iii.   Now, select a generic depreciation area (say, 0) and double-click on 'Account Assignment Objects' on the left-hand side 'Dialog Structure'.

iv.   On the next screen, click on 'New Entries'. Per account assignment object ('AcctAsgnOb'), enter the transaction type ('Tra'), select the 'Account Assignment Type' (whether it is 'APC Values Posting' or 'Depreciation Posting') and select the 'AcctAssgnt' check-box if required (Figure 13.36).

Figure 13.36 Account Assignment Type Specifications

You may enter * to allow all transactions in 'Tra' field. In case you want to assign both the account assignment types for an account assignment object, then make two entries for that account assignment object. Use the 'AcctAssgnt' check-box to specify if the account assignment to the given account assignment object is active or inactive. When selected, the system updates the values on the account assignment object. Do not select this, if you do not want an update for this combination of depreciation area, transaction type, and account assignment type for that account assignment object.

However, you will be able to select this check-box only for 'Active' account assignment objects (refer Figure 13.31, in the previous Section).

v.   'Save' the settings when completed. Go back, select the generic depreciation area 1 and make the settings, again, as described in (iv) above.

vi.   You can also make these settings to specific company codes (say, 1110), specific / generic depreciation areas and specific/generic transaction types (as outlined earlier in Figure 13.33). In that case, the system will proceed as outlined in Figure 13.32 to find a suitable record for the account assignment object.

With this we are now ready to make the settings for processing the error table.

13.4.4.12.3 Process Error Table

You have to configure this step only when you have set the 'Agreement' indicator for the account assignment objects while configuring the IMG node 'Activate Account Assignment Objects'. Since we have selected that indicator for a number of account assignment objects, vide Section 13.4.4.12.1, let us complete this configuration step. As you are aware, when this indicator is set, then the account assignment object at posting has to be the same as that of the one entered in the asset master record. The settings we make here will not apply to the account assignment objects for which we have not selected this 'Agreement' check-box.

Specify, here, which error message you want the system to output when the account assignment object entered during posting is different from the one entered in the asset master record. We recommend that you select 'Warning' wherever you have selected the 'Agreement' check-box. Then, the system issues this message and makes appropriate account assignment to the account assignment object entered in the asset master record, ignoring what is entered in the posting.

Use the menu path: SAP Customizing Implementation Guide > Financial Accounting > Asset Accounting > Integration with General Ledger Accounting > Additional Account Assignment Objects > Process Error Table.

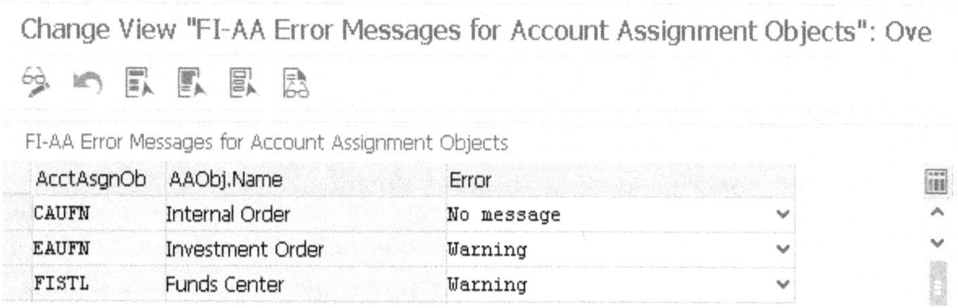

Change View "FI-AA Error Messages for Account Assignment Objects": Ove

FI-AA Error Messages for Account Assignment Objects

AcctAsgnOb	AAObj.Name	Error	
CAUFN	Internal Order	No message	
EAUFN	Investment Order	Warning	
FISTL	Funds Center	Warning	

Figure 13.37 Error Message Configuration for Account Assignment Object

On the resulting screen, select the appropriate 'Error' message per account assignment object in line with the settings that you have made for the 'Agreement' flag for that object (Figure 13.37).

With this you can, now, move on to discuss how to display the active account assignment objects in the system.

13.4.4.12.4 Display of Active Account Assignment Objects

Use the menu path: SAP Customizing Implementation Guide > Financial Accounting > Asset Accounting > Integration with General Ledger Accounting > Additional Account Assignment Objects > Display of Active Account Assignment Objects. You may also use Transaction AACCOBJ, to display the active account assignment objects.

On the resulting screen, maintain the required parameters and run the report. The system will bring up the active account assignments, in SAP List Viewer table (Figure 13.38).

Display of Active Account Assignment Objects

CoCode	Short Name Dep.Area	Account Assignment Object Name	AcctAssignType	TType	Transact. Type Text
1110	Book Deprctn	Functional Area	APC Values Posting	*	Generic Transact.Type
	Book Deprctn		Depreciation Run		Generic Transact.Type
	Book Deprctn	Funds Center	APC Values Posting		Generic Transact.Type
	Book Deprctn		Depreciation Run		Generic Transact.Type
	Book Deprctn	Funds Center for Investment	APC Values Posting		Generic Transact.Type

Figure 13.38 List of Active Account Assignment Objects

This completes our discussion on the configuration settings required for additional account assignment. With this, we have also completed the discussion on configuration settings required for FI-AA integration with SAP G/L Accounting.

Let us, now, move on to discuss the settings required for general valuation.

13.5 General Valuation

Using the basic functions in FI-AA, you can determine the values of all fixed assets - at a given point in time – to meet the statutory and legal requirements of the country and also your own business needs. The valuation provides you not only with the current value of an asset, but also helps in timing your asset replacement, asset retirement etc.

You manage valuation of fixed assets through the various depreciation areas in FI-AA. In this Section, we shall make all the configurations that you may need for the valuation of fixed assets. We can group and discuss the configuration activities, as shown under:

- Depreciation Areas
- Amount Specifications (Company Code/Depreciation Area)
- Fiscal Year Specifications
- Currencies
- Group Assets

Let us start with the settings that you need to make for the depreciation areas.

13.5.1 Depreciation Areas

When you create a chart of depreciation, from a reference chart of depreciation, the system copies the depreciation areas from the reference to the new chart of depreciation. However, you can also create new depreciation areas, by copying an existing depreciation area in your new chart of deprecation. Through various configuration steps, you shall define the characteristics of the depreciation areas in this step.

Let us, first, start with the definition of depreciation areas.

13.5.1.1   Define Depreciation Areas

We have already created the required depreciation areas vide Section 13.2.2. Since we have used a country-specific chart of depreciation (0US and 0IN) to create the new chart of depreciation (BEUS and BEIN respectively), we have already defined the various depreciation areas for (a) valuation according to local laws, (b) tax depreciation, (c) cost-accounting, depreciation, (d) special reserves and (e) investment support.

When you need parallel valuation, you can define real depreciation areas and derived depreciation areas. The values in the *'derived depreciation areas'* are calculated from the values of two or more real depreciation areas, using a formula that you define. For a derived depreciation area, the system does not store the derived values permanently, but determines the same, dynamically, during a request. The derived depreciation areas cannot manage any parallel currencies and as such are not allowed to have any parallel currency areas. While denoting a derived depreciation area, ensure that the key of the derived depreciation area (say, 50) is higher than the keys of the depreciation area (say, 01 & 20) from it is derived.

You can use derived depreciation areas for (a) reserve for special depreciation or (b) reporting purposes:

- In the case of 'reserve for special depreciation', you can use the same functions for derived depreciation areas as that of the real depreciation areas. Hence, these derived depreciation areas can be evaluated in the same way, as that of the real depreciation area, and posted to a ledger in the G/L.
- In the case of 'derived depreciation areas for reporting', you cannot post to them.

Project Dolphin

The BESTM management, after a detailed discussion with the implementation team, has decided not to create any new depreciation areas other than the ones that were copied from the country-specific chart of depreciation. It was also decided that all the company codes will use the book depreciation area (1) for updating the quantity information of LVAs.

To create any new depreciation area, or change an existing one, use the menu path: SAP Customizing Implementation Guide > Financial Accounting > Asset Accounting > General Valuation > Depreciation Areas > Define Depreciation Areas.

 i.   Set the 'Chart of Depreciation' on entering the Transaction (BEUS). To change chart of depreciation, use IMG activity 'Set Chart of Depreciation' or Transaction OAPL.

 ii.   On the resulting 'Select Activity' pop-up screen, double-click on, 'Define Depreciation Areas'. On the next screen (use Transaction OADB to reach this screen directly), you will see the list of depreciation areas that have already been copied. You can copy and create a new depreciation area, or you can change the parameters that you have already defined for a depreciation area.

 iii. Go back to the 'Select Activity' pop-up screen, and double-click on 'Specify Area Type'. On the resulting screen (you may also reach this screen directly by using Transaction OADC), per depreciation area, enter the type of depreciation area ('Typ'). You will assign the 'Typ' according to the primary purpose of a depreciation area (Figure 13.39): for example, area 01 (or 1) will be of type 01 - B/S valuation, area 20 will be of type 07 – cost accounting valuation etc. If you use SAP IM, then, the type 07 has a special significance, as you are not allowed to settle differences, due to capitalization as non-operating expense, in this depreciation area. This to ensure that all non-capitalized debits in a capital investment measure are recognized in cost accounting.

Change View ""Actual depreciation areas: area type"": Overview

Chart of dep.   BEUS   Chart of Depreciation USA (BESTM)

Ar.	Name of Depreciation Area	Typ	Description
01	Book Depreciation	01	Valuation for trade bal. sheet
10	Federal Tax ACR / MACRS	10	US: Federal tax ACRS / MACRS
11	Alternative Minimum Tax	12	US: ALTMIN - Alternative minimum tax
12	Adjusted Current Earnings	13	US: ACE - Adjusted Current Earnings
20	Cost Accounting Depreciation	07	Cost-acc. valuation

Figure 13.39 Assigning 'Depreciation Area Type' to Depreciation Areas

With this let us understand how to implement depreciation areas, subsequently.

13.5.1.1.1   Subsequent Implementation of a Depreciation Area

Recommended that you define all the required depreciation areas before you 'go-live'. However, you can implement new depreciation areas (for example, to create a new depreciation area for insurable values) in an existing valuation, later, even after the 'go-live'.

Use the menu path: SAP Customizing Implementation Guide > Financial Accounting > Asset Accounting > General Valuation > Depreciation Areas > Subsequent Implementation of a Depreciation Area > Implement Depreciation Area Subsequently or Transaction FAA_AREA_COPY.

The system uses the program RAFAB_COPY_AREA to implement the new depreciation areas and the related settings. This program uses the default implementation of the 'Subsequent Implementation of a Depreciation Area' BAdI (FAA_AA_COPY_AREA). In case you need to have customized influence on source depreciation area, depreciation terms, and the transaction data, then, you need to implement your own BAdI.

With the subsequent implementation of depreciation areas, you can:

- Add a newly created depreciation area (target depreciation area) to the existing asset master records.
- Copy the depreciation terms from the source to the target depreciation area.
- Copy, by default, the balance c/f values and the transaction data of the current fiscal year from the source to the target depreciation area.

> **i** With subsequent implementation of depreciation area(s), note that the system does not copy (a) the depreciation postings of the current fiscal year, and also (b) the data from the previous fiscal years.

Now that we have understood about subsequent implementation of new depreciations areas, let us discuss about the subsequent deletion of depreciation areas.

13.5.1.1.2   Subsequent Deletion of a Depreciation Area

SAP allows you to delete the depreciation areas that you do not need, at a later point of time. When you delete the depreciation area, the system deletes the depreciation area marked for deletion from (a) the chart of depreciation and (b) the depreciation data of all affected assets and asset classes, in the system.

When you want to delete a depreciation area subsequently, note that:

- You are not allowed to delete the depreciation area that posts in real time to the leading ledger group.

- You cannot delete an area if it is acting as a reference area for another area.
- You cannot use the area that is to be deleted, in the calculation formula for a derived depreciation area. If you use that area in the calculation formula for a derived area, but still want to delete the area, then, you have to change the calculation formula of the derived depreciation area.
- The area, to be deleted, should not have been defined for automatic posting of APC values to the G/L.
- If the depreciation area, to be deleted, is used for investment support, then, you first need to delete all investment support keys that reference this depreciation area, before deleting the area.

Use the menu path: SAP Customizing Implementation Guide > Financial Accounting > Asset Accounting > General Valuation > Depreciation Areas > Define Depreciation Areas.

i. On the resulting pop-up screen, select 'Define Depreciation Areas' activity and click on 'Choose'.
ii. On the next 'Change View "Depreciation Areas": Overview' screen (you can reach here directly by using Transaction OADB), select the depreciation area row that you want to delete and click on 'Delete'.

With this, let us continue with the configuration of depreciation areas. The next step is to define the depreciation area for quantity update.

13.5.1.2   Define Depreciation Area for Quantity Update

Required for managing LVAs on a collective basis, here, you will specify which depreciation area you want to use for updating quantities. The system updates the quantities in the asset master record only when posting is made to this specified deprecation area. As in the case of SAP's standard settings, you need to use depreciation area 1 (book depreciation) for updating the quantities.

In cases where you subsequently change the depreciation area for quantity update, the system will not update these changes in the respective master records. Accordingly, any asset sub-ledger posting that was done before the area change retains the original quantity information and the same is reflected in the asset master. When you reverse such an earlier document (with the original quantity information), after the change of the depreciation area, then, the system adjusts the quantity regardless of whether postings are made to the depreciation area that is now being used for quantity update.

Use the menu path: SAP Customizing Implementation Guide > Financial Accounting > Asset Accounting > General Valuation > Depreciation Areas > Define Depreciation Area for Quantity Update.

On the resulting screen, select the 'Update Quantity' radio-button against the 'Book Depreciation' area (1) for the chart of depreciation BESTM (Figure 13.40).

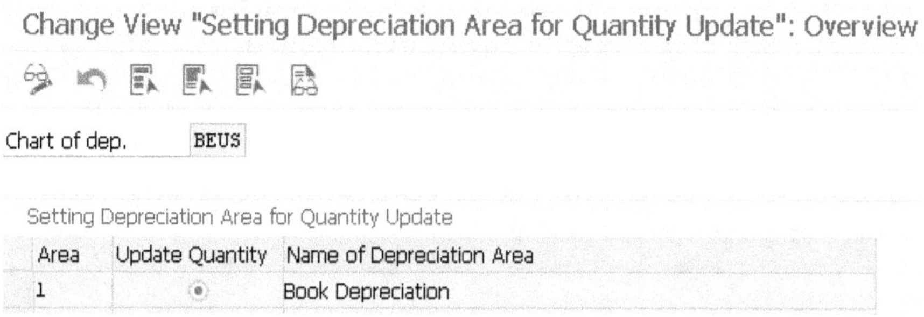

Change View "Setting Depreciation Area for Quantity Update": Overview

Chart of dep.   BEUS

Setting Depreciation Area for Quantity Update

Area	Update Quantity	Name of Depreciation Area
1	⦿	Book Depreciation

Figure 13.40 Specifying Depreciation Area for Quantity Update of LVAs

The next task is to make the settings for transferring APC values.

13.5.1.3   Specify Transfer of APC Values

Use this configuration step to define the transfer rules for posting the values of depreciation areas. These rules enable the system to have certain depreciation areas the identical asset values. This you will achieve, by specifying the reference depreciation area that provides values to another depreciation area. Then, the, system transfers the posting amounts of any transactions that affect APC from this area to the dependent area. You can also decide if the transfer is mandatory or optional: if optional, you will be able to manually enter the posting values, for that depreciation area, during posting.

> **i** When you want to transfer APC values from one depreciation area to another, you need to be aware of the fact that such a transfer is only possible when the 'from' depreciation area and the 'to' depreciation area have the same accounting principle.

Project Dolphin

BESTM has indicated that, when posting values are transferred from the book depreciation area (01) to other areas, all the APC-relevant values should be transferred in a manner that the user will have no option to make any change, later, during posting so as to minimise errors in the transferred values.

Use the menu path: SAP Customizing Implementation Guide > Financial Accounting > Asset Accounting > General Valuation > Depreciation Areas > Specify Transfer of APC Values. You may also use Transaction OABC.

On the resulting screen, specify the reference depreciation area (say, 01) that will provide the values to another depreciation area (say, 10,11 etc) in the field 'ValAd'. Accordingly, the system transfers the posting amounts of any transactions that affect APC from this area (01) to the dependent area (say, 10). If you want to ensure that the system transfers all APC-relevant posting values to the dependent depreciation area(s) from the transferring depreciation area without any change in value, later, during posting, then, you need to select the 'Ident.' check-box for each of these depreciation areas (Figure 13.41).

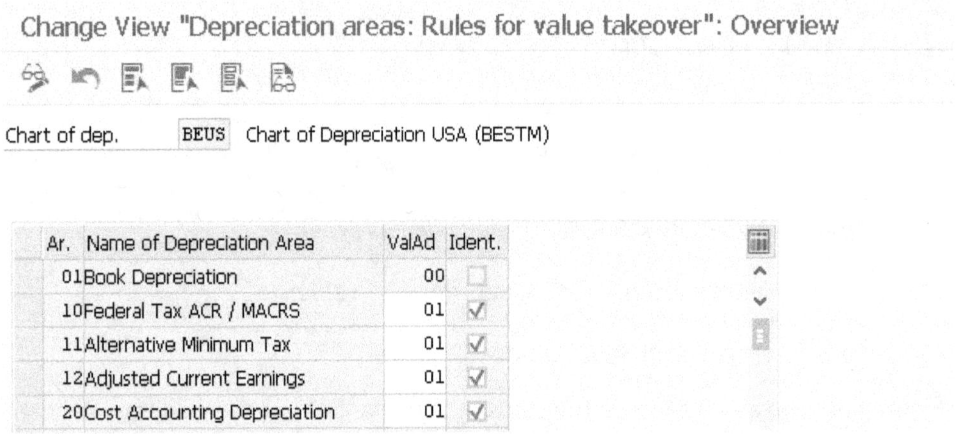

Change View "Depreciation areas: Rules for value takeover": Overview

Chart of dep.   BEUS   Chart of Depreciation USA (BESTM)

Ar.	Name of Depreciation Area	ValAd	Ident.
01	Book Depreciation	00	☐
10	Federal Tax ACR / MACRS	01	☑
11	Alternative Minimum Tax	01	☑
12	Adjusted Current Earnings	01	☑
20	Cost Accounting Depreciation	01	☑

Figure 13.41 Rules for Transferring APC Values

ℹ️ When a depreciation area takes over the values from another depreciation area, the taking over depreciation area (say, 12) should have the depreciation key that is higher than that of the area from which the values are being taken over (say, 01). This precisely the reason that you will never be able to transfer values for the book depreciation area (01).

The next step is to define the settings for transferring depreciation terms.

13.5.1.4   Specify Transfer of Depreciation Terms

You need to specify, here, how the system adopts the depreciation terms, for a depreciation area, from another depreciation area. As in the case of transfer of APC values, here also you can specify if the adoption of values is optional or mandatory. If you specify that the transfer is optional, then you can change the proposed depreciation terms in the dependent areas in the asset master record. Else, if you specify that as a mandatory transfer, then, you cannot maintain any depreciation terms in the asset master record. This is to ensure that depreciation is uniform in certain depreciation areas.

ℹ️ You will be able to adopt depreciation terms, from one area to another, only when the depreciation areas use the same ledger group. In the case of depreciation areas posting APC values to SAP G/L in real-time, the system will not allow to adopt depreciation terms from another depreciation area. However, the system allows adopting the depreciation terms in case of other depreciation areas that post in real time (as in the case of investment support or revaluation), as long as both areas have the same ledger group.

Unlike derived depreciation area, the depreciation area (say, 11) that adopts depreciation terms from another area (say, 12) can have a smaller key.

Project Dolphin

BESTM has requested the project team to configure adoption of depreciation terms from one depreciation area to another in such a way that the adopted depreciation terms cannot be changed, manually, later in the asset master.

Use the menu path: SAP Customizing Implementation Guide > Financial Accounting > Asset Accounting > General Valuation > Depreciation Areas > Specify Transfer of Depreciation Terms. You may also use Transaction OABD.

i.   On the resulting screen, per depreciation area, enter the area from where the depreciation terms will be transferred (Figure 13.42).

ii. Select 'Identical' check-box, so that the depreciation terms of the selected depreciation area are always identical to that of the referenced area. When selected, the system transfers all changes in the reference depreciation area to the dependent depreciation areas, and it will not possible to change them in the master records, later.   When you do not select the 'Identical' check-box, you can change the depreciation terms, in the dependent depreciation areas, in the asset master records.

Figure 13.42 Rules for Adoption of Depreciation Terms

Let us move on to discuss the depreciation area settings in the asset classes.

13.5.1.5   Determine Depreciation Areas in the Asset Class

Normally, all the assets in an asset class will use the same depreciation terms (depreciation key, useful life, etc). Hence, once maintained at the level of the asset class, you do not need to maintain them in the asset master record as they are offered as the default values from the respective asset classes. Using this configuration activity, you can determine the depreciation terms that are to be used in your asset classes.

> **i** If you make changes to the asset class, they only affect the assets that are created after the change. For all the assets that are already existing in the system, and are affected by the changes made at the asset class level, use mass change procedures. As far as the changes made to the depreciation terms, note that the system automatically re-calculates depreciation for the assets affected.

Project Dolphin

BESTM management decided to have a uniform economic life policy for the asset classes across company codes, both in US and India. Accordingly, for example, the useful life of vehicles has been set at 10 years, computer hardware at 5 years, computer software at 2 years, furniture & fittings at 5 years, office equipments at 5 years and so on.

Use the menu path: SAP Customizing Implementation Guide > Financial Accounting > Asset Accounting > General Valuation > Determine Depreciation Areas in the Asset Class. You may also use Transaction OAYZ.

    i.   On the resulting screen, select or highlight the appropriate 'Asset Class' (say, B3000 – Vehicles) and double-click on 'Depreciation areas' folder on the left-hand side 'Dialog Structure'. The system takes you to the 'Change View "Depreciation areas": Overview' screen (Figure 13.43).

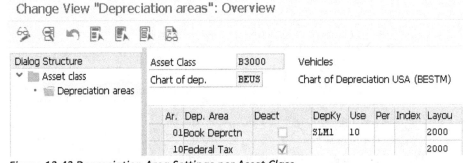

Figure 13.43 Depreciation Area Settings per Asset Class

   ii.   You will notice that the system has copied the standard settings from the reference chart of depreciation. You may change the values, if required by double-clicking on a depreciation area ('Ar.').

iii.   On the resulting screen Figure 13.44):

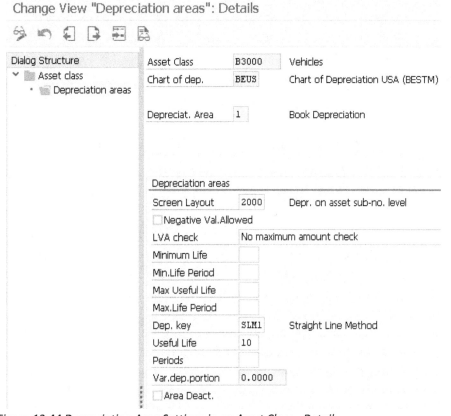

Change View "Depreciation areas": Details

Figure 13.44 Depreciation Area Settings in an Asset Class - Detail

- Enter the appropriate 'Screen Layout'. You shall enter 2000 for depreciating the asset at the subnumber level.
- Select 'Negative Val.Allowed' check-box, if you want negative APC and positive depreciation to be allowed for assets like, investment support, AuC (if you need to post a subsequent credit memo after the AuC has been completely settled) etc.
- Select the appropriate value for 'LVA check': select 'No maximum amount check' for all the assets other than LVA. In case of LVAs, you can select 'Value based maximum amount check' when you manage those assets on 'individual management' (that, is each LVA has it is own asset mater record); else, select 'Check maximum amount with quantity' when you manage them 'collectively' in a single asset master record.

> **i** In the case of *'individual maintenance'*, for each acquisition posting, the system checks whether or not the value for the asset exceeds the 'LVA maximum amount' defined for the company code/depreciation area. If yes, the system will not allow the posting.
>
> In the case of *'collective management'*, for every acquisition posting, the system checks whether or not the 'asset value' divided by the 'quantity managed' on the master record exceeds the 'LVA maximum amount' defined for the company code/depreciation area. If yes, the system will not allow you to post.

- You may enter the 'Minimum Life' and 'Maximum Useful Life'. If the life of the asset is in fraction, then enter the fraction (say, 0.5 years) as a period (say, 6) in 'Min. Life Period' / 'Max. Life Period'.
- Select the appropriate depreciation key ('Dep. key'). The 'depreciation key' consisting of (a) the calculation method for the automatic calculation of interest, ordinary and special depreciation, (b) a possible a cutoff value key and (c) various control parameters, controls the asset valuation in the particular depreciation areas (we shall discuss depreciation key, in detail, in Section 13.6.5.1). The key SLM1, for example, denotes 'Straight Line Method' of depreciation. You will enter the key 0000 for 'no depreciation no interest'.
- Enter the 'Useful Life', in whole number of years, over which the asset needs to be depreciated. If you do not enter the useful life in the asset class, but use depreciation keys that calculate depreciation automatically, the system marks this field is as a 'required entry' field irrespective of other settings in the screen layout control.

> **i** The asset class usually provides a default useful life when you create the asset master record. However, if the system cannot determine useful life for the asset, and if you are using a depreciation method that always operates independently of the useful life, you can enter a very long useful life: say, 100 years!

- If the 'Useful Life' of an asset includes a part of a year in addition to whole years, then, you need to enter the additional time in the form of period in the 'Periods' field, besides entering the whole years in the 'Useful Life' field. You can enter 000 to 365 for 'Periods' field.

> **i** Consider that an asset's useful life is 5.5 years. Now, you need to enter the whole years (5) in the 'Useful Life' field, and 6 in the field 'Periods'; the 6 entered in 'Periods' field represents 6 periods that is nothing but 0.5 years.

- Select 'Area Deact.' check-box, if you want the depreciation area(s) to be inactive in this asset class or asset (although it appears in the chart of depreciation).
- 'Save' the settings and repeat the steps for other depreciation areas for the selected asset class.

iv. Go back to the initial screen and select the other asset classes, and complete the settings, as described above, for all the asset classes and for all the depreciation areas.

The next step is to lock an asset class for asset creation.

13.5.1.6   Deactivate Asset Class for Chart of Depreciation

It is possible that you can lock asset classes, for entire charts of depreciation, so as prevent someone from using that asset classes inadvertently, in the given chart of depreciation, for creating the fixed assets.

Use the menu path: SAP Customizing Implementation Guide > Financial Accounting > Asset Accounting > General Valuation > Deactivate Asset Class for Chart of Depreciation. You may also use Transaction AM05.

On the resulting screen (Figure 13.45), select the 'Lock' check-box for the required asset classes. When selected, the system prevents creation of new assets in that asset class, specific to the given chart of depreciation. We are not locking any of the asset classes, for BESTM.

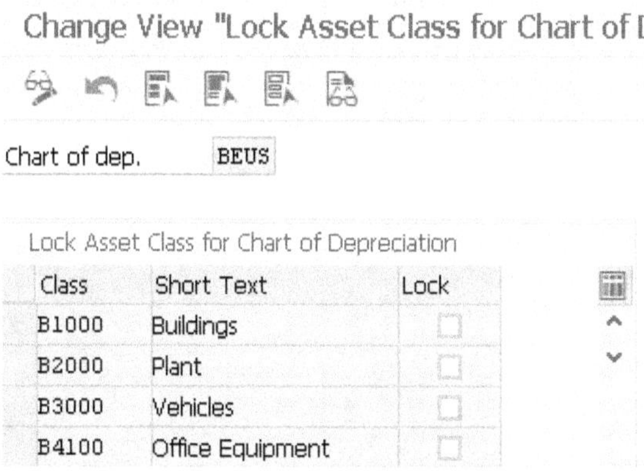

Change View "Lock Asset Class for Chart of Depreciation": Overview

Chart of dep.   BEUS

Lock Asset Class for Chart of Depreciation

Class	Short Text	Lock
B1000	Buildings	☐
B2000	Plant	☐
B3000	Vehicles	☐
B4100	Office Equipment	☐

Figure 13.45 Locking an Asset Class in a Chart of Depreciation

> **i** Even if you lock an asset class in one depreciation, you can still use the same asset class in other charts of depreciation.

This completes our discussion on the configuration settings that you need to make for depreciation areas, as a part of general valuation settings. With this, we are, now, ready to move on to the next topic: configuring the amount specifications.

13.5.2 Amount Specifications (Company Code/Depreciation Area)

In this Section, let us discuss about some of the settings like, (a) rules for rounding off, (b) memo value and (d) changeover amount, that you need to make, for the calculation of depreciation and/or net book value (NBV) per company code/depreciation area.

Let us start with the specification of maximum amount for LVAs.

13.5.2.1   Specify Max. Amount for Low-Value Assets + Asset Classes

Use this step, to determine the maximum amount for LVAs (Low-Value Assets) for each company code/depreciation area. Once configured, the system checks this maximum amount limit, during every acquisition posting, provided that you have set the indicator for LVA in the corresponding asset class(es) We have already defined (refer Section 13.3.1.4) two asset classes for LAVs for BESTM: one for collective management (B7000) and the other for individual management (B7100).

Project Dolphin

As configured in the country-specific parameters, for all BESTM company codes in USA, the LVA cut-off amount will be $5,000, and INR 5,000 for India-based company codes. The project team has been asked to configure for both individual and collective management of LVAs using the respective asset classes and account determinations.

Use the menu path: SAP Customizing Implementation Guide > Financial Accounting > Asset Accounting > General Valuation > Amount Specifications (Company Code/Depreciation Area) > Specify Max. Amount for Low-Value Assets + Asset Classes:

   i.   On the resulting pop-up screen (Figure 13.46), double-click on 'Specify LVA asset classes':

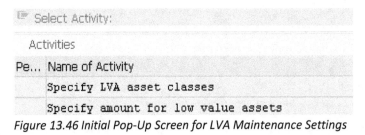

Figure 13.46 Initial Pop-Up Screen for LVA Maintenance Settings

- On the next screen (you may use or Transaction OAY2 to reach this screen directly), highlight the appropriate LVA asset class (say, B7000) and double-click on 'Low-val. asset check' on the left-hand side 'Dialog Structure'.
- On the 'Change View "Low-val. asset check": Overview' screen, enter the suitable option under 'LVA' for each of the depreciation areas. We have entered the option 2 (Check maximum amount with quantity) as the asset class B7000 is for collective management of LVAs. The other options are: 0 – No maximum amount check and 1- value based maximum amount check.
- Go-back to the initial screen, and now select the other LVA asset class B7100. Repeat the steps, and assign the value 1 in the 'LVA' field for this asset class, as this is for individual management of LVAs.

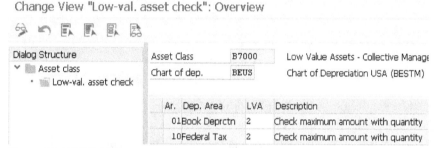

Change View "Low-val. asset check": Overview

Dialog Structure	Asset Class	B7000	Low Value Assets - Collective Manage
∨ Asset class	Chart of dep.	BEUS	Chart of Depreciation USA (BESTM)
• Low-val. asset check			

Ar.	Dep. Area	LVA	Description
01	Book Deprctn	2	Check maximum amount with quantity
10	Federal Tax	2	Check maximum amount with quantity

Figure 13.47 LVA Maintenance Settings

ii. Now, go back to the initial pop-up screen, and double-click on 'Specify amount for low value assets':

- On the resulting screen (use Transaction OAYK to reach this screen directly), select the company code (say, 1110) and double-click on 'Amount for low-value assets' on the left-hand side 'Dialog Structure'.
- On the next screen, you will notice that the system has already populated the amounts based on the country-specific settings that we made earlier in Section13.2.1 wherein we had maintained the 'Max. LVA Amount: for Posting' as $5,000 for USA.

Change View "Amount for low-value assets": Overview

Dialog Structure	Company Code	1110	BESTM Farm Machinery
∨ Company code selection			
• Amount for low-value assets			

Ar.	Name of Depreciation Area	LVA Amount	MaxLVA Pur	Crcy
01	Book Depreciation	5,000.00	5,500.00	USD
10	Federal Tax ACR / MACRS	5,000.00	5,500.00	USD

Figure 13.48 Amount Limit for LVAs

- The value in the 'LVA Amount' field, denotes the maximum amount for checking posting to low value assets. When set, this applies to all postings that would cause the acquisition value of the asset not to exceed the specified maximum amount. In the case of collectively managed LVAs, this amount is the acquisition amount divided by the quantity.
- The value in the 'MaxLVA Pur.' Field, specifies the maximum amount for checking purchase orders (PO) for assets. When set, the system applies this maximum limit when you create POs for assets in the SAP MM component. The system prevents the creation of a PO if the acquisition value of the asset exceeds this limit. Again, if you manage LVAs managed collectively, then, this is the acquisition value divided by the quantity.
- Repeat the settings for all the deprecation areas, and for all the company codes, and 'Save' the details.

The next activity is to specify the rounding off rules, per company code / depreciation area.

13.5.2.2   Specify Rounding of Net Book Value and/or Depreciation

You may define here, the rounding off specifications for (a) year-end net book value (NBV) and (b) for the automatically determined depreciation, per company code and per depreciation area. The system will round off only the decimal places. In the standard system, the NBV is rounded off to the whole currency unit.

Project Dolphin

BESTM wants to round off, using arithmetic rounding method, the year-end net book value, and also the automatically calculated replacement value of assets.

Use the menu path: SAP Customizing Implementation Guide > Financial Accounting > Asset Accounting > General Valuation > Amount Specifications (Company Code/Depreciation Area) > Specify Rounding of Net Book Value and/or Depreciation, or Transaction OAYO:

i.   On the resulting screen, select the company code (say,1110) and double-click on 'Rounding specifications' on the left-hand side 'Dialog Structure'.
ii.   On the next screen, you will notice that the system has brought up all the depreciation areas defined for the company code. Double-click on the appropriate area, (say, 01) and maintain the settings on the 'Change View: "Rounding specifications: Detail' screen (Figure 13.49):
- Select all the appropriate check-boxes under 'Rounding specifications' block:
  a. Select 'Net Book Value at Year End' check-box, to specify that the net book value of an asset should be rounded off to whole units of currency at the end of the fiscal year.

b. By selecting 'Automatically Calculated Depreciation' check-box, you specify that the automatically calculated depreciation (ordinary / special depreciation) should be rounded to whole units of currency.

c. Select the 'Replacement Value' check-box, to specify if you want to round the decimals in the replacement value that you calculate using an index series.

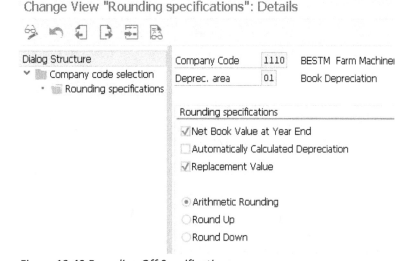

Figure 13.49 Rounding Off Specifications

- Select the appropriate rounding off method:
  - a. The 'Arithmetic Rounding' specifies that the rounding off should take place according to the rule that tenths up to and including 4 are rounded downward to the next whole number, starting with 5 they are rounded upward to the next whole number. For example, 7.07 or 7.49 is rounded off to 7, and 7.50 or 7.87 is rounded off to 8
  - b. With the 'Round Up', you indicate that the system always rounds off to the next highest whole number: for example, 7.07 or 7.47 or 7.88 is rounded off to 8.
  - c. The 'Round Down', when selected, indicates that you want to round off to the next lowest whole number: for example, 7.07 or 7.47 or 7.88 is rounded off to 7.

iii. 'Save' and make similar settings for all the depreciation areas of the selected company code and repeat for all the company codes.

The next activity to configure is specifying the changeover amount.

13.5.2.3   Specify Changeover Amount

Here, you specify the amount (per depreciation area) at which the system will change the depreciation calculation to the 'changeover key' specified in the depreciation key. The changeover takes place as soon as the net book value (NBV) of the asset goes below the changeover amount. This will work only when you use a depreciation key defined with changeover method 3 ('Changeover when NBV is less than the changeover amount'). In all other changeover methods, the system will not recognize this changeover amount.

Use the menu path: SAP Customizing Implementation Guide > Financial Accounting > Asset Accounting > General Valuation > Amount Specifications (Company Code/Depreciation Area) > Specify Changeover Amount, or Transaction OAYJ.

On the resulting screen, select the appropriate company code, double-click on 'Changeover amount' on the left-hand side 'Dialog Structure' and enter the amount in 'Chnge.NBV' field for all the required depreciation areas.

The last and final configuration step, under amount specifications, is to make the required settings for taking care of memo value.

13.5.2.4   Specify Memo Value

The 'memo value' function has been provided in FI-AA, by SAP, to allow for managing memo values from a previous system. When you specify a memo value, it is mandatory that all of the affected assets have a book value at least equal to the memo value at all times, even when the planned expected useful life has already been exceeded. It is not normally required to manage memo values. When you do not maintain a memo value, the system always depreciates the assets till the net book value becomes zero.

> **i** The *memo value* is the residual book value of an asset that appears in the in your balance sheet. When you maintain a memo value, per depreciation area/company code, for an asset, the system does not depreciate any further when the net book value of the asset becomes equal to the memo value. In general, you do not need to manage memo values in FI-AA, as the system always records the gross values: both the acquisition value and accumulated depreciation of assets. By this, the system ensures that even the fully-depreciated fixed assets appear in all legal reports, even when they have a net book value = 0.
>
> It may, sometimes, be necessary that you want to depreciate assets not to their zero book value, but only up to a specified *scrap value* or *cutoff value*. The system does not depreciate the asset, as soon as this value is reached. You can set up the (time-dependent) scrap value for assets, in two ways: (a) by assigning a *cutoff value key* to the depreciation key used in the depreciation area or (b) by entering an absolute scrap value or a percentage of APC in the

asset master data for the depreciation area; when you maintain both an absolute scrap value and a percentage scrap value, the system uses the percentage value. Refer Section 13.6.5.1.4, for understanding how to configure the scrap value / cutoff value.

If you maintain both scrap value and cutoff value key for an asset, at the same time, then, the system accords priority to the scrap value even if the cutoff value (determined from the cutoff value key) is smaller than the scrap value. Accordingly, the system will stop depreciation when the book value of the asset reaches the scrap value.

If all the three values (memo value, scrap value and cutoff value) exist for an asset, then, (a) when the memo value is the smallest amount, it becomes the residual value of the asset, or (b) when the memo value is not the smallest of all the three amounts, then, the system will consider the biggest amount, of all three, and make that as the residual value for the asset.

Project Dolphin

BESTM has indicated that they want to depreciate, all the fixed assets, until the book values become zero. Accordingly, the project team has decided not to use the 'memo value' functionality in the system.

Use the menu path: SAP Customizing Implementation Guide > Financial Accounting > Asset Accounting > General Valuation > Amount Specifications (Company Code/Depreciation Area) > Specify Memo Value.

i.   On the resulting pop-up screen (Figure 13.50), double-click on 'Specify Asset Classes without Memo Value' activity

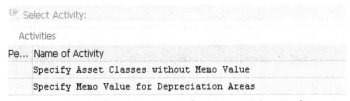

Figure 13.50 Initial Pop-Up Screen for Memo Value Configuration

ii. On the next screen (you may reach here directly using Transaction OAAW), select the 'Do not take memo value into account' check-box for all the asset classes for which you do not want the memo value functionality. We have selected this check-box for all the asset classes of BESTM (Figure 13.51).

Change View "Asset class: Ignore memo value": Overview

Class	Name of asset class	Do not take memo value into account
B1000	Buildings	☑
B2000	Plant & Machinery	☑
B3000	Vehicles	☑
B4100	Office Equipment	☑
B4200	Furniture & Fixtures	☑

Figure 13.51 Memo Value Configuration for BESTM

iii.   However, should you want to configure memo value, then you do not need to carry out the above step (ii). Instead, you need to double-click on the 'Specify Memo Value for Depreciation Areas' activity on the initial pop-up screen (Figure 13.50), and select the appropriate company code on the next screen (use Transaction OAYI to reach here directly). Then, double-click on 'Memo value' on the left hand-side 'Dialog Structure'. Now, enter the amount in the 'Memo value' field, per depreciation area on the next screen.

With this, we have completed all the configuration steps that are required for configuring the amount specifications. We are, now, ready to discuss the settings required for fiscal year specifications for general valuation in FI-AA.

13.5.3 Fiscal Year Specifications

FI-AA, generally, uses the same fiscal year variant (FYV) as that of SAP FI (G/L). Accordingly, the depreciation periods of FI-AA correspond to the posting periods in FI, but without considering the special periods. The system, therefore, automatically defaults the FYV of the G/L when you define the FI-AA system settings for a company code. You do not need to make any additional system settings if your depreciation periods and G/L posting periods are identical.

Project Dolphin

BESTM company codes will use the same FYV that has been defined in SAP FI (G/L) in FI-AA as well. However, the project team has been asked to configure use of half months to take care of mid-month acquisition / depreciation of assets for all the US-based company codes.

However, you may come across situations in which the G/L posting periods are not suitable for determining depreciation in FI-AA. In those cases, you need FI-AA-specific fiscal year variants. You can use FI-AA specific FYV (of course, you need to define them in SAP FI G/L Customizing before you can use that here in FI-AA):

i. At the level of the company code (use the menu path: SAP Customizing Implementation Guide > Financial Accounting > Asset Accounting > General Valuation > Fiscal Year Specifications > Fiscal Year Variants > Specify Other Variants on Company Code Level, or

ii. Below the company code level and for each of the depreciation areas:

- You first need to specify in the company code(s) that you will be going in for a differing FYV by using the menu path: SAP Customizing Implementation Guide > Financial Accounting > Asset Accounting > General Valuation > Fiscal Year Specifications > Fiscal Year Variants > Allow Differing Variants for Depreciation Areas with G/L Integration.

- Later, you need to specify the FYV for each of the depreciation areas by using the menu path: SAP Customizing Implementation Guide > Financial Accounting > Asset Accounting > General Valuation > Fiscal Year Specifications > Fiscal Year Variants > Specify Other Variants on Depreciation Area Level.

> **i** You can change the FYV in FI-AA for as long as the company code is not 'productive'.

With this, let us understand how to configure the system to consider mid-month or mid-quarter acquisition of fixed assets.

13.5.3.1   Use of Half Months in the Company Code

'Half-periods' or 'half-months' are necessary to represent the 'mid-quarter/month rule'. Used widely in the USA, it helps in determination of depreciation when an acquisition takes place in the first or the second half of a period.

Here, you determine the company codes for which you want to use half periods, so as to calculate depreciation on the basis of half months or half periods. Using this method, you can work with 24 periods in FI-AA, even if the FYV in SAP FI has only 12 normal periods, without resorting to defining a different fiscal year version in FI-AA.

> **i** To use half-periods in asset accounting, ensure that the number of posting periods in the fiscal year variant used correspond to the number of calendar months (12). You cannot use half-periods with non-calendar fiscal months. Once specified, you cannot take back the use of half-periods as the system notes the same internally in the asset master records

Use the menu path: SAP Customizing Implementation Guide > Financial Accounting > Asset Accounting > General Valuation > Fiscal Year Specifications > Use of Half Months in the Company Code. On the resulting screen, enter 15 in 'MidMon' field to specify the middle of month for all the required company codes, and 'Save' the details (Figure 13.52).

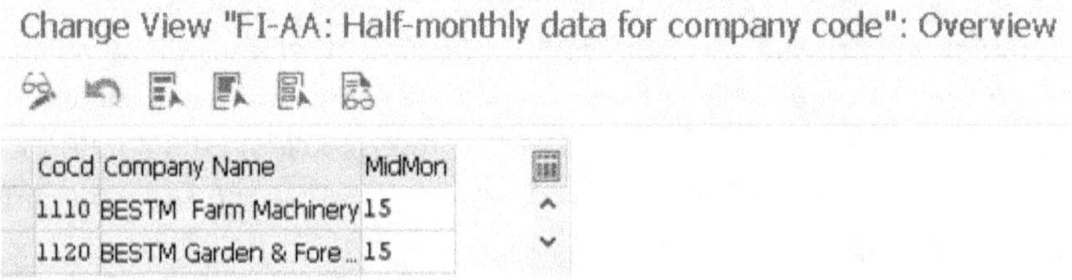

Change View "FI-AA: Half-monthly data for company code": Overview

CoCd	Company Name	MidMon
1110	BESTM Farm Machinery	15
1120	BESTM Garden & Fore...	15

Figure 13.52 Configuring Half Months for US-based Company Codes of BESTM

This completes our discussion on the settings required for fiscal year specification in FI-AA. We shall now discuss the settings required for managing fixed assets in foreign currencies.

13.5.4 Currencies

You need to make appropriate settings in the system that will allow (a) valuation of fixed assets in FI-AA, in separate depreciation areas with foreign currencies and (b) management of parallel currencies at the G/L level, from the point of asset view point. Essentially, you will define depreciation areas for foreign currencies besides specifying the use of parallel currencies.

Let us start with the depreciation areas for foreign currencies.

13.5.4.1   Define Depreciation Areas for Foreign Currencies

SAP allows you to manage depreciation areas in various currencies. You can then use the values, from these depreciation areas, for group consolidation or analysis. Here, in this activity, you define depreciation areas that manage asset values in a foreign currency, per company code. When in place, during acquisitions, the system makes the foreign currency translation, at the exchange rate prevailing on the posting date. The system calculates the depreciation and proportional value adjustments, for asset retirements, directly in the foreign currency

When you manage depreciation areas in the currency of the corporate group for legal consolidation, we recommend you to set up separate depreciation areas in the group currency for the historical management of values. This is particularly required, when the valuation of assets at the group level is different from the local valuation.

Project Dolphin

Managing depreciation areas in the currency of corporate group, for legal consolidation, is a requirement for all the India-based company codes of BESTM as the local valuation will be in INR but the group consolidation in USD. Accordingly, suitable depreciation areas need to be defined for the chart of depreciation BEIN which will be used by the India-based company codes1210 and 1220.

Use the menu path: SAP Customizing Implementation Guide > Financial Accounting > Asset Accounting > General Valuation > Currencies > Define Depreciation Areas for Foreign Currencies, or Transaction OAYH.

On the resulting screen, select the appropriate company code (say, 1210) and double-click on 'Depreciation area currency' on the left-hand side 'Dialog Structure'. On the next screen (Figure 13.53), you need to enter the foreign currency (USD) for the required depreciation areas (say, 33).

Figure 13.53 Foreign Currency Specification for Depreciation Area

The next step is to specify the parallel currencies.

13.5.4.2   Specify the Use of Parallel Currencies

For the legal consolidation of your fixed assets, you need only foreign currency amounts, but not a different basis for valuation (APC/depreciation terms) than the one used in the local currency. That being the case, you can use the functions of SAP FI wherein you can manage all values of a company code in parallel on the same accounts in several currencies. As you can define three local currencies, for each combination of company code and ledger in FI, even the values that are posted within FI-AA, are updated in several currencies along with the local currency in FI.

To ensure that the currency type and currency of the depreciation area are identical to those of the corresponding parallel currency in the company code in question, and that the depreciation area manages depreciation terms and acquisition values that are identical with those of the reference area, use the menu path: SAP Customizing Implementation Guide >

Financial Accounting > Asset Accounting > General Valuation > Currencies > Specify the Use of Parallel Currencies. On the resulting screen, select the appropriate 'Currency Type' against the appropriate depreciations area: for example, 30 for area 33. (Figure 13.54).

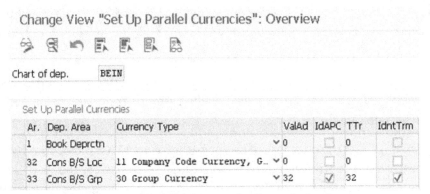

Figure 13.54 Setting up of Parallel Currency for Depreciation Area

This completes our discussion of currency settings required for general valuation. Let us, now, move on to discuss the settings relating to group assets.

13.5.5 Group Assets

The system, generally, calculates depreciation at the level of individual assets. However, you can calculate depreciation at a higher level (at the level of group asset) to meet certain tax requirements (as in the case of USA). To make the necessary system settings for group assets, you need to specify depreciation area(s) for group assets besides specifying the asset classes for group assets.

Let us start with the specification of depreciation areas for group assets.

13.5.5.1   Specify Depreciation Areas for Group Assets

If required, you can specify which are the depreciation that you also want to manage at the group asset level. Then, in these depreciation areas, you can make an assignment to a group asset in the respective asset master record. Later, when you post an acquisition to this kind of asset, the system duplicates the line items from this depreciation area on the given group asset.

Project Dolphin

To meet some of the tax requirements in USA, BESTM has requested to specify the appropriate depreciation areas for managing the group assets as well. However, it has been indicated that there is no need for creating exclusive asset classes for group assets, instead any of the defined asset classes can be used to create a group asset as well.

Use the menu path: SAP Customizing Implementation Guide > Financial Accounting > Asset Accounting > General Valuation > Group Assets > Specify Depreciation Areas for Group Assets, or Transaction OAYM:

i.   On the resulting screen, select the company code, double-click on 'Group assets' on the left-hand side 'Dialog Structure', and select the 'Grp. asset' check-box against the required depreciation areas (Figure 13.55).

ii.   Repeat the settings for other company codes as well.

We have configured this for all the US-based company codes of BESTM.

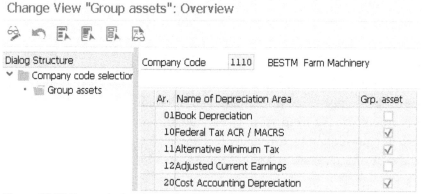

Figure 13.55 Depreciation Areas for Group Assets

The next step is specifying the asset classes, exclusively for group assets.

13.5.5.2   Specify Asset Classes for Group Assets

Though it is generally possible to use all asset classes for creating group assets, you can set aside particular asset classes for use in conjunction with group assets. These asset classes are then reserved solely for group assets, and are not allowed to be used for normal assets. It is not mandatory to specify asset classes exclusively for group assets.

Use the menu path: SAP Customizing Implementation Guide > Financial Accounting > Asset Accounting > General Valuation > Group Assets > Specify Asset Classes for Group Assets, or Transaction OAAX.

On the resulting screen, to designate an asset class exclusively for group assets, select the 'Class consists entirely of group assets' check-box against those asset classes (Figure 13.56). BESTM does not want any exclusive asset class for group assets.

Change View "Asset class: Indicator for group assets only": Overview

Class	Name of asset class	Class consists entirely of group assets
B1000	Buildings	☐
B2000	Plant & Machinery	☐
B3000	Vehicles	☐
B4100	Office Equipment	☐

Figure 13.56 Specifying Asset Classes Exclusively for Group Assets

This completes our discussion on the settings required for group assets, and this also completes our discussion on the configuration settings for general valuation. Let us move on to discuss depreciation, next.

13.6 Depreciation

The 'depreciation' represents the decrease in value of a fixed asset (other than land), over its economic life, due to its usage including wear and tear. In accounting, this is referred to as the reduction of recorded cost of a fixed asset, in a systematic manner, until the value of that asset becomes zero or a pre-defined scrap value. By depreciating an asset, you are assigning or allocating of the cost of a fixed asset, to an expense account, in the accounting periods encompassing its useful life.

Let us start our discussion with the understanding of depreciation types, in SAP.

13.6.1 Depreciation Types

SAP supports two depreciation types, (a) automatically calculated depreciation (you can plan this manually as well) and (b) manually planned depreciation (Figure 13.57).

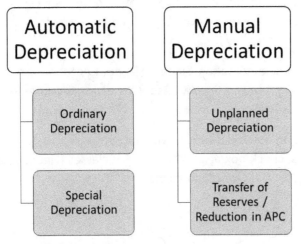

Figure 13.57 Depreciation Types

The system controls the automatic calculation of depreciation through 'depreciation keys' which you can modify to define your own method of calculation, if required. SAP treats the 'interest' calculation (for cost-accounting purposes) also as a depreciation type, and controls the same by depreciation keys and calculation methods.

Let us understand more on the depreciation types:

- *Ordinary Depreciation*: This is the planned deduction for wear and tear during normal use of an asset.
- *Special Depreciation*: This represents the deduction for wear and tear of an asset from a purely tax-based point of view. This allows for a percentage depreciation, normally staggered within a period allowed by the tax authority, without considering the actual wear and tear on the asset.
- *Unplanned Depreciation*: While the ordinary depreciation reflects the deduction for wear and tear during the normal use of the asset, the unplanned depreciation covers the permanent decrease in an asset's value due to certain unusual / unforeseen influence or occurrence like damages to the asset because of fire, flood etc.
- *Transfer of Reserves/Reduction of APC*: By reducing the APC, you can reduce the depreciation base of an asset by a given amount. You cannot post this automatically, using depreciation keys, but only manually.
- *Interest*: It is required, for internal accounting, that you evaluate the fixed capital tied up in an asset, besides the depreciation. You do this by calculating the 'imputed interest' on the capital so tied up and the system treats this also as a depreciation type, and uses the depreciation keys / calculation methods similar to depreciation calculation.

With this let us see how the system handles manual depreciation.

13.6.1.1   Manual Depreciation

The system, in general, determines the planned depreciations for the current financial year using the depreciation key entered in the master record. However, the system enables to manually change the planned depreciation for an asset: you can enter the depreciation amount, manually, for all depreciation types; but, usually, you will manually enter only the unplanned depreciation and the transfer of reserves. You will resort to such a manual intervention when (a) there is an unexpected permanent reduction in the value of an asset that needs to be posted as unplanned depreciation, or (b) you need to use the special tax depreciation only partially or (c) you need to schedule the 'unit-of-production' method of depreciation manually instead of scheduling the same using the depreciation keys.

> **i** You can post ordinary depreciation and special depreciation, manually, only if the depreciation key that you entered in the respective depreciation area uses a base method in which no automatic calculation has been specified as the depreciation calculation method.

When you undertake manual depreciation:

- You can use the standard posting transaction of FI-AA, to forecast the manual depreciation. You can also use the special transaction types that enable you to forecast depreciation for specific or all the depreciations areas.
- While posting, the transaction does not initially affect the G/L accounts in SAP FI. The system creates only asset line items, but no FI journal entries. The system updates the G/L accounts and creates the corresponding FI documents only with the periodic depreciation posting run.
- Though the system creates the journal entries, with the depreciation posting run, you can still specify an asset value date so that journal entries thus generated, in the posting period, falls within that value date.

With this we are now ready to configure the system for various types of depreciation. Let us start with the ordinary depreciation.

13.6.2 Ordinary Depreciation

We already know that the ordinary depreciation is a form of planned depreciation that you will use to take care of the normal wear and of an asset during its economic life. The first task is to determine the depreciation areas for handling ordinary depreciation in the system.

13.6.2.1   Determine Depreciation Areas

Here, you determine the depreciation areas in which you want to manage ordinary depreciation. In the detail screen per area, you can also determine which sign (+ or -) the ordinary depreciation is allowed to have in the respective area.

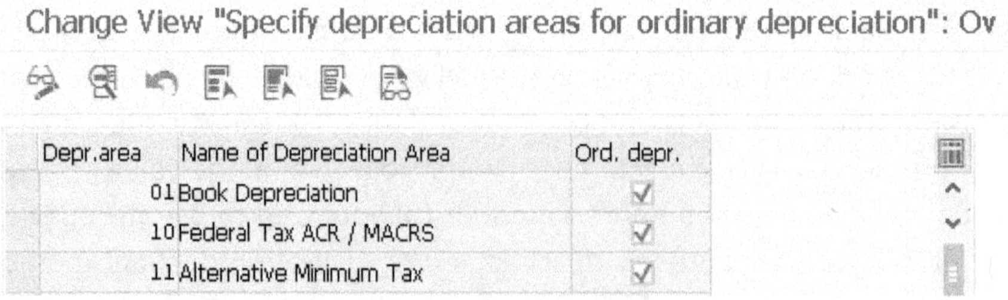

Change View "Specify depreciation areas for ordinary depreciation": Ov

Depr.area	Name of Depreciation Area	Ord. depr.	
01	Book Depreciation	☑	
10	Federal Tax ACR / MACRS	☑	
11	Alternative Minimum Tax	☑	

Figure 13.58 Specifying Areas for Ordinary Depreciation

Use the menu path: SAP Customizing Implementation Guide > Financial Accounting > Asset Accounting > Depreciation > Ordinary Depreciation > Determine Depreciation Areas, or Transaction OABN

On the resulting screen (Figure 13.58), select the 'Ord. depr.' check-box against the all the required depreciation areas. You may double-click on any of the areas, and see the detailed settings on the next screen (13.59). For normal depreciation in the book depreciation area (01), you need to select the 'Only negative values and zero allowed' radio-button under the 'Rule for pos./neg. sign for ord. depreciation' data block.

Change View "Specify depreciation areas for ordinary depreciation": De

| hart of dep. | BEUS | Chart of Depreciation USA (BESTM) |
| Depreciat. Area | 01 | Book Depreciation |

Rule for pos./neg. sign for ord. depreciation

○ Ordinary depreciation not desired
○ Only positive values and zero allowed
◉ Only negative values and zero allowed
○ All values allowed

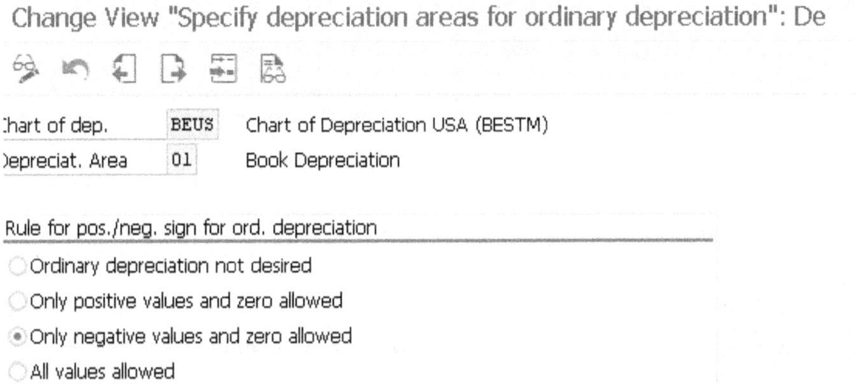

Figure 13.59 Specifying Areas for Ordinary Depreciation – Detailed Settings

The next activity is to assign the G/L accounts for ordinary depreciation

13.6.2.2   Assign Accounts

Use the menu path: SAP Customizing Implementation Guide > Financial Accounting > Asset Accounting > Depreciation > Ordinary Depreciation > Assign Accounts, or Transaction AO93:

i.   On the resulting screen, select the chart of accounts (BEUS, in our case) and double-click on 'Account Determination' on the left-hand side 'Dialog Structure'.

ii. On the 'Change View "Account Determination"; Overview' screen, select the required account determination (say, B1000 – Buildings), and double-click on 'Ordinary Depreciation' on the left-hand side 'Dialog Structure'.

iii. On the resulting 'Change View "Ordinary Depreciation"; Overview' screen, double-click on the row containing 1 ('Area') – 'Book Depreciation', and enter the appropriate G/L accounts on the next screen in 'Ordinary depreciation account assignment' and 'Account assignment for revaluation on depreciation' data blocks (Figure 13.60), and 'Save' the details.

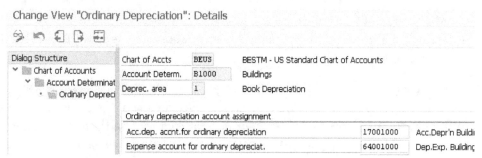

Figure 13.60 G/L Account Assignment – Ordinary Depreciation

iv.   Complete the G/L account assignment for the rest of the account determinations, for the chart of accounts BEUS, and 'Save' when fully completed.

With this we are now ready to configure the settings for special depreciation.

13.6.3 Special Depreciation

In 'special depreciation', you depreciate an asset from the point of taxation (staggered within the taxation period) without considering the actual wear and tear of the asset. Here, you define the system settings for determining and posting special depreciation. The first task, as in the case of ordinary depreciation, is to determine the depreciation areas for special depreciation.

13.6.3.1   Determine Depreciation Areas

Using this configuration activity, you will determine the depreciation areas in which you want to manage special depreciation. This specification informs the system that this value type is allowed in that depreciation area so that there is no error message when you enter corresponding depreciation terms in the asset master record.

As in the case of ordinary depreciation areas, use the menu path: SAP Customizing Implementation Guide > Financial Accounting > Asset Accounting > Depreciation > Special Depreciation > Determine Depreciation Areas, or Transaction OABS.

On the resulting screen, select the 'Spec. depr.' check-box against all depreciation areas wherein you want to manage special depreciation. Double-click on a depreciation area, and select the appropriate radio-button ('Only negative values and zero allowed') under the 'Rule for pos./neg. sign for ord. depreciation' data block, on the next screen (Figure 13.61).

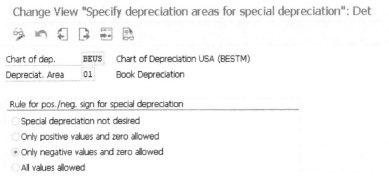

Figure 13.61 Specifying Areas for Special Depreciation – Detailed Settings

The next configuration activity is to define the settings for calculating ordinary depreciation before special depreciation.

13.6.3.2   Calculate Ordinary Depreciation before Special Depreciation

Though the order in which the system determines different types of depreciation is somewhat flexible, the system always determines the 'transfer of reserves' first, and the 'unplanned depreciation' at the last. However, you can decide the order in which ordinary depreciation and special depreciation should be determined. When you specify, per depreciation area, that the system should determine ordinary depreciation before special depreciation, then, the sequence of depreciation determination will be as shown in Figure 13.62.

Figure 13.62 Depreciation Sequence

When there is a need for reduction in depreciation, then, the system determines the depreciation exactly in the reverse order, starting with 'unplanned depreciation' and finally with the 'transfer of reserves' as shown in Figure 13.63.

Figure 13.63 Reduction in Depreciation - Sequence

> **i** In the standard SAP system, the system calculates the ordinary depreciation before the special depreciation.

Project Dolphin

As in line with the standard settings, BESTM wants to calculate the ordinary depreciation before the special depreciation.

Use the menu path: SAP Customizing Implementation Guide > Financial Accounting > Asset Accounting > Depreciation > Special Depreciation > Calculate Ordinary Depreciation before Special Depreciation, or Transaction AOBK.

On the resulting screen, select, per depreciation area, the 'O.dep. before sp.dep.' check-box so that the system calculates ordinary depreciation first, before calculating the special depreciation (Figure 13.64).

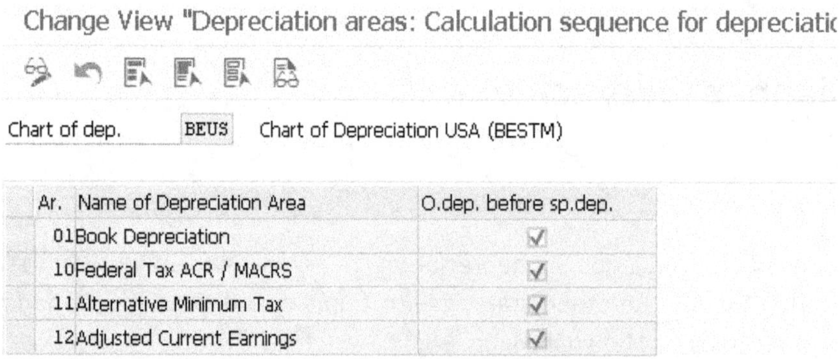

Change View "Depreciation areas: Calculation sequence for depreciatic

Chart of dep.   BEUS   Chart of Depreciation USA (BESTM)

Ar.	Name of Depreciation Area	O.dep. before sp.dep.
01	Book Depreciation	✓
10	Federal Tax ACR / MACRS	✓
11	Alternative Minimum Tax	✓
12	Adjusted Current Earnings	✓

Figure 13.64 Specifying Calculation Sequence for Ordinary Depreciation

The last configuration for special depreciation, is to assign the G/L accounts.

13.6.3.3   Assign Accounts

As in the case of assigning G/L accounts for ordinary depreciation, use the menu path: SAP Customizing Implementation Guide > Financial Accounting > Asset Accounting > Depreciation > Special Depreciation > Assign Accounts, or Transaction AO94 and assign the required G/L accounts for the special depreciation areas. Unlike ordinary depreciation, wherein you have to assign G/L accounts for both 'Ordinary depreciation account assignment' and 'Account assignment for revaluation on depreciation' data block, here, you will assign G/L accounts only for the 'Special depreciation account assignment' data block.

With this, let us move on to discuss the settings required for unplanned depreciation.

13.6.4 Unplanned Depreciation

As you are already aware, you may need to resort to 'unplanned depreciation' in certain special situations like flooding of the factory or a fire mishap making an asset unusable. You need to use the depreciation key MANU ('Manual depreciation only'), for undertaking unplanned depreciation. Besides (a) determining the depreciation areas for unplanned depreciation, and (b) assigning the appropriate G/L accounts, you also need to (c) define the required transaction types to handle unplanned depreciation.

13.6.4.1   Determine Depreciation Areas

The determination of depreciation areas to handle unplanned depreciation is similar to what we have already discussed for ordinary depreciation (in Section 13.6.2.1) and special depreciation (in Section 13.6.3.1). Use the menu path: SAP Customizing Implementation Guide > Financial Accounting > Asset Accounting > Depreciation > Unplanned Depreciation > Determine Depreciation Areas, or Transaction OABU, and specify the areas for unplanned depreciation by selecting the 'UDep' check-box against the required areas.

13.6.4.2   Assign Accounts

The other configuration activity of assigning G/L accounts, is also similar to the one that we have already discussed for ordinary and special depreciation in Section 13.6.2.2 and Section 13.6.3.3, respectively. Use the menu path: SAP Customizing Implementation Guide > Financial Accounting > Asset Accounting > Depreciation > Unplanned Depreciation > Assign Accounts, or Transaction AO95, and enter the appropriate G/L accounts per account determination for the chart of accounts BEUS.

Now, we can define the transaction types for unplanned depreciation.

13.6.4.3   Define Transaction Types for Unplanned Depreciation

You will use different 'transaction types' for various postings to manually correct the value of assets, in case of unplanned depreciation, other manually scheduled depreciation (ordinary or special depreciation) and write-ups. SAP provides you with the standard transaction types for all these three purposes, which you can use as such.

Project Dolphin

BESTM does not want to define any new transaction types for unplanned depreciation. Instead, they have indicated that, they want to use the SAP supplied standard ones.

Use the menu path: SAP Customizing Implementation Guide > Financial Accounting > Asset Accounting > Depreciation > Unplanned Depreciation > Define Transaction Types for Unplanned Depreciation, or Transaction AO78.

On the resulting 'Change View "FI-AA: Transaction types": Overview' screen (Figure 13.65) you will see the standard transactions defined by SAP for manual (ordinary & special) depreciation postings, unplanned depreciation postings and for posting write-ups (relating to ordinary, special and unplanned depreciation).

Change View "FI-AA: Transaction types": Overview

   New Entries

Transact. type	Transaction Type Name
600	Manual ordinary depreciation on prior-yr acquis.
610	Manual ordinary depreciation on current-yr acquis.
620	Manual spec. dep. on prior-yr acquis per dep. key
630	Manual spec. dep. on curr-yr acquis per dep. key
640	Unplanned depreciation on prior-year acquisitions
650	Unplanned depreciation on current-yr acquisition
6J1	Adjust cut-off value check (Japan)
700	Write-up ordinary and special depreciation
710	Write-up ordinary book and tax depreciation
720	Write-up special tax depreciation
730	Write-up general unplanned depreciation

Figure 13.65 Standard Transaction Types

You will notice that there are three transaction types for handling unplanned depreciation postings:

- 640 - Unplanned depreciation on prior-year acquisitions
- 650 - Unplanned depreciation on current-yr acquisition
- 730 - Write-up general unplanned depreciation

You may double-click on any of the rows in Figure 13.65, to see the detailed settings for the transaction type (Figure 13.66). You will notice that the transaction type (say, 650) has been grouped under the transaction type group 65. In 'Account assignment', you will see the settings relating to the type of transaction (credit, debit etc). In 'Other features', you will see some more characteristics that can be configured for the transaction type. You will notice that the corresponding 'Consolidation transaction type' is 925 for the transaction type 650.

If you need to create a new transaction type, we recommend you do that by copying an existing entry and making the required changes instead of creating on anew.

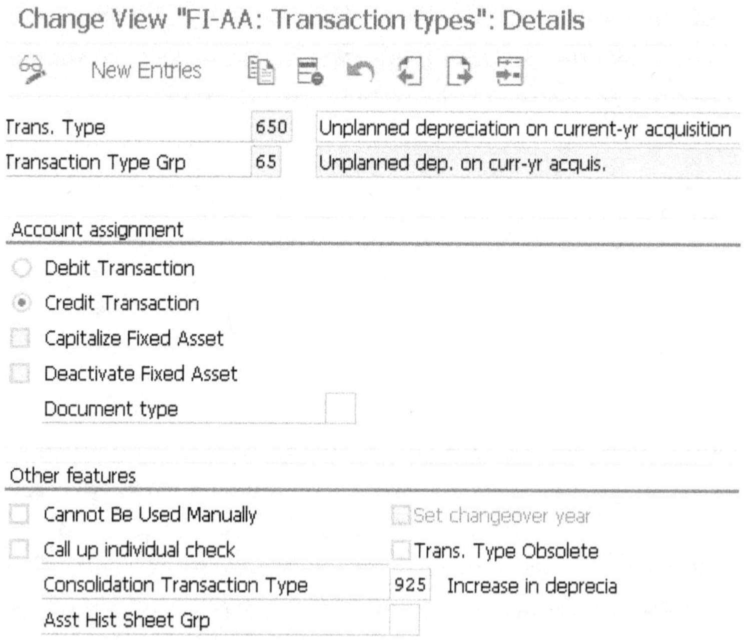

Change View "FI-AA: Transaction types": Details

 New Entries

| Trans. Type | 650 | Unplanned depreciation on current-yr acquisition |
| Transaction Type Grp | 65 | Unplanned dep. on curr-yr acquis. |

Account assignment

○ Debit Transaction
◉ Credit Transaction
☐ Capitalize Fixed Asset
☐ Deactivate Fixed Asset
  Document type

Other features

☐ Cannot Be Used Manually   ☐ Set changeover year
☐ Call up individual check   ☐ Trans. Type Obsolete
  Consolidation Transaction Type   925 Increase in deprecia
  Asst Hist Sheet Grp

Figure 13.66 Transaction Type 650 – Details

---

i Now, in FI-AA, it is not required (and also not possible) to restrict the transaction types to depreciation areas. This has become unnecessary because, when you enter a transaction, you can restrict the same to a depreciation area or accounting principle. Besides, in a posting transaction, you can also select the depreciation areas to be posted. This approach vastly reduces the number of transaction types that you need to be define in the system. However, for some reason, if you have restricted certain transaction types to depreciation areas (by making entries in table TABWA or view cluster V_TABWA), the system rejects the same.

This completes our discussion on the settings for unplanned depreciation. Let us move on to discuss the valuation methods in the next Section.

13.6.5 Valuation Methods

As already indicated, you can modify the depreciation keys in the system to create your own calculation method for asset valuation as the standard methods, in the system, are not hard-coded. Based on a number of flexibly-definable calculation keys, you can easily define your own calculation methods and control parameters, to have your own specific depreciation methods in the system. Of course, you can also use the pre-defined calculation methods and parameters, that come delivered with the standard SAP system, for the most commonly used depreciation methods.

The depreciation calculation, in the system, is based on the 'valuation method' and the 'planned useful life' of the asset that you maintain in the asset master record. Pre-defined in the system, the valuation methods are based on the following variables:

- *Depreciation Key*
  The '*depreciation key*' (also known as 'valuation key') contains all the control data (or control indicators) that the system needs for calculating the planned annual depreciation. Entered in each of the depreciation areas of an asset master record, the depreciation key also contains the 'calculation method'. Refer Section 13.6.5.1.5 to understand how to define a depreciation key.

  - *Calculation Methods*
    The '*calculation method*' (also known as 'control functions') defined within the depreciation key, is used for the calculation of different types of automatically calculated depreciation (ordinary and special depreciation, and interest). The calculation method is very important for defining the 'depreciation calculation method'. You may refer Section 13.6.5.1.1, for more details on calculation methods.

    The *depreciation calculation method* is the most important characteristic of the 'base method', as it makes possible to carry out the different types of depreciation calculation in the system. Depending on how you set up the depreciation calculation method, the system determines which further 'control parameters' (or '*control indicators*') that you need to specify in the depreciation key.

    - *Base Method*
      The '*base method*' (of a calculation method) contains general control parameters that the system needs for calculating the depreciation. Refer Section 13.6.5.1.1.1, for more details.

- Further Parameters like *'cutoff value' (scrap value)*. You may refer Section 13.6.5.1.4 for more details on scrap value / cutoff value.

Let us understand, in detail, about the depreciation key, next.

13.6.5.1   Depreciation Key

Defined at the level of the chart of depreciation, the depreciation keys are valid in all company codes. As mentioned earlier, the 'depreciation key' contains the value settings that are necessary for determining depreciation amounts (Figure 13.67).

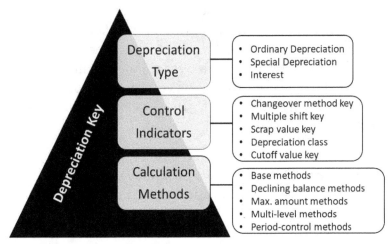

Figure 13.67 Depreciation Key

The depreciation key contains information on the depreciation types, besides a combination of calculation methods and control indicators:

- It has information as to the automatically calculated 'depreciation types' viz., the ordinary depreciation, special depreciation and imputed interest.
- It contains several 'control indicators' as indicated below, besides the ones that are shown in Figure 13.67:
    o No ordinary depreciation with special depreciation
    o No interest if no depreciation is planned
    o Period control according to fiscal years
    o Depreciation to the day
    o Depreciation calculation in shortened fiscal years
    o Number of places for rounding
    o Effect of scrap value on base value for depreciation
- The 'calculation method' in each depreciation key determines the depreciation amounts.

With this, let us discuss the calculation methods, in detail.

13.6.5.1.1   Calculation Methods

The system uses 'calculation methods' (also known as, 'control functions') for the calculation of depreciation and (imputed) interest, and they provide the parameters for the 'Depreciation Calculation Program' (DCP); we shall discuss the DCP in detail, in Section 13.6.5.2. You will assign a calculation method to a depreciation key. Together with the control parameters of the depreciation key, and the cutoff value keys, the calculation method controls the depreciation calculation.

You will maintain the calculation methods separately, independent of the depreciation keys. In this way, you can assign the same calculation method in more than one depreciation key. These individual calculation methods, with the exception of the base method, are dependent on the chart of depreciation: you can represent your country-specific depreciation requirements by means of calculation methods that are chart-of-depreciation-specific. The system offers, for selection, only the methods that apply to your chart of depreciation. If you want a changeover to other calculation methods, during the duration of depreciation, then, you need to define that in the depreciation key.

> **i** You will not be able to alter the standard calculation methods in the SAP system. However, you can modify, any one of them, by copying and making the necessary changes on the copy which need to begin with X, Y or Z.

The following are the various depreciation calculation methods supported in the standard SAP, which can be grouped into two categories:

- A. Chart-of-depreciation-independent calculation methods
  - Base methods
- B. Chart-of-depreciation-dependent calculation methods
  - Declining-balance methods
  - Maximum amount methods
  - Multi-level methods
  - Period control methods

> **i** When you are maintaining chart-of-depreciation-dependent calculation methods, you get a display of the existing calculation methods in accordance with the chart of depreciation that has been set.

Let us see each of the calculation methods in detail, and how to maintain the same in the system. Let us start with the base methods.

13.6.5.1.1.1 Define Base Methods

The *'base method'* contains the general control parameters that the system needs for calculating depreciation. Independent of the chart of depreciation, it does not contain any country-specific settings and hence you can use them across charts of depreciation.

For a base method, you have to specify:

i. The depreciation type (say: ordinary, special or interest)
ii. The depreciation calculation method (say: 0001-ordinary: sum-of-the-year-digits, 0002-no automatic depreciation, 0014-ordinary: explicit percentage, after end of life, 0021-special: total percentage rate, 0028-interest: leasing, 0029-interest: explicit percentage etc)
iii. The treatment at the end of the depreciation (for example, continuing depreciation even after the end of the planned life, curb, depreciation below zero etc)

You may not need to define any new base method, as the SAP-supplied based methods are several and will be more than sufficient.

Use the menu path: SAP Customizing Implementation Guide > Financial Accounting > Asset Accounting > Depreciation > Valuation Methods > Depreciation Key > Calculation Methods > Define Base Methods, or Transaction AFMR.

On the resulting 'Change View "Base Method": Overview' screen (Figure 13.68), you will see a listing of all the default base methods supplied by SAP. Should you ever need a new based method to be defined, you may use the 'New Entries' button or 'Copy in same chart of depreciation' button to create a new one.

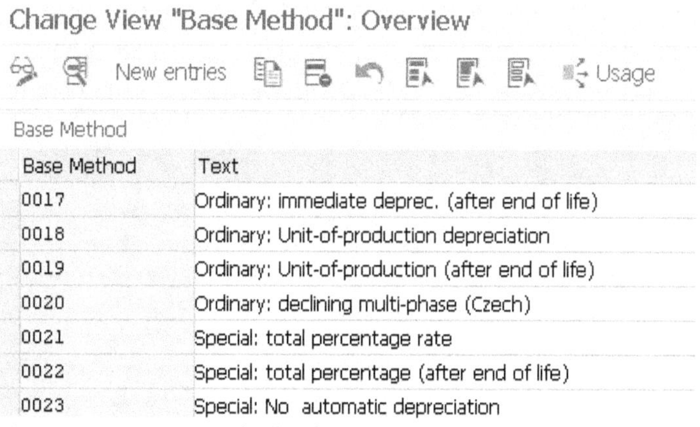

Change View "Base Method": Overview

New entries Usage

Base Method

Base Method	Text
0017	Ordinary: immediate deprec. (after end of life)
0018	Ordinary: Unit-of-production depreciation
0019	Ordinary: Unit-of-production (after end of life)
0020	Ordinary: declining multi-phase (Czech)
0021	Special: total percentage rate
0022	Special: total percentage (after end of life)
0023	Special: No automatic depreciation

Figure 13.68 Base Methods of Depreciation

To understand the detailed settings of a base method, you may double-click on any of the rows and see the settings on the next screen (Figure 13.69).

Change View "Base Method": Details

New entries

Base Method	0001	Ordinary: sum-of-the-years-digits

Type of Depreciation	Ord.depreciation
Dep. Method	Sum-of-the-years-digits method of depreciation
Reduce Use.Life at FY End	☐

Treatment of end of depreciation

Dep. After Plnd.Life End	No
Dep.Below NBValue Zero	No
Curb	No

Figure 13.69 Base Method of Depreciation: 0001 – Details

With this, let us move on to discuss / maintain declining-balance methods.

13.6.5.1.1.2 Define Declining-Balance Methods

The normal '*declining-balance method*' of depreciation (the other variation being 'sum-of-the-years-digits-method') multiplies the straight-line percentage rate resulting from the useful life, by a given factor. Since a relatively short useful life may result in a very large depreciation percentage rate, you can specify a maximum percentage rate as the upper ceiling limit in the declining-balance method. A similar principle applies for a very long useful life. When you enter a minimum percentage rate, the system prevents the percentage rate from sinking below a given level. In this method, you can never make the NBV equal to zero.

Use the menu path: SAP Customizing Implementation Guide > Financial Accounting > Asset Accounting > Depreciation > Valuation Methods > Depreciation Key > Calculation Methods > Define Declining-Balance Methods, or Transaction AFAMD, to view / create declining-rate depreciation methods (Figure 13.70):

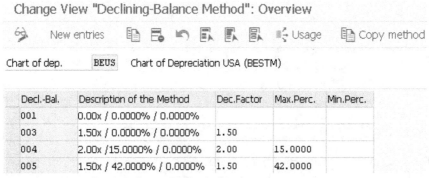

Change View "Declining-Balance Method": Overview

New entries   Usage   Copy method

Chart of dep.	BEUS	Chart of Depreciation USA (BESTM)

Decl.-Bal.	Description of the Method	Dec.Factor	Max.Perc.	Min.Perc.
001	0.00x / 0.0000% / 0.0000%			
003	1.50x / 0.0000% / 0.0000%	1.50		
004	2.00x /15.0000% / 0.0000%	2.00	15.0000	
005	1.50x / 42.0000% / 0.0000%	1.50	42.0000	

Figure 13.70 Declining-Balance Method of Depreciation

- The multiplication factor ('Dec.Factor') is used in determining the depreciation percentage rate for declining-balance depreciation. The system multiplies the depreciation percentage rate resulting from the total useful life by this factor.
- The 'Max.Perc.' is the upper limit for the depreciation percentage rate. If a higher depreciation percentage rate is produced from the useful life, multiplication factor or number of units to be depreciated, then, the system uses the maximum percentage rate specified here.
- The 'Min.Perc.' is the lower limit for the depreciation percentage rate. Similar to 'Max.Perc.', if a lower percentage rate is produced from the useful life, multiplication factor, or number of units to be depreciated, then, the system uses the minimum percentage specified here.

With this, let us move on to the maximum amount methods.

13.6.5.1.1.3 Define Maximum Amount Methods

Here, you specify the maximum amount up to which the system should calculate depreciation until a certain calendar date. During the specified time period, the system calculates depreciation only until this amount is reached. If the system arrives at a depreciation that is greater than this maximum amount, then, it reduces the depreciation appropriately so that the overall depreciation is not exceeding the maximum allowed for that time.

You can specify how the maximum amount applies within the time period specified for it. It can either apply to each individual year in the specified time period, or to the accumulated depreciation.

> **i** The 'maximum amount method' does not function in the same way as a maximum 'base value'. With the maximum base value, the system calculates depreciation based on the acquisition value (which may be below the actual acquisition value). But in 'maximum amount method', it calculates the depreciation without any dependency on the acquisition value.
>
> The 'base value' for depreciation is closely linked to the depreciation calculation method that you select. Since it is not logical to use every depreciation method with every base value, the base value is often already determined by the depreciation method. SAP has already defined several base values in the system including, acquisition Value, acquisition value less unplanned depreciation, half of acquisition value, replacement value, half of replacement value, current net book value without special depreciation, average net book value, average net book value without special depreciation, current net book value, accumulated ordinary depreciation, accumulated special depreciation, sum of accumulated ordinary and special depreciation and limited base value. You can also define your own custom base value using a customer enhancement (BAdI method FAA_EE_CUSTOMER: Set_BASE_VALUE).

Use the menu path: SAP Customizing Implementation Guide > Financial Accounting > Asset Accounting > Depreciation > Valuation Methods > Depreciation Key > Calculation Methods > Define Maximum Amount Methods, or Transaction AFAMH:

i.   On the resulting 'Change View "Maximum Amount Method": Overview' screen, click on 'New Entries'.

ii.   On the next screen (Figure 13.71), enter the identifier for the depreciation key for the new maximum amount method in 'Max. Amt.' field, and provide a 'Description of the Method'. Use the 'Annual' check-box to specify if the maximum amount for depreciation should be based on accumulated depreciation or on annual depreciation; when selected it will be on annual depreciation.

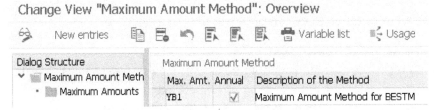

Figure 13.71 New Maximum Amount Method YB1

iii. Now, select the row YB1 and double-click on 'Maximum Amounts' on the left-hand side 'Dialog Structure' and maintain the settings on the next screen (Figure 13.72):

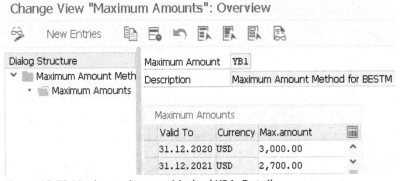

Figure 13.72 Maximum Amount Method YB1: Details

- Enter the 'Valid To' date, enter the 'Currency' and enter the 'Max.amount'. The amount in 'Max.amount' field denotes the maximum amount of depreciation allowed up to the calendar date entered in 'Valid To'. If the depreciation amount is below or equal to this maximum, then, the system posts the calculated value; else, if the system-calculated depreciation amount is above the maximum, then the system posts the fixed maximum entered in this field.

With this, let us move on to understand and maintain the next calculation method, the multi-level method.

13.6.5.1.1.4 Define Multi-Level Methods

In the base methods, for example, in 'stated percentage' method you use a total percentage, throughout the life, to depreciate the asset. But, in a multi-level method, you divide the entire life into different periods (phases) using different calculation keys. A level, in this sense, represents the period of validity of a certain percentage rate. This percentage rate is then replaced by the next percentage rate when the period's validity expires. You will determine the validity period, for the individual levels of a key, by specifying the length of time in years and months. You can specify when the defined validity period begins with the: (a) capitalization date, (b) start date for ordinary or tax depreciation, (c) original acquisition date of the AuC, or (d) the changeover year.

The defined time periods, of a key, always have a common start date. This means that the period from the start of one key to its end will overlap with the next period, which has the same start date but a longer validity period. Therefore, you have to enter the validity periods, for the levels, in cumulative form.

When you use 'Total percentage in concessionary period' as the depreciation calculation method, then, you need to enter the depreciation percentage rate in cumulative form. On the other hand, when using the 'Stated percentage method', you do need not enter the percentage rate in cumulative form (see Table 13.1).

Validity (Absolute) Period in Year	Validity (Cumulative) Period in Year	Total Percentage in Concessionary Period Method (%)	Stated Percentage Method (%)
1	1	40	40
1	2	60	20
1	3	80	20
1	4	90	10
1	5	100	10

Table 13:1 Multi-Level Depreciation Method: Periods and Percentages

Use the menu path: SAP Customizing Implementation Guide > Financial Accounting > Asset Accounting > Depreciation > Valuation Methods > Depreciation Key > Calculation Methods > Define Multi-Level Methods, or Transaction AFAMS. You will see a list of default multi-level calculation methods on the resulting screen (Figure 13.73).

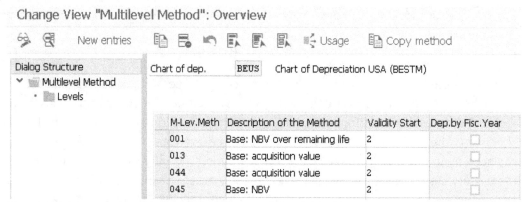

Figure 13.73 Standard Multi-Level Calculation Methods

Project Dolphin

BESTM wants to the project team to define a multi-level depreciation method, with three levels for special depreciation. The three levels will correspond to three periods being first 5 years, next 3 years and the last 2 years. The depreciation percentage for these corresponding phases will need to set at 10%, 7% and 3% respectively.

You may also define your own multi-level methods, if required:

i. Click on 'New Entries' and enter the key (say, YB1) for the new multi-level method ('M-Lev.Meth'), enter the 'Description of the Method' and select a 'Validity Start'; we have selected 3 as BESTM wanted this to be start from the special depreciation. You need to select the 'Dep.by Fisc. Year' check-box, only when the fiscal year end or period ends are different and they depend on the year (Figure 13.74).

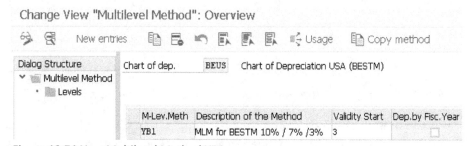

Figure 13.74 New Multilevel Method YB1

ii. Now, select the YB1 row and double-click on 'Levels' on the left-hand side 'Dialog Structure'. On the next screen (Figure 13.75):

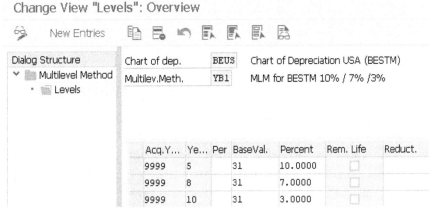

Change View "Levels": Overview

| | New Entries | | | | | | | |

Dialog Structure

- ∨ Multilevel Method
  - Levels

Chart of dep.	BEUS	Chart of Depreciation USA (BESTM)
Multilev.Meth.	YB1	MLM for BESTM 10% / 7% /3%

Acq.Y...	Ye...	Per	BaseVal.	Percent	Rem. Life	Reduct.
9999	5		31	10.0000	☐	
9999	8		31	7.0000	☐	
9999	10		31	3.0000	☐	

Figure 13.75 New Multilevel Method YB1: Details

- Entering 9999 in 'Acq. Year' makes the asset's year of acquisition as valid for ever.
- Specify the validity period, for a percentage rate, in calendar 'Years' field. Enter the 'Years' in cumulative form: for example, if 10% is to be applied for the first 5 years, 7% for the next 3 years, and 3% for the last 2 years, then, for level 1 (first row), the 'Years' entry will be 5, level 2 will be 8 and level 3 will be 10.
- You may specify the validity period ('Per'), in calendar months also.
- Select the appropriate base value 'BaseVal.': 31 represents 'cumulative special depreciation'. Besides the base values supplied by SAP, you can also use your own base value (define this user-specific base value using a customer enhancement). Refer the previous Section 13.6.5.1.1.3, for more details on base value.
- Enter the depreciation percentage in 'Percent' field. Only when you use 'Total percentage in concessionary period' depreciation calculation method, then, you need to enter the rates in cumulative form. Else, you need to enter them in absolute values.
- You need to set 'Rem. Life' flag, only if you want the system to determine the periodic depreciation percentage based on the remaining life, as in the case of depreciation keys wherein the base method makes use of 'percentage from the useful life' depreciation calculation method.
- By using the 'Reduct.' Field, you can reduce the base value for the calculation of depreciation by entering a reduction percentage rate. For example, if you enter 25.0000, then, the system reduces the base value by 25% for that level.

ii. 'Save' the details, when completed.

With this, we are ready, now, to discuss and maintain the last calculation method, namely, period control method.

13.6.5.1.1.5 Maintain Period Control Methods

You can set an appropriate period control in the 'period control method', for determining the depreciation start and end date for asset transactions, for the four transaction categories: acquisitions, subsequent acquisitions/post-capitalization, transfer Postings and retirements. By defining a period control method, you can set the depreciation start date for all acquisitions within the same year to the beginning of the year, for example. You can also set the depreciation start date for retirements to the first or last day of each period. Using the asset value date of a transaction (acquisition or retirement), the system determines the start date or end date of depreciation calculation using the period control.

Use the menu path: SAP Customizing Implementation Guide > Financial Accounting > Asset Accounting > Depreciation > Valuation Methods > Depreciation Key > Calculation Methods > Maintain Period Control Methods, or Transaction AFAMP to view the default methods (Figure 13.76). You may click on 'New Entries' to create new period control methods.

Change View "Period Control": Overview

    New entries   Usage   Copy method

Chart of dep.   **BEUS** Chart of Depreciation USA (BESTM)

Period Control

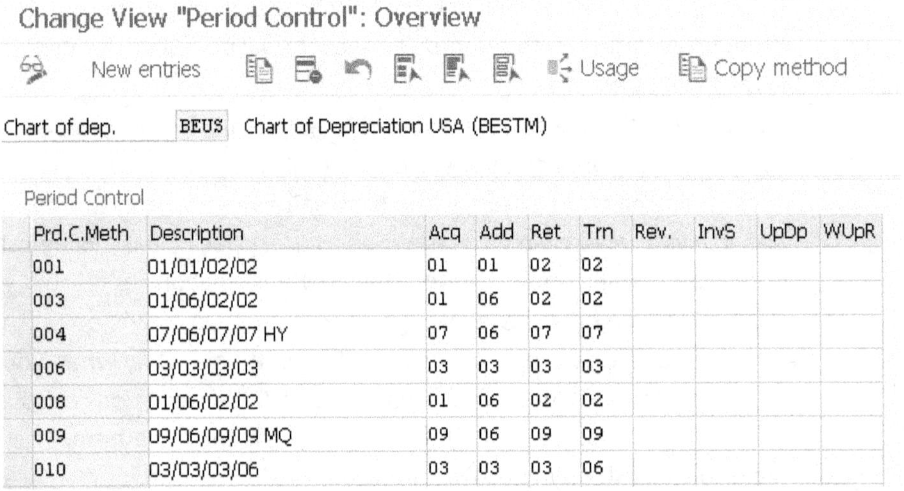

Prd.C.Meth	Description	Acq	Add	Ret	Trn	Rev.	InvS	UpDp	WUpR
001	01/01/02/02	01	01	02	02				
003	01/06/02/02	01	06	02	02				
004	07/06/07/07 HY	07	06	07	07				
006	03/03/03/03	03	03	03	03				
008	01/06/02/02	01	06	02	02				
009	09/06/09/09 MQ	09	06	09	09				
010	03/03/03/06	03	03	03	06				

Figure 13.76 Period Control Methods

Per period control method, you need to select the appropriate start date for the four transaction categories: acquisitions ('Acq'), subsequent acquisitions ('Add') / post-capitalization, transfer Postings ('Trn') and retirements ('Ret'). Consider the period control method 003, where 'asset acquisition' is set for 01 – pro rata at period start date, 'subsequent additions' at 06 – at the start of the year, 'asset retirement' and 'transfer postings' at 02 – pro rata up to mid-period at period start date.

With this, let us understand some of the important depreciation methods, next.

13.6.5.1.2   Depreciation Methods

The depreciation keys, with their calculation methods and parameters, enable representing several depreciation methods in the system. Let us understand the most important depreciation methods, and how the system handles them during depreciation calculation.

- *Straight-Line Depreciation over Total Useful Life*: Here, the system depreciates the asset, uniformly, over the specified useful life of the asset, so that at the end of the life the NBV = 0.

  Depreciation = APC / Expected Useful Life

- *Straight-Line from the Book Value over Remaining Useful Life*: Here, the system distributes the NBV of the fixed asset, uniformly, over the remaining life. This method, unlike straight-line depreciation over total useful life, ensures that post-capitalization and subsequent acquisitions do not lead to an extension of expected useful life.

  Depreciation = NBV / Remaining Life

- *Declining-Balance Method of Depreciation*: Here, the system depreciates the asset by a progressively falling rate. A constant percentage rate is calculated, from the expected useful life and a given multiplication factor, which is multiplied with the falling NBV of the asset. Accordingly, the NBV can never reach zero in this method. Therefore, the system changes the method to straight-line or complete the depreciation under certain conditions when (a) declining-balance method of depreciation < straight-line depreciation or (b) NBV < x percent of acquisition value, or (c) NBV < fixed amount, or NBV < straight-line depreciation, or (d) the changeover method is specified in the internal calculation key. Also refer Section 13.6.5.1.1.2.

  Depreciation = NBV* Percentage Rate from Useful Life and Factor

  > **i** Consider that the asset's APC is 20,000, scrap is estimated at 15% and the useful life is 10 years. Now, the 'Percentage Rate from Useful Life and Factor' is arrived at using the formula = $1 - \{3000/20000\}^{1/10}\} = 17.28\%$

- *Declining Multi-Phase Depreciation:* By specifying rate of depreciation and validity period, you can determine a course of depreciation that changes in levels over time (usually decreasing). The validity period can be based, either on the capitalization date or on the depreciation start date. The change between the levels of depreciation does not have to take place at the start or end of a fiscal year. You can also change to another rate of depreciation during the fiscal year. Also refer Section 13.6.5.1.1.4.

  Depreciation = APC * Percentage Rate of the Level

> **i** Consider an asset with an APC of 10000, and useful life of 20 years. Assume that the useful life has been divided into 4 phases of 5 years each with the depreciation at 10% for years 1-5, 5% for years 6-10, 3% for years 11-15 and 2% for 16-20.

- *Sum-of-the-Years-Digits Method of Depreciation (Digital)*: Here, the total of the remaining life, of an asset, is mapped in each individual year over the entire useful life. The depreciation percentage rate of a fiscal year is then derived from the respective remaining life, divided by this total. The result of this method leads to depreciation amounts that are reduced by the same amount in each period. As the remaining useful life is no longer defined, after the end of the planned useful life, you can no longer depreciate the asset, using this method once the planned useful life has expired. However, you can changeover to another method once the expected useful life is reached.

  Depreciation = APC * Remaining Useful Life (Current Period) / Total of Remaining Useful Life (Over all Periods)

> **i** Consider that the APC of an asset is 10000, and the useful life is 5 years. The sum-of-year-digits = 5+4+3+2+1 = 15. The depreciation of 1st year = 10000*5/15 = 3333, 2nd year = 10000*4/15 = 2667 and so on.

- *Mean Value Method*: You will use this method when you want to have the mean value of two depreciation methods, in a derived depreciation area that links the values of the two depreciation areas. For this, you have to identify the derived depreciation area as a 'mean value area'. Instead of using the arithmetic mean, you can also link the areas proportionally.

  Depreciation = (Depreciation in Area 1) / 2 + (Depreciation in Area 2) / 2

- *Depreciation for Multiple-Shift Operation and Shutdown*: When you use an asset in multiple shifts, then you need to calculate additional or increased depreciation. Likewise, when you shut down an asset, you will not calculate any depreciation on that asset. SAP provides you with the 'Shift Factor' field and the 'Asset shutdown' check-box (in 'Time-dependent' tab) in the asset master record (Figure 13.77) for handling these situations.

  Depreciation Amount = Fixed Depreciation + (Variable Depreciation * Shift Factor)

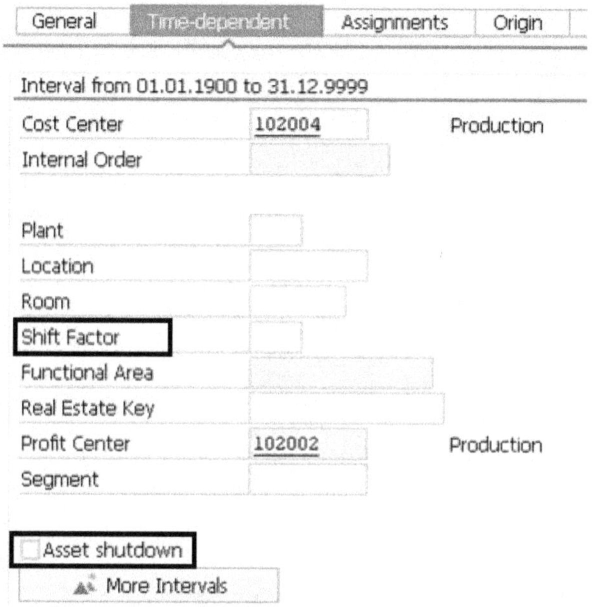

| General | Time-dependent | Assignments | Origin |

Interval from 01.01.1900 to 31.12.9999

Cost Center	102004		Production
Internal Order			
Plant			
Location			
Room			
Shift Factor			
Functional Area			
Real Estate Key			
Profit Center	102002		Production
Segment			

☐ Asset shutdown

⬥ More Intervals

Figure 13.77 Fields for Multiple Shift / Asset Shutdown Specifications

> **i** You can calculate increased depreciation due to multiple-shift operation for all types of depreciation except 'unit-of-production', because the unit-of-production depreciation is by definition 100% variable.

This completes our discussion and maintenance of different calculation / depreciation methods. Let us move on to define the default values.

13.6.5.1.3 Default Values

You can maintain default values for depreciation keys (a) at the level of company codes and depreciation areas, and (b) at the company code level. Let us, first, understand what are the values you can propose as default values for depreciation areas and company codes

13.6.5.1.3.1 Propose Values for Depreciation Areas and Company Codes

You can enter default values, valid for certain company codes and depreciation areas, so as to configure depreciation keys in such a way that the system uses a different interest key or a special treatment of the end of depreciation, for example, in certain specific company codes and depreciation areas. Applicable to depreciation areas that manage interest, the system uses this default interest key if there is no interest method entered in the depreciation key.

Use the menu path: SAP Customizing Implementation Guide > Financial Accounting > Asset Accounting > Depreciation > Valuation Methods > Depreciation Key > Default Values > Propose Values for Depreciation Areas and Company Codes, or Transaction AFAM_093B. On the resulting screen, click on 'New Entries', enter the 'Company Code' and depreciation area ('Deprec. area'). You my maintain the default parameters as required.

Project Dolphin

BESTM requested the project management team not to define default values for the company codes and depreciation areas. Also, BESTM does not want to impose the condition that the acquisitions are allowed only in the year in which depreciation started.

The system uses these default values only if you explicitly set 'Default value from company code' in the depreciation key or 'Default value from company code and depreciation area' in the base method of depreciation calculation (Figure 13.78).

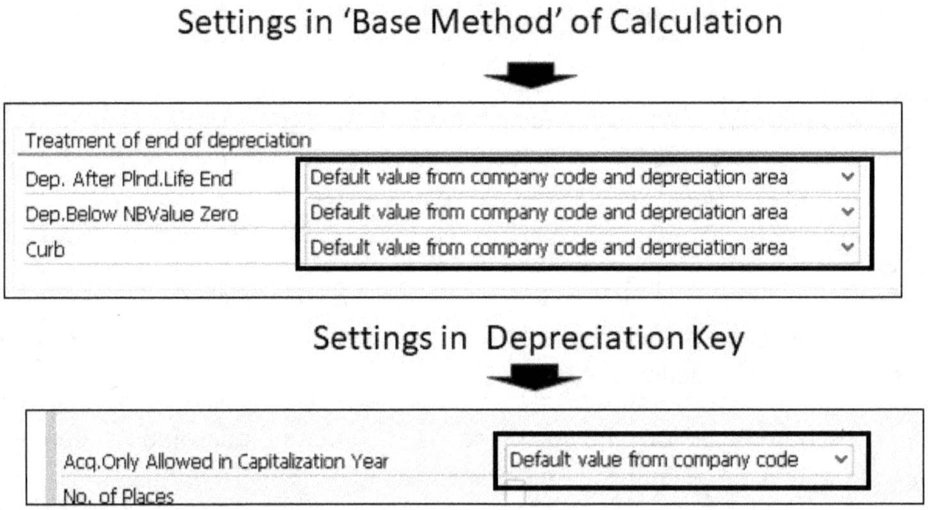

Settings in 'Base Method' of Calculation

Treatment of end of depreciation	
Dep. After Plnd.Life End	Default value from company code and depreciation area ⌄
Dep.Below NBValue Zero	Default value from company code and depreciation area ⌄
Curb	Default value from company code and depreciation area ⌄

Settings in Depreciation Key

Acq.Only Allowed in Capitalization Year	Default value from company code ⌄
No. of Places	

Figure 13.78 Default Value Settings in Base Method of Calculation / Depreciation Key

You can also make default settings at the company code level so that the system proposes acquisition in capitalization year, for the company codes.

13.6.5.1.3.2 Propose Acquisition Only in Capitalization Year for Company Codes
Here, you set, as a default, for certain company codes that acquisitions in this company code are only allowed in the year in which depreciation started. This setting may be necessary for technical reasons, for example, if you use sum-of-the-years-digits depreciation method. It is also possible to use this function for organizational purposes. The system uses these default values only if you explicitly set 'Default value from company code' in the depreciation key (Figure 13.78).

Before we move on to define the depreciation keys, let us understand how to handle scrap / cutoff value in the system

13.6.5.1.4 Scrap Value / Cutoff Value

You may come across situations wherein it may be necessary not to depreciate till the asset's NBV = 0, but only up to a pre-determined value which is known as a 'scrap value' or 'cutoff value'. You can manage scrap value in two ways:

i. By entering a scrap value in percentage (using the 'cutoff value key') in the depreciation key (Figure 13.79) used in the depreciation area, or

Figure 13.79 Cutoff Value Key in Depreciation Key

ii. By entering an absolute 'scrap value' in the asset master data for the depreciation area (in the detail screen) as shown in Figure 13.80. When you maintain the scrap value in absolute terms, either in the form of percentage and/or amount, in the asset master, note that the system does not depreciate this amount. When you specify both, the system uses the percentage by default.

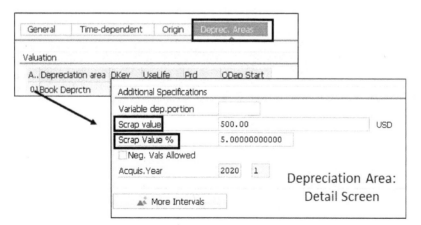

Figure 13.80 Entering Scrap Value in Asset Master

> **i** SAP recommends that you enter scrap value as a percentage, in the asset master per depreciation area.

If you have defined a cutoff value key and also have entered the scrap value in the asset master, then, the system ignores the cutoff value percentage of the key, and treats the amount entered in the asset master record as the scrap value (refer Section 13.5.2.4).

Let us understand how to define the cutoff value key.

13.6.5.1.4.1 Define the Cutoff Value Key

Here, you define the 'cutoff value' calculation key for automatically determining scrap values. For each calculation key, you can specify:

- The percentage of the depreciation base that should be used as the cutoff value percentage.
- Whether the cutoff value percentage should be deducted at the start or the end of the calculation of depreciation.
- At what point in time the system should start calculating the validity period.

You can maintain several cutoff percentages for each cutoff value key. You can define the cutoff percentages/levels per acquisition year, and the validity period can be of any length. You have to enter the validity period of the individual percentages or levels of a scrap value key in cumulative form.

Use the menu path: SAP Customizing Implementation Guide > Financial Accounting > Asset Accounting > Depreciation > Valuation Methods > Further Settings > Define the Cutoff Value Key, or Transaction ANHAL. You will see, on the resulting screen, the standard cutoff value keys defined in the system (Figure 13.81).

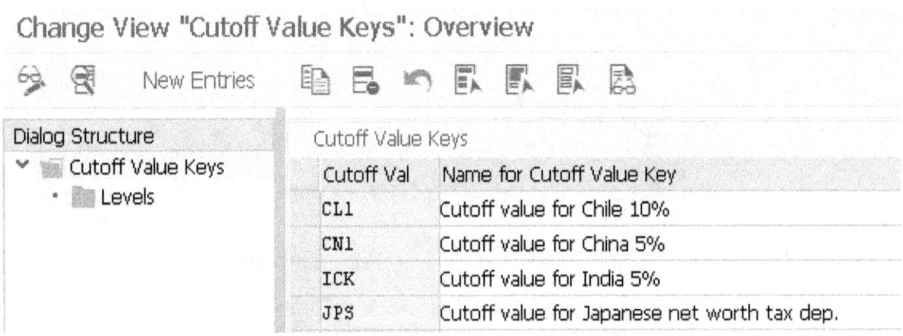

Change View "Cutoff Value Keys": Overview

Cutoff Val	Name for Cutoff Value Key
CL1	Cutoff value for Chile 10%
CN1	Cutoff value for China 5%
ICK	Cutoff value for India 5%
JPS	Cutoff value for Japanese net worth tax dep.

Figure 13.81 Standard Cutoff Value Keys

You may double-click on a row to see the settings for that cutoff value key (Figure 13.82). Depending on the settings, the system deducts the scrap value from the base value of the asset, with the start of date calculation being the asset capitalisation date or start of ordinary depreciation or start of special depreciation or original acquisition date for AuC.

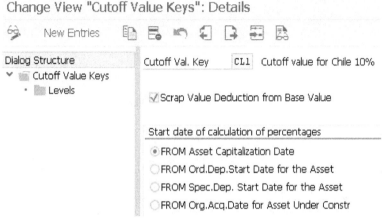

Figure 13.82 Standard Cutoff Value Key CL1 - Details

You can double-click on 'Levels' on the left-hand side 'Dialog Structure' and see the settings associated with the levels (Figure 13.83). What you see is the default entries by SAP; you can customize this to suit your own needs.

Figure 13.83 Standard Cutoff Value Key CL1 - Levels

Project Dolphin

BESTM has decided to have a cutoff value key defined for depreciating vehicles with 10 year validity. The scrap value percentage will vary at 5% for the first 5 years, 3% for the next 3 years and 2% for the last 2 years. The scrap value needs to be deducted from the base value and the start of calculation will be from the asset capitalization date.

You can define your own cutoff values keys, by clicking on 'New Entries' on the initial screen, and maintaining the appropriate validity in cumulative period (years). You can have different cutoff percentages for different levels, with each level defined in cumulative years. Consider

BESTM's requirement as an example wherein you want to define a cutoff value key for depreciating assets with a validity period of 10 years, with three different percentages: 5%, 3% and 2%. In this case, you may define a scenario like the one depicted in Figure 13.84.

Figure 13.84 New Cutoff Value Key YB1 – Multiple Levels

With this, we are now ready to discuss how to define the depreciation keys.

13.6.5.1.5   Maintain Depreciation Key

We have discussed the depreciation key, in detail, in Section 13.6.5.1. Use this configuration activity, to maintain the required depreciation keys and assign the appropriate calculation methods to them.

> ℹ️ We recommend using the standard pre-defined depreciation keys (like LINS – Straight line over remaining life pro rata to zero, M150 - MACRS 15, 20 years property, CWG - LVA 100 % Complete write off etc) that are designed to meet country-specific depreciation needs.

Project Dolphin

BESTM has decided to make use of the standard depreciation keys that are pre-defined in the system. However, while handling multiple shift operations, it needs to be configured that the result is increased depreciation / expired useful life. Also, there need not be any stopping of depreciation during asset shutdown.

Use the menu path: SAP Customizing Implementation Guide > Financial Accounting > Asset Accounting > Depreciation > Valuation Methods > Depreciation Key > Maintain Depreciation Key, or Transaction AFAMA. You will see, for the given chart of accounts (BEUS), the system supplied default depreciation keys on the resulting screen (Figure 13.85).

Figure 13.85 Maintaining Depreciation Keys – List of Standard Keys

You may double-click on any of the keys (say, LINS), to see the detailed settings (Figure 13.86).

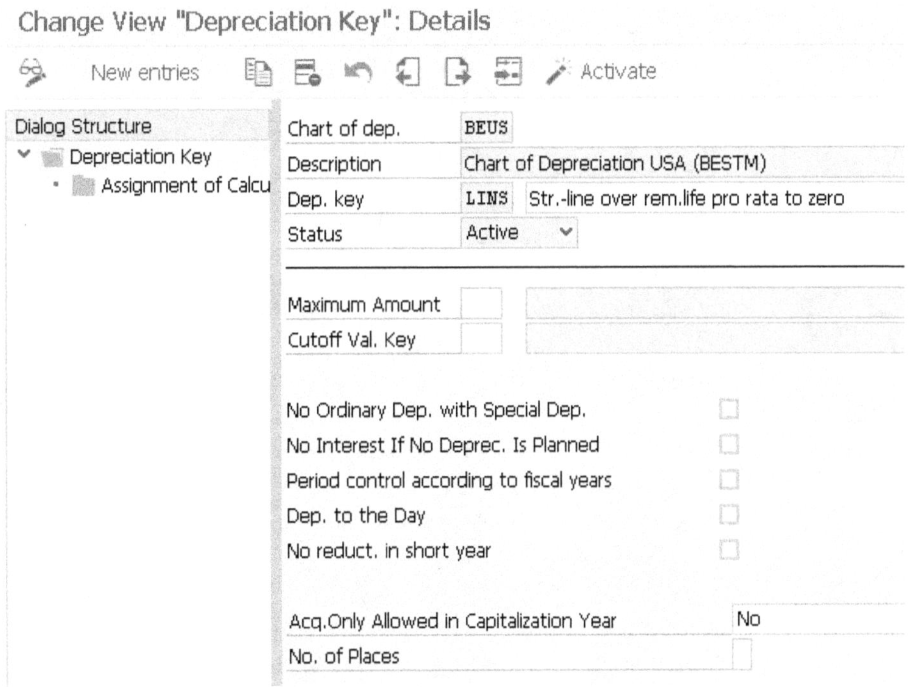

Figure 13.86 Maintaining Depreciation Key LINS – Initial Configuration

On the next screen, you will see the 'Status' of the depreciation key. It can have one of three statuses: (a) 'Active': the depreciation key has no errors, and can be used in asset master records, (b) 'Inactive': either the depreciation key or one of its calculation methods has errors, you cannot use the key and (c) 'Migrated': the depreciation key has been migrated from the old table to the new table; the old depreciation key is still valid. Let us look at other fields:

i.   You will use the 'Maximum Amount' field to enter the appropriate maximum amount method's depreciation key for calculating depreciation or imputed interest.

ii. You may enter the appropriate 'Cutoff Val. Key', if required, for controlling the calculation of the cutoff value for depreciation.

iii. You may maintain the other control parameters, if required, for the various check-boxes like 'No Ordinary Dep. with Special Dep.', 'Dep. to the Day' etc.

iv. Enter the 'No. of Places', for rounding off the percentage rates internally, to the number of decimal places that you enter here. The standard setting for this field is 0 or blank: the system calculates with 10 decimal places.

Now, double-click on 'Assignment of Calculation Methods' on the left-hand side 'Dialog Structure'. Click on 'New Entries' and maintain the settings (Figure 13.87), on the next screen:

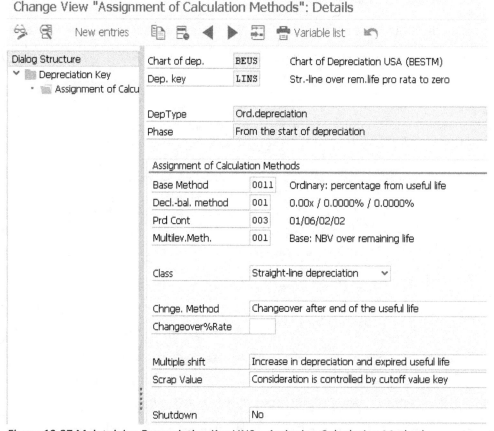

Figure 13.87 Maintaining Depreciation Key LINS – Assigning Calculation Methods

i.   Note that the system defaults to 'Ord.depreciation' in 'DepType' field and to 'From the start of depreciation' for the 'Phase' field. You will use 'Phase' to configure the system appropriately, when you divide the duration of depreciation into several phases, during each of which the depreciation key uses different calculation methods for calculating depreciation. You have three options like 'from the start of the depreciation', or 'changeover with planned life' or 'changeover after end of the useful life'.

ii.   Under 'Assignment of Calculation Methods':

- Maintain the appropriate calculation methods in 'Base Methods', 'Decl.-bal. Method'. 'Prd. Cont' and 'Multilev.Method' that we have defined earlier in 'Calculation Methods' Section 13.6.5.1.1.

- Enter appropriate classification of ordinary depreciation in the 'Class' field.

- Enter a changeover method, if required in 'Chnge.Method' and also maintain the changeover rate in 'Changeover%Rate' field.

- Select the appropriate value for 'Multiple shift'.

- Enter how the system handles the 'Scrap Value'. Refer to the previous Section 13.6.5.1.4, for more details on scrap value / cutoff value.

- If you do not want the system to calculate depreciation during asset shutdown, enter 'Yes' in the 'Shutdown' field. We have entered 'No' as we do not want to halt the depreciation during asset shutdown for BESTM. By specifying shutdown periods when maintaining the asset master record, you ensure that depreciation is suspended during the shutdown periods.

iii.   'Save' the details when completed.

Repeat the steps and maintain the settings for other required depreciation keys.

This completes our discussion on valuation methods, and the settings required to configure the same. Let us now understand the Depreciation Calculation Program (DCP) in the next Section.

13.6.5.2   Depreciation Calculation Program

The 'Depreciation Calculation Program' (DCP) is a back-end solution that does not require any special or extra configuration. However, you can the SAP-provided Business Add Ins (BAdI) to modify the calculation of values.

The DCP is made up two components (Figure 13.88):

- An external component, that is application-specific (business-oriented).
- An internal component, ('Evaluation Engine'), which controls the calculation logic for depreciation calculations.

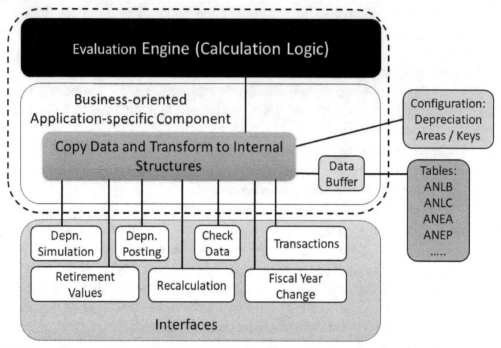

Figure 13.88 Depreciation Calculation Program (DCP)

The *'business oriented, application-specific external component'* provides an interface to other applications. It transfers asset master data and transaction data to internal work structures, besides grouping transactions together, based on calculation periods. It reads all configuration settings needed for the depreciation calculation, and transfers them to internal work structures. It specifies the depreciation start date and updates the total asset values.

The internal *'Evaluation Engine'* is based on the work structures created by the application-specific part of the program. It calculates replacement values, depreciation, and interest, as well as revaluation (both upward and downward) as part of an automatic calculation of inflation. It determines the base value or net value, as well as the shutdown value of the assets besides correcting the values and amounts when derived depreciation areas are used.

The DCP, now, provides the following new and improved functions for calculating depreciation, under the following functionality groups:

A. *Period-Based Calculation*
   - The calculation of depreciation is now based on periods, instead of individual transactions, as it was previously. Now, the system groups the transactions for an asset together by the calculation period.

- o The system uses the asset value date and the period control group of the transaction type group to determine the calculation period. The system assigns each transaction to a calculation period.
  - Then, the system creates period intervals from the calculation periods that are determined. Based on these intervals, the system calculates the depreciation.

B. *Time-Dependent Depreciation Terms*

Now, you can make 'time-dependent changes to depreciation terms' (that include useful life, depreciation key, scrap value, scrap value percentage, and variable depreciation portion) in the asset master data. The changes to the depreciation terms become effective on the key date that you specify for the given depreciation area. A mid-year change to depreciation terms, causes the system to set up new calculation period intervals.

C. *Mid-year, Period-Dependent Changeover*

With the new depreciation calculation, you have new options for changeover of the depreciation method. Instead annual changeover, you can, now, specify a mid-year automatic changeover of the depreciation method. The system uses the UMPER field in table ANLB for this function. To make use of this mid-year changeover, you need to use the FAA_DC_CUSTOMER BAdI (method: DEFINE_USE_OF_MAX_PERIODS), and set the CB_USE_MAX_PERIODS parameter to X.

With this, we can, now, move on to discuss the special valuations, in the next Section.

13.7 Special Valuations

Use 'special valuations' for special value adjustments to assets (like, investment support, special depreciation reserves etc) and for meeting some of the special valuation purposes, like, cost-accounting replacement values, interest, revaluation for the balance sheet etc.

Using special valuations, you can take care of:

- Special Reserves
- Transferred Reserves
- Investment Support
- Revaluation of Fixed Assets
- Interest
- Net Worth Tax
- Preparations for Consolidation
- Leasing Processing

Let us start with the special reserves.

13.7.1 Special Reserves

You are allowed to use tax valuation approaches, in some of the countries, in the B/S. That being the case, you should make it possible for the person looking at the B/S, to know, that a different approach was used in depreciation calculation. Hence, you carry out both book depreciation and tax depreciation (which exceeds book depreciation) and show the difference as 'special reserves' on the liabilities side of the B/S. Showing the difference between book depreciation and tax depreciation, in a derived depreciation area, you can use the values from this derived area to create special depreciation reserves for the B/S.

To configure the system to handle special reserves, you need to complete the following steps:

- Specify Gross or Net Procedure
- Assign Accounts

Let us understand how to specify gross or net procedure.

13.7.1.1   Specify Gross or Net Procedure

You need to determine, using this configuration step, if you want the system to balance the amounts from the allocation and writing off of special reserves on the same asset in the same posting run against each other (net procedure).

Project Dolphin

In the case of special reserves, BESYM has asked the project team to configure the system, to use the net procedure, so that it posts the allocation amounts and write-off amounts, for the same asset, offsetting against each other instead of the gross method.

Use the menu path: SAP Customizing Implementation Guide > Financial Accounting > Asset Accounting > Special Valuations > Special Reserves > Specify Gross or Net Procedure, or you may use Transaction OAYQ.

On the resulting screen, select the appropriate company code (say, 1110) and double-click on 'Net reserve for special depreciation' on the left-hand side 'Dialog Structure'. On the next screen, against the appropriate depreciation area(s), select the 'Net' check-box indicating that the system will post allocation amounts and write-off amounts, for the same asset, offsetting against each other instead of the 'gross' method (in which the system allocates special depreciation amount to the reserves and writes off the balance of ordinary depreciation of the two depreciation areas).

The next step is to assign the G/L accounts, to handle special reserves.

13.7.1.2   Assign Accounts

Use this activity, to determine the G/L accounts for the write-off or allocation of special reserves.

If you enter gain/loss accounts for a depreciation area, the system does not post any revenue from the write-off of special items for reserve. Instead, the system includes that revenue, resulting from an asset sale, in the calculation of gain/loss itself. The system, then, balances the loss in the book depreciation area against an offsetting posting, and posts the total or the difference (between the write-off of special items for reserve and the book loss) to these accounts.

Use the menu path: SAP Customizing Implementation Guide > Financial Accounting > Asset Accounting > Special Valuations > Special Reserves > Assign Accounts, or Transaction AO99.

On the resulting screen, select the chart of accounts (say, BEUS), and double-click on 'Account Determination' on the left-hand side 'Dialog Structure'. On the next screen (Figure 13.89), select the required 'Account Determination' (say, B2000) and double-click on 'Special Reserves' on the left-hand side 'Dialog Structure' and enter the appropriate G/L accounts, on the next screen, for the required depreciation areas, under 'Special Reserve Balance', 'Allocation to Special Reserves (Expenses)', and 'Write-off Special Reserves after Retirement' data blocks.

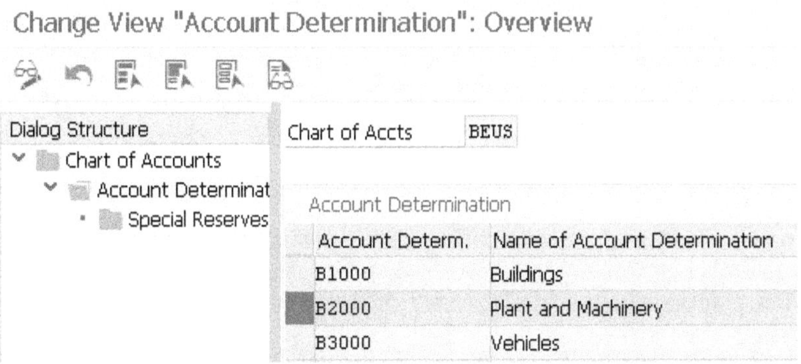

Change View "Account Determination": Overview

Dialog Structure	Chart of Accts	BEUS	
∨ Chart of Accounts			
∨ Account Determinat	Account Determination		
• Special Reserves	Account Determ.	Name of Account Determination	
	B1000	Buildings	
	B2000	Plant and Machinery	
	B3000	Vehicles	

Figure 13.89 Configuring Account Determination for Special Reserves

This completes our discussion on special reserves. We can move on to discuss the settings required for transferred reserves.

13.7.2 Transferred Reserves

The tax legislation, of many countries, allows you to transfer the entire undisclosed reserves or a part thereof, created by the sale of assets, to replacement acquisitions. The gain on the sale, then, reduces the depreciation base of the newly acquired assets. If you cannot transfer such undisclosed reserves, in the year they are formed because there are no suitable new acquisitions, you can set up a reserve in the year in question to prevent the gain on the sale influencing your profit. You can transfer these reserves, in the next few years, to assets acquired during this time period.

Here, you define the configuration settings that are necessary for transfer of reserves (also called as transferred reserves, undisclosed reserves, deferred gain, balancing charges) to newly acquired fixed assets.

The first activity is to determine the depreciation areas for enabling transfer of reserves.

13.7.2.1   Determine Depreciation Areas

Use the menu path: SAP Customizing Implementation Guide > Financial Accounting > Asset Accounting > Special Valuations > Transferred Reserves > Determine Depreciation Areas, or Transaction OABM. On the resulting screen, select the 'Res.' Check box against the appropriate depreciations area(s). These are all the areas into which you will transfer reserves for fixed assets.

The next activity is to assign the relevant G/L accounts.

13.7.2.2   Assign Accounts

Use the menu path: SAP Customizing Implementation Guide > Financial Accounting > Asset Accounting > Special Valuations > Transferred Reserves > Assign Accounts, or Transaction AO96. On the resulting screen, for the given chart of accounts, select the 'Account Determination' and double-click on 'Reserves' on the left-hand side 'Dialog Structure'. On the next screen, per depreciation area, enter the relevant G/L account for value adjustment of transfer of reserves, for the contra account etc, under the 'Account assignment for transfer of reserves' data block.

The third and final step is to define the transaction types of transfer of reserves.

13.7.2.3   Define Transaction Types for Transfer of Reserves

You have to transfer reserves in FI-AA using manual posting. Here, in this activity, you can define transaction types for the transfer of reserves. In fact, you do not need to define any new transaction type, but use the SAP supplied transaction types 680 / 690.

Project Dolphin

The project team has suggested to the BESTM management to use the SAP supplied standard transaction types for handling transfer of reserves in FI-AA.

Use the menu path: SAP Customizing Implementation Guide > Financial Accounting > Asset Accounting > Special Valuations > Transferred Reserves > Define Transaction Types for Transfer of Reserves, or Transaction AO80. On the resulting screen, you shall see the standard transaction types from SAP, for transfer of reserves to current / previous year acquisitions (Figure 13.90).

Change View "FI-AA: Transaction types": Overview

New Entries

Transact. type	Transaction Type Name
680	Transfer of reserves to prior-year acquisitions
690	Transfer of reserves to curr-yr acquis.

Figure 13.90 Transaction Types for Transfer of Reserves

With this, we are, now, ready to discuss revaluation of fixed assets.

13.7.3 Revaluation of Fixed Assets

It may be required that you need to revalue your fixed assets either to compensate for inflation or to account for the changed replacement values to meet (a) management accounting requirements and/or (b) tax obligations. Using an index series, you can periodically revalue assets' APC and cumulative value adjustments, to arrive at the 'indexed replacement values'. Or, you can carry out revaluation for balance sheet (B/S) once every few years. Let us understand more about these two valuations:

1) *Indexed Replacement Values*

   Using index series, you can automatically account for periodic changes in the value of the assets. When the system posts the depreciation, these changes get reflected in the specific asset (or asset class). The indexed replacement value is influenced by (a) the replacement value of an asset changes due to inflation and/or (b) technical progress resulting in changed price for an appropriate replacement acquisition. Accordingly, you can specify two index series to cover these two situations, for each asset, for determining replacement value in FI-AA. The system, then, determines the replacement value by multiplying the index figures in the two index series.

2) *Revaluation for the Balance Sheet*

   You may need to carry out a single revaluation of the entire fixed asset portfolio, at intervals of every few years. Also known as '*B/S revaluation*', this enables you to comply with the country's tax requirements for a single revaluation of all fixed assets to offset the effects of inflation. The system does not calculate this single revaluation automatically; you need to define and carry that out manually. Of course, you can use collective processing to carry out this revaluation.

Though you can manage revaluation values in any depreciation area, you must be able to separately identify such changes in value, to meet the country's legal requirements. In this case, you must use a separate depreciation area for each revaluation.

With this, let us look at the configuration settings required for revaluation of fixed assets.

13.7.3.1   Maintain Accounts for Revaluation

Here, you will specify the G/L accounts for changes to APC or accumulated depreciation due to revaluation, in order to determine the asset replacement value.

Use the menu path: SAP Customizing Implementation Guide > Financial Accounting > Asset Accounting > Special Valuations > Revaluation of Fixed Assets > Maintain Accounts for Revaluation:

i.   On the resulting pop-up screen, enter the chart of depreciation (BEUS), and select the chart of accounts (BEUS) on the next screen.

ii.   Double-click on 'Account Determination' on the left-hand side 'Dialog Structure' and select an 'Account Determination' (say, B2000).

iii.   Now, select the depreciation area ('Area') on the resulting screen and double-click on 'Revaluation of APC' on the left-hand side 'Dialog Structure', and maintain the required G/L account on the next screen.

iv.   Similarly, double-click on 'Revaluation of Depreciation' on the left-hand side 'Dialog Structure', and maintain the required G/L account on the next screen, for same account determination.

v.   Repeat and maintain the settings for all the required asset determinations.

13.7.3.2   Revaluation for the Balance Sheet

SAP offers two ways of for carrying out the revaluation for B/S:

1)   For a *'one-time revaluation'*, you need to configure the system using the IMG node 'Revaluation for the Balance Sheet' but without carrying out the transaction in the 'Inflation Accounting' node.

   To execute one-time revaluation, use the SAP Easy Access menu path: SAP Menu > Accounting > Financial Accounting > Fixed Assets > Periodic Processing > Revaluation for the Balance Sheet > Post Revaluation and New Valuation, or Transaction AR29N.

2)   For *'periodic revaluation'*, you need to configure all the nodes under 'Revaluation for the Balance Sheet' including the IMG node 'Inflation Accounting'.

To execute periodic revaluation, use the SAP Easy Access menu path: SAP Menu > Accounting > Financial Accounting > Fixed Assets > Periodic Processing > Revaluation for the Balance Sheet > Inflation, or Transaction J1AI.

Let us, now, look at the configuration settings for revaluation for the B/S. The first task is to determine the depreciation areas for this purpose.

13.7.3.2.1   Determine Depreciation Areas

Use the menu path: SAP Customizing Implementation Guide > Financial Accounting > Asset Accounting > Special Valuations > Revaluation of Fixed Assets > Revaluation for the Balance Sheet > Determine Depreciation Areas, to specify the depreciation areas in which you want to manage revaluation of fixed assets. You may also use Transaction OABW.

Project Dolphin

BESTM, while configuring the depreciation area for revaluation of fixed assets, wants only the APC to be revalued but not the accumulated depreciation that had been debited to the asset in the earlier years.

On the resulting screen (Figure 13.91), select the 'RevlAPC' and/or 'RevlDep' check-boxes against the depreciation area (say, 20 – cost accounting depreciation) wherein you want to manage the revaluation. You will select the 'RevlDep' check-box, if you want the system to use not only the APC, when determining the replacement value, but to also revalue the value adjustments made to the asset, in the past; else, you will select only the "RevlAPC' check-box.

Change View "Asset Accounting: Management of replacement values": Over

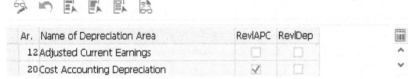

Ar.	Name of Depreciation Area	RevlAPC	RevlDep
12	Adjusted Current Earnings	☐	☐
20	Cost Accounting Depreciation	☑	☐

Figure 13.91 Depreciation Area for Revaluation of Assets

The next step is to define the revaluation measures.

13.7.3.2.2   Define Revaluation Measures

Here, you define the revaluation measures like the key, description, depreciation areas and posting data in the system. Besides the revaluation measures, you also need a special depreciation area for each revaluation. While making the required settings, you need to create the calculation rule for the revaluation using a user exit and include the calculation rule in the function module 'EXIT_RAAUFW01_001'.

Use the report RAAUFW02 ('Post Revaluation and New Valuation'), to carry out the revaluation. The report determines the posted depreciation, writes it back, and posts the required adjustment to the net book value (NBV) for both individual and mass revaluations. You can also use this report to update a nominated evaluation group/user field with a specified characteristic, such as revaluation year, for reporting purposes.

Project Dolphin

The revaluation of fixed assets for balance sheet purposes, will happen on 31st December, every five years, starting with 31-Dec-2020. The revaluation IDs will be numbered serially and the revaluation will be handled in the cost accounting depreciation area.

Use the menu path: SAP Customizing Implementation Guide > Financial Accounting > Asset Accounting > Special Valuations > Revaluation of Fixed Assets > Revaluation for the Balance Sheet > Define Revaluation Measures, or Transaction AUFW:

i.   Enter the chart of depreciation (BEUS) on the resulting pop-up screen, and 'Continue'.

ii.   On the resulting 'Change View "Revaluation Measures": Overview' screen, click on 'New Entries'.

iii. On the next screen (Figure 13.92), enter the 'Revaluation' ID (say,1) and provide the description. Under 'Date specifications', specify the date on which the system posts the one-time revaluation to fixed assets. The system uses this date as the posting date in FI and as the asset value date in FI-AA.

iv.   Enter the 'Area specifications': enter the 'Base Area' (01) that provides the APC and also the 'Revaluation Area' (20), and 'Save' the settings.

Figure 13.92 Specifying Revaluation Measures

The next and final task in configuring the settings for revaluation for balance sheet is to define the transaction types for asset revaluation.

13.7.3.2.3   Define Transaction Types for Revaluation

Use the menu path: SAP Customizing Implementation Guide > Financial Accounting > Asset Accounting > Special Valuations > Revaluation of Fixed Assets > Revaluation for the Balance Sheet > Define Transaction Types for Revaluation:

Project Dolphin

BESTM does not want to create any new transaction types for handling asset revaluations in the system. They have decided to use SAP supplied standard transaction types, instead.

i.   On the resulting 'Select Activity' pop-up screen, double-click on 'Define Transaction Types for Revaluation'.

ii. On the resulting screen (use Transaction AO84 to reach here, directly), you will see a list of standard transaction types that are available as default (Figure 13.93). You do not need to define anything new, and can use the appropriate standard transaction types.

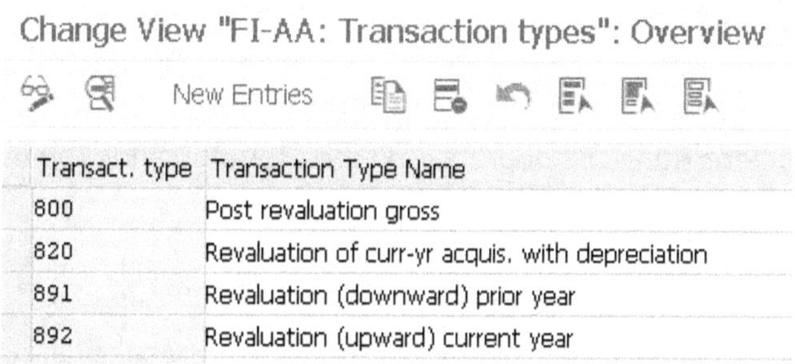

Change View "FI-AA: Transaction types": Overview

Transact. type	Transaction Type Name
800	Post revaluation gross
820	Revaluation of curr-yr acquis. with depreciation
891	Revaluation (downward) prior year
892	Revaluation (upward) current year

Figure 13.93 Standard Transaction Types for Asset Revaluation

iii. Now, go back to the initial 'Select Activity' pop-up screen, and double-click on 'Limit Transaction Types to Depreciation Areas'.

iv. On the resulting 'Change View "Transaction type selection": Overview' screen (you may use Transaction OAXJ to come to this screen directly), select a transaction type (say, 800) and double-click on 'Depreciation area specification' on the left-hand side 'Dialog Structure'.

v.   On the next screen, select the depreciation area (say, 20) and 'Save'. Essentially, you use this step to restrict certain transaction types to certain depreciation areas, if required.

This completes our discussion on revaluation of fixed assets. Let us discuss, the settings required for interest, in the next Section.

13.7.4 Interest

You may need to calculate (imputed) interest on the capital tied up in assets, for cost accounting purposes. In FI-AA, you can calculate this interest, per depreciation area, in addition to ordinary depreciation, special depreciation, unplanned depreciation etc.

The system calculates the interest, as that of automatically calculated depreciation, using the calculation method in a depreciation key. The account assignment is to the G/L accounts that you specify for interest in the respective account determination/depreciation area. In addition, you can make an additional assignment to the cost center of the respective asset, if required.

The calculation of interest to be posted, depends mainly on the base value of the interest key: if the key uses the current net book value (NBV) as the base value, for example, then, the system takes this NBV into account to the exact period during depreciation posting. The system calculates the interest either until book value = 0, or up to the end of expected useful life, or for an unlimited period. And, it then posts interest together with depreciation when you perform a periodic depreciation posting run.

Let us configure the system for calculating interest on the fixed assets. As in the previous Sections, the first step is to determine the depreciation area for managing the interest.

13.7.4.1   Determine Depreciation Areas

The interest calculation, in general, in most of the countries, is allowed only for cost accounting purposes. Here, in this step, you will make the necessary specification to denote a cost account depreciation area for managing interest.

Project Dolphin

As in practice, the interest calculated on the capital tied up on fixed assets needs to be managed in the cost accounting depreciation area, 20 in the case of BESTM.

Use the menu path: SAP Customizing Implementation Guide > Financial Accounting > Asset Accounting > Special Valuations > Revaluation of Fixed Assets > Interest > Determine Depreciation Areas, or Transaction OABZ.

On the resulting screen, select the 'Int.' check-box against the cost accounting depreciation area (20) for the chart of depreciation, BEUS (Figure 13.94).

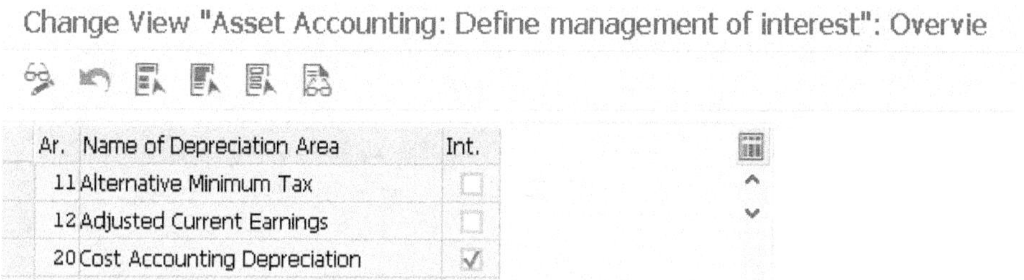

Change View "Asset Accounting: Define management of interest": Overvie

Ar.	Name of Depreciation Area	Int.	
11	Alternative Minimum Tax	☐	
12	Adjusted Current Earnings	☐	
20	Cost Accounting Depreciation	✓	

Figure 13.94 Depreciation Area for Managing Interest

The next activity is to assign the appropriate G/L accounts to manage interest.

13.7.4.2   Assign Accounts

Use the menu path: SAP Customizing Implementation Guide > Financial Accounting > Asset Accounting > Special Valuations > Revaluation of Fixed Assets > Interest > Assign Accounts, or Transaction AO98:

i. Select the chart of depreciation (say, BEUS), on the resulting screen and double-click on 'Account Determination' on the left-hand side 'Dialog Structure'.

ii. Select an 'Account Determination' (say, B3000 – Vehicles) and double-click on 'Interest' on the left-hand side 'Dialog Structure'.

iii. Now, select the depreciation area on the next screen, and enter the G/L accounts in 'Expense account for interest' (say, 71100400) and 'Clearing interest posting' (contra account) fields under 'Interest account assignment' data block on the next screen. 'Save' the details.

iv. Repeat and maintain the required accounts for all the other account determinations.

The last configuration activity for interest determination, is to define the required depreciation key.

13.7.4.3   Maintain Depreciation Key

You may use the menu path: SAP Customizing Implementation Guide > Financial Accounting > Asset Accounting > Special Valuations > Revaluation of Fixed Assets > Interest > Maintain Depreciation Key, or Transaction AFAMA, to make the required specifications for interest calculation in a depreciation key.

This is exactly similar to the configuration step ('Maintain Depreciation Key') that we have discussed in <u>Section 13.6.5.1.5</u>. Here, for a given, depreciation key, in the 'DepType', you will select 'Interest', instead of any other values ('ordinary depreciation' or 'special depreciation'). Besides, you also need to assign the appropriate calculation method for 'Base Method' (say, 0029) and other calculation methods (Figure 13.95).

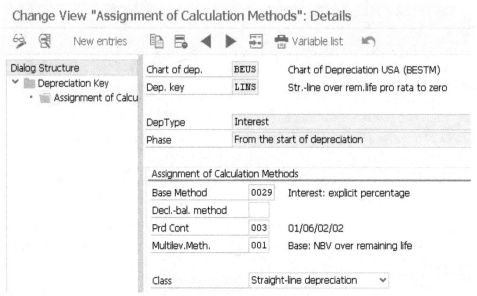

Figure 13.95 Depreciation Key for Interest Calculation - Details

Once defined and activated, the overview screen will show this depreciation key for interest calculation with the appropriate calculation methods already assigned. (Figure 13.96).

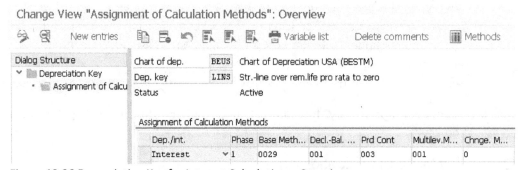

Figure 13.96 Depreciation Key for Interest Calculation – Overview

This completes our discussion on configuring the system for interest calculation. Let us now understand the settings required for legal consolidation, from asset accounting side.

13.7.5 Preparations for Consolidation

These settings, for preparation for consolidation from asset accounting side, mostly concern the features of transaction types, besides specifying the depreciation areas for handling legal consolidation.

Let us start with the consolidation transaction types of APC transactions.

13.7.5.1   Specify Consolidation Transaction Types for APC Transactions

Here, you can group FI-AA transaction types together for legal consolidation. You can make this grouping by assigning a common transaction type to all FI-AA transaction types in a transaction category, for consolidation purposes. This consolidation transaction type is generally the FI-AA transaction type used for the corresponding transaction category.

SAP supplied transaction types will be adequate to meet your business needs. And, you just need to go ahead with the default grouping of the consolidation transaction types; there is, in general, no need to define your own grouping.

Use the menu path: SAP Customizing Implementation Guide > Financial Accounting > Asset Accounting > Special Valuations > Revaluation of Fixed Assets > Preparations for Consolidation > Specify Consolidation Transaction Types for APC Transactions.

On the resulting screen (Figure 13.97), you will notice the standard transaction types that are already categorised into consolidation transaction types ('Cons TType'). For example, the consolidation transaction type 900 denotes 'opening balance', 920 indicates 'increase/ purchase', 930 'decrease /disposal' etc.

Change View "Asset transaction types -> Consolidation": Overview

Trans. Type	Transaction Type Name	Cons TType
1A1	CYr Acq: Accum APC, Acq Not Affect P&L	920
1A2	PYr Acq, Aff.Comp: Accum APC, Acq Not Affect ...	920
1A3	CYr Acq, Aff.Comp: Accum APC, Acq Not Affect ...	920
1W0	PYr Acq: Accum Depr, Acq Not Affect P&L	900
1W1	CYr Acq: Accum Depr, Acq Not Affect P&L	900
1W2	PYr Acq, Aff.Comp: Accum Depr, Acq Not Affect...	900
1W3	CYr Acq, Aff.Comp: Accum Depr, Acq Not Affect...	900
200	Retirement without revenue	930
201	Retirement due to catastrophe, without revenue	930

Figure 13.97 Consolidation Transaction Types for APC Transactions

The next task is to specify the transaction types for proportional value adjustments.

13.7.5.2   Specify Transaction Types for Proportional Value Adjustments

For consolidation purposes, you need to post the 'APC retirement' and the 'retirement of proportional value adjustments', with different transaction types, for a fixed asset retirement. This is to ensure that these two items remain separable, for the legal consolidation, even though they are posted to the same consolidated item.

Here, in this step, you define, for each retirement transaction type, from which transaction types the system should derive the consolidation transaction type with which the system posts the proportional value adjustments.

Use the menu path: SAP Customizing Implementation Guide > Financial Accounting > Asset Accounting > Special Valuations > Revaluation of Fixed Assets > Preparations for Consolidation > Specify Transaction Types for Proportional Value Adjustments. You may also use Transaction OAYT.

On the resulting screen, select the appropriate transaction type (say, 200 - Retirement without revenue) and double-click on 'Value adjustment procedure' on the left-hand side 'Dialog Structure'. On the next screen, you will see the standard transaction types for proportional value adjustments for each of the transaction like ordinary depreciation, special depreciation etc (Figure 13.98). We strongly recommend that you use the standard settings, instead of defining your own.

Figure 13.98 Transaction Types for Proportional Value Adjustments

The last configuration activity for consolidation preparation is to specify the group depreciation areas.

13.7.5.3   Specify Group Depreciation Areas

The asset transfers, between affiliated companies, represent either an acquisition or a retirement from the point of view of the participating individual companies. From the point of view of the corporate group, it is a transfer. The business transaction is posted as an acquisition or a retirement, and that should appear as a transfer from a consolidation point of view.

Hence, you can specify the group depreciation areas, so that the system represents transfers between affiliated companies correctly as transfers in reports, using these areas, for the corporate group.

Use the menu path: SAP Customizing Implementation Guide > Financial Accounting > Asset Accounting > Special Valuations > Revaluation of Fixed Assets > Preparations for Consolidation > Specify Group Depreciation Areas. You may also use Transaction OABE.

Select the 'GrossTrnsf' check-box for the appropriate depreciation areas, on the resulting screen. Once done, now, the asset transfers are not represented in these areas as acquisitions or retirements but as transfers (particularly in the asset history sheet; you may refer to Section 13.10.7 for details on asset history sheet).

This completes our discussion on the settings required for legal consolidation from asset accounting side; and this also completes our discussion on special valuation for fixed assets. Let us, now, move on to discuss the settings required for managing asset master data, in the next Section.

13.8 Master Data

You need to make the necessary system settings, relating to master data maintenance in FI-AA System. This will, for example, help you define your own evaluation groups. SAP provides you with several functions, for asset master data maintenance, including control of the screen layout, validation / substitution of entries, mass changes to master record fields etc. Before we look at configuring some of these functions, let us, first understand how the asset information is stored in an asset master record.

13.8.1 Asset Master Record

To enable easy creation, management and evaluation of asset master data, SAP has structured the asset data according to its use and function. Accordingly, an asset master record consists of two data areas: (a) general master data and (b) data for calculating asset values (Figure 13.99).

The *'general master data'* contains the information about the fixed asset. This includes general information (description, serial number, account determination, quantity etc), time-dependent assignments (cost center, internal order, plant, location, shift factor, profit center, segment, asset shutdown etc), origin data (vendor, manufacturer, country of origin, original acquisition year etc), entries for net worth tax, information on real estate, information on investment support measures, insurance data, leasing information (leasing company, agreement number, lease start date, payment cycle etc), and user fields/evaluation groups. Besides, there are long texts, that you can create, for the individual field groups belonging to the general data part of the asset master record.

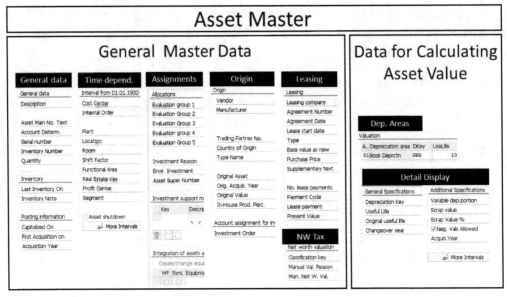

Figure 13.99 Data Sections of an Asset Master

In the *'data for calculating asset values'*, you can specify depreciation terms in the asset master record, for each depreciation area. When doing so, you can get into the 'detailed display' for each depreciation area wherein you can maintain, for example, the depreciation key, useful life, changeover year, variable depreciation proportion, scrap value etc. If there are depreciation areas proposed from the asset class that you do not need for a specific asset, you can deactivate these depreciation areas at the asset level.

With this, let us see the settings required for screen layout.

13.8.2 Screen Layout

We have already discussed the screen layout rules in <u>Section 13.3.1.2</u>.

Here, you will define the structure of your asset master records with the help of screen layout rules. In these screen layout rules, you can assign the field status to individual master record fields (for example, if the fields can be changed, or if they are to be suppressed completely etc). Besides, the screen layout also determines whether you can copy the fields as reference fields, for example. You can define screen layout for master records and also for depreciation areas. Also, you can maintain the settings for individual tabs on a master record screen.

Let us configure the screen lay out for asset master data.

13.8.2.1   Define Screen Layout for Asset Master Data

The *'screen layout control'* contains the specifications for the field groups in the asset master record. By entering the screen layout control in the asset class, you may structure the master record individually per asset class.

Project Dolphin

BESTM, to make physical inventory easier, requires that all the assets be identified with the valid 'Inventory number' in their respective asset master records. Accordingly, this field is to be made mandatory for data input. Also, to keep track of asset history, they want the 'History indicator' field to be enabled, but not mandatory to input. Besides, they also insisted that the 'Cost center', 'Business area' and 'Maintenance order' fields be made as a 'optional entry' field. During this discussion, the project team suggested to synchronize all the equipments with SAP Plant Maintenance application.

Use the menu path: SAP Customizing Implementation Guide > Financial Accounting > Asset Accounting > Master Data > Screen Layout > Define Screen Layout for Asset Master Data. On entering the transaction, you will see the 'Select Activity' pop-up screen:

i.   First, double-click 'Define Screen Layout for Asset Master Data' on the pop-up or use Transaction S_ALR_87009044. On the resulting 'Change View "Screen layout": Overview' screen (Figure 13.100), you will see several screen layout rules (that we have defined earlier in Section 13.3.1.2) listed.

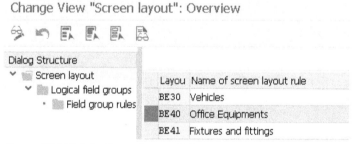

Figure 13.100 Selecting a Layout Rule

ii.   Now, select a rule (say, BE40), and double-click on 'Logical field groups' on the left-hand side 'Dialog Structure' (Figure 12.2). The system will display the logical field groups, on the next screen (Figure 13.101).

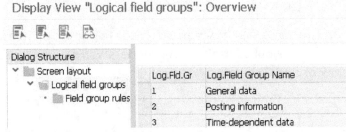

Figure 13.101 Logical Field Groups

iii.   Select the appropriate field group, and double-click on 'Field group rules' on the left-hand side 'Dialog Structure'. Since BESTM has requested to make 'Inventory number' as a mandatory field, and also enable 'History indictor', you need to select the logical field group 1 ('General data') and double-click on 'Field group rules' on the left-hand side 'Dialog Structure'.

iv.   On the resulting screen, you make changes so that the 'Inventory number' field becomes a 'required entry' ('Req.') from optional ('Opt.'). And, change the field status of 'History indicator' from suppressed ('No') status to 'optional entry' ('Opt.'), as shown in Figure 13.102.

Screen Layout   BE40   Office Equipments
Logical Fld Grp   1   General data

FG	Field group name	Req.	Opt.	No	Disp	Class	MnNo.	Sbno.	Copy	Mult
01	Description 1	●	○	○			✓	✓	✓	☐
02	Description 2	○	●	○			✓	✓	✓	☐
03	General long text	○	●	○			✓	✓		
04	Inventory number	● ←	○	○			✓	✓	✓	☐
05	Unit of measure	○	●	○		☐	✓	✓	✓	☐
06	Quantity	○	●	○	○		✓	✓	✓	☐
07	Asset main no. text	○	●	○			✓	✓	✓	☐
09	Account allocation	●				☐				
75	Serial number	○	●	○			✓	✓	☐	☐
79	Longtxt.:C-acc.view	○	●	○			✓	✓		
80	Longtxt.:Tech.view	○	●	○			✓	✓		
82	History indicator	○	● ←	○		☐	✓	✓	✓	☐

Figure 13.102 Field Status Change for Field Group 04 / 82

v.   Similarly, to make the required field status changes to 'Cost center', 'Business area' and 'Maintenance order' fields, use the logical field group 3 ('Time-dependent data'), and change the status from 'suppressed' ('No') status to 'optional entry' ('Opt.').

vi.   To enable synchronization of all the equipment assets with SAP Plant Maintenance application, use the logical field group 13 ('Equipment') and change the status of the 'Synchronize Asset' field to 'required entry'.

If you want to disable a field from maintenance, then you need to select the 'Disp' radio button against the field, so that the screen layout rule makes the corresponding field group as display only which you cannot be maintain. When you select 'MnNo.' check-box, then, the screen layout rule defines the asset main number as the maintenance level for the field group. Accordingly, when the system creates a subnumber for the asset, then, the values for this field group in the subnumber are supplied by the asset main number. However, when you select 'Sbno.' check-box, the screen layout rule defines the subnumber as the maintenance level for the corresponding field group. The 'Copy' check-box, when selected, makes the screen layout rule to indicate that when you create a new asset, using another as reference, the system copies the values, automatically from the referenced asset, for this specified field group.

vii. Now, go back to the initial 'Select Activity' pop-up screen, and double-click on the 'Create Screen Layout Rules for Asset Master Record' activity if you need to define any more screen layout rules. This is the same Transaction S_ALR_87009209, that we maintained in Section 13.1.3.2.

viii. On the initial 'Select Activity' pop-up screen, you may, finally, double-click on the 'Configurable Entry Screen for Creating Multiple Assets' activity, to activate configurable entry screen for creating multiple assets (13.103).

Change View "Activate Config. Input Screen When Creating Multiple Asse

Activate Config. Input Screen When Creating Multiple Assets
✓ Config. Entry Screen for Creating Multiple Assets

Figure 13.103 Activating Configurable Input Screen for Creating Multiple Assets

With this, we can move on to define the screen layout for depreciation areas.

13.8.2.2   Define Screen Layout for Asset Depreciation Areas

Use this configuration step, to define the screen layout control for the depreciation terms (depreciation key, useful life etc) in the asset master record. Similar to the screen layout control of general master data section of asset master, that we discussed in the previous Section 13.8.2.1, you can use this to control the features of the depreciation areas in the asset master record. You can make different specifications in each depreciation area.

ℹ SAP delivers two standard versions: (a) 1000 - depreciation on main number level and (b) 2000 - depreciation on subnumber level. Recommended that you use these screen layout controls, as such, without making any changes.

Project Dolphin

As regards the screen layout control of depreciation areas is concerned, BESTM has decided to make use of the standard versions supplied by SAP, without changing any of the field status thereon.

Use the menu path: SAP Customizing Implementation Guide > Financial Accounting > Asset Accounting > Master Data > Screen Layout > Define Screen Layout for Asset Depreciation Areas, or Transaction AO21.

On the resulting screen, you will notice the two standard layout versions, 1000 and 2000. You may select any one of them, and double-click on 'Field group rules' on the left-hand side 'Dialog Structure' to view the field status of various field groups (Figure 13.104). We are not making any changes to the standard versions, as BESTM wants to use them as such.

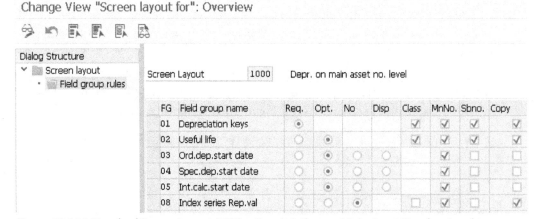

Figure 13.104 Standard Screen Layout 1000 – Depreciation on Main Asset Number Level

With this, we are now ready to define the layout for tabs on a screen of an asset master.

13.8.2.3   Specify Tab Layout for Asset Master Record

As you are aware, the asset master record is split over several tab pages, due to its large number of possible fields. Here, in this configuration step, you define the layout of these tab pages: specify which tab pages are seen for each asset class (or if needed, by chart of depreciation within the asset class); then, for each tab page, specify which field groups appear in which positions on the tab page.

Use the menu path: SAP Customizing Implementation Guide > Financial Accounting > Asset Accounting > Master Data > Screen Layout > Specify Tab Layout for Asset Master Record:

i.   On the resulting 'Select Activity' pop-up screen, double-click on 'Define Tab Layout for Asset Master Data'. On the next screen (you can reach this directly through Transaction AOLA), you will see the list of standard layouts (Figure 13.105).

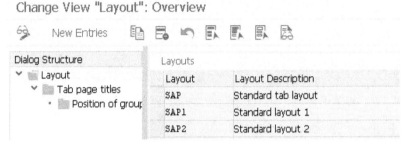

Figure 13.105 Standard Layouts for Tabs

ii. Select any of the standard layouts (say, SAP), and double-click 'Tab page titles' on the left-hand side 'Dialog Structure', to view list of tabs / tab names (Figure 13.106).

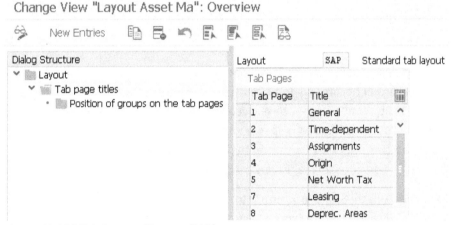

Figure 13.106 Tab Pages of Layout 'SAP'

iii. You may select a 'Tab Page' and double-click 'Position of groups on the tab pages' on the left-hand side 'Dialog Structure' to view the field group placement on that tab page (Figure 13.107).

iv. You may also create a new tab layout, if required, by clicking on 'New Entries' on the screen (Figure 13.105) under step (i) above. Once defined, then, you need to go back to the initial 'Select Activity' pop-up screen, and double-click on the 'Assign Tab Layouts to Asset Classes' activity, to assign the newly defined tab layout to the required asset classes. You may also use Transaction AOLK to accomplish this.

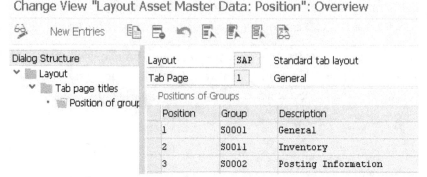

Figure 13.107 Field Group Position on Tab Page 1, for Layout 'SAP'

With this, we are ready to process selection criteria, for web transactions.

13.8.2.4   Process Selection Criteria

Here, using this step, you can make specifications for the 'My Assets' and 'Assets on my Cost Center' web transactions (internet / intranet). Per transaction, you can specify the 'selection criteria' that are available for selecting assets when you call up the Transaction. Besides, you can also specify the standard selection criteria that are presented when you start each of these Transactions.

Project Dolphin

For making the selection screen specifications for some of the web transactions including 'my assets', the project team has indicated that it will use most of the common fields, such as asset, asset sub number, asset class, account determination, acquisition year, capitalized on, evaluation group 1/2/3, asset super number, vendor, manufacturer, description, lease start date etc, as the selection fields for the 'cost accountant' role. Similar definitions will be created for 'cost center manager' and 'employee self-service'.

Use the menu path: SAP Customizing Implementation Guide > Financial Accounting > Asset Accounting > Master Data > Screen Layout > Process Selection Criteria:

i.   On the resulting 'Select Activity' pop-up screen, double-click on 'Process Selection Options for List Box'.

ii. On the next screen (you can also reach this directly through Transaction CUSTSEL_FIAA), you will see the list of Transactions like 'Cost center manager', 'Employee Self-Service' and 'Asset accountant'.

iii. Select a transaction, and double-click on 'Selectable Selection Criteria' on the left-hand side 'Dialog Structure'. On the next screen, use 'New Entries' and build the selection criteria fields for that selected transaction (Figure 13.108).

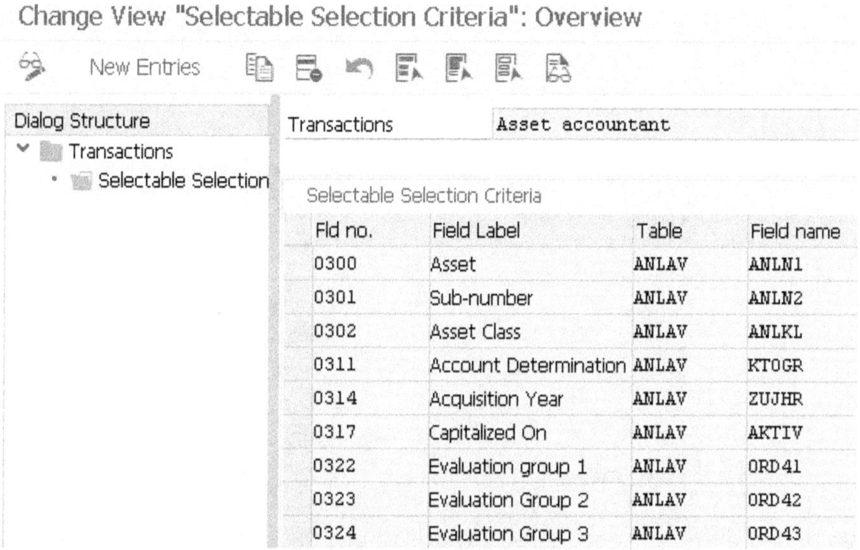

Change View "Selectable Selection Criteria": Overview

New Entries

Transactions		Asset accountant	

Selectable Selection Criteria

Fld no.	Field Label	Table	Field name
0300	Asset	ANLAV	ANLN1
0301	Sub-number	ANLAV	ANLN2
0302	Asset Class	ANLAV	ANLKL
0311	Account Determination	ANLAV	KTOGR
0314	Acquisition Year	ANLAV	ZUJHR
0317	Capitalized On	ANLAV	AKTIV
0322	Evaluation group 1	ANLAV	ORD41
0323	Evaluation Group 2	ANLAV	ORD42
0324	Evaluation Group 3	ANLAV	ORD43

Figure 13.108 Defining Selectable Selection Criteria

This completes our discussion on screen layout, and let us move on to discuss asset views.

13.8.3 Asset Views

FI-AA makes use of a 'view' concept for the protection of authorizations and also to provide access to some of the data in asset master data to certain employees who have only occasional and/or limited contact with fixed assets. The 'asset view', then, allows such employees only a limited view of asset data and values, whether or not they formally have access to every other master record. With the 'Purchasing asset view', for example, you can grant a person responsible for purchases, access only to the data that is purchase-relevant.

> **i** The 'asset view' determines which fields and depreciation areas can be processed from that particular view. The standard system comes delivered with 8 pre-defined asset views; you can use them as such, or you can adopt them to meet your specific needs. However, you cannot add more views or delete the pre-defined ones.

Use the menu path: SAP Customizing Implementation Guide > Financial Accounting > Asset Accounting > Preparations for Going Live > Authorization Management > Process Asset Views. You may also use Transaction ANSCHT.

On the resulting screen, you will see a list of all the eight pre-defined asset views, numbered 1 to 8, as shown in Figure 13.109.

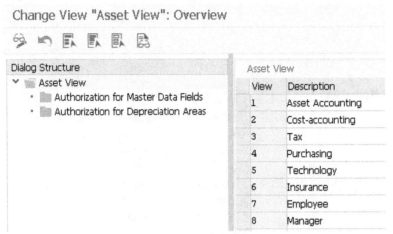

Figure 13.109 Standard Asset Views

You can assign different processing authorizations, for each asset view, to every field group of the asset master record. For that, you need to select a view (say, 1) and double-click on 'Authorization for Master Data Fields' on the left-hand side 'Dialog Structure' (Figure 13.110). On the resulting screen, you may change the processing authorization per field group, as required.

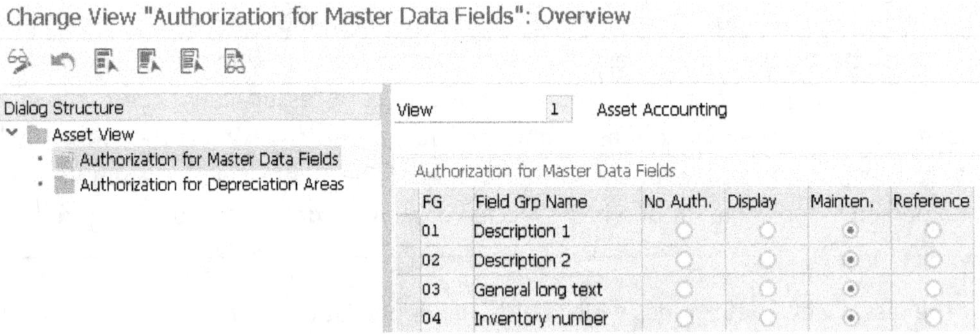

Change View "Authorization for Master Data Fields": Overview

Dialog Structure
∨ Asset View
  • Authorization for Master Data Fields
  • Authorization for Depreciation Areas

View   1   Asset Accounting

Authorization for Master Data Fields

FG	Field Grp Name	No Auth.	Display	Mainten.	Reference
01	Description 1	○	○	●	○
02	Description 2	○	○	●	○
03	General long text	○	○	●	○
04	Inventory number	○	○	●	○

Figure 13.110 Authorization for Master Data Fields, for a given View

You may also manage authorizations as the depreciation area level. For that, you need to select a field group, say 04, and then, double-click on 'Authorization for Depreciation Areas' on the left-hand side 'Dialog Structure' (Figure 13.111). On the resulting screen, you may change the default processing authorization per depreciation area, as you may require.

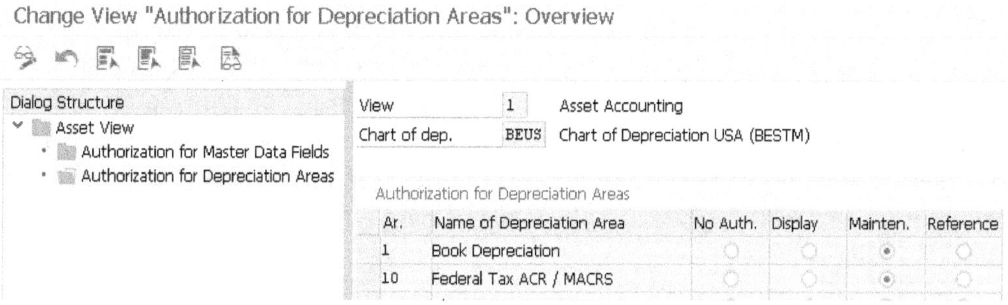

Change View "Authorization for Depreciation Areas": Overview

Figure 13.111 Authorization for Master Data Fields, for Depreciation Areas

> **i** Note that creating complete assets is only possible with asset view 1 ('Asset Accounting view'). The users who do not have this view cannot create any assets, in the system.

This completes our discussion on configuring for master data maintenance in FI-AA. In the next Section, let us discuss the settings required for configuring the most important transactions in FI-AA.

13.9 Transactions

The 'transactions' component, in FI-AA, enables you to carry out all accounting transactions that occur during the life of a fixed asset in your organization, and include – for example - acquisitions, retirements, intracompany / intercompany transfers, and capitalizations of AuC.

The asset 'transaction types', in FI-AA, identify individual business transactions, and you need to associate a transaction type, manually or automatically, with each transaction that affects the assets in the system. Besides controlling the account assignment (debit / credit entry, document numbering etc), the transaction type also takes care of posting type (gross or net, for example) and other features. You can assign the business transactions to an 'asset history sheet' using these transaction types.

Each transaction type is assigned exactly to one 'transaction type group'. The transaction type group, determines, among others, which value fields are updated in year segments, whether the transaction refers to the past (for example, write-ups) or to the current fiscal year, whether the total of transactions of a group is positive or negative with reference to a fiscal year, according to which rule the start period for the depreciation calculation is determined, in which G/L accounts posting is to take place, whether the acquisition date of the fixed asset is set on the date of the first transaction of a group, whether proportional accumulated depreciation can be entered for a transaction (for example, during post-capitalization), or is to be determined by the system (for example, with asset retirements) and so on.

> **i** It is not possible to change either the number of transaction type groups or their characteristics, in the standard system. However, unlike transaction type groups, you can add new transaction types in the system to meet your exact business needs: when you create your own transaction types, make sure to enter the letter x, y, or z at any position in the three place transaction type key so that SAP does not over-write them with the future release updates.

On the basis of transaction type groups, you can segregate the asset business transactions into various categories, like:

- Transactions that influence the APC of fixed assets
  o Acquisitions
  o Retirements
  o Transfer postings
  o Post-capitalization
- Downpayments
- Investment support measures
- Manual depreciation
- Write-ups

Let us start discussing the configuration settings that are required for asset acquisitions.

13.9.1 Acquisitions

The 'acquisition' is the primary business process in FI-AA relating to the purchase of assets and/or the capitalization of in-house produced goods or services. The system supports three distinct methods of asset acquisition:

1. *Direct Capitalization*: This refers to asset acquisitions that do not have an AuC phase. Hence, the assets are capitalized and you begin the depreciation immediately on such assets. You can represent acquisitions of this kind using the following three options:
   - Direct account assignment to the final asset and possible statistical updating to an order or work breakdown structure (WBS) element. This includes:
     ✓ External asset acquisitions
     ✓ Processing asset acquisitions in Purchasing (FI-AA/MM)
     ✓ Goods Receipt (GR) and Invoice Receipt (IR) with reference to asset
   - Account assignment to an order or WBS element (with allocation cost element) and settlement to the final asset:
     ✓ Acquisition from internal activity
   - Account assignment to a clearing account and transferring from this account to the final asset.

2. *Assets under Construction (AuC):* These are acquisitions to fixed assets that are not permitted to be capitalized and depreciated immediately. You can represent acquisitions of this kind using the following options:
   - Collect the costs using an investment measure (an order or a WBS element) with an AuC linked to it.
   - Collect the costs on an independent AuC in FI-AA.
3. *Budget Monitoring using Statistical Orders or WBS Elements:* The system offers the option of automatic statistical updating to an order or WBS element of all acquisitions posted to an asset as this may be required for CO purposes that you monitor spending on asset acquisitions for the budget.

A *'subsequent acquisition'* is an addition or enhancement, to an already capitalized asset, in the current fiscal year with the depreciation start date for the enhancement in the current fiscal year. You can post a subsequent acquisition to an already existing asset either to the existing asset master record or to a new subnumber. When you post to an already existing asset master record, the system creates separate line items for each acquisition; however, it cannot display the depreciation from the subsequent acquisition after the end of the current fiscal year separately from the historical original acquisition. If you need to separately display the depreciation, then, you need to use a separate subnumber for the subsequent acquisition.

An *'acquisition resulting from extraordinary revenue'* is an asset acquisition that you post in FI-AA without any reference to a valuated GR or IR. You may need this type of transaction because (a) you have discovered a new fixed asset, requiring capitalization, during a physical inventory and /or (b) you receive an asset as a gift.

With this background in asset acquisition, let us look at the various configuration steps to set up the functionality.

13.9.1.1   Define Transaction Types for Acquisitions

You can use the standard transaction types, from SAP, without making any changes to them, for asset acquisitions. However, you may want to define your own transaction types (a) if you want to have certain types of acquisitions appear in different asset history sheet items; to meet this, define new acquisition transaction types and assign them to exceptional history sheet groups (in the IMG), (b) that do not lead to the capitalization of the assets posted; for this, you need to uncheck the 'Capitalize Fixed Asset' check-box while defining the new one, or (c) to monitor a budget using statistical orders/projects; here, you need set the flag for statistical updating of an order/project.

Project Dolphin

BESTM does not want to define any new transaction types for asset acquisitions; they are good with the standard ones supplied by SAP. However, while defining the account assignment category of asset purchase orders, BESTM has indicated to make the settings in such a way to have the 'Business Area' and 'Cost Center' as optional entry fields (from their original status of 'suppressed') to have the details captured, wherever possible.

Use the menu path: SAP Customizing Implementation Guide > Financial Accounting > Asset Accounting > Transactions > Acquisitions > Define Transaction Types for Acquisitions. You may also use Transaction AO73.

On the resulting screen, you can view the standard transaction types for various functions in asset acquisition (Figure 13.112). You may use 'New Entries' button, if you need to define a new transaction type.

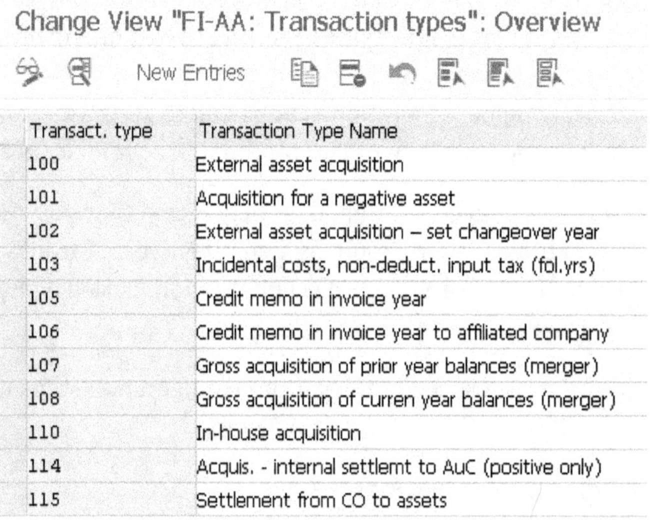

Change View "FI-AA: Transaction types": Overview

New Entries

Transact. type	Transaction Type Name
100	External asset acquisition
101	Acquisition for a negative asset
102	External asset acquisition – set changeover year
103	Incidental costs, non-deduct. input tax (fol.yrs)
105	Credit memo in invoice year
106	Credit memo in invoice year to affiliated company
107	Gross acquisition of prior year balances (merger)
108	Gross acquisition of curren year balances (merger)
110	In-house acquisition
114	Acquis. - internal settlemt to AuC (positive only)
115	Settlement from CO to assets

Figure 13.112 Standard Transaction Types for Asset Acquisition

The next configuration step is to define the account assignment category for asset purchase orders.

13.9.1.2   Define Account Assignment Category for Asset Purch. Orders

You can post asset acquisitions during the processing of purchase orders (POs) in SAP MM (see also Section 13.4.1 for FI-AA integration with SAP MM). You can post a PO or a purchase requisition (PR) with account assignment to an asset. In order to make this assignment, however, you should have already created the asset in the system. Then, the system, automatically capitalizes the asset when the GR or IR is posted.

When you create a PO, you need to enter an 'account assignment category' (in the standard system, account assignment category A is pre-defined for valuated GR): entering account assignment category A tells the system that you are entering a PO for a fixed asset. The account assignment category also has specification as to whether the GR should be valuated (as in the case of standard account assignment category A) or not: if the GR is valuated, then, the asset is capitalized at the time of the GR; else, (that is, when it is non-valuated), the asset is capitalized at the time of the IR.

Use the menu path: SAP Customizing Implementation Guide > Financial Accounting > Asset Accounting > Transactions > Acquisitions > Define Account Assignment Category for Asset Purch. Orders. You may also use Transaction OME9.

On the resulting screen, you will see a list of account assignment categories including the standard account assignment category A for asset POs. Double-click on account assignment category A to see the detailed settings, on the next screen (13.113).

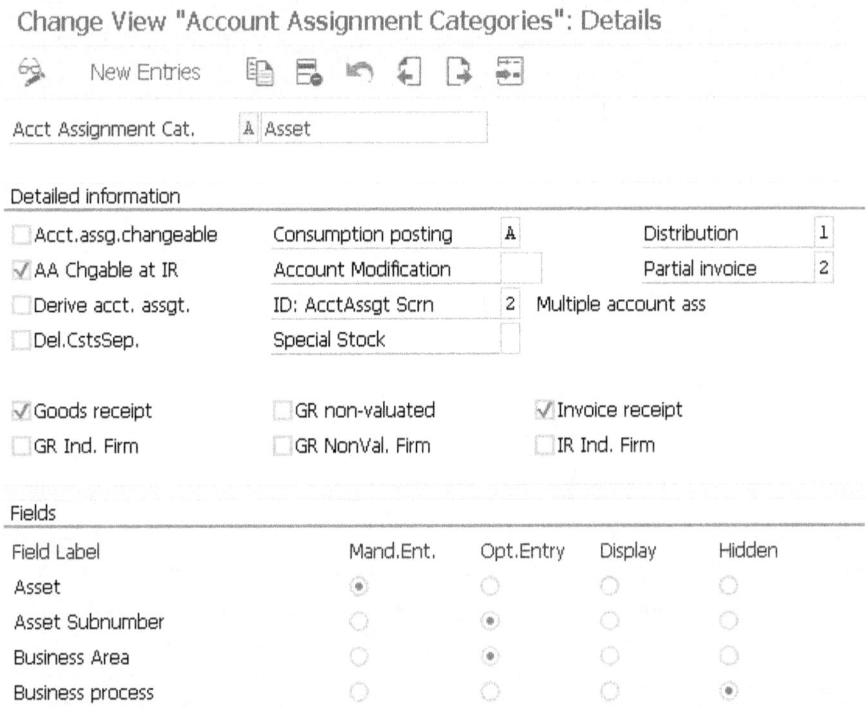

Figure 13.113 Standard Account Assignment Category (A) for Asset POs

Make changes, if required:

- Use the 'Acct.assg.changeable' check-box to determine if the account assignment of an item with the specified account assignment category can be changed following a

GR or IR. Do not select this, when you want no changes for the account assignment following a GR/IR.

- Ensure that the value A ('Asset') has been selected for 'Consumption posting' field. In case of sales-order-related production, this field determines whether the costs of sales-order-related production are collected under a sales order item. For that you need to select E (Accounting via sales order).

- The entry in the 'Distribution' field determines how the quantity and value of a PO item are to be distributed among the individual account assignment items: by quantity (1) or on a percentage basis (2) or) or by amount (3). The value you enter here will be pre-set on the multiple account assignment screen.

- Use the 'AA Chagble at IR' check-box to decide if you need the flexibility to change the account assignment of a PO item at the time of IR during invoice verification.

- Select 'Goods receipt' to specify if the item involves a GR.

- Select 'Invoice receipt' to specify if an IR is linked to the PO item. If not set, the goods are to be delivered free of charge.

- Select 'GR non-valuated' check-box, to determine if the GR for this item is to be valuated or not. When selected (= GR is valuated), the asset is capitalized at the time of the GR; when not selected (= GR is non-valuated), the asset is capitalized at the time of the IR.

- You may also make the required changes to the field status of any of the fields that is listed at the bottom of the screen: we have changed the field status of 'Business Area' and 'Cost Center' fields from 'Hidden' to 'Opt.Entry'.

The next step is to specify the asset class for creating asset form POs.

13.9.1.3   Specify Asset Class for Creating Asset from Purchase Order

As you can create an asset directly from the purchasing transaction for PO, you can enter an asset PO, without creating an asset beforehand in FI-AA. This asset, thus created, will, then, serve as the account assignment object for the PO. Here, in this configuration step, you can specify the asset classes that the system should use, as defaults, when you create an asset from within a PO. You need to specify the asset class for each of the material groups for fixed assets.

Use the menu path: SAP Customizing Implementation Guide > Financial Accounting > Asset Accounting > Transactions > Acquisitions > Specify Asset Class for Creating Asset from Purchase Order. You may also use Transaction OMQX.

On the resulting screen, enter the appropriate asset 'Class' against all the material groups ('Mat. Grp') for fixed assets (Figure 13.114).

Change View "Default Asset Class": Overview

Mat. Grp	Mat. Grp Descr.	Class	Short Text
YBFA05	Machinery Equipment	B2000	Plant
YBFA06	Fixtures Fittings	B4200	Furniture
YBFA07	Vehicles	B3000	Vehicles
YBFA08	Computer Hardware	B5100	Computer Hardware
YBFA09	Computer Software	B5200	Computer Software
YBFA10	Low Value Assets	B7000	LVA - Collective
YBFA11	Other Intangibles	B8000	Intangible Assets
YBFA12	Office Equipment	B4100	Office Equipment

Figure 13.114 Asset Class Specification for Creating Asset from PO

The next step is to assign the G/L accounts for asset acquisitions.

13.9.1.4   Assign Accounts

Use the menu path: SAP Customizing Implementation Guide > Financial Accounting > Asset Accounting > Transactions > Acquisitions > Assign Accounts, or Transaction AO85 to assign the appropriate G/L accounts for posting acquisition-related asset transactions:

i.   Maintain the chart of depreciation (BEUS), and select the chart of accounts (BEUS) on the resulting screen.

ii.   Select an 'Account Determination' (say, B1000 Buildings) and double-click on 'Balance Sheet Accounts' on the left-hand side 'Dialog Structure'.

iii.   On the next screen, double-click on the depreciation area (say, 01) and maintain the required G/L accounts on the next screen. We have already completed assigning of accounts for acquisitions in Section 13.4.4.2 when we discussed the FI-AA integration with SAP G/L Accounting. Here, in this activity, you may add the G/L accounts for 'Account assignment of cost portions not capitalized' which we did not set up earlier.

iv.   Repeat assigning the G/L accounts for 'Account assignment of cost portions not capitalized', for all the account determinations.

The next configuration activity is to define the technical clearing account for integrated asset acquisition.

13.9.1.5   Define Technical Clearing Account for Integrated Asset Acquisition

We have completed this setting in Section 13.4.4.3 when we discussed the FI-AA integration with SAP G/L Accounting. However, you may use the menu path: SAP Customizing Implementation Guide > Financial Accounting > Asset Accounting > Transactions > Acquisitions > Technical Clearing Account for Integrated Asset Acquisition > Define Technical Clearing Account for Integrated Asset Acquisition, to verify the same.

With this, let us see how to configure a different technical clearing account for required field control, in the next Section.

13.9.1.6   Define Different Technical Clearing Account for Required Field Control

We have already seen, vide Section 13.4.4.3, that in an integrated asset acquisition posting, the system divides the business transaction into an operational part and a valuating part. When you enter the posting, initially, only the operational part (that is, the posting against the technical clearing account) is visible. The properties of the account assignment fields, such as cost center or profit center, are derived from the field control of the technical clearing account. Hence, if you require different field control behaviour, depending on the asset balance sheet account to be posted to, you, then, need to reflect this using different technical clearing accounts for integrated asset acquisition.

We have, vide the pervious Section 13.9.1.5, already defined a technical clearing account of integrated asset acquisition. Here, in this activity, you differentiate between technical clearing accounts for integrated asset acquisition using their account determination. You can then assign the required field status variant to the different technical clearing accounts for integrated asset acquisition. In the process, you also need to make sure that the FSV of the technical clearing accounts and the relevant asset accounts (that are posted to in the valuating part of the transaction) match. Especially in the field control of the technical clearing account, you need to ensure that no 'required entry' fields of asset accounts are with 'hidden' field status.

For example, when you want the system to post the asset in, say, 'Independent AuC' asset class with the account assignment to the 'Order' field, then, that field is to be set to 'required entry' status; for all other asset classes it is to be set as 'optional entry' status. Here, as you need different field control behaviour, you need to make the required configuration settings. To achieve this, you need two G/L accounts, defined, to be used as technical clearing accounts for integrated asset acquisition: for the first account, you enter a field status with the setting 'optional entry' for the 'Order' field, and for the second account, you enter a field status with the setting 'required entry' for the 'Order' field.

You may achieve this configuration by using the menu path: SAP Customizing Implementation Guide > Financial Accounting > Asset Accounting > Transactions > Acquisitions > Technical Clearing Account for Integrated Asset Acquisition > Define Different Technical Clearing Account for Required Field Control.

On the resulting screen, you assign an FSV with 'Order' field set to 'optional entry' to the G/L account that you have already defined in the previous configuration activity 'Define Technical Clearing Account for Integrated Asset Acquisition' (Section 13.9.1.5). Now, create another entry, enter another G/L account for the specific asset class ('Independent AuC') and assign another FSV with the field status of 'Order' set to 'required entry'.

Project Dolphin

In the case of integrated asset accounting, BESTM does not want to use differing technical clearing accounts, but wants the system to use the one defined at the chart of accounts level. Accordingly, the project team has decided not to configure the IMG node 'Define Different Technical Clearing Account for Required Field Control'.

The next configuration is to make the required settings for allowing down payment transaction types in the appropriate asset classes.

13.9.1.7   Allow Down Payment Transaction Types in Asset Classes

Using this configuration step, you can determine the asset classes, like AuC, for which downpayments made may be capitalized in the system.

Use the menu path: SAP Customizing Implementation Guide > Financial Accounting > Asset Accounting > Transactions > Acquisitions > Allow Down Payment Transaction Types in Asset Classes. You may also use Transaction OAYB.

On the resulting screen, for each of the transaction type groups ('TTG') like 15 (down payment), 16 (down payment balance from previous years), 38 (retirement transfer previous year acquisition - AuC summary) and 39 (retirement transfer current year acquisition - AuC summary), you need to specify the asset classes. Select a 'TTG' (say, 15), double-click on 'Specification of asset classes' on the left-hand side 'Dialog Structure' and specify the asset class(es) on the next screen (say, B6000), by clicking on 'New Entries' (Figure 13.115). And, repeat this for all the transaction type groups, and 'Save' your details.

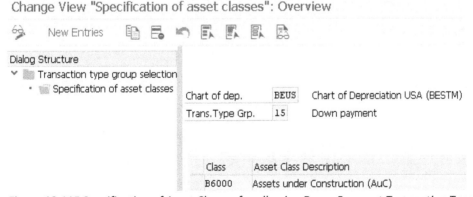

Figure 13.115 Specification of Asset Classes for allowing Down Payment Transaction Types

The next task is to make the appropriate configuration to prevent subsequent capitalization of discounts.

13.9.1.8 Prevent Subsequent Capitalization of Discounts

When an asset acquisition posting has been integrated with FI-A/P, you can specify, through the appropriate document type, if the invoice should be posted 'gross' (without deducting discount) or 'net' (with discount deducted). In 'net' posting, the system automatically determines the cash discount to be deducted (on the basis of the payment terms), capitalizes the invoice amount (less tax and cash discount), on the fixed asset. However, should there be a difference in discount (too much or too little), which you find out later during the payment run, you can subsequently adjust / correct the APC (through collective processing) in SAP G/L Accounting. But, using this configuration step, and selecting the 'No Discount' check-box, you can prevent these subsequent adjustments to APC.

Project Dolphin

BESTM wants the project team to configure the system to prevent subsequent adjustments made to APC of an asset arising out of incorrect discount charged in 'net' invoice posting, relating to assets, in FI-A/P and the resulting capitalization.

Use the menu path: SAP Customizing Implementation Guide > Financial Accounting > Asset Accounting > Transactions > Acquisitions > Prevent Subsequent Capitalization of Discounts.

On the resulting screen, select the 'No Discount' check-box for all the required company codes to prevent subsequent adjustments to APC on account of incorrect discount during 'net' posting capitalization (Figure 13.116).

Figure 13.116 Preventing Subsequent Capitalization of Discounts

This completes our discussion on configuration for acquisition transactions. Let us move on to discuss the settings required for asset retirement, in the next Section.

13.9.2 Retirements

The *'asset retirement'* is the removal of an asset or part of an asset from your asset portfolio. The asset retirement ca be complete or partial. It can happen with or without revenue. Based on the organizational considerations, or business transaction leading to asset retirement, you will come across with the following types of asset retirement in the system:

- You sell an asset and realise some revenue. You post the sale with a customer.
- You sell an asset and realise some revenue. You post the sale against a clearing account.
- You scrap an asset and do not realise any revenue.
- You sell an asset to your affiliated company (manual posting).

SAP provides you with the standard transaction types to take care of asset sale (with or without customer) and asset retirement due to scrapping. Let us understand each of the asset retirements in brief:

- *Asset Sale with Customer*
  In cases of *'asset sale with customer'*, the system enables posting the entry to FI-A/R, the revenue posting and asset retirement in one step. During posting, first, you need to enter the revenue posting (debit A/R, credit revenue from asset sale), and, then, enter the asset retirement. An indicator in the posting transaction denotes that the system posts the asset retirement with the revenue posting. The system posts a separate accounting-principle-specific document, per posting depreciation area, provided that the depreciation area manages APC.

- *Asset Retirement without Revenue*
  When you use the *'asset retirement without revenue'* (for example, asset scrapping) posting option, the system does not create revenue and gain/loss postings; instead, it creates a 'loss made on asset retirement without revenue' posting in the amount of the NBV of the asset that is getting retired.

- *Complete / Partial Retirement*
  The asset retirement can refer to an entire fixed asset (*'complete retirement'*) or part of a fixed asset (*'partial retirement'*). In both cases, the system automatically determines, using the asset retirement dates entered, the amounts to be charged off for each depreciation area. You can initiate the partial retirement of a fixed asset by entering (a) the APC that is being retired or (b) a retirement percentage or (c) a quantity:

- o When you enter the amount of APC that is being retired, the system determines, per accounting principle, the percentage to be retired from the asset using the first depreciation area of the respective ledger group in which posting is to take place. It, then, uses the same percentage for other depreciation areas. You can enter a quantity, provided that you have not specified a retirement amount or percentage rate: then, the system interprets the quantity as a ratio to the total quantity of the asset and thereby determines the asset retirement percentage rate.

- o The complete retirement of a fixed asset is only possible if all transactions to the asset were posted with a value date before the asset value date of asset retirement. You must clear or reverse downpayments and investment support measures, which are in the same posting year as the retirement, before you post the complete retirement.

> **i** Select the correct transaction type, for both partial and complete retirement. For the complete retirement of a fixed asset acquired in previous years, always select a transaction type intended for prior-year acquisitions. A partial retirement can always relate either to prior-year acquisitions or to current-year acquisitions. The system shows prior-year asset acquisitions and current-year acquisitions, separately from one another in the document.

- *Retirement of LVAs*
  It is not necessary to actually post the retirement of LVAs, due to the large number of assets that are being retired, in order for the assets transactions to be displayed correctly in the asset history sheet. You can simulate the retirements during a time period that you specify in the initial screen of the asset history sheet. However, if you want to actually post the retirement of LVAs, use the usual procedure for asset retirements. Refer Section 13.10.7 for details on asset history sheet.

- *Simultaneous Retirement of Several Asset Subnumbers*
  You can post the complete retirement of several subnumbers of a fixed asset in one step by using the generic entry using an * in the 'Subnumber' field.

- *Mass Retirement*
  When you sell a large portion of its fixed assets (such as a plant or a building), it is necessary to post the retirement of all the individual assets which make up the whole asset. Since the number of affected assets can be very large, FI-AA enables making the necessary postings using mass processing. For the selection of the assets involved and the basic procedure for mass retirement, you will be using the same functions as that of 'mass change' to asset master data. When you create a worklist for mass

retirement, enter the purpose as either 'retirement with revenue' or 'retirement without revenue (scrapping)'. Besides you also need to make the entries including the posting date, transaction type, revenue and type of revenue distribution.

> **i** When you retire an asset, the system records the value date of the retirement in the asset master record. Once this is done, you cannot, then, post any transactions with a value date before the value date of the last retirement. However, if need to post such a transaction, you must first reverse all retirements that lie after the value date of the belated posting, post the belated transaction, then, finally then re-post the asset retirements.

With this background in asset retirement, let us now understand the configuration that is required to use the retirement functionality in the system.

Let us start with the transaction types for asset retirements.

13.9.2.1   Define Transaction Types for Retirements

Use the menu path: SAP Customizing Implementation Guide > Financial Accounting > Asset Accounting > Transactions > Retirements > Define Transaction Types for Retirements. On the resulting 'Select Activity' pop-up, double-click on 'Define Transaction Types for Retirements'. You will see the standard transaction types, for asset retirement transactions, on the next screen (Figure 13.117). You may also use Transaction AO74 to reach this screen directly.

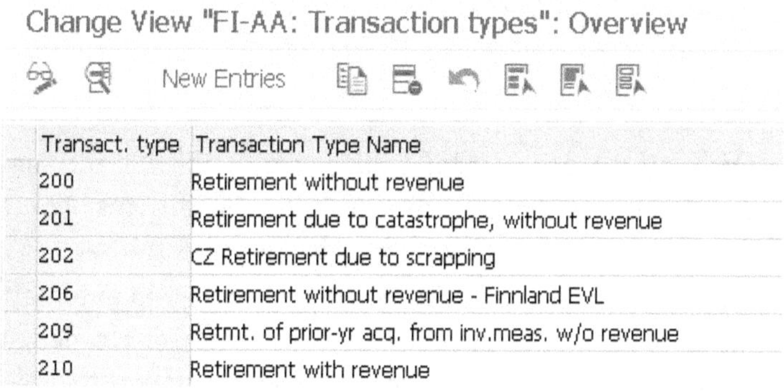

Change View "FI-AA: Transaction types": Overview

New Entries

Transact. type	Transaction Type Name
200	Retirement without revenue
201	Retirement due to catastrophe, without revenue
202	CZ Retirement due to scrapping
206	Retirement without revenue - Finnland EVL
209	Retmt. of prior-yr acq. from inv.meas. w/o revenue
210	Retirement with revenue

Figure 13.117 Transaction Types for Asset Retirement

When you double-click on a particular transaction type (say, 210), you will be able to see the detailed settings on the next screen (Figure 13.118):

- You will notice that the 'Deactivate Fixed Asset' check-box has been selected under 'Account assignment'. This indicates that the asset will be deactivated when you make a posting that results in an acquisition value = zero. The system sets the asset retirement date and the status.

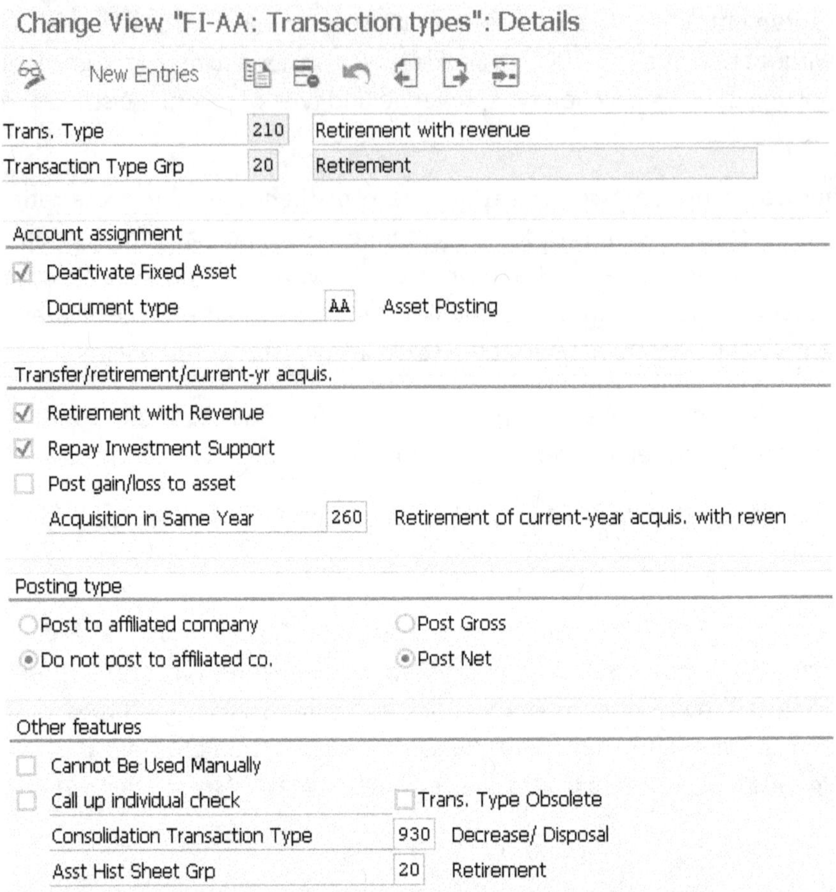

Change View "FI-AA: Transaction types": Details

   New Entries   📋 📑 ↩ ⏎ ⏏ ⏩

| Trans. Type | 210 | Retirement with revenue |
| Transaction Type Grp | 20 | Retirement |

Account assignment

☑ Deactivate Fixed Asset

   Document type   AA   Asset Posting

Transfer/retirement/current-yr acquis.

☑ Retirement with Revenue

☑ Repay Investment Support

☐ Post gain/loss to asset

   Acquisition in Same Year   260   Retirement of current-year acquis. with reven

Posting type

◯ Post to affiliated company   ◯ Post Gross

◉ Do not post to affiliated co.   ◉ Post Net

Other features

☐ Cannot Be Used Manually

☐ Call up individual check   ☐ Trans. Type Obsolete

   Consolidation Transaction Type   930   Decrease/ Disposal

   Asst Hist Sheet Grp   20   Retirement

Figure 13.118 Transaction Type 210: Detailed Settings

- Under 'Transfer / retirement / current-yr. acquis.' data block, you will see that the 'Retirement with Revenue' check-box has been selected indicating that you must enter revenue when posting a retirement of a fixed asset using this transaction type.
- The 'Repay Investment Support', when selected, results in the system automatically posting the repayment of the investment support, if any, that has been claimed, when the asset is retired. However, if you claimed the investment support in the same year in which the asset is retired, you have to reverse the investment support before posting the retirement.
- The 'Post gain/loss to asset' check-box, when selected, denotes that the gain/loss made on an asset retirement will not assigned to a P&L account, but to a specific asset as a value adjustment.

You may go back to the initial pop-up and double-click on 'Define Transaction Types for Subsequent Costs/Revenues' to view the associated transaction types (285 and 286) for subsequent costs and revenues. You can reach this screen directly by using Transaction AO81.

Change View "FI-AA: Transaction types": Overview

Transact. type	Transaction Type Name
285	Subsequent costs from asset retirement
286	Subsequent revenue from asset retirement

Figure 13.119 Transaction Types for Subsequent Costs / Revenues from Asset Retirement

The next activity is to determine the posting variants for gain/loss posting, arising out of asset retirements.

13.9.2.2   Determine Posting Variants

Here, you define how to manage gain/loss with asset retirement for each depreciation area. The standard asset retirement transaction types use variant 0, and is the variant prescribed by tax/commercial law in most countries. The variants 1 and 2 are, for example, necessary for *group assets* in USA, to meet the with American ADR legislation.

Use the menu path: SAP Customizing Implementation Guide > Financial Accounting > Asset Accounting > Transactions > Retirements > Gain/Loss Posting > Determine Posting Variants. You may also use Transaction OAYS.

On the resulting screen, select the transaction type (say, 210) and double-click on 'Special treatment of retirement' on the left-hand side 'Dialog Structure'. On the next screen, select the depreciation area, and enter the appropriate posting variant for that. We have selected the variant 0 for the 'Ret.type' field which is suitable for most of the countries (Figure 13.120). Repeat and assign the variant for all the required transaction types / depreciation areas.

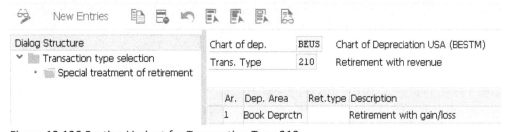

Change View "Special treatment of retirement": Overview

New Entries

Dialog Structure
- Transaction type selection
  - Special treatment of retirement

Chart of dep.	BEUS	Chart of Depreciation USA (BESTM)
Trans. Type	210	Retirement with revenue

Ar.	Dep. Area	Ret.type	Description
1	Book Deprctn		Retirement with gain/loss

Figure 13.120 Posting Variant for Transaction Type 210

With this, let us move to define the transaction types for write-up due to gain/loss.

13.9.2.3   Define Transaction Types for Write-Up Due to Gain/Loss

You need to configure this step only if you do not post gain/loss to P&L accounts, but instead want to collect gain/loss on *'special assets'* as in USA. The system uses the transaction types, you define here, to post gain/loss to specified assets as a write-up. You can use SAP supplied standard transaction type 770, without making any changes, for this purpose. This is not required for BESTM and hence we are not configuring the same.

Project Dolphin

As BESTM uses P&L accounts to post the gain/loss arising out of asset retirements, the project team has been asked not to configure the transaction types to collect gain/loss on an asset itself. Also, BESTM does not want to configure this for asset classes as well.

The next step is to determine the asset for gain/loss posting per asset class

13.9.2.4   Determine Asset for Gain/Loss Posting per Class

Similar to the previous activity, you will need this implementation step only when you do not post gain/loss to profit and loss accounts, but instead want to collect gain/loss on *'special assets'* (using asset retirement variant 3) In that case, you enter the asset ('Asset No.' and 'SNo.'), for each asset class, to which the system should post gain/loss from asset retirement. Not required for BESTM.

Let us now define the how to distribute the revenue for asset retirement.

13.9.2.5   Define Revenue Distribution for Fixed Asset Retirement

You can specify, here, at company code level, how the system is to distribute revenue arising from asset retirements: whether it is to be distributed based on APC or based on NBV. However, when you create a worklist of mass retirement, you can still opt for an alternative type of revenue distribution, irrespective the settings you make here.

Project Dolphin

BESTM has indicated that the revenue distribution method, in company code, should be based on NBV instead of APC, for all the company codes, both in US and India.

Use the menu path: SAP Customizing Implementation Guide > Financial Accounting > Asset Accounting > Transactions > Retirements > Gain/Loss Posting > Determine Posting Variants, to configure the settings.

On the resulting screen, select the appropriate value ('By Net Book Value') for 'Rev. Dist.' field (Figure 13.121). The other option is 'By APC'.

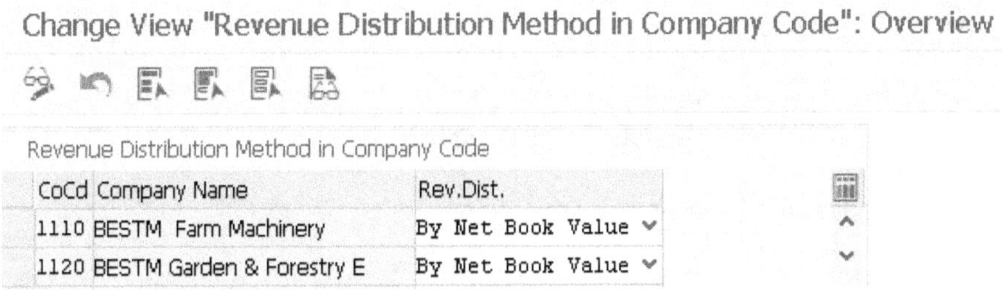

Change View "Revenue Distribution Method in Company Code": Overview

Revenue Distribution Method in Company Code

CoCd	Company Name	Rev.Dist.
1110	BESTM Farm Machinery	By Net Book Value ∨
1120	BESTM Garden & Forestry E	By Net Book Value ∨

Figure 13.121 Revenue Distribution Method per Company Code

The last configuration activity under asset retirement is to assign the G/L accounts.

13.9.2.6   Assign Accounts

Use the menu path: SAP Customizing Implementation Guide > Financial Accounting > Asset Accounting > Transactions > Retirements > Assign Accounts or Transaction AO86, to enter the appropriate G/L accounts for posting asset retirements. On the resulting screen:

i. Select the chart of accounts (say, BEUS) and double-click on 'Account Determination' on the left-hand side 'Dialog Structure'.

ii. On the next screen, select an 'Account Determination' (say, B1000) and double-click on 'Balance Sheet Accounts' on the left-hand side 'Dialog Structure'

iii. On the resulting screen, double-click on the depreciation area ('Area') and maintain the appropriate G/L accounts, under 'Retirement account assignment' data block, on the next screen (Figure 13.122).

iv. Repeat for all the account determinations and appropriate depreciation areas.

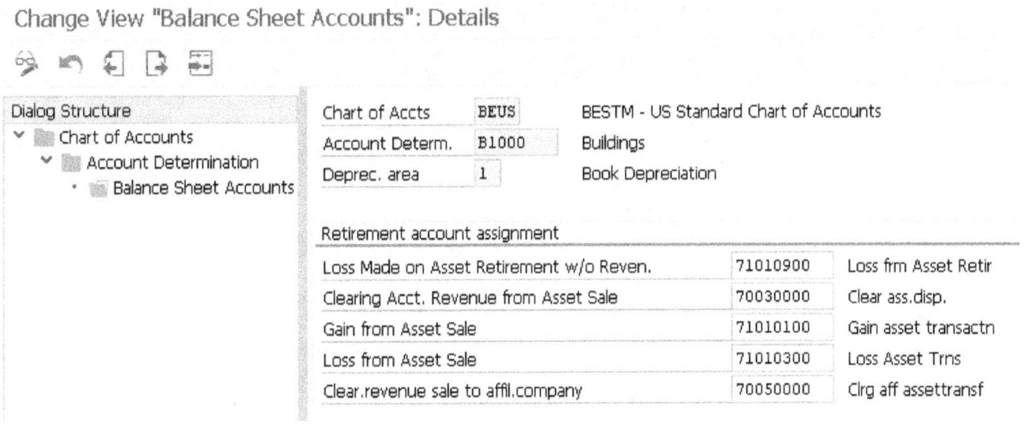

Change View "Balance Sheet Accounts": Details

Dialog Structure
∨ Chart of Accounts
  ∨ Account Determination
    · Balance Sheet Accounts

Chart of Accts	BEUS	BESTM - US Standard Chart of Accounts
Account Determ.	B1000	Buildings
Deprec. area	1	Book Depreciation

Retirement account assignment

Loss Made on Asset Retirement w/o Reven.	71010900	Loss frm Asset Retir
Clearing Acct. Revenue from Asset Sale	70030000	Clear ass.disp.
Gain from Asset Sale	71010100	Gain asset transactn
Loss from Asset Sale	71010300	Loss Asset Trns
Clear.revenue sale to affil.company	70050000	Clrg aff assettransf

Figure 13.122 Assigning G/L Accounts for Asset Retirements

This completes our discussion on configuring the settings for asset retirements. Let us move on to discuss the settings for asset transfers.

13.9.3 Transfer Postings

In this Section, we shall be discussing the configuration settings for asset transfers. The first activity is to define the transaction types for such transfers.

13.9.3.1   Define Transaction Types for Transfers

You need two transaction types for transfers between assets: (a) a transaction type for retirement from the sending asset and (b) a transaction type for the acquisition on the receiving asset. The system performs the posting transaction from the point of view of the sending asset.

We recommend using the SAP supplied standard transaction types which you can view using the menu path: SAP Customizing Implementation Guide > Financial Accounting > Asset Accounting > Transactions > Transfer Postings > Define Transaction Types for Transfers.

You will see the 'Select Activity' pop-up screen, when you enter the transaction. Double-click on the 'Define Transaction Types for Retirement Transfers' activity to view the list of standard transaction types (300, 306, 320, 338, 339, 340 etc) for retirement transfers (Figure 13.123). You can also reach this screen, directly, by using Transaction AO76.

Change View "FI-AA: Transaction types": Overview

New Entries

Transact. type	Transaction Type Name
300	Retirmt transfer of prior-yr acquis. frm cap.asset
306	Retmt transfer prior-yr acquis. from cap.asset FI
320	Retirmt transfer of curr-yr acquis.
338	Retirmt transfer of prior-yr acquis from inv.meas.
339	Acquirg transfer of curr-yr acquis from inv.meas.
340	Retmt transfer of prior-yr acquis f. AuC, line itm
345	Retmt transfer of curr-yr acquis f. AuC, line itm
348	Retmt transfer of prior-yr acquis from AuC,summary

Figure 13.123 Standard Transaction Types for Retirement Transfers

When you go back to the initial pop-up and double-click on 'Define Transaction Types for Acquisition Transfers', you will be taken to another set of standard transaction types (310, 330, 331, 336 etc) for acquisition transfers. You may reach this screen (Figure 13.124), directly, using Transaction AO75.

Change View "FI-AA: Transaction types": Overview

New Entries

Transact. type	Transaction Type Name
310	Acquirg transfer of prior-yr acquis. frm cap.asset
330	Acquiring transfer of curr-yr acquis.
331	Acquirg transfer of prior-yr acquis from inv.meas.
336	Acquirg transfer of curr-yr acquis from inv.meas.
341	Acquirg transfer of prior-yr acquis from AuC
342	Bal.forward AuC after partial settlmt pr-yr acquis
346	Acquirg transfer of curr-yr acquis. from AuC

Figure 13.124 Standard Transaction Types for Acquisition Transfers

The next step is to specify the posting variant for retirement transfers.

13.9.3.2   Specify Posting Variant for Retirement Transfers

Here, in this step, you shall define the way retirement transfers are to be treated in the system, per depreciation area, whether to:

a) Transfer of APC and proportional value adjustments, or

b) Transfer of APC <u>without</u> proportional value adjustment.

In most of the countries, you will use the option (a) unless you need to take care of group assets in accordance with ADR legislation in USA wherein you will use the option (b).

Use the menu path: SAP Customizing Implementation Guide > Financial Accounting > Asset Accounting > Transactions > Transfer Postings > Specify Posting Variant for Retirement Transfers, or Transaction OAY1:

i. On the resulting screen, per transaction type ('Tra'), you need to specify how to handle the retirement transfers. Select the transaction type and double-click on 'Special handling of transfer posting' on the left-hand side 'Dialog Structure'.

ii. On the next screen, ensure that you do not select 'Trans. APC Only' check-box, for the depreciation areas, if you want to transfer APC and proportional value adjustments (Figure 13.125). If you select this check-box, then, the system transfers only the APC and <u>not</u> the proportional value adjustments. You will select the check-box only when you want to take care of *group assets* in accordance with ADR legislation in USA.

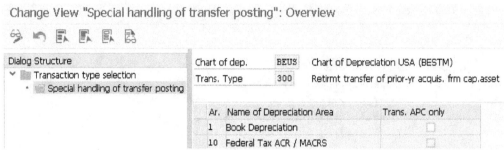

Figure 13.125 Posting Variant for Retirement Transfers

With this, we are, now, ready to discuss the configuration settings for intercompany asset transfers.

13.9.4 Intercompany Asset Transfers

You use *'intercompany asset transfer'* to carry out asset transfers between company codes. In the case of individual companies, an intercompany transfer represents a retirement for one company code and an acquisition for the other. However, from corporate groups' view point, it represents a transfer that balances to zero in the group asset history sheet. Refer Section 13.10.7 for details on asset history sheet.

An intercompany asset transfer results when (a) there is a change in the physical location of the asset which leads to assigning of the asset to a new company code and/or (b) there is a change in the organizational structure of the corporate group calling for re-assigning the asset to a different company code.

You cannot just change the organizational assignment of the asset by changing the asset master record: for each asset that you want to transfer, you have to create a new master record in the target company code, or you use an existing asset master record. This way, the system preserves the unique identity of the asset using the inventory number in the asset master record.

The intercompany asset transfers can be of the following types:

- *Client-internal transfer*
  Also known as *'automatic intercompany transfer'*, here, you post the retirement transfer and the acquisition transfer in a single step.

  You can reverse automatic intercompany asset transfers, using the normal reversal functions in FI-AA: the system reverses the 'retirement document' in the sending company code and the 'acquisition document' in the target company code. If the transfer has resulted in a new asset creation in the target company code, you can block the asset for any additional acquisition postings.

- *Cross-client transfer*

  Also known as the *'manual intercompany transfer*, here, you process the transfer across clients / systems; you post the retirement transfer and the acquisition transfer in two separate steps. While you can integrate the posting with FI-A/P and FI-A/R in the manual transfer, you cannot do so in the automatic transfer.

  In the case of manual intercompany asset transfer, you can reverse the retirement and the acquisition, separately, in the company code in which you made the respective postings.

With this background, let us understand the control parameters that you need to define for intercompany asset transfer (both automatic and manual).

Let us understand first, the settings, for automatic transfer.

13.9.4.1   Automatic Intercompany Asset Transfers

Towards automatic intercompany asset transfer, you need to complete the following tasks:

- Define Cross-System Depreciation Areas
- Define Transfer Variants

Let us start with the first activity of defining the cross-system depreciation areas.

13.9.4.1.1   *Define Cross-System Depreciation Areas*

Using *'cross-system depreciation areas'*, you can assign a meaning to the local depreciation areas that is then valid in all charts of depreciation throughout your system. The cross-system depreciation area makes this possible, although the different depreciation areas have different keys in different charts of depreciation. For each cross-system depreciation area, you can specify its own transfer methods in a transfer variant.

Project Dolphin

BESTM does not need a cross-system depreciation areas to handle intercompany asset transactions, when asset transfer happens among the company codes situated either within US or within India, as all the US-based company codes use the same chart of depreciation BEUS and all the company codes in India use the same chart of depreciation BEIN. In each case, the chart of depreciation is the same and the depreciation areas have the same numbering and meaning (Figure 13.126).

However, BESTM requires the cross-system depreciation areas, to facilitate intercompany asset transfers between a company in US and another in India, as these company codes use two different charts of accounts (BEUS for US-based company codes and BEIN for India-based company codes). In this case, the depreciation areas, though have the same keys (for some of the areas), their meaning are different across the systems.

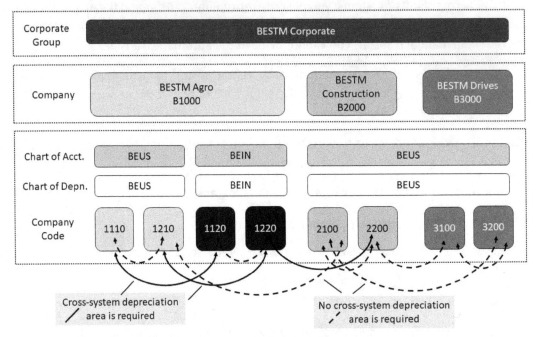

Figure 13.126 BESTM - Intercompany Asset Transfer: Overview

You do not need cross-system depreciation areas, if all company codes in your client use the same chart of depreciation, or if the depreciation areas (in your charts of depreciation) have the same purpose and meaning, across the system, and also have the same keys.

You need global cross-system depreciation areas only when (a) you use different charts of depreciation (with the individual depreciation areas having the same meaning), or (b) a depreciation area that is not intended to be transferred during intercompany transfer, or (c) you have individual depreciation areas with the same name, but their meanings are different.

Use the menu path: SAP Customizing Implementation Guide > Financial Accounting > Asset Accounting > Transactions > Intercompany Asset Transfers > Automatic Intercompany Asset Transfers > Define Cross-System Depreciation Areas.

On the resulting 'Select Activity' pop-up screen, double-click on 'Define Cross-System Depreciation Areas'. On the next screen, click on 'New Entries' and define the new cross-system depreciation area (Figure 13.127).

Change View "Define Cross-System Depreciation Areas": Overview

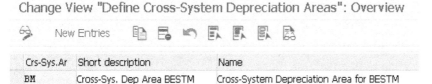

Crs-Sys.Ar	Short description	Name
BM	Cross-Sys. Dep Area BESTM	Cross-System Depreciation Area for BESTM

Figure 13.127 New Cross-System Depreciation Area for BESTM

Now, go back to the initial pop-up screen, and double-click on 'Assign Local to Cross-System Depreciation Areas'. On the next screen (you can reach here, directly, by using Transaction OATB), for your chart of depreciations (say, BEUS and BEIN) enter the cross-system depreciation area's key in the 'Crs-Sys.Ar' field against the appropriate depreciation area(s), and 'Save' the details (Figure 13.128).

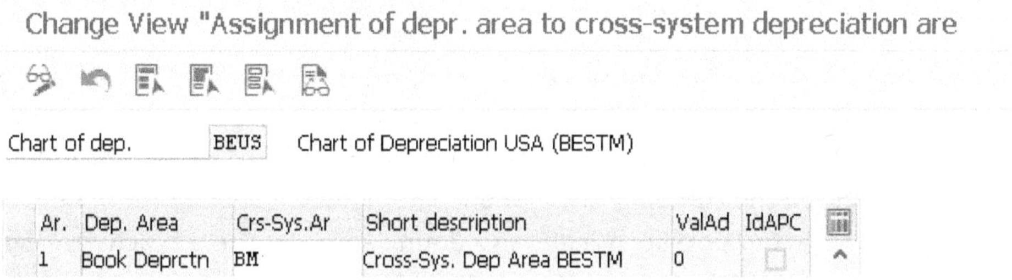

Change View "Assignment of depr. area to cross-system depreciation are

Chart of dep.   BEUS   Chart of Depreciation USA (BESTM)

Ar.	Dep. Area	Crs-Sys.Ar	Short description	ValAd	IdAPC	
1	Book Deprctn	BM	Cross-Sys. Dep Area BESTM	0	☐	^

Figure 13.128 Assigning Depreciation Area to Cross-System Depreciation Area

The next step is to define the transfer variants.

13.9.4.1.2   Define Transfer Variants

Here, in this step, you will define the *'transfer variants'*. These variants contain the appropriate control parameters for intercompany asset transfers including (a) the transaction types for posting the transactions that belong to an intercompany transfer (retirement / acquisition) and (b) the transfer method for the capitalization of the transferred assets in the target company code. Besides these two, you can also specify, in each transfer variant, which master data fields should be copied from the transferred asset to the target asset, if a new asset has to be created in the target company code.

> **ℹ** You can use SAP supplied standard transaction types without creating your own. The retirement transaction type specifies whether the retirement affects current-year acquisitions or prior-year acquisitions. Accordingly, you need two different transfer variants (with different transaction types, such as 230 and 275) for the transfer of prior-year acquisitions and current-year acquisitions.

Use the menu path: SAP Customizing Implementation Guide > Financial Accounting > Asset Accounting > Transactions > Intercompany Asset Transfers > Automatic Intercompany Asset Transfers > Define Transfer Variants.

On the resulting screen, you will see a 'Select Activity' pop-up screen, with three activities listed there on (Figure 13.129).

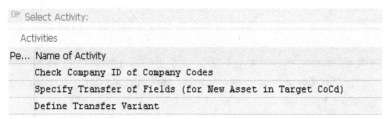

Figure 13.129 'Select Activity' Pop-up Screen for defining Transfer Variants

i.   Double-click on the 1st activity ('Check Company ID of Company Codes'). The system takes you to the next screen wherein you can view / change company code global parameters. You can also reach this screen directly using Transaction OAY6. We have already configured the company code global parameters in Section 6.8 of Chapter 6.

ii. Go back to the initial pop-up screen, and double-click on the 2nd activity, 'Specify Transfer of Fields (for New Asset in Target CoCd)'.

   a)   On the resulting screen, you will see the list of variants (Figure 13.130).

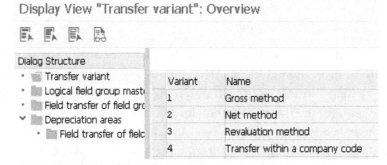

Figure 13.130 List of Transfer Variants

   b)   Select a variant (say, 2 Net method) and double-click on 'Logical field group master data' on the left-hand side 'Dialog Structure'. The system will bring up the logical field groups, on the next screen (Figure 13.131).

Display View "Logical field group master data": Overview

Dialog Structure
- Transfer variant
- Logical field group mast
- Field transfer of field grc
- ✓ Depreciation areas
  - Field transfer of fielc

Log.Fld.Gr	Log.Field Group Name
1	General data
2	Posting information
3	Time-dependent data
4	Allocations
5	Leasing
6	Net worth valuation
7	Real estate and similar rights

Figure 13.131 List of Logical Field Groups

c) Select a logical field group (say, 1 General Data) and double-click on 'Field transfer of field groups' on the left-hand side 'Dialog Structure'. The system brings up the next screen, with the field group details. Select the 'Copy' checkbox against the required field groups, if you want the system to copy the contents of fields, of the corresponding field group, from the asset being retired to the new asset, during intercompany asset transfer (Figure 13.132).

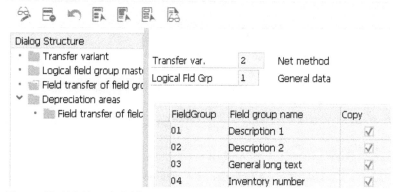

Change View "Field transfer of field groups": Overview

Dialog Structure
- Transfer variant
- Logical field group mast
- Field transfer of field grc
- ✓ Depreciation areas
  - Field transfer of fielc

| Transfer var. | 2 | Net method |
| Logical Fld Grp | 1 | General data |

FieldGroup	Field group name	Copy
01	Description 1	✓
02	Description 2	✓
03	General long text	✓
04	Inventory number	✓

Figure 13.132 List of Field Groups

d) Now, select a field group (say, 04 Inventory number) and double-click on 'Depreciation areas' on the left-hand side 'Dialog Structure'. The system brings up the 'Change View "Depreciation Areas": Overview' screen. You will notice that there are two entries: one with * and another with BM (Figure 13.133).

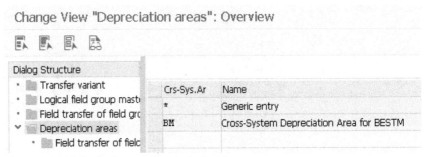

Figure 13.133 Cross-System Depreciation Area

e) Now, select the BM row and double-click on 'Field transfer of field groups' (under 'Depreciation areas') on the left-hand side 'Dialog Structure'. You will reach the 'Change View "Field transfer of field groups": Overview' screen. Select the 'Copy' check-box against the required field groups and 'Save' your settings (Figure 13.134). The 'Copy' check-box, when selected, enables the system to copy the field content, of the corresponding fields in the field group, from the asset being retired to the new asset, during intercompany asset transfer.

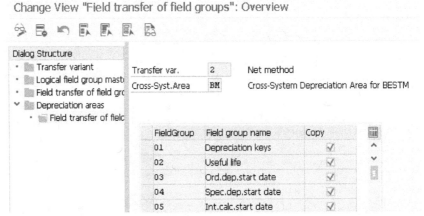

Figure 13.134 Field Group Activation for Cross-System Depreciation Area BM

f) Repeat the steps (a) to (e) for the other variants / logical field groups / field groups for the cross-system depreciation area BM and 'Save' the details.

iii. Now, again, go back to the initial pop-up screen, and double-click on 3rd activity, 'Define Transfer Variant':

a) On the resulting screen, the system brings up all the transfer variants (Figure 13.135).

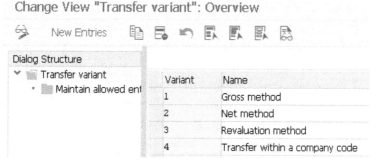

Figure 13.135 Transfer Variants

b) Select the variant (say, 2 Net method) and double-click on 'Maintain allowed entries' on the left-hand side 'Dialog Structure'. The system will, now, bring up the next screen, 'Change View "Maintain allowed entries": Overview' screen, with two generic entries. Copy those two * entries and create the new entries for BM (Figure 13.136).

Figure 13.136 Maintaining Allowed Depreciation Areas for Transfer Variant 2

c) Repeat the steps (a) and (b) and complete the configuration for the other transfer variants also.

This completes our settings for automatic intercompany asset transfer. The next configuration is to specify gross/net transfer method for manual intercompany transfer.

13.9.4.2 Specify Gross or Net Transfer Method for Manual Transfer

You need to make the system settings, here in this step, only if you plan to post intercompany asset transfers manually between systems or clients, as in the case of BESTM when asset transfer happens between a US-based company code and an India-based company code. In all other cases intercompany asset transfers for BESTM, that is between company codes within US / India, you can use the automatic intercompany transfer procedure that we have described in the previous Section 13.9.4.1.

You are already aware that the intercompany transfers between systems or clients are posted in two steps: (a) retirement of the sending asset and (b) acquisition on the receiving asset. Now, using this configuration step, you shall define the features of the transaction types that you will use in these manual asset transfers. You will specify (a) a sending or receiving company for the postings belonging to a transfer (posting with affiliated company), and (b) that cumulative value adjustments can be entered along with the APC being acquired, when making the acquisition posting (gross posting). You can also specify that the affiliated company can be entered in receiving transfers from affiliated companies, but that accounting transaction, however, will be posted net in all areas (regardless of the indicator in the area definition).

Use the menu path: SAP Customizing Implementation Guide > Financial Accounting > Asset Accounting > Transactions > Intercompany Asset Transfers > Specify Gross or Net Transfer Method for Manual Transfer:

i.   On the resulting 'Select Activity' pop-up screen, double-click on 'Define Characteristics of Transfer Transact. Types (Acquis.)'.

ii.   The system takes you to the 'Change view "FI-AA: Transaction types": Overview' screen. You can also reach this screen directly using Transaction AO67. You will see a list of asset acquisition transaction types on this screen.

iii. Double-click on a transaction type (say, 151), and ensure that the standard settings are correct (Figure 13.137).

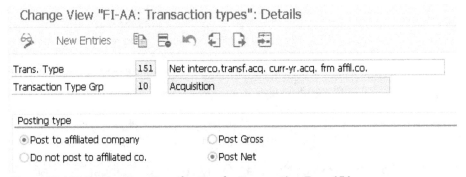

Figure 13.137 Posting Type Specification for Transaction Type 151

iv.   Now, go back to the initial pop-up screen, and double-click on 'Define Characteristics of Transfer Transact. Types (Retirmt)'. You will see the list of transaction types associated with asset retirement, on the next screen (you can also reach this screen, directly, through Transaction AO68).

v.   Double-click on a specific transaction (say, 230) to view the settings for intercompany retirement posting on the next screen (Figure 13.138).

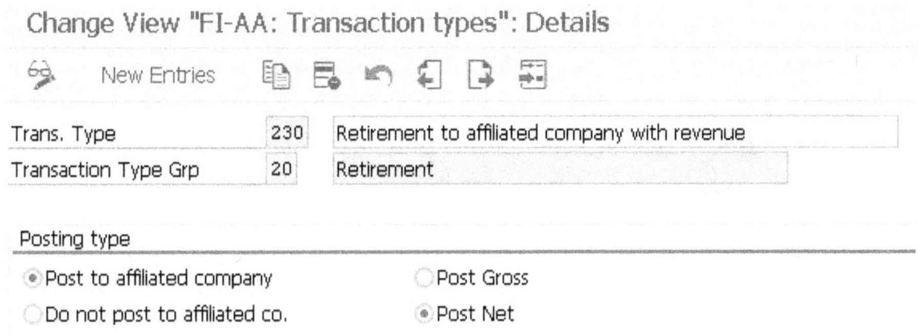

Change View "FI-AA: Transaction types": Details

⟳   New Entries   🗎 🗐 ↩ ⟵ 📤 ⬚

| Trans. Type | 230 | Retirement to affiliated company with revenue |
| Transaction Type Grp | 20 | Retirement |

Posting type

◉ Post to affiliated company   ○ Post Gross
○ Do not post to affiliated co.   ◉ Post Net

Figure 13.138 Posting Type Specification for Transaction Type 230

This completes our discussion on configuring the system for intercompany asset transfers. Let us, now, move on to discuss how to configure the transactions for AuC.

13.9.5 Capitalization of Assets under Construction (AuC)

We have already seen in <u>Section 13.3.1</u>, that AuC is a special form of tangible asset that you usually display as a separate B/S item and therefore it needs a separate account determination in the asset class.

The AuC that you produce in-house has two stages in its life that is relevant for accounting: (a) under construction phase and (b) useful life (Figure 13.139). You need to show AuC as a different B/S item, based on the phase that it is in. Hence, you need to manage this asset as a separate object or asset master record during the construction phase. The transition from the construction phase to the other phase is called as the 'capitalization of AuC'.

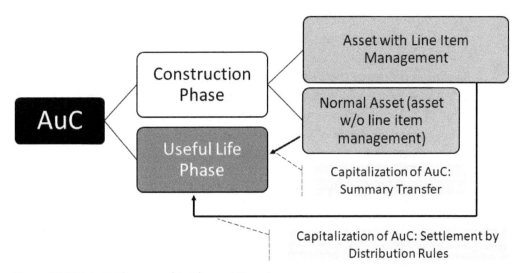

Figure 13.139 AuC: Phases and Settlement Overview

During the under *'construction phase'*, you can manage these assets either in a normal asset master record or in an asset master record with line item management. As a result, you can handle the transfer from the AuC to completed fixed assets in one of two ways: (a) summary transfer from a normal asset master record to the receiver assets (transaction type 348/349) or (b) as an asset master record with line item management, that you settle by line item to the receivers.

Let us understand more on AuC with line item management / without line item management (summary transfer):

- *AuC without Line Item Management (Summary Transfer)*
  The procedure corresponds to the procedure for the transfer between two assets within the same company code. Before carrying out a full transfer of an AuC, reverse any downpayments that you have already posted in the current fiscal year. You can ignore downpayments for a partial transfer. To display transfers in asset history sheet as acquisitions, you need to use special transaction types for the transfer of AuC.

- *AuC with Line Item Management (Collective Management)*
  As FI-AA allows you to accumulate costs, under purely technical aspects, in an AuC, you do not need to consider the later creation of fixed assets at this point, during construction. Accordingly, you can accumulate all acquisitions for an investment in a single asset, during the construction phase. These acquisitions can include (a) external activity (acquisition from vendor), (b) internal activity (internal order) and/or (c) stock material (withdrawal from warehouse).

  When you use this *'collective management'* of AuC, it is possible that you can manage the individual acquisitions as open items over the course of several fiscal years. However, at completion, you need to clear these line items and distribute them to the various receivers. The system activates open item management when you create AuC, if you have set the corresponding indicator in the asset class (Refer Section 13.3.1.4). Besides, for open item settlement, you need to assign a settlement profile to the company codes involved (Refer Section 13.9.5.4); using the settlement profile, you can specify the allowed receivers (such as, assets or cost centers).

During the *'settlement phase'*, for AuCs with line item settlement, the system carries the settlement by using *'distribution rules'*. These are asset-specific, and they contain a distribution key and a receiver. You can bundle several distribution rules to form a *'distribution rule group'*. You can, then, assign these groups to one or more line items of an asset. You can have the distribution key either as equivalence numbers or percentage rates, so that you can distribute any number of combinations of line items to any number of combinations of receivers.

> ℹ️ You can set up the settlement rules at a given point in time, and then carry out the corresponding update of the line items at a later point in time, since a separate transaction exists for the actual settlement (Transaction AIBU). This transaction triggers the settlement posting for the selected AuC, and creates the necessary posting documents. Here, the system automatically separates the transfer of asset acquisitions from prior fiscal years from acquisitions that took place in the year of capitalization. When the system transfers the prior-year acquisitions, it also transfers the (special) depreciation and investment support proportionally. The system automatically generates carryforward postings for partial capitalization.

With this background on AuC, let us understand the configuration settings that are required for setting up the system for capitalizing AuC. Let us start with the first task of defining the transaction types.

13.9.5.1   Define Transaction Types

Here, using this configuration step, you shall define the transaction types for capitalizing AuC. As in other cases of asset transaction types, here also, you can use the standard ones supplied by SAP without defining a new transaction type.

Use the menu path: SAP Customizing Implementation Guide > Financial Accounting > Asset Accounting > Transactions > Capitalization of Assets under Construction > Define Transaction Types. You may also use Transaction OAXG.

On the resulting screen, you will see the list of standard transactions (like 331, 336, 338 etc) associated with AuC (Figure 13.140). You may select any of the transaction types and view the detailed settings.

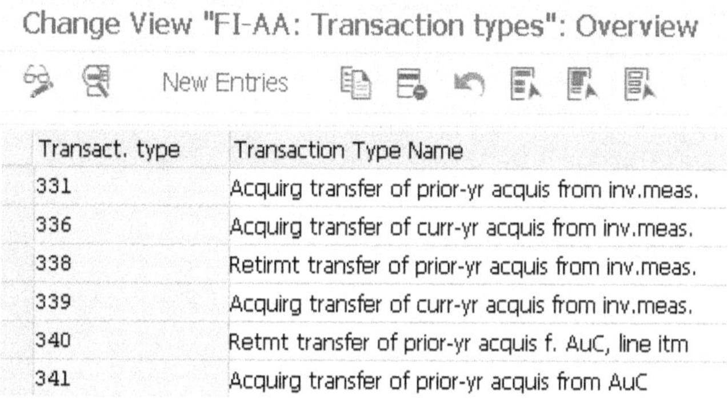

Change View "FI-AA: Transaction types": Overview

🔍 🔍   New Entries   ▤ ▤ ↻ ▤ ▤ ▤

Transact. type	Transaction Type Name
331	Acquirg transfer of prior-yr acquis from inv.meas.
336	Acquirg transfer of curr-yr acquis from inv.meas.
338	Retirmt transfer of prior-yr acquis from inv.meas.
339	Acquirg transfer of curr-yr acquis from inv.meas.
340	Retmt transfer of prior-yr acquis f. AuC, line itm
341	Acquirg transfer of prior-yr acquis from AuC

Figure 13.140 AuC: Transaction Types

We can, now, move on to specify the asset classes for enabling transfer posting, from AuC to completed assets, in the next step.

13.9.5.2   Allow Transfer Transaction Types for Asset Classes

In this step, you will specify the asset classes, in which posting is allowed using the transaction type groups, for transfers from AuC to completed assets.

Use the menu path: SAP Customizing Implementation Guide > Financial Accounting > Asset Accounting > Transactions > Capitalization of Assets under Construction > Allow Transfer Transaction Types for Asset Classes. You may also use Transaction OAYB:

i.   On the resulting screen, select a transaction type group (say, 15 Down payment) and double-click on 'Specification of asset classes' on the left-hand side 'Dialog Structure'.

ii.   On the resulting screen (Figure 13.141), you will see that the system has already populated the asset class B6000 (AuC) as the specified asset class for allowing transfer postings for AuC.

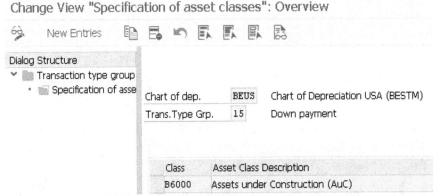

Figure 13.141 AuC: Specification of Asset Classes for Transaction Type Group 15

iii. Go back to the previous screen and select another transaction type group (say, 38) and double-click on 'Specification of asset classes' on the left-hand side 'Dialog Structure'.

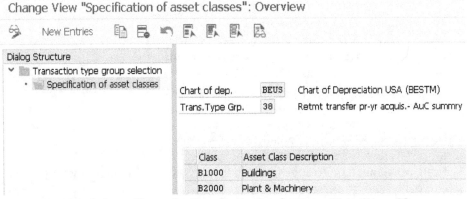

Figure 13.142 AuC: Asset Classes for Transfer Posting for Trans. Type Group 38

iv.   Click on 'New Entries' on the next screen, and enter the appropriate asset classes (Figure 13.142).

v.   Repeat the steps for the other two transaction type groups (16 and 39), if required.

The next step is to specify the cost element for AuC's settlement to CO receiver.

13.9.5.3   Determine Cost Element for Settlement to CO Receiver

When you settle AuC with line item management, you can settle debits to CO receivers (particularly, cost centers). You may need this if debits were capitalized to the AuC by mistake. To make this settlement to CO receivers, the system requires a cost element that you will define in this step.

Use the menu path: SAP Customizing Implementation Guide > Financial Accounting > Asset Accounting > Transactions > Capitalization of Assets under Construction > Determine Cost Element for Settlement to CO Receiver. You may also use Transaction AO89:

i.   On the resulting screen, select the chart of accounts (say, BEUS) and double-click on 'Account Determination' on the left-hand side 'Dialog Structure'.

ii.   Select an account determination (say, B1000) and double-click on 'Assign Accounts to Areas' on the left-hand side 'Dialog Structure'.

iii.   Now, double-click on the depreciation area (say, 01) on the resulting screen, and enter the cost element for settlement of AuC to Co objects on the next screen.

The next step is to define / assign settlement for profiles.

13.9.5.4   Define/Assign Settlement Profiles

Here, in this step, you can define the *'settlement profiles'* for settling AuC. You can store one profile in the Customizing definition of each asset company code. The system, then, uses this key when there is an AuC to be settled in that company code. SAP provides the settlement profile 'AI' as the default one which you can use as such, or you can create a new one by copying this and changing settings appropriately.

Project Dolphin

The project team has suggested to the BESTM management to copy the standard profile and create a new one so that settlement is made optional to some of the CO receivers like cost center, order etc. This is required to take care of settling debits to these receivers when debits were capitalized to AuC by mistake. Also, BESTM wants to have the flexibility of settling by percentage, equivalence numbers and amount. Besides, it was suggested to have a validation to ensure that the settlement does not exceed 100% in a percentage settlement; above, or below, the system should issue a warning accordingly.

Use the menu path: SAP Customizing Implementation Guide > Financial Accounting > Asset Accounting > Transactions > Capitalization of Assets under Construction > Define/Assign Settlement Profiles:

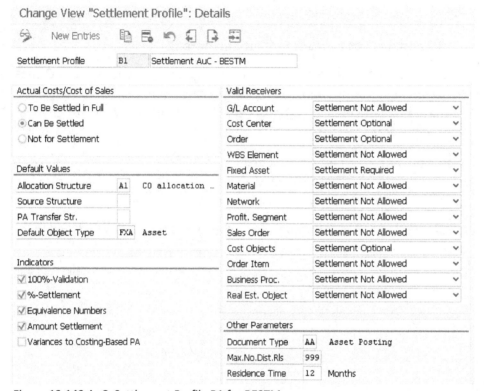

Figure 13.143 AuC: Settlement Profile B1 for BESTM

i.   On the resulting pop-up screen, double-click on the 'Define Settlement Profile' activity.

ii. On the next screen, you will see the standard settlement profile, AI, supplied by SAP (you may directly reach this screen using Transaction OKO7). Select that row and click on 'Copy As' and create a new one (B1) for BESTM.

iii. Double-click on B1 to change the default settings, appropriately, on the next screen (Figure 13.143):

    a.   Under 'Actual cost/ Cost of Sales', endure that you have selected the default 'To be settled in full' radio-button. If you try to close the object, or set the delete flag, the system displays an error message if the balance in the object is not zero.

    a.   Under 'Valid Receivers', the default setting is 'Settlement Required' for 'Fixed Asset'. As we want to settle the debits that would have been mistakenly capitalized to AuC, you need to select the value 'Settlement Optional' for 'Cost Center' and 'Order'.

b. Under 'Indicators':

- When you select '100%-Validation', if you have defined percentage distribution rules for a particular settlement rule, then, the system checks the total percentage either when you save the settlement rule or when you use the percentage check function. The indicator only affects periodic settlement. In overall settlement, the percentage must always be 100%. When set, the system issues a warning, if the total is <> 100%. When NOT set, the system issues a warning only when the total is >100%. In both cases, you can ignore the warning and save the settlement rule. However, to run the settlement, you must first correct the settlement rule.

- When you select '%-Settlement', then, you can use the settlement rule to determine the distribution rules governing the percentage costs to be settled.

- When you select 'Equivalence Numbers', then, you can define distribution rules in the settlement rule, according to which costs are settled proportionally.

> **i** For example, if you have a settlement rule to distribute to four cost centers, in the ratio of 1:2:3:4, then as per equivalence, the first cost center will receive 1/10 of the costs, the second cost center at 2/10, and so on.

- Select 'Amount Settlement' check-box, so as to define distribution rules in the settlement rule, which allow costs to be settled by amount.

iv. Now, go back to the initial pop-up screen, and double-click on 'Assign Settlement Profile to Company Code'.

v. On the resulting screen, enter the settlement profile ('SProf.') against the asset accounting company codes and 'Save' the details (Figure 13.144). You may also reach this screen, directly, by using Transaction OAAZ.

Change View "FI-AA: Settlement profile": Overview

CoCd	Company Name	SProf.	Text
1110	BESTM Farm Machinery	B1	Settlement AuC - BESTM
1120	BESTM Garden & Forestry E	B1	Settlement AuC - BESTM

Figure 13.144 AuC: Assignment Settlement Profile

The next task is to specify the depreciation areas for capitalization of AuC / downpayment.

13.9.5.5   Specify Capitalization of AUC/Down-Payment

Here, you can determine how the system deals with down payments on AuCs, and their closing invoice during capitalization (=settlement) of the AuC. The settings you make here are particularly relevant for representing the downpayments, from previous years, in the asset history sheet.

> **i** In the standard system, when you capitalize downpayment (from the previous year), and the closing invoice (from the current year) together, the system transfers (a) the downpayment amount, with the transaction type for old asset data from previous years, and (b) only the difference between the closing invoice and the downpayment, with the transaction type for current (new) acquisitions.

Project Dolphin

BESTM, in AuCs, does not want to ignore the downpayments during line item settlement. Instead, they want capitalization of downpayments from the previous year, and the closing invoice from the current year, together.

Use the menu path: SAP Customizing Implementation Guide > Financial Accounting > Asset Accounting > Transactions > Capitalization of Assets under Construction > Specify Capitalization of AUC/Down-Payment, or Transaction OAYU:

i.   On the resulting screen, select the company code (say, 1110), and double-click on the 'Capitalization rule' on the left-hand side 'Dialog Structure'.

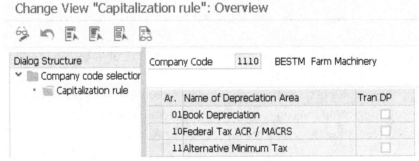

Figure 13.145 AuC: Capitalization Rule

ii.   On the next screen, the system displays all the depreciation areas with the 'Trans DP' check-box selected against them, by default.

With this setting, the system ignores downpayments during the line item settlement of AuC. The total amount of the closing invoice is, then, transferred to the capitalized asset using the transaction type based on the year of the closing invoice. However, if you want to capitalize downpayment (from the previous year), and the closing invoice (from the current year) together, as in for BESTM, then, you should de-select the 'Trans DP' check-box for the appropriate depreciation areas (Figure 13.145).

iii.   Repeat the settings for other company codes, and 'Save' the details.

The next task is to maintain the number ranges for line item settlement documents.

13.9.5.6   Maintain Number Ranges for Documents for Line Item Settlmt

As in the case of every settlement (in cost accounting) that is uniquely numbered by a settlement document, under a separate number (per settlement), the system creates a CO settlement document in the CO area, to which the asset or the investment measure belongs, for the line item settlement of an AuC. Hence, if you plan to use line item settlement of AuC (or investment measures), then, you need to define the number range intervals for the settlement documents in one or more CO areas.

> **i** Define separate number range intervals for settlement documents for each CO area, if you use more than one CO area, so as to improve performance when you carry out settlements in different CO areas simultaneously.

Use the menu path: SAP Customizing Implementation Guide > Financial Accounting > Asset Accounting > Transactions > Capitalization of Assets under Construction > Maintain Number Ranges for Documents for Line Item Settlmt:

i.   On the resulting 'Select Activity' pop-up screen, double-click on the first activity: 'Maintain Number Ranges for Controlling Documents'.

    a.   On the next screen, enter the controlling area (say, B100). You can come to this screen directly by using Transaction KANK.

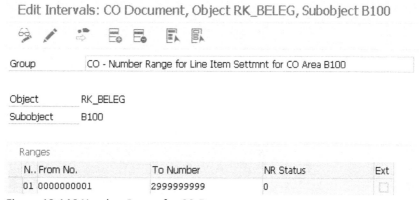

Figure 13.146 Number Range for CO Documents

b. Now, click on 'Change Groups' and click on 'Create Group' on the next screen.

c. On the resulting screen, enter the details to create a new group and assign the appropriate number ranges (Figure 13.146).

d. Go, back to the initial 'Edit Intervals: CO Document, Object RK_BELEG' screen, and click on 'Change Groups'.

e. On the next screen, you will see the 'Non-Assigned Elements' for the controlling area B100 (Figure 13.147).

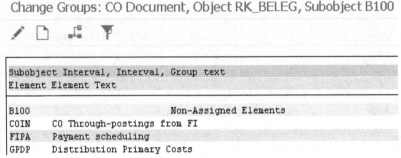

Figure 13.147 Non-Assigned Elements for CO Area B100

f. Place the cursor on an 'Element' and click on 'Assign Element to Group', to add the appropriate elements to the newly created number interval group for CO area B100.

ii. Go back to the initial pop-up screen, double-click on 'Change Number Ranges for Settlement Document':

a. On the resulting screen (you can also reach this screen using Transaction SNUM), click on 'Change Groups'. On the next screen, click 'Create Group' and define a new number range group (say, B1) for settlement documents.

b. Once defined, assign this group the CO area B100.

c. Now, from the 'Edit Intervals: CO object Settlement, Object CO_ABRECHN' screen, you can click on 'Change Intervals' and see the newly added group B1 (Figure 13.148).

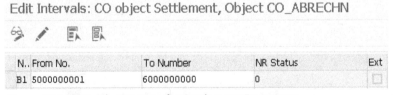

Figure 13.148 Number Ranges for Settlement Document

iii. Again, go back to the initial pop-up and double-click on 'Check Assignment of Controlling Area to Company Code':

a. On the resulting screen (you can reach here directly by using Transaction OKKP), select the controlling area (say, B100) and double-click on 'Activate components/control indicators' on the left-hand side 'Dialog Structure'.

b. On the resulting screen, you will see the CO components that have already been activated. You can reach this screen (Figure 13.149) directly by using Transaction OKKP.

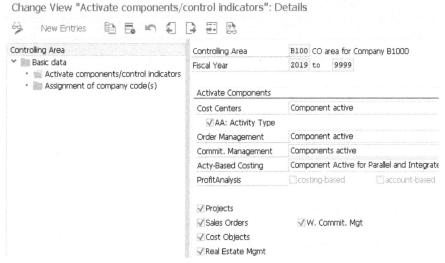

Figure 13.149 Activation of CO Components / Control Indicators – CO Area B100

c. Now, double-click on 'Assignment of company code(s)', and you will see the company codes assigned to the controlling area B100 on the next screen (Figure 13.150). We have already completed this step when we did the 'CO Area-Company Code' assignment vide Section 5.4.4 of Chapter 5.

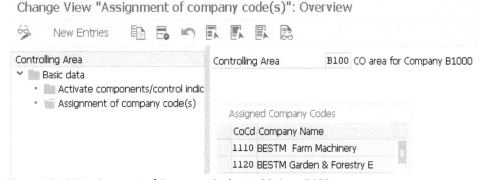

Figure 13.150 Assignment of Company Codes to CO Area B100

iv. Repeat and complete the above steps, for all other controlling areas of BESTM.

This completes our discussion on configuring the system for capitalizing AuC. Let us now look at a few more settings that are required for putting through some of the asset transactions. Let us start with the transaction types for post-capitalization

13.9.6 Define Transaction Types for Post-Capitalization

Here, you will define the transaction types for post-capitalization activities. If you plan to use SAP's standard transaction types, you do not need to define anything new here. You can view the standard transaction types for post-capitalization (Figure 13.151) by using the menu path: SAP Customizing Implementation Guide > Financial Accounting > Asset Accounting > Transactions > Define Transaction Types for Post-Capitalization, or Transaction AO77.

Change View "FI-AA: Transaction types": Overview

New Entries

Transact. type	Transaction Type Name
400	Post-capitalization
401	Post-capitalization in following year
490	Post-capitalization: TTY for proportional values

Figure 13.151 Standard Transaction Types for Post-Capitalization

The next step is to define the transaction types for manual depreciation.

13.9.7 Define Transaction Types for Manual Depreciation

You already know that you can use manual postings to correct the value of assets, for example, when there is a need for unplanned depreciation, or write-ups or handling other manually scheduled depreciation (ordinary or special depreciation). Here in this step, you can define the transaction types for handling manual depreciation. As in other cases of transaction types, here also, you can use SAP supplied standard transaction types without going in for your own transaction types. In that case, you do not define anything new here.

Change View "FI-AA: Transaction types": Overview

New Entries

Transact. type	Transaction Type Name
600	Manual ordinary depreciation on prior-yr acquis.
610	Manual ordinary depreciation on current-yr acquis.
620	Manual spec. dep. on prior-yr acquis per dep. key
630	Manual spec. dep. on curr-yr acquis per dep. key
640	Unplanned depreciation on prior-year acquisitions
650	Unplanned depreciation on current-yr acquisition
6J1	Adjust cut-off value check (Japan)
700	Write-up ordinary and special depreciation

Figure 13.152 Standard Transaction Types for Manual Depreciation

You can use the menu path: SAP Customizing Implementation Guide > Financial Accounting > Asset Accounting > Transactions > Define Transaction Types for Manual Depreciation or Transaction AO78, to view the standard transaction types (Figure 13.152).

With this, let us specify the default transaction types for FI-AA postings.

13.9.8 Specify Default Transaction Types

Here, in this step, you can determine the transaction types that the system defaults to, for the standard posting transactions in FI-AA. Again, go with SAP's standard settings unless you have a very specific reason to change the transaction type for a given asset transaction.

If you have defined any new transaction type, then you may need to change the defaults in the "TType" field. Else, you do not need to take any action here, except viewing the details (Figure 13.153) using the menu path: SAP Customizing Implementation Guide > Financial Accounting > Asset Accounting > Transactions > Specify Default Transaction Types.

Change View "Default transaction types for FI-AA posting transactions"

New Entries

Default transaction types for FI-AA posting transactions

Acct. transact. ID	Description	TType	Transact. Type Text
ABAA	Unplanned depreciation	640	Unplanned depreciation on prior-year acquisitions
ABA0	Asset sale without customer	210	Retirement with revenue
ABAV	Asset retirement by scrapping	200	Retirement without revenue
ABAW	Balance sheet revaluation	800	Post revaluation gross
ABGF	Credit memo in year after invoice	160	Credit memo in following year
ABGL	Enter credit memo in year of invoice	105	Credit memo in invoice year
ABMA	Manual depreciation	600	Manual ordinary depreciation on prior-yr acquis.

Figure 13.153 Default Transaction Types for FI-AA Posting Transactions

The next step is to determine the default transaction types for internal transactions.

13.9.9 Determine Transaction Types for Internal Transactions

Here, in this step, you can determine the default transaction types that the system uses for postings that are initiated (a) in other SAP modules / applications (like, SAP MM), and (b) automatically (like, depreciation). You can, of course, go along with the defaults from SAP.

You can use menu path: SAP Customizing Implementation Guide > Financial Accounting > Asset Accounting > Transactions > Determine Transaction Types for Internal Transactions, to view the standard settings, and change, if required (Figure 13.154). Note to make an entry here in 'Tra' field, if you have defined your own transaction type for any of the transaction postings.

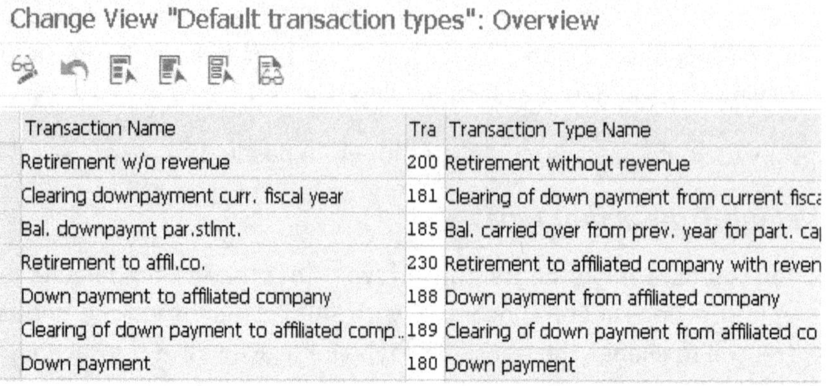

Change View "Default transaction types": Overview

Transaction Name	Tra	Transaction Type Name
Retirement w/o revenue	200	Retirement without revenue
Clearing downpayment curr. fiscal year	181	Clearing of down payment from current fisca
Bal. downpaymt par.stlmt.	185	Bal. carried over from prev. year for part. ca
Retirement to affil.co.	230	Retirement to affiliated company with reven
Down payment to affiliated company	188	Down payment from affiliated company
Clearing of down payment to affiliated comp..	189	Clearing of down payment from affiliated co
Down payment	180	Down payment

Figure 13.154 Default Transaction Types for Internal Transactions in FI-AA

With this, let us understand the last configuration activity of specifying how the system should determine the default value date for an asset.

13.9.10   Specify How Default Asset Value Date is Determined

The default asset value date is particularly important for transactions that are initiated in applications that are integrated with FI-AA (such as, acquisition from GR, from SAP MM). In those transactions, the default asset value date is not displayed, and you cannot, therefore, manually change that, when you post.

Normally, you do not need to configure this step unless you have some special needs in regard to the asset value date, since the standard rules, in the system, can meet most the needs for setting the asset date. In case you need to define, you will define the 'value date variant' (per company code) which contains the rules for determining the default asset value date.

You can use menu path: SAP Customizing Implementation Guide > Financial Accounting > Asset Accounting > Transactions > Specify How Default Asset Value Date is Determined, to make the required settings.

First, you will assign a value date variant for each of the company codes. Later, for the variant entered, you will define the business transactions with the primary / alternate rules for determining the asset value date (Figure 13.155). For example, for the transaction 'Current-value depreciation' the primary rule determines the default asset value data as 'capitalization date' (9) and the alternate rule as 'earlier of either the document or posting date' (4); for the transaction 'retirement', the primary rule stipulates that the asset value date to be entered manually (1).

Figure 13.155 Determining Default Asset Value Date for Business Transactions

> **i** SAP supplies the value date variant SAP_DEFAULT, that contains the rules for determining the asset value date for all Asset Accounting transactions. The system uses this variant, in all company codes, to which you do not assign a specific value date variant.

This completes our discussion on configuring the system for FI-AA transactions. We are now ready to discuss the settings relating to information system, in the next Section.

13.10 Information System

The *Information System* component, of FI-AA, contains several standard reports and functions to meet your specific reporting needs. The reports are offered in the form of a *report tree*. You can freely define the hierarchical structure of the report tree through Customizing. The system makes use of the logical database ADA for these reports.

You can pre-define all of the reports, in the standard report selection tree, using the report variants. All the standard report variants begin with 'SAP...'; you can copy them, if needed, and make the required changes. Or, you can create new variants, from scratch, and enter them in the report tree.

Here, in this Section, we shall define (a) the report selection in FI-AA Information System, (b) sort versions for the asset reports, (c) the structure of the asset history sheet, (d) currency translation methods and (e) any other system configurations, for reporting.

Let us start with the sort versions for asset reports.

13.10.1 Define Sort Versions for Asset Reports

You use '*sort versions*' for sorting and totalling the data records in report lists in FI-AA. You need to enter the sort version, as a parameter, before running the report. The system offers a standard sort as a default for each report; you can, of course, change this default. When you choose the 'input help' on the 'Sort version' field, the system displays an overview of the existing sort versions from which you can select the required one.

You may use SAP-delivered standard sort versions, as such. Or you can use them as reference to create your own sort versions. The standard ones include:

- Classification for Transaction Data Reports
- Book Depreciation Classification
- Cost-Accounting Classification
- Net Worth Tax Classification
- Classification for Insurance Values

Project Dolphin

BESTM wants to use the standard sort versions without defining anything new.

Use the menu path: SAP Customizing Implementation Guide > Financial Accounting > Asset Accounting > Information System > Define Sort Versions for Asset Reports, to view the standard sort versions (Figure 13.156) or create your own (starting with X, Y or Z). You can also use Transaction OVAI.

Change View "Sort Versions for Asset Reporting": Overview

New Entries

Sort Versions for Asset Reporting

Sort Vers.	Explanation
0001	Co. code/bus. area/bal. item/B/S account/class
0002	Co code/ plant / cost center
0003	Co. code / B/S acccount / asset class
0004	Co. code / property classif. /asset class
0005	Co. code / insurance type / ins. company

Figure 13.156 Standard Sort Versions

You may double-click on a row (say, 0001), to see the detailed settings of a sort version (Figure 13.157):

i.   The 'Total' check-box, when selected, indicates that values will be totalled at this sort level for, reports using this sort version.
ii.   Select the 'Page' radio-button, against a field name, at which you want a page break to occur, in the printed report. The system, then, makes a page break as soon as the sort level has new field contents. This setting guarantees that a page break occurs after high sort levels (such as, plant or business area), and that there is no page break after lower sort levels (such as, asset class).

iii.   The other parameters, under 'Processing subnumbers', help you to, for example, sort the asset subnumbers in the reverse order, making the totals line to stand out from the rest, and enabling totals per main number.

iv.   You can use the 'From subnumber(s)' field to control the totals of the values of subnumbers per asset. In this field, you can specify the number of subnumbers after which the system should provide a total. For example, if you enter 3 here in this field, then the system totals assets with more than 2 subnumbers; you can enter a value between 0 and 9.

Figure 13.157 Standard Sort Version 0001 – Details

The next step is to define simulation variants for depreciation reports.

13.10.2   Define Simulation Variants for Depreciation Reports

SAP offers two simulation options with which (a) you can execute standard reports with simulated depreciation terms and (b) you can analyze changes in the value of individual assets using simulated depreciation terms and transactions. The simulation enables planning the future development value your fixed assets portfolio.

When starting a standard list report, you can enter a defined *'simulation version'* to generate the list using simulated depreciation terms. For example, you can simulate how depreciation would look like if you used declining-balance depreciation instead of straight-line depreciation for your assets.

All depreciation lists that allow the use of simulation versions show the simulation version that was used, in the page header of the list. You can also request a list of all the replacement rules that were used in the simulation by pressing F2.

You can define these simulation versions anew, specifying the rules for the simulation. In this case, you need to specify (a) the depreciation area for the simulation, (b) the asset class (generic entry from right to left with '+'), (c) the depreciation key to be replaced in the simulation, and (d) a valid-to date, which means that for an asset to be included in the simulation, it has to have a capitalization date on or before this date.

Project Dolphin

BESTM wants to create a new simulation version to simulate the depreciation in all asset classes, for book depreciation, to understand what happens when the depreciation key is LINS and the useful life is increased by 10% across asset classes.

Use the menu path: SAP Customizing Implementation Guide > Financial Accounting > Asset Accounting > Information System > Define Simulation Variants for Depreciation Reports or Transaction OAV7, to define a simulation version:

i.   On the resulting screen, click on 'New Entries' and enter the identifier for the simulation version (say, B1) and provide a description in 'Simulation Version'. 'Save'.
ii.   Select this row B1, and double-click on 'Simulation Rules' on the left-hand side 'Dialog Structure'.
iii. On the next screen (Figure 13.158), click on 'New Entries' and make the required settings:

Figure 13.158 New Simulation Version B1

- Enter the depreciation area ('Area'); let that be 01.
- Enter the asset class in 'Class'. You can make a generic entry here instead of specifying the individual asset classes.

> **i** You can use the generic entry in several ways: enter a '+' sign, starting from the right and moving to the left. The '+' sign always represents a single character.
> Asset Class: B++++: B1000 to B8000
> Asset Class: B4+++: B4100 to B4200

- Enter the actual depreciation terms. Here also, you may use a generic entry.
- Enter 'Valid To' and 'Valid From' dates.
- Enter the simulation depreciation key (say, LINS).
- Enter the percentage by which you want to increase the useful life of assets in 'Diff.%rate UL' field. When you enter, 110, it means that the useful life will be increased by 10% during the simulation.
- 'Save' the settings. You have now created a simulation version (B1) with the required simulation rules.

When you execute the simulation, if the system finds several possible entries, it follows the following logic: (a) all the unmasked entries always take precedence, (b) when there is more than one masked entry, the system uses the first appropriate entry and finally (c) if the system finds only masked entries and no unmasked entries, it uses the entry that has the least number of masks.

With this, let us move on to discuss the SAP Queries.

13.10.3   Define SAP Queries

Some of the FI-AA reports, in the report tree, have been created using *ABAP Query*. SAP provides you with several standard queries (Figure 13.159) that you can use as such, or copy / modify them to meet your specific requirements. All these standard queries for FI-AA are provided in the global application area, and hence are not client-specific; you do not have to transport them.

> **i** ABAP or *SAP queries* are either limited to a given client, or are not client-specific. Whether they are client-specific or not depends on where you define them: in the standard application area or in the global application area. When you define them in the standard application area, then, you need to transport them (Transaction SQ02) as they are client-specific queries, so that they are available in other clients.

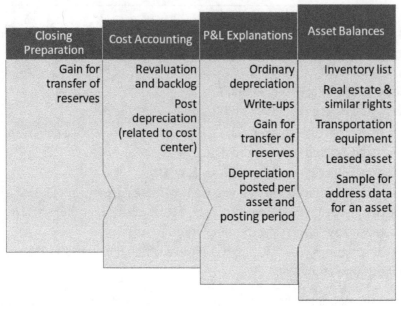

Figure 13.159 Standard SAP Queries in FI-AA - Categorization

Use the menu path: SAP Customizing Implementation Guide > Financial Accounting > Asset Accounting > Information System > Define SAP Queries, to view the standard queries (Figure 13.160) and/or creating your own. You may also use Transaction SQ01.

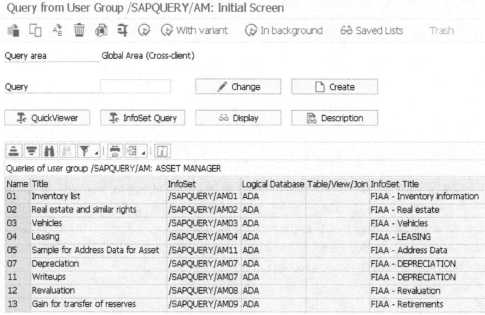

Figure 13.160 Standard SAP Queries in FI-AA

> **i** When you define your own queries, you can decide if you want to create them in the global application area (not client-specific) or in the standard application area (client-specific). However, we recommend that you define your own queries in the global application area (not client-specific). However, you should use your own user group. To create your own user group, copy the user group AM with all of its queries, and then, name your user group using a name in the allowed name range (with X, Y or Z).

With this, let us understand some of the settings for Fiori apps for FI-AA.

13.10.4   Display Key Figures for Asset Accounting (Fiori)

SAP provides all the required *'key figures'* for use in SAP Fiori apps in FI-AA. You can use this step to display them (you cannot define new key figures). Additionally, you can display, which analytical transaction type categories and subledger line item types, are assigned to a key figure. This assignment determines which line items are combined in a key figure. You can assign the key figures to a *'key figure group'*. With the assignment of the key figures to the key figure group, you define which key figures are displayed in an analytical Fiori app of FI-AA, such as Asset History Sheet or Asset Transaction List.

Use the menu path: SAP Customizing Implementation Guide > Financial Accounting > Asset Accounting > Information System > Display Key Figures for Asset Accounting (Fiori), to display the key figures and also the assigned business transactions per key figure.

On entering the Transaction, you will see the list of key figures (Figure 13.161).

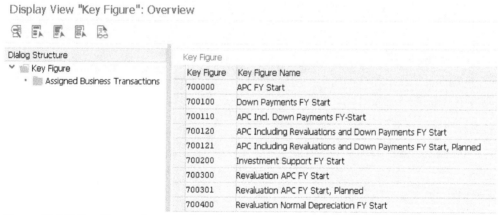

Figure 13.161 Key Figures for FI-AA (Fiori)

Select a key figure row (say, 700100), and double-click on 'Assigned Business Transactions' on the left-hand side 'Dialog Structure' to view the assigned business transactions for that key figure, on the next screen (Figure 13.162.)

Key Figure	700100			
KF Name	Down Payments FY Start			

Assigned Business Transactions

Category	Analytical Trans. Type Category Name	Subldgr LItm Type	Subledger Line Item Type De...	VT AA	
00	Balance Carry Forward	7001	Cumulative Down Payments	Exclusive Planned Value	⌄
87	Legacy Data Transfer AuC Down Payment	7001	Cumulative Down Payments	Exclusive Planned Value	⌄
C7	Legacy Data Transfer FY Start	7001	Cumulative Down Payments	Exclusive Planned Value	⌄
E7	Legacy Data Transfer FY Ending Balance	7001	Cumulative Down Payments	Exclusive Planned Value	⌄

Figure 13.162 Assigned Business Transactions for the Key Figure 700100

The next step is to define the key figure groups for Fiori app 'Asset Balances'.

13.10.5   Define Key Figure Groups for Asset Balances (Fiori)

SAP provides all the necessary key figure groups for the asset balances. By default, these are the key figure groups ABS_DEF (asset balances, planned values) and ABS_POSTED (asset balances, posted values). These key figure groups are, then, available as parameters when you execute the Fiori app 'Asset Balances' (Figure 13.163).

Figure 13.163 Entry Screen of Fiori App 'Asset Balances'

Here, in this configuration step, you can define your own key figure groups for the Fiori app 'Asset Balances'. Essentially, you define the key figures and their sequence for the asset balances.

> **i** You do not, in general, need to define your own key figure groups. However, you may do that when you want to display key figure digits in the asset balances that are different to the standard or when you want a different sequence of key figure digits.

Project Dolphin

BESTM wants to use the default key figure groups, without going in for any new key figure group definition for the Fiori app 'Asset Balances' and 'Asset Transactions'.

Use the menu path: SAP Customizing Implementation Guide > Financial Accounting > Asset Accounting > Information System > Define Key Figure Groups for Asset Balances (Fiori):

i. On the resulting screen, you see the default key figure groups with their description (Figure 13.164).

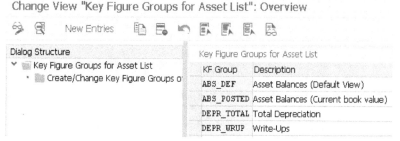

Figure 13.164 Standard Key Figure Groups for the Fiori App 'Asset Balances'

ii. Select a 'KF Group' row, and double-click on 'Create/Change Key Figure Groups of Asset Accounting' on the left-hand side 'Dialog Structure' to view the key figures and their sort sequences, on the next screen (Figure 13.165).

Key Figure Group   ABS_DEF

Create/Change Key Figure Groups of Asset Accounting (ABS)

Key Figure	Key Figure Name	Sequence
10700110	APC at Reporting Date	1
10700300	Revaluation APC at Reporting Date, Posted	10
10700302	Revaluation APC at Reporting Date, to be Posted	11
10700400	Revaluation Ordinary Depreciation at Reporting Date, Posted	12
10700402	Revaluation Ordinary Depreciation at Reporting Date, to be Posted	13
10700500	Ordinary Depreciation at Reporting Date, Posted	2
10700502	Ordinary Depreciation at Reporting Date, to be Posted	3

Figure 13.165 Key Figures and Sort Sequence of Key Figure Group ABS_DEF

iii.   In case you want a different sort sequence of the key figures in a key figure group, you can define a new one by copying from the standard ones.

The next step is defining the key figure groups for the Fiori app 'Asset Transactions'.

13.10.6   Define Key Figure Groups for Asset Transactions (Fiori)

As in the case of key figure groups for the Fiori app 'Asset Balances', SAP provides all the necessary key figure groups for the app 'Asset Transactions' (Figure13.166). By default, this comprises the following key figure groups:

- Asset Acquisitions: TRANS_ACQ
- Asset Retirements: TRANS_RET
- Intracompany Asset Transfers: TRANS_TRN
- All Asset Transactions: TRANS_ALL

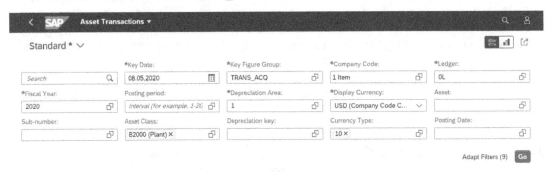

Figure 13.166 Entry Screen for Fiori App 'Asset Transactions'

Here also, you generally do not need to define your own key figure groups. However, if you want to have a display of transactions different to the standard, then, you may define your own key figure groups. Use the menu path: SAP Customizing Implementation Guide > Financial Accounting > Asset Accounting > Information System > Define Key Figure Groups for Asset Transactions (Fiori):

i.   On the resulting screen, you will see the default key figure groups for the Fiori app 'Asset Transactions' (Figure 13.167).

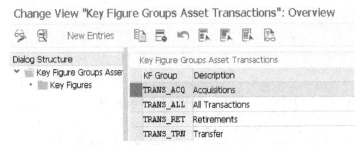

Figure 13.167 Standard Key Figure Groups for the Fiori App 'Asset Transactions'

ii. Select a key figure group (say, TRANS_ACQ) and double-click on 'Key Figures' on the left-hand side 'Dialog Structure' to view the transaction types associated with this group, on the next screen (Figure 13.168).

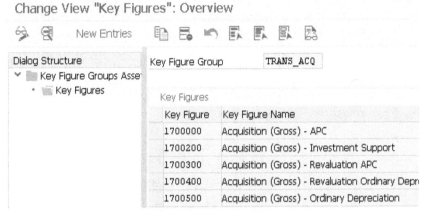

Figure 13.168 Key Figures of Key Figure Group TRANS_ACQ

iv. In case you want to display transactions different to that of the standard, then you may define your own key figure groups and /or key figures.

With this, we are now ready to discuss how to configure asset history sheets.

13.10.7   Asset History Sheet

The 'asset history sheet' is the most important and most comprehensive report, for the year-end closing or for an interim financial statement. Like other reports, you can set this up with any sort versions, and total on any group level. You can, also, create a compact totals list without individual asset information.

> **i** SAP enables you to freely define the line and column structure of the asset history sheet, to meet your specific requirements. You can also define, which values should be displayed, in which lines of the report.

Let us now understand the different steps in configuring asset history sheet.

13.10.7.1   Define History Sheet Versions

The structure of the asset history sheet varies from country to country, depending on tax laws. Hence, SAP provides you with country-specific versions of the asset history sheet, known as 'asset history sheet versions'; you also get additional history sheet versions. The system uses the asset history sheet version in the report, RAGITT01.

When you create an asset history sheet, the system notes (in the header of every screen) whether the asset history sheet version was created using a 'complete' or 'incomplete' version. An asset history sheet version is only complete when (a) every transaction type relevant to the asset history sheet is assigned to a 'history sheet group' and (b) the allocation indicator in column 1 to 5 is set (that is, contains either an X or a period) for every history sheet group except for the special groups YA, YY or YZ (more details in Section 13.10.7.2). When the asset history sheet version is complete, the indicator for completeness automatically appears in the definition for the version, on the overview screen. You can do a completeness check in Customizing, and see the log to identify the reason why the asset history sheet version is incomplete.

> **i** The transactions relevant to the asset history sheet are the posting of acquisition and production costs, downpayments, investment grants and write-ups.
>
> The completeness of the asset history sheet version can only be guaranteed with the standard transaction types and groups provided by SAP. If you have defined your own transaction types, then, that could influence the completeness of the asset history sheet. Of course, an 'incomplete' history sheet version, from the system's point of view, does not necessarily mean that the asset history sheet is incorrect for accounting purposes.

Use the menu path: SAP Customizing Implementation Guide > Financial Accounting > Asset Accounting > Information System > Asset History Sheet > Define History Sheet Versions or Transaction OA79, to display the standard asset history sheet versions and to define your own, if required:

Choose Asset History Sheet Version

  Details   New Entries

Asset hist. sheet versions

Language	Hist.Sht.Vers.	Asset History Sheet Name
EN	0001	In compl. w/EC directive 4 (13 col., wide version)
EN	0002	In compliance with EC directive 4 (13 col.)
EN	0003	Depreciation by depreciation type
EN	0004	Acquisition values
EN	0005	Asset Register (Italy)
EN	0006	Cost-accouting w/revaluation (derived from HGB2)
EN	0007	Transferred reserves
EN	0008	History of res.for spec.depr.
EN	0009	History version for data-collection program in EIS
EN	0010	Asset history sheet - Denmark

Figure 13.169 Standard Asset History Sheet Versions (asset history sheet version)

i.   You can see the standard asset history sheet versions on the resulting screen (13.169). You can use these versions without making any changes.

ii.   You may double-click on a version row (say, 0003), and see the detailed settings, on the next screen (13.170).

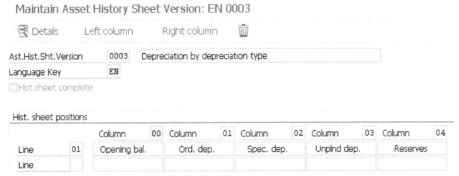

Figure 13.170 Initial Screen of Asset History Sheet Version 0003

iii.   Let us understand the asset history sheet version 0003 (Figure 13.170), for example, before proceeding to discuss how to create a new one. On the initial 'Maintain Asset History Sheet Version: EN 0003' screen:

   •   You will see the 4-digit identifier for the asset history sheet version (0003, in this case) and a description for the version

   •   You will see the maintenance language as EN.

   > ℹ️ A history sheet item created in another language, but which has not yet received a description in the maintenance language, will be marked with *.

   •   You will also notice if the asset history sheet version is 'complete' or 'incomplete' ('Hist. sheet complete' check-box). This information appears in the header of every screen.

   •   This particular asset history sheet version contains 6 columns; you see only 5 columns, 00 (Opening bal.) to 04 (Reserves) in the Figure 13.170; but, when you press 'Right column', the system scrolls to the right and shows the last column, that is 99 (Closing bal.). When you have scrolled to the right using the 'Right column' button, you need to press 'Left column' to come back to the initial position.

iv.   Let us understand more details about this asset history sheet version. Let us bring up the details, by double-clicking the column 01 (Ord. dep.). You can see these details on the next screen 'Maintain Items In Asset History Sheet Version 0003' (Figure 13.171):

- What you see in the Figure 13.171, is actually the 2nd page of the details (you can press 'Previous page' to see the 1st page). If there are several pages, you can navigate across pages using 'Previous page' and 'Next page'.
- You will see that the column 01 (Ord. dep.) is made up of several *'history sheet groups'* viz., 70, 71…YA, YY and YZ. These groups control the sheet items into which the transaction amounts, their transaction types, and the proportional values flow. We shall discuss more about asset history sheet groups, in the next Section 13.10.7.2.
- Per group, you will see 8 subgroups (= indicators or flags) like 'Trn', 'Ord', 'Spc' etc, to the right of the group, that you need to configure for the flow of the transaction amount.
- A blank cell, in a subgroup, denotes that you have not allocated that transaction to the history sheet item; a '.' (period or dot) shows that the transaction has been allocated to another history sheet item, and X indicates that the transaction has been allocated to the current asset history sheet item.

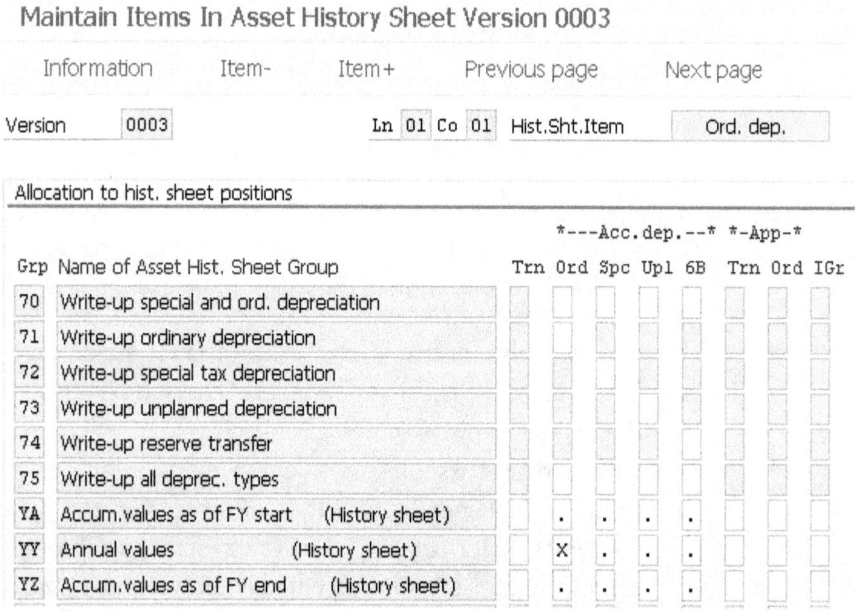

Maintain Items In Asset History Sheet Version 0003

| Information | Item- | Item+ | Previous page | Next page |

Version   0003   Ln `01` Co `01`   Hist.Sht.Item   Ord. dep.

Allocation to hist. sheet positions

		---Acc.dep.--					*-App-*		
Grp	Name of Asset Hist. Sheet Group	Trn	Ord	Spc	Upl	6B		Trn	Ord	IGr
70	Write-up special and ord. depreciation									
71	Write-up ordinary depreciation									
72	Write-up special tax depreciation									
73	Write-up unplanned depreciation									
74	Write-up reserve transfer									
75	Write-up all deprec. types									
YA	Accum.values as of FY start (History sheet)		.	.	.	.				
YY	Annual values (History sheet)	X	.	.	.					
YZ	Accum.values as of FY end (History sheet)		.	.	.	.				

Figure 13.171 Asset History Sheet Version 0003 – Details for Column 01

v.   If at all you need to create your own asset history sheet version, it is recommended that you copy an existing version and adapt the same suitably:

- To define a new asset history sheet version, you must first name it using a 4-digit identification code (starting with X, Y, or Z).

- When you define a new asset history sheet version, you need to set up the structure of the lines and columns of the asset history sheet. A maximum of 10 lines (rows) and 8 columns is possible, but a history sheet version must have at least 2 columns. The first column is always 00, the last one 99. All other columns must be between 01 and 80.

- The first step is to consider which lines and columns you need; enter these into free line or column fields.

- If you need more than 5 columns, you must scroll to the right. When you press 'Enter', the lines and the columns are positioned correctly.

- To delete existing lines/columns, you have to over-write the line or column number with blanks.

- You can also duplicate lines/columns by over-writing the existing line or column number with the new number.

- You must enter all headings for the history sheet items that you have created.

- To define which asset transactions should flow into which history sheet items, you can go through the individual history sheet items one by one, using 'Edit > Choose' function.

- To check, if the asset history sheet version is complete, use 'Edit > Completion Check' or use F8. The system will bring up the log with the details (Figure 13.172).

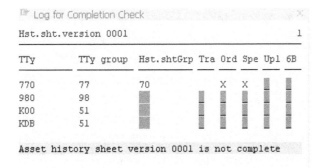

Figure 13.172 Asset History Sheet Version 0001 – Log for Completion Check

With this, we are ready to discuss (asset) history sheet groups.

13.10.7.2   Define History Sheet Groups

You will see a list of 'history sheet groups' in the detail screen of each history sheet position. SAP delivers all the necessary history sheet groups for the standard version of the asset history sheet. In the standard system, these are all nothing but the transaction type groups that are relevant for the asset history sheet (every transaction type group corresponds to a history sheet group), and they bring in the values for APC, downpayments, investment grants and write-ups. Besides, you will also notice three special history sheet groups: YA (values at the beginning of the fiscal year), YY (values during the fiscal year) and YZ (values at the end of the fiscal year).

Every history sheet group contains 8 indicators, with each of them representing a *'history sheet subgroup'*. By setting these indicators, in the selected history sheet position, you specify that the value fields associated with this group will flow into the selected history sheet position. The history sheet subgroups that are already allocated to a different (not the current one) history sheet position are identified with a period (.). You may press F7 on the indicator to determine the history sheet position into which the transaction type subgroup flows. The history sheet groups that are delivered with the standard system guarantee uniformity by ensuring that all transactions that belong to the same transaction type group are handled uniformly.

The meaning of the history sheet subgroups is not always uniform. The history sheet group YA (cumulative values at start of fiscal year), for example, has the following history sheet subgroups with the corresponding definitions:

- Trn = accumulated acquisition value, start of fiscal year
- Acc.dep-Ord = accumulated ordinary depreciation, start of fiscal year
- Acc.dep-Spc = accumulated special depreciation, start of fiscal year
- Acc.dep-Upl = accumulated unplanned depreciation, start of fiscal year
- Acc.dep-6B = accumulated transfer of reserves, start of fiscal year
- App-Trn = accumulated appreciation, start of fiscal year
- App-Ord = accumulated appreciation ordinary depreciation, start of fiscal year
- IGr = accumulated capital investment grants, start of fiscal year

Use the menu path: SAP Customizing Implementation Guide > Financial Accounting > Asset Accounting > Information System > Asset History Sheet > Define History Sheet Groups, to view the standard history sheet groups (Figure 13.173). You may also use Transaction OAV9.

Change View ""Asset History Sheet Group and Name"": Overview

New Entries

Grp	Name of Asset Hist. Sheet Group
10	Acquisition
12	Reverse acquisition in following years
15	Down payment
20	Retirement
25	Retirement of curr-yr acquisition
30	Retirmt transfer of prior-yr acquis.
31	Acquiring transfer of prior-yr acquis.

Figure 13.173 Standard History Sheet Groups

In general, you do not need to define your own asset history sheet groups. You should do this only if you want transaction types from the same transaction type group to flow into different positions of the history sheet. In this way, you can assign a newly defined transaction type to a special position in the asset history sheet, without having to define an individual transaction type group for it.

Click on 'New Entries' when you are in Transaction OAV9 (Figure 13.173) and define the new asset history sheet groups ('Grp') and ensure that you the group identifier starts with Z.

The last activity, under configuring asset history sheet, is to define the key figures for the Fiori app 'Asset History Sheet'.

13.10.7.3   Define Key Figure Groups for Asset History Sheet (Fiori)

SAP delivers all the necessary key figure groups for the standard version of the asset history sheet. By default, these are the key figure groups AHS (asset history sheet, book value) and AHS_PLAN (asset history sheet, planned values).

Use the menu path: SAP Customizing Implementation Guide > Financial Accounting > Asset Accounting > Information System > Asset History Sheet > Define Key Figure Groups for Asset History Sheet (Fiori), to view the default key figure groups for the Fiori app 'Asset History Sheet' (Figure 13.174). These key figure groups are available as parameters, when you execute the Fiori app, 'Asset History Sheet'.

Change View "Key Figure Groups Asset History Sheet": Overview

New Entries

Dialog Structure	Key Figure Groups Asset History Sheet	
⌄ Key Figure Groups Asset History Shee	KF Group	Description
• Create/Change Key Figure Groups	AHS	Asset History Sheet (Posted Values, No Hierarchy)
⌄ Fixed Asset Key Figure Hierarchy	AHS_AT	Asset History Sheet (AT)
• Fixed Asset Key Figure Hierarc	AHS_EFS	Asset History Sheet (Electronic Financial Stmnt)
• Movement category determinatior	AHS_HRY	Asset History Sheet (Posted Values, Wth Hierarchy)
	AHS_HRY_PL	Asset History Sheet (Plan Values, With Hierarchy)

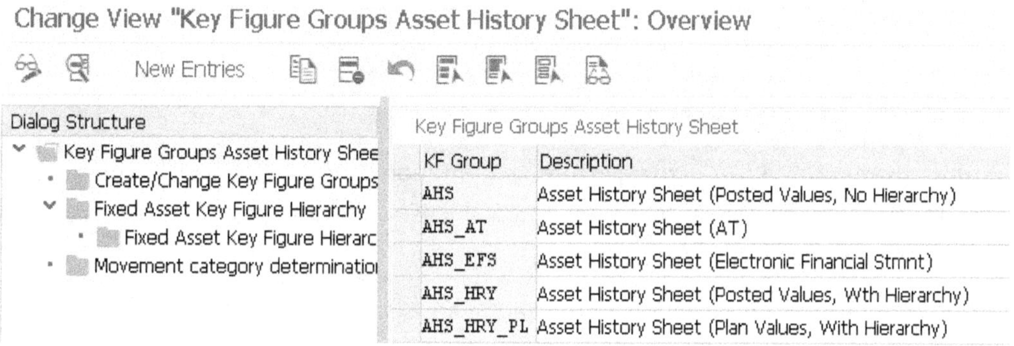

Figure 13.174 Key Figure Groups for Fiori App 'Asset History Sheet'

Select a 'KF Group' and double click on 'Create/Change Key Figure Groups of Asset Accounting' on the left-hand side 'Dialog Structure'. Now, on the resulting screen, you will see the key figures and their sequence (Figure 13.175).

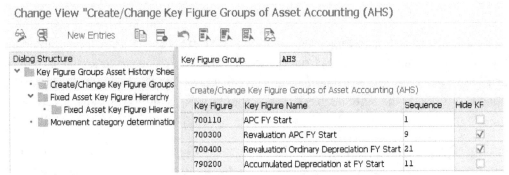

Figure 13.175 Details for Key Figure Group 'AHS'

Normally, you do not need to define your own key figure groups. However, you may need to define new key figure groups, when you want to display key figures in the asset history sheet that are different to the standard or when you want a different sequence of key figure digits. Use 'New Entries' or 'Copy As' on the initial screen to create your own key figure groups.

This completes our discussion on configuring the asset history sheet as a part of FI-AA Information System. There are a few more settings that we need to complete for FI-AA Information System, starting with the option to rename the value fields for asset explorer.

13.10.8   Rename Value Fields for the Asset Explorer

Here, in this step, you can change the default short texts of value fields that are displayed in the *Asset Explorer* (Transaction AW01N / AW01). You can specify this per depreciation area.

Project Dolphin

BESTM will not be renaming any of the value fields meant for the asset explorer. They are good with the short text supplied by SAP.

Use the menu path: SAP Customizing Implementation Guide > Financial Accounting > Asset Accounting > Information System > Rename Value Fields for the Asset Explorer. You may also use Transaction OAWT.

On the resulting screen, select the depreciation area (say, 01) and double-click on 'Value field texts' on the left-hand side 'Dialog Structure'. On the next screen (Figure 13.176), you will see the value fields along with their default short names and description. You may change the 'Short name' and 'Description', if required.

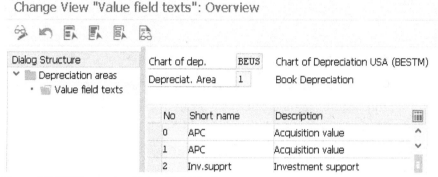

Figure 13.176 Renaming Value Field Texts

The next step is to define currency translation methods, for the asset reports.

13.10.9   Define Currency Translation Methods

You can specify the currency translation methods, when starting a report. The system, then, determines the asset values for the report, according to the defined method and in the corresponding currency. SAP delivers two translation methods as default, (a) historical conversion at the capitalization date and (b) key date translation. If these are not sufficient, you can define the new currency translation methods, in this configuration step.

Project Dolphin

BESTM will not be requiring any new currency translation methods as they will use the standard ones supplied by SAP as default.

Use the menu path: SAP Customizing Implementation Guide > Financial Accounting > Asset Accounting > Information System > Define Currency Translation Methods, or Transaction OAW3, to define new currency translation methods.

The last and final step in configuring FI-AA Information System is to define / assign forms (layout sets) for asset history sheet and asset labels.

13.10.10   Define or Assign Forms

Here, you can define layout sets (forms) for (a) the evaluation of 'asset history' (*asset chart*) and (b) printing of labels with asset information (*barcodes*) using the inventory list. The layout sets determine the layout of the list printout of reports.

You can store a separate layout set, per asset class, for the asset chart. The report then uses this layout set for the fixed assets of this class and creates a corresponding asset chart. You can enter the layout set for the inventory list when you start the report. SAP supplies the layout set FIAA_F001 as a default for the asset chart and the layout set FIAA_0003 for the inventory labels.

Project Dolphin

BESTM has decided to create new layout sets for both asset chart and asset information, and they will engage the ABAP development team to complete the task.

Use the menu path: SAP Customizing Implementation Guide > Financial Accounting > Asset Accounting > Information System > Define or Assign Forms, or Transaction SE71, to define the new forms. Once defined, you may use Transaction OAAY, later, to assign the new form (layout set), per asset class, for the asset chart.

This completes our discussion on configuring FI-AA Information System. Let us move on to discuss asset data transfer.

13.11   Asset Data Transfer

The 'asset data transfer' or 'legacy data transfer' refers to transferring of existing asset data from a previous system or from a file maintained outside the accounting system. Normally, it is the first action that you do, after configuring (including classification of assets) FI-AA in SAP.

The legacy data transfer consists of transferring of (a) asset master records, (b) asset values and the accumulated prior-year acquisitions and (c) transactions, starting from the beginning of the fiscal year up to the time of the transfer, if legacy data transfer is during the year.

SAP provides you with multiple options for asset data transfer, as shown in Figure 13.177.

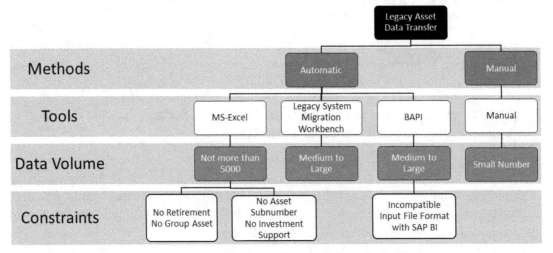

Figure 13.177 Legacy Data Transfer – Methods, Tools, Data Volume & Constraints

Let us now discuss the various settings that you need to make in Customizing in FI-AA, for legacy data transfer. Let us start with the parameters for data transfer.

13.11.1   *Parameters for Data Transfer*

Let us specify the various parameters for data transfer. This includes (a) defining the data transfer date and the associated parameters, (b) specifying the offsetting G/L account for legacy data transfer and (c) defining the transaction types for transferring open items.

The first activity is to define the transfer date and the additional parameters.

13.11.1.1   Define Transfer Date and Additional Parameters

The *'transfer date'* is the cut-off date for the transfer of legacy asset data. The transfer will only include data up to this point in time. There are two scenarios: (a) transfer at the end of the fiscal year – here, the transfer date is the end of the last closed fiscal year; when you transfer at the end of the year (YYYY-1), then, you can only open the fiscal year (YYYY) after the transfer date, and (b) transfer during the fiscal year – here, the transfer date can be in the fiscal year that directly follows the last closed fiscal year; when you transfer during the year, in year YYYY, then, you can open only the fiscal year of the transfer (YYYY). The system adopts the transfer date in the master record of the legacy asset as the value date. Once you have created the first legacy fixed asset, in SAP, you will not be able to change the transfer date in the segment.

The transfer date is, generally, not the same date in which you actually enter the data. Normally, you create legacy data after the transfer date. This could be due to the fact that you may have to perform a closing in your legacy system, between the transfer date and the date of the actual transfer. You can also transfer legacy assets to the SAP System before the transfer date: you, then, have to make sure that the transactions that you posted in your legacy system, up until the transfer date, are also later posted in the FI-AA in SAP.

Use the menu path: SAP Customizing Implementation Guide > Financial Accounting > Asset Accounting > Asset Data Transfer > Parameters for Data Transfer> Define Transfer Date and Additional Parameters, or Transaction FAA_CMP_LDT.

Upon entering the Transaction, you will see a tree structure on the left of the screen showing asset accounting company codes, and the relevant ledgers for each of the company codes. SAP displays only the representative ledgers for the various accounting principles and not the extension ledgers.

To define settings for a company code or ledger, you need to select the company code/ledger below the company code from the left-hand side tree structure. Here, in this Transaction, you can configure three different group of settings for company codes and ledgers that are relevant for FI-AA:

i.   Select the required company code (say, 1110) on the left-hand side 'FI-AA Company Codes' tree-structure. Highlight 'General Settings' tab on the right-hand side screen. Here, you set the company code status as to whether the company code is in testing status ('For Testing') or 'Productive' or 'Deactivated' (Figure 13.178). Since company code 1110 is still in testing phase, select the value 'For Testing' for 'Company Code Status'. You can also specify if the company code is locked, using the 'Company Code Locked' flag; when locked, you will not be able to make postings on fixed asset accounts or changes to the asset master record in that particular company code.

General Information						
Company Code	1110	BESTM	Farm Machinery		Chart of Accounts	BEUS BESTM - US :
Country Key	US					

General Settings	Legacy Data Transfer

General Settings for Company Code	
Company Code Status	For Testing ∨
Company Code Locked	☐

Figure 13.178 General Settings for FI-AA Company Code Status

ii. The second group of settings, you can make here, relates to year-end closing. By selecting the appropriate ledger (say, 0L), on the left-hand side tree structure, under the company code, you can close or re-open a fiscal year. You will be doing these settings in 'Ledger Settings' tab (Figure 13.179). Refer Section 13.12.5.1 for more details on closing / re-opening a fiscal year.

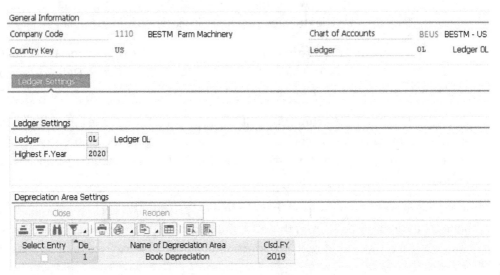

Figure 13.179 Fiscal Year Settings for FI-AA Company Code

iii. You can specify transfer date and other parameters, for legacy data transfer. Highlight the company code (say, 1110) on the left-hand side tree structure. In 'Legacy Data Transfer' tab, click on 'Create legacy transfer segment' and create the segment. Then, enter the details under 'Current Settings for Legacy Data Transfer' data block: specify the 'Transfer Date', select the appropriate value for 'Legacy Data Transfer Status' and select the appropriate 'Document Type' (Figure 13.180).

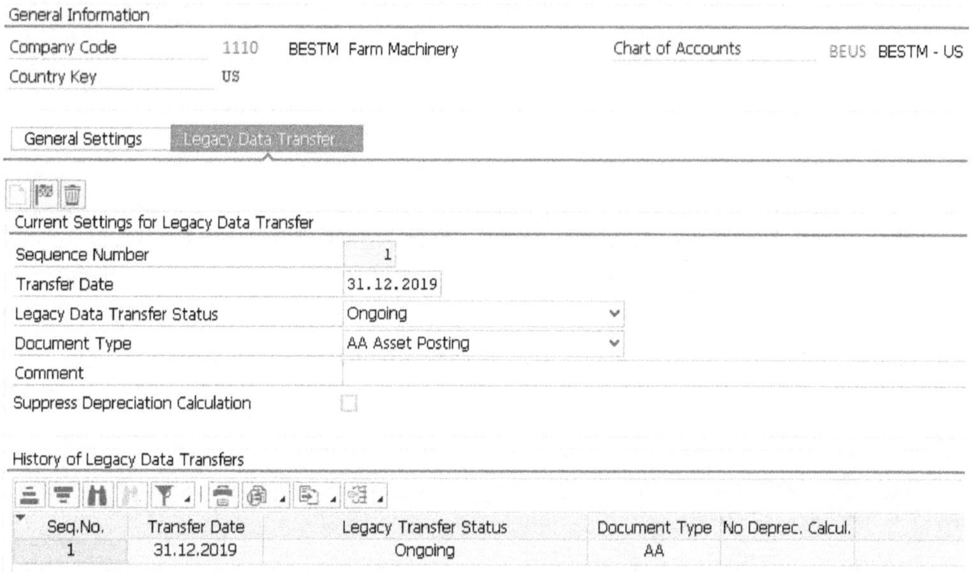

Figure 13.180 Legacy Data Transfer Settings for FI-AA Company Code

For 'Legacy Data Transfer Status', you can have three possible values: 'In Preparation' – here the system allows incomplete Customizing settings for legacy data transfer, 'Ongoing' - only legacy data transfer postings are permitted; other postings (like, acquisition, asset retirement etc) are not permitted, and 'Ongoing (Other Postings Allowed)' - both legacy data transfer and other postings are permitted; you will select this when you perform further legacy data transfers in a company code that is already productive. Select 'Ongoing' if your company code status is 'For Testing', and 'Ongoing (Other Postings Allowed)' when the company code status is 'Productive'.

You need to select 'Suppress Depreciation Calculation' check-box, to supress the calculation of planned values for depreciation, during legacy data transfer, purely on performance reasons. However, you need to perform this calculation, separately, using Transaction AFAR, later, once you have completed the legacy data transfer.

> **i** You should set the 'Suppress Depreciation Calculation' indicator only during mass data transfers. If you are transferring individual assets, manually, then, you should not set this.

The next configuration step is to specify the offsetting G/L account for legacy data transfer.

13.11.1.2   Specify Offsetting Account for Legacy Data Transfer

Here, you need to specify a G/L account that you will use with legacy data transfer, for transferring the asset balances. You need to make sure that you have defined this G/L as B/S account with line item management. Ensure that you use this account only for data transfer purposes, and the balance of this account is zero, once you complete the data transfer.

Use the menu path: SAP Customizing Implementation Guide > Financial Accounting > Asset Accounting > Asset Data Transfer > Parameters for Data Transfer> Specify Offsetting Account for Legacy Data Transfer. Enter the offsetting G/L account number, for legacy data transfer, against the chart of accounts (BEUS) as in Figure 13.181.

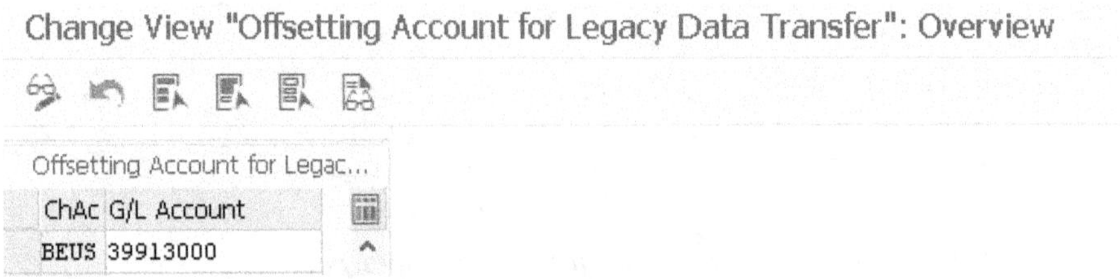

Figure 13.181 Offsetting G/L Account for Legacy Data Transfer

With this, we are ready to define the transaction types for transfer of open items.

13.11.1.3   Define Transaction Types for Transfer of Open Items

Here, you define the transaction types for the takeover of asset open items from a previous system. If you do not have AuC with line item management, you do not need this kind of transaction type. As in other cases of transaction types, go along with the SAP-supplied transaction types without defining your own.

Use the menu path: SAP Customizing Implementation Guide > Financial Accounting > Asset Accounting > Asset Data Transfer > Parameters for Data Transfer> Define Transaction Types for Transfer of Open Items, or Transaction AO79, to view the standard transaction types for transfer of open items (Figure 13.182).

Change View "FI-AA: Transaction types": Overview

   ⚙   New Entries   📄 📑 ↰ 📑 📑 📑

Transact. type	Transaction Type Name
900	Takeover open items APC (AuC)
910	Takeover open down payments
970	Asset Data Transfer

Figure 13.182 Standard Transaction Types for Transfer of Open Items

With this, we are now ready to discuss the manual asset data transfer.

13.11.2   Manual Data Transfer

You will normally resort to manual data transfer when the volume is small, mainly in case of individual assets and for subsequent maintenance. When you transfer the asset values and transactions, the system updates the balances in G/L and hence no separate balance transfer is required. You can use various functions, under this Customizing node in the IMG, to manually create legacy assets in the system.

Though you create master data for legacy assets exactly the same way as you create regular asset master data, you need to consider the following special features of legacy assets:

- The 'Capitalization date' is always a required entry. Using the capitalization date, the system determines the depreciation start date and the expired useful life, based on the period control in the depreciation key. If you had acquired an asset, previously at a time when the company code had a different fiscal year variant, the system's determination of the useful life will be correct only if the period calendar assignments have been maintained historically.
- The 'Planned useful life' is a required entry when a depreciation key for automatic depreciation calculation has been entered. You can also account for increased wear and tear on an asset, in the past, as the result of multiple shift use. You can do this, by manually correcting the expired useful life that was automatically calculated by the system.
- You can only transfer the current values of time-dependent data (such as the assignment to a cost center) as on the transfer date. To create new time intervals, you have to use the function for changing master data.

There are separate functions for creating normal legacy fixed assets and legacy group assets:

13.11.2.1   Legacy Fixed Assets

Let us see the various Transactions associated with the creation / change of master data for legacy assets, posting transfer values etc in the following Table 13.2.

Menu Path: **SAP Customizing Implementation Guide > Financial Accounting > Asset Accounting > Asset Data Transfer > Manual Data Transfer > Legacy Fixed Asset >**	Transaction
Create Master Data for Legacy Asset	AS91
Change Master Data for Legacy Asset	AS92
Display Master Data for Legacy Asset	AS93
Create Master Data for Subnumber for Legacy Asset	AS94
Post Transfer Values*	ABLDT
Data Transfer During the Fiscal Year: Transfer Line Items**	AB01L
AUC with Line Item Management: Transfer Line Items***	ABLDT_OI

Table 13:2 Legacy Fixed Assets -Manual Data Transfer – Transactions

Post Transfer Values
The system posts a journal entry for the asset with this Transaction; it also updates the G/L accounts. The system creates, for each asset, a transfer document that posts the transfer values, for example, on the APC and accumulated depreciation account and against the offsetting account for the legacy data transfer

** *Data Transfer During the Fiscal Year: Transfer Line Items*
If you enter a posting date, in the current fiscal year, that is before the transfer date, the system recognizes this business transaction as a transfer document; it does not calculate depreciation, posts the document against the offsetting account for the legacy data transfer.

*** *AUC with Line Item Management: Transfer Line Items*
To ensure that the line item-managed AuC is included, the transfer values are not allowed to be entered as accumulated values, in Transaction ABLDT. Instead, you must enter the values individually using transaction ABLDT_OI. You must use the specific transaction types 900 and 910 for the transfer. If you have proportional depreciation on the AuC, then, enter this as proportional depreciation from the previous years' using the Transaction.

13.11.2.2   Legacy Group Assets

Similar to that of the legacy fixed assets, let us see the various Transactions associated with the creation / change of master data for legacy group assets, posting transfer values etc in the following Table 13.3.

Menu Path: **SAP Customizing Implementation Guide > Financial Accounting > Asset Accounting > Asset Data Transfer > Manual Data Transfer > Legacy Group Asset >**	**Transaction**
Create Master Data for Legacy Group Asset	AS81
Change Master Data for Legacy Group Asset	AS82
Display Master Data for Legacy Group Asset	AS83
Create Master Data for Subnumber for Legacy Group Asset	AS84
Post Transfer Values	ABLDT

Table 13:3 Legacy Fixed Assets -Manual Data Transfer – Transactions

With this, we can now move on to discuss the legacy data transfer using MS-Excel.

13.11.3 *Legacy Data Transfer using Microsoft® Excel*

You can use Microsoft® Excel, to transfer legacy asset data in combination with Transaction AS100. This Transaction is adjusted completely to be in line with the universal journal entry's logic. Using this Transaction, you can process about 5,000 assets in a single file upload. The amount of data, you transfer using this method, is limited by the maximum number of rows in your Excel version; you can, if necessary, split the data into several files.

> **i** You cannot use this method to transfer data relating to group assets, asset subnumbers, investment support and retirements.

The first step, when you use this method, is to load or manually enter the legacy asset data and values (from your legacy system) into an Excel sheet, in a pre-defined format. To ensure that you can transfer the data correctly, you need to adhere to certain guidelines when creating the Excel spreadsheet:

- Set the Excel format to 'General' for the entire document before you enter any data. You can, however, enter the dates, using the 'Custom' format.
- The Excel spreadsheet consists of two parts:
  - Header section: here, you specify the type of data you want to transfer for all the assets (for example, company code, description, and so on).
  - Asset section, you enter the information relating to individual assets and their values.

The Excel worksheet needs to contain cells for the legacy asset number, company code, asset class and capitalization date, and you need to supply the values in these cells for each asset. The same applies for any 'required' entry fields that are defined in the asset class in the system.

Header Section

In the 'header section', you need to specify the field descriptions that are to be transferred. The first 5 rows in the Excel worksheet are reserved for this header information. Do not to use them for asset master data or asset values. The fields are organized in *record types*. Enter these record types in the first column of the worksheet. The next columns should contain the field descriptions assigned to these record types. SAP recommends that you follow the structure as shown in Table 13.4. If you do not need certain record types (for example, record type 4 – Transactions), then, you can omit them when creating your worksheet.

Record Type	Explanation	Remarks
0	Identifier (legacy asset number); record type 0 is reserved solely for the number of the asset from the legacy system, and is not allowed to be used for any other purpose. The system needs this identifier, in order to assign them to the correct assets, if there are errors.	Header data
1	Asset master data, general data and inventory data	Header data
2	Posting information, time-dependent data	Time-dependent data
3	Depreciation areas, cumulative values, posted values	Depreciation areas, cumulative values, posted values
4	Transactions	Transactions

Table 13:4 Legacy Asset Transfer using MS- Excel – Header Section

Asset Section

In the 'asset section', you will be entering the asset values, below the header data, in the Excel worksheet. Enter the asset data, as per the structure of the field descriptions in the header.

> **i** For example, you specify in the header for record type 1 that the company code is in column B and the asset class is in column C. The system, then, will recognize the field contents of all fields of record type 1 in column B as company codes and in column C as asset classes. Hence, you have to make sure that for each asset, which is in a row specified as record type 1, that its company code is always in column B and its asset class in column C. The fields with leading zeroes in the system (for example, company code 0001), should have leading zeroes in the format. Always enter the asset class with 8 places and leading zeroes (for example, asset class 1000 needs to entered as 00001000). You need enter all values specifying if they are positive or negative (unlike when you create legacy asset data manually); for example, enter accumulated ordinary depreciation in the Excel worksheet with a negative sign.

The Figure 13.183 shows an example of a MS-Excel spreadsheet with header and asset data.

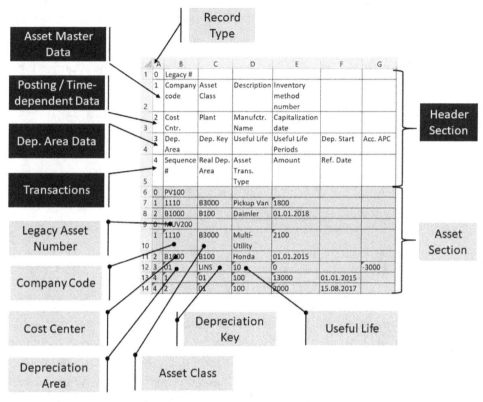

Figure 13.183 Sample Microsoft Excel Worksheet with Legacy Asset Data

You will notice, in Figure 13.183, that:

- Column A represents the record type: 0, 1, 2 etc.
- Rows 1 to 5 (records 0 to 4) represents the header data that contains the details of field for each of the cells; Record 0 (row 1) identifies the legacy or old asset number, record 1 (row 2) represents the asset master data including the company code, asset class and so on.
- From row number 6, you have the asset details.
- Rows 6, 7 and 8 together denotes a single asset record: row 6 has the legacy asset number in cell B6 (value = PV100).
- Rows 9 to 14 represent another asset data (the legacy asset number MUV200 is shown in cell B9). For this asset, the 'Company Code' (1110) value is in cell B10, Cell C10 denotes the 'Asset Class' (B3000), Cell B11 indicates the 'Cost Center' (B1000), Cell B12 denotes the 'Depreciation Area' (01), Cell C12 is the 'Depreciation Key' (LINS), Cell D12 shows the 'Useful Life' and so on.

- Rows 13 and 14(record 4) represent the transaction details: 'Sequence #' denotes the sequence number of transaction (1, for example), 'Real Dep. Area' is the depreciation area (say, 01), 'Asset Trans. Type' is the asset transaction type (say, 100) and so on.

With this background on using MS-Excel for legacy data transfer, let us, now, understand how you can transfer legacy data in the system:

Use the menu path: SAP Customizing Implementation Guide > Financial Accounting > Asset Accounting > Asset Data Transfer > Legacy Data Transfer using Microsoft® Excel. You may also use Transaction AS100.

i. On the resulting screen (Figure 13.184), select the 'Input file' and click on 'Start'.

Legacy Data Transfer in Asset Accounting

Start   [i]

Input file   C:\USERS\S4H1809U51\DOCUMENTS\ASSET TRANSFER - CO COD 1110 - 1.X…

Figure 13.184 Legacy Data Transfer using Microsoft Excel – Initial Screen

ii. On the next screen (Figure 13.185), you will see the details for mapping the fields of your input Excel file to the fields of asset master record in SAP. Under 'Assignment of table fields', you will see two tables on the screen: on the left-hand side, you will see the fields from the input file ('Field of file') and on the right, you will see a table with 'Fields of asset master record' as it appears in SAP with the fields arranged in various tabs like 'Header Data', 'General Data' Inventory' and so on. At the bottom of the screen, you will see table that will show the 'Results of assignment'.

To start assigning the fields from your Excel input file to that of SAP's asset master record fields, you need to highlight a row on the left-hand side input table (say, 'Cost Cntr') and highlight the corresponding field on the right-hand side SAP table (say, 'Cost Center' on 'Time-dependent' tab), and click on the 'Assign' button located at the middle of these two tables. Now, the system will populate the bottom table ('Results of assignment') with this assignment. Continue to make all the assignments (you may need to search the fields on various tabs on the SAP table).

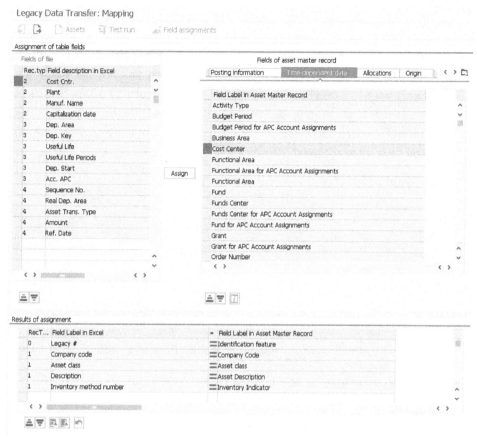

Figure 13.185 Legacy Data Transfer using Microsoft Excel – Field Mapping & Assignment

iii.   Once completed, you may 'Save' the assignments. Enter the details on the resulting 'Field Assignments: Maintain Attributes' pop-up screen. This way you do not need to do assignments every time to make a transfer, using a similar file format but for uploading, say, another tranche of legacy assets.

iv.   Now, click on the 'Next screen (create assets)' button at the top of the 'Legacy Data Transfer: Mapping' screen. The system takes you to the 'Legacy Date Transfer: Creation of Assets' screen. Here, go to 'Settings > Date format...' and set the appropriate date format (European, American, SAP format). Unless you do this, you may encounter an error (like, 'Fiscal year of legacy data transfer could not be determined'), later, when you do the 'Test run' or the actual 'Creation of asset(s)'.

v.   Now, while on this screen, you may click on 'Test run' (before actually creating the assets using the 'Creation of asset(s)' button). At this point, the system will bring up errors, if any, without transferring the legacy data. At any time, you can click on 'Field assignments' to view or modify the assignments that you have already made.

vi.   When satisfied, you can create the assets in SAP system by clicking on the 'Creation of asset(s)' button). The system issues suitable confirmations, on the table under

'Creation of asset(s)'. You can display incomplete or incorrect data that could not be processed; export them to a new MS-Excel file that you can correct and use for upload, later.

vii.   Next time, when you start the Transaction, you will see the existing assignment of fields with the previous 'Assignment' name (Figure 13.186). You can use the same assignments or modify later when you do another transfer, by selecting another 'Input file'. This way, you can save your time on making new assignments every time you do a legacy data transfer using MS-Excel.

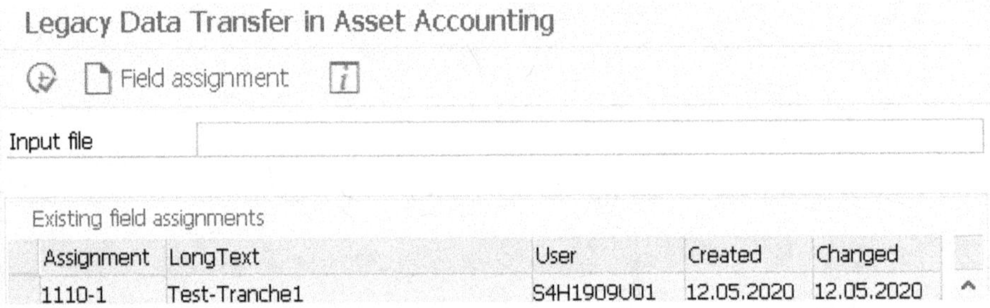

Legacy Data Transfer in Asset Accounting

Field assignment

Input file

Existing field assignments

Assignment	LongText	User	Created	Changed
1110-1	Test-Tranche1	S4H1909U01	12.05.2020	12.05.2020

Figure 13.186 Legacy Data Transfer using Microsoft Excel – Existing Field Assignment

With this, we are now ready to discuss the preparations required for 'going live' with FI-AA.

13.12   Preparations for Going Live

In the previous Sections, you have configured the system to meet your functional requirements of FI-AA, in SAP. You can, now, carry out the more technically-oriented activities that are necessary for going live with FI-AA. The first of such activity is to take care of the authorization management in the system.

13.12.1   Authorization Management

SAP's authorization protection is based on 'authorization objects' defined in the system. Using these objects, you can define 'authorizations'. Later, you can group these authorizations into 'authorization profiles' and assign the same to individual users. Here, in this Section, we shall be discussing the following configuration tasks for authorization management:

- Maintain Authorizations
- Assign Workflow Tasks
- Process Asset Views

Let us start with the first task of maintaining authorizations.

13.12.1.1   Maintain Authorizations

SAP comes delivered with several standard authorization objects (Table 13.5) that you can straightaway use in authorization management. However, should you decide to maintain your own authorizations, you may do so by using the menu path: SAP Customizing Implementation Guide > Financial Accounting > Asset Accounting > Asset Data Transfer > Preparations for Going Live > Authorization Management > Maintain Authorizations. You may also use Transaction PFCG.

Authorization Objects	Functions
Asset View	Assets in General
Company Code/Asset Class	Asset Postings
Asset Class/Transaction Type	
Asset Classes	Asset Class Maintenance
Authorizations for Periodic Processing	Asset Accounting
Company Code, Asset Class	Asset Master Record Maintenance
Company Code, Business Area	
Company Code, Cost Center	
Company Code, Plant	
Group Asset	Group Asset Maintenance
Chart of Depreciation, Company Code	Asset Customizing

Table 13:5 Standard Authorization Objects for FI-AA

Project Dolphin

BESTM will not be creating any new authorizations; rather, they will be using the standard ones supplied by SAP.

The next task is to assign the workflow tasks to appropriate organizational objects, and then to the required users.

13.12.1.2   Assign Workflow Tasks

Here, in this configuration task, you will be making the system settings for workflow control. You will need these settings for taking up some of the activities in FI-AA including (a) making mass changes to master data using workflow, (b) posting mass retirement using workflow and (c) completing assets that were not fully created.

However, you can carry out the above three activities without using workflow. For example, you can complete the activities (a) and (b) through mass changes and mass retirements; and you can complete activity (c) by processing incomplete assets using normal asset reporting. In such a situation, you do not need to complete this configuration task.

When you want to use workflow, then, you need to (a) assign the task by linking the same with an organizational object (like, asset accountant), (b) link the organizational objects (from you company's organization structure) to appropriate user (as owner) and finally (c) activate the event linkage for the standard tasks.

> **i** You can also assign a Workflow task directly to a user, but this option is available if you use workflow only in FI-AA, and when you have not defined your organizational plan in the system. Then, in this case, you do not need any other organizational objects.

Use the menu path: SAP Customizing Implementation Guide > Financial Accounting > Asset Accounting > Asset Data Transfer > Preparations for Going Live > Authorization Management > Assign Workflow Tasks. You may also use Transaction OAWF.

i.   On the next screen, you will see the various application components for FI-AA (Figure 13.187).

Task Customizing Overview

Application Component Abbreviati...	Application Component Description	Agent Assignment	Event Linkage
FI-AA-AA	Basic Functions	Assign Agents	Activate event link
FI-AA-AA-MA	Asset Maintenance		
FI-AA-AA-BV	Basic Valuation Functions		
FI-AA-AA-BV-DA	Depreciation Areas		
FI-AA-AA-BV-DD	Derived Depreciation Areas		
FI-AA-AA-BV-CI	Calculation of interest		
FI-AA-AA-BV-PC	Period Control		
FI-AA-AA-BV-GA	Group Assets		
FI-AA-AA-BV-VM	Valuation Methods		
FI-AA-AA-FY	Fiscal Year Specifications		
FI-AA-AA-FY-AV	Alternative Fiscal Year Variants		
FI-AA-AA-FY-SF	Shortened Fiscal Years		
FI-AA-AA-FY-HM	Half Months		
FI-AA-AA-FY-PW	Period Weighting (4-4-5 Rule)		
FI-AA-AA-DE	Depreciation		

Figure 13.187 Initial Screen for Assigning Workflow Tasks

ii.   Click on 'Assign Agents', and on the next screen (Figure 13.188), you will see the standard catalog of workflow tasks associated with FI-AA.

Tasks of an Application Component: Assign Agents

Attributes...   Org. assignment

Name	ID	Assigned a...
Basic Functions	FA FI-AA-AA	
Process incomplete asset	TS 00001003	01.01.1900
Correct worklist	TS 00008010	01.01.1900
Release worklist	TS 00008011	01.01.1900
Change asset in forgrnd:synchr.to equip.	TS 03100037	01.01.1900
Change asset in bckgrnd:synchr.to equip.	TS 03100039	01.01.1900
Create asset for equip. in foreground	TS 03100042	01.01.1900

Figure 13.188 Workflow Tasks Catalog

iii.   Select the task (say, 'Process incomplete asset') and click on 'Create agent assignment' button (on the left corner of the screen, just above 'Name').

iv.   On the resulting 'Choose agent type' pop-up screen (Figure 13.189), highlight the object type (say, 'Role') and assign the appropriate object (say, 'Asset Accountant') to the task.

Figure 13.189 'Choose agent type' Pop-Up Screen

v.   Now, assign the appropriate user(s) to the 'Role' ('Asset Accountant') that you have just linked with the task (Figure 13.190).

vi.   Repeat and link all the required tasks with the appropriate object, and assign the appropriate users in each case.

vii.   Once you have assigned the users, you need to 'activate' (Figure 13.190) the same.

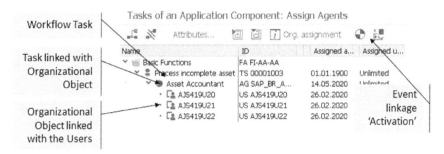

Figure 13.190 'Workflow Task – Organization Object – User' Linkage and Activation

The final configuration activity, under authorization management, is to process the asset views.

13.12.1.3   Process Asset Views

Besides the standard SAP authorization functions, FI-AA component provides you with the *'asset view'* for additional authorization protection. The asset view authorization object (A_A_VIEW) controls master data maintenance to a certain extent. You can use this object to assign users limited views of asset data and asset values.

We have already discussed asset views, in detail in <u>Section 13.8.3</u>

With this, we are now ready to discuss how to check consistency of the system settings that you have made so far, in the next Section.

13.12.2   Check Consistency

Now that you have completed the configuration settings for FI-AA, you should carry out this step for checking the consistency of your system as to the settings that you have made under various configuration activities and tasks.

Use the menu path: SAP Customizing Implementation Guide > Financial Accounting > Asset Accounting > Asset Data Transfer > Preparations for Going Live > Check Consistency.

On the resulting pop-up screen (Figure 13.191), you will see several individual tasks to check for consistency of, say, asset class definition, chart of depreciation, company codes, depreciation area etc. At the end, you will see the activity 'Consistency Report: FI-AA Customizing' that will provide the overview of all the settings for FI-AA. Complete all the activities, as listed on the screen (Figure 13.191).

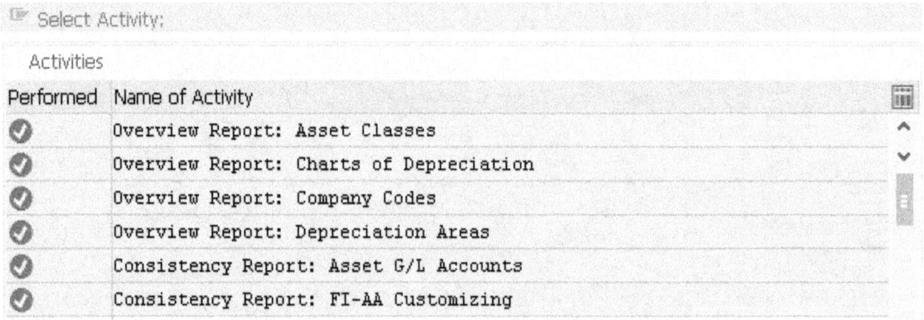

Select Activity:		
Activities		
Performed	Name of Activity	
✓	Overview Report: Asset Classes	^
✓	Overview Report: Charts of Depreciation	∨
✓	Overview Report: Company Codes	
✓	Overview Report: Depreciation Areas	
✓	Consistency Report: Asset G/L Accounts	
✓	Consistency Report: FI-AA Customizing	

Figure 13.191 Consistency Check – Overview of Activities

For example, when you double-click on the activity 'Overview Report: Company Codes', you will get the details, on the next screen, for all your asset accounting company codes as shown in Figure 13.192.

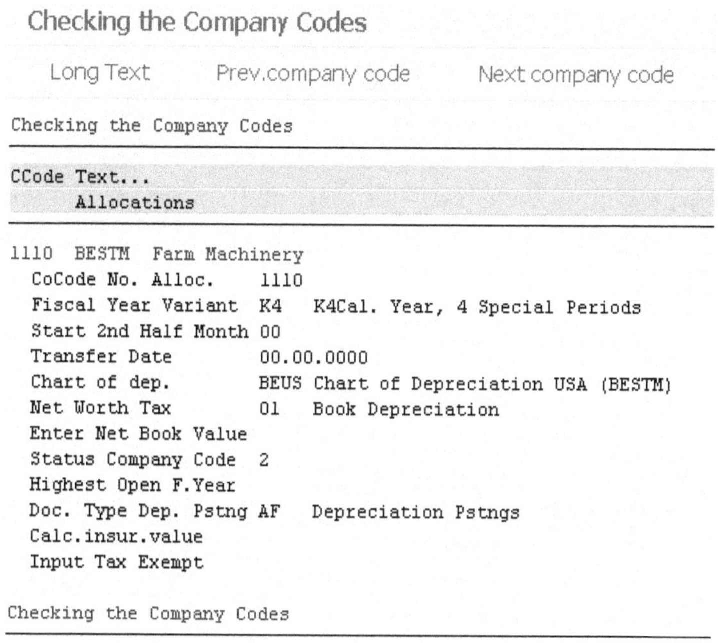

Checking the Company Codes

Long Text   Prev.company code   Next company code

```
Checking the Company Codes
_____

CCode Text...
     Allocations
_____

1110  BESTM  Farm Machinery
  CoCode No. Alloc.    1110
  Fiscal Year Variant  K4   K4Cal. Year, 4 Special Periods
  Start 2nd Half Month 00
  Transfer Date        00.00.0000
  Chart of dep.        BEUS Chart of Depreciation USA (BESTM)
  Net Worth Tax        01   Book Depreciation
  Enter Net Book Value
  Status Company Code  2
  Highest Open F.Year
  Doc. Type Dep. Pstng AF   Depreciation Pstngs
  Calc.insur.value
  Input Tax Exempt
_____

Checking the Company Codes
_____
```

Figure 13.192 Consistency Check – Company Codes

Instead of going through the menu path shown here, in this Section, you can also reach the individual screens directly using the corresponding Transactions as listed below, in Table 13.6:

Activity	Transaction
Overview Report: Asset Classes	ANKA
Overview Report: Charts of Depreciation	OAK1
Overview Report: Company Codes	OAK2
Overview Report: Depreciation Areas	OAK3
Consistency Report: Asset G/L Accounts	OAK4
Consistency Report: FI-AA Customizing	OAK6

Table 13:6 Transaction Codes for Consistency Check

The next activity is to reset the company code before making the settings for going live.

13.12.3 Reset Company Code

You can delete test data (asset master records and transactions) for a company code. You may need to do this activity, for example, following a test legacy data transfer. To reset, the 'Company Code Status' should be in 'For Testing' status (refer Section 13.11.1.1).

> **i** Once deleted, you will not be able to retrieve the deleted data back. The system deletes data only in FI-AA component and not in any of the integrated applications. The system does not delete the configuration settings.

Use the menu path: SAP Customizing Implementation Guide > Financial Accounting > Asset Accounting > Asset Data Transfer > Preparations for Going Live > Tools > Reset Company Code. You may also use Transaction OABL:

i.   On the resulting screen, enter the 'Company Code' (say, 1110). If you select 'Line items only' check-box, then, the system deletes only the transactions and not the asset master data (Figure 13.193).

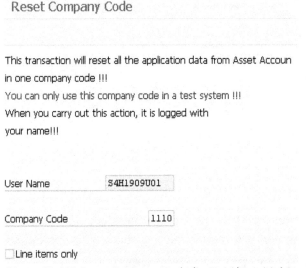

Figure 13.193 Reset Company Code (in FI-AA) – Initial Screen

ii. Press 'Yes' on the 'Reset company code' pop-up screen. Now, the system deletes all the test data in the selected company code for FI-AA and resets the company code. The system displays a message on the status bar informing that the company code has been reset (Figure 13.194).

iii. Repeat for all other company codes.

Figure 13.194 Reset Company Code (in FI-AA) - Confirmation

With this, we are now ready for making the settings for production startup.

13.12.4   Production Startup

Towards making the settings for production startup, you need to complete three configuration steps:

- Accounts Approach: Set/Reset Reconciliation Accounts for Parallel Valuation
- Define Settings for Company Code
- Activate New Asset Accounting (New Customers)

Let us start with the first step of setting / resetting reconciliation accounts for parallel valuation if you use account approach.

13.12.4.1   Accounts Approach: Set/Reset Reconciliation Accounts for Parallel Valuation

You need to complete this setting only if you use accounts approach (instead of ledger approach) for parallel accounting. In that case, you can define G/L accounts, as reconciliation accounts, for depreciation areas of a parallel valuation of FI-AA, or define them again as accounts for normal posting.

Use the menu path: SAP Customizing Implementation Guide > Financial Accounting > Asset Accounting > Asset Data Transfer > Preparations for Going Live > Production Startup > Accounts Approach: Set/Reset Reconciliation Accounts for Parallel Valuation, to set /reset the required reconciliation account(s) for parallel valuation.

On the resulting screen, select the required 'Company code' and double-click on 'Change Control of Reconciliation Accounts' on the left-hand side 'Dialog Structure'. On the next screen, set / reset the required G/L account(s) as the reconciliation accounts for parallel valuation. Since BESTM uses ledger approach for parallel accounting, we will not be configuring this step.

The next step is to assign the 'Productive' status to the asset accounting company codes as you have completed all the configuration and also reset the company code to delete all the test data.

13.12.4.2   Define Settings for Company Code

To change the status from 'For Testing' to 'Productive' for the required asset accounting company codes, use the menu path: SAP Customizing Implementation Guide > Financial Accounting > Asset Accounting > Asset Data Transfer > Preparations for Going Live > Production Startup > Define Settings for Company Code, or Transaction FAA_CMP. You will notice that this is the same Transaction that we have already discussed in Section 13.11.1.1 when we defined the transfer data and other parameters for asset data transfer.

You need to select the required company code on the tree-structure on the left, and change the 'Company Code Status' to 'Productive' on the 'General Settings' tab (Figure 13.195).

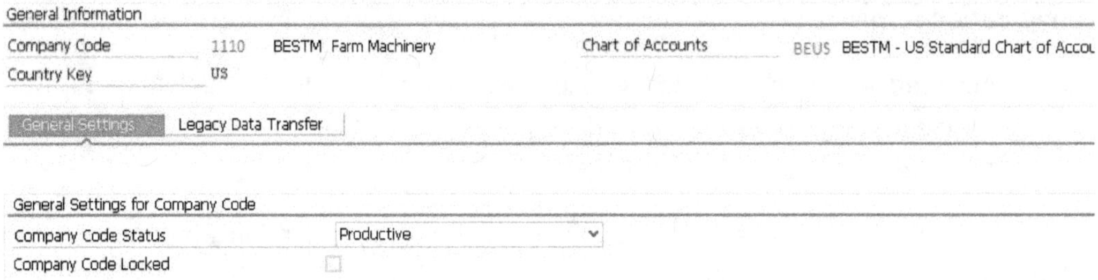

General Information

| Company Code | 1110 | BESTM Farm Machinery | Chart of Accounts | BEUS BESTM - US Standard Chart of Accou |
| Country Key | US | | | |

General Settings   Legacy Data Transfer

General Settings for Company Code

| Company Code Status | Productive | ✓ |
| Company Code Locked | ☐ | |

Figure 13.195 Making the Company Code 'Productive'

Repeat and change the status to all other company codes, one by one.

> **ℹ** You may also change the 'Legacy Data Transfer Status' (on the 'Legacy Data Transfer' tab) to 'Ongoing (Other Postings Allowed)' to allow both legacy data transfer postings and other postings. You will need this kind of status if you plan to perform further legacy data transfers the company code that is already productive.
>
> When you have completed legacy data transfer, you can set this status to 'Completed'.

With this, we are ready complete the final step in production startup, namely, activating the new Asset Accounting, in case you are a new customer for SAP.

13.12.4.3   Activate New Asset Accounting (New Customers)

You need to complete this activity if you have not yet used FI-AA in SAP S/4HANA. You will use this configuration step to activate new Asset Accounting in SAP S/4HANA. You must perform this activation per client. Before activating, you must first make the relevant settings in Customizing for new Asset Accounting. When activated, the system checks whether the settings in Customizing have been made correctly.

When you activate, the system activates the new Asset Accounting in downstream systems (test system and production system) by importing the active Customizing switch and the normal Customizing settings. Once the import to the downstream system has been carried out, the system performs the same checks here as in the Customizing system with the activation. If these checks are not successful, the switch for this activity gets the status 'Active (Posting in client not possible)'.

Use the menu path: SAP Customizing Implementation Guide > Financial Accounting > Asset Accounting > Asset Data Transfer > Preparations for Going Live > Production Startup > Activate New Asset Accounting (New Customers). On the resulting screen, select the value '2 Active' to activate new Asset Accounting in the client (Figure 13.196).

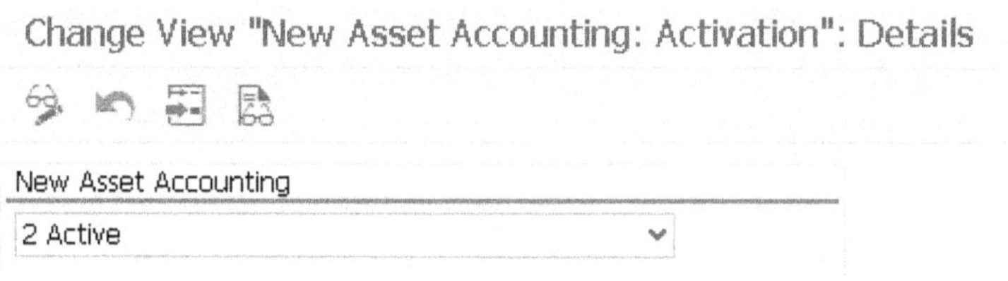

Figure 13.196 Activating New Asset Accounting

This completes our discussion on the settings required for production startup. Let us, now, understand the tools that are available for preparing the system for go-live.

13.12.5   Tools

There are two tools that are made available for preparations for go-live:

- Reset Company Code
- Execute/Undo Year-End Closing

As we have already discussed 'Reset Company Code' activity vide Section 13.12.3, let us look at the other activity that you can use for executing year end closing.

13.12.5.1   Execute/Undo Year-End Closing

You can use this configuration step to close / re-open a fiscal year. We have already touched upon this configuration activity in Section 13.11.1.1 when we were discussing the transfer date (and the related parameters) for legacy asset transfer.

13.12.5.1.1 Closing a Fiscal Year

You can close a fiscal year from an accounting view for a ledger or for a depreciation area. Then, you will not be able to make postings or change values (for example, by recalculating depreciation) in FI-AA for that closed fiscal year.

Let us understand the difference between closing a fiscal year at the ledger level and depreciation area level:

- *Year-End Closing at Ledger Level*
  The year-end closing at ledger level involves closing the fiscal year for all depreciation areas of the ledger. The prerequisite, for this, is that all depreciation areas have the last closed fiscal year.

- *Year-End Closing at the Level of Individual Depreciation Areas*
  If you want to do this, you must choose one or more depreciation areas and close it/them. If you choose all depreciation areas, it is the same as performing a year-end closing at ledger level. This option makes sense when you expect that you will have to re-open some depreciation areas and close them again later (for tax reasons, for example).

> **i** The fiscal year that is closed is always the year following the last closed fiscal year. You should not close the current fiscal year unless you want to 'Deactivate' the company code in FI-AA.

You will execute year-end closing only when (a) the system has found no errors (such as, incorrectly defined depreciation keys) during the calculation of depreciation, (b) all assets (excluding AuC) acquired in the fiscal year have already been capitalized and (c) all incomplete assets (master records) have been completed.

Use the menu path: SAP Customizing Implementation Guide > Financial Accounting > Asset Accounting > Asset Data Transfer > Preparations for Going Live > Production Startup > Define Settings for Company Code, or Transaction FAA_CMP to close a fiscal year. As you can close a fiscal year at the ledger level or at the depreciation area level, you need to decide at what level you want to close the fiscal year.

To close a fiscal year at the ledger level:

i.   On the resulting screen, select the company code (say, 1110) on the left-hand side tree structure.
ii. Select the appropriate ledger, below the selected company code (say, OL).
iii. Now, on the right-hand side of the screen, on the 'Ledger Settings' tab (Figure 13.197), you will notice that the 'Highest F.Year' is 2019 with the fiscal year 2018 already closed (you can see that there is an entry under 'Depreciation Area Settings' block as to the closed fiscal year = 2018).

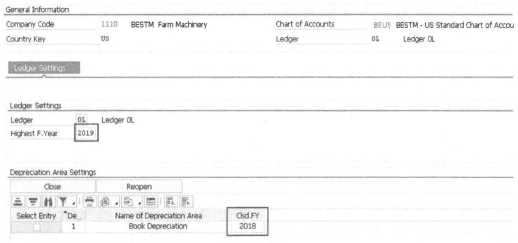

Figure 13.197 Closed Fiscal Year 2018

iv. With the fiscal year 2018 already closed, if you want to close the next fiscal year (2019), select the check-box ('Select Entry') against the all the depreciation areas, and then click on 'Close' button.

v. Now, you will see that the closed fiscal year ('ClsdFY') is 2019, and you can enter the highest fiscal year as 2020 (Figure 13.198).

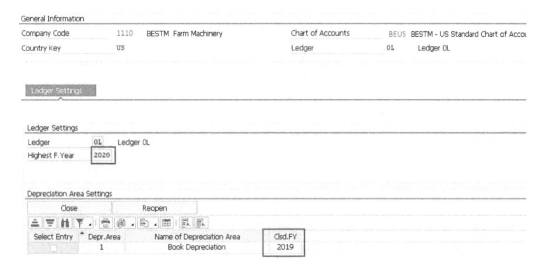

Figure 13.198 Closed Fiscal Year 2019

To close a fiscal year at the depreciation area level:

i. On the resulting screen, select the company code (say, 1110) on the left-hand side tree structure.

ii. Select the appropriate ledger, below the selected company code.

iii.   Now, on the right-hand side of the screen (Figure 13.197), on the 'Ledger Settings' tab, you will notice that the 'Highest F.Year' is 2019 with the fiscal year 2018 already closed (you may see entries under 'Depreciation Area Settings' block as to the closed fiscal year (2018), for various depreciation areas)

iv.   If you want to close the next fiscal year (2019), for a particular depreciation area(s), select the appropriate check-box(es) against the depreciation area(s) under 'Select Entry', and then click on 'Close' button.

v.   Now, the system closes the fiscal year 2019 for the selected depreciation area(s).

vi.   If you select all the check-boxes (meaning, all the depreciation areas) then it is as good as closing that fiscal year at the ledger level.

Let us now understand how to undo a year-end closing or re-open a closed fiscal year.

13.12.5.1.2   Re-open a Fiscal Year / Undo Year-end Closing

You may resort to re-open the last closed fiscal in FI-AA, if you have closed it by mistake. This way, you open that fiscal year, again, for postings. As in the case of closing a fiscal year, you can re-open the fiscal year, for individual depreciation areas of a ledger or for all depreciation areas of the ledger.

> **i** You cannot, in general, open a fiscal year that is already closed from an accounting point of view if that has already been certified by an external auditor.

Use the menu path: SAP Customizing Implementation Guide > Financial Accounting > Asset Accounting > Asset Data Transfer > Preparations for Going Live > Production Startup > Define Settings for Company Code, or Transaction FAA_CMP, to re-open a fiscal year.

As in the case of closing a fiscal year, select the company code, and select the ledger (one or more depreciation areas if the fiscal year is to be re-opened only for selected depreciation area(s) and not for the entire ledger). You will, then, select appropriate check box(es) under the 'Depreciation Area Settings' data block, and click on 'Reopen' button. Here, as shown in Figure 13.198, we are trying to re-open the last closed FY (2019). Now, the system brings up a pop-up screen confirming that the closed fiscal year is reset to 2018 (Figure 13.199).

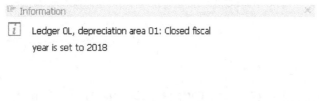

Figure 13.199 Closed Fiscal Year set to 2018

Press 'Continue' and you can see now that closed fiscal year is se to 2018, fiscal year 2019 is re-opened and the highest fiscal year at 2020 (Figure 13.200).

General Information

Company Code	1110	BESTM Farm Machinery	Chart of Accounts	BEUS	BESTM - US Standard Chart of Accou
Country Key	US		Ledger	OL	Ledger OL

Ledger Settings

Ledger Settings

Ledger	OL	Ledger OL
Highest F.Year	2020	

Depreciation Area Settings

Close	Reopen

Select Entry	Depr.Area	Name of Depreciation Area	Clsd.FY
☐	1	Book Depreciation	2018

Figure 13.200 Closed Fiscal Year set to 2018, Fiscal Year 2019 Re-opened

---

ℹ️ You can also perform the year-end closing by using the SAP Easy Access menu path: SAP Menu > Accounting > Financial Accounting > Fixed Assets >Periodic Processing > Year-End Closing > Execute/Undo, instead of using the Customizing activity using the IMG. The Transaction FAA_CMP is the same.

This completes our discussion on the preparations for going live. With this, let us move on to discuss the overview for experts.

13.13   Overview for Experts

The *'overview for experts'* provides a one-stop review of the settings that you made in different sections of IMG while configuring the system for FI-AA. Using the various activities under this IMG node, you can re-check the configuration settings, at a glance; and, go back to the respective IMG node to correct, if necessary. The various activities include:

- Assign Accounts
- Assign Selected G/L Accounts per Chart of Accounts
- Check Depreciation Areas
- Check Real Depreciation Areas
- Check Active Charts of Depreciation for Asset Accounting
- Check Company Code
- Check Depreciation Areas of Company Codes
- Check Account Assignments

- Check Transaction Types
- Check Asset Classes

Let us see these activities one-by-one:

13.13.1   Assign Accounts

Here, you can display the G/L accounts that you have already determined for the write-off or allocation of special reserves.

Use the menu path: SAP Customizing Implementation Guide > Financial Accounting > Asset Accounting > Asset Data Transfer > Overview for Experts > Assign Accounts, or Transaction AO99.

On the resulting screen, for your chart of accounts, you can display the G/L accounts that have already been determined for special reserves per account determination.

13.13.2   Assign Selected G/L Accounts per Chart of Accounts

In this activity, you can display the G/L accounts that you have already determined for the following account assignments. If required, you may also maintain the same here.

- Offsetting of revenue from sale of asset
- Gain with sale of asset
- Acquisition offsetting account, acquisition value
- Offsetting account, revaluation APC
- Loss with sale of asset
- Loss from asset retirement without revenue (scrapping)

Use the menu path: SAP Customizing Implementation Guide > Financial Accounting > Asset Accounting > Asset Data Transfer > Overview for Experts > Assign Selected G/L Accounts per Chart of Accounts.

Change View "Assign Selected G/L Accounts per Chart of Accounts": Over

Chart of Accts   BEUS

Assign Selected G/L Accounts per Chart of Accounts

Account Determination	Ar.	Gain frm Ret.	Asset Ret.Loss	Rev.Clear.Acct	Scrapping	Contra act.Acq. APC	Offst.Act. Rev.
B1000	1	71010100	71010300	70030000	71010900	16014100	16015000

Figure 13.201 Determining G/L Accounts for Various Account Assignments

On the resulting screen, for your chart of accounts, you can display / maintain the G/L accounts for each of the account assignments listed above, per account determination and per depreciation area. This is very convenient as all these assignments are shown in a tabular format (Figure 13.201).

13.13.3   Check Depreciation Areas

Here, in this step, you can display depreciation areas that you have defined for your chart of depreciation. Besides, you can view the settings associated with the depreciation areas for ordinary depreciation, special depreciation, unplanned depreciation, transfer of reserves, interest, investment support and replacement values. You can also view the settings for cross-system depreciation area.

Use the menu path: SAP Customizing Implementation Guide > Financial Accounting > Asset Accounting > Asset Data Transfer > Overview for Experts > Check Depreciation Areas.

13.13.4   Check Real Depreciation Areas

Here, you can check the various settings like depreciation area type, currency type, value copy rules, copy rules for depreciation terms, gross transfer for intercompany asset transfer, sequence of depreciation calculation and capitalization version for the real depreciation areas.

Use the menu path: SAP Customizing Implementation Guide > Financial Accounting > Asset Accounting > Asset Data Transfer > Overview for Experts > Check Real Depreciation Areas.

13.13.5   Check Active Charts of Depreciation for Asset Accounting

You have already activated, vide Section 13.12.4.3, new Asset Accounting in Customizing in the IMG activity 'Activate New Asset Accounting (New Customers)'. Now, in this activity, you can check if the Customizing settings for your depreciation areas are correct for new Asset Accounting, as correct configuration (of the depreciation areas) is a prerequisite for activating the Customizing switch (FAA_PARALLEL_VAL) for new Asset Accounting. Of course, the individual checks of this program are already contained in the various IMG activities for the depreciation areas. Here, using this program, however, you can start the individual checks together. The check is carried out per chart of depreciation.

Use the menu path: SAP Customizing Implementation Guide > Financial Accounting > Asset Accounting > Asset Data Transfer > Overview for Experts > Check Active Charts of Depreciation for Asset Accounting. You may also use Transaction FAA_CHEK_AREA_4_PARV.

On the resulting screen, enter the chart of depreciation (say, BEUS) and click 'Execute'. On the next screen, the system brings up the log displaying the details (Figure 13.202). If everything is fine, you will see a green coloured square against the message 'No error found; requirements to activate Customizing switch have been met'.

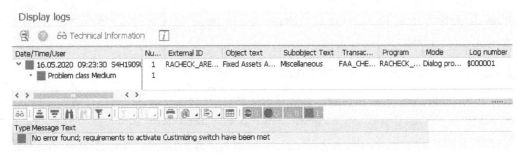

Figure 13.202 Checking Customizing for Depreciation Areas, for Chart of Depreciation BEUS

13.13.6   Check Company Code

Here, you can check the various settings like chart of depreciation, number range, posting of net value, fiscal year variant etc for an asset accounting company code (Figure 13.203).

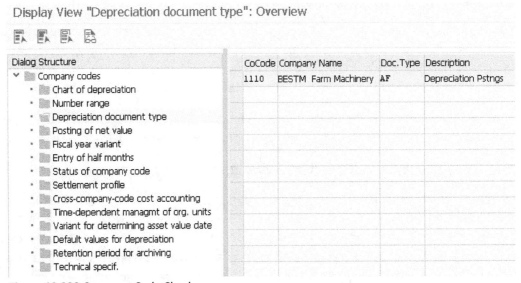

Figure 13.203 Company Code Check

Use the menu path: SAP Customizing Implementation Guide > Financial Accounting > Asset Accounting > Asset Data Transfer > Overview for Experts > Check Company Code.

13.13.7   Check Depreciation Areas of Company Codes

In this activity, you can check the various settings for depreciation areas of company codes.

Use the menu path: SAP Customizing Implementation Guide > Financial Accounting > Asset Accounting > Asset Data Transfer > Overview for Experts > Check Depreciation Areas of Company Codes.

Here, you can check the settings relating to period version, currency, memo value, changeover amount, LVA amount, period weighting, B/S version, capitalization of downpayments, posting rules and net reserve for special depreciation (Figure 13.204).

Figure 13.204 Checking Depreciation Areas for Company Codes

13.13.8   Check Account Assignments

Here, you can check, for the given chart of accounts, the various account assignments (B/S accounts, depreciation accounts and accounts for special reserves), per account assignment and per depreciation area.

Use the menu path: SAP Customizing Implementation Guide > Financial Accounting > Asset Accounting > Asset Data Transfer > Overview for Experts > Check Account Assignments (Figure 13.205).

Figure 13.205 Checking Account Assignments

13.13.9   Check Transaction Types

Here, you can check various settings associated with the transaction types. You can also check, for example, if there is a limitation of depreciation areas that can used with specific transaction types, is there a need for special handling of transfer posting and so on.

Use the menu path: SAP Customizing Implementation Guide > Financial Accounting > Asset Accounting > Asset Data Transfer > Overview for Experts > Check Transaction Types (Figure 13.206).

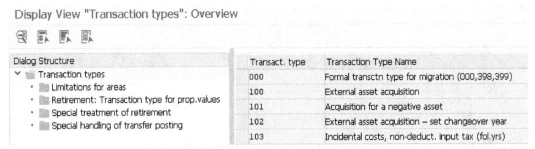

Figure 13.206 Checking Transaction Types

13.13.10   Check Asset Classes

In this activity you can see an overview of all settings that you have made, up to now, for asset classes. Per asset class, you can view the settings relating to net worth tax, leasing specifications, user fields, asset history form, capitalization key etc (Figure 13.207).

Use the menu path: SAP Customizing Implementation Guide > Financial Accounting > Asset Accounting > Asset Data Transfer > Overview for Experts > Check Asset Classes.

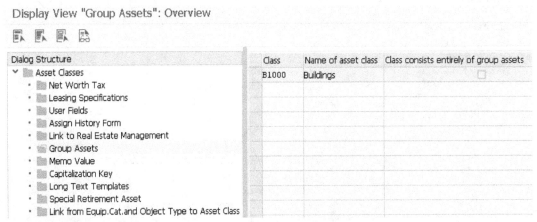

Figure 13.207 Checking Asset Classes

This completes our discussion on overview for experts. This also completes our discussion on various topics of FI-AA.

13.14   Conclusion

You learned that you can use SAP Asset Accounting (FI-AA) to manage your business entity's fixed assets internationally, in any country and in any industry. You learned that you need to portray your organizational structure in FI-AA - by defining organizational objects like chart of depreciation, FI company code, asset class etc., - to classify your fixed assets according to asset accounting criteria.

You understood that the 'chart of depreciation' is a list of 'depreciation areas' arranged according to business and legal requirements, to manage the rules for depreciation and valuation of assets in a particular country. You also understood that, once defined, you can assign the chart of depreciation to the appropriate company codes, so as to make them available for asset accounting.

You learned that you can structure fixed assets, in FI-AA, at three different levels: at balance sheet (B/S) structure level, at classification structure level and at asset-related structure level. For example, at 'classification structure level', you learned that you can use the 'asset classes' (like buildings, vehicles, AuC, machinery etc) in structuring the fixed assets. With every asset belonging to an asset class, you noticed, that the asset class establishes the link (through the account determination key) between asset master records and the G/L accounts in SAP FI.

You learned that FI-AA is tightly integrated with other application components like SAP MM (Materials Management), PM (Plant Maintenance), SAP PP (Production Planning) and IM (Investment Management). With its integration with SAP G/L Accounting, you learned, that you can automatically update all asset accounting transactions including depreciation, to SAP G/L, in real-time, for the leading depreciation areas of an accounting principle.

You learned that you can manage valuation of fixed assets through 'depreciation areas'. You learned that you need different depreciation areas for valuation according to local laws (book depreciation), tax depreciation, cost-accounting depreciation, special reserves and investment support. You also learned about the differences between a 'real depreciation area' and a 'derived depreciation area', and how to derive the values for the derived area.

You learned that SAP supports both automatically calculated depreciation (ordinary & special depreciation) and manually planned depreciation (unplanned depreciation & transfer of reserves / reduction in APC). You understood that the depreciation calculation is based on the 'valuation method' and the 'planned useful life' of the asset. You further understood that the valuation methods are based on two variables: the depreciation key and the cutoff value. You learned that the 'depreciation key' (defined at the level of the chart of depreciation) contains all the control indicators for depreciation calculation, besides the calculation methods. You learned that the 'calculation methods' - defined within the depreciation key - supply the required parameters to the 'Depreciation Calculation Program' (DCP).

You learned that you will use 'special valuations' for special value adjustments to assets (like, investment support, special depreciation reserves etc) and for meeting some of the special valuation purposes like, cost-accounting replacement values, interest, revaluation for the balance sheet etc.

You learned that an asset master record, in SAP, consists of two data areas: (a) general master data and (b) data for calculating asset values. You further learned that while the 'general master data', contains the concrete information about the fixed asset, the 'data for calculating asset values', contains the depreciation terms in the asset master record, for each depreciation area.

You learned that the system makes use of asset 'transaction types', for carrying out all accounting / business transactions that occur during the life of a fixed asset (like acquisitions, retirements, intracompany / intercompany transfers, capitalization of AuC etc). You also learned that each transaction type is assigned exactly to one 'transaction type group', with the group determining the characteristics and parameters for a transaction.

Later, you learned how to configure the FI-AA Information system to suit your own reporting requirements. You learned about the sort versions, simulation variants and SAP Queries in asset reporting. You also learned about the key figures / key figure groups for some of the SAP Fiori apps relating to assets. You finally learned about configuring asset history sheets, especially the history sheet versions and history sheet groups.

In asset data transfer, you learned about the parameters for data transfer including the definition of transfer date, offsetting account for legacy data transfer and the associated transaction types. You also learned about manual data transfer of legacy fixed assets and legacy group assets. You understood how to carry out legacy asset transfer using Microsoft Excel.

As a part of preparations for 'going live', you learned about maintenance of authorizations, assignment of workflow tasks and processing asset views. You learned how to check the consistency of FI-AA configuration settings. You learned how to reset the company codes and how to make them 'productive' in the system. You also learned that you can use the 'overview for experts' functionality to check and verify the configuration settings at a glance.

***

In this book:

You learned about the *'Accounts Receivable'* (FI-A/R) and *'Accounts Payable'* (FI-A/P) components of SAP, that deal with your customers and vendors for managing the amounts that your business would receive from (customers) and pay to (vendors). In the process, you learned about customer / vendor master data and the preparations for creating those records in the system. You understood the configuration settings that are required for various business transactions, in FI-A/R and FI-A/P, like incoming & outgoing invoices, release for payment, outgoing & incoming payments, payments with payment cards, dunning, open item clearing, down payment processing, interest calculation and closing operations. You also learned about the standard evaluations, in FI-A/R and FI-A/P, as a part of information system, and how to leverage them for your specific reporting requirements.

You, then, moved on to learn *'Contract Accounts Receivable and Payable'* (SAP FICA) application component: its functionality, when to go in for this application etc. You learned about the various organizational units of FICA and how to configure them in SAP. You, also, learned about the configuration settings of the basic functions and some of the important business transactions including security deposits, payments, dunning and interest calculation. You understood how SAP FICA is integrated with SAP G/L Accounting, and the associated settings for the integration.

In *'Bank Accounting'* (FI-BL), you learned about bank master data, multi-stage payment methods and payment transactions. In bank master data, you learned about bank directories, house banks, business partner's bank, bank distribution and checks for bank master data. While discussing multi-stage payment methods (bank chains), you learned about the various scenarios that determine the bank chain. You also learned about creating general bank chain, bank chain for customers / vendors, bank chains for house banks and how to include the bank chain information on payment lists. In payment transactions, you learned about the configuration settings for manual & electronic bank statements, lockbox processing, setting up of cash journal and configuring for online payments.

Finally, you learned about *'Asset Accounting'* (FI-AA), in detail, towards the end of this book. You learned about the difference between classic and new asset accounting functionalities, in SAP. You learned how to define the asset accounting organizational structure to model your enterprise's fixed assets. You learned how to structure your fixed assets in FI-AA and how to create the asset master records. You learned about the depreciation types, depreciation areas, and general and special valuations. You learned about the various asset transactions including acquisitions, transfers, retirements, and capitalization of assets under construction. You, also, learned how to complete legacy asset data transfer, preparations for going 'live' and how to leverage FI-AA information system to suit your reporting needs.

***

Together with Vol. I and Vol. II of this title, we are confident that you are now familiar with the configuration required for setting up of *SAP Financial Accounting* in SAP S/4HANA Finance, for a business enterprise, to leverage the application's functionality in the areas of G/L accounting, bank accounting, accounts receivable & accounts payable, asset accounting etc.

About the Author

Narayanan Veeriah is a Chartered Financial Analyst (CFA), a PMP (from Project Management Institute), and IBM Certified Executive Project Management Professional, having more than 35 years of work experience, in finance, project management and information technology (IT), including 20+ years of experience in SAP implementation and consulting. A member of Certified Associate of Indian Institute of Bankers (CAIIB), he brings along with him a strong domain expertise in Banking and Finance with core competencies in retail banking and credit management, along with SAP.

Narayanan has worked with several multi-national clients for consulting, implementing and supporting SAP, across industries including automotive, banking & finance, electronics, manufacturing, multimedia, pharmaceuticals etc. He has worked with several versions of SAP right from SAP R/3 3.1H to the latest SAP S/4HANA, in new implementations, upgrades and support.

Till recently, he was leading SAP practice, for a couple of industry verticals in a leading multinational IT consulting company. He has authored several books on SAP Finance, besides being a regular guest faculty at management institutions for ERP, SAP, banking & finance and project management.

He is currently a freelance SAP consultant.

You can reach him at vdotn@yahoo.com.

Index

List of Figures

List of Tables

Latest Book by the Author

Configuring SAP Financial Accounting – Vol. I
(SAP S/4HANA Finance)
(1st Edition)

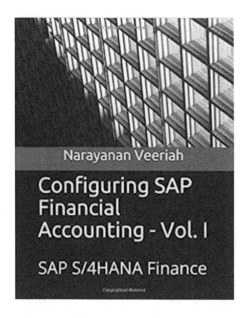

Configure SAP Financial Accounting, in SAP S/4HANA Finance (1909), to suit your exact business needs! Understand the concepts and learn configuring your SAP system step-by-step, through case-studies, with numerous screenshots and illustrations covering:

- SAP HANA
- SAP S/4HANA
- SAP S/4HANA Finance
- Case Study
- FI Global Settings I (Ledgers, Field Status, Fiscal Year, Company Code Global Parameters etc.)
- FI Global Settings II (Documents, Inflation Accounting and Correspondence)
- FI Global Settings III (Taxes including Withholding Tax)
- General Ledger Accounting

564 pages, 1st edition 2020
Formats: Kindle & Paperback
ISBN: 979-8657784145
https://www.amazon.com/dp/B08C4DHF8Z

Latest Book by the Author

Configuring SAP Asset Accounting
(SAP S/4HANA Finance)
(1st Edition)

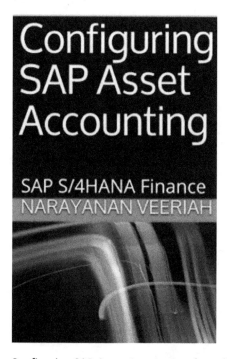

Configuring SAP Asset Accounting, based on the latest version of SAP S/4HANA Finance, is a complete guide to comprehend and configure SAP Asset Accounting (FI-AA). This book follows a case-study approach to make your learning easy. Efforts have been taken, throughout the book, to guide you step-by-step in understanding how to configure your SAP system, to meet your exact business needs. Each configuration activity has been discussed with appropriate screen shots and illustrations to help you 'see' what is being discussed in that activity / step. You will see a lot of context-based additional information across Chapters, for better assimilation of concepts / settings. The entire content of the book has been presented as in SAP Implementation Guide with appropriate menu paths and Transactions.

324 pages, 1st edition 2020
Formats: Kindle & Paperback
ISBN: 979-865383115

https://www.amazon.com/Configuring-SAP-Asset-Accounting-Finance/dp/B08B333BY6/ref=tmm_pap_swatch_0?_encoding=UTF8&qid=&sr=

Latest Book by the Author

Configuring Financial Accounting in SAP ® ERP
(3rd Edition)

This is your comprehensive guide to configuring Financial Accounting in SAP ERP! Brush up on the old standbys—Accounts Payable, Account Receivable, SAP General Ledger, and Asset Accounting—and then dive in to Contract Accounts Receivable and Payable, Consolidation, Lease Accounting, Travel Management, SAP Fiori, and much more. You'll learn to set up your enterprise structure, use maintenance tools, and ensure your implementation works for your unique business.

916 pages, 3rd, updated edition 2018
E-book formats: EPUB, MOBI, PDF, online
ISBN 978-1-4932-1723-6

https://www.sap-press.com/configuring-financial-accounting-in-sap-erp_4674/

Other Books by the Author

Title: *SAP ERP: Quick Reference Guide*
Edition: 2
Publisher: Mercury Learning & Information, 2020
ISBN: 1683920961, 9781683920960
Length: 500 pages

Title: *SAP FI: Financial Accounting ERP ECC6, R/3 4.70*
Edition: 2
Publisher: Mercury Learning & Information, 2017
ISBN: 1683921003, 9781683921004
Length: 350 pages

Title: *SAP CO: Controlling*
Edition: 2
Publisher: Mercury Learning & Information, 2017
ISBN: 168392102X, 9781683921028
Length: 350 pages

Title: *Configuring Financial Accounting in SAP*
Edition: 2, illustrated
Publisher: Galileo Press, 2014 (SAP Press)
ISBN: 1493210424, 9781493210428
Length: 907 pages

Title: *Implementing SAP ERP Financials: A Configuration Guide*
Edition: 2
Publisher: Tata McGraw Hill Publishing Co Ltd, 2013
ISBN-13: 978-0-0701-4297-8
Length: 965 pages

Title: *SAP FI Financial Accounting: SAP ERP ECC 6.0, SAP R/3 4.70*
Edition: 1, illustrated, reprint
Publisher: Mercury Learning & Information, 2013
ISBN   1937585646, 9781937585648
Length: 338 pages

Title: ***Customizing Financial Accounting in SAP***
Edition: 1, illustrated
Publisher: Galileo Press, 2011 (SAP Press)
ISBN   1592293778, 9781592293773
Length: 792 pages

Title: ***Mastering SAP CO: Controlling***
Edition: 1, illustrated
Publisher: BPB Publications, 2007
ISBN: 9788183333344
Length: 297 pages

Title: ***SAP FI***
Edition: 1, illustrated
Publisher: BPB Publications, 2010
ISBN: 9788183333238
Length: 302 pages

Title: ***SAP FI/CO Demystified***
Edition: 1, illustrated
Publisher: BPB Publications, 2008
ISBN: 8183332315, 9788183332316
Length: 370 pages

Title: ***SAP R/3 FI Transactions***
Edition: 1, illustrated
Publisher: Jones & Bartlett Learning, 2007
ISBN: 1934015016, 9781934015018
Length: 530 pages

Title: ***Mastering SAP R/3 FI: Transaction Made Easy***
Edition: 1, illustrated
Publisher: BPB Publications, 2007
ISBN: 8183331319, 9788183331319
Length: 472 pages

***